Studying Politics

An Introduction to Political Science

Third Edition

Edited by Rand Dyck

Carleton University

NELSON / EDUCATION

Studying Politics: An Introduction to Political Science, Third Edition
by Rand Dyck

Associate Vice President, Editorial Director:
Evelyn Veitch

Editor-in-Chief:
Anne Williams

Publisher:
Cara Yarzab

Acquisitions Editor:
Bram Sepers

Marketing Manager:
Ann Byford

Senior Developmental Editor:
Linda Sparks

Photo Researcher:
Indu Arora

Permissions Coordinator:
Indu Arora

Content Production Manager:
Christine Gilbert

Production Service:
Newgen

Copy Editor:
Rodney Rawlings

Proofreader:
Matt Diedrich

Indexer:
Mauri Baggiano

Manufacturing Coordinator:
Ferial Suleman

Design Director:
Ken Phipps

Managing Designer:
Katherine Strain

Interior Design:
Dianna Little

Cover Design:
Jennifer Leung

Cover Image:
top center, A.G.E. Foto Stock / First Light; top left, Chris Hondros/Staff / Getty Images News; bottom left, Ezra Shaw/Staff / Getty Images News; top right, Majid/Stringer / Getty Images News; bottom center, Watts/Hall Inc / First Light; bottom right, © William S. Kuta / Alamy

Compositor:
Newgen

Printer:
RR Donnelley

Library and Archives Canada Cataloguing in Publication

Studying politics : an introduction to political science / edited by Rand Dyck.—3rd ed.

Includes bibliographical references and index.
ISBN 978-0-17-610539-6

1. Political science—Textbooks.
I. Dyck, Rand, 1943-
JA66.S84 2008 320
C2008-905976-X

ISBN 13: 978-0-17-610539-6
ISBN 10: 0-17-610539-5

We dedicate this book to those who are about to experience the joys and rigours of studying politics, in the hope and expectation that they will emerge stimulated by and committed to the subject, and thus become citizens capable of dealing with the domestic and global challenges of the 21st century.

Brief Contents

Contents

PART FIVE   Political Participation

PART SIX   Political Development and Change

PART SEVEN International Politics

Preface

That this text is entering its third edition is a sign it is holding its own among many other good introductory texts available in the field of political science in Canada. It is obviously fulfilling the hopes of its creators—to produce a fresh new text for the new century. In 2002 we saw the need for a text that incorporated the best of the traditional approaches and subject matter of the discipline, but at the same time acknowledged how patterns of domestic and global politics and the ways they are studied were changing at a rapid pace. The market was asking for a text designed for Canadian students, one that opened their eyes to important developments around the globe. In retrospect, we were correct in thinking that the resulting work would have wide appeal among students and professors alike.

The Development of *Studying Politics*

We originally canvassed a large number of professors of first-year political science courses and asked them what they wanted included in such a text. We then assembled an impressive array of leading Canadian political scientists from across the country, most of whom also taught the introductory political science course at their respective institutions, and asked each to write a chapter in the area of his or her expertise. We also put them together in a room and asked them to come up with common themes, common approaches, and a common format, so that their chapters would speak to each other and there would be a seamless transition from one to the next. Numerous other political science professors were then asked to review their work and to suggest revisions. One of the exciting things about politics, however, is that it is never static, and so we are now presenting a third, updated edition.

A Text Written for Students

We believe this to be the most student-friendly text on the market today. *Studying Politics* starts out with a gentle introduction to the subject of politics and political science, mindful of the fact that many students will not have formally encountered this discipline before. We have tried to write at an appropriate level and avoid confusing jargon, even when we get into more difficult subject matter. Basic concepts are defined at the end of each chapter and again in a glossary at the end of the book. Moreover, we have integrated into the text a large number of tables, figures, photographs, cartoons, and discussion boxes to clarify, stimulate, and amuse, and to add to the visual appeal of the book. Each chapter also begins with a list of its learning objectives, and ends with discussion questions, the aforementioned key terms (basic concepts), web links, and suggestions for further reading. In addition, at the opening of each of the parts into which this book is divided, we have offered profiles, with photographs, of several political science graduates, illustrating how their study of politics contributed to their exciting and varied careers.

A Text Written for Professors

As for professors, *Studying Politics* provides the content and approaches that teachers of introductory political science courses are looking for, combining traditional and newer concepts. The book has a comparative/conceptual approach, but remains Canadian. *Studying Politics* is accompanied by a wide array of ancillary materials, including a comprehensive instructor's manual, test bank, PowerPoint® slides, and a video. The book has its own website at http://www.studyingpolitics3e. nelson.com, which contains a variety of other features.

Acknowledgments

With such guidance from the political science community, with such expert and enthusiastic contributors involved, and with a top-notch publishing team at Nelson, it was not a difficult job for me to coordinate the project. By way of acknowledgment, I must first thank the contributors to this book. It was a joy to work with these impressive and accomplished people. Busy as they were with their teaching and administrative duties and other writing and research projects, they were all most faithful and cooperative in making this work a reality. We welcome Christopher G. Anderson to the group with this edition.

Then I wish to acknowledge the contributions of the many other political science professors who were asked for advice in the planning of the book or in reviewing draft chapters. Their recommendations led to many valuable changes. Among these reviewers over the years were Christopher Dunn, Memorial University; Syed S. Islam, Lakehead University; James Kelly, Brock University; Dan W. Middlemiss, Dalhousie University; Eric Mintz, Sir Wilfred Grenfell College; Ross Rudolph, York University; David Winchester, Capilano College; Ken Woodside, University of Guelph; James Ferguson, University of Manitoba; John Sutcliffe, University of Windsor; Josie Hernandez de Leon, Laurentian University; Chaldeans Mensah, Grant MacEwan College; Logan Masilamani, Kwantlen Polytechnic University; Brian Tanguay, Wilfrid Laurier University; and Myron Galan, Dawson College.

Next, we thank the organizations, publishers, newspapers, photographers, and cartoonists who gave us permission to reproduce their work, which has so complemented our written words. We are also very pleased at the calibre of seven individuals who agreed to be profiled as political science graduates to demonstrate the range of careers to which this discipline is open.

Finally, as a veteran author attached to Nelson Education Ltd., I wish to thank the wonderful people at that organization, whose daily assistance, encouragement, support, and advice have brought the three editions of this book to fruition. In this edition, I worked most closely with Linda Sparks and Bram Sepers, but they were supported by many talented, artistic people in the production department and beyond.

Rand Dyck
Carleton University

About the Authors

Yasmeen Abu-Laban is an Associate Professor in the Department of Political Science at the University of Alberta. Her research interests centre on the Canadian and comparative dimensions of gender and ethnic politics, nationalism and globalization, immigration policies and politics, and citizenship theory. In addition to publishing over 40 articles and chapters, she is the co-author of *Selling Diversity: Immigration, Multiculturalism, Employment Equity and Globalization* (2002); the co-editor of *Politics in North America: Redefining Continental Relations* (2008); and the editor of *Gendering the Nation-State: Canadian and Comparative Perspectives* (2008).

Christopher G. Anderson is an Assistant Professor in the Department of Political Science at Wilfrid Laurier University and received his Ph.D. from McGill University. He researches and has published on Canadian immigration, refugee, and citizenship policies, especially in terms of situating contemporary debates within a more extensive historical context, and exploring how the liberalness of the Canadian political system shapes policies toward noncitizens.

James Busumtwi-Sam is an Associate Professor in the Department of Political Science at Simon Fraser University, where he was a recent recipient of the Excellence in Teaching Award. He specializes in international relations and comparative development. He has published work on the politics of development finance and the role of international financial institutions; international organizations and regional security; the political economy of conflict and peacebuilding in Africa; and the politics of macroeconomic policy reform and financial liberalization in developing countries.

William D. Coleman is Distinguished University Professor and holds the Canada Research Chair on Global Governance and Public Policy at McMaster University. He has written five books and edited five others. Among his awards are Lauréat Trudeau Fellow, the Konrad Adenauer Research Award from the Alexander von Humboldt-Stiftung in Bonn, the 3M Teaching Fellowship, and the Ontario Confederation of University Faculty Associations (OCUFA) Teaching Award. Since 2002, he has headed a team that received a Major Collaborative Research Initiatives grant from the Social Sciences and Humanities Research Council of Canada (SSHRCC) to study globalization and autonomy.

Rand Dyck retired as Professor Emeritus in the Department of Political Science at Laurentian University, where he won the Teaching Excellence Award along with the OCUFA Teaching Award in 2002, and served as Vice-Dean of Social Sciences and Humanities. He is the author of several widely used textbooks in Canadian political science: *Provincial Politics in Canada* (1996), *Canadian Politics: Critical Approaches*, 5th ed. (2008), and *Canadian Politics*, concise 4th ed. (2008). He has also taught at Memorial University of Newfoundland and the University of Victoria, and is currently an Adjunct Professor at Carleton University.

Peter A. Ferguson is an Assistant Professor at the University of Western Ontario, where he teaches international relations and American politics. His research is devoted to the study of democratization, specifically the breakdown of democratic regimes. He has published a number of chapters and articles addressing democratization, as well as public opinion polls and the media.

Andrew Heard is an Associate Professor at Simon Fraser University and an Honorary Adjunct Professor at Dalhousie University. He was a parliamentary intern in the House of Commons before completing his graduate work. His research interests and publications include topics in Canadian constitutional law, parliamentary government, judicial behaviour, electoral systems, and theories of human rights.

Heather MacIvor teaches Canadian politics and political theory at the University of Windsor. She has published articles and book chapters about electoral systems, women's political participation, and party leadership selection. Her numerous books include *Parameters of Power: Canada's Political Institutions*, 4th ed. (2005) and *Canadian Politics and Government in the Charter Era* (2006). Her current research interests include the impact of the *Charter of Rights* on Canadian political parties, the comparative study of election and party finance laws, and the political thought of Machiavelli.

Kim Richard Nossal is a professor in the Department of Political Studies at Queen's University, where he teaches international relations and the first-year introduction to political science. He is the author of a number of books and articles on Canadian foreign and defence policy; his most recent book, co-authored with Stéphane Roussel and Stéphane Paquin, is *Politique international et défense au Canada et au Québec* (2007). He is a past president of the Canadian Political Science Association.

Brenda O'Neill is an Associate Professor of Political Science at the University of Calgary. Her research is devoted to the study of Canadian political behaviour, specifically gender, political opinions, and youth engagement. Recent publications include *Citizen Politics: Research and Theory in Canadian Political Behaviour* (with Joanna Everitt), *Gender and Social Capital* (with Elisabeth Gidengil, 2006), and articles in the *International Journal of Canadian Studies*, the *Canadian Journal of Political Science*, and the *International Political Science Review*.

Stephen Phillips teaches Political Science at Langara College in Vancouver and is a past president of the British Columbia Political Studies Association. Trained in law as well as political science, he teaches Canadian government and comparative politics. His current research interests centre on electoral reform and on the role of the Crown in Canada. In recent years he has made formal submissions to the Berger Commission on Vancouver's civic electoral system and to the BC Electoral Boundaries Commission.

Richard Sigurdson is Dean of Arts at the University of Manitoba, where he is also Professor of Political Studies. He teaches primarily in the fields of Canadian politics and political theory. He is the author of *Jacob Burckhardt's Social and Political Thought* (University of Toronto Press, 2004) and a forthcoming book on nationalism.

Miriam Smith is a Professor in the School of Public Policy and Administration at York University. She specializes in Canadian and comparative politics, especially social movements, public law, and lesbian and gay politics in Canada and the United States. Among many other works, she is the author of *Lesbian and Gay Rights in Canada* (1999), *A Civil Society? Collective Actors in Canadian Political Life* (2005), editor of *Group Politics and Social Movements in Canadian Politics* (2008), and co-editor of *Critical Policy Studies* (2007). She also serves as President of the Canadian Political Science Association.

Part

1

Introduction

DEIRDRA McCRACKEN

Deirdra McCracken completed a BA in Political Science at Laurentian University (Sudbury, ON) in 2004, and, being fluently bilingual, followed that with an MA in Political Science at Université Laval (Quebec, QC).

While studying at Laurentian, Deirdra participated in the annual Model Parliament held in the House of Commons chamber in Ottawa. In 2003, she was named Deputy Prime Minister and received an award for the best speech of the day. The final year of her undergraduate degree was spent as an exchange student at the University of Limerick, Ireland. While in Ireland she was published in the *Journal of Historical Studies* and was a member of the UL Debating Union, representing the university at various intervarsity competitions and making it to the quarterfinal round of the Irish Times Debates. Following her year abroad, Deirdra was the sole Canadian chosen to participate in the 2004 American–European Summer Academy held in Austria.

At Laval University, she was the recipient of a Canada Graduate Scholarship through the SSHRC in support of her master's thesis which focused on whether Canadian journalists are properly equipped to deal with public opinion polls.

In February 2006, Deirdra was named "Canada's Next Great Prime Minister" on the first edition of the eponymous national television program that aired on the CTV network, by a panel of 4 former Prime Ministers. While only five finalists were included in the television program, some 700 young Canadians had participated in earlier rounds, suggesting what they would do to create a better, more prosperous country. The program is now an annual production on CBC-TV.

Since March 2006, Deirdra has been working in Ottawa as Press Secretary to the Honourable Jim Prentice, Minister of Industry (previously Minister of Indian Affairs and Northern Development). Part of studying political science involves keeping track of current affairs, and Deirdra has always made a point of reading newspapers and news magazines, as well as watching news broadcasts.

She credits this discipline with helping her to settle in as press secretary quite easily, since much of her job consists of reading, analyzing, and summarizing the media daily for the Minister. She is also constantly checking updates of news stories all day, not to mention responding to those that concern her files. In short, "it's fair to say that much of what I learned throughout six years of studying political science comes to mind and is put into practice on a regular basis."

Chapter One

STUDYING POLITICS

Rand Dyck

CHAPTER OBJECTIVES

After you have completed this chapter, you should be able to:

- provide several good reasons to study politics

- describe the breadth of the discipline of political science

- discuss the changing nature of studying politics

- outline the basic fields of study within political science

- define such basic concepts as politics, government, power, influence, coercion, and authority

Why Study Politics?

Before you commit yourself to studying politics, even in an introductory course in political science, you may well be asking the following three questions:

- Is it interesting?
- Is it important?
- If I decide to major in political science, is there a job at the end of the line?

This chapter and this book seek to assure you that the answer to all three questions is an unequivocal "YES!"

Politics Is Fascinating

That politics is important is the basic reason to study it, of course, but let us start with the fact that the subject is interesting—often fascinating and even entertaining. This is partly because politics involves prominent individuals, with all their strengths, weaknesses, foibles, and idiosyncrasies, and we cannot help but be captivated by such colourful, intriguing people. A few current examples are control-freak Stephen Harper, Hillary Clinton and Barack Obama, competing for the U.S. presidential nomination, Newfoundland and Labrador's aggressive premier, Danny Williams, and a number of interesting Canadian mayors. Political leaders who have arguably left more meaningful legacies include Winston Churchill, in his determination to defeat the Nazi threat in World War II; Nelson Mandela, in his gracious stature as President of South Africa, devoid of bitterness even after having spent 27 years in prison for fighting against apartheid; Margaret Thatcher, with her "Iron Lady" determination to reduce the role of the state in the 1980s; Tommy Douglas, who as premier of Saskatchewan brought public health insurance to Canada; Pierre Elliott Trudeau, with his stylish, debonair, and often arrogant demeanour as Canadian prime minister; Martin Luther King, whose courageous leadership of the fight for racial integration in the United States had a tremendous impact; Mahatma Gandhi, in his effective pacifist resistance to British rule in India; and even Eva Peron, immortalized in the musical *Evita*, who fought for the rights of women and the poor in Argentina, however opportunistic her motives. One might also mention political leaders who had a devastating impact on their own countries or the world: Attila the Hun, Adolf Hitler, Joseph Stalin, Augusto Pinochet (in Chile), Ferdinand and Imelda Marcos (in the Philippines), and Saddam Hussein.

Part of the reason the subject is so interesting is that egos and ambition abound in political life, and the leading participants are usually involved in antagonistic relationships, either with colleagues or opponents. The daily oral question period in the Canadian and British Houses of Commons and in provincial legislatures is usually a great show. The prolonged animosity between Jean Chrétien and Paul Martin within the Liberal Party titillated Canadians for years, and Brian Mulroney is still fighting against the legacy of Pierre Trudeau.

The personal characteristics of political leaders, their personality conflicts, and the peculiarity of many of their decisions provide daily fodder for cartoonists, comedians, and satirical radio and television shows. Every daily newspaper features a cartoon on its editorial page, and more often than not such cartoons reflect the humorous (or tragicomic) nature of politics. To brighten and lighten up the material in this text, we have included throughout some of the best recent editorial cartoons. Canadians excel at political satire; two of the most popular television programs in the country are *The Royal Canadian Air Farce* and *This Hour Has 22 Minutes*. If you are not already familiar with these programs on CBC television, we strongly encourage you to give them a try.

While political events and personalities are interesting and often entertaining to observe, many people prefer to take an active part rather than passively follow political developments. Politics offers many exciting opportunities for participation. Joining a political party or interest group, collecting names on a petition, going to a public meeting to discuss an issue of political importance, getting involved in an election campaign at any level, or taking part in a political demonstration—all of these can combine meaningful political participation with camaraderie, excitement, and fun.

Sue Dewar/Artizans

Politics Is Important

More importantly, politics is important: it has significant implications for how we live our lives. At its core, politics is about government actions and **public policies** that affect everyone in one way or another. When we consider water policy in Walkerton, Ontario, environmental policy in the Alberta oil sands, or the American invasion of Iraq, for example, we can see that policies are often deadly serious. But there is even more to it than that. Because government actions and policies usually offer support for some people at the expense of others, they are normally accompanied by controversy and inevitably involve conflict. Such policy conflicts can be just as fascinating as the peculiarities of the individual policymakers involved.

Perhaps it is time to define the term *politics*. One of the classic and catchy definitions is Harold Lasswell's "who gets what, when, and how?"[1] Another widely used definition is that politics is "the struggle for power"; alternatively, we could call it the struggle for dominance or advantage. Lasswell adds that "the study of politics is the study of influence and the influential," the influential being those who get the most of what there is to get. Canadian-born political scientist David Easton defined politics as "the authoritative allocation of values for a society."[2] There is a good deal of similarity among these varied definitions, although they use different terminology. For example, to talk about the allocation of values is basically to discuss the distribution of things that are valued in a society. Such desirable things include money, goods, services, jobs, favours, health, education, security, comfort, freedom, and so on. These are the "what" of who gets what, when, and how. They are also the things of which those who are influential want to get the most.

We should reemphasize that at its core, politics involves a difference of opinion, a conflict, or interests that are opposed to each other. It does not arise where there is complete harmony between two or more individuals, two or more states, or two or more actors of any kind.

The other unstated premise here is that there is usually a desire to resolve such conflict, at least on the part of some of the actors involved. Politics is sometimes said to be "the art of the possible," or to be marked by compromise. Regardless of whether such a description is meant as praise or criticism, it is true that the public policies adopted are frequently designed to incorporate conflicting interests or to seek a middle ground. It is not always such a bad thing to develop a compromise policy that tries to bring together as many conflicting interests as possible, and it adds to the policy's legitimacy.

Politics thus seems to arise in a situation marked by conflict, in which attempts are made to resolve that conflict. Let us therefore define **politics** as "that activity in which conflicting interests struggle for advantage or dominance." In the context of government, we can add "in the making and execution of public policies." (The definitions used in this book are meant to be helpful to your understanding of the concepts involved, but you will likely encounter alternative definitions in other texts and from other authors.)

There is not much dispute about the idea that government should guarantee law and order in society by passing laws to make certain types of behaviour a crime and by hiring police officers and building jails. But beyond this basic consensus, political controversies immediately begin to arise. You may well have your own opinion on these matters. Does the Canadian government's antiterrorism legislation infringe upon civil liberties? Is it a crime to kill a severely disabled daughter, as in the case of Robert Latimer, or to demonstrate against the government, as in the case of some young people at the Quebec City Summit of the Americas who spent two months in jail? You may be hoping for a career in policing, and whether the government should hire more women and visible-minority police officers may be of personal interest to you. Should private companies be given contracts to operate jails? Should the penalty for murder be capital punishment?

It is usually assumed that national governments should establish armed forces to protect the country from external threats. But how large should such armed forces be? What kinds of armaments and equipment should be provided? Should the United States build a new missile defence shield that it claims will protect itself and its friends from the weapons of terrorists and "rogue" states? Should a country require military training of all its citizens, especially those about the age of most readers of this book? Even in the case of internal and external security—a seemingly straightforward issue—politics becomes quite complicated because there are many different and conflicting ways of proceeding.

Beyond the commonly accepted notion of providing for law, order, and security, the question arises as to whether the government should intervene in society any further. Generally speaking, government action was limited until about 1900; the extent of government intervention then increased over the first eight decades of the 20th century, but after 1985 or so it began to recede. In the early part of the 21st century, most governments seem to be less reluctant to spend or otherwise intervene, but if a government decides to get more involved, what form should such intervention take? We are all familiar with myriad government regulations that constrain individual, group, and corporate behaviour, for example, and with government programs that provide many kinds of services and money transfers to individuals, groups, communities, provinces, and corporations. In order to finance such regulation, services, and transfers, the government normally has to engage in taxation. Occasionally, though less frequently than in the past, governments go beyond regulation, services, transfers, and taxation; they actually buy or establish corporations and have them function as public- or state-owned enterprises. In Canada, these are called Crown corporations.

There is still virtual unanimity that government provision of a public education system is beneficial for society as a whole. But the consensus immediately breaks down around questions of what should be taught in such schools. For example, whether to teach evolution or creationism remains an issue for some people. This also leads to the question of whether there should be only one public education system or whether private institutions can be established. What about religious schools and home schooling? Should public funds be available for schools that are not part of the public system? As a recent secondary school graduate, you may well have opinions on these matters. Postsecondary education issues include the level of tuition fees, grants, and loans and the idea of private universities.

As costs escalate, the role of government in the provision of health services has also become particularly controversial. To what extent should there be a universal, public healthcare system, or what health services should people have to pay for outside that system: Chiropractors? Physiotherapy? Circumcisions? Eyeglasses? Should people who can afford it be allowed faster or superior service, as the proponents of the so-called two-tier system believe? Should the universal system be extended to cover pharmaceuticals and dental care? What about deterrent fees?

Education and health are two of the most expensive public services provided by governments today, but the array of other social services is also extensive, although far from unanimously supported. Should the government ensure that no one goes hungry, through initiatives such as public pensions for the elderly and disabled, child benefits, employment insurance, or social assistance? Should the government ensure that no one is homeless? Should single mothers who want to pursue postsecondary education be provided with childcare services? Should governments establish a reasonably priced universal childcare system, as in Quebec?

The preceding sketch of public programs leads to the question of how to finance the operations that government decides to undertake. Who should pay what kinds of taxes? Should there be a flat rate for everyone, or should richer people pay at a higher rate? Should all forms of income be taxed equally, or should capital gains, for example, be taxed at a lower rate? What about lottery winnings? Should business people be allowed to deduct entertainment expenses from their income tax? What about individual charitable donations, political contributions, and interest paid on loans to buy stocks and shares?

The implications of the issues just raised are of considerable importance. Political decisions on these issues influence, if not determine, what kind of lifestyle a person or a family may possess; they can certainly make life easier or more difficult, as you yourself, as a student, can attest. While they are significant, such decisions, actions, and policies rarely constitute matters of life and death in the generally comfortable Canadian context. Canada ranked first for seven consecutive years in the United Nations **Human Development Index (HDI)** in terms of life expectancy, literacy, and income, as Prime Minister Chrétien never tired of pointing out. By 2006, however, Canada had fallen to sixth place on the general index, and it ranked eleventh on the gender empowerment index and eighth in terms of reducing human poverty. Some of these statistics are revealed in Table 1.1.

When one looks beyond Canada and the other industrialized democracies, the decisions made by governments often have much more serious implications. Huge portions of the global population suffer from the insecurities of poverty, malnutrition, illness, and homelessness. In many cases, national governments might improve the situation with a fairer distribution of income, an internal political decision. Other cases require a helping hand from richer, industrialized countries. Many corners of the world are engaged in civil wars or military conflicts with external enemies, in which government decisions or terrorist retaliations put lives in danger daily. These include Afghanistan, Iraq, the neverending Israeli–Palestinian conflict, and many parts of Africa. In short, politics is a matter of life and death in a large part of the globe. The study of this important subject may serve as the first step in trying to solve such problems.

The Question of Citizenship Another aspect of the importance of politics revolves around the obligations of citizenship. Simply put, citizens of a democracy are expected to develop the best understanding they can of the political system in which they live, in return for the right of having a say in its governance. Studying politics is hard intellectual work that will make students better thinkers and better citizens.

The concept of citizenship has changed considerably over time. In ancient Athens, for example, citizenship was severely restricted, excluding women, labourers, slaves, and foreigners. But those propertied males who were citizens were expected to play a direct, almost full-time part in the governing of their city-state.

Early in the 20th century, in most civilized countries, women and the working class forced their way into becoming part of the electorate, and other exclusions from the right to vote were gradually eliminated. **Citizenship** became virtually universal, and it came to mean membership in a nation-state that entailed rights and responsibilities, including that of political participation. On

Table 1.1 Top 15 Rankings in Various United Nations Human Development Indexes, 2006

Human Development	Gender Empowerment	Least Poverty
1. Norway	1. Norway	1. Sweden
2. Iceland	2. Sweden	2. Norway
3. Australia	3. Iceland	3. Netherlands
4. Ireland	4. Denmark	4. Finland
5. Sweden	5. Belgium	5. Denmark
6. Canada	6. Finland	6. Germany
7. Japan	7. Netherlands	7. Switzerland
8. United States	8. Australia	8. Canada
9. Switzerland	9. Germany	9. Luxembourg
10. Netherlands	10. Austria	10. France
11. Finland	11. Canada	11. Japan
12. Luxembourg	12. United States	12. Belgium
13. Belgium	13. New Zealand	13. Spain
14. Austria	14. Switzerland	14. Australia
15. Denmark	15. Spain	15. United Kingdom

Source: United Nations, Human Development Report, 2006; available at http://hdr.undp.org/hdr2006/statistics; accessed October 25, 2007. © 2006 by the United Nations Development Programme. Used by permission of Oxford University Press.

the other hand, a very small proportion of citizens made political life a full-time preoccupation. The direct democracy of ancient Greece evolved into a representative democracy, in which periodic elections became the main focus of political activity for the general population. In an ideal case, everyone would at least cast an informed vote in such elections.

In the period between 1945 and 1985, often called the period of the **welfare state**, the concept of citizenship in industrialized countries changed again. Citizens came to expect the state to provide universal programs of social security to overcome the negative effects of economic uncertainty associated with private-sector market forces. After 1985, however, an increasing consensus developed throughout the Western world that citizens should be more self-reliant. Led by Margaret Thatcher in Britain and Ronald Reagan in the United States, the balance between individual and collective responsibility underwent a major shift, as governments balanced their budgets by dismantling social programs while also lowering taxes. In almost every state, the government plays a smaller role today than it did in 1985, be it in terms of regulation, ownership, taxation, or social services.

A rather dramatic development in such industrialized democracies as Canada, the United Kingdom, and the United States is the declining voter turnout rate in recent elections. Although this trend has many causes, it may be partially attributed to the fact that as the government becomes less involved in society, citizens decide that it is not as important to vote.

In this book, on the contrary, we take the position that governments continue to make a wide range of crucial decisions for society, even in the advanced, industrialized democracies such as Canada. Therefore, it is still an important obligation of citizens to cast an informed vote in elections, as well as to try to influence government decisions during the inter-election period. Studying politics is the most logical route to developing an understanding of our political system and of how to make an impact upon it.

Moreover, besides being a citizen of a specific state, we are all now citizens of the world, and we are all subject to unprecedented global forces. The question is often raised as to whether individual states are still as capable of providing for their own citizens as in the past. We are all affected by worldwide environmental developments, massive migrations of dispossessed people, and the concentration of capital in an ever-decreasing number of rapidly expanding **transnational corporations**. By studying politics, global citizens can help meet their obligation to understand as much as they can about the condition of the globe, and to do their part to try to improve it.

Political Science Graduates Get Jobs

But does anybody hire students who decide to study and graduate with a degree in political science? The answer is yes, and the diversity of the jobs would probably astound you. This book will introduce you to several young people who have gone beyond the introductory course to specialize in political science in Canadian universities and show you the range of their career experiences.

When you tell someone that you are studying political science, chances are they will jump to the conclusion that you plan to become a politician! That may well be your intention, and a noble calling it is, however much abuse politicians take in the media and in public discussion. Many political science graduates *do* become politicians, and many politicians are political science graduates. Speaking only of Canada, many of those elected to the House of Commons, provincial legislatures, municipal councils, and other political posts have graduated in this field. We give you the example of Keith Hutchings, a member of the Newfoundland and Labrador House of Assembly, in the introductory vignette to Part 5 of this text.

The number of politicians is fairly limited, however, and not all political science graduates can or want to choose this option. Many are employed as assistants to politicians, be they MPs, senators, members of provincial legislatures, or cabinet ministers. We have already presented the example of Deirdra McCracken as an example of a ministerial assistant. Very often, a period of employment in this capacity leads people to seek political office on their own, as in the case of Keith Hutchings.

Another career avenue is to work for the government—federal, provincial, or municipal. These three levels of government employ over a million people in Canada, and a good proportion of these employees are political science graduates. Such graduates typically work in management positions or are involved in policy development. That is, they advise on which policies should be pursued and work to implement these policies once they are adopted. Kathryn Royal, profiled in the introductory vignette to Part 4, is an excellent example. With government downsizing and privatization characteristic of the post-1985 period, few such positions have been available, but if you are graduating in the early years of the 21st century, your prospects are much brighter. In the next 10 years or so, governments at all levels will be replacing thousands of employees who have reached retirement age.

In addition to jobs at regular government departments, there are many employment opportunities in semi-independent government agencies, boards, commissions, and Crown corporations, such as Elections Canada, Statistics Canada, or indeed, the House of Commons or the Senate.

One aspect of government employment that many political science graduates find attractive is the foreign service—the diplomatic corps. Some people are particularly excited about the prospect of serving at embassies, consulates, or high commissions around the world and of advising on Canada's foreign policy. Once again, a degree in political science is the most appropriate entry to such a career, although a postgraduate degree in international relations and the ability to speak at least two languages is an additional asset. We give the example of Katrina Burgess in the introductory vignette to Part 7. Related to this career is work for an international organization, such as the United Nations, or for a **nongovernmental organization (NGO)**, such as Greenpeace, the Red Cross, Amnesty International, Oxfam, or others involved in Third World development.

In addition to NGO employees, many political science graduates prefer to work *close* to the government rather than *for* the government. They are employed by political parties, for example, as researchers, recruiters, organizers, policy advisors, and campaign managers. Political science graduates also possess the skills to seek employment in the media as radio, television, and newspaper reporters and commentators, or with polling firms, as public opinion

Public Service Goes on Youth Hiring Spree | BOX 1.1

In a bid to rejuvenate Canada's aging public service, the country's top federal bureaucrat has ordered the hiring of at least 3,000 new university and college graduates into full-time jobs by the end of March.

The recruitment drive, the biggest in decades, is a key piece of Privy Council Clerk Kevin Lynch's "renewal action plan" to help bring in new blood and groom the next generation of bureaucrats to take over from retiring baby boomers. . . .

About 40 percent of the public service is eligible to retire by 2011. More than half of all public servants are now between the ages of 45 and 64 and another 40 percent are between 25 and 44. . . .

SOURCE: Kathryn May, "PS goes on youth hiring spree," *Ottawa Citizen*, December 27, 2007, p. 1. Reprinted with permission.

and voting analysts. Another, related line of work is with interest groups, advocacy groups, and think tanks. In their attempt to analyze or influence government policy, these organizations also value the knowledge and skills acquired in the course of obtaining a political science degree. Some graduates actually establish their own lobbying and consulting firms, providing policy advice for a fee. Jonathan Ross, a freelance political commentator who has also established a political consulting firm, is profiled in the introductory vignette to Part 6.

Political science is also an appropriate background for a career in law. Although law schools welcome applicants from a wide range of disciplines, it is safe to say that they accept more applicants with political science degrees than from any other educational background. A large proportion of political science graduates from every university in Canada have gone on to law school.

Political science graduates can also become teachers. Some provinces hire political science graduates in their secondary schools, but all teach a certain amount of political science at the college level. Individuals dedicated to political science can also become university professors. We provide 13 examples in the form of contributing authors of this book!

So far, we have mentioned careers that put a premium on a specific *political* component, but political science is so broad in its scope and in the skills the graduates of this discipline develop that such a degree is valuable in a much wider range of occupations. Renny Khan, for example, whom we profile in the introductory vignette to Part 2, works as the International Relations Officer at the University of Alberta. Political science graduates also find a ready market in business—in corporations of all kinds, national and multinational, from banks and insurance companies to public relations firms. Alan Boras, profiled for Part 3, provides a wonderful example of a political science graduate who finds his degree of great usefulness as the manager of media relations in one of Canada's leading petroleum companies.

The political science curriculum that you are about to embark upon, both in this book and possibly beyond, will help to open your eyes to what is happening at home and abroad. You will be required to analyze public issues from a variety of points of view, and in the process you will learn to think clearly and communicate effectively. Your studies will also make you a valuable commodity to an array of employers whose focus is not strictly political. The Brock University Department of Political Science website once identified the skills acquired in pursuing a degree in political science; they are listed in Box 1.2.

You will often hear that in the modern world few people will retain a job with a single employer or even have the same kind of job with different employers until retirement and that you will have to be flexible in today's labour market. That is another way of saying that employers are not so much seeking job-specific abilities as skills that allow an employee to adapt to the changing workplace and the changing world. The skills listed in Box 1.2 will be among the most valuable of all in this exciting but unpredictable environment.

The Breadth of the Study of Politics

If we have convinced you that you are on the right track in thinking about studying politics, let us spend the rest of this chapter introducing the subject of politics. Let us show you the breadth of the field and the central concerns of the discipline, and let us provide greater proof that the subject is both interesting and important. We will do so in terms of the organization of this book.

Governments, States, and Nations

Governments, states, and nations have always been core subjects of politics, and remain so today. Part 2 of this book, incorporating Chapters 2 and 3, deals primarily with these three concepts. We will leave it to those chapters to define *state* and *nation*, but here we will connect the definition of **government** to that of politics, cited above. Government is the set of institutions and practices that makes and enforces collective public decisions for a society. Government is the body that decides who will get what, when, and how; government reflects the interests of the influential; government represents those who have succeeded in the struggle for power; government makes the authoritative allocation of values for a society. Although the two terms—government and state—usually go together, some governments in the world are not closely identified with a state. Thus, Chapter 2 elaborates on all aspects of government, including those that do not take the form of the government of a state.

Chapter 3 concerns itself to a great extent in distinguishing between states and nations and clarifying the concepts of nationalism and cultural pluralism. We seem to have moved from a world made up of nation-states, in which the population was quite homogeneous, to a situation where most states are characterized by ethnic diversity. The world has seen huge waves of migration in the past 50 years, leaving few states without the problem of accommodating a variety of cultural groups within them. In many countries, Aboriginal populations have also become much more self-conscious and assertive. Such cultural groups that exist within a society often wish to practise as much self-government as possible. This is true even in a traditional multiethnic state, the United Kingdom, as Scotland and Wales are granted more autonomy. The place of Quebec in the Canadian federation also comes to mind.

Typical Research Question: Will the various religious and ethnic groups within Iraq ever be able to work together in a common government, or should the country be divided into several small homogeneous states?

Political Values, Ideas, and Ideologies

Studying politics also means studying political values, ideas, and ideologies, and these concepts are the subject of Part 3 of this book, which comprises Chapters 4 and 5. Values, ideas, and ideologies can be seen as the inspiration for much of what takes place in the realm of politics, even when it seems to centre on more trivial issues.

Political Socialization and Political Culture Most citizens have certain political values and ideas whether they realize it or not. Where do these values come from? Political science uses the term **political socialization** to refer to the process of acquiring such values and ideas. Think about your own case: What are some of your own political values and ideas? Can you figure out where they came from? Common agents of political socialization are families, schools, peers, and the mass media, although there are many other sources.

Political science focuses primarily on those values and ideas that relate to the role of government in society. Figure 1.1 indicates an interesting difference of opinion on this role among Canadians of different party preferences. What this figure shows is that New Democrats are more committed to spending on social programs, while Liberals and supporters of the two parties that later combined to form the new Conservative Party of Canada emphasize reduction of the public debt. (The figure also indicates a subtle difference between those two partners.)

If we can find values and ideas that are widely held in any political system, we call such a collection the **political culture**. The politics of any society takes place within an often distinctive context of values and attitudes. Switzerland, for example, prefers to have citizens make many decisions by way of referendums. Chapter 4 deals with both political socialization and political culture.

Political Ideas and Philosophy Just as we can ask where an individual's basic values and ideas came from, so we can inquire about the origins of the basic concepts in the study of politics. This inquiry usually takes us back to ancient Greece. There we find philosophers such as Socrates, Plato, and Aristotle asking questions such as "What is justice?"; "What is the best form of the state?"; "Who should govern?"; and "What are the obligations of citizenship?" When

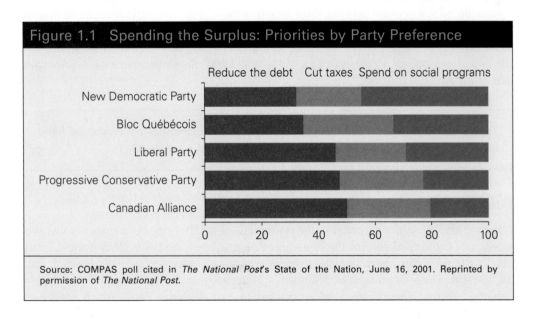

Figure 1.1 Spending the Surplus: Priorities by Party Preference

Source: COMPAS poll cited in *The National Post*'s State of the Nation, June 16, 2001. Reprinted by permission of *The National Post*.

you start to think about them, none of these questions is easy to answer, but the ancient Greeks were among the first ones to try.

Later on, other political philosophers added their thoughts on these and other questions. Machiavelli told us how he thought a prince should govern, and Jean-Jacques Rousseau, Thomas Hobbes, John Locke, and John Stuart Mill all contributed profound ideas about the relationship between the individual and the state and about the concepts of citizenship, equality, freedom, and liberty, among others. Even if these writers were not widely read by the general public, some of their ideas greatly influenced political developments such as the French and American Revolutions and the evolution of democracy. Similarly, Karl Marx's call for a working-class revolution to overthrow the alleged evils of capitalism had an enormous impact on the shape of the world in the 20th century. The ideas of subsequent political philosophers also influenced the way in which that century ended, and the new century will doubtless produce political philosophers of its own.

Studying politics, therefore, includes studying the ideas of the great minds that have addressed various concepts central to political thought over the centuries. It cannot be complete without examining what these thinkers had to say, and hence some of their views are discussed in Chapter 5.

Political Ideologies When a person or group holds a consistent set of ideas about the objectives of political life, we often call it an **ideology**. An ideology usually includes a collection of related thoughts on the respective roles of the individual and the government in the state. In the daily battle among politicians and among political parties, we expect their respective words, promises, and decisions to reflect a basic ideological framework. The labels we apply to such sets of ideas include liberalism, conservatism, socialism, communism, fascism, nationalism, individualism, collectivism, feminism, environmentalism, populism, and radicalism, among others,[3] and political scientists are always on the lookout to classify politicians and parties in terms of such ideologies.

It is often expected, for example, that democratic political systems will be characterized by two or more political parties with at least slightly different ideological orientations. In a two-party system, one party might emphasize equality and collectivism, while the other might favour individualism and privilege. In a three-party system, there might be a third party occupying a central ideological position between these two. In a multiparty system, there might be four or more parties, each claiming a narrow part of the ideological continuum: communists, socialists, social democrats, liberals, conservatives, neoconservatives, and so on. Even if such ideological clarity and consistency are often lacking in the real world, the subject remains an important part of the study of politics.

Typical Research Question: Do social democratic Scandinavian countries have models of healthcare policy worthy of North American emulation?

Political Institutions

Politics is also about the operation of the institutions of government. In fact, historically, this aspect was the very essence of the discipline. Although studying politics has a wider focus now, we must never forget that the ways in which government institutions function and the ways in which they might be reformed in order to operate more effectively are highly important topics. These subjects are contained in Part 4 of this book, which comprises Chapters 6, 7, 8, and 9.

Constitutions Government institutions are normally provided for in a state's **constitution**, which is the subject of much study in itself. In some countries, such as the United States of America, the constitution is a single comprehensive document. In contrast, as Chapter 6 of this book shows, the Canadian constitution is an unusual combination of written and unwritten parts.

Another interesting aspect of constitutions is the ease or difficulty with which they can be amended. The process of amending the Canadian constitution is rather complex, and after the experiences of the Meech Lake and Charlottetown Accords, we know that it is almost impossible to get agreement on comprehensive changes.

Most modern constitutions also contain some kind of bill or charter of rights that prohibits the government from interfering with the basic freedoms or liberties of its citizens. Canada added the Charter of Rights and Freedoms to its Constitution in 1982, but that did not mean that Canadians had no such rights beforehand. When there is a question about whether the government has overstepped its bounds, for example in curtailing freedom of expression in terms of terrorism or pornography, it is usually up to the courts or judiciary to decide the issue.

The Political Executive and the Bureaucracy The constitution normally establishes institutions that embody four branches of government: the executive, the bureaucracy, the legislature, and the judiciary. The **executive** branch of government usually consists of a head of state—a president or a monarch—who may be largely ceremonial, as in Britain and Canada, or imbued with great power, as in the United States or Mexico. In the case of a country with a ceremonial head of state, there is also an effective decision-making body, often called a prime minister and cabinet. As in the case of any organization, as you may know from your own experience, the executive provides leadership and makes many of the key decisions. Studying politics includes examining how such executive bodies function, including the question as to who *really* makes the big decisions in running a government.

Nobody expects those politicians who make up the executive branch of government to be able to solve all of society's problems single-handedly. For the most part, they are fairly ordinary mortals without a profound knowledge of the issues they are called upon to address. But in modern political systems, these politicians are assisted and advised by permanent, professional employees of the state whose job it is to be able to answer whatever questions the politicians ask. The members of the public service or **bureaucracy** advise the politicians on which policies to pursue and how to pursue them, and then administer the policies adopted. The bureaucracy is the largest branch of a 21st-century government, and no successful politician would go very far without asking the bureaucrats for advice. Studying politics therefore means spending considerable time in assessing the role of the bureaucracy in the policy process. Chapter 7 of this book examines both the political executive and the bureaucracy.

The Legislature Almost every political system has a legislative chamber made up of the elected representatives of the people, variously called the House of Commons, House of Representatives, Chamber of Deputies, etc. If chosen in free and fair elections, this chamber is a defining sign of a democracy. In some countries, including Canada, the members of the executive branch also sit in the **legislature**, but in others, as in the United States, they are separately elected. In either case, it is essential that the legislative branch give approval to laws, whatever their origin. Many Canadian members of parliament, feeling that they have little influence in the making of government policies, look longingly south of the border at the real power of members of the American House of Representatives and Senate. On the other hand, American observers often envy the efficiency with which the government of Canada can make decisions, at least in a majority government situation. Studying politics means examining legislative chambers and assessing the functions they perform, as well as understanding the logic of single-chamber and dual-chamber legislatures. These topics will be covered in Chapter 8 of this text.

The Parliament Buildings in Ottawa are the seat of the Government of Canada.

CP Photo/Peter Bregg

The Judiciary Ideally, every state should have an independent **judiciary**, a system of courts that aim to make impartial decisions when it becomes necessary to interpret the law in cases of dispute. Studying politics has not always involved paying much attention to judicial interpretation, but this may have been a serious oversight. Nowadays, the judiciary has become intensely scrutinized as an integral part of the political process. The courts seem to be making more significant decisions than previously, partly because most states have some version of a bill of rights that has to be interpreted. Are judicial decisions impartial? How should judges be chosen? When should they be removed? Such questions are discussed in Chapter 9.

Studying politics thus includes examining how presidents, prime ministers, cabinets, councils of ministers, houses of commons or representatives, senates, bureaucracies, and courts function individually and how they interact with each other. It involves looking for the strengths and weaknesses in each national set of government institutions and tackling the question of whether what has proved successful in one country might be adopted or adapted elsewhere.

Typical Research Question: In which states do the courts have most power to overturn decisions of elected politicians?

Political Behaviour and Participation

Many observers would regard political behaviour and participation as the most interesting part of the study of politics. Whether or not this includes you, these subjects are addressed in Part 5 of the book, which comprises Chapters 10, 11, and 12.

Voting and Elections In large part, politics is about political behaviour and participation. One main aspect of this domain is voting and electing candidates to public office. Politics is also about deciding what kind of electoral system to use, and nearly every country has a distinctive process to choose its politicians. Especially in countries where **elections** are free and fair (a characteristic of democracy), they are usually exciting, entertaining experiences. If you have not been involved in an election campaign, you might wish to track down a candidate and volunteer for action! Of course, you might even become a candidate yourself.

But elections are also very serious events, since the leader or the political party that emerges victorious can have a profound effect on the public policies later adopted. The winning party normally proceeds to reward its supporters, whether in the appointments it makes or in the policies it adopts. When George W. Bush succeeded Bill Clinton as president of the United States, for example, his reversal of many of his predecessor's policies had implications far beyond American borders: he reneged on the Kyoto Protocol, denied federal aid to groups that promoted abortion overseas, went to war in Afghanistan and Iraq, and generally threw American weight around throughout the world.

Since the **mass media** play a major role in the election campaigns in most countries, political science also studies the media. Do they give equitable coverage to all parties? Do they encourage an emphasis on image rather than substance? Does television advertising make elections too expensive and take away from their democratic character? Somewhat similarly, public opinion polls have come to figure prominently in election campaigns. Political science is interested in whether they are accurate, whether they favour one party over another, and whether they influence the results.

While being intensely interested in political participation, political science is also concerned with nonparticipation. As mentioned, the voter turnout rate in Canada, the United States, and the United Kingdom seems to be dwindling. Who is not voting, and why? Table 1.2 provides the voter turnout rates in selected countries in the post–World War II period, and in most cases the rate has decreased somewhat over this period.

Table 1.2 Voter Turnout Rates in 20 Selected Countries, 1945–2001

Country	Percent	Country	Percent
Australia	94.5	Greece	79.9
Belgium	92.5	Finland	76.0
Austria	91.3	United Kingdom	75.2
New Zealand	90.8	Canada	73.9
Italy	89.8	France	73.8
Netherlands	87.5	Spain	73.6
Sweden	87.1	Ireland	73.3
Denmark	85.9	Japan	69.5
Germany	85.4	U.S.A.	66.5
Norway	80.4	Switzerland	56.5

Source: International Institute for Democracy and Electoral Assistance, Voter Turnout Since 1945: A Global Report; available at http:// www.idea.int/publications/vt/index.cfm; accessed October 26, 2007. Reprinted by permission of International IDEA. These figures are based on percentage of registered voters who voted.

Political Parties Politics is also about **political parties**, which seem to crop up in virtually every political system. In most cases, candidates run for office on a party banner and as a member of a party team. Studying politics involves investigating the number of parties (one, two, three, or more) present in what is usually referred to as the party system. Political science is also interested in why established parties sometimes founder and why new parties form. In Canada, for example, we are interested in whether the Liberal Party will regain its traditional dominant position or whether we have moved to a new era of party competition with a stronger presence of Conservatives and Greens.

Studying politics involves examining how democratic political parties are organized, how they choose their candidates, how they choose or get rid of their leaders, and how they develop their policies. Has increased public financial support affected their operations?

All of these aspects of political parties are discussed in Chapter 11 of this text. Again, most parties would welcome your own participation, and you might even want to become involved in the creation of a new one.

Interest Groups and Social Movements Many people join together with others who share similar interests to establish organized groups. They may organize simply to promote their common interests without any thought of becoming political. But even if this is the case, such groups often find themselves drawn into the political process when they begin to see defects in government policies. Thus, countries that value freedom of association are characterized by hordes of **interest or advocacy groups** that at least occasionally try to put pressure on the government to change public policies. Other groups may be formed with a more deliberate political purpose, and they may spend most of their time trying to influence such policies. The Canadian Federation of Students (CFS), for example, provides certain services for its members, but it is concerned primarily with influencing the policies of federal and provincial governments that affect postsecondary students. More active participation in the CFS by a greater number of students would no doubt make it a stronger political force. On the local level, the student organization at your college or university may often function as a pressure group on your own campus.

The Summit of the Americas meeting in Quebec City in April 2001 attracted thousands of protesters from both Canada and abroad—often young people who could be said to be part of the antiglobalization movement. Similar **social movements** include the women's movement, the environmental movement, the gay and lesbian movement, and the animal rights movement, among many others. Studying politics also means studying such social movements, whether they operate in a single country or, as is increasingly the case, network with each other around the world. Possessing such resources as information and time, professors and students are often active in their communities in organizing demonstrations to articulate their opinion on contentious issues. Engaging in pressure group activity or protests can be a rather enjoyable social activity at the same time as it seriously tries to influence public policies that are felt to be detrimental. Interest groups and social movements are the subject of Chapter 12 in this book.

Typical Research Question: Do proportional electoral systems generally result in higher voter turnout rates and a larger representation of women and minorities?

Political Development and Change

At one point in time, studying politics may have been largely confined to studying political ideas, institutions, and behaviour in the advanced, industrialized, often democratic states. But it cannot be so restricted any longer. Today, the study of politics must include what is often called the

Third World or developing world, the concern of Chapter 13. Why are some countries rich and others poor? Why are some advanced and others underdeveloped? Is it a question of resources, distribution, or colonialism and exploitation? Should we expect every country to embrace the kind of democracy that we think is best? Perhaps the events of September 11, 2001 provided the most dramatic impetus for everyone to become more familiar with that part of the world.

As for political change, we seem to be seeing a general movement from nondemocratic to democratic regimes around the world. Is this really true, and if so, what are the factors behind this fundamental transformation? How are democratic regimes consolidated in such situations, and what are the consequences? On the other hand, is there any movement in the opposite direction? Another aspect of political change relates to questions of dissent, protest, rebellion, and violence, including terrorism and revolution. Why do some countries manage to change in a peaceful fashion, while others resort to radical, often violent change? These questions are addressed in Chapter 14.

Typical Research Question: Why are a number of Asian states undergoing massive economic development, while generally speaking, African states are not?

International Politics and Globalization

So far, we have concentrated primarily on domestic politics, that is, politics within any given country or state. But studying politics has always gone beyond the internal operation of individual states to include the international dimension. If we define politics as the activity in which conflicting interests struggle for advantage or dominance, then there is probably just as much politics involved between states as within them.

International politics has always been important, partly because conflict between states has often led to war, a dimension of violence usually much more serious than what is experienced within a single state. Studying politics involves examining the factors that lead to conflict between states and searching for mechanisms to moderate or prevent international violence, as shown in Chapter 15. The first half of the 20th century witnessed the two most horrible wars in human history, while the second half was dominated by the Cold War between the United States and the Soviet Union, in a kind of balance of terror. But if the Cold War is over, what are the new dimensions of international security in the 21st century? Was U.S. President George W. Bush correct in proposing that an expensive new missile shield was the best way to protect peace-loving states or that the United States should try to extend its brand of democracy throughout the Arab/Muslim world? Or is the war against terrorism, especially after September 11, 2001, more a matter of improving intelligence capabilities?

Finally, as we have mentioned, individual states in the 21st century are increasingly subject to the forces of **globalization**, the subject of Chapter 16. One aspect of globalization is that the global economy is increasingly dominated by huge multinational or transnational corporations. They operate around the world, have little or no allegiance to a specific state, and are often so mobile that they can move operations from one state to another. To minimize costs and maximize profits, such firms pressure the countries in which they operate to sign free trade deals with each other. Such agreements prevent the states involved from protecting their own interests and prohibit them from imposing barriers that would reduce the worldwide flow of the corporations' goods and services. Transnational companies also abhor taxation, ownership restrictions, and regulations such as environmental controls and labour standards. The 10 largest transnational corporations in the world in 2007 are ranked in Table 1.3 by total revenue. The annual revenues of some of these companies equal or exceed the total value of all goods and services produced (the gross domestic product) in many industrialized countries, such as Belgium ($370.8 billion), Switzerland ($367.0 billion), Sweden ($357.7 billion), Greece ($225.2 billion), Ireland ($201.8 billion), and Finland ($195.7 billion), not to mention most underdeveloped countries.[4]

Thus, pressured by such transnational corporations, organizations such as the World Trade Organization (WTO) and treaties such as the North American Free Trade Agreement (NAFTA) can force states to repeal laws and policies that favour their own companies and residents or that otherwise infringe the principles of the trade agreement. It is these aspects of globalization that are so controversial and that have led to violent clashes between demonstrators and police officers at many recent international gatherings.

Studying politics includes assessing the benefits and drawbacks of such globalizing forces, as well as inquiring about how much discretion states continue to possess in designing their own policies. Since up to now politics has been studied primarily in terms of the internal or external functioning of sovereign states, globalization requires quite a shift in our orientation. It raises the basic question of whether electorates can still hold their governments democratically accountable.

> **Typical Research Question:** What would be the consequences of enlarging the Security Council of the United Nations?

The Changing Nature of the Study of Politics

The study of politics is now a much broader enterprise than it used to be. Today it embraces the whole world, paying attention to developing countries as well as advanced, industrialized democracies. It now must contend with multinational states, that is, states that are no longer embodiments of a single ethnic group, language, or culture, but instead are characterized by cultural pluralism. In many cases, Aboriginal peoples are part of these pluralistic states, and in almost all cases, the question of gender is of increasing significance. Studying politics now must address questions of political change, especially the general move toward democracy in the developing world. At the same time, it must examine the breakdown of former multinational states (often called "state failure") and the role of rebellion, terrorism, and civil war. Finally, studying politics means coping with all the forces of globalization that impinge upon states as they try to make collective decisions for their own citizens. Who could deny that this broad undertaking is both fascinating and important?

Table 1.3 The 10 Largest Transnational Corporations in the World, 2007

Corporation	Revenues (millions of US$)
1. Wal-Mart Stores	351,139.0
2. Exxon Mobil	347,254.0
3. Royal Dutch Shell	318,845.0
4. BP	274,316.0
5. General Motors	207,349.0
6. Toyota Motor	204,746.4
7. Chevron	200,567.0
8. DaimlerChrysler	190,191.4
9. ConocoPhillips	172,451.0
10. Total Petroleum	168,356.7

Source: Fortune 500 Companies, Global Edition 2007. "Global 500: World's Largest Corporations," Fortune Magazine. Used with permission.

The Study of Political Science

Most university departments in this field call themselves **political science**, but some prefer the label *political studies*. This is a point that requires elaboration. Most teachers and researchers attached to the discipline believe that they should be as "scientific" as possible in the sense of searching for explanations, being as unbiased as possible, employing numerical measures wherever practicable, looking for causal relations between variables, and even enunciating theories. Few believe, however, that all aspects of the discipline can be subject to the same stringent "scientific method" standards as are practised in the natural sciences. You will regularly encounter the debate between political science and political studies if you proceed with further courses in the discipline.

In the process of discussing the breadth of the discipline, we have, to a large extent, already outlined the subfields within political science or political studies. Not every university department breaks the subject down in the same way, and many are changing their traditional organization. At least until recently, however, there has been a general consensus about the chart below. Studying politics involves examining most or all of these aspects of the subject, usually in specialized upper-year courses.

Political Science					
Canadian Politics	Comparative Politics	Political Development	International Relations	Public Administration	Political Theory

For people who are studying politics in Canada, one of the subfields of the discipline is obviously *Canadian politics*. If you were studying politics in another country, such as the United States or Britain, that country's politics would substitute as this first field. We have already seen the breadth of the discipline as it relates to a single state, as well as what is involved in the study of international relations. *Comparative politics* compares a number of states instead of concentrating on only one. *Political development* is essentially the study of the Third World or developing countries.

Studies in the stream called *political theory* begin with an examination of the evolution of political philosophy or political thought, and then branch out into various aspects of modern political theory and analysis. *Public administration* is often separated out from a study of national politics and concentrates on the operation of the bureaucracy and the policymaking process. This is probably a sign of the significance of the bureaucracy in the making of public policy.

Political science is, of course, one of the social sciences, and it can be easily combined with any of its cognate disciplines, such as political economy, political sociology, political psychology, or political geography (or geopolitics). Of these combinations, *political economy* is probably most common, as it studies the close connection between the political and economic realms of life. This connection can be seen at both the national and the global level.

Basic Concepts in the Study of Politics

One of the charms (or curses!) of the discipline of political science is that almost every concept is open to debate. Not everyone agrees on what the basic concepts of the subject are, and not everyone agrees on how to define them. Nevertheless, we do need a common starting point.

We have already defined "politics" as the activity in which conflicting interests struggle for advantage or dominance in the making and execution of public policies, and "government" as the set of institutions that makes and enforces collective public decisions for a society. The central concepts that emerge from these key definitions of politics and government are power, coercion, influence, and authority, so let us focus on these four terms.

Power is often defined as the ability of one actor to impose its will on another, to get its own way, to do or get what it wants. Such an imposition of will can be readily seen in the relations between states: for example, when Hitler's Nazi forces invaded Poland, or when Canada succumbed to American pressure to open up its magazine industry to foreign competition. Within a single state, we can witness a power relationship when a government extracts taxes from its citizens, imposes environmental controls on corporations, or rewards its friends. In all of these cases, those in a position of power impose their will, whether on another country, on society in general, or on individuals or other entities within that society. In Jean Chrétien's memoirs, he comments as follows on the question of power:

> To be frank, politics is about wanting power, getting it, exercising it, and keeping it. Helping people comes with it naturally, because you'll never be elected if you treat people badly. But no one will ever convince me, with all the experience I've had, that the motivations are strictly altruistic.[5]

Most political scientists are inclined to subdivide the concept of power into three parts.[6] The first kind of power is **coercion**, which involves threats of harm, penalties, violence, or punishment. This is the kind of power that Russia uses to put down separatist sentiment in Chechnya or that George W. Bush employed in spearheading an armed invasion of Afghanistan and Iraq. When the United States pressures Canada to change its policies on any matter, what is left unsaid is that economic penalties might follow if Canada resists. Coercion is also what Canadian governments do when the police break up a demonstration or when people are put in jail, or what governments in the United States do when they carry out an execution. While democratic countries are entitled to use coercion in imposing their will on dissident citizens, they are expected to do so only as a last resort.

The second kind of power is **influence**, which is usually seen as involving persuasion and voluntary compliance. One actor imposes its will on another by making arguments that the latter finds convincing. Within a single state, a bureaucrat tries to influence a minister to adopt a certain policy, a party member tries to persuade a party leader to resign, or the government pays for television advertising to try to convince smokers that it is time to quit. On the international level, the Secretary General of the United Nations appeals to the United States to pay the arrears in its dues, for example, and states regularly try to persuade each other to change their policies. It is now common in international relations to distinguish between "hard power" such as military threats and invasions, and "soft power," in which one state tries to persuade another of the superiority of its approach. It is often said that Canada has primarily relied on soft power in its foreign policy, at least in the past, and that the United States should follow our example.

The third aspect of power is **authority**. This is often called **legitimate** power; that is, one actor imposes its will on another because the latter regards the former as legitimate, as having a right to impose its will.[7] It is a kind of power that we have agreed to be bound by because it comes from a respected source; it stems from the acceptance of an obligation to obey. Such authority is particularly relevant to democratic governments because, having had a say (by way of elections) in who makes the decisions, citizens generally accept the decisions even when they do not entirely agree with them. When governments extract taxes, most people pay them, however reluctantly, because elected politicians have a right to make such decisions. To some extent, this kind of power is less evident at the international level, where raw coercion or hard power is more often apparent than it is in domestic politics. But even there, states have voluntarily joined a multitude of international organizations and made treaties with each other, and they usually respect the authority of such agreements.

We can witness power, coercion, influence, and authority in our daily lives in areas that do not necessarily involve government. The Mafia and other criminal elements, for example, are infamous for committing crimes and causing injury and death in order to impose their will. Parents sometimes resort to coercion by grounding their children in their room. Friends influence each other about what movie to see; transnational corporations try to influence what clothes we buy; and you yourself may have pleaded with someone to go out on a date. We obey our parents because we feel that they have a right to make certain decisions; we do what our bosses or union leaders demand because they are legitimately in control; and we follow the dictates of respected religious authorities. The "politics of the family," the "politics of the workplace," "corporate politics," "union politics," the "politics of religion"—all such activity may involve power, coercion, influence, or authority. Politics surrounds us! Everywhere we turn we see relationships involving power, coercion, influence, and authority.

Generally speaking, however, if for no other reason than to keep the subject within manageable proportions, it is advantageous to develop a narrower concept of politics for the purposes of this book. What political science is mostly interested in are the conflicts in society that need a society-wide, authoritative resolution and that result in the authoritative distribution of valued things. That is, in fact, what we mean by public policies: an authoritative distribution of things that are valued, such as wealth, freedom, and security.

In making and enforcing public policies, government draws on all three aspects of power: coercion, influence, and authority. Government has the ability to impose its will by means of sanctions or penalties, relying on the armed forces, the police, and punishments such as fines or jail. Indeed, as a general rule, *only* the government is allowed to use force or coercive power in society. But, especially in democratic societies, governments try to minimize their use of coercion in seeking compliance with their decisions. They would prefer to have citizens respond voluntarily, after they have been persuaded or influenced. Merely asking citizens, corporations, or other groups to refrain from smoking, from polluting, from discriminating, or from asking for too much money may sometimes have an effect, but such voluntary compliance is not usually effective.

That leaves authority as the leading ground on which democratic governments rely to impose their will. If the citizens have had a hand in choosing the government, if the government at least appears to listen to the electorate, if the government gives the impression that it is taking all interests into account in its public policies, then the people will probably feel that the government is legitimate and that they should abide by its authority. Canadians have been seen as particularly deferential to authority and are almost always ready to obey whatever policies the government adopts. Whether or not such deference is on the decline, as is now commonly claimed,[8] we are instinctively inclined to do what the government says because we have put it there and because we feel it has a right to make such decisions. Of course, we may also remind ourselves that if we disobey such policies, whether by speeding, stealing, or not paying taxes, the government can come down on us with coercive measures involving police, fines, and prison.

These definitions of politics, government, and power may betray a bias in favour of peaceful, domestic, democratic political systems. When political science turns its attention to such subjects as political change, political violence, state failure, and international politics, some of the wider definitions previously outlined may be more appropriate. There are many aspects of political activity, especially in relations between states, in which authority—agreement on who has a right to make collective decisions—is severely lacking. It may sometimes be more appropriate to revert to the idea of politics as a struggle for power or dominance, but in any case, we have now established a focus for our study of politics in this book.

This Book

This book seeks to meet the demand for an introductory political science textbook for the 21st century—fresh and yet classic in its approach. It aims to be a definitive introductory text, marrying traditional and contemporary approaches and appealing directly to the learning demands of modern students.

We have already outlined the basic contents of the book. Every effort has been made to provide a solid background in the traditional subjects, while at the same time offering material that covers emerging themes and issues in political science. Chapters that deal with these newer issues include Chapter 3 (Cultural Pluralism, Nationalism, and Identity), Chapter 13 (The Politics of Development and Underdevelopment), Chapter 14 (Regime Change in an Era of Globalization), and Chapter 16 (The Politics of Globalization). We wish to emphasize the cultural pluralism of most modern states; we try to promote a greater understanding of the Third World; we want to ensure that students are aware of the massive aspects of political change currently taking place around the world; we have included women's issues wherever relevant; and we insist that the entire study of politics be enveloped within the context of globalization. Yet going farther in unorthodox directions would probably have disturbed those who value the important material contained in the other chapters. We have tried to make the material relevant to Canadian students' lives with stimulating examples, and we are conscious of the fact that many of the students using the book will be relatively recent immigrants to Canada. We also profile a number of recent graduates in political science to show what kinds of careers they are pursuing and how their degree in this discipline got them to where they are today.

The chapters are intended to be discrete units, so professors who use this text can cover the material in a different sequence or omit certain chapters entirely. Nevertheless, we hope that the chapters jibe with each other, having certain common themes and coverage but minimal overlap. The book might be said to have a conceptual/comparative approach, working outward from Canada to other industrialized, developed democracies, then to the developing world, and finally to the global scene.

We have put considerable effort into the visual attractiveness of this text. These visual features—colour, photographs, cartoons, graphs, charts, and boxes of various kinds—will animate the material and allow an examination of alternative viewpoints. We have also tried to include many pedagogical features that make the book more interesting: learning objectives for each chapter; discussion questions; and web links. At the end of the book is a full-fledged glossary of all the key terms used.

For the benefit of professors selecting this text, we have also prepared an Instructor's Manual and a Test Bank, PowerPoint slides, and an accompanying video. There is also a book-specific website—http://www.studyingpolitics3e.nelson.com, supplemented by Nelson's comprehensive, general political science website.

In other words, this is a cutting-edge textbook, supplemented by helpful teaching materials and ready to meet the demands of 21st-century students and instructors.

CONCLUSION

This chapter has tried to show you that studying politics is both interesting and important, and that if you go beyond a single course, it also leads to jobs. The chapter has sketched the broad lines of the scope of the discipline of political science, outlined how the field is changing, and detailed its subfields. It concluded with definitions and explanations of some of the key concepts in political science, namely politics, government, power, coercion, influence, and authority.

DISCUSSION QUESTIONS

1. Think about your most recent personal experiences (unrelated to government) involving relationships of power. Did they involve coercion, influence, or authority?

2. Think about your most recent experiences involving government. Did any of them include aspects of coercion, influence, or authority?

3. Consider the question posed in Figure 1.1: How should government divide a budget surplus among cutting taxes, reducing the debt, or spending on social programs? Why?

4. In what kinds of political activity have you been engaged in the past, and in what kinds do you see yourself involved in the future? Why?

5. What do you think are the most pressing public issues facing Canada in the early 21st century?

6. What do you think are the most pressing issues facing the rest of the world?

KEY TERMS

AUTHORITY: The imposition of one's will on another by reason of legitimacy—because the subject regards the decision-maker as having a right to make such a binding decision. (22)

COERCION: The imposition of one's will on another by the use of penalty, force, or the threat of force. (22)

GOVERNMENT: The set of institutions and practices that make and enforce collective public decisions for a society. (12)

INFLUENCE: The imposition of one's will on another through persuasion and voluntary compliance. (22)

POLITICS: That activity in which conflicting interests struggle for advantage or dominance in the making and execution of public policies. (6)

POWER: The ability of one actor to impose its will on another, to get its own way, to do or get what it wants. (22)

WEB LINKS W W W

This book:
http://www.studyingpolitics3e.nelson.com

Nelson Political Science Resource Centre:
http://www.polisci.nelson.com

Government of Canada:
http://canada.gc.ca

Government of the United States:
http://www.firstgov.gov

Government of Mexico:
http://www.presidencia.gob.mx

The Globe and Mail:
http://www.globeandmail.com

United Nations:
http://www.un.org

World Trade Organization:
http://www.wto.org

FURTHER READING

Barber, Benjamin R. *Jihad vs. McWorld*. New York: Ballantine, 1996.

Bateman, Thomas, et al. *Braving the New World: Readings in Contemporary Politics*, 4th ed. Toronto: Nelson, 2008.

Chrétien, Jean. *My Years as Prime Minister*. Toronto: Knopf Canada, 2007.

Huntington, Samuel P. *The Third Wave: Democratization in the Late Twentieth Century*. Norman: University of Oklahoma Press, 1992.

Miliband, Ralph. *The State in Capitalist Society*. London: Weidenfeld and Nicolson, 1969.

Sens, Allen, and Peter J. Stoett. *Global Politics: Origins, Currents and Directions*, 3rd ed. Toronto: Thomson Nelson, 2005.

Simpson, Jeffrey. *The Friendly Dictatorship*. Toronto: McClelland and Stewart, 2001.

ENDNOTES

1. Harold Lasswell, *Politics: Who Gets What, When, How* (New York: Meridian Books, 1958).

2. David Easton, *The Political System: An Inquiry into the State of Political Science* (New York: Knopf, 1967).

3. Roger Gibbins and Loleen Youngman, *Mindscapes: Political Ideologies Towards the 21st Century* (Toronto: McGraw-Hill Ryerson, 1996).

4. Although the comparison between corporations and countries can be problematic, recent GDP figures can be found at "OECD in Figures, 2006–2007," available at http://www.oecdobserver.org/news/printpage.php/aid/1988/OECD_in_Figures_.html; accessed April 27, 2008.

5. Jean Chrétien, *My Years as Prime Minister* (Toronto: Knopf Canada, 2007), p. 2.

6. Mark O. Dickerson and Thomas Flanagan, *An Introduction to Government and Politics: A Conceptual Approach*, 5th ed. (Toronto: Nelson Thomson Learning, 1998).

7. Discussions of authority almost always centre on Max Weber's distinction among rational-legal, charismatic, and traditional authority. The first is based on rules, the second on personal devotion and trust, and the third on unwritten custom.

8. Neil Nevitte, *The Decline of Deference* (Peterborough: Broadview Press, 1996).

Part 2

Governments, States, and Nations

RENNY KHAN

Renny Khan is the Associate Director, International Relations and Recruitment (Europe) at the University of Alberta. Through collaboration internally with senior administration, faculty, and staff, and externally with organizations, foundations, and governments, Renny works to facilitate the international strategies and initiatives of the university.

Renny works to advance the university's strategic plan for the United States and Europe. He has played a key role in negotiating and implementing successful agreements between the University of Alberta and several leading European and U.S. institutions, and foundations, leading to the creation of innovative and successful research partnerships, visiting professorships, student fellowships, and innovative international curriculum. Over the past four years, Renny has served as project leader of a multisector provincial science and technology team to promote Alberta's national leadership in nanotechnology in Europe. In 2005, Renny received a European Union Visitors Award, co-sponsored by the European Union Commission and the European Parliament. In 2001, he also received an International Visitors Award from the U.S. State Department.

Renny joined the University of Alberta in 1999 after working in the United States/ Mexico Division of the Alberta Ministry of International and Intergovernmental Relations. He continues to work closely with governments, industries, businesses, and not-for-profit organizations to help ensure that institutional links result in comprehensive and long-term partnerships.

Renny holds a bachelor's degree in Political Science and History from McGill University, where he studied on an entrance scholarship, and a master's degree in International Relations from the University of Alberta.

Chapter Two

GOVERNMENTS AND STATES: Perpetual Works in Progress

Christopher G. Anderson

CHAPTER OBJECTIVES

After you have completed this chapter, you should be able to:

- discuss the general concept of government
- explain how classical scholars classified governments
- trace the evolution of the concepts of democracy and the state
- enumerate the principal features of the modern state
- discuss the principal features of democratic government
- discuss the principal features of nondemocratic government
- explain and exemplify forms of non-state governments
- identify the possible conditions and consequences of state failure

Introduction

Imagine a political system in which there is no government and no state, a society where everyone has an equal say over decisions that affect individuals, groups, or the full community, in which people hammer out the details of these decisions in person and on a regular basis. Although there have been repeated attempts throughout history to create such political systems based on the principles of **anarchy**, in which authority is not entrenched in established institutions and routine practices but rather is made to justify itself over and again, they have proved to be quite difficult to set up, much less maintain, and therefore have remained more of a philosophical ideal than a practical reality.[1] Instead, governments and states—structures of **governance**—have long been prevalent in the lives of human beings, locally, nationally, and even internationally.

Certainly, it is difficult to think about modern life without coming across the presence of governments and states. Consider what you do on a daily basis. The hour at which you wake up is defined, in part, by whether there is legislation concerning Daylight Saving Time. The ingredients in your breakfast are subject to bureaucratic regulation. The clothes that you wear were taxed by the state when they were purchased. The frequency with which the bus arrives to take you to university or work is affected by the level of public funding that the transit system receives. The list goes on. If you lived in a less democratic political system, the nature of government and state intervention in your life would probably be even more dramatic, censoring the news that you could read, limiting the range of jobs that you could hold, curtailing your ability to travel freely inside or outside the country, and—in the extreme—determining whether you live or die because of who you are and what you believe. No matter where we live, then, governments and states are fundamental and fundamentally important aspects of our very existence.

For this reason, they are an essential point of focus when we engage in studying politics, as you will see not only in this chapter but throughout the remainder of this book. In part we study governments and states because we want to understand why some things happen, and why others do not. In short, we hope to create and accumulate knowledge about the world around us. In doing so, we can become better informed as citizens, whether locally or globally, and gain the potential not only to interpret the world but to change it as well. Indeed, in studying governments and states, we soon learn that no political system is perfect, that each has strengths and weaknesses in varying proportions, but that all of them can be improved. Governments and states can be and often are powerful vehicles for positive change, but this seems at least to require that we constantly ask what they do, why they do it, and how they might do it better.

As we consider these questions, we will constantly encounter the fact that governments and states are often—and often quite justifiably—subject to considerable criticism. For example, in many of the long-established democracies of the world, including Canada, there is evidence of a **democratic deficit**, in which citizens feel that the actions of the government and the state do not meet their expectations, either in terms of the accountability of the political system to "the people" or its responsiveness to their interests. In nondemocratic regimes, where there are few mechanisms through which public opinion can be brought to bear on those who rule, serious concerns exist over the prevalence of human rights abuses. In some countries, there is talk of failed or failing states, where violent conflicts rage between state and non-state forces, and central governments are unable to provide even basic services in such areas as education and health. Sometimes such conflict is rooted in the demands of people who are looking to create their own state in order to meet certain group-based needs as part of a process of liberating themselves from oppression. At the global level, in turn, there are increasing discussions about the necessity—or even inevitability—of a system of **global governance** to bind governments and states more closely to a commonly derived set of laws and norms of behaviour.

In this chapter, we will explore these and many other features of governments and states at the outset of the 21st century, and it will be important to think of them as part of a broader historical process. Governing institutions do not appear before us wholly formed, and neither do they remain the same for very long—rather, they evolve within a variety of economic, social, and political contexts. In a global age, when the barriers between states are understood to be ever more permeable, the task of tracing such patterns of continuity and change has become all the more difficult and important. Moreover, in an increasingly interconnected world, we need to think more about the foundations of governing institutions and practices that differ from our own, that originate in alternate political traditions, such as those that predominate in China or Iran. A historical perspective will also serve to remind us that the institutions and practices under which we live are not set in stone, but have evolved and will continue to do so in myriad ways. As the Canadian political scientist Alan C. Cairns suggests, societies, governments, and states can be understood to be embedded in one another, both nationally and internationally, and an important aspect of studying politics is determining the nature of this embeddedness and its effects on politics.[2] While we cannot do justice to the sheer variety and complexity of forms this might take, we can establish some general terms and ideas to help us study governments and states in a more systematic manner.

Studying Governments

Human beings and **government** are related in close, complex, and enduring ways. Indeed, everyone in the world today falls under the purview of some governing authority. Even those who have been rendered stateless, or who live in one of the estimated 100 "uncontacted" tribes left in the world, fall within the ambit of one government or another, even if they are not aware of it! Because governments can affect most every aspect of our lives, the ways in which they are set up and in which we interact with them are multiple and complex. An important first step, therefore, is to make some sense of what governments do—their functions within the political system.

Let us turn to the work of the political scientist Gabriel Almond (1911–2002), who proposed a checklist of functions performed by any government: rule-making, rule-application, and rule-adjudication.[3] Although governments take on a great number of forms, they all share certain tasks involving the creation of rules, their implementation, and their interpretation, especially when there are disputes. Although Canadians and citizens of other democracies can readily connect these three functions with the three main branches of government—the legislature, the executive, and the judiciary—in many other political systems these functions may not be so clearly divided and allotted to such easily identifiable institutions. For example, in an absolute monarchy such as Swaziland, the king has complete power to make and unmake any rule and expects his orders to be implemented. Even among democracies, there can be significant differences in terms of how these functions are institutionalized, as can be seen in the contrasting cases of parliamentary (as can be found in Canada) and presidential (as can be found in the United States) systems, details of which can be found in Part 4 of this book, "The Structure and Operations of Government."

This diversity can be explained by the fact that each system of government has evolved within its own set of historical conditions and political traditions, some of which stretch far back in time. Indeed, in some parts of the world—such as China, India, and the Middle East—we can trace histories of government for several millennia. Thus, the forms that governments have taken, and the justifications that have been used to support them, have varied greatly over time, and continue to do so today. One way to appreciate this diversity at the outset of the 21st century, then, is to look back in time and to trace its roots.

Sue Dewar/Artizans

A Brief History of Government

Our knowledge of how people have been governed only really stretches as far back as the written word in human history. We can certainly speculate about what happened before that time—based, for example, on archaeological evidence or more contemporary forms of ancient tribal societies—but this leaves us with enormous gaps in our understanding of the economic, social, and political life of such communities, and of the institutions and practices through which they were governed. Even where written records and archaeological findings coexist—as they do for the first time with the Sumerian and Egyptian civilizations as early as c. 3500–3000 BCE (in what we today call the Middle East)—our knowledge remains quite impressionistic.[4] In both cases, we know that absolute monarchs with a mandate that was said to come from the gods ruled over large peasant populations with the support of a relatively small number of court officials and temple priests, as well as a select and well-trained staff of accountants and scribes. While some features of these early governments hold a certain familiarity for us in present-day Canada—there were, for example, repeated concerns over corruption and attempts at reform to improve the administration of government—there were also significant differences. Perhaps most importantly, these governments did not rule *for the people* but ruled *over the people* to ensure that they obeyed the gods. Thus, the people were subjects, not citizens, and they had little or no say over how they were governed. Although the precise configurations would change over time, and while new governments emerged, evolved, and disappeared in the Middle East (e.g., in Assyria, Babylonia, and Persia) and beyond (e.g., in present-day India and China), each presents us with a variation on this original form—**absolute monarchy**. It was not until the formation of the **republics** of ancient Greece that a radically different type of relationship between the rulers and the ruled appears in the historical record.

The Legacy of Government in Ancient Greece

Within the broad scope of the history of government, from the Sumerian city-states of 3500 BCE to the acceptance of the Republic of Montenegro as the latest (and 192nd) member state of the United Nations in 2006, the rise and fall of democracy in the Greek republics from about 600 BCE to 300 BCE constitutes a relatively brief moment in time—but it has nonetheless had a profound influence on how we think about and practise government in this day and age.[5] Most of the 1,500 or so city-states that existed within ancient Greece were already notable for having instituted and developed republican governments, in which subjects (at least some of them) were transformed into citizens who participated in collective decision-making for society. Thus, government in the Greek city-states had generally shifted from the palace of the monarch to the *polis*, which consisted of both the city (along with the lands surrounding it) and its citizens. This was in and of itself a radical break with the past. The Greeks, however, also originated the word as well as the practice of democracy, both of which have come to permeate the political world today, albeit with a number of important modifications. Although it is quite possible that governments with democratic features had existed prior to this time, it is with the ancient Greeks that we first see it named, described, analyzed, debated, and even celebrated (see Box 2.1).

In broad strokes, the institutional arrangement of the *polis* consisted of an executive, a select council, and a general assembly, and as democracy took hold, decision-making increasingly shifted toward the Assembly. For example, in Athens, which was considered to be the centre of democratic life in ancient Greece, all citizens could participate in the Assembly, where they could discuss and judge proposed legislation, decide questions of war and peace, and, indeed, debate any issue they deemed proper.[6] Moreover, they might be chosen by lot to participate in the select Council of 500 or the Law Courts. Although similar to modern democracy in privileging the voice of "the people" in the political process, this was nonetheless a very different democracy than that which we find in the world today in a number of important respects. First, it occurred on a much smaller scale: at the height of democratic Athens there were perhaps 30,000 citizens, and only a few thousand would take part in the meetings of the general assembly or would be selected by lot each year to serve as potential jury

In *The History of the Peloponnesian War*, Thucydides (460–395 BCE) recounts a speech given by Pericles (495–429 BCE), who ruled in Athens for more than 30 years, in memory of those who had died during the first year of what would become a 27-year war between Sparta and Athens.

> *Our constitution does not copy the laws of neighbouring states; we are rather a pattern to others than imitators ourselves. Its administration favours the many instead of the few; this is why it is called a democracy. If we look to the laws, they afford equal justice to all in their private differences; if to social standing, advancement in public life falls to reputation for capacity, class considerations not being allowed to interfere with merit; nor again does poverty bar the way, if a man is able to serve the state, he is not hindered by the obscurity of his condition. The freedom which we enjoy in our government extends also to our ordinary life. There, far from exercising a jealous surveillance over each other, we do not feel called upon to be angry with our neighbour for doing what he likes. . . . But all this ease in our private relations does not make us lawless as citizens. Against this fear is our chief safeguard, teaching us to obey the magistrates and the laws . . . whether they are actually on the statue book, or belong to that code which, although unwritten, yet cannot be broken without acknowledged disgrace.*

SOURCE: Robert B. Stassler, *The Landmark Thucydides: A Comprehensive Guide to the Peloponnesian War* (New York: Touchstone, 1996), 112.

members, and just a few hundred would serve in various public posts. Second, citizen involvement was much more extensive and intensive—this was **direct democracy**, in which citizens were expected to participate as rulers as well as the ruled within the political system. Third, citizenship was limited to adult males whose parents were both Athenians, thereby excluding some 220,000 foreigners, women, slaves, and children. Furthermore, just because the *polis* was democratic did not mean that everyone agreed it was the best system of government (indeed, it was overthrown for a period in Athens), and while the historian Thucydides provides us with a glimpse of the pride democracy could engender in its advocates, it was not uncommon to hear it denounced as a dangerous form of government.

Although numerous figures from ancient Greece discussed and wrote on the nature of government (along with Thucydides we could add Sophocles the playwright and Plato the philosopher, for example), Aristotle is generally understood to have provided the first (or at least the most) systematic analysis of the different forms of government known to the Greeks during this period. In *The Politics*, he famously states that "man is a political animal in a sense in which a bee is not, or any other gregarious animal," because men possess a "power of speech" that allows them "not only to feel pleasure and pain but to communicate these feelings to each other."[7] As a result, they have a unique ability to consider what is right and what is wrong, what is just and what is unjust, and do so to greatest effect in association with one another. While this leads Aristotle to claim that government is, therefore, a natural phenomenon—indeed, that it is the means by which men can not only live but also pursue the "good life"—there remains the vital question of which form of government is best.

To address this issue, Aristotle undertook a political analysis to determine which form was most likely to produce the stability required for the contemplation and achievement of the good life. He did so by collecting the political constitutions of 158 city-states and then organizing and comparing them across certain core characteristics. Specifically, he separated his cases according to whether they were defined by the rule of one, a few, or the many, and then he distinguished between systems in which those in power ruled in the common interest from those in which they ruled in their own particular interests. This produced a sixfold classification (see Table 2.1) from which—after having considered the nature of the cases in each—he drew a number of conclusions. While democracy was not considered by Aristotle to be the worst form of government (this was tyranny, which replicated a master–slave relationship between ruler and ruled), neither was it the best, because it was prone to instability when demagogues courted popular support against the wealthy few, eventually leading to an **oligarchy** as the rich seized power and governed to protect their own interests. Aristotle did, nonetheless, speak of the need to incorporate democratic elements into any stable system of government. As for monarchy and **aristocracy**, they were ideal forms only when controlled by people truly able to define and reflect the common interest. However, when this was not the case, these forms were likely to slide into tyranny and oligarchy. Instead, Aristotle pointed to the benefits of a **polity**, with the rule of the many, on the grounds that its deliberations were more likely to reflect the common interest consistently over time: "As a larger amount of water is less easily polluted, so the multitude is less easily corrupted than the few."[8] Thus, Aristotle saw in a polity the potential to balance the interests of the many who were poor with those of the few who were wealthy, integrating the best features of both oligarchy and democracy, and thereby increasing the likelihood of political stability.

Because of the systematic way he approached the study of government—as a comparative examination of political institutions—Aristotle's work is often seen as an early example of political science in action. Moreover, as was the case with other Greek thinkers of the day such as Plato, the vocabulary he employed and the ideas he explored have influenced political thinkers through the ages to the present. As just one example, we can look at the term *oligarchy*. Robert Michels (1876–1936), a German sociologist, was confronted with an important puzzle when he noticed that all the political parties that he studied—even those that were democratically structured—wound up being dominated by party leaders. In an effort to explain this, he proposed the existence of an "iron law of oligarchy," in which all organizational forms eventually become oligarchic, not simply because leaders seek to consolidate their power but also because those who are led permit them to do so, among other factors. This idea, while it seeks to explain a particular aspect of organizational behaviour, speaks directly to the study of governments and states, especially those that are democratic, for it challenges the idea that modern democracies are simply based in the will of the people and suggests instead that power may more often reflect the narrower interests of leaders and political parties.

Table 2.1 Aristotle's Typology of Government Forms

	RULE IN THE INTERESTS OF:	
Number of Rulers	**All Citizens** (common interests)	**The Rulers** (particular interests)
One	Monarchy	Tyranny
A few	Aristocracy	Oligarchy
The many	Polity	Democracy

Other Ancient Government Traditions

What is most surprising about ancient Greek democracy is not that it ended, as the various city-states were eventually subsumed within the expanding power of Rome around 150 BCE, but that it so completely disappeared as a form of political organization for centuries before rising to such prominence in the recent past. While Rome itself emerged with a republican form of government, it would never be a democracy but would perhaps resemble more an oligarchy, with an elite dominating public affairs, before taking on a more tyrannical form with the arrival of emperors claiming to descend from the gods. Nonetheless, Rome also left its mark on the subsequent development of government, initially at least in Europe. Aside from providing the staging ground for the eventual expansion of Christianity as a major religious and political force in the world, the Romans developed complex systems of both public and private law—the former giving definition to government, and the latter setting out rights and obligations between persons—that were both secular and rationally developed. As well as contributing to the expansion of the legal profession, this began the process of transforming government from something personal (i.e., embodied in a monarch or particular individuals) to something more abstract. Thus, the essence of political authority was increasingly seen to exist in the laws, rather than in the individuals who participated in collective decision-making. When European nation-states began to emerge in the 16th century, they would draw considerably upon this tradition.

However, with the decline and eventual fall of the Roman Empire from about the 5th to 7th centuries, political life in Europe generally became quite fragmented and local, while alternative forms of political organization elsewhere in the world thrived, some of which continue to shape the nature of governments and states, and thus politics, at the outset of the 21st century. For example, the roots of Chinese political life can be traced back thousands of years to around 2000 BCE, after which time it became one of the most developed and durable forms of political organization until the late 18th century. By the time of the Han dynasty (206 BCE–220 CE), the basic contours of a form of government that combined an absolute monarchy with a Confucian system of belief were in place, from which have evolved a number of democratic and nondemocratic governments in East Asia today (see Box 2.2).

Confucianism is not a religion or a systematic code of law, but instead is rooted in a set of ethical assertions originating with the Chinese sage or philosopher Confucius (551–479 BCE) concerning the correct ordering of society, and therefore of politics as well. According to the teachings of Confucius, the best way to achieve social harmony, and therefore the best form of government, is through rituals that reflect and reinforce ordered and hierarchical relationships—between government and the people, between parents and children, and between friends, for instance. Those in positions of authority are duty-bound to lead by example and to care for those under their charge, while those subject to such authority are obliged to revere and obey those in command. As opposed to the ancient Greeks, then, there is no sense of individual equality or political power residing with the people; at the same time, the power of the rulers was much more clearly articulated than was the case in other monarchical systems of the day. In part, this stemmed from another distinctive feature of government in China, which was the elevation of scholars into the highest ranks of social and political life on the basis of merit, which provided them with a relatively privileged position from which to influence decision-making. In comparison, the idea of a merit-based bureaucracy would not really take hold in the West until the 19th century—some 2,000 years later. Of course, the history of Chinese government reveals periods of both relative stability and instability (both through civil war and external conflicts), and many Confucian ideas were explicitly rejected with the rise to power of the Communist Party in 1949. Nonetheless, in recent years, they have

Although there is a tendency in the West to see liberal-democratic traditions as providing the key to successful economic and political organization, other traditions continue to prevail in much of the world, some of which—such as Confucianism—can also lay claim to having achieved considerable accomplishments in these areas.

The East Asian countries that have been strongly influenced by Confucianism . . . offer an interesting variation on the theme of halting development in the so-called Third World. Consider how they have fared as regards the three modern challenges of unity, prosperity, and democracy. First, all the Confucian countries of the region, including massive China as well as the smaller societies of Taiwan, the two Koreas, Vietnam, and Singapore, have succeeded in establishing powerful, centralized bureaucratic states under-girded by robust national sentiments. Second, many of them have succeeded, often dramatically, at the task of generating economic growth: Taiwan, South Korea, and Singapore have become famous as "tigers" while more recently China has been astonishing the world in this field. Third, South Korea and Taiwan have not only maintained stable governance and economic development, but have made full-fledged transitions to democracy. . . . If one puts Japan back into the picture, it becomes apparent that, aside from Western Europe and the lands of its wider historic ambit, no region has been more successful than East Asia when it comes to achieving political and economic modernization.

SOURCE: Quotation from Chae-bong Ham, "The Ironies of Confucianism," *Journal of Democracy* 15(3) (July 2004): 93–94.

experienced resurgence, as an emphasis on harmony and order, as well as hierarchy and responsibility, have been seen to offer the possibility of a greater sense of certainty as China undergoes a massive social upheaval with its rise to prominence as one of the foremost economic and military powers in the world today.

Elsewhere, with the emergence and consolidation of Muhammad (570–632 CE) as a prophet and political leader at the outset of the 7th century, the roots of a new religion and a new form of political organization took hold. From its origins in present-day Saudi Arabia, Islam rapidly spread within 100 years to encompass the Middle East, Northern Africa, parts of South and Central Asia, as well as Portugal and Spain, and in doing so it provided the foundations to one of the most extensive empires in human history. Although the Empire of the Caliphate lasted for just about 250 years (c. 630–870 CE), it has had a profound influence on politics and government in these regions of the world and beyond through to the present. This can be seen in the fact that there are today nearly 50 countries in the world in which Muslims represent a majority of the population, mostly in the Middle East, Northern Africa, Central and South Asia, and Southeast Asia, constituting almost a third of the world's population, and a number of these countries—such as Indonesia and Mali—are relatively stable democracies. Probably the most distinctive feature of Islam's influence on government has been the role of

sharia law, which—as the command of God—regulates aspects of both public and private life, including features of worship and interpersonal relations. Since its inception, the existence of sharia law, and the role of religious scholars in interpreting its meaning, have raised a question of great political significance, namely, that of the appropriate role for a political governing authority. In practice, from the Empire of the Caliphate to modern-day Islamic republics such as Iran and Pakistan, this issue has not been easy to settle: should a more secular political authority exist, and, if so, should its authority be higher than or merely different from that of religious authorities? As with political systems based on Confucianism, there have been periods of relative stability and instability in the Islamic world over time, but we can certainly contrast the often high degree of sophistication of its government forms up until the 17th century with those prevalent in Europe during these centuries.

European Nation-States

Indeed, the contrast with Europe (with the exception of the Byzantium Empire, which from its base in Constantinople would last almost 1,000 years as an absolute monarchy after the fall of the Roman Empire) was stark. It was not really until the late Middle Ages that government began to coalesce around a series of feudal kingdoms on the continent, which despite their diversity shared several common characteristics. Although the pinnacle of political authority resided with kings, they depended very much on the support of local landholders, who were powerful and armed, and who could choose with whom they wished to align themselves. Within such a relatively decentralized system of power, towns came to take on a greater role, often acting as essentially self-governing republics. The general population had, however, reverted from being citizens to become subjects of their respective feudal lords. Alongside this secular system of political organization, Christianity was becoming an integral thread in the weave of political life in Europe during this period, as the Catholic Church worked hard to carve out and develop a political space for itself that was superior to that of kingly governments, representing—in the person of the Pope—a higher authority. Thus, the Middle Ages were defined by a complex and evolving patchwork of relations of authority, responsibility, and rights, and it was far from democratic. Indeed, it was only in a few small areas, such as a handful of Swiss cantons, that democracy could be found.

Nonetheless, within a few centuries, key features of modern democratic government would emerge and challenge the political authority of established monarchies as well as the papacy, and a new form of political organization—the **nation-state**—would appear. This would occur at a time when European governments were beginning once again to become active on the world stage, and when European society was experiencing an incredibly dynamic period of economic, social, and political development. It is difficult to do justice to the breadth and speed of the changes that took place in Europe from the 14th to 18th centuries. With the rise of Protestantism, the religious and political authority of the Catholic Church came under attack. When combined with a new age of secular thought that blossomed throughout the Reformation and Renaissance, radical transformations took place in terms of how the authority of governments was conceptualized. This process was facilitated by the invention of the printing press, which resulted in the widespread debate of competing economic, political, religious, and social ideas. The emergence of capitalism and industrialization, urbanization, and a period of rapid technological development in such areas as transportation and weaponry can be added to this mix, which facilitated both commerce and conquest. Indeed, during this period European governments began not only to centralize and institutionalize their authority as nation-states, but also to expand their economic and political ambitions vis-à-vis the rest of the world, and by the 19th century much of Africa, the Americas, and South and Southeast Asia would come under their control under the aegis of **colonialism**. Altogether, this constituted perhaps the most rapid and extensive spread of political ideas and influence since the Empire of the Caliphate.

Nowhere was this perhaps more apparent than in 17th-century England. A number of ingredients came together to challenge the domination of the English political scene by the monarchy. First, the enclosure movement produced profound changes in English society. Landlords were allowed to "enclose" or fence off lands that had been formerly available for public use, so that they could be used for increased agricultural production. This "tragedy," as it is referred to by some historians, forced the displacement of people from the country to the city centres of England, providing a ready-made working class for developing industry. Indeed, it was through this process that the seeds of the Industrial Revolution were sown in England. Second, the new entrepreneurial or bourgeois class began to oppose the power of the monarchy to tax and to control lands at will. As their demands for the greater protection of their private property increased, so did the tensions between them and the landed aristocracy, who had long benefited from close proximity to the crown. As they mobilized against one another, and vis-à-vis the crown, the origins of the party system that defines modern democratic government can be seen. Third, religious toleration became socially and politically acceptable. The uncoupling of England and other emerging nation-states from the power of the Catholic Church in Rome led to an increasing awareness of the power of new ideas. Along with this spiritual liberation came a scientific liberation that assisted in shifting attention away from the divine right of kings and toward the terrestrial and rational interests (individual and collective) of the population.

These ingredients came together to form a new political culture, one that the traditional political institutions associated with the monarchy could not represent. Although the power of the crown had been circumscribed—and many of the rights of the people asserted—through the *Magna Carta* as early as 1215, it would take centuries for the institutions and practices of government to reflect more accurately this shift in power. The calls and struggles for political reform that emerged from both workers and the bourgeoisie from the 17th century onwards, and that were encouraged by the air of toleration and liberation of the times, put into motion a series of important parliamentary transformations. The concepts of representative democracy, free speech, the right to rebel against a bad government, freedom for the accumulation of profit, human rights—all of which are now the hallmarks of our modern systems of government— were reborn in a political renaissance that owed its inspiration to the ancient thinkers and its innovation to a new intellectual class that embodied the values of the new age of democracy. A prime example would be John Locke, a philosopher and activist whose ideas would be reflected in both the American Revolution and its *Declaration of Independence*. In his *Two Treatises on Government*, Locke contested the notion of the divine right of kings, and argued instead that against the uncertainty inherent in a "state of nature," a people will submit to government as long as it is directed toward "the mutual preservation of their lives, liberties and estates, which I call by the general name, property."[9] When such property rights were not respected, however, Locke argued that the people had the right to rebel against the government—that is, the right of **revolution**.

Two of the most significant political revolutions of the period were those that took place during the late 18th century in the American colonies and France, respectively. In each, a fiery rhetoric arose in which the rights of citizens within and over the government were to be placed at the foundation of the political system (see Box 2.3). Moreover, as can be seen in the American case in particular, this was to be a democratically elected government, a notion that resonated with the democracy of the ancient Greeks but also altered it in significant ways. On the one hand, the commitment to what Abraham Lincoln would one day call in his famous Gettysburg Address "government of the people, by the people, for the people" harked directly back to the ideas of the Greeks, as did the notion that only a select group of citizens (in this

BOX 2.3

The American *Declaration of Independence* of 1776 is quite a radical document, both for its time and in the present day. Building on the ideas of philosophers such as John Locke, its authors provided a justification for the removal of any government that did not adequately reflect the people's will:

> We hold these truths to be self-evident, that all men are created equal, that they are endowed by their Creator with certain unalienable Rights, that among these are Life, Liberty and the pursuit of Happiness.—That to secure these rights, Governments are instituted among Men, deriving their just powers from the consent of the governed,—That whenever any Form of Government becomes destructive of these ends, it is the Right of the People to alter or to abolish it, and to institute new Government. . . .

A similar commitment to the sanctity of political rights can be seen in the French *Declaration of the Rights of Man and of the Citizen* of 1789:

> Law is the expression of the general will. Every citizen has a right to participate personally, or through his representative, in its foundation. It must be the same for all, whether it protects or punishes.

case, property and/or taxpaying white males) should participate. It was radically different, however, in two related ways: first, it was to be a large-scale political system, and second, it would be based on indirect or **representative democracy** rather than direct democracy. Thus, the vast majority of citizens would be ruled but not rulers as well. Although it would take some time, democratic forms of government would increasingly take hold in Europe after the American and French revolutions, and while the paths would vary considerably, they would all exist within a new form—the nation-state.

Studying States

Just as it is difficult to imagine modern life without governments, it is hard to overlook the presence of states in our world, especially when we discuss international politics. However, the historical survey undertaken in the preceding pages underlines the point that the world has not always been organized into a system of states. Indeed, for centuries—millennia, even—vast areas of the globe were left relatively unstructured in political terms, even during the rule of some of the most highly developed governments of the ancient world. This began to change with the emergence and expansion of European nation-states from the 17th century onwards, although, as will be seen further below, a degree of uncertainty remains to this day. What, then, are the basic features of a state?

First and foremost, a **state** needs a constitutive population; there must be a people over which rulers can rule. In the contemporary period, we can point to the need for there to be a body of citizens whose status as such links them to a particular state, creating unique ties of responsibilities and rights between them. Often, the people are seen to be the equivalent of a **nation**, but in reality very few states have ever existed within such a singular ethnocultural environment (although some, such as Iceland, North and South Korea, and Portugal, probably come close). For example, at Confederation it was understood that four national cultures made up the Canadian people: English, French, Irish, and Scottish. It is now generally accepted that numerous Aboriginal peoples also existed as nations at that time, even if they were not recognized as such, while the process of immigration has produced a reality of diversity—or **multiculturalism**—that is now thought to give definition to what it means to be a Canadian. In other parts of the world, colonialism and the subsequent process of decolonization often resulted in borders being drawn in such a way as to create numerous multiethnic if not **multination states**, sometimes with tragic consequences. For example, while a range of economic, social, and political factors can be drawn on to explain the 1994 genocide in Rwanda, during which an estimated 800,000 Tutsis were killed by Hutus within a period of about 100 days, as hundreds of thousands more fled to neighbouring countries as refugees, the uneasy coexistence of these two groups both during and after the colonial period that preceded the country's independence in 1961 remains a central factor. The politics of national identity, then, can affect both the behaviour and the form of a state.

Second, a state also requires an established territory over which to govern. Although conflicts have probably always arisen over land, it is only relatively recently in human history that set boundaries have become such a defining feature of political organization. We can trace this at least as far back as the *1648 Treaty of Westphalia* that brought an end to the Thirty Years' War in Europe, which was fought against the backdrop of the competing religious claims of Catholicism and Protestantism. One of the major outcomes of the treaty was the principle that each ruler could determine the religion for the territory over which he or she ruled. It followed, then, that a ruler would no longer need to submit to an external religious or political authority. Thus, the **sovereignty** of the state became a legal condition, with political authority being embedded in domestic political institutions and practices. This has not, however, resulted in an absence of disputes over just where the precise boundaries lie between various sovereign states of the world. Indeed, even Canada still has a number of unresolved maritime boundary disagreements with the United States (in the Beaufort Sea, at the Dixon Entrance between Alaska and British Columbia, and in the Strait of Juan de Fuca between Washington State and British Columbia, as well as around Machias Seal Island and North Rock, both of which lie between Maine and New Brunswick). More recently, the issue of Arctic sovereignty has come to the fore in Canadian politics, as Canada, the United States, Denmark, Norway, and Russia all lay claim to parts of the Arctic (see Box 2.4). While many border disputes are maintained or resolved peacefully, others can explode into violence, as occurred in 1982 when Argentina forcibly occupied the Falkland Islands in the South Atlantic Ocean, which had been under British control since their own forcible occupation in 1833. By the time the British subsequently retook the islands, 900 combatants on both sides were dead.

Third, a state requires a range of political institutions to govern the population within its territory. As noted at the outset of this chapter, these are often associated with the rule-making, rule-enforcing, and rule-adjudicating tasks of governance. In order for such functions to be undertaken in a well-ordered manner, a capable **bureaucracy** (or civil service) is required, some form of public administration that can advise decision-makers on policy and both interpret and implement their decisions. While the politics of a given country will give more precise definition to the purposes to which such activities are turned, at some general level there is an expectation that a sovereign state will possess the appropriate institutions and use them at least to meet the needs of (and thereby act on behalf of) the people. All states, however, will tend to claim to have the interests of the people at heart, when clearly there are instances where this is not true. As a result, greater attention has been turned recently to the question of what responsibilities states have to their own citizens, and whether under certain circumstances the international community ought to take it upon itself to violate the sovereignty of a state to protect the people from that state. This debate over the international community's "responsibility to

As long as it remained frozen, it seemed possible to contain Canada's long-standing disagreement with the United States over who had sovereignty over the Arctic, especially the Northwest Passage. As with other border disputes between the two countries, they had, since the 1988 Arctic Co-operation Agreement, more or less agreed to disagree for the time being. More recently, however, a number of other states have begun to weigh in more heavily with claims of their own. Although Canada's 2005 diplomatic dispute with Denmark over who controls tiny Hans Island (which lies between Ellesmere Island and Greenland) often generated amusement if not bewilderment, Russia's 2007 decision to lay a flag on the seabed floor beneath the North Pole was seen by many as an aggressive attempt to bolster its claims over the Arctic. The economic payoff in this sovereignty game for all concerned might be quite significant. With ice sheets melting, control over the previously hidden bounty of up to one-fourth of the untapped energy resources in the world, along with a wealth in minerals, is at stake.

protect" was brought into sharp focus by the failure of the world to intervene in the face of the 1994 Rwandan genocide, and it arises today within the context of the human tragedy unfolding in the Darfur region of Sudan.

Fourth, a state must have, as sociologist Max Weber famously phrased it, a "monopoly of the legitimate use of physical force within a given territory."[10] Such force can be used not only to defend the country's interests but as well to enforce collective decisions. This usually involves the military and the police, although a small number of states only have the latter, such as Costa Rica, which abolished its standing army in 1948 after a civil war that left some 2,000 dead. The relationship between the development of the modern state and the military has been, some argue, quite close. For example, American sociologist Charles Tilly proposes that the emergence and development of European nation-states occurred as they extended their military control and their control over the military.[11] As they increasingly came to rely on standing armies to preserve and expand their political authority, large bureaucracies were created to extract the funds necessary to maintain national armies and to administer the territories that had been conquered. Moreover, with the state drawing ever more heavily on the resources of the people, Tilly suggests, over time the people came to feel that they had the right, in turn, to make increasing demands upon the state—especially with respect to some form of participation within collective decision-making. At more than $1 trillion (U.S.) a year at present, it is worth considering whether global military expenditures and the arms trade continue to shape the nature of the state.[12] After all, while it pales in comparison to the $62 billion apiece spent by China and Russia, or the $420 billion allocated to military expenditures in 2005 by the United States, Canada nonetheless ranked 14th in the world at $10.9 billion.

Finally, a state must be able to function within a community of states at the international level. Certainly, without international recognition, an entity that possesses all the other characteristics of a state already noted will not be able to engage as an equal on the world stage, whether at the United Nations or with respect to other international institutions. As can be seen in the case of East Timor (Box 2.5), not only can statehood result in the ability of a people to overcome oppression and determine its own future, but the status that it provides under international law can result in such tangible benefits as gaining control over local resources, and

Situated between Indonesia and Australia, East Timor became a Portuguese colony in the 16th century. When a process of decolonization that would have likely resulted in independence began to unfold in the mid-1970s, however, Indonesia invaded and annexed the territory, which subsequently resulted in the death of an estimated 150,000 of a population of 650,000. Indonesia's occupation was tacitly if not explicitly supported by the international community until the 1993 Dili Massacre, when Western journalists filmed the Indonesian military as it opened fire on and subsequently killed some 400 protesters in the capital city. By 1999, a United Nations– brokered agreement between Indonesia, Portugal, and the United States resulted in a successful referendum on independence and by the end of 2002 East Timor had become an independent state and a member of the United Nations. Although it remains heavily dependent on foreign assistance, as an independent state, East Timor now has a say over the potentially rich petroleum and natural gas resources in the Timor Sea. As Xanana Gusmao, East Timor's first president, observed on the day of his country's independence: "We wanted to be ourselves, we wanted to take pride in being ourselves—a people and a nation . . . standing on equal footing with all other people in the world."

SOURCE: BBC News, "E. Timor Independence: Gusmao's Speech"; available at http://news.bbc.co.uk/2/hi/asia-pacific/1997437.stm.

the possibility of receiving international assistance on a bilateral (i.e., country-to-country) or multilateral basis. In a sense, international recognition provides a state with the legitimacy to act as a sovereign state, giving a de facto state a de jure or legal status under international law. Table 2.2 lists the member states of the United Nations in 2008.

Although all states share these basic features, few states possess all of them fully. Indeed, even though some states clearly do not meet these standards, they are still considered to be such. This underlines the point that not all states take a similar form. In today's world, there is a tendency to separate states into **regimes** that are democratic and ones that are authoritarian. Although each type raises certain definitional difficulties—for example, concerning the point at which a particular regime crosses over from one to the other—they nonetheless possess fundamental and distinguishing characteristics that are important to the study of politics.

Modern Democratic Governments

One thing that we can say about the world is that it is more democratic than at any other time in human history. For example, in its 2002 *Human Development Report*, the United Nations Development Program observed that an incredible burst of democratization had occurred since the 1980s: "Some 81 countries took significant steps towards democracy, and today 140 of the world's nearly 200 countries hold multiparty elections—more than ever before."[13] Notwithstanding the progress that can be tracked (see Figure 2.1), the report recommends caution in considering whether this marks an irreversible turn toward democracy. Not only has the expansion of democracy flatlined during the past decade, but the strength of democracy remains weak in a number of recently converted countries, and thus the possibility of a return

Table 2.2 The 192 Member States of the United Nations

Afghanistan	Djibouti	Liechtenstein	Principe
Albania	Dominica	Lithuania	Saudi Arabia
Algeria	Dominican Republic	Luxembourg	Senegal
Andorra	Ecuador	Madagascar	Serbia
Angola	Egypt	Malawi	Seychelles
Antigua and Barbuda	El Salvador	Malaysia	Sierra Leone
Argentina	Equatorial Guinea	Maldives	Singapore
Armenia	Eritrea	Mali	Slovakia
Australia	Estonia	Malta	Slovenia
Austria	Ethiopia	Marshall Islands	Solomon Islands
Azerbaijan	Fiji	Mauritania	Somalia
Bahamas	Finland	Mauritius	South Africa
Bahrain	France	Mexico	Spain
Bangladesh	Gabon	Micronesia, Federated	Sri Lanka
Barbados	Gambia	States of	Sudan
Belarus	Georgia	Moldova	Suriname
Belgium	Germany	Monaco	Swaziland
Belize	Ghana	Mongolia	Sweden
Benin	Greece	Montenegro	Switzerland
Bhutan	Grenada	Morocco	Syrian Arab Republic
Bolivia	Guatemala	Mozambique	Tajikistan
Bosnia and	Guinea	Myanmar	Thailand
Herzegovina	Guinea-Bissau	Namibia	The former Yugoslav
Botswana	Guyana	Nauru	Republic of
Brazil	Haiti	Nepal	Macedonia
Brunei Darussalam	Honduras	Netherlands	Timor-Leste
Bulgaria	Hungary	New Zealand	Togo
Burkina Faso	Iceland	Nicaragua	Tonga
Burundi	India	Niger	Trinidad and
Cambodia	Indonesia	Nigeria	Tobago
Cameroon	Iran, Islamic	Norway	Tunisia
Canada	Republic of	Oman	Turkey
Cape Verde	Iraq	Pakistan	Turkmenistan
Central African	Ireland	Palau	Tuvalu
Republic	Israel	Panama	Uganda
Chad	Italy	Papua New Guinea	Ukraine
Chile	Jamaica	Paraguay	United Arab Emirates
China	Japan	Peru	United Kingdom of
Colombia	Jordan	Philippines	Great Britain and
Comoros	Kazakhstan	Poland	Northern Ireland
Congo, Republic of	Kenya	Portugal	United Republic of
the	Kiribati	Qatar	Tanzania
Costa Rica	Kuwait	Republic of Korea	United States of
Côte d'Ivoire	Kyrgyzstan	Romania	America
Croatia	Lao People's	Russian Federation	Uruguay
Cuba	Democratic	Rwanda	Uzbekistan
Cyprus	Republic	Saint Kitts and Nevis	Vanuatu
Czech Republic	Latvia	Saint Lucia	Venezuela, Bolivarian
Democratic People's	Lebanon	Saint Vincent and	Republic of
Republic of Korea	Lesotho	the Grenadines	Viet Nam
Democratic Republic	Liberia	Samoa	Yemen
of the Congo	Libyan Arab	San Marino	Zambia
Denmark	Jamahiriya	Sao Tome and	Zimbabwe

Source: United Nations, "List of Member States"; available at http://www.un.org/New/Press/docs/2006/ORG/1469.doc.htm; accessed November 30, 2007.

to authoritarianism remains. Indeed, despite popular aspirations for more democratic rule in many parts of the world where democracy does not prevail, there is growing evidence in both long-established and more recent democracies that publics are growing disillusioned with the seeming inability of the institutions of democratic governance to fulfil their expectations, even to the point, in some countries, of favouring more authoritarian forms of government.[14]

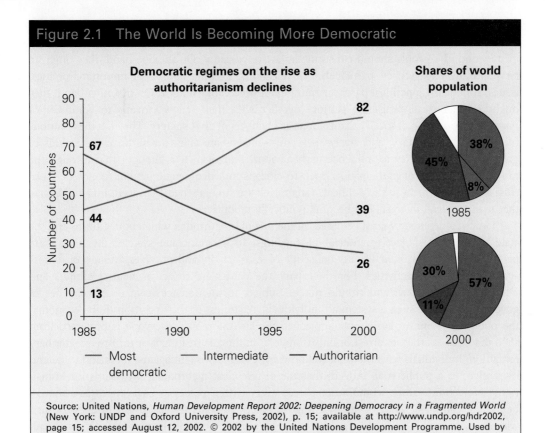

Figure 2.1   The World Is Becoming More Democratic

Democratic regimes on the rise as authoritarianism declines

Shares of world population

1985

2000

— Most democratic   — Intermediate   — Authoritarian

Source: United Nations, *Human Development Report 2002: Deepening Democracy in a Fragmented World* (New York: UNDP and Oxford University Press, 2002), p. 15; available at http://www.undp.org/hdr2002, page 15; accessed August 12, 2002. © 2002 by the United Nations Development Programme. Used by permission of Oxford University Press.

The need to probe in greater detail how to make democracies work is not simply a question of addressing the perception of a democratic deficit in our own part of the world, or in order to test the democratic claims of other states, although these are valuable undertakings in their own right; it has also emerged as a question of considerable international importance. In recent years, **democratization** has become a component part of the foreign policies of a number of countries, including Canada, and recent efforts to export democracy to Afghanistan and Iraq have underlined how difficult this process can be. Moreover, the language of democracy has come to permeate if not dominate political discourse, even in those countries where it is practised the least. So what do we mean when we talk about a democracy?[15]

First, as noted in Chapter 14, the government must be established, and it must be possible to replace it, through free and fair elections. It is in this way that, at a fundamental level, it can be said that power resides with the citizenry. Moreover, it is through their elected representatives that the people can be said to (indirectly) govern. The rulers, therefore, have power on loan from the people, and must return it when asked to do so. For elections to be free and fair, several conditions need to be met, including the possibility of competition between different political parties, accessible information on both party and candidate positions as well as the issues, and the regulation of the election itself by a nonpartisan agency whose job it is to ensure that everyone adheres to the law. Furthermore, votes should be cast through a secret ballot, and people should not be intimidated or harassed at the polls. Thus, an election in and of itself is not democratic if it is not free and fair, and even established democracies can have difficulties in administering such contests, as the United States found in 2000, when the election between President George W. Bush and former Vice-President Al Gore ultimately had to be settled (and not without controversy) by the Supreme Court.

Second, the people should constitute an active citizenry. On the one hand, they ought to be politically engaged, by participating in elections, keeping abreast of important political issues, supporting a political party, or running for office, for example. On the other hand, they ought to be civically engaged, getting together with their fellow citizens to volunteer or participate in a range of social organizations as members of **civil society**. Through these various means—often voluntary, and always peaceful—citizens are able to scrutinize the actions of government, and to try to influence its behaviour. Moreover, it is thought that through the multitude of forms of participation open to citizens in a democratic system, bonds of social trust and commitment to the political system itself are strengthened.[16] Indeed, it is in this way that many societal interests can become politically mobilized.

Finally, a democracy must be based on the rule of law, through which both citizens and the state are equally subject to judicial proceedings. In a democratic system, the people are protected by the law, which limits the scope of state activity and provides avenues of redress against illegal state activities. For their part, the courts are to act as neutral arbiters and interpreters of the law, and should not be subject to interference from other branches of government. Under such a system all individuals, regardless of their position in the economy, the political system, or society are subject to the law. Moreover, everyone is protected from such practices as arbitrary arrest or imprisonment, inhumane treatment or torture, or summary execution. Individuals have the right to know any charges brought against them and to defend themselves in a public trial. Indeed, the rule of law must incorporate provisions for human rights protections. Thus, within a democracy every citizen possesses basic rights as a human being that cannot be taken away by the government or state. Often these will be enshrined within a constitution, and they may be supported under international law as well. Of course, no country, even the most democratic, fulfils all **human rights** all the time. Indeed, this can be seen by a quick look through Amnesty International's annual report, the latest edition of which lists human rights violations in 153 countries, many of which—such as Canada—are long-standing and established democracies.[17]

Modern Nondemocratic Governments

Clearly, then, while a democracy contains several basic institutional features, and requires a normative commitment on the part of the population to sustain it over time, it is no simple matter to create one. This complexity is increased by the fact that most states in the world make some kind of claim to be democratic. Indeed, if you examine the constitutions of all the member states of the United Nations, most make reference to democracy. For example, the constitution of the People's Republic of China states that "the Chinese people of all nationalities will continue to adhere to the people's democratic dictatorship and the socialist road, steadily improve socialist institutions, develop socialist democracy, improve the socialist legal system, and work hard and self-reliantly . . . to turn China into a socialist country with a high level of culture and democracy." While China nonetheless lacks most of the institutional features commonly associated with a democracy, it underlines the point that many governments we call authoritarian have some element or elements we can associate with democracy. In the Islamic Republic of Iran, for example, there are competitive elections. Such regimes also possess, however, numerous characteristics that are fundamentally undemocratic.

Such states are often called dictatorships and are commonly divided into **authoritarian** and **totalitarian** states.[18] Both authoritarian and totalitarian governments are concerned with the maintenance, at almost any cost, of their position of power. There are generally no constitutional limitations on the government, there is no authorized process to change the government, and citizens have few (if any) rights. Lacking popular support, both types of government frequently resort to political violence to maintain their rule, using excessive force to control the populations that they "serve." Indeed, they are typically dominated by a strong and vocal military presence. Authoritarian and totalitarian governments glorify their leadership to the point of absurdity; this phenomenon is sometimes reflected in a written law, which specifies that the only public display of political prominence is to be the face of the leader, often a charismatic, self-appointed dictator for life. Moreover, there is a tendency in these regimes to control all aspects of the **mass media** in order to consolidate and control the flow of information. In fact, what has perhaps led to the downfall of these styles of government more than anything is the penetration of communications into the country from outside sources that affirm human rights and freedom.

Hitler and Mussolini—two totalitarian leaders—confer with each other.

© Corbis.

But authoritarian and totalitarian regimes have their differences. For example, authoritarian regimes usually exercise power in a more limited sphere, focusing primarily on their control over state institutions. Totalitarian regimes seek control over all aspects of political, social, economic, and intellectual life; no activity is beyond the power of the government. Moreover, while authoritarian governments may merely want power for its own sake, totalitarian regimes are based on a single party and ideology—a mission to mould society in some way. The three most prominent totalitarian regimes in history are Nazism in Hitler's Germany, **fascism** in Mussolini's Italy, and Soviet **communism**, especially under Stalin. In each case, the party had an ideology to change the society in some ideal fashion that the leadership claimed, however falsely, was in the public interest. Although the number of authoritarian or totalitarian governments has been in decline over the past 25 years, they still have a marked presence in the international system of states. For some examples, see Box 2.6.

Indeed, "authoritarian state" is the designation more commonly applied today to any nondemocratic state, and great variations among the members of this category can be found. Many of the newly emerged "democracies" during the past few decades, in fact, have retained attributes of their former authoritarian selves, which probably helps to explain the tenuousness of the more general turn toward democracy during the past few decades. Moreover, the growth of legislation and policies to counter terrorist threats in recent years—which frequently involve the suspension of certain liberties that otherwise remain central to democratic political life—has opened up an increasing debate over a "creeping authoritarianism" in the more established democracies of the world.

Non-state Governments and De Facto States

If you take a map of the world and overlay it with the 192 member states of the United Nations, some of them more democratic than others and some of them more authoritarian, you would not have an accurate representation of the full range of either governments or state-like entities

China is, of course, the most populous country in the world, and currently houses one of the most rapidly expanding economies. It is a one-party communist state, and among its more notorious legacies is the Tiananmen Square massacre of student dissidents in 1989. Although its record of human rights violations has improved somewhat since then, it continues to be under pressure from Western trading partners to move faster in this direction. Among other authoritarian features of its government are rampant corruption; government control of the judiciary, including wholesale executions of people convicted of nonviolent crimes such as tax fraud; arrest and imprisonment of labour activists, journalists, human rights defenders, and political and religious dissidents; government control of the media; and severe restriction of freedom of expression and religion in Tibet.

Iran is an Islamic Republic located next to Iraq; it is a leading example of a theocratic state. The constitution gives supreme authority to the Spiritual Leader, and requires that the precepts of Islam be the basis for political, social, and economic relations. As a result of a strong reform movement in recent years, religious rule has loosened somewhat, but reforms are resisted by the Council of Guardians, which vetoes legislation that is not in accordance with Islamic principles. Among other authoritarian features of the government are the shutting down of reformist newspapers and jailing of journalists; political organizations and demonstrations are not allowed to criticize ("insult") Islamic values; judicial abuses abound, including arbitrary arrests and holding people in secret detention; and the penal code provides for widespread executions and a range of penalties that violate fundamental human rights. In recent years, there has been increasing talk of the likelihood of a U.S. attack, especially within the context of Iran's advanced nuclear industry.

North Korea, formally the Democratic People's Republic of Korea, is another state whose nuclear ambitions have raised concerns in recent years—especially after it conducted a nuclear test in October 2006. Commonly labelled a Stalinist dictatorship and totalitarian state, the country is under the control of Kim Jong-il, who—as chair of the National Defense Commission—wields more power than either the President or the Premier. Although there are elections, there is effectively only one political party in existence. In the 1950s, North Korea instituted a "self-reliance" or isolationist policy in an effort to distance itself from the former Soviet Union and China, and it has long had antagonistic relations with the United States. Nonetheless, in the face of widespread famines that have likely killed some 2 million people since the 1990s and left millions others malnourished, the country has relied on international food aid from the United States, among others. According to both Amnesty International and Human Rights Watch, North Korea has one of the worst human rights records in the world, with reports of enforced disappearances and political executions, among numerous other human rights abuses.

Zimbabwe, in southern Africa, has been under the increasingly authoritarian control of Robert Mugabe since 1980. Inheriting a difficult problem of land reform (in which most of the land was owned by whites), his controversial plan to redistribute land has precipitated much violence, and the beneficiaries have often been his friends and supporters rather than landless black Zimbabweans. Much of the criticism of Mugabe's authoritarianism has centred on repeated electoral irregularities. However, Zimbabwe also features the common authoritarian state restrictions on the media, including closure of the only independent daily newspaper; corruption; limits on public assembly and criticism; repression of human rights defenders, including arbitrary arrests, assaults, and torture; and uncontrolled security forces. Moreover, the country faces one of the worst HIV/AIDS crises, and the government has not shown much interest in solving it. World reaction to the violent 2008 election, however, may lead to regime change.

SOURCE: Reports from Amnesty International, Human Rights Watch, Freedom House, *The Europa World Year Book*, *The Statesmen's Yearbook*, *Political Systems of the World*, *The International Year Book and Statesmen's Who's Who*, *Political Handbook of the World 2000–2002*, and *The Oxford Companion to Politics of the World*.

in the world. Not only would you miss areas where it is not quite clear who is sovereign, but you would also miss areas where other types of government or state-like entities operate. In order to understand more fully the nature of governments and states at the outset of the 21st century, it is worth taking some time to consider a few of these situations.

Traditional Governments

One of the founding principles of European colonization throughout the world was the doctrine of *terra nullius*. According to this doctrine, any land that was not already claimed by a recognized and sovereign state was available for conquest. Furthermore, such "empty land" could be taken over when the colonizers deemed that no system of law or property—no system of government—was in place to rule the population in question. Thus, when Indigenous peoples (people "native" to the areas under consideration for settlement) were encountered, they were considered to be living in a "state of nature" without a government, not unlike the state described by John Locke. In reality, however, Indigenous peoples never lived under the principles established by the doctrine of *terra nullius*. Instead, just as different traditions and conditions provided a foundation for governance in ancient China and the Middle East, Indigenous peoples possessed their own forms of institutions and practices through which collective decisions were both made and enforced, and these are increasingly shaping politics in many parts of the world today—including Canada.

At the outset of the 21st century, such traditional governments are those that practise rule-making, rule-application, and rule-adjudication according to the customs and traditions that their own peoples have passed down through generations of occupancy of a particular territory. For some time now, many Indigenous peoples have been reviving their traditional ideas about governance and justice in a way that provides a new context for discussion of Indigenous worldviews in contrast to Western European worldviews. There is, moreover, great variation in terms of the forms that this has been taking, as there exist around 370,000 Indigenous people in the world today, constituting some 5,000 different groups in more than 70 countries. For example, large parts of territories of Pakistan are governed by tribal authorities, which are composed of tribal chiefs ruling over their traditional land with minimal intervention by the national government. Some of these traditional forms of government are based on matrilineal succession; others, on consensus decision-making; and still others, on principles that are hard to describe because they are expressed in languages that defy effective translation into the dominant languages of the developed world. However, as a result of the legacy of colonialism and the emergence of an international system of states since the 16th century, such traditional governments have often been marginalized if not actively suppressed. Nonetheless, in recent years a revival of traditional forms of government has been occurring. Indeed, there is a world movement of Indigenous peoples that meets on a regular basis to discuss and recommend political actions that could result in the recognition of spheres of independent Indigenous political authority in many countries of the world.

Before the arrival of Europeans in what is now Canada, Aboriginal peoples governed themselves, although their "first nations" did not take the form of modern states. Before long, however, many Indigenous peoples were relocated to lands "reserved" for them by the Crown or by the new Canadian state, forced into a residential school system that denied their heritage, and dispossessed of territory through a process of flawed if not fraudulent treaty-making. Although it was long expected that Aboriginal peoples would eventually become assimilated into the majority population and thereby die out as distinct groups, and while government policies were often designed to facilitate this process, by the 1960s it had become apparent that this would not occur. Indeed, since that time Aboriginal peoples have become increasingly organized and involved in Canadian politics, examples of which can be seen with the Mohawk Council in Akwesasne or the Cree Grand Council in northern Quebec. Although there has been some progress on the recognition of Aboriginal rights and Aboriginal title to land in recent years, increasingly the debate is revolving around the recognition and implementation of an inherent right to **Aboriginal self-government**. What forms such governments will assume and what powers they will have are currently subject to heated debate. According to some, such governments would possess sovereignty and be similar to states. For many, however, Aboriginal self-governments would be more like provinces or municipalities, with certain guaranteed powers, but not all the characteristics of a state. A recent model was created with the *Nisga'a Treaty* of 2000, which recognized the authority of a Nisga'a government in British Columbia within the context of the Canadian constitutional structure.

Aside from such governments without states, there is also one area of the globe with neither government nor state—Antarctica, which has no permanent population but nonetheless is the fifth-largest continent in the world. Although seven countries claim parts of the Antarctic, these have been laid aside for the time being under the *1959 Antarctic Treaty*, the purpose of which is to ensure that Antarctica remains demilitarized and accessible for peaceful scientific research. There are also various entities around the world that have state-like attributes but do not possess state sovereignty. For example, there are numerous colonies, dependencies, and external territories that are linked and in some way subordinate to an established state. Often, such relationships have emerged out of a particular colonial history, while at other times it can reflect a certain geographic proximity. At present, there are more than 50 dependencies and areas of special sovereignty in the world (according to the U.S. State Department), including such well-known examples as Bermuda, the Cayman Islands, and Puerto Rico. Although they tend to be associated with western states such as Australia, France, the Netherlands, New Zealand, Norway, the United Kingdom, and the United States, a few are linked to China. For its part, Canada does not possess any such territories, but we can nonetheless point to the case of the islands that make up the Territorial Collectivity of Saint Pierre and Miquelon, which lies just off the coast of Newfoundland and has been under the control of France since the *1763 Treaty of Paris*, through which the territories of New France (now Quebec) were transferred to the British.

There also exist de facto states that have not received de jure recognition from the United Nations. For its part, Palestine is recognized at the United Nations as a non-member entity that, like the Holy See of the Catholic Church in Vatican State, maintains a permanent mission at UN headquarters in New York and is allowed to participate as an observer in the General Assembly.

Other cases are much less clear-cut, such as those of Taiwan, which is claimed by China, and the Sahrawi Arab Democratic Republic, which effectively controls a significant amount of territory otherwise claimed by Morocco in the Western Sahara. Only a minority of states have been willing to establish diplomatic relations with either entity. Meanwhile, while the United States and many European countries support statehood for Kosovo, this is opposed both by Serbia and Russia, among others. There are also several possible de facto states that are not really recognized by anyone else. These include the areas of Northern Cyprus (which is recognized only by the Turkish government), Abkhazia and South Ossetia (in Georgia), Nagorno-Karabakh (in Armenia-Azerbaijan), Somaliland (in Somalia), and Transnistria (in Moldova). By challenging the authority of governing authorities from within, such state-like entities might one day become sovereign in their own right, but they might also foster a condition of state failure.

Failed States

The issue of state failure has become particularly acute in the post–Cold War era, and even more so in the wake of September 11, 2001. Although the international system of states had seen major shakeups before, what has happened in the aftermath of the Cold War has been especially dramatic. For example, with the demise of the Soviet Union, 16 new states were recognized by the United Nations, while the breakup of the former Yugoslavia has resulted in six new member states and Kosovo could constitute a seventh. In some instances, this process was fairly peaceful—as in the 1989 Velvet Revolution in Czechoslovakia. In others, however, it was extremely turbulent, as in the former Yugoslavia, which was beset by violent interethnic conflict between 1991 and 2001, resulting in the death of perhaps 120,000 and the displacement of more than two million. The issue of state failure took on heightened resonance, however, following September 11, when a more explicit connection was made between failing states and **terrorism**. In short, it became accepted that failed or failing states could provide a safe haven for terrorists to the extent to which there was no central authority that was willing or able to confront them. For these and other reasons, the international community (along with those who study politics) has been paying increased attention to identifying the conditions of state failure and trying to determine how best to respond.

The conditions of state failure might at first seem to be fairly obvious: a state is no longer a state when it loses one or more of the five characteristics covered above. Thus, a **failed state** would be one, for example, that no longer had "a monopoly of the legitimate use of physical force within [its] given territory." This answer, however, does not take us very far, because as we saw above, in the real world of politics very few states match the ideal of statehood, and even states that clearly do not meet this standard are still considered to be states by the international community. For example, despite its inability to control its sovereign territory, the international community has not ceased to recognize the Republic of Sudan as a state. As opposed to stateless governments, those in power in a recognized state at least nominally have a territory over which they possess jurisdiction under international law.

Indeed, the factors at play in state failure are diverse and can combine in various ways. This has led the researchers behind the Failed States Index, a joint project of *Foreign Policy Magazine* and the Fund for Peace, to suggest that "Just as there are many paths to success, there are many paths to failure for states on the edge."[19] In constructing the index, a variety of economic, political, and social indicators are gauged (see Box 2.7), and in 2007, the five states deemed to be most likely to fail were Sudan, Iraq, Somalia, Zimbabwe, and Chad. As can be seen, each indicator represents a range of complex issues that defy easy solution, and in order to address any of them a certain degree of political will from both the state in question and the

BOX 2.7

Social Indicators

1. Mounting demographic pressures

2. Massive movement of refugees or internally displaced persons creating complex humanitarian emergencies

3. Legacy of vengeance-seeking group grievance or group paranoia

4. Chronic and sustained human flight

Economic Indicators

1. Uneven economic development along group lines

2. Sharp and/or severe economic decline

Political Indicators

1. Criminalization and/or delegitimization of the state

2. Progressive deterioration of public services

3. Suspension or arbitrary application of the rule of law and widespread violation of human rights

4. Security apparatus operates as a "state within a state"

5. Rise of factionalized elites

6. Intervention of other states or external political actors

SOURCE: Fund for Peace, "Failed States Index Scores 2007"; available at http://www.fundforpeace.org/web/index.php?option=com_content&task=view&id=229&Itemid=366; accessed April 30, 2008.

international community is required, but this is not always easy to attain. Moreover, as can be seen in Box 2.8, a new twist has been added to the issue of state failure with the rise to prominence of the issue of global warming.

While state failure is generally discussed in terms of countries in the developing world, the concept can also speak to "pockets of state failure" that can occur in any political system. For example, when Hurricane Katrina hit New Orleans in 2005, the United States was unable to

BOX 2.8

As public attention increasingly turns to the question of global warming, new potential patterns of state failure have been identified. Take, for example, the case of the tiny island state of Tuvalu (consisting of four reef islands and five atolls), which is the least populated and fourth-smallest member state of the United Nations. This Polynesian nation, located between Australia and Hawaii, became independent of Britain in 1978 and has survived mainly on foreign aid ever since. Although it is a fully functioning constitutional monarchy, with a democratically elected parliament, the state faces the prospect of failure due to rising sea levels. Tuvalu is one of a number of island states whose very physical existence as a territory is threatened in this way.

SOURCE: United Nations High Commissioner for Refugees, *Refugees*, 147 (2007).

mount an effective reaction for several days; that same year, France declared a state of emergency after weeks of rioting in Paris and beyond. More generally, there have been concerns that the emergence of a pandemic, such as the outbreak of influenza that killed an estimated 50 million persons worldwide between 1918 and 1920, might produce situations of state failure in many countries as hospital systems become overloaded. By expanding the concept of state failure, of course, the point is not to equate the political situation in Canada, for example, with that of Sudan, for clearly the differences in the degree, nature, and consequences of failure are ones of apples and oranges. It does, however, remind us that all states have the potential to fail for reasons of external intervention, internal combustion, or both, while history suggests that over the long term, all states are likely to confront such challenges eventually.

Postnational States?

While questions of state failure still seem remote for the more established states of the world, there has been considerable talk of their transformation since the late 20th century, often in the context of a process of **globalization**. According to one scenario, in an era of increased international migration, the old notion of the *nation*-state, while never an accurate depiction, has become an especially inappropriate term for the increasingly diversified societies in the West today. This might, in fact, change the meaning of citizenship that lies at the heart of the definition of a state. In another scenario, states are being challenged both from within and from without, as the power generally associated with the national state is transferred upwards to international governing structures or devolved downwards to regional or municipal levels. With respect to the former, analysts often focus on institutions such as the **World Trade Organization**, which works to ensure that national economic activities conform to certain shared standards of behaviour, or the **European Union**, through which a range of administrative, executive, judicial, and legislative functions have been passed from member states to a higher political authority. With respect to the latter, the focus often shifts to the rise of "global cities" such as New York, London, and Tokyo, which—while existing within sovereign states—operate within global economic and social networks that create powerful political interests and forces within national capitals. In either case, interesting and challenging questions are raised as to the nature of governments and states, and it suggests that their evolution is far from over.

CONCLUSION

As will become evident as you work your way through this book, governments and states do not define the entire scope of the study of politics, but they are often important factors and are rarely very far removed from modern political life. Clearly, whether we live under a democratic or an authoritarian regime quite literally shapes our prospects for living—as Aristotle noted—the good life. It also affects the types of politics that surround us and in which we become engaged. It is important, therefore, that we study the governments under and the states within which we live in order to understand how they operate, determine whether they work well, and decide if they need to be altered. Indeed, history reminds us that no political regime is perfect, and that each might be improved. In an age of increasing globalization, moreover, it is ever more difficult to isolate ourselves from what is going on in the rest of the world, and therefore we need to study as well the nature of other governments and states, how they are similar to or different from our own and why, and what kinds of ties —whether of self-interest or shared responsibility—bind us together.

DISCUSSION QUESTIONS

1. Is Aristotle's scheme for classifying governments only appropriate for the ancient world, or is it still relevant today? Where would you place Canada?

2. In what ways are modern democracies less democratic than they might be, and how might they become more democratic?

3. Should the international community intervene in or put pressure on authoritarian states in order to effect a regime change toward democracy?

4. Should we be concerned about state failure in countries halfway around the world? If so, what should we do about it?

5. What kind of Aboriginal self-government should Canada seek to achieve?

KEY TERMS

ABORIGINAL SELF-GOVERNMENT: A demand by Aboriginal or Indigenous groups that they be able to govern themselves, as they did before colonial rulers removed such power. (50)

ABSOLUTE MONARCHY: A system of government ruled, at least in name, by one individual whose authority is unchecked, final, and permanent. (33)

AUTHORITARIAN GOVERNMENT: A nondemocratic form of government that rules without public input, glorifies the leader, allows no dissent, strictly controls the mass media, relies on the police and military to root out opposition, and is dedicated to remaining in power at all costs. (46)

GOVERNMENT: The set of institutions and practices that make and enforce collective public decisions for a society. (32)

OLIGARCHY: A system of government ruled by a few and, according to Aristotle, in their own interests. (35)

POLITY: A system of government ruled by the many but not—as in a democracy—by all; according to Aristotle, this was the most stable system of government when it was able to balance the interests of the wealthy with those of the poor. (35)

REGIME: The whole decision-making apparatus of the state; the constitutional principles and arrangements according to which government decisions are made; the fundamental rules of the game. (43)

REPUBLIC: A system of government ruled by a head of state who is not a monarch (generally, in modern times, a president), in which citizens are entitled to participate in decision-making. (33)

SOVEREIGNTY: The final or ultimate power over a population and a piece of territory, commonly claimed by the government of a state but ultimately sanctioned by the international system of states. In other contexts, sovereignty can be said to reside in the people or in parliament; in all cases, however, it has probably been eroded by global forces. (41)

STATE: A modern form of organizing political life that is characterized by a population, territory, governing institutions, and a government that claims a monopoly of legitimate force; recognition by the international community of states (most prominently by the United Nations) may also be key. (40)

TOTALITARIAN GOVERNMENT: A nondemocratic form of government—most notably Nazism, fascism, and Soviet communism—that is based on a single party and ideology, takes control of all aspects of political, social, economic, and intellectual life, and mobilizes its mass public into active support of the government. (46)

WEB LINKS

Inter-Parliamentary Union:
http://www.ipu.org

**The United Nations' 2002
Report Human Development:**
http://hdr.undp.org/en/reports/global/hdr2002

Fund for Peace:
http://www.fundforpeace.org/web/index.php

International Workgroup for Indigenous Affairs:
http://www.iwgia.org

Amnesty International:
http://www.amnesty.org

FURTHER READING

Berger, Mark T., ed. *From Nation-Building to State-Building*. New York: Routledge, 2007.

Diamond, Larry, Marc F. Plattner, and Philip J. Costopoulos, eds. *World Religions and Democracy*. Baltimore: The Johns Hopkins University Press, 2005.

Dunn, John. *Democracy: A History*. Toronto: Penguin Canada, 2005.

Europa World Year Book. London: Europa Publications, 2007.

Finer, S.E. *The History of Government from the Earliest Times, Vols. I–III*. Oxford: Oxford University Press, 1997.

Hawkesworth, Mary, and Maurice Kogan, eds. *Encyclopedia of Government and Politics*. New York: Routledge, 2003.

Krieger, Joel, ed. *The Oxford Companion to Politics of the World*, 2nd ed. Oxford: Oxford University Press, 2001.

Monture-Angus, Patricia. *Journeying Forward: Dreaming First Nations' Independence*. Halifax: Fernwood Press, 1999.

ENDNOTES

1. A comprehensive account can be found in Peter Marshall, *Demanding the Impossible: A History of Anarchism* (London: Fontana Press, 1993).

2. Alan C. Cairns, "The Embedded State: State-Society Relations in Canada," in D.E. Williams, ed., *Reconfigurations: Canadian Citizenship & Constitutional Change, Selected Essays by Alan C. Cairns* (Toronto: McClelland & Stewart Inc., 1995), pp. 31–61, 358–61.

3. Gabriel A. Almond, "A Functional Approach to Comparative Politics," in G.A. Almond and J.S. Coleman, eds., *The Politics of the Developing Areas* (Princeton: Princeton University Press, 1960), pp. 3–64.

4. "In a world-historical perspective, then, the Middle East is the cradle of organized government, and it was to retain its cultural, political, and military supremacy . . . for over 2,000 years." S.E. Finer, *The History of Government from the Earliest Times, Vol. I* (Oxford: Oxford University Press, 1997), p. 99.

5. See John Dunn, *Democracy: A History* (Toronto: Penguin Canada, 2005).

6. For a detailed examination of what we know of democratic life in Athens, see Mogens Herman Hansen, *The Athenian Democracy in the Age of Demosthenes: Structure, Principles and Ideology*, trans. J.A. Crook (Oxford: Blackwell Publishers, 1991).

7. Aristotle, *The Politics*, trans. T.A. Sinclair, revised and re-presented by Trevor J. Saunders (London: Penguin Books, 1981 [1962]), p. 60. Aristotle viewed men to be by nature superior to women, and on this ground he justified the rule of the former over the latter, and the exclusion of women from politics.

8. *Ibid.*, p. 222.

9. John Locke, *Second Treatise of Government*, ch. 9, sec. 123, originally published in 1689 and accessible online through *Project Gutenberg*, at http://www.gutenberg.org/etext/7370.

10. Max Weber, "Politics as a Vocation," originally delivered as a speech in 1918 and accessible online through Wikisource, at http://en.wikisource.org/wiki/Politics_as_a_Vocation. He defines a state as "a human community that (successfully) claims the monopoly of the legitimate use of physical force within a given territory."

11. See Charles Tilly, *Coercion, Capital and European States, AD 900–1990* (Cambridge, Massachusetts: Basil Blackburn, 1990).

12. Petter Stålenheim, Damien Fruchart, Wuyi Omitoogun, and Catalina Perdomo, "Military Expenditure," in Stockholm International Peace Research Institute, *Yearbook 2006: Armaments, Disarmament and International Security* (Stockholm: SIPRI, 2006).

13. United Nations Development Program, *2002 Human Development Report* (New York: Oxford University Press, 2002), p. 1.

14. See, for example, the regional reports on the state of popular support for democracy included in *Journal of Democracy* 18(3) (July 2007).

15. See Larry Diamond, "What Is Democracy?," lecture at Hillah University for Humanitarian, Scientific and Religious Studies, January 21, 2004, available at http://www.stanford.edu/%7Eldiamond/iraq.html, accessed April 30, 2008. Diamond advised the Coalition Provisional Authority in Baghdad in its efforts to establish a democratic political system in Iraq, and delivered this speech on the basic characteristics of a democracy to some 1,500 Iraqi leaders in 2004.

16. This is the basic thrust of Robert Putnam, *Bowling Alone: The Collapse and Revival of American Community* (New York: Simon & Schuster, 2000).

17. Amnesty International, *Amnesty International Report 2007*, available at http://www.amnesty.org/en/library/asset/POL10/007/2007/en/dom-POL100072007en.html, accessed April 30, 2008.

18. See James Malloy, "Contemporary Authoritarian Regimes," in M. Hawkesworth and M. Korgan, eds., *Encyclopedia of Government and Politics, Vol. I* (London: Routledge, 1992), pp. 229–46.

19. "The Failed State Index," *Foreign Policy*, 161 (July/August 2007), p. 56.

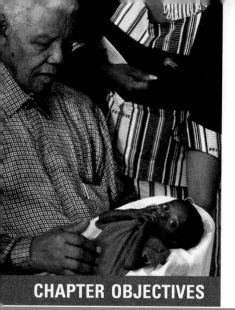

Chapter Three

CULTURAL PLURALISM, NATIONALISM, AND IDENTITY

Yasmeen Abu-Laban

CHAPTER OBJECTIVES

After you have completed this chapter, you should be able to:

- define the key concepts of nationalism, state, nation, multination state, genocide, ethnic cleansing, diaspora, race, globalization, dominant conformity, and cultural pluralism

- outline and evaluate two different approaches to the study of nationalism (universalizing and individualizing comparisons)

- discuss the debate over the impact of contemporary globalization on national identity

- describe some contemporary expressions of nationalism and other identity-based claims

Why Study Cultural Pluralism?

According to demographic statistics, only about 10 percent of countries can be said to be ethnically homogeneous.[1] The fact that cultural pluralism is a reality in most countries has important implications for politics. As noted in Chapter 2, modern government has come to rest largely with the state. Given that 90 percent of the countries of the world are characterized by having a heterogeneous population (see Table 3.1), it is easy to see why political scientists are interested in cultural and ethnic diversity. The sense of identity people have, relations between different cultural and ethnic groups, and the possibility of different and even conflicting demands made by groups can all affect the terrain of state governance. A better understanding of these issues has considerable practical significance, affecting people's quality of life and helping decision-makers who wish to enact effective public policies.

In this way, the attempt to describe ethnic, cultural, and other forms of diversity is not merely an abstract theoretical exercise. The research findings of political and other social scientists on issues pertaining to diversity are extremely relevant. This fact has been recognized at the highest levels internationally, as exemplified by the mandate of the Management of

Table 3.1 Diversity in Selected Countries

Drawing on national census data and other statistical information, *The World Factbook* of the U.S. Central Intelligence Agency lists ethnic groups present in all countries of the world. Below is a selection from the 2007 edition.

Afghanistan	Pashtun 42%, Tajik 27%, Hazara 9%, Uzbek 9%, Aimak 4%, Turkmen 3%, Baloch 2%, other 4%
Australia	White 92%, Asian 7%, Aboriginal and other 1%
Belgium	Fleming 58%, Walloon 31%, mixed or other 11%
Brazil	White 53.7%, mulatto (mixed white and black) 38.5%, black 6.2%, other (includes Japanese, Arab, Amerindian) 0.9%, unspecified 0.7%
China	Han Chinese 91.9%, Zhuang, Uygur, Hui, Yi, Tibetan, Miao, Manchu, Mongol, Buyi, Korean, and other nationalities 8.1%
Finland	Finn 93.4%, Swede 5.7%, Russian 0.4%, Estonian 0.2%, Roma (Gypsy) 0.2%, Sami 0.1%
Germany	German 91.5%, Turkish 2.4%, other 6.1% (made up largely of Greek, Italian, Polish, Russian, Serbo-Croatian, Spanish)
India	Indo-Aryan 72%, Dravidian 25%, Mongoloid and other 3%
Iraq	Arab 75%–80%, Kurdish 15%–20%; Turkoman, Assyrian, or other 5%
Iran	Persian 51%, Azeri 24%, Gilaki and Mazandarani 8%, Kurd 7%, Arab 3%, Lur 2%, Baloch 2%, Turkmen 2%, other 1%
Israel	Jewish 76.4% (of which Israel-born 67.1%, Europe/America-born 22.6%, Africa-born 5.9%, Asia-born 4.2%), non-Jewish 23.6% (mostly Arab); Gaza Strip: Palestinian Arab and other 99.4%, Jewish 0.6%; West Bank: Palestinian Arab and other 83%, Jewish 17%
Mexico	Mestizo (Amerindian-Spanish) 60%, Amerindian or predominantly Amerindian 30%, white 9%, other 1%
South Africa	Black African 79%, white 9.6%, coloured 8.9%, Indian/Asian 2.5%
Sudan	Black 52%, Arab 39%, Beja 6%, foreigners 2%, other 1%
Switzerland	German 65%, French 18%, Italian 10%, Romansch 1%, other 6%
United Kingdom	White 92.1% (of which English 83.6%, Scottish 8.6%, Welsh 4.9%, Northern Irish 2.9%), black 2%, Indian 1.8%, Pakistani 1.3%, mixed 1.2%, other 1.6%
United States	White 81.7%, Black 12.9%, Asian 4.2%, Amerindian and Alaska native 1%, native Hawaiian and other Pacific Islander 0.2%*

* Note: the U.S. Census Bureau does not have a separate listing for Hispanic or Latin American descent.

Source: Central Intelligence Agency, The World Factbook 2007; available at https://www.cia.gov/library/publications/the-world-factbook/index.html; accessed November 9, 2007.

Social Transformations (MOST) program, launched in January 1994 by the United Nations Educational, Scientific and Cultural Organization (UNESCO). MOST is an ongoing project designed to promote international comparative social science research, with the aim of transferring policy-relevant findings to governmental and nongovernmental decision-makers. A central goal of the MOST project in its first phase of operation (1994–2003) was to better understand multicultural and multiethnic societies, precisely because of the potential implications for a host of policy areas. Accordingly, it was argued,

> *The major challenge facing policy-makers in the fields of education, health, social welfare, and justice is to formulate policies in such a way as to promote and sustain peaceful multi-ethnic and multi-cultural co-operation and to rebuild such co-operation in societies undergoing post-war political, social and economic reconstruction.*[2]

This quest continues in the second phase of operation (2004–13) with an explicit focus on "International Migration and Multicultural Policies." To highlight "best practices" and to facilitate effective policymaking, the MOST project has developed a series of publications and electronic databases to provide relevant information to policymakers grounded in evidence-based social science research.

This chapter examines the internal diversity of nation-states in light of a belief system that profoundly shaped politics and events in the 20th century: nationalism. For political scientists today, a major research question concerns the salience of nationalism in the 21st century, given contemporary patterns of globalization. The economic, cultural, and technological processes associated with globalization now seem to challenge both national identity as the only or main form of identity experienced by people and the nation-state as a form of political organization. In this chapter, it is argued that while national identity is not disappearing, its primacy is being challenged by contemporary globalization.

In the first section of this chapter, key concepts pertaining to nationalism are explained. The second section contains an overview of theories of nationalism with reference to historic nationalist liberation struggles in the developing world. In the third section, the tension between nationalism and other forms of identity (especially gender) is examined in light of recent developments in South Africa. Finally, the tension between nationalism and globalization is addressed, and contemporary expressions of nationalism and identity claims that are not based on a single national identity are explored in relation to Canada.

Key Concepts in the Study of Nationalism
Connotation of Nationalism

What comes to mind when you see the word *nationalism*? Are your reactions positive or negative? No matter how you answer these questions, you will enter into a debate that has raged among analysts and historians for over two centuries. This momentous force has been viewed as the root cause of such diverse events as the emergence of the European state system, World War I, the rise of fascism in Europe, Third World anti-colonial struggles, reassertions of national identity by minorities in industrialized countries (e.g., in Scotland and in Quebec), and post–Cold War conflict in the former Soviet bloc countries (e.g., the Balkans and Central Asia).

Some see nationalism as a positive force. It has been suggested, for example, that the existence of nations is associated with the existence of ties of love or kinship.[3] Frequently, we may speak of nations as "motherlands" and "fatherlands." Citizens form a national "family." Immigrants are said to "adopt" countries that are not their native homes. In the United States, the president and the president's spouse are referred to as the "First Family." In Canada, the first two lines of the national anthem (at least in English, as the Canadian anthem's meaning is different in French!) are "O Canada! Our home and native land! True patriot love in all thy sons command." When Nelson Mandela became the first president of post-apartheid South Africa, his wife at the time, Winnie Mandela, was honoured as South Africa's "Mother of the Nation."

Probably more often, however, nationalism has been associated with hatred. Some have seen nationalism as the most destructive force of the 20th century—the cause of violence, atrocity, and incalculable human misery.[4] The Nazi regime in Germany and the evils of the Holocaust stood as the mid-century's horrifying example of this scourge. Responding to the tragedy of the Holocaust, Polish jurist Raphael Lemkin coined the term **genocide** (from the Greek word *genos*, meaning race, and the Latin word *caedere*, meaning to kill).[5] An international prohibition against genocide was established in 1948 when the United Nations adopted the Convention on the Prevention and Punishment of the Crime of Genocide.

In the 1990s, the violence, bloodshed, and killing that occurred among rival ethnic and religious groups in the former Yugoslavia (Serbs, Croats, and Muslims) and also in Rwanda (Hutus and Tutsis) emerged as new horrors that led many to reaffirm that nationalism was one of the most destructive forces imaginable and to refocus international attention on genocide. The Rwandan genocide began on April 6, 1994, when a small group of Hutu political and military leaders targeted and began the slaughter of more than a half a million Tutsis—a group that constituted about 10 percent of the population—along with thousands of Hutus who opposed the elite in power. This genocide differed from others in its rapidity (lasting about a hundred days) and in the number of ordinary people who were mobilized by a small elite to kill.[6]

The 1992–95 war in Bosnia-Herzegovina was the most destructive segment in the dissolution of Yugoslavia, which began when the republics of Croatia and Slovenia seceded in 1991, leaving open the possibility of an independent Bosnia. There was no clear ethnic majority in Bosnia; the three constituent peoples (as defined by earlier Yugoslav constitutions) were the Muslims (most numerous at 42 percent of the population), followed by the Serbs and the Croats.[7] In this climate of uncertainty in Bosnia, President Slobodan Milosevic of Serbia used the crisis to consolidate his power by sending in his paramilitary troops bent on ethnic cleansing.[8] While the United Nations attributes violence in Bosnia-Herzegovina to all sides, the term **ethnic cleansing** was used specifically to refer to a slate of violent measures and policies designed to eliminate or dramatically reduce the Muslim and Croat populations in Serb-held territory.[9] Ethnic cleansing included the systematic rape by Serbian soldiers of Muslim and Croat women, whose captivity, torture, and forced pregnancies were designed to reproduce "Serbians."[10] The term is controversial because it is seen as somewhat euphemistic (in contrast to *genocide*) and serves to mask the impact of this nationalist violence.

The travesties in both Rwanda and the former Yugoslavia, which clearly included both the direct and indirect involvement of governments, led to renewed calls within the international community for more effective means to prosecute such crimes. To this end, the United Nations convened an International Criminal Court, whose jurisdiction includes the ability to prosecute the crime of genocide, as defined in the 1948 Convention on the Prevention and Punishment of the Crime of Genocide. These tragic events of the 1990s also had an impact on the study of nationalism. Indeed, in 1993, Michael Ignatieff wrote an international bestseller, tellingly entitled *Blood and Belonging*, in which he argues that the end of the Cold War has been replaced by a new age of violence based on nationalism and ethnic particularism.[11] Some see the continuation of this age of violence in the 2003 escalation of violence between Arabs and black Africans in the Sudan—to the point that by 2004 Darfur, Sudan's western region, was described by many government and UN officials as the world's worst humanitarian crisis, with conservative estimates suggesting at least 200,000 deaths and 2 million people displaced.[12] While there have been debates in the UN about classifying the conflict as a "genocide," in July 2007 the UN Security Council approved deploying a peacekeeping force to Darfur to protect civilians.

Denotation of Nationalism

While there are radically different readings of the impact of nationalism as a force, political scientists are on less contentious ground in delineating what nationalism is. At root, **nationalism** may be defined as an ideology or belief system that contains three major assumptions.[13] The first assumption is that certain identified populations contain characteristics that make them nations. The second is that the world is divided into nations. The third is that a nation should be able to establish its own institutions, laws, and government and to determine its future—this is really what lies behind the idea of self-determination. The doctrine of self-determination holds that a group of people who call themselves a nation have a right to have control over territory or domains that immediately concern them, normally through statehood. The idea of self-determination may be traced back to the emergence of the European state system in the middle of the 17th century. In the 20th century, it became enshrined in the principles of international institutions such as the United Nations, and self-determination is now considered a human right under international law.[14]

Other Associated Concepts: State, Nation, Multination State, Diaspora

Unpacking the ideology of nationalism requires a closer examination of several associated concepts. The first concept is that of the state. Political scientists have theorized much about the state, but there is no clear consensus about whose interests it promotes. For example, the 19th-century thinker Karl Marx (1818–83) argued that in a capitalist society the state was a class instrument that served the interests of the owners of the means of production (the bourgeoisie) over the interests of the workers (the proletariat). For Marx, the state was central in the functioning of the capitalist system and the perpetuation of class inequality. This is why Marx called on workers to unite, overthrow the state, and usher in a more egalitarian (in this case, communist) society. More recently, radical feminists have argued that the state is central in perpetuating patriarchy (the rule of males) by privileging men in law and public policy.[15] Other (mainly liberal) theorists assert that the state operates in the interests of different individuals or groups at different times.

Although there is considerable debate about whose interests are represented by the state, most political scientists do agree on what the state is and use the definition first provided by Max Weber (1864–1920), as noted in Chapter 2. Weber argued that the "**state** is a human community that (successfully) claims the monopoly of legitimate use of physical force within a given territory."[16] For Weber, the state is characterized by territory (existing in a given geographical boundary), by sovereignty (the state is the highest authority and can back up its claims with force), and by institutions (including the bureaucracy, the military and the police, and the legislature).

It should be noted that the way political scientists use the term *state* to refer to territory, sovereignty, and institutions is very comprehensive and precise; the term *state* is not synonymous with *country* or *government*. The term *country* describes geographical units of the globe. When you look at the divisions of the world in an atlas, you are looking at countries. As discussed in Chapters 1 and 2, the term *government* refers to the set of institutions that makes and enforces collective public decisions for a society, a society that usually takes the form of a state.

The ideology of nationalism holds that territory, sovereignty, and institutions must be allocated to people of a single nation. While belonging to a state may be a simple matter of citizenship, belonging to a **nation** rests on a subjective sense of identity and of belonging to an ethnic group (usually marked by a distinct culture or language).[17] A leading theorist of nationalism, Benedict Anderson, refers to nations as "imagined communities" precisely because the idea of a nation rests on a subjective sense of belonging to a community that is neither voluntary nor organizationally defined. Joining an organization such as an undergraduate students' association (which likely holds elections for those willing to run for president, vice-president, and the like) is not like being part of a nation. In contrast, belonging to a nation is somewhat similar to belonging to a family—it is seemingly "natural" and involuntary.[18] For this reason, according to Anderson, dying for one's nation "assumes a moral grandeur which dying for the Labour Party, the American Medical Association, or perhaps even Amnesty International cannot rival, for these are all bodies one can join or leave at easy will."[19] Undoubtedly, we could put campus student associations in this same "voluntary" category as political parties or interest groups.

Although the ideology of nationalism implies that there ought to be an easily definable correspondence between territory, a single nation, and rule, this is not the case with most countries. Some states contain more than one nation; such a state is called a **multination state**. For example, Canada has been variously described as containing two nations (the French and the British), three nations (the French, the British, and Aboriginal peoples), and even numerous nations (particularly when the multiple traditions and languages among all Aboriginal peoples in Canada are considered). This is where the problems of the doctrine of self-determination become apparent. Often, in real-world politics, the same territory is claimed by more than one

Nationalistic Americans fear "dangerous" Arab nationalism.

Kirk Anderson/Artizans

group. This is especially apparent in a country such as Canada—a settler colony with an Indigenous population and a minority francophone population located primarily in Quebec. During the 1995 Quebec referendum on sovereignty, separation from the rest of Canada was rejected by a very narrow margin (50.6 percent to 49.4 percent). Aboriginal peoples have land claims all over Canada, including in the province of Quebec. For this reason, when the referendum was called, some Aboriginal groups, including the Cree and the Montagnais, held their own referendums on the issue of sovereignty, in which the proposal was rejected by a wide margin. A prime international example of nations laying claim to the same land is the Israeli–Palestinian conflict. Both sides have insisted for decades on the legitimacy of their claim on historic grounds, and a solution has not been found (see Box 3.1).

A further complication to the doctrine of nationalism is the fact that nations may spill out across state boundaries—a feature encapsulated in the concept of **diaspora**. The term was originally applied to Jewish people, but today it is used to describe any ethnic group that has experienced or currently experiences dislocation across multiple states, and yet typically nurtures narratives and political projects about a "homeland" as a place of eventual return at some opportune time.[20] In contemporary usage it has been applied to such diverse groups as Palestinians, Armenians, and Cubans.[21]

Racial Discrimination and the Politics of Multiculturalism

Finally, as part of understanding nationalism, it should also be noted that ethnic groups can have many different political demands and points of mobilization that do not take the form of nationalism and self-determination, but instead stress gaining acceptance and equality.[22] In particular, some groups may struggle against discrimination based on race.

Both Palestinian Arabs (Muslims and Christians) and Israeli Jews lay claim to the territory of Palestine/Israel as their national home on the basis of long residence, history, and religion. The area known as Palestine was, until World War I, part of the Turkish Ottoman Empire. Following the war, the League of Nations (the forerunner to the United Nations) granted Britain a mandate over Palestine. Flowing from the 1917 Balfour Declaration, the British government viewed "with favour the establishment in Palestine of a national home for the Jewish people," and promised to use immigration to support this objective.

While Palestinian Arabs remained a majority in the area until the late 1940s, the goal of creating a Jewish state in Palestine was further developed in the United Nations Partition Plan in 1947. The Partition Plan sought to divide Palestine into an Arab state and a Jewish state, with the city of Jerusalem designated as an international zone. The Partition Plan was viewed as unacceptable and unfair by Arab Palestinians, who believed it threatened the geographical integrity of Palestine and disagreed with the manner in which Palestine was divided. Hostility between Arabs and Jews mounted in Palestine, and civil war broke out. On May 14, 1948, an independent state of Israel was declared, and the British mandate came to an end. As a result, open warfare between the surrounding Arab states and Israel erupted. By the end of the war, there was more land taken by Israel than had been allotted under the Partition Plan. However, Israel rapidly gained the recognition of both the world's superpowers, the United States and the Soviet Union. Israeli leaders immediately indicated that the new state belonged to all the Jewish people around the world and invited immigration from the Jewish diaspora. This is codified as the Israeli state's "law of return."

The events of 1948 are subject to very different national narratives on the parts of Palestinians and Israelis. For many Israelis, the years 1947 and 1948 are seen as a period in which the birth of a national state was made possible after the Holocaust and after what Israelis call the War of Independence of 1948. This accounts for the jubilant celebrations in Israel in 1998 of 50 years of statehood. In contrast, for most Palestinians, the year 1948 represents a disaster (in Arabic *Al-Nakba*) characterized by half of the Arab population losing homes and property and becoming stateless refugees outside of historic Palestine. Today Palestinians make up the world's largest and one of the oldest refugee groups. Indeed, from 1949, Palestinian national identity crystallized around the loss of homeland, the longing to return, and the desire for self-determination. This is symbolized in the quest for a "right of return."

A series of wars in the region (in 1956, 1967, 1973, and 1982) has served to reconfigure control of the land in favour of the state of Israel. For example, after the 1967 war, the territories of the West Bank and Gaza (known as "the occupied territories") came under Israeli control. The Oslo agreement signed in 1993 by Israel and the Palestine Liberation Organization (PLO) allows for parts of these two territories to be handed over to Palestinian rule. Nonetheless, peace remains elusive between Israelis and Palestinians, as well as in the larger region. This case provokes the following question: Can competing claims to the same territory be adequately resolved in a framework emphasizing self-determination?

In the past, the term **race** has been used in many different ways. During the 19th century, biologists used it to refer to different "subspecies" of humans. The inspiration behind eugenics movements—which advocated the use of "scientific" breeding techniques to improve the genetic potential of humans—was the supposed existence of biological differences between different "racial" groups. In the early 20th century, the term *race* was often used as a synonym for *nation* and *ethnic group*. This can be seen in the metaphor of America as a "melting pot," popularized in the 1908 play *The Melting Pot* by Israel Zangwill. Zangwill spoke of different "races" (by which he meant Germans, Russians, the English, the French, and the Irish) jumping into a common melting pot and emerging as Americans.[23] By the middle of the 20th century, as a result of the atrocities of the Holocaust, the use of *race* to refer to biological differences between people was completely discredited; instead, many began to talk about "the human race" to indicate that eugenics was wrong, as all people are of the same species.

Today, social scientists use the term *race* to refer to socially constructed rather than biologically inherited differences. In other words, race is viewed as significant only because of socially created beliefs about differences between people, not because biology itself determines culture or personality. In particular, social scientists are interested in how the processes of racism (or racialization) are manifested in practices and institutions to the detriment of particular groups in particular times and places. Some have advocated rejecting the term *race* altogether, or at least putting it in quotation marks to signify that there are no inherent differences between people.[24]

The idea that race and processes of racism are socially constructed and temporally specific can be readily documented. For example, historically, the Irish were held to be a separate and inferior "race" to the British; they experienced discrimination in a host of spheres in Britain, Canada, and the United States. Today groups struggling with racial discrimination include African-Americans in the United States. African-Americans overcame slavery in the 1800s, and through the civil rights movement in the 1950s and 1960s successfully challenged segregation in public schools and private establishments, yet discrimination against them remains a fact of life.

The continued inequality in employment and earnings between African-Americans and all other groups has led to public policy measures such as affirmative action. **Affirmative action** is designed to equalize the chances of members of minority groups or groups traditionally discriminated against, such as African-Americans, women, and people with disabilities, in accessing education and jobs by setting goals for ensuring the statistical representation of these groups. Affirmative action has become increasingly controversial in the United States. Critics charge that it is "reverse discrimination," while proponents argue that it helps put into practice the principle that all people are of equal worth. In the United States, affirmative action has tended to be supported by African-Americans more than by other groups.[25] Given the historical and contemporary social context of that country, categories such as "black" and "white" (and increasingly, "mixed race") are important politically.

Contemporary theoretical discussions of racism are further complicated by the fact that analysts have increasingly sought to identify the relationship between culture (not just biology) and processes by which groups can experience differentiation, discrimination, and disadvantage. For example, British political theorist Tariq Modood distinguishes "colour racism" (as seen in hierarchically distinguishing "black" and "white") and "cultural racism." For Modood, the primary example of cultural racism today can be seen in how Muslims in Britain face discrimination and their religion is vilified (also captured in the more popularized concept of Islamophobia).[26] Modood states as well that this tendency predates the events of September 11, 2001.

Whether looking at African-Americans in the United States or British Muslims, the projects of such groups tend to be different from groups seeking national self-determination. Political theorist Will Kymlicka suggests that in Canada and elsewhere many minority and immigrant groups have mobilized to demand **multiculturalism**. Kymlicka points out that this pursuit of multiculturalism is geared primarily to achieve inclusion in the dominant culture, rather than to attempt to live separately from it. For Kymlicka, multicultural responses to minority and immigrant group claims might involve such diverse policies as affirmative action, guaranteed seats in legislatures, curriculum changes in schools, work schedule changes to accommodate diverse religions, flexible dress codes, literacy programs in the first language of immigrants, and bilingual education programs for the children of immigrants.[27] In this way, multiculturalism may be seen as a very different kind of demand than national self-determination.

Explaining Nationalism: National Liberation Movements and Decolonization

So far in our discussion, two main themes have emerged. First, nationalism has been associated with many different—even opposite—phenomena in the 20th century: war, violence, hate, oppression, liberation, family, and love. Second, political scientists have defined the ideology of nationalism and related concepts in a precise way that seems to capture the essence of most, if not all, expressions of nationalism. The areas of agreement and disagreement help account for two very distinct approaches to studying nationalism that political scientists have used in explaining its emergence in very different times and locales.

Because the ideology of nationalism is fairly consistent across its various expressions, political scientists have tried to determine whether there is one primary factor that can explain the emergence of nationalism in so many different places. Those searching for this all-purpose general explanation have engaged in *universalizing comparisons*; that is, they have attempted to show how all instances of nationalism follow the same patterns. In contrast, other political scientists have postulated that, partly because of the sheer variety of phenomena associated with nationalism (from oppression to liberation), there may be many different explanations for why nationalism emerges in different locales—that is, that there is no universal explanation. Those searching to discover such differences have engaged in *individualizing comparisons*, which attempt to show the unique characteristics of a given instance of nationalism.

To evaluate these two different approaches, it is helpful to consider how each might account for the same manifestation of nationalism, namely that of 20th century Third World anti-colonial movements. During the 19th century, **imperialism**—in the form of **colonization** of other countries and the establishment of empires—led to the expansion of Western power over the rest of the world. However, during the 20th century, the formal control of Western states in different parts of the world largely came to an unexpected end in a relatively short period of time. Consider that in 1945, when the United Nations emerged as the primary international organization to promote peace and human rights, 51 states obtained membership. Out of these 51 states, only three were located in Africa (Ethiopia, Liberia, and South Africa), three in Asia (of which only China was independent of colonial rule), and seven in the Middle East, as can be seen in Table 3.2. Initially, then, the great majority of member states in the United Nations were the countries of North America, the Commonwealth, and Europe, including the former Soviet Union. Notably, most observers in the 1950s did not expect European power to end in their lifetime.[28] However, by the end of 1965, 66 new states had joined the United Nations, bringing the number up to 117; in 2006, with the addition of Montenegro, the number reached 192.

The addition of 66 new states by 1965 symbolized a dramatic political change: the formal transfer of power from Europeans to non-Europeans and the liberation of some 1 billion people from colonial rule in Asia and Africa. The emergence and successes of Third World nationalist anti-colonial movements might be explained in different ways depending on the approach one uses.

Table 3.2 The Original 51 Member States of the United Nations, 1945

Argentina	Czechoslovakia	Honduras	Panama	United Kingdom of Great Britain and Northern Ireland
Australia	Denmark	India	Paraguay	United States of America
Belgium	Dominican Republic	Iran	Peru	Uruguay
Bolivia		Iraq	Philippines	Venezuela
Brazil	Ecuador	Lebanon	Poland	Yugoslavia
Belarus	Egypt	Liberia	Russian Federation	
Canada	El Salvador	Luxembourg		
Chile	Ethiopia	Mexico	Saudi Arabia	
China	France	Netherlands	South Africa	
Colombia	Greece	New Zealand	Syrian Arab Republic	
Costa Rica	Guatemala	Nicaragua	Turkey	
Cuba	Haiti	Norway	Ukraine	

Universalizing Comparisons

Traditionally, many political scientists used universalizing comparisons to try to establish that all forms of nationalism follow the same patterns or rules. This approach was widely accepted during the 1950s, 1960s, and 1970s, and there are still people who use it today. Its popularity may be related to how political science, as a discipline, has been influenced by developments in the United States. In the United States, during the first two to three decades after World War II, political analysts were very much concerned with developing generalizations that could be applied to all societies at all times. This was part and parcel of developing a "science" of social and political life.[29]

The accounts that address nationalism from the vantage point of universalizing comparisons generally suggest that nationalism was rooted in the European experience, dating from the French Revolution and gaining speed with the unification of Germany and Italy in 1870. In this view, nationalism was somehow related to the processes of industrialization. What exactly is highlighted as important about industrialization varies in different accounts that make use of universalizing comparisons. Some have argued that technological developments in mass communication and the introduction of mass education made it possible for people to easily communicate with each other across vast distances.[30] As a result, people started to identify with one another in a new way—as part of national communities. Others have proposed that capitalism accompanied industrialization, and with capitalism came uneven development, and, when there were pockets of poverty in distinct regions, expressions of nationalism emerged.[31] Both of these scenarios that use industrialization to explain nationalism have a universalizing quality to them—a sense that the ideology of nationalism developed in Europe and was simply exported to Africa and Asia on the back of European colonialism.[32]

More recently, such universalizing explanations have been criticized for being Eurocentric— that is, focused only on the experience of Europe. Critics also argue that they are ahistorical—that is, they tend to ignore the unique historical context of different countries outside of Europe in accounting for nationalism. There is value to these criticisms, since political scientists have never been able to produce one general theory that accounts for the emergence of nationalism everywhere and for all time.

Individualizing Comparisons

Individualizing comparisons, then, take into account both historical and geographical specificity. They seek to uncover that which is unique about a given form or instance of nationalism. Broadly speaking, the suggestion that comes out of such accounts is that many expressions of Third World nationalism may be viewed as a political reaction against colonialism.[33] This political reaction occurs in societies where traditional modes of social and political organization have collapsed as a result of the changes introduced by colonialism.

One way to understand how Third World expressions of nationalism were a reaction against the oppressive effects of colonial rule is to consider how colonized people were treated and depicted by colonial powers. The famous lines by British poet Rudyard Kipling on "The White Man's Burden" provide a literary example of this broader phenomenon. Kipling's poem, written in 1899, describes the need for British men, and more broadly white men, to go out to the colonial world and rule the peoples there, whom Kipling describes as "half devil and half child."[34]

Unequal power relations that rested upon the dehumanized depiction of the colonized by the colonizer are key to understanding the motivation behind Third World nationalist movements for liberation. Imperialism and colonialism worked to erode the dignity of peoples of the Third World, but nationalism formed a part in the recovery of that dignity.[35] Consequently, one of the things that tend to surface in such expressions of Third World nationalism aimed at liberation is an attempt to invert and put value on the identity of the colonized. For example, Léopold Sédar Senghor, a poet who became the first president of Senegal after it achieved independence from France in 1960, is associated with a literary and political movement known as négritude. The négritude movement, which began in the 1930s and reached its zenith in the 1960s, launched a critique of Western society for suppressing blacks and for cutting African blacks off from their roots. Négritude aimed to rediscover ancient African values so that Africans could feel pride and dignity in their heritage and culture.

Likewise, Frantz Fanon, a West Indian–born psychoanalyst and philosopher who spent time in Algeria when it was under French colonial rule, went on to write about the necessity of creating or recreating a national cultural consciousness as a means of achieving true independence. In contrast to the négritude movement, however, Fanon saw an important, almost redemptive, role to be played by violence. He describes this idea in his famous 1963 book *The Wretched of the Earth*, which deals with the situation in Algeria. Between 1954 and 1961, there was a bitter and violent war between France and Algeria, as a result of which Algeria gained its independence in 1962. For Fanon, the lessons of the Algerian war of independence suggest the value of violent struggle as a means to empower colonized people. Violence, he argues, is a cleansing force that "frees the native from his inferiority complex and from his despair and inaction."[36] Yet ultimately, the development of a genuine national consciousness leading to real liberation is difficult to achieve, Fanon points out, because the forces of domination are internalized by indigenous elites.[37] Even after decolonization, the unequal social and economic structures inherited from colonialism might well continue. Fanon sensed very early on that the national liberation movements in countries that experienced colonization might be successful in overthrowing foreign rulers, but that this might not necessarily in and of itself lead to an egalitarian future.

The basic idea behind individualizing comparisons is that while nationalism might be a single ideology, it contains several subvarieties.[38] From the vantage point of individualizing comparisons, manifestations of nationalism in the Third World in the context of national struggles for liberation may be seen as unique because the factors that motivated nationalism were unique. Universalizing explanations, in contrast, fail to take into account the specificity of the situation in the Third World. In an attempt to fit all manifestations of nationalism into one pattern, they fail to consider the historical effects of imperialism and colonialism in the countries of the developing world. Individualizing comparisons do not have these limitations, suggesting the general necessity of attending to context when trying to understand nationalism in the contemporary period.

The Nation Versus Other Forms of Identity: Considering South Africa

The advantages of individualizing comparisons do not completely negate the need to theorize about the nation in relation to internal forces. The warnings of Frantz Fanon about the future of liberated (postcolonial) states highlight the complexities present in any nation. Any population that calls itself a nation is inevitably internally diverse and divided along some combination of class, gender, age, and rural–urban lines. As one prominent example of the relevance of this kind of internal diversity within nations, it is useful to consider the recent work of feminist scholars who have insisted on the importance of gender diversity in the study of national identity and relations of power. We have noted how nationalist discourses often make use of metaphors relating to kinship—motherlands, fatherlands, and the like. Such "familial" depictions of the nation have been the starting point for the work of these feminist scholars who stress that nationalist movements can act to subordinate women. For example, whether women have children, how women socialize children, and even how women dress are often extremely important to most nationalist movements.[39]

Because women frequently play a central role in transmitting and reflecting cultural traditions across generations, the argument has been made that it is women who play the primary role as "bearers of the nation," rather than schools or forms of mass communication (as has been suggested by some accounts focusing on explaining the rise of nationalism in relation to industrialization).[40] In this way, women can become specific targets as both the "property of men" and the "embodiment of the nation," as attested to by the systematic use of rape in the name of ethnic cleansing.[41] While, typically, nationalist movements themselves are tied to gendered relations, this does not always mean that they specifically improve the position of women. Indeed, according to feminist scholars, those who assume that nationalist movements generally improve the lot of the disadvantaged often neglect to attend to specific social and political structures and belief systems that can keep women in subordinate positions.[42]

In the context of nationalist movements aimed at liberation, South Africa provides a noteworthy recent example of a country where gender equality had to be considered explicitly. The history of the African National Congress (ANC) illustrates this point. The ANC was created in 1912 as the principal organization reflecting black South African interests. Although it was outlawed in 1960, the ANC was later instrumental in ending the racist policies of apartheid (or apartness) that had supported white colonial political and economic dominance. Nelson Mandela emerged from a long prison term to lead a successful anti-apartheid movement and then become the first president of post-apartheid South Africa in 1994.

The history of politics in South Africa and the reaction of black women there to the long years of resistance and hope for liberating the country from white control demonstrate that black women's relation to nationalism has undergone changes.[43] Initially, when the ANC was created, women were denied formal representation in the organization, yet gradually, as a result of women's own insistence, they were granted full participation. Nevertheless, calls for women's emancipation were generally seen as secondary to national revolution, sometimes even by women themselves. Over the late 1970s and 1980s, however, the issue of women's empowerment began to be raised as a project distinct from national, democratic, and social revolution. By the early 1990s, female ANC nationalists carried placards with the slogan "A nation will never be free until women are free."[44]

Such women's demonstrations were successful in leading to formal recognition of women's rights within the ANC, which in 1990 issued a Statement on the Emancipation of Women. The statement argued that the experience of other societies with successful national liberation struggles showed that the emancipation of women does not necessarily follow from national

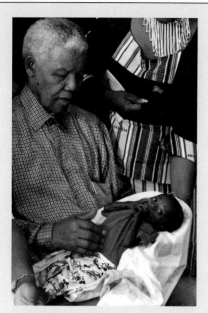

Former South African President Nelson Mandela holds a six-month-old baby infected with HIV during his visit to Beautiful Gate, a home that looks after children in Crossroads township, outside of Cape Town, South Africa; Saturday, December 1, 2001.

CP Photo/Obed Zilwa

liberation. The statement asserted that, given this historical record, women's emancipation had to be addressed within the ANC, the mass democratic national movement, and society as a whole. It went as far as to say that all "laws, customs, traditions and practices which discriminate against women shall be held unconstitutional."[45] Indeed, under Nelson Mandela a new constitution was passed that emphasized not only formal but also substantive equality for women.[46] Formal equality refers to the idea that everyone has the same rights; substantive equality refers to the idea that everyone is able to actually access the same opportunities by holding and exercising those rights.

While it has been observed that no other country has a constitution with such progressive ideas to eliminate sexism,[47] constitutions do not in and of themselves necessarily guarantee all the rights they may proclaim. For this reason, gender equality in the context of national liberation in South Africa is still on the agenda for analysts to explore, and also for women's organizations to address in what is proving to be an ever-changing political environment.[48] Nevertheless, the case of South Africa and the ANC demonstrates how nationalism still matters, how nations are internally diverse, and how national movements may be affected by these phenomena.

Nationalism Versus Globalization

Given the internal diversity of nations and the fact that what motivates nationalism might vary depending on the time period and geography, it seems clear that the idea of a universal theory of nationalism is problematic. The limitations of universalizing explanations should be kept in mind as we turn to the grand question concerning the future of national identity and nationalism in light of contemporary globalization.

In an important way, as attested to by the examples of imperialism and colonialism, **globalization** is not a completely new phenomenon. For centuries, people, money, ideas, goods, and corporations have crossed geopolitical boundaries. But the processes associated with contemporary globalization (since 1945) have some distinct features. Globalization before the end of World War II was based on imperialism, colonialism, and coercion practised by institutions of empires (such as the British or French). Contemporary globalization processes rest on a multitude of multilateral institutions (such as the World Trade Organization and gigantic **transnational corporations**) and, since the collapse of the Soviet Union, the political and economic dominance of the United States.[49] As well, the contemporary economic, technological, and cultural flows associated with globalization are more intense than in earlier periods.[50] Money can flow from one country to another via e-mail and the Internet, computer technology has spread around the world, and electronic communications (including satellites) transmit popular culture to every corner of the globe. The unprecedented speed with which capital (in the form of cash, stocks, and shares, for example) can move around the world as a result of new information technologies illustrates how economic flows have changed in the past several decades; and the speed with which information can flow across the planet as a result of the Internet and other developments in communications (such as the advent of CNN, which is based in Atlanta in the United States but has overseas operations and services) means that information flows are not simply national but global. As well, while people may always have moved from place to place, the flows are now much more widespread and multidirectional. Currently all regions and countries both send and receive people.[51]

The combination of all of these developments has led some political scientists to question the future viability of the state as a form of organization, because one of its key aspects (as identified by Weber) is sovereignty, the assumption that it is the highest authority. But sovereignty may be eroding in the face of the contemporary worldwide reorganization of economic, technological, and cultural flows. For example, states now have much more difficulty controlling the flow of information.

Globalization and National Identity

Globalization also raises questions concerning national identity. Stuart Hall, a leading British analyst of culture, has argued that the developments associated with contemporary globalization that appear to challenge the state and its sovereignty also raise issues about the future of nationalism. Hall argues that the seemingly "natural" priority given to national culture (and identity) is in fact a historical phenomenon tied to the emergence of the nation-state. He suggests that contemporary globalization appears to have the effect of "contesting and dislocating the centred and 'closed' identities of a national culture."[52] Globalization raises many uncertainties about the future of national identity, not only because people who move across national boundaries may bring with them different cultural influences, but also because there are forms of culture (from Mickey Mouse to world music) that are not simply national but global. Furthermore, there are elements of identity (gender, for example) that may assume as much importance for some people as national identity, if not more.

According to Stuart Hall, the 21st century carries three possibilities for national identity.[53] One possibility is that national identity may actually be strengthened in response to globalization. Another possibility is that national identity may be weakened. The third possibility is that new, shifting, and even hybrid forms of identity may emerge to challenge a singular national identity.

Drawing from our discussion on the advantages of individualizing comparisons, it is probably more useful to attend to specific cases when considering these propositions rather than to attempt to make universal claims. We will therefore turn our attention to the cases of the **European Union (EU)** (see Box 3.2) and Canada to gain insight into the possibilities that contemporary globalization raises for the future primacy of national identity.

The Canadian Case

In Canada, the daily news reminds us that people of many different backgrounds reside here—that is, that Canada is a country that reflects a reality of cultural pluralism. Among a host of possible demographic statistics that might be utilized to illustrate this reality are those on ethnic diversity (Table 3.3) and religious diversity (Table 3.4). A dominant issue that structured Canada's history as a settler-colony concerned the rights of Catholics versus those of Protestants. For example, the 1774 *Québec Act* granted the freedom to practise the Catholic faith, and retained the French civil law and seigneurial landholding systems. While the *Québec Act* did not say anything about the use of French, the appointed council (overseen by a colonial governor) allowed for Roman Catholics to hold office. Today, this particular division has less obvious resonance, and instead, Canadian electoral and other political debates have revolved around the future of the province of Quebec, where many francophones (who constitute the majority of the population) are committed to the idea of sovereignty for their province.

The modern nation-state system arose in Europe, so it is particularly relevant to consider developments in this region when examining the question of whether national identity is weakening. The European Union (EU) is an international organization dating back to the 1950s, created with the specific goal of weakening national rivalries (especially between France and Germany) through greater economic cooperation. Initially consisting of only West European countries, in May 2004 the EU gained 10 new members, including for the first time former Soviet-bloc countries of Central Europe. As of 2007, membership stands at 27, Austria, Belgium, Denmark, Finland, France, Germany, Greece, Ireland, Italy, Luxembourg, Spain, Sweden, the Netherlands, Portugal and the United Kingdom having been joined in 2004 by Cyprus, the Czech Republic, Estonia, Hungary, Latvia, Lithuania, Malta, Poland, Slovakia, and Slovenia and in 2007 by Bulgaria and Romania.

Over the 1980s and 1990s, economic cooperation in Europe deepened significantly, also affecting the political sphere. A European flag, anthem, and parliament were created, and in 1993 the **Maastricht Treaty** introduced a citizenship of the European Union. The rights associated with EU citizenship include the right of free movement; for example, a Dutch citizen has the right to move to and work in Belgium or any other member country. EU citizens also have the right to vote and stand for elections at the local level and at the European level in any member state. Finally, EU citizenship entitles one to consular protection when abroad from any embassy of a member country.

Every citizen of an EU member state is considered to be an EU citizen. However, the rights of EU citizenship, and especially the right of free movement, will not be fully implemented across all EU countries for a period of anywhere from two to seven years for citizens of the countries that joined in 2004 and 2007.

The EU and its citizenship raise many interesting questions. Does EU citizenship contribute to a new form of belonging or identity—that of being "European"? If so, how does that differ from national identity? Does EU citizenship really weaken national citizenship? Should EU citizenship be automatically and fully granted to the citizens of the 12 countries that joined between 2004 and 2007, or is it reasonable to do this over time? Should EU citizenship be granted to any person who permanently lives in Europe regardless of citizenship (including some 12 million legally residing migrant workers and their families who have come mainly from countries of the developing world)?

Beyond the potential secession of Quebec, other issues related to cultural identity cause heated debates. For example, what about the right of francophones outside of Quebec to speak French in public institutions? What about Aboriginal peoples and their quest for self-government and cultural preservation? What about non-French or non-British immigrants and their offspring—to what extent should the maintenance of languages other than French and English be encouraged and to what extent should Canadian institutions change to reflect and accommodate peoples of all backgrounds? And what about those who want to define themselves as simply "Canadian"—should the Canadian state foster only this kind of allegiance?

Table 3.3   Top 15 Ethnic Origins in Canada, 2006

The following are the results of the 2006 census, based on the responses to the question "To which ethnic or cultural group(s) did [your] ancestors belong?" People were allowed to name more than one origin.

	Total Response	Single Responses	Multiple Responses
Total population	**31,241,030**	**18,319,580**	**12,921,445**
Canadian	10,066,290	5,748,725	4,317,570
English	6,570,015	1,367,125	5,202,890
French	4,941,210	1,230,535	3,710,675
Scottish	4,719,850	568,515	4,151,340
Irish	4,354,155	491,030	3,863,125
German	3,179,425	670,640	2,508,785
Italian	1,445,335	741,045	704,285
Chinese	1,346,510	1,135,365	211,145
North American Indian	1,253,615	512,150	741,470
Ukrainian	1,209,085	300,590	908,495
Dutch	1,035,965	303,400	732,560
Polish	984,565	269,375	715,190
East Indian	962,665	780,175	182,495
Russian	500,600	98,245	402,355
Welsh	440,965	27,115	413,855

Source: Statistics Canada, Census of Population, "Population by Selected Ethnic Origins, By Provinces and Territories (2001 Census)" (April 21, 2004). Adapted from Statistics Canada website http://www40.statcan.ca/l01/cst01/demo26a.htm?sdi=ethnic%20origins.; accessed May 7, 2008.

Table 3.4   Major Religious Denominations in Canada, 2001 (as % of population)

Christian Faith Communities	
Roman Catholic	43.2
Protestant	29.2
Christian Orthodox	1.6
Christian, not included elsewhere	2.6
Non–Christian Faith Communities	
Muslim	2.0
Jewish	1.1
Buddhist	1.0
Hindu	1.0
Sikh	0.9
No Religious Affiliation	
No Religion	16.2

Source: Statistics Canada, "2001 Census: Analysis Series Religions in Canada," Catalogue No. 96F0030XIE2001015 (2003).

All of these questions lie at the heart of the politics of multiculturalism, national recognition, and nationalism in Canada, and there is an ebb and flow to which ones assume prominence in public debate. Since the events of September 11, 2001, and the fallout from the U.S.-led "war on terrorism," there has been a strong shift to thinking of accommodation and multiculturalism through the lens of religious difference, and to the question of accommodating religious minorities (i.e., non–Christian faith groups, in contrast to the historic focus on Catholics versus Protestants), especially Muslims. The focus on religious minorities was in evidence in Ontario during the 2005 debate over religious-based arbitration (especially as it concerned Sharia law) as well as the 2007 electoral discussion over faith-based schools. In

Quebec in 2007, Premier Jean Charest formed a commission, headed by the prominent historian Gérard Bouchard and prominent political theorist Charles Taylor, to address the question of "reasonable accommodation" as it concerns religious minorities and practices in relation to public institutions. Irrespective of the outcome of the Bouchard-Taylor Commission, religion will likely continue to assume prominence in Canadian discussion over the first and second decade of the 2000s, but it is only one facet of diversity that has entailed questions of governance.

Prior to European colonization in the early 17th century, Aboriginal societies were characterized by a rich range of cultural, linguistic, social, and political practices.[54] When the French and the British established their settlements and expropriated land from Aboriginal peoples, they brought with them their own cultures and languages. Since then, there have been many waves of immigration from other European countries, and increasingly, since the late 1960s, from countries outside of Europe. For much of Canada's history, government policies reflected an emphasis on the model of **dominant conformity** and, specifically, Anglo conformity. The idea behind dominant conformity is that all groups should assimilate to the language, culture, and values of the dominant group, and in the case of Anglo conformity in Canada, that all groups should conform to the British group.

In the last few decades, as a result of pressures from different minority groups, the Canadian state has adopted a series of **public policy** measures designed to deal with diversity in a different way. In 1969, a national policy of official bilingualism (French and English) was introduced. In 1971, a national policy of official multiculturalism within a bilingual framework was established, giving recognition to the multiplicity of ethnic groups represented in the country. In recent years, both the federal and provincial governments have been involved in discussions pertaining to settling Aboriginal land claims and fostering forms of Aboriginal self-government. Canadian human rights commissions and courts have also followed suit, for example by highlighting the need for employers, landlords, and public officials to make "reasonable accommodation" for a range of groups (including persons with disabilities and religious minorities) in such areas as job duties and expectations, building design, or even school rules. For instance, in March 2006 the Supreme Court of Canada ruled that a Quebec schoolboy, who is an orthodox Sikh, could wear the *kirpan* (ceremonial dagger) to school, and that refusing to allow this on the basis of a general prohibition against students carrying "weapons" was a violation of the religious freedom guaranteed by the Canadian Charter of Rights and Freedoms.[55]

Does the shift since the 1960s suggest that national identity is weakening? If that identity is defined in terms of Anglo conformity, then the answer is yes. These kinds of initiatives reflect Canada's commitment to a variant of the model of cultural pluralism. While the term **cultural pluralism** refers to the existence of diverse ethnic and cultural groups within a country, the cultural pluralism model specifically aims at promoting peaceful cooperation and recognition among these groups. The model of cultural pluralism suggests that groups can maintain distinct features without being marginalized economically or socially. Moreover, it contends that the cultivation of differences does not necessarily produce conflict; rather, it can produce peaceful coexistence through overarching values and institutions. Canada's official policy of multiculturalism within a bilingual framework is a variant on the model of cultural pluralism.

The models of dominant conformity and cultural pluralism represent opposite methods of dealing with ethnic and cultural diversity within a country. While many federal policies in Canada today reflect the model of cultural pluralism, it should also be noted that these policies have been controversial. For example, members of the Conservative Party (and its precursors, the Reform Party and Canadian Alliance) and some intellectuals have argued that multiculturalism is leading to the fragmentation of Canada and should therefore not be publicly recognized or funded. In a related way, it has been suggested that a policy emphasis on "being Canadian" would contribute to the unity of the country and the loyalty of citizens toward the Canadian state.[56] These developments illustrate that there are those who would like to see the strengthening of a singular national identity in Canada.

Finally, there is evidence that Canadians identify in many ways that are not captured completely by the idea of belonging to any one group, whether defined by gender, ethnicity, or other factors. Indeed, the National Action Committee on the Status of Women, the main umbrella association for women's groups outside Quebec, has increasingly taken the position that there is a complex heterogeneity among Canadian women along racial, ethnic, class, and other lines. Likewise, we see that Canadians self-identify in complex ways. For example, in the 2001 census, 38 percent of Canadians gave multiple responses to the ethnic origin question.[57] It

Fans show their support for Team Canada during their game against Team USA at the Women's World Hockey Championships in Winnipeg on April 7, 2007.

Source: CP Photo/Adrian Wyld

is clear that many Canadians describe themselves as having multiple ethnic origins, such as writer Lawrence Hill who has referred to himself as a "zebra" to describe the hybrid experience of having a white mother and a black father.[58] It could be anticipated that such kinds of multiple and mixed identities might increase as a result of contemporary globalization, since people may migrate several times in a lifetime, and since a growing number of people appear to be at ease with multiple national attachments and fluid and shifting identities.[59]

The case of Canada therefore suggests that an argument can be made for saying that the salience of a single national identity (particularly in the form of Anglo conformity) has lessened with time. Although there are still debates about the desirability of having one dominant national identity, there is evidence that many Canadians see themselves as having multiple origins and identities. This suggests that while national identity is not about to disappear, it may be increasingly less dominant in the 21st century. In light of this tension, this may be why the politics associated with diversity—as seen in the recent turn to looking at "reasonable accommodation" in Canada—has been so vexed.

CONCLUSION

This chapter examined key terms and concepts pertaining to the politics of cultural pluralism. It surveyed different theoretical approaches to the study of nationalism, arguing that helpful insights are gleaned by attending to specific cases and using contemporary approaches that consider issues such as gender and different forms of identity. The central question raised in this chapter concerns the future of the nation-state and the salience of national identity in the era of globalization. It was suggested that there are three possib... national identity may be strengthened; national identity may be eroded; or ne... and even hybrid forms of identity may emerge. The chapter tested these three poss... examining the case of Canada. The findings suggest that while national identi... disappearing, its primacy is indeed being challenged by contemporary globalizatio...

Given the internal diversity of most countries around the world today, and given the fact that contemporary globalization itself may create the conditions for new and evolving forms of identity, it seems that political scientists will have much to examine in the years ahead. As well, because the already heterogeneous national populations are increasingly (and perhaps differently) affected by the larger international context, policymakers will have to think creatively to enact effective public policies.

DISCUSSION QUESTIONS

1. Is nationalism primarily a negative or a positive force? Why?

2. It has been suggested that the gendered aspects of nationalism are particularly apparent when it comes to war, the transmission of culture, and dress. Can you provide examples supporting this idea? Can you think of other ways in which men and women are called upon differently in the name of "the nation," or ways in which they are called upon similarly?

3. Are people attached primarily to a singular national identity, or is there another form (or other forms) of identity to which people are attached?

4. Does contemporary globalization weaken or strengthen nationalism? What examples would you use to support your position?

5. Are the demands made by minority ethnic groups for policies such as affirmative action, or flexible work or dress codes, easier or more difficult to resolve than claims for self-determination?

KEY TERMS

CULTURAL PLURALISM: The coexistence of many ethnic and cultural groups within a country. Such diversity is the starting point in arguing that all groups in a society can maintain their linguistic, cultural, and religious distinctiveness without being relegated to the economic or cultural margins, and is achieved through the creation of a common set of values and institutions. (74)

DIASPORA: An ethnic group that has experienced or currently experiences dislocation across multiple states, yet typically nurtures narratives and political projects about a specific "homeland" as a place of eventual return. (63)

DOMINANT CONFORMITY: A model of ethnic group integration holding that all groups in a society should conform to the language and values of the dominant group. In the case of Canada, this is the idea behind historical policies emphasizing Anglo conformity, which aimed to have all groups assimilate by speaking English and holding the values of the dominant British-origin group. (74)

ETHNIC CLEANSING: The removal of one or more ethnic groups from a society by means of expulsion, imprisonment, or killing. The term entered the political lexicon in reference to the former Yugoslavia; it was first used to describe the violent measures and policies designed to eliminate or dramatically reduce the Muslim and Croat populations in Serb-held territory. (61)

GENOCIDE: The deliberate and systematic extermination of a national, ethnic, or religious group. The term was developed in response to the horrors of the Holocaust. (60)

GLOBALIZATION: The movement of goods, capital, ideas, and people across geopolitical boundaries today and in the past. Contemporary patterns of globalization involve a deepening constellation of economic, technological, and cultural changes that are worldwide in scope and that challenge the sovereignty of the state. (70)

MULTICULTURALISM: A policy sometimes adopted in a state characterized by cultural pluralism that supports ethnic and cultural groups in maintaining their customs and traditions, often with public financial assistance. (66)

MULTINATION STATE: A state that contains more than one nation. (62)

NATION: A community of people, normally defined by a combination of ethnicity, language, and culture, with a subjective sense of belonging together. (62)

NATIONALISM: An ideology that holds that certain populations are nations, that the world is divided into nations, and that a nation should be self-determining (i.e., able to establish its own institutions, laws, and government and to determine its future). (61)

RACE: Historically, the term *race* was used to speak about differences between people that were supposedly biologically based. Today social scientists completely reject the idea that there are any significant biological differences between people that warrant the use of the term. While some suggest that in light of this the term should not be used at all, many contemporary social scientists put the term in quotation marks to refer to differences that are socially constructed and historically specific, but have important consequences in the form of racism. Contemporary discussions of racism assume that it involves a biological and/or cultural assertion of superiority by one group over another. (65)

WEB LINKS W W W

UNESCO's Management of Social Transformations Programme:
http://www.unesco.org/shs/most

The Nationalism Project:
http://www.nationalismproject.org

The International Forum on Globalization:
http://www.ifg.org

Citizenship, Democracy and Ethnocultural Diversity Newsletter:
http://queensu.ca/cded/newsletter.html

Major Collaborative Research Initiative: Ethnicity and Democratic Governance:
http://www.queensu.ca/edg/links.html

FURTHER READING

Abu-Laban, Yasmeen, ed. *Gendering the Nation-State: Canadian and Comparative Perspectives.* Vancouver: University of British Columbia Press, 2008.

Banting, Keith, Thomas J. Courchene, and F. Leslie Seidle, eds. *Diversity, Recognition and Shared Citizenship in Canada.* Montreal: Institute for Research on Public Policy, 2007.

Gagnon, Alain-G, Montserrat Guibernau, and François Rocher, eds. *The Conditions of Diversity in Multinational Democracies.* Montreal: Institute for Research on Public Policy, 2004.

Green, Joyce, ed. *Making Space for Indigenous Feminism.* London: Zed Books: 2007.

Kymlicka, Will. *Multicultural Odysseys: Navigating the New International Politics of Diversity.* Oxford and New York: Oxford University Press, 2007.

Modood, Tariq. *Multicultural Politics: Racism, Ethnicity and Muslims in Britain.* Minneapolis: University of Minnesota Press, 2005.

ENDNOTES

1. *MOST Newsletter* 3 (June 1995): 1; available at http://www.unesco.org/most/newlet3e. htm; accessed August 22, 2001.

2. *MOST Newsletter* 1 (December 1994): 5; available at http://www.unesco.org/most/ newlet1e.htm; accessed August 22, 2001.

3. See Benedict Anderson, *Imagined Communities: Reflections on the Origin and Spread of Nationalism*, rev. ed. (London: Verso, 1991).

4. See Elie Kedourie, *Nationalism* (London: Hutchinson, 1985).

5. Danilo Türk, "Genocide," in Joel Krieger, ed., *The Oxford Companion to Politics of the World* (Oxford: Oxford University Press, 2001), p. 316.

6. Allison Des Forges, "Rwandan Genocide," in Krieger, *The Oxford Companion to Politics of the World*, p. 749.

7. Srda Trifkovic, "Bosnian War," in Krieger, *The Oxford Companion to Politics of the World*, p. 79.

8. *Ibid.*

9. Elizabeth Philipose, "Ethnic Cleansing," in Lorraine Code, ed., *Encyclopedia of Feminist Theories* (London: Routledge, 2001), pp. 192–93.

10. *Ibid.*, p. 193.

11. Michael Ignatieff, *Blood and Belonging: Journeys into the New Nationalism* (Toronto: Penguin Books, 1993).

12. BBC News, "Q&A: Sudan's Darfur Conflict" (October 10, 2007); available at http:// news.bbc.co.uk/2/hi/africa/3496731.stm; accessed June 2, 2008.

13. E. Ellis Cashmore, *Dictionary of Race and Ethnic Relations* (London: Routledge and Kegan Paul, 1984), p. 182.

14. Pereket Hablte Selassie, "Self-Determination," in Krieger, *The Oxford Companion to Politics of the World*, pp. 760–61.

15. Janine Brodie, "State Theory," in Code, *Encyclopedia of Feminist Theories*, p. 462.

16. Quoted in Ronald H. Chilcote, *Theories of Comparative Politics: The Search for a Paradigm Reconsidered* (Boulder: Westview Press, 1994), p. 98.

17. Sometimes the term *civic nationalism* is used to refer to an inclusive form of national belonging based on participation in a shared public sphere, as contrasted with *ethnic nationalism*, which is based on a belief in shared ethnicity or blood ties. However, the utility of this dichotomy has been called into question on a number of grounds, including the claim that *civic nationalism* can serve to mask the power of the dominant ethnic group(s) in organizing public life in the first place. See Claude Couture, *Paddling*

with the Current: Pierre Elliott Trudeau, Etienne Parent, Liberalism and Nationalism in Canada (Edmonton: University of Alberta Press, 1998), p. 112.

18. Walker Connor, "A Nation Is a Nation, Is a State Is an Ethnic Group Is a . . . ," *Ethnic and Racial Studies* 1(4) (October 1978): 381.

19. Anderson, *Imagined Communities*, p. 144.

20. James Clifford, "Diasporas," in Montserrat Guibernau and John Rex, eds., *The Ethnicity Reader: Nationalism, Multiculturalism and Migration* (Cambridge: Polity Press, 1997), pp. 283–90.

21. *Ibid.*, p. 284.

22. Tomas Hylland Eriksen, "Ethnicity, Race and Nation," in Guibernau and Rex, *The Ethnicity Reader*, pp. 33–41.

23. Yasmeen Abu-Laban and Victoria Lamont, "Crossing Borders: Interdisciplinary, Immigration and the Melting Pot in the American Cultural Imaginary," *Canadian Review of American Studies* 27(2) (1997): 33.

24. Robert Miles and Rudy Torres, "Does 'Race' Matter? Transatlantic Perspectives on Racism after 'Race Relations,'" in Vered Amit-Talai and Caroline Knowles, eds., *Re-situating Identities: The Politics of Race, Ethnicity and Culture* (Peterborough: Broadview Press, 1996), pp. 25–46.

25. Lucius J. Barker and Mack H. Jones, *African Americans and the American Political System* (Englewood Cliffs: Prentice Hall, 1994), pp. 30–49.

26. Tariq Modood, *Multicultural Politics: Racism, Ethnicity and Muslims in Britain* (Minneapolis: University of Minnesota Press, 2005).

27. Will Kymlicka, *Finding Our Way: Rethinking Ethnocultural Relations in Canada* (Don Mills: Oxford University Press, 1998), p. 42.

28. John Isbester, *Promises Not Kept: The Betrayal of Social Change in the Third World* (West Hartford: Kumarian Press, 1995), p. 109.

29. For an example, see Karl W. Deutsch, *Nationalism and Social Communication: An Inquiry into the Foundations of Nationality* (New York: John Wiley, 1953).

30. See Ernest Gellner, *Nations and Nationalism* (Oxford: Basil Blackwell, 1983) on these points, and see Anderson, *Imagined Communities*, regarding the significance of the printing press.

31. See Tom Nairn, *The Break-up of Britain* (London: NLB, 1979).

32. See especially Kedourie, *Nationalism*, p. 145.

33. Isbester, *Promises Not Kept*, p. 106.

34. *Ibid.*, p. 102.

35. *Ibid.*, pp. 105–48.

36. Frantz Fanon, "The Wretched of the Earth," in Omar Dahbour and Micheline R. Ishay, eds., *The Nationalism Reader* (New Jersey: Humanities Press, 1995), p. 283.

37. *Ibid.*, pp. 274–83.

38. Anthony D. Smith, *Theories of Nationalism*, 2nd ed. (London: Gerald Duckworth, 1983), p. 193.

39. Nira Yuval-Davis and Floya Anthias, *Woman-Nation-State* (Basingstoke, U.K.: Macmillan, 1989).

40. Nira Yuval-Davis, "Gender and Nation," in Rick Wilford and Robert L. Miller, eds., *Women, Ethnicity and Nationalism* (London: Routledge, 1998), pp. 23–35.

41. Elizabeth Philipose, "Ethnic Cleansing," in Code, *Encyclopedia of Feminist Theories*, p. 183.

42. For a discussion of these issues, see Deniz Kandiyoti, "Identity and Its Discontents: Women and the Nation," in Patrick Williams and Laura Chrisman, eds., *Colonial Discourse and Post-Colonial Theory: A Reader* (New York: Columbia University Press, 1994), pp. 376–91.

43. For an overview, see Sheila Meintjes, "Gender, Nationalism and Transformation: Difference and Commonality in South Africa's Past and Present," in Wilford and Miller, *Women, Ethnicity and Nationalism*, pp. 62–86.

44. This account of women's organizing and example of the placard is adapted from Anne McClintock, *Imperial Leather: Race, Gender and Sexuality in the Colonial Context* (New York: Routledge, 1995), pp. 379–86.

45. McClintock, *Imperial Leather*, p. 384.

46. Meintjes, "Gender, Nationalism and Transformation," pp. 82–83.

47. *Ibid.*, p. 83.

48. *Ibid.*, p. 84.

49. David Held et al., *Global Transformations: Politics, Economics and Culture* (Stanford: Stanford University Press, 1999), pp. 425–26.

50. *Ibid.* See Chapter 16 of this book.

51. *Ibid.*, p. 297.

52. Stuart Hall, "The Question of Cultural Identity," in Stuart Hall et al., eds., *Modernity: An Introduction to Modern Societies* (Cambridge: Polity Press, 1995), p. 628.

53. *Ibid.*, pp. 596–634.

54. Olive Patricia Dickason, *Canada's First Nations: A History of Founding Peoples from Earliest Times* (Toronto: McClelland and Stewart, 1992), pp. 63–83.

55. Yasmeen Abu-Laban and Baha Abu-Laban, "Reasonable Accommodation in a Global Village," *Policy Options* 28(8) (September 2007): 28–33.

56. For this position, see Rhoda Howard-Hassmann, "Canadian as an Ethnic Category: Implications for Multiculturalism and National Unity," *Canadian Public Policy* 25(4) (1999): 523–37. For a critique of this position, see Yasmeen Abu-Laban and Daiva Stasiulis, "Constructing 'Ethnic Canadians': The Implications for Public Policy and Inclusive Citizenship," *Canadian Public Policy* 26(4) (December 2000): 477–87.

57. Statistics Canada, "Canada's Ethnocultural Portrait: The Changing Mosaic," *The Daily*, January 21, 2003, p. 14; available at http://www12.statcan.ca/english/census01/products/analytic/companion/etoimm/contents.cfm; accessed June 2, 2008.

58. Lawrence Hill, "Zebra: Growing Up Black and White in Canada," in Carl E. James and Adrienne Shadd, eds., *Talking About Difference: Encounters in Culture, Language and Identity* (Toronto: Between the Lines, 1994), pp. 41–47.

59. See, for example, Parminder Bhachu, "The Multiple Landscapes of Transnational Asian Women in the Diaspora," in Vered Amit-Talai and Caroline Knowles, eds., *Re-situating Identities: The Politics of Race, Ethnicity and Culture* (Peterborough: Broadview Press, 1996), pp. 283–303, and Ayse S. Caglar, "Hyphenated Identities and the Limits of 'Culture,'" in Tariq Modood and Pnina Werbner, eds., *The Politics of Multiculturalism in the New Europe* (London: Zed Books, 1997), pp. 169–85.

Part

3

Political Values

ALAN BORAS

Political discourse and public policy matters have long permeated the home and energy industry career of Alan Boras. His father John, a southern Alberta lawyer with a lifelong passion for politics, ran in one federal and four provincial elections. Many a Sunday brunch discussion with his family was grounded in debate of a variety of public policy matters.

Alan attended the University of Lethbridge before transferring to St. Francis Xavier University in Nova Scotia to complete an arts degree in Political Science and History. Following a backpack trip through Asia and Europe, Alan earned a second degree in journalism and communications at the University of Regina. A political education, travel, and journalism formed a solid foundation for 12 years of print reporting, two years at the Regina *Leader-Post* writing news features, followed by a decade at the *Calgary Herald*, the last five years as a business writer covering Canada's oil and gas industry. Alan then sought an opportunity to work in communications in Canada's energy sector, first at PanCanadian Petroleum Limited and later at Alberta Energy Company Ltd. The two firms merged in 2002 to form EnCana Corporation, creating the nation's largest oil and gas producer. "While a political science education may sometimes be cast as having modest practical applications in private enterprise, the reality is that the politics and development of public policy influence the operations of any business or corporation," he says.

Businesses receive their operating licence from civil authorities, operations are highly regulated, profits are taxed, and governments and public policymakers at all levels set the rules for how business will function. In the resource industries, one of the most fundamental public and economic policies is the determination of royalty rates and the government rent applied to the extraction of resources. Government leaders seek to secure the highest resource rent over the long term for the public while creating an investment climate that attracts development capital and the opportunity to earn competitive returns. Having an understanding of government, of how public policy is determined, and of the role of politics and public opinion in the making of those decisions impacts every aspect of business, and can only benefit companies dealing with governments and regulators seeking to serve the public interest.

In his daily work of writing and delivering EnCana's business and operational story to the media and the public, Alan Boras and his colleagues always consider the political implications of what the company does and says. Earning and maintaining a reputation for integrity and reliable performance is essential for success beyond the bottom line. Understanding politics and democratic governance is fundamental for all business leaders as they endeavour to work with governments, public interest groups, and all stakeholders to fashion policies that balance the interests of investors and the public, and achieve the economic vitality to grow and develop society.

Chapter Four

POLITICAL CULTURE AND SOCIALIZATION: The Media and Other Mind Shapers

Andrew Heard

CHAPTER OBJECTIVES

After you have completed this chapter, you should be able to:

- outline the relationship between a society's culture and its politics

- discuss the nature of political culture

- explain the significance of identity politics

- describe how deep divisions between groups in a society may be handled

- understand the processes through which we acquire our political knowledge and beliefs

What Is Political Culture?

Politics is all about things we value and wish to see respected and protected, whether they are specific material benefits, such as health care, or higher moral principles, such as freedom of speech. What we think about the society we live in, the government that rules over us, and the other groups of people who live alongside us are all matters of personal attitude that can have profound political effects. One will know very little indeed about politics without an appreciation of the broader cultural context within which it occurs. Ultimately, the politics of a society is a reflection of that society's culture. The depth of differences among groups within a society and the way they are dealt with can profoundly shape the nature of political discourse and conflict. For example, the difference between a stable, harmonious society and one wracked by a bloody civil war can flow from answers to such basic cultural questions as "To which group do I most strongly identify myself as belonging?" and "How is my group treated by others in my country?" These concepts were introduced in Chapter 3.

Comparisons of Canadian political phenomena with those from around the world can provide an idea of the practical consequences of the cultural values people hold. A large number of francophones in Quebec have supported separation throughout most of the last three decades, while there is no significant separatist movement within the United States, despite its enormous ethnic diversity. Canada does not have the death penalty, while China not only executes people but often does so in public settings. Most women have had the vote in Canadian national elections since 1918, while women in Kuwait only won the right to vote in 2005.[1] In the end, the differences between Canada and the other countries mentioned in these examples stem fundamentally from different values in the cultures of those societies.

Quite clearly, the variations in cultural values in societies can have a significant effect on these societies' politics. In order to understand the politics of any state or the variations and similarities between states, one has to appreciate the framing role of cultural values in political objects, principles, and processes. To understand politics, we need to grasp the essence of political culture, realize how the predominant values of that culture come to be passed on among its members, and discover whose values come to be accepted as the norm. Political scientists are interested in how deeply individuals identify with different social groups, what enduring cleavages may exist between these groups within a given society, and how political systems accommodate, foster, and suppress conflicts between them.

We all have a sense of what culture means, but the concept of culture is highly contentious; there are literally hundreds of definitions. In a general sense, culture consists of the shared values, beliefs, practices, and symbols relating to the food, clothing, social relations, language, religion, literature, music, and so on that are practised or favoured among a particular group of people. But culture in a larger sense relates to the fundamental values of communities and their beliefs about how life should be lived, how people should behave, and how society should be organized. Political culture is essentially this social phenomenon applied to politics. Indeed, political culture is really just a particular aspect of a society's broader culture.

Political culture is the collection of the understandings, values, attitudes, and principles of a community or society that relate to its political organization, processes, disputes, and public policies. Out of a society's political culture come important beliefs and values that structure the citizens' attitudes and expectations toward such basic political concepts as legitimacy, power, authority, and obedience. These attitudes play an important background role in the success and effectiveness of the government in that society. The extent to which citizens acquiesce in or defer to their political leaders has a significant bearing on whether the government feels it necessary to use more force and coercion than influence in order to exercise authority and secure compliance with its decisions. As well, these attitudes can shape the informal processes through which a society manages to direct and settle disputes outside the formal political institutions.

Some powerful consequences can flow from as seemingly simple an attitude as "We should respect and defer to the political leaders of our country. They are the elders of our group. They know things that I do not know." One can expect a very different relationship between the citizens and their political leaders in a democracy where the culture encourages people to believe "My view is as good as the prime minister's (or president's)," an attitude more typical in Canada. A 2007 opinion poll found that only 15 percent of Canadians said that they trust politicians; that figure contrasts with the 35 percent who trusted new-car salespeople and 89 percent who trusted teachers (see Figure 4.1).[2]

Political culture is not just about those things explicitly related to the political system; it is also about general social attitudes that can have political ramifications. For example, attitudes toward sexual practices are largely a matter of personal, private behaviour in Western countries, but they become political when issues of government censorship of pornography arise or when debates over the promotion of gay rights come up. Whether the government should ban homosexual behaviour or allow same-sex marriages has been strongly debated at different times in many countries, and an individual's attitudes toward the role of the state in this matter are deeply connected to his or her beliefs about what types of sexual behaviour are to be prohibited, tolerated, or even celebrated. The position taken by different groups on many

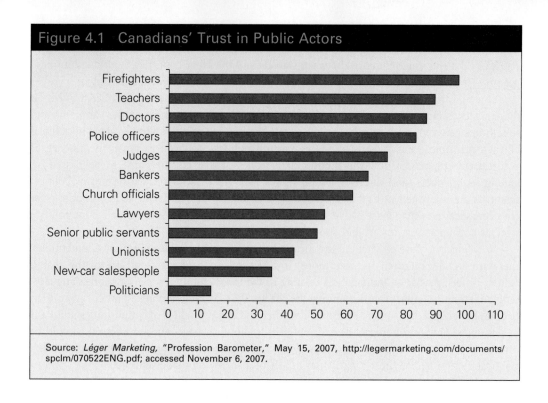

Figure 4.1   Canadians' Trust in Public Actors

Source: *Léger Marketing,* "Profession Barometer," May 15, 2007, http://legermarketing.com/documents/spclm/070522ENG.pdf; accessed November 6, 2007.

political issues is often largely determined by their broader social beliefs and principles. The "social" becomes "political" as members of a society who hold opposing views compete over whose beliefs should be embodied in their government's laws and policies.

The values and beliefs of individuals regarding their governments and about their own sense of responsibility toward their governments can have a crucial impact on those governments' abilities to function properly. One example is people's attitudes toward paying taxes. Canadians may take taxes for granted because of a high rate of compliance; there may be a certain amount of fiddling, but only a small minority of Canadians refuse to report the bulk of their earnings and pay taxes on them. People in different parts of the world have very different attitudes toward paying taxes to their governments; yet governments cannot function effectively without an adequate tax base. Without enough tax revenue, a government simply will not have the capacity to fulfil the functions required of it. The Swiss are the most likely to pay their taxes, with just 6 percent of the country's economic activity going untaxed. In Canada, only about 15 percent goes untaxed, in contrast to 27 percent in Italy.[3] The problem is chronic in many other countries. For example, Russia's uncollected tax bill was estimated at US$100 billion in 1997.[4] This is a staggering figure when one realizes that the Russian government was set to collect only US$26 billion in total in 1999.[5] In Kenya, almost 64 percent of the workers are estimated to be employed in the informal sector, beyond state taxation.[6] Attitudes of people in a variety of countries on questions of employment policy are another example of different values and beliefs; they are compared in Table 4.1.

Political Subcultures and the Power of Elites to Shape Ideas

Political cultures are almost never homogeneous or monolithic; indeed, the political cultures of most societies contain many different subgroups or **subcultures**. Even in liberal democracies, political culture is often a majoritarian phenomenon—the majority within any group essentially

Table 4.1 Attitudes Toward Employment Policies

An international survey asked people if they agree with the following questions: "When jobs are scarce . . ."

Country	MEN HAVE MORE RIGHT TO A JOB THAN WOMEN		PRIORITY SHOULD BE GIVEN TO "CO-NATIONALS" OVER IMMIGRANTS	
	Agree	Disagree	Agree	Disagree
Argentina	25.8	61.0	73.3	15.9
Canada	15.6	77.2	51.4	38.5
Egypt	89.6	0.4	98.6	0.0
France	21.7	68.3	53.6	36.1
Germany	26.6	55.9	64.3	23.2
India	57.2	31.3	85.4	8.3
Italy	27.0	56.8	61.4	20.3
Japan	31.8	63.1	60.6	7.6
Mexico	31.1	58.9	79.9	11.2
Philippines	67.3	16.3	84.8	4.7
Russia	36.0	52.9	73.5	20.6
South Africa	36.2	52.5	83.2	9.4
Sweden	2.3	93.4	11.2	77.8
United Kingdom	21.0	66.9	58.8	31.6
United States	9.7	82.3	50.2	39.6

Source: Data are from the European Values Study Group and World Values Survey Association.

gets to determine and foster the views that are taken as representative of that group. As a result, it is important to keep in mind the distinction between generalization and universalization: just because most members of a society believe something does not mean that everybody believes it. It is equally important to ask whose ideas are accepted as the "norm" in a society and why. Political culture is every bit as much a creation as it is an organic phenomenon.

By delving more deeply into particular aspects of a society's culture, one can often find that it is not even a majority but rather a small powerful group or **elite** that is able to dominate or even totally control the values propagated publicly in that society. This is most clearly seen in states with totalitarian regimes, where ruling elites mould most aspects of the society's public values; Nazi Germany, Stalinist Russia, and China under Mao are some examples of this phenomenon. However, one can also suggest that even in liberal democratic societies, powerful cliques are able to set the tone and range of public discussion for the general community. For example, those who control the media have an enormous influence, as discussed later in this chapter. Critics of Western democracies argue that even in these supposedly free cultures, dominant socioeconomic groups not only assert their preferred values as the "ideals" but also create an attitudinal environment that leads the members of the various lower strata of society to accept their exploitation. Predominant attitudes taught to the poor thus lead them away from openly questioning the distribution of benefits within their society and toward acquiescing in the prevailing order.

In most societies one finds significant distinctions between the values widely held among the elites and those held by the mass population. But because elites are the ones who make most of the public policies for a society, it is their values that are often embodied in government policies; furthermore, it is their values that are usually reflected in public descriptions of what their society believes in. Examples of the mass–elite division of values and beliefs are easy to find in Canada. For example, a majority of Canadian members of parliament have voted against capital punishment on three occasions: in 1967, 1976, and 1987. Opinion polls, however, showed that a majority of the general adult population consistently favoured the death penalty right up until the early 21st century; only in 2004 did a national survey reveal that Canadian public opinion had caught up with the decisions of their elites with only 42 percent in favour of the death penalty in Canada.[7]

The **ideologies** favoured by a society's elites are usually reflected in the dominant political culture of a country as well. The elites' general understandings about how a country's economy and political system should be organized end up forming the basis of the public policies and political debate in the state. In a telling critique of human societies, Antonio Gramsci has developed an important notion of a hegemony of ideas that describes particular values and beliefs so ingrained in people that they not only do not question them but also think of them as pure common sense. Furthermore, Gramsci has argued that political rulers would succeed in the long run only to the extent to which the masses they ruled accepted the elite's worldview.[8] Perhaps the ultimate exercise of political power by elites in a society is the ability to structure the beliefs of those they rule in such ways that the masses neither question the elites' rule nor understand that their own interests may lie in a different political order or set of public policies.

Michel Foucault has also argued that elites in society are able to structure even our most basic conceptions of who we are and what actions or benefits are truly in our own interest.[9] One does not have to take these perspectives to the point of asserting some deliberate conspiracy of mind control to appreciate the enormous potential that the various agents of political socialization have in shaping and moulding members of a society into sharing a vast array of common beliefs and perspectives. Furthermore, as students of politics, we can ask ourselves what interests and values particular to women, minority groups, or even the majority of "ordinary people" are not being articulated and embraced in the general political culture of a society.

Political Trust, Efficacy, and Alienation

Several types of personal attitudes can deeply affect a political system when they are aggregated among all the members of a society. How individual members feel about their political system and even how they think about it can have very significant effects on the political culture of groups in society.

Affective attitudes and orientations are those we hold because of the way we feel about something; they are an emotional response to issues and events. *Cognitive* attitudes and orientations are those we hold because of what we know about the issues and events, or at least what we think we know about them. (Remember here that just because we believe something to be a fact does not mean it is true.) *Evaluative* attitudes and orientations are ones that combine emotion and knowledge—that is, where we combine what we know with what we feel about something to make judgments about political phenomena and events. A subtle but important part of our personal maturation process as we grow up, as well as the political socialization process in general, lies in how we learn to think about events and issues. Our behaviour in the political world will be very different depending on whether we are guided by affective, cognitive, or evaluative attitudes.

How we think is very much influenced by how we have been taught to think, by role models as well as by implicit instruction. What we believe we know about our political system and how we feel about it greatly influence our own sense of where we personally fit into our society. If we feel that we have political representatives or other leaders who generally act honestly, in good faith, and use good judgment in furthering our collective well-being, then we may have a strong sense of **political trust** in our political elites. **Political efficacy** is the belief that we as individuals can have some influence upon the decisions that affect our lives. If, however, we have a low degree of trust in our political leaders and have little sense of political efficacy, then we may well feel **political alienation**.

Civic Culture and Democracy

Two American political scientists, Gabriel A. Almond and Sidney Verba, first coined the term *civic culture* to describe the group of attitudes and beliefs needed in a political culture in order for a stable, liberal democracy to thrive.[10] Many of Almond and Verba's views have since come under severe criticism, particularly their belief that America was an example of the virtues of a civic culture, but some of their observations have spawned a continuing debate over the cultural requirements for a peaceful, democratic society, now termed **civil society**. Not only is representative democracy predicated upon the general population having significant trust in their elected representatives, but citizens must also have a sense of efficacy in order to participate in many of the society's political processes. Thus, a stable democracy with a civic culture is most likely to be found in societies where the political culture reflects high levels of trust and efficacy but low levels of political alienation.

Civic culture and civil society do not *cause* stable democracy, but they do appear to be an essential precondition for a stable liberal democracy.[11] A lack of a civic culture or strong civil society might explain the significant difficulties some countries have when they try to adopt a democratic form of government after many decades of a system of government that fostered political alienation and distrust of political elites. (This issue is addressed in Chapter 14.) It is also important for the political culture to embrace a spirit of genuine compromise and an ability to lose out from time to time. After all, the essence of a democracy is that different factions are willing to reach a compromise and not remain rigidly demanding that all of their claims be met; furthermore, a group has to be willing to lose in elections and allow another group to take office.

Willingness to compromise and an ability to lose may seem rather vague and distant attitudes, but they are essential cultural values for a democratic form of government to survive more than one party's term in office. Samuel P. Huntington described the fate of newly minted democracies in the late 20th century as follows:

> *Threats to third-wave democracies are likely to come not from generals and revolutionaries who have nothing but contempt for democracy, but rather from participants in the democratic process. These are political leaders and groups who win elections, take power, and then manipulate the mechanisms of democracy to curtail or destroy democracy.*[12]

What is important, however, is that Western political scientists do not simply suppose that their own perceived virtues of Western liberal democracies are necessary for other countries to adopt in their entirety or that they are readily transferable to other, ancient cultures.

Identity Politics

An individual's self-identification is profoundly personal and yet has enormous political relevance. How we view ourselves and who we believe ourselves to be are matters of complex psychological evolution over the course of our lives. One of the strongest human inclinations we develop is to identify ourselves with some group, or several groups, to which we feel we belong. Humans are social, gregarious animals, and most of us are naturally inclined to interact with others. Speaking in general terms, we seem to have a need to be part of a group. Most of us have many sides to our personalities and a range of interests, and as a result we associate with different groups at different times to match different aspects of our character. Some of the groups we identify ourselves with have little political significance, such as a group of friends who share a love of snowboarding. But we may also identify ourselves with other groups that can at times have real political significance.

Identity politics draws attention to ways in which political power is structured around group politics in society. The term **identity politics** (or the politics of difference) describes political activity by particular groups looking for recognition of their status and identity, as introduced in Chapter 3; such groups wish to see acknowledgment of the ways their beliefs and value systems differ from others in their society. Thus, Canadian philosopher Charles Taylor has argued that a "number of strands in contemporary politics turn on the need, sometimes demand, for *recognition*."[13] Examples include women's rights movements, minority rights groups, Aboriginal movements, movements for the rights of disabled persons, and gay and lesbian rights movements. Another example is seen in the political debate launched in Canada when the 1987 Meech Lake Accord proposed that Quebec be recognized as a "distinct society."

Of particular importance is a group's belief about how its members are treated, as a group, by the rest of society (see Box 4.1). For many groups, a prime struggle is to create and project a positive identity to counteract negative stereotypes of them created by other groups in their society. This process may involve finding ways for individual members of the group to develop a new positive self-esteem, as well as the group acting collectively to create in others a positive, respectful image of them.

For many people, group identity and membership creates the framework for meaningful choices made by an individual: who we are, the values and goals we possess, and where we stand in society are given to us by our culture and history. Culture, therefore, is not simply the

---

Class Identity and False Consciousness — BOX 4.1

Class is a concept that describes the hierarchical layers within a society that result from different levels of wealth, income, occupation, and social status. Social scientists distinguish between objective class levels, which are often measured based on income, and subjective class, which is the class people say they identify themselves as belonging to. The difference between objective class and subjective class is striking in Canada, where there are enormous disparities in income spread across the population, but where the overwhelming majority of citizens identify themselves as "middle class." As a result, class conflict is largely absent from Canada's political scene. Countries such as France or Italy, where a significant number of people identify themselves as "working class" and possess **class consciousness**, have much more polarized political systems and much higher levels of support for left-wing political parties than in North America.

Marxists talk about "false consciousness" in situations where poor people have been socialized into believing they are middle class so that they are unlikely to organize and change the existing social and economic order. The Marxist critique is that members of the objective working class falsely identify with a higher class and therefore are not aware of the "true interests" of the group to which they really belong.

The issue of false consciousness and ignorance of one's own group's true interests is a controversial one, but it can be applied to most characteristics upon which identity is based. For example, does each group based on ethnicity, gender, sexual orientation, religion, and so on have an objective set of true interests that everyone who belongs to the group should be aware of and pursue? If so, who gets to decide what those interests are?

sum of individual values. Attachments such as gender, sexual orientation, class, and ethnicity define an individual's place in society, and as such constitute part of one's culture (see Box 4.2). This is a very different view from the dominant liberal view of culture and groups. Liberalism separates the individual from his or her community and culture; it treats culture as an aggregate of the beliefs and values of individuals. From the perspective of liberalism, communities exist only insofar as they find expression in the values and beliefs of individuals.[14]

The politics of identity is about more than merely wanting to be valued. Achieving the respect of others is just the first step in trying to participate in the political system on a more equal basis. In many respects, identity groups are reacting against existing political structures in which a dominant culture, espousing the language of universalism, attempts to deny the importance of the particular circumstances and values—particularism—of those groups. This denial of difference is a way for the dominant culture to exercise political power and control over these groups. Identity politics and the politics of difference, in effect, represent a demand for greater political power by groups in society through the recognition of their different identities and value systems. This demand for political power is usually framed in the language of "rights."

Universalism does not recognize differences among people in the granting of rights and maintains that everyone should be treated equally and in exactly the same manner, irrespective of differences in gender, religion, sexual orientation, ethnicity, and history. The focus is on

---

Check Your Own Identity

BOX 4.2

Pause a few moments and think about how you think of yourself. The questions that follow and your answers to them should give you some idea of how important your own view of yourself is—your identity. You should also have a clearer idea of the impact on you of other people's views of who you are.

- Your parents gave you a name at birth. Do you like it, dislike it, or not care much? Why? Are you still called by that name, or do people call you by a short form of it (e.g., Jo instead of Joanne) or a nickname? If the name you are called has changed, did you initiate the change or have you lived with what others decided to call you? Do different groups of people call you different variations of your name? What significance would there be in that?

- How many different defining characteristics do you think of yourself as

having? For starters, think about religion, language, gender, sexual orientation, ethnic background(s), body size and shape, attractiveness, physical abilities, the neighbourhood or town you grew up in, how much money you have, etc.

- Have you ever felt you have received privileged treatment because of who you are? Have you been singled out for poor treatment because of some personal characteristic someone else did not like?

- What sorts of negative things that people have said about who or what you are have hurt you? How difficult has it felt to try to change other people's negative views of you?

- What things about yourself would you not change, even if it meant putting up with abuse from other people?

individual rights—rights that apply to all individuals equally. The purpose of these rights is to guarantee that everyone gets equal treatment in politics and in law. The particularism advocated by many identity groups, on the other hand, is based on the argument that real equality cannot be achieved without recognizing the value of differences and according differential rights on the basis of group membership. The focus here is on collective rights or group-differentiated rights. The purpose is to overcome the vulnerability and disadvantage of certain groups—to help them acquire the ability to make choices.

Historically marginalized groups such as African-Americans, people with disabilities, or Aboriginal people have not just striven for recognition and respect from the larger society—they also desire to be full participants in their society and to effectively pursue their own interests. The politics of identity involve groups seeking political goals related to fostering those things that give them a distinct identity. For example, francophone parents across Canada have sought the establishment of French-language schools, so that their children may learn the language and cultural heritage of their group. These parents believe that French schools will help preserve and foster the most important things that set their group apart from the rest of society.

Thus, there is a continuing controversy in modern politics about how to balance individual equality with special treatment for particular groups. Should a group receive special benefits to foster the characteristics that give its members their identity, or should all groups be treated equally? Some advocates argue that to treat different groups in very different circumstances with absolute equality only serves to perpetuate the existing inequalities between the groups. To achieve substantive equality between groups, one has to treat them in ways that account for their differences. A current example of this dilemma in Canada relates to Aboriginal self-government. Many critics of self-government argue that it offends the principle of equality by creating a particular form of government for one "race" when all other races in Canada belong to a common political system. (Note the discussion on the contemporary and historical usage of the term *race* in Chapter 3.)

Others counter that it is race that has created the disadvantages that so many Aboriginal people face, and a "race-based" government is actually the best solution to a cultural problem. Will Kymlicka has forcefully argued that modern liberalism can and should adapt equality to allow for special treatment that fosters a group's cultural identity.[15] This is justified on the grounds that individuals fully develop only within the context of their group memberships, and thus by providing different benefits required by the circumstances of different groups (particularly minority groups), one is fostering the development of all individuals in society. The difficulty that modern politicians face in many countries is finding a way to accommodate the claims and needs of different groups while still ensuring that the common good is furthered. As Kenneth Hoover has written, "democracy becomes an exercise in balancing particular sources of distinctiveness and individual difference against the universal needs of all citizens."[16]

Many feminist writers have argued that women can be truly free only if public policies take into account the inherent differences between the genders. The social context and basic characteristics of women are said to be so different from those of men that to treat men and women exactly the same would perpetuate the subordination of women and deny them the ability to develop. Carole Pateman puts it this way: "Women's equal standing must be accepted as an expression of the freedom of women *as women*, and not treated as an indication that women can be just like men."[17]

However, there is a lively political and academic debate over just what really are the distinguishing characteristics of women that should be accommodated. The social, economic, and political discrimination faced by women can be assessed, but it is much more difficult to determine whether there are innate attitudinal and behavioural characteristics that define women that go beyond those acquired through millennia of socialization into caregiver roles. Carol Gilligan is one feminist theorist who believes there are essential characteristics that are part of women's nature and identity.[18] Simone de Beauvoir, however, has written, "One is not born a woman, but rather becomes a woman."[19] The key point here is the enormous political significance of current debates about the identity of women.

The most potent aspect of the politics of identity and difference arises when a group believes that it is a distinct cultural nation that needs greater political control over its own affairs. Most states today are **multination states**, in that they contain more than one distinct cultural nation. A group's pride in their cultural nation—nationalism—can be a powerful force if it does not have an effective outlet within the political structures of their country. Many groups demand greater political autonomy to control matters of direct importance to them, usually because they believe their interests are continually sacrificed in favour of other, more dominant groups in their country. The drive for self-determination, and ultimately political independence, is founded on a very strong national identity and a belief that members of the nation cannot develop their group's identity, values, and needs by remaining just as one of several other groups within the existing state. Quebec nationalism is a staple of Canadian politics, and Quebec's quest for independence has become an established part of Canadian politics ever since the Parti Québécois was first elected as the provincial government in 1976. Canada is lucky that most of the politics of self-determination for Quebec has played out relatively peacefully. Many civil wars have broken out across the globe as one minority group or another struggled to establish a separate state of its own. Bangladesh and Eritrea are only two examples of many states that arose from civil wars aimed at the independence of a group.

While identity politics is a potent force, it is important not to overstate the phenomenon. The difficulty is that since all individuals have many characteristics that form their identity, they may belong to a wide variety of groups. A particular issue, such as abortion or affirmative action, may incline one to identify with the group most relevant for the moment, but another issue will find most of us identifying with a different group—or none at all. Postmodernism is a perspective on society that underlines the complexity of both individuals and society taken as a whole. In this view, it is unsound to reduce political behaviour to simple, enduring categories. Since identities are multidimensional, many people are motivated to find new ways of expressing and identifying themselves over time and across issues. Whole new social movements, such as environmentalism, are spawned as a result.

Political Cleavages

Some group identities endure, and the prevailing attitudes and beliefs of that group are relevant across a wide range of public policy issues. As noted in Chapter 11, political **cleavages** arise in a society when there are enduring differences between groups within a society over political values, perspectives, and objectives. Many cleavages may occur at the same time in a society, according to gender, religion, socioeconomic class, language, ethnicity, and even ideology. Depending on what causes these cleavages, how deeply entrenched they are, and how opposed they are in outlook, a country may simply have a richly diverse political culture or be destabilized into civil war. Much also depends on the reaction to the political cleavages of political leaders of both the larger society and of the groups involved. In general, there are four broadly different strategies for reacting to political cleavages in a society.

First, there may be an attempt to actively foster a single overarching culture. While subgroups may continue to exist, their members may come to identify even more strongly with the general culture. The melting pot of the United States is one example: significant cleavages exist within American society, but they are minimized by the overarching patriotism and attachment to America as a whole. A common "American" identity is layered on top of other group identities.

A second strategy may be to recognize the cleavages and try to accommodate them by fostering mutual tolerance and respect. In essence, the multicultural policies of Canadian federal governments have successfully defused the most negative resentment toward immigration by hailing as a virtue the cultural diversity brought by immigrants to the country. This approach fosters **cultural pluralism**, which means not only that are there strong subcultures within a society, but also that they are fostered and accommodated as a positive aspect of the political culture.

A third approach involves designing the country's political structures to accommodate the most significant cleavages within the institutional framework. In this way, the subgroups are more inclined to pursue their objectives within the existing state structure than to aim for independence and the breakup of the country. **Federal** systems of government are a common choice of institutional design in countries where significant cleavages coincide with geographic regions. The main idea of federations is to allow considerable variation at the regional level of the public policies most important to the different provincial or state societies. In essence, as in the case of the division of powers between the federal and provincial governments in Canada, control of issues central to the regional cultures can be given to those communities while still ensuring common national policies for other matters.

A fourth approach to political cleavages involves actively repressing the subgroups in violent or nonviolent ways, which means trying to stamp out the cleavages. This may take the form of prohibiting the use of a language or practice of a particular religion. In Canada's history, there is a shameful reminder of this approach, where for several generations Canadian governments tried to eliminate the Aboriginal cultures by teaching Native people to behave like white people. Thousands of children were taken away from their families at a young age and taught to dress, act, and speak like those of European descent. **Genocide** or **ethnic cleansing** by forcible expulsion are the most extreme forms of dealing with cultural cleavages, aimed at simply eliminating all those who belong to the subgroup.

Another important issue arising from deep political cleavages is the question of how the groups involved respond to the approaches taken by the government. If a group believes strongly that the current situation is likely to lead to its continued subordination or even extinction by dominant groups, then a country will in all likelihood face significant political turmoil.

Political Socialization: Moulding the Mind

If political cultures and identities are so important, the following questions arise: How are they formed? What processes create dominant beliefs and attitudes among large groups of people? The answers lie in one of the most important social phenomena of human existence. The sharing and propagating of attitudes, knowledge, values, and other beliefs are fundamental processes that create human societies. While the net result may be measured on a collective, group-wide level, the process occurs bit by bit on each individual member of the society. Wide ranges of influences and forces are at work throughout our lives to shape us into the people we become. The sum of those forces on all of the members of a community is what eventually creates its general culture.

Most of us would like to think of ourselves as essentially self-made individuals. We might recognize and appreciate the influence of parents and perhaps of a few key teachers and friends along the way, but overall we would like to believe that we are the people we are principally because of choices we have made for ourselves. But are we really self-made? What kinds of influences, both direct and unseen, have really moulded us and structured the range of choices that we feel we have made for ourselves? How many of our individual beliefs and attitudes are actually the product of other people's choices about what we should or should not believe? In reality, it is clear that individual members of any society are shaped by a lifelong process through which cultural, moral, and political values are shared and passed on and through which a group's culture is fostered.

Political socialization is the process through which political knowledge, attitudes, and beliefs are transmitted within a society. It is important to note that political socialization is not necessarily only about explicitly political attitudes and values, such as "Capitalism is good." It also involves broader cultural and social values, such as views of the role of women, which can also have political implications. Through this process, most of us come to share certain core values and identify ourselves as members of a larger group or community. It is also through political socialization that the preferred values of particular groups and individuals within society are acquired by or even imposed on others.

The values of a political culture are passed on as new people enter the society, either as immigrants or as children born into and raised in that society. People born and raised in Argentina, China, India, Kenya, Russia, Taiwan, and Canada likely have had a different upbringing, which results in adults with many different attitudes. The whole environment and context in which we grow up has a tremendous effect on what we believe to be right and wrong and on the principles we regard highly and value above others. This socialization has its most profound impact during childhood years, but our political values and knowledge continue to be shaped throughout the rest of our lives.

Political socialization can work through several processes, with knowledge and beliefs being either deliberately expounded or passively transmitted. The deliberate sharing of ideas might occur, for example, when a parent or teacher tells a child how to behave or what to think. The lesson might be as benign as "Share your lunch with someone who doesn't have any," or it might be a more potent one such as "Remember who your people are and that the rulers are our enemies." Knowledge and beliefs can also be spread through imitation. It is common for people to imitate, sometimes unconsciously, role models whom they admire. Charismatic political and religious leaders, or even peers, are often imitated in how they treat others and in what they have to say about society. Many people also learn ideas about gender roles simply from seeing how their parents interact over the years.

Agents of Political Socialization

There are countless ways in which political socialization occurs, but specific **agents of political socialization** can be identified as having a role to play in an individual's life. It is primarily through these that an individual acquires particular knowledge, attitudes, and beliefs about the political world. Given the potential impact on political systems, it is perhaps curious that political scientists do not undertake more serious study of the socialization process; indeed, political sociology is more usually the province of sociologists, anthropologists, and psychologists.[20] Political scientists, however, do concern themselves quite frequently with the consequences of socialization. For example, studies of voting patterns often examine whether there are correlations between the choice of political party and the specific social attributes of the voters, such as income, education, religion, or gender, as discussed in Chapter 10. A brief examination of the principal agents of political socialization, which follows, will give you an idea of the powerful forces that can mould our views of society throughout the course of our lives, and it will illustrate how relevant political socialization can be to the study of politics.

The Family Undoubtedly, one of the most fundamental influences on an individual's outlook on politics is the family. Children learn all sorts of political lessons from their families in both direct and indirect ways. The most overt way in which families may act as agents of political socialization is through explicit training, when parents engage in active, deliberate instruction on the political values to hold, the political parties or leaders to support, and the ways to participate in the political process. From an early age, children are aware of their parents' partisan preferences, and parents who are politically active become clear role models. Such politically active parents may also take their young children along to party functions or political demonstrations. In many families, countless hours around a dining table are spent discussing views about the political leaders and events of the day.

Children also acquire important beliefs from their families about their group identities and common enemies, both of which can have profound political implications later in life. From their family upbringing, individuals may develop strong views about the place of their group in the larger society and the wrongs their group has suffered. Nationalist movements have as their basis a commonly held belief among a large collection of individuals that they form a distinctive group; this belief is usually created and instilled on the family level. It is not an exaggeration to say that many civil wars started because of what children learned from their families.

The political socialization role of families, however, is not limited to such overt political instruction. Children also learn in subtle ways an enormous amount about how decisions are made within a group. The parental figures in the family may make authoritative decisions without consulting the children, or children may learn from an early age that they are entitled to voice their opinion and participate in a "family conference," in which important decisions are reached collectively. In either case, the children are learning about decision-making. In countless ways, children learn from their families which social and moral principles they should value and uphold, and these in turn have many political dimensions. For example, some children may be actively taught to engage in acts of charity toward strangers; they may be given to understand that it is a good thing for those with more to share with those who have less. On the other hand, family members may believe and teach their children that it is only important to help one's relatives and close friends; they may feel they have no responsibility to help others in need, as those people must be responsible for themselves. These opposing views are examples of how children learn from their families about their relationship and responsibility to others in their community.

Everyday family dynamics also teach children a great deal about social hierarchy, deference to authority, obedience to rules, and acquiescence in judgments they do not support. There is a kernel of truth to the charge that all children are born into totalitarian regimes. Parents and other caregivers have total control over the lives of infants, and many only reluctantly and incompletely give up trying to exercise that degree of control as the children grow older. Just about every child cries out at some point in complaint against a parent's decision, "That's not fair!" And in doing so, children are expressing volumes about a conception of justice and fair process they have started to develop from a very tender age. Most children in Western families today are raised in an environment where they are encouraged, as they grow older, to voice their own opinions and question the views of their adult caregivers. Freedom of expression and a sense of personal autonomy are usually ingrained into Canadian children as a matter of course.

Families around the world lay the foundation for different understandings of gender roles—for example, on the question of how active and vocal females should be in their society—by

"This is America, son. You can grow up to be anything I want you to be."

Mark Anderson/Artizans

the role taken by the mother in relation to the father (if present in the family) or by the different opportunities given to the sons rather than daughters. Patriarchy has its social roots in the family, but those roots spread out in many ways into the political system. The Victorian-era family supposedly gave the father total final decision-making powers, and that reflected the predominant male view of the time that women were simply unsuited to vote in elections, let alone hold political office. As the patriarchal family model has begun to erode in Western countries, the place of women in society has also changed.

The life lessons that children learn in the family can flow directly into the general political culture. Table 4.2 shows quite a range in views about family life that came from international surveys conducted in 1999 and 2000. At one extreme, 90 percent of Mexicans believe that parents should be loved and respected regardless of what they do. Mexicans also placed relatively high importance on teaching children to be obedient and unselfish in the family. By contrast, 40 percent of Germans felt that parents need to earn the love and respect of their children, and they placed very little emphasis on teaching children obedience and selflessness in the family. One would expect Mexican and German political cultures, then, to reflect these differences in family life, with the Mexicans more deferential and obedient to government authority and the Germans much more individualistic. Indeed, the modern history of authoritarian politics in Mexico and hotly contested elections in Germany are consistent with these divergent sets of values. In the same surveys, 54 percent of Mexicans agreed that it was a good idea to have "a strong leader who does not have to bother with parliament and elections," while only 19 percent of Germans agreed.

Educational Institutions The next major influence on a person's development is usually the school. Educational institutions can be very powerful agents of political socialization. In the most transparent instance, schools deliver a curriculum developed by the government to deliberately indoctrinate children with a particular set of views. This is clearly seen in communist countries, where the ruling party ensures that the official dogmas of the party are taught throughout the school years. Yet similar processes occur in democratic countries—even

Table 4.2 Attitudes Toward Families

An international survey asked people questions about the following beliefs:

Country	DUTY TO LOVE AND RESPECT PARENTS		IMPORTANT QUALITIES FOR CHILDREN TO LEARN AT HOME INCLUDE:		
	Always	If Earned	Independence	Obedience	Unselfishness
Argentina	87.9	13.2	37.0	37.0	12.7
Britain	64.6	35.4	53.4	46.8	60.3
Canada	79.2	20.8	62.0	31.1	45.6
Egypt	95.2	4.8	72.6	53.2	21.6
France	75.2	24.8	29.0	36.4	40.2
Germany	60.0	40.0	69.7	13.9	8.7
India	88.8	11.2	56.2	55.7	36.6
Italy	79.4	20.6	41.4	20.3	41.4
Japan	71.6	28.4	81.6	4.3	53.2
Mexico	90.0	10.0	44.4	58.6	48.7
Philippines	93.6	6.4	68.2	44.4	38.3
Russia	84.6	15.3	29.6	34.4	20.6
South Africa	90.8	9.2	58.4	55.4	32.2
Sweden	43.0	57.0	68.6	12.2	33.2
United States	77.3	22.7	62.0	32.3	39.1

Source: Data are from the European Values Study Group and World Values Survey Association.

if the indoctrination is far less visible and not implemented to the same degree. State school authorities usually set the official curriculum guidelines for material taught in the main subjects offered in public schools—and often in private schools as well. This curriculum includes not just a sanctioned view of the society's history but also much material that has political implications, even if it is not directly political.

Students in Canada are exposed to many different messages during their school years that lead them to accept the importance of individual freedoms and personal autonomy. Tolerance of diverse cultures and religions is another social norm instilled in students that has significant implications for political culture in both Canada and the United States. Just as significant is what is not taught in school. For example, few American or Canadian secondary school graduates will have ever studied Marx and Engels' *The Communist Manifesto*; capitalist free enterprise is simply accepted as the norm in North American schools, and only a few students are exposed to teachings that seriously envision alternative forms of organizing society and the economy. Instead, many corporations are making inroads into schools through product placement and advertising.

Schools have important socializing effects in many informal ways as well. The structure of classroom time and the interaction between students and their teachers can both serve as political models. A class that is structured in an informal setting, with students able to get up and move around or talk to other students, provides a very different sense of liberty than does a classroom where students may never move or speak without permission. Students who use a teacher's first name will have a different notion of equality and social hierarchy than those who must call their teachers "master," "madam," or "sir." The degree to which discipline is kept in the school through verbal abuse or corporal punishment can leave strong impressions on school children about the importance of deferring to or obeying authority. For that matter, however, overly strict or cruel discipline may incline students to grow up resentful of authority and make them ready to rebel.

Something as simple as teaching students to inquire and make up their own minds, rather than simply learn by rote memorization, can have consequences for the political culture. In schools and universities in many authoritarian states, students have been taught from a single thick book that contains all they need to memorize about that subject. Learning becomes a matter of simply absorbing, accepting, and repeating the official position. Citizens in such countries have a very different starting point from which to assess their government's actions than people who have grown up learning that there are many different views and interpretations on important subjects and that their own opinion is valued.

The influence of the school is so significant that across the Western industrialized world increasing education levels correlate with greater political interest and participation, as well as with more liberal attitudes on civil rights and social welfare issues.[21] However, this raises the question of whether it is education per se that has this effect, or whether these liberal values are so common among Western educators and so consistently propagated that the longer individuals are exposed to these views, the more likely they are to absorb them. Some of the most important differences in attitudes relate to the amount (if any) of postsecondary education that individuals have had. This makes particular sense in Western democracies, where universities and colleges usually present quite a different style of learning and intellectual inquiry than students experienced in their earlier schooling.

The Media The **mass media**, in their broadest sense of "the means of mass communication," include radio, television, and newspapers, as well as books, movies, music, and the Internet. Taken together, a country's media have the power to provide an important part of the cultural glue that defines that society's culture. The media provide some of the most powerful means of reinforcing common values and beliefs that create a nation's sense of identity. The media play a central role in conveying political attitudes, beliefs, and knowledge among not just the members of one society, but also across societies around the world. Whether it is news broadcasts of political developments or debates over opposing views, much of what we come across on television, radio, and in newspapers frames what we think we know about political issues and causes. In media coverage of political issues, what is not said is just as important as what is said. An enormous amount of filtering occurs as to what issues or events are reported in the first place, as well as in the kind of coverage they receive. To understand the role of the media in modern society is to understand a lot about that society. As Marshall McLuhan (1911–80) put it, "The medium is the message."

Noam Chomsky is the best-known living critic of the media and their ability to shape a society's knowledge and understanding of political events. In a series of stinging commentaries, Chomsky has argued that one of the principal roles of the media is to manufacture consent among the masses for the existing social and political order and to control what people are told about the world around them.[22]

Lloyd Robertson is probably Canada's most recognized news anchor, having presided over the CBC's The National for six years before taking over the CTV National News with Lloyd Robertson in 1976.

Courtesy of CTV; photographer Geoff George

The power of the media to influence society's political views is most clearly demonstrated in different relationships between the media and the government found across the globe (see Table 4.3). In many countries of the world, the state owns and controls all media organizations, so that the only views and information that get publicly disseminated are those that the rulers of that society want people to know. In other countries, media corporations may be in private hands, but the government still exercises close supervision and censorship of the content, again

Table 4.3 Ranking of Selected Countries on Press Freedom

Freedom House ranks the countries of the world according to the freedom under which the news media operate. The categories indicate the level of restrictions put on journalists and media companies by governments, as well as other factors, such as the concentration of ownership.

FREE (1–30)		PARTLY FREE (31–60)		NOT FREE (61–100)	
Finland	9	India	35	Egypt	62
Sweden	11	Brazil	42	Pakistan	63
Belgium	11	Panama	43	Armenia	64
Switzerland	12	Philippines	46	Malaysia	68
New Zealand	13	Mexico	48	Singapore	69
Jamaica	15	Argentina	49	Afghanistan	69
United States	16	Turkey	49	Iraq	70
Germany	16	Albania	50	Venezuela	74
Canada	17	Tanzania	51	Russia	75
Britain	19	Ukraine	53	Vietnam	77
Taiwan	20	Indonesia	54	Saudi Arabia	82
Australia	21	Nigeria	55	China	84
Japan	21	Kuwait	56	Iran	84
Ghana	26	Colombia	57	Burma	96
Italy	29	Guatemala	59	Cuba	96
South Korea	30	Haiti	59	North Korea	97

Source: Freedom House, Freedom of the Press 2007, Table of Global Press Freedom Rankings; available at http://www.freedomhouse .org/uploads/fop/2007/pfscharts.pdf; accessed October 22, 2007.

to prevent the publication of facts and opinions that undermine the rulers' control of their society. At the other end of the scale is the value placed in established democracies on ensuring that the state does not censor or control the media in a general way. In these countries, because of an acceptance of the media's ability to profoundly shape people's knowledge and perceptions, freedom of expression in the media is a cornerstone of the society's culture. The more sources of information and the more perspectives citizens can draw from, the better they are able to form their own opinions on political events and issues.

Events in early 2002 show that the importance of getting the right message across in the media is not lost on either autocratic or democratic governments. Zimbabwe enacted legislation barring foreign news agencies from basing reporters in that country; in addition, local journalists are required to apply each year to the Minister of Information for a permit, which can be refused if the government disapproves of their work. In the United States, the Department of Defense was forced to close down its Office of Strategic Influence after only two months of operations, once it became clear that one of its prime missions was to provide disinformation to foreign news agencies as part of the campaign against terrorism.

Given the important role that the media have in informing people about political events and opinions, it is crucial to understand that the coverage of news and views that actually does occur is very incomplete, even within democracies. Only a relatively small number of stories can be covered in any one radio or TV broadcast. Newspaper editors have a finite number of column inches to devote to news items. On any given day, news editors must face choices about which stories to cover, which to ignore, and how much coverage to give to the stories they do choose to report on; they also have to find a balance between local, provincial or state, national, and international stories. Inevitably, many stories that do get reported are greatly simplified to fit time or space constraints. The creation of news reports is far too often a matter of producers deciding what "take" their reporters should follow on the story so that the finished report will reflect the views of those producers.

A number of studies reveal that the media consistently fail to report on certain newsworthy issues and that their coverage often favours one side of an issue over another. For example, the views of business may predominate over the views of unions. Furthermore, from time to time editors kill stories initiated by individual reporters because they cast a negative light on associates of the media corporation's owners or—more often—on those who pay for advertising. Journalists often engage in self-censorship because of a fear of repercussions, as they may become targets of intimidation or death threats if they investigate widespread corruption in the corridors of power or the activities of organized crime. In many countries of the world, journalists are arrested, beaten, or killed by government forces if their stories become too critical of the ruling party. Self-censorship may also occur because a reporter does not want to lose important contacts and informants. Reporters who cover their local police forces are particularly vulnerable, since a negative story on some police officers' activities can quickly dry up their sources for the inside scoops they rely on when covering general criminal activity.

High value is put on a free press, and in Canada we also value impartiality in news reporting. The freedom of the press is usually seen as freedom from government control and censorship. Even where all the media organizations are not owned by the government in some countries, potential media owners or journalists must get the permission of the government. This permission is not simply the technical broadcast licensing we think of in Canada, but actually provides the real opportunity for a government to stifle those who would be critical. At various times many countries have practised official censorship, where scripts of news and even entertainment shows must be approved by government censors; material that is considered either immoral or politically controversial would not be allowed. However, freedom from government control does not mean that a newspaper or TV station will be fair and impartial in its coverage of current events. Where the media are privately owned, the companies aim first and foremost to make a profit; the editors will publish the news that sells and overlook or ignore material that would lead to a drop in public viewers or advertisers. Few media owners would allow their companies to champion for long positions that vilify the owners' personal political or economic interests. Such biases are, in a sense, inevitable, and may be balanced in a competitive media market by alternative perspectives and stories covered by different media.

In many countries, the concentration of media ownership can provide very little competition in news reporting. Where the main media sources are owned by one or two companies, the public will be presented with little range of news stories and perspectives. For example, by the late 1990s, three media chains controlled two-thirds of all daily newspaper circulation in Canada,[23] and many dailies had a complete monopoly on local news in their communities. A significant shift in media ownership occurred in Canada in 2000, when CanWest Global bought most of the newspapers and Internet sites owned by Conrad Black's Hollinger and Southam companies, transforming itself into Canada's largest owner of daily newspapers. As Table 4.4 shows, CanWest accounted for 28 percent of total daily newspaper circulation in 2006. CanWest also owns the Global television network and other stations, which raises the spectre of one company controlling both the major TV and newspaper sources of information in many communities. Perhaps tellingly, the only government review of this media concentration centred not on the potential for one company's control over the news coverage in any particular community but instead on whether the new concentration would adversely affect the advertising market. Even where there are competing media outlets, one radio or TV station may have a crushing lead in terms of listeners and viewers. As a result, the tangible value of the freedom of the press and multiple news outlets is eroded as most citizens rely on only one or two sources for their news. These few sources then end up having an enormous influence over the public.

Surveys show that public attitudes toward the media involve a mixture of trust and wariness and that the public are more likely to believe news from some sources than from others. For example, a 1998 poll of Canadians found that only 20 percent distrusted TV news anchors to some degree, while 41 percent distrusted newspaper journalists.[24] The significance of this discrepancy is all the more important because Canadians rely far more heavily on TV

Table 4.4 Daily Newspaper Market in Canada, 2006

Corporation	Average Weekly Circulation	Percentage of Total
CanWest	8,7070,656	28.0
Quebecor	6,532,498	21.0
Torstar	4,393,579	13.8
Power	3,096,041	10.0
Bell Globemedia	2,014,441	6.5
Osprey Media	1,780,529	5.7
Transcontinental Media	951,879	3.1
F.P. Canadian Newspapers	973,177	3.1
Halifax Herald	732,541	2.4
Brunswick	604,116	1.9
Continental Newspapers	370,154	1.2
Independents	309,018	0.9
Glacier Canadian	281,947	0.9
Alberta Newspaper Group	221,079	0.7
Black Press	106,896	0.3
Total	31,075,551	100.0

Source: Canadian Newspaper Association, "Canadian Daily Newspaper Circulation Data," p. 16; available at http://www.cna-acj.ca/Client/CNA/cna.nsf/object/CircData06/$file/CIRCULATION%20DATA%202006.pdf; accessed October 22, 2007.

than on newspapers as their primary news source. There are indications that some people are becoming more skeptical of the media over time. Gallup surveys in the United States show an increase in the number of Americans who distrust the media to report events fairly and accurately, from 26 percent in 1976 to 44 percent in 1998.[25] Table 4.5 provides an interesting comparison of attitudes toward the press in a number of countries. A comparison of Tables 4.3 and 4.5 shows that freedom from state control and censorship does not necessarily translate into public confidence that journalists are depicting events in a country fairly. It may also be that a more educated and politically aware population simply expects more from their media.

The tremendous globalization of mass communication in the late 20th century has also created a situation in which the media have a powerful role in eroding the traditional distinctiveness of some nations' cultures by spreading "alien" ideas, beliefs, and knowledge around the world. National cultures are constantly being reshaped by the adoption of ideas spread by the media. Starting in the mid–20th century, radio was deliberately used as a **propaganda** tool by both Western and communist states to beam broadcasts to each others' citizens, in hopes of providing a fresh view of the world to the other side. The later growth of television has superseded the impact of short-wave radio in reaching into the homes of people around the world. CNN now provides live TV broadcasts by satellite to every continent, and countless entertainment programs are dubbed into foreign languages to be watched by global audiences.

Television, however, is being supplanted in many ways by the Internet, which has a potential for global communication that can only be described as staggering. An estimated 1.2 billion people worldwide made use of the Internet by 2007, when 70 percent of North Americans had access to the Internet. The growth in Internet usage has exploded since the early days when the majority of world users were in the United States. By 2007, Asia and Europe counted more Internet users than North America; the worldwide patterns of Internet usage will continue to change significantly as the vast populations of Africa and Asia come on line in increasing numbers. (See Figures 4.2 and 4.3.)[26]

The Internet already serves as an alternative source for news and information, and there is speculation that a kind of global cyber culture is emerging that may cause us to rethink basic ideas about the territorial basis of society. People's access to news used to be largely limited to

Table 4.5 Attitudes Toward the Media

An international survey asked people how much confidence they have in the press.

Country	A Great Deal	Quite a Lot	Not Very Much	None at All
Argentina	10.9	27.6	45.5	15.9
Britain	1.2	13.2	48.3	37.3
Canada	4.4	31.6	50.8	13.2
Egypt	22.6	46.7	23.3	7.4
France	2.4	33.7	41.2	23.4
Germany	4.2	33.0	48.0	14.8
India	28.8	42.3	22.8	6.9
Italy	5.2	30.1	51.4	13.4
Japan	7.4	65.6	24.9	2.1
Mexico	13.0	29.7	36.1	21.1
Philippines	21.8	48.0	26.6	3.6
Russia	5.0	25.1	43.4	26.5
South Africa	13.8	41.5	35.7	8.9
Sweden	4.4	42.3	47.5	5.8
United States	6.4	20.0	55.6	18.0

Source: Data are from the European Values Study Group and World Values Survey Association.

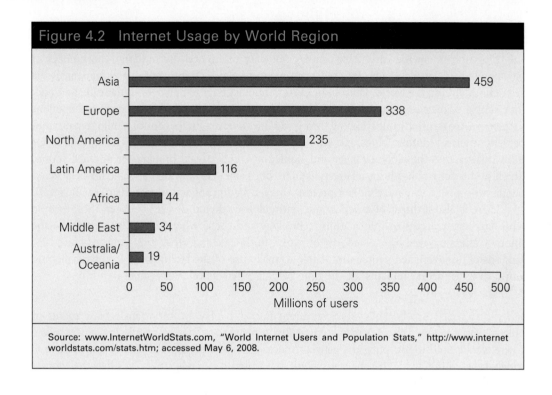

Figure 4.2 Internet Usage by World Region

Source: www.InternetWorldStats.com, "World Internet Users and Population Stats," http://www.internet worldstats.com/stats.htm; accessed May 6, 2008.

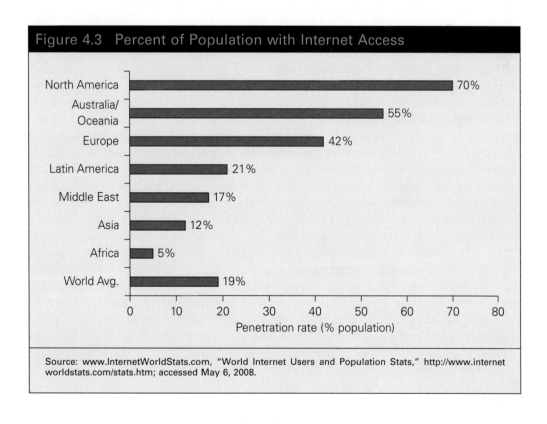

Figure 4.3 Percent of Population with Internet Access

Source: www.InternetWorldStats.com, "World Internet Users and Population Stats," http://www.internet worldstats.com/stats.htm; accessed May 6, 2008.

their own community's media, but the Internet was created a whole wave of "citizen-journalists" who record their views for the world to read on their blogs. The rapid emergence of the "blogosphere" in the early 21st century not only multiplied, by millions, the number of viewpoints made available for all to read, but blogs have also circumvented government media restrictions around the world. During the current military engagements in Afghanistan and Iraq, for example, soldiers from most countries there have been recording their experiences and opinions on personal blogs, greatly undermining their governments' former tight control of information from battlefront areas.[27] Public blogs and more private discussion forums have created places for individuals across the globe to meet and, sometimes, collectively prepare for political action. Much of this activity has been relatively benign, but some has provided a locale for disaffected people who wish to organize violent protests or even significant acts of terrorism (see Box 4.3).

There is also a threat of an economic and cultural "digital divide" between those people who have ready access to information technology and those who do not. In contrast to the Internet access enjoyed by the majority of people in Canada and other industrialized countries, millions of impoverished people are unable to make use of the technology. In the developing world, Internet access remains for the time being a privilege of a very small minority.

Religious Institutions Religious institutions may also play an important role as agents of political socialization. This idea may seem at first somewhat strange to people in Canada today, where we are used to accepting the general principle of the separation of church and state. It is widely believed in Canada that the state should not embrace one religion as the official religion of the society that is promoted above or to the exclusion of others. Furthermore, the separation of church and state means that religious institutions and leaders do not play an active role in the administration of government. Through religious teachings, however, individuals can learn about their role in society, their responsibility to others, the importance of tradition, tolerance or intolerance of other faiths, and the existence of higher duties that transcend any that secular authorities might try to impose. All of these beliefs have political implications. As well, followers of some religions acquire a very strong sense of group identity based on that religion, with strong cultural understandings of the history of that group and its place in the larger society. Perceived and actual wrongs inflicted by others in the same society on that religious group can have direct political consequences, such as providing a basis for nationalist aspirations. As Table 4.6 shows, significant numbers of people in many countries regularly partake in religious services. Attending church, temple, or synagogue on a regular basis, one is much more likely to be influenced by the values espoused by one's religious leaders; after all, if one disagrees one is likely to stop attending.

Even with the formal separation of church and state in North America, we still see the interplay of religion and politics. In Canada, prayers are still part of many official functions, the Christian Lord's Prayer is still recited in some public schools, and ordained ministers and priests do occasionally hold elected office. In the United States, religion is an even bigger part of everyday politics, with many organized religious groups actively funding or campaigning for their favourite candidates and against their perceived enemies. These situations are nevertheless quite different from that in Great Britain, where the Church of England is the official church, and where the queen or king, as head of state, is also the head of the church. Ironically, a majority of British hardly ever or never attend religious services. Nor can the North American situation compare with the one in Iran, where religious leaders have an official place in the constitution and are able to exercise political power. In some Latin American countries, social liberation theology leads many priests and their followers to expose brutal tactics of repression used by the government and wealthy landowners. As a result, some local Catholic churches become centres of political activity in ways not seen in Canada or the United States, and security forces actively target priests for intimidation or even assassination.

LONDON (Reuters)—From behind a computer keyboard at his London home, student Younes Tsouli used the Internet to spread al Qaeda propaganda, recruit suicide bombers and promote Web sites that encouraged the killing of non-Muslims. The Moroccan-born student and two accomplices, one of whom he had never met in person, went on to become the first to be jailed in Britain for inciting terrorism over the Internet. In September, a Scottish student described as a "wannabe suicide bomber" was imprisoned for eight years for owning terrorism material and distributing it via Web sites.

The two cases are examples of what Western authorities believe is the dangerous and growing role the Internet plays in spreading extremist propaganda and recruiting sympathisers to Islamist militant causes. But can the West censor radical Web sites and, indeed, is it morally right to do so?

The perceived threat has prompted much talk from governments of the need for action. The European Commission urged the EU's 27 states to crack down on militant sites. "The Internet serves . . . as one of the principal boosters of the processes of radicalisation and recruitment and also serves as a source of information on terrorist means and methods, thus functioning as a virtual training camp," the Commission's proposal said. . . .

However, many governments disagree about what should actually be done and experts express serious doubts about what would be effective, saying little research has been carried out.

Johnny Ryan, Senior Researcher at Dublin's Institute of International and European Affairs, said users could easily circumvent any restrictions imposed by the authorities. Web sites could relocate from one country to another unless there was international agreement, while the controversial content was often distributed through services that are hard to block, such as legitimate chat rooms. "In China, where censorship is a more serious business, users have developed a series of tools to break through government Internet blocks," said Ryan. . . .

Dr. Akil Awan, of the Royal Holloway, University of London, another of the few academics to have studied the issue, agrees. "The virtual jihadists are very net-savvy and generally are always two steps ahead of the authorities," he told Reuters, adding it would be morally questionable to censor jihadist Web sites that presented an alternative world view. "These accounts may be skewed, tendentious and indoctrinating, but then so is a lot of other material on the Internet," he said. . . . A simple search of the Internet shows how easy it is to find material that could concern the authorities, from speeches by Osama bin Laden and al Qaeda leaders to inflammatory videos. . . . However, it is also not clear whether messages, videos or sermons on the Internet alone can radicalise individuals.

"It is only the means through which individuals can become aligned with jihadist ideologies and causes. Other factors are equally important," the Royal Holloway's Awan said, adding it is estimated there are more than 5,000 extremist Web sites.

SOURCE: Michael Holden (Reuters), "Experts Say West Cannot Stop Web Radicalization," November 06, 2007; available at http://www.canada.com/topics/technology/story.html?id=7ee9be0c-3e07-42f1-b663-61c7e95b8626; accessed May 6, 2008. Reprinted with permission.

Table 4.6 Attendance at Religious Services

An international survey asked people how frequently they attend religious services.

Country	At Least Monthly	Occasionally	Hardly Ever/Never
Argentina	42.4	29.6	28.4
Britain	18.7	26.2	55.1
Canada	38.3	35.3	26.4
Egypt	44.7	30.3	25.1
France	12.3	27.2	60.4
Germany	24.2	35.6	40.1
India	51.3	45.6	3.1
Italy	53.6	32.5	13.9
Japan	12.4	79.1	8.6
Mexico	13.0	29.7	36.1
Philippines	79.6	19.4	1.0
Russia	9.6	41.0	49.4
South Africa	71.8	18.8	9.4
Sweden	9.1	45.2	45.7
United States	61.1	24.5	14.4

Source: Data are from the European Values Study Group and World Values Survey Association.

The power of religion has been well understood in states that try to prohibit all organized religion. Karl Marx once said religion is the opiate of the people; he believed religion merely ensured that the workers of the world accepted their oppressed lot in society in anticipation of a better life after death. More practically, however, the belief in a higher divine authority may lead many devotees to disobey the laws of man. Thus, organized religions were banned in many communist countries as insidious elements that would otherwise undermine the creation of a socialist society. After all, a quest for freedom of religion might very easily snowball into demands for other freedoms, such as freedom of expression, that have a direct bearing on the stability of the political regime.

Religious beliefs also provide a framework for people to understand and form opinions on a wide variety of controversial political issues, from abortion to same-sex marriage. For example, a 2005 COMPAS poll found that gay marriage was opposed by 80 percent of Canadians who said that religion was "very important" to them, as against only 35 percent of those for whom religion is "not at all important."[28]

Perhaps the most vivid example of the political impact of religious values came when Islamic extremists hijacked four planes in September 2001 and crashed two of them into the World Trade Center towers in New York City and another into the Pentagon in Washington. Although the geopolitical circumstances of the Middle East were part of the motivation behind those actions, the hijackers became a new version of suicide bombers only because of their religious conviction that they were fighting a holy war and would be rewarded in the afterlife for their martyrdom. Anti-Americanism moved from being a political sentiment to a holy cause.

Peer Groups Peer groups can be very important agents of socialization, even though they remain unorganized. Once children enter school, most of their experiences are shared by their friends. Throughout the rest of our lives, we share with our friends our thoughts and reactions, and their reactions, in turn, become an important framing for our assessment of what is right and wrong. By the late teenage and early adult years, peer groups come to play an increasingly important role in an individual's life. At election time, people end up having most of their discussions with their friends about political events and candidates. As a result, our peer groups become a crucial social context from which we learn new information about political events and where we debate political alternatives.

In our interactions with friends, we practise important political principles, such as freedom of expression, but we also practise group conformity and exclusion of "others"; we may even defer to the unofficial leader of the group. While we may have a broad collection of different types of individuals within our groups of friends, there are strong pressures on individuals with a circle of friends to "go with the flow" and do what is considered popular with the group. In addition, we tend to exclude or even ostracize individuals who "go too far" and stray beyond what the group tends to think of as acceptable attitudes and behaviour. These pressures are strongest and most visible in the teenage years, but carry on to some degree into later life.

The Workplace In North America, the workplace is not often thought of as being a political arena, yet there is much in our work life that has political import. Although it very much depends on the particular place of work, we can be exposed to many situations in our jobs that carry over into our political world.[29] For example, a rigidly hierarchical workplace gives people a very different sense of the importance of the individual, depending on whether they are at the top or at the bottom. If the lesson from work is to defer to the boss and acquiesce in authoritative decisions, we may carry this attitude with us into society in general. In contrast, based on experiences in a workplace where we are actively consulted and where we feel we can have meaningful input into collective decisions, we may be more inclined to become actively involved in the political affairs of our society.

An important minority of Canadians and Americans work in situations that are highly charged by adversarial union–employer dynamics. An active belief in the power of collective action through unions translates directly to the political world. Unions can be important sources of funds and volunteers for political parties that seek to change society and economic relations in ways that favour the workers. Pro-business parties and governments may inspire trade unions to actively support parties and governments that promise to implement policies favouring the country's workers instead of the country's industrialists. For example, there have been historically strong ties between organized labour in Canada and the New Democratic Party (NDP); in fact, trade unions even get to exercise formal votes in NDP conventions. A highly polarized workplace that pits rich bosses against poorly paid workers may actually have a politically energizing influence on the workers; the latter may see their poverty and exploitation as resulting from a political regime that ensures the continuing dominance of business people and corporate interests. Indeed, it was the highly exploitative setting of industries in the 19th century that provided the inspiration for Karl Marx and others after him to argue that the entire political, economic, and social orders must be swept away and replaced by ones organized on socialist or communist principles. The workplace may breed, not just political activism, but **revolution**!

State Actors State actors can act as agents of political socialization, propagating official views of the society in hopes of garnering support or acquiescence in government policies. Schools are one such state institution, as are state-owned media. All governments engage to some degree in publicity and propaganda, spreading their messages to the populace about what is good and proper in a political sense through pamphlets, media advertising, and public events. For example, successive Canadian governments since the 1970s have actively (and quite successfully) campaigned for Canadians to embrace multiculturalism as a central part of Canada's political culture.

A crucial part of most governments' mission is to foster—and sometimes even create—a distinct national identity for their country. An important part of this is the selection and promotion of symbols (such as flags and national anthems) and rituals (public holidays and celebrations) that promote a sense of pride in the country. American governments have been particularly successful in developing a strong sense of **patriotism**. The Canadian federal government took a series of measures in the 1960s and 1970s to develop a new set of Canadian symbols that distinguished Canada from its colonial past. In 1965, in a very controversial move at the time, the flag was changed from the one based on the British Union Jack to one focused on the maple leaf. Over the next few years, the government eliminated virtually all references to "Royal" in government institutions; for instance, the Royal Mail became Canada Post. One criticism of the Canadian government is that our problems with national unity may stem in part from a failure to develop an effective sense of Canadian patriotism (which some say would be rather un-Canadian anyway).

In some countries—democratic as well as nondemocratic—the military plays a crucial socialization role, because almost every male is required to do a compulsory period of military service. In Israel, even women have to join. The military is able to indoctrinate, in both subtle and overt ways, vast numbers of citizens with views about the nature of the state, its society, and the duties of citizens to obey and defend.

Political parties also act as important agents of socialization. In communist countries in particular, where only the communist party is allowed to exist and is made a part of everyday life, the party can engage the citizens in many ways—for example, through newspapers, youth groups, neighbourhood activities, and sports clubs. In democratic countries, we do not tend to think of political parties as official state actors, and yet they are intimately tied to the political system and the process of governing. Political parties in every country can come to play central roles in the lives of those who are politically active, and these individuals acquire many beliefs and much information through party activities.

It should be clear by this point that there are many forces at work within a society that combine to mould individuals and ensure that most members of society come to accept common attitudes and beliefs. Where the same set of messages is reinforced by multiple agents—such as the family, school, friends, and the media—it is far more likely that people within a particular community will hold common attitudes and beliefs without serious questioning. Socialization may be a straightforward process of indoctrination, effectively brainwashing people to revere certain beliefs and revile others, but the socialization process that any one individual goes through usually is as much about the individual's reaction to the messages as it is about the messages themselves. This explains why members of the same family raised in much the same way and living within the same community can have very different views about political issues and principles. Nevertheless, we are all shaped by a multitude of agents of political socialization to become in some ways very much what others have wanted us to become, while still becoming in other ways what we ourselves have actually chosen to become. Political socialization is a process of absorbing information and ideas presented by others, observing role models, and internalizing our reactions to these inputs. Individuals within a group who are exposed to the same upbringing can and do react differently, but they also share many predominant views.

The Consequences of Political Socialization

Political socialization creates a political culture. A general culture is generated and perpetuated through the accumulated effects on each individual in society. Cultures can and do change over time, but even that change occurs as new ideas spread through agents of political socialization. For example, women have struggled for political and social rights for a very long time, but feminism made significant headway only once agents of socialization in the late 20th century dealt with women's issues.

It is crucial to understand who is spreading what values and beliefs, and how easily new ideas can get circulated within an established society to spark new ways of thinking about politics. For example, research has shown very strong correlations between authoritarian views in a country's populace and the extent of authoritarian measures practised by their government. In short, authoritarian governments rely on state-orchestrated socialization to impart widespread support for the values that the government wishes to enforce and how they are enforced. By the same token, a population that strongly supports democratic values would not voluntarily tolerate authoritarian measures by their government.

A great deal depends on the type of values propagated through the various agents of socialization, on how deliberate the process of indoctrination is, and on the degree to which the various agents of political socialization reinforce the same messages. The political socialization process in the People's Republic of China, for example, involves massive, overt indoctrination that provides a stark contrast to the seemingly haphazard and uncoordinated process in Canada or the United States. However, it would be a mistake to conclude that the Canadian or American political socialization processes are not as effective as the Chinese in instilling widespread support for and belief in the values that the most important elites in the country wish the majority of citizens to hold. Indeed, Ralph Miliband has decried the political socialization process in Western democracies as "very largely a process of mass *indoctrination*" aimed at instilling support for the existing social order and capitalist economy.[30] The belief in diversity and freedom of expression provides a more heterogeneous political culture in Canada and the United States, but that diversity and the expression of opposing points of view do not contradict the existence of many values deeply shared by most citizens that result in mass acceptance of the existing social order.

Political socialization has many important consequences for a society and for individuals and groups within a society. Essential to any stable community is a large degree of acceptance of shared values about the structure of political institutions, about the processes used to settle political disputes and issue authoritative decisions, and about the basic parameters of social and economic policies to be pursued by those who hold political office. Socialization allows the spread of beliefs, attitudes, and knowledge needed for a widespread sharing of that acceptance. In short, political socialization underlies any stable society by ensuring that enough new members who are born into or immigrate to it come to hold many values and attitudes in common with those already present. Through socialization, a society of many different subgroups can also be melded into sharing one overarching culture. The United States is often taken as a prime example of the successful creation of a single nation despite enormous regional differences in culture and ethnic background. The *melting pot* is an expression often used to describe American cultural history and socialization.

Yet the process of political socialization may have many different outcomes. Existing divisions and tensions within a society may be perpetuated and even exacerbated over time. For example, there have always been tensions between French- and English-speaking people in Quebec, but the political socialization processes in Quebec in the past four decades have amplified the nationalist sentiments that a minority had long held. By the 1990s, a large number of francophones in Quebec were in favour of separation or "sovereignty-association," and this growth in nationalist fervour was fostered through schools and peer groups, in the arts, and in the media. The growth of Quebec nationalism can even be seen to have occurred in the workplace, through provincial legislation and policies designed to enhance the use and predominance of the French language in business.

The enduring power of political socialization is vividly highlighted in theories about the character of political cultures in societies that are largely made up of immigrant settlers. In the 1960s, Louis Hartz developed a theory of political culture known as the *fragment theory*, which was also explored by Seymour Lipset.[31] Hartz argued that the contemporary political culture of an immigrant society reflects the dominant views of the different groups of immigrants who settled there. Each wave of immigrants is usually recruited from a specific place in their original country and thus represents only a fragment of the original country's political culture. Each different wave of immigrants can establish an enduring set of beliefs and attitudes that will be reflected in the modern politics of the new society. Gad Horowitz adapted this theory to explain some of the most significant differences between Canadian and American political cultures, particularly the wider range of ideologies that have popular appeal in Canada, as opposed to the United States.[32] If true, the survival of these original fragments of political culture is a testament to the political socialization process that passed the values down from generation to generation. It should be noted, however, that the contemporary values of these groups have indeed evolved significantly over time, and are not simply time capsules of the values of bygone European cultures.

Further significance of political socialization lies in the ways in which political scientists study politics. For several decades, political behaviour has been studied by conducting surveys in an attempt to correlate the social background of individuals with their support for particular policies or political parties. It was thought that if religion, education, and occupation can have an impact on an individual's beliefs, one might be able to explain people's political behaviour by studying their social, economic, and cultural backgrounds. This approach to studying politics started out trying to concentrate on developing statistical models of political behaviour. In recent years, however, an appreciation of the complexity of human behaviour and of the strong interplay of the various forces in our lives has uncovered serious puzzles for political scientists to unravel.

CONCLUSION

Political culture—the set of beliefs, values, attitudes, and principles widely held among members of a society—may be a concept formulated by academics, but it has enormous practical implications. Political culture provides the foundation upon which any political system is created and operates. The degree of consensus on fundamental values, and what those values actually are, can have a profound effect on the stability of the political order in a particular country. Identity politics, which stems from individuals' identification with groups within a society and involves those groups' pursuit of their perceived needs, has important political ramifications. The depth and causes of political cleavages and how the political elites react to accommodate or suppress members of subgroups can lead not only to the creation of a healthy, vibrant political pluralism but also to separatist movements, civil war, and the disintegration of the state.

At the heart of understanding political culture lies our awareness of the process of political socialization, through which attitudes, knowledge, and beliefs are passed on within a society. Political socialization occurs through a variety of agents, including the family, schools, peer groups, religious institutions, the media, the workplace, and various state actors. The power of ideas is tremendous, and in every society a wide variety of groups and individuals act, sometimes in very subtle ways and at other times in strikingly forceful ways, to try to ensure that others embrace their values.

DISCUSSION QUESTIONS

1. Do you think that the courts should protect citizens' rights? Try to think of all the different sources of information that have led you to give an answer to that question. Could you name several or none? Does your answer strike you simply as common sense?

2. Think of a particular issue such as clearcut logging, strip mining, trade union rights, universal medicare, or trade between Canada and some state with an authoritarian regime. Ask yourself what your views on it are and what you think the government should do about it. Then ask yourself how you came to learn about this issue and develop an opinion. Who informed and influenced you, and how?

3. Think about the various agents of political socialization that you have read about in this chapter. How would you rank them in order of the effects you believe each has had in forming your own political beliefs and attitudes?

4. Which agent of political socialization do you think you have reacted negatively to the most? Have other agents positively reinforced your negative reactions?

5. How deeply divided by political cleavages do you think our society is? What do you think are the main causes of those cleavages? Do you think our political system tries to accommodate subgroups or meld them into a single, national culture?

KEY TERMS

AGENTS OF POLITICAL SOCIALIZATION: Those groups of people or institutions that convey political attitudes and values to others in society. (95)

ELITE: A small group of individuals who have significantly more power than other members of their community. They are either in a position to make authoritative decisions or have privileged access to decision-makers. (87)

IDEOLOGY: A fairly coherent set of beliefs that not only explains what may be wrong with society, but also provides a vision of what society should be like. (88)

PATRIOTISM: A sense of pride in one's country. (108)

POLITICAL CULTURE: The collection of the understandings, values, attitudes, and principles of a community or society that relate to its political organization, processes, disputes, and public policies. Out of a society's political culture come important beliefs and values that structure the citizens' attitudes and expectations toward such basic political concepts as legitimacy, power, authority, and obedience. (85)

POLITICAL SOCIALIZATION: The process through which attitudes toward and knowledge about political matters are passed on within a society. (95)

PROPAGANDA: An organized attempt to spread beliefs through a communications campaign. It implies the use of exaggerated facts. (102)

SUBCULTURE: A cluster of people who share the same basic political values and attributes that are distinct from those of other groups in society or from the predominant values and attributes of society as a whole. (86)

WEB LINKS W W W

Columbia Journalism Review: Who Owns What:
http://www.cjr.org/owners

Nelson Education: Political Culture:
http://polisci.nelson.com/intropc.html

The Noam Chomsky Archive:
http://zmag.org/chomsky

A Sociological Tour Through Cyberspace:
http://www.trinity.edu/~mkearl

Voice of the Shuttle: Cultural Studies:
http://vos.ucsb.edu/browse.asp?id=2709

FURTHER READING

Almond, Gabriel A., and Sidney Verba. *The Civic Culture: Political Attitudes in Five Democracies*. Princeton: Princeton University Press, 1963.

Herman, Edward, and Noam Chomsky. *Manufacturing Dissent*. New York: Pantheon, 1986.

Kymlicka, Will. *Multicultural Citizenship*. Oxford: Clarendon Press, 1997.

Miliband, Ralph. *The State in Capitalist Society*. London: Weidenfeld and Nicolson, 1969.

Nevitte, Neil. *The Decline of Deference*. Peterborough: Broadview Press, 1996.

ENDNOTES

1. BBC News, "Kuwait Women Win Right to Vote"; available at http://news.bbc.co.uk/2/hi/middle_east/4552749.stm; accessed November 6, 2007.

2. Léger Marketing, "How Canadians Perceive Various Professions," February 16, 2004, p. 3; available at http://www.legermarketing.com/documents/spclm/040216eng.pdf; accessed May 6, 2008.

3. The information for Canada and Italy is from Government of New Zealand, "Tax Compliance"; available at http://executive.govt.nz/96-99/compliance/chapter7.htm; accessed June 2, 2008.

4. "Russia's Ever Mounting Back Taxes," *Washington Post*, December 26, 1997, p. A31; available at http://www.washingtonpost.com/wp-srv/inatl/longterm/russiagov/stories/taxes122697.htm; accessed July 17, 2002.

5. BBC News, "Russia Cuts Taxes," November 27, 1998; available at http://news.bbc.co.uk/hi/english/business/the_economy/newsid_223000/223266.stm; accessed July 17, 2002.

6. Hans Christiaan Haan, "Training for Work in the Informal Sector: New Evidence from Kenya, Tanzania and Uganda," p. 14, International Labour Organization website; available at http://www.ilo.org/public/english/employment/infeco/download/haan.pdf; accessed August 6, 2002.

7. Ipsos Reid, "How We See Each Other: Part II," December 1, 2004; available at http://www.ipsos-na.com/news/pressrelease.cfm?id=2480; accessed October 22, 2007.

8. Antonio Gramsci, *Letters from Prison* (New York: Columbia University Press, 1994).

9. Michel Foucault, *Ethics: Subjectivity and Truth* (New York: New Press, 1997).

10. Gabriel A. Almond and Sidney Verba, *The Civic Culture: Political Attitudes in Five Democracies* (Princeton: Princeton University Press, 1963). For a more recent discussion of related issues that have since been discussed in terms of civil society, see John Keane, *Civil Society and the State* (London: Verso, 1988).

11. For a discussion of the importance of civil society, as well as the limits of its political effects, in transitions from authoritarian regimes to democratic societies, see Emmanuel Gyimah-Boadi, "Civil Society in Africa," *Journal of Democracy* 7 (1996): 118.

12. Samuel P. Huntington, "Democracy for the Long Haul," *Journal of Democracy* 7(2) (April 1996): 8.

13. Charles Taylor, "The Politics of Recognition," in Amy Gutmann, ed., *Multiculturalism and the Politics of Recognition* (Princeton: Princeton University Press, 1992).

14. Iris M. Young, *Justice and the Politics of Difference* (Princeton: Princeton University Press, 1990); Will Kymlicka, *Multicultural Citizenship* (Oxford: Clarendon Press, 1997).

15. Will Kymlicka, *Liberalism, Community and Culture* (Oxford: Oxford University Press, 1989), pp. 182–205; see also Will Kymlicka, *Finding Our War: Rethinking Ethnocultural Relations in Canada* (Toronto: Oxford University Press, 1998).

16. Kenneth Hoover, *The Power of Identity: Politics in a New Key* (Chatham: Chatham House, 1997), pp. 37–38.

17. Carole Pateman, *The Sexual Contract* (Stanford: Stanford University Press, 1988), p. 231.

18. Carol Gilligan, *In a Different Voice: Psychological Theory and Women's Development* (Cambridge: Harvard University Press, 1982).

19. Simone de Beauvoir, *The Second Sex* (New York: Vintage Press, 1973), p. 301.

20. Richard G. Niemi and Mary A. Hepburn, "The Rebirth of Political Socialization," *Perspectives on Political Science* 24 (Winter 1995): 7–16.

21. Neil Nevitte, *The Decline of Deference* (Peterborough: Broadview Press, 1996).

22. See Edward Herman and Noam Chomsky, *Manufacturing Dissent* (New York: Pantheon, 1986); Noam Chomsky and David Barsamian, *Chronicles of Dissent* (Monroe, ME: Common Courage Press, 1992); and Noam Chomsky, "Media Control," available at http://www.zmag.org/zbooks/224, accessed June 2, 2008.

23. James Winter, *Democracy's Oxygen: How Corporations Control the News* (Montreal: Black Rose Books, 1997).

24. POLLARA, "Public Trust Index"; available at http://www.pollara.ca/Library/Reports/intro~1.html; accessed June 2, 2008.

25. Gallup, "Public Trust in Federal Government Remains High"; available at http://www.gallup.com/poll/releases/apr990108.asp; accessed January 8, 1998.

26. "World Internet Users and Population Stats"; available at http://www.internetworldstats.com/stats.htm; accessed November 6, 2007.

27. See "Soldier-Reporters Rewrite the Rules," *Toronto Star*, August 11, 2007; available at http://www.thestar.com/sciencetech/Ideas/article/245204; accessed November 6, 2007.

28. COMPAS, "Same Sex: Public Embraces Gay Rights, Opposes Gay Marriage, Advocates National Referendum," February 2, 2005, p. 9, available at http://www.compas.ca/data/050202-SameSex-EPC.pdf; accessed October 3, 2006.

29. For an examination of the relationship between the workplace and political attitudes in America, see Steven A. Peterson, *Political Behaviour: Patterns in Everyday Life* (Newbury Park: Sage, 1990), ch. 8.

30. Ralph Miliband, *The State in Capitalist Society* (London: Weidenfeld and Nicolson, 1969), p. 181.

31. Louis Hartz, *The Founding of New Societies* (New York: Harcourt Brace, 1964). See also Seymour Martin Lipset, "Canada and the United States: A Comparative Review," *Canadian Review of Sociology and Anthropology* 1 (1964): 173–85.

32. Gad Horowitz, "Conservatism, Liberalism, and Socialism in Canada: An Interpretation," *Canadian Journal of Economics and Political Science* 32 (1966): 143–71.

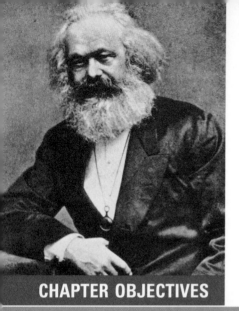

Chapter Five

THINKING ABOUT POLITICS: Ideas, Philosophies, and Ideologies

Richard Sigurdson

Introduction

Political *theory* (or political *philosophy*) is the subfield of the discipline of political science that involves theoretical or philosophical reflection on the "big ideas" about things political: the nature and function of the state; the role, legitimacy and proper ends of government; the relationship between the individual and society; the meaning of liberty, obligation, and rights; and the connections between law, justice, authority, and power. Political theory has been practised by thinkers in various eras and cultures—whenever and wherever people have given their collective condition and governance structures philosophical consideration. As an academic discipline in the Western world, political philosophy dates at least as far back as the ancient Greeks, whose philosophers contemplated the merits of most of the forms of government still known to us today: monarchy, aristocracy, democracy, tyranny, and oligarchy. As noted in Chapter 2, it was Aristotle (384–322 BCE) who famously classified types of government according to the number of rulers (the one, the few, or the many), as well as the ends pursued by the rulers (illegitimate rule is for the benefit of the rulers alone and legitimate for the benefit of all).[1] Political philosophers in the East struggled with similar issues related to politics and statecraft. In ancient China, Confucius (551–471 BCE), Mencius (372–289 BCE), Han Fei (280–33 BCE), and others produced vibrant philosophies during an era of political chaos and constant warfare. In ancient India, notable figures such as Kautilya (also known as Chanakya, 350–283 BCE) also pondered the practical and philosophical issues of political life. In the West from the fall of the Roman Empire in the 4th and 5th centuries CE to the Renaissance in the 15th century, most political philosophy was closely tied to Christianity—indeed, most leading Medieval philosophers in Europe were men of the church, such as Augustine (354–430) and Thomas Aquinas (1225–74). They were highly interested in the relationship between church and state, but also worked through many of the questions left them by the ancient Greeks. At around the same time, Islamic philosophers al-Farabi (872–951) and Ibn Khaldun (1332–1406) studied the same Hellenic writers and proposed their own versions of the ideal or most virtuous city-state. In the early modern period, political thinking in Europe increasingly focused on the foundations of power and the relative merits of monarchical and constitutional authority. Beginning in the 19th century, political philosophers took up the issues of social welfare and equality, and these and other general concerns have continued to motivate contemporary political thinkers around the world and in many cultures.

Reading these classic works of political philosophy is not always easy. For the most part, the people writing political theory were addressing a scholarly rather than a popular audience. Their texts are not particularly user-friendly, the manner of argument is often foreign to the non-specialist reader, and the ideas themselves are challenging. Indeed, it can be quite a struggle to determine what exactly Cicero (106–43 BCE) or Marsilius of Padua (1275–1342) or G.W.F. Hegel (1770–1831) meant in this or that text or what is really the most important thing to understand about their arguments. What is more, it is usually not possible to get the most out of the study of political theory without some knowledge of the long tradition of social and political ideas within a civilization or culture. In the Western tradition, for instance, the major political ideas were developed over a long period of time and through the interaction of different thinkers from various periods and countries. Indeed, one way to conceptualize this tradition is as a "conversation" about the big ideas carried out over the centuries, primarily found today in a limited number of major historical texts with which most everyone writing political theory is familiar. (See Box 5.1 for a list of important primary texts.)

Knowledge of this "canon" of Western political philosophy is generally regarded as fundamental to the discipline of political science in the Anglo-American academy. Yet some contemporary students might wonder why they should have to spend the time and effort to understand philosophical texts that were written centuries ago, sometimes in obscure languages, and by people long dead. How, some might ask, is this going to help them come to grips with the intricacies of contemporary international relations or the workings of the domestic politics of their own countries? And in any case, political philosophy is just too abstract and far removed from the nitty-gritty of political life to provide us with any insights about a world dominated by practical considerations, not idealistic theory. Why, then, should we study the history of political thought?

For one thing, the ideas of many now-dead political philosophers profoundly shaped the strategies and practices of actual political leaders, and their philosophizing became manifest in the ideologies that underlie all modern political systems: liberalism, conservatism, socialism, feminism, anarchism, political Islam, and so on. Sun Tzu (544–496 BCE), for instance, greatly influenced military strategists over the centuries, and many a politician has read attentively the short book *The Prince* by Niccolò Machiavelli (1459–1527). As we will see later, the views of Augustine, the Bishop of Hippo, continue to influence political attitudes centuries after his death. In an even more direct fashion, the ideas of John Locke (1632–1704) and Baron de Montesquieu (1689–1755) were profoundly influential in the rise of the liberal democratic nation-state, helping to shape such founding documents as the Constitution of the United States. The writings of Adam Smith (1723–90) not only helped create the modern discipline of political economy but provided the intellectual foundations for capitalism, free trade, and libertarianism. Jean-Jacques Rousseau's (1712–78) contemplations on freedom and equality inspired many of the key figures behind the French Revolution of 1789, which had as its slogan the Rousseauian phrase: "*liberté, égalité, fraternité.*" A direct line can be drawn between the advocacy of women's equality of opportunity by Mary Astell (1666–1731) and Mary Wollstonecraft (1759–97) and the feminist movement of the contemporary era. The radical ideas of Karl Marx (1818–83) and Friedrich Nietzsche (1844–1900) aroused, often unwittingly, political movements, communist and fascist respectively, that had a tremendous impact on the 20th century. Mao Zedong's (1893–1976) adaptation of Marxist notions to the Chinese context provided the blueprint for the creation of the People's Republic of China in 1949. Frantz Fanon (1925–61) used his knowledge of psychotherapy to develop the most influential theory on colonialism, becoming the inspiration for anticolonial liberation movements throughout the Third World. Current attempts to reconcile rational philosophy with Islamic theology have their roots in the interpretations of both Western and Eastern traditions by philosophers such as Avicenna (980–1037). And more recently, Sayyid Qutb (1906–66), who argued that sharia law should be the sole basis for government and who defended a broad application of jihad, can be seen as an author of the political version of Islam prominent in the 21st century among various political actors, including those in al Qaeda.

But there is more to studying political theory than linking the meaning of what philosophers said with the role their ideas have played in social or political struggles, or with identifying the historical consequences for which this or that political philosopher's ideas are commonly held responsible. The study of political ideas can also afford us the opportunity to think through, in our own mind and with our own experiences as points of reference, the big political questions that face humankind in all ages and territories. By so doing, we can come to our own conclusions about issues such as how political institutions should best be arranged and for what purpose. Our engagement with the writings of major political philosophers of the past is simply one way to help clarify in our own minds the precise meaning and utility of notions such as equality, freedom, and justice. And we can ask ourselves whether these key concepts that are still relevant today are coherent or contradictory with each other: Can we have equality without limiting freedom? Is allowing everyone to be free going to lead to justice? Such questions are more than merely abstract thought experiments. They represent conflicts which are at the root of contemporary political life everywhere on the planet. Over the past two centuries, we have taken to see political disputes as primarily involving clashes between competing ideologies: liberalism, conservatism, socialism, communism, fascism, and so on. We need to try to identify our own perspectives on these world historical political movements, and can do so in part by studying their philosophical roots. More recently, some scholars speak of a "clash of civilizations" whereby powerful and all-encompassing worldviews come into conflict.[2] Underlying these world historical confrontations, too, are sets of ideas and theories about the nature of human beings, the concept of equality, the nature of freedom and authority, and the uses of power. The critical investigation of these matters illuminates the values and principles that inform contemporary social, cultural, or economic policy.

The goal of this chapter is to introduce some of these key ideas about politics and to explore their meaning and impact. In the latter part of the chapter, we will look at how political ideas form the foundation for major world ideologies. But first we will examine some of the perennial issues and topics in political thought, organizing the material thematically in an effort to provide a broad survey of the subject. While the specific theories of individual philosophers cannot be given the space they deserve in a single chapter, it is hoped that students will take up the challenge of reading in their own words not only some of the great historical political thinkers from the distant past but also some of the most prominent political philosophers of our own day. (See Box 5.2 for a list of some of the most influential political philosophers from the past century.) Political theory is by no means a field of merely historical study. Ideas are alive today and the debates over them are as important and lively as they have ever been.

Prominent Political Theorists of the Past Century   BOX 5.2

Hannah Arendt (1906–75). Key works: *The Origins of Totalitarianism* (1951); *Eichmann in Jerusalem: A Report on the Banality of Evil* (1963)

Michel Foucault (1926–84). Key works: *Madness and Civilization* (1961); *Discipline and Punish* (1975)

Jürgen Habermas (1929–). Key works: *Legitimation Crisis* (1973); *The Theory of Communicative Action* (1981)

Friedrich Hayek (1899–1992). Key works: *The Road to Serfdom* (1944); *The Constitution of Liberty* (1960)

Leo Strauss (1899–1973). Key works: *The City and Man* (1962); *Political Philosophy: Six Essays by Leo Strauss* (1975)

Catherine MacKinnon (1946–). Key works: *Towards a Feminist Theory of the State* (1989); *Only Words* (1993)

Herbert Marcuse (1898–1979). Key works: *Eros and Civilization* (1955); *One-Dimensional Man* (1964)

Robert Nozick (1938–2002). Key works: *Anarchy, State, and Utopia* (1974); *Philosophical Explanations* (1981)

John Rawls (1921–2002). Key works: *A Theory of Justice* (1971); *Political Liberalism* (1993)

Charles Taylor (1931–). Key works: *Hegel* (1975); *The Politics of Recognition* (1992)

Perennial Issues in Political Thought

Human Nature and Politics

It is sometimes said that the history of political philosophy is one long meditation on the question of human nature. Indeed, whether it is acknowledged or not, the starting point for all thinking about politics is a probing into the very nature of human beingness. What does it mean to be human? What is our human essence? Are we by nature social animals, as Aristotle said, or are we solitary and isolated creatures, as Thomas Hobbes (1588–1679) assumed? Is the desire for power intrinsic to human nature, as Nietzsche believed, or are we by nature benign beings, capable of mutual love and cooperation, as Mencius suggested? Our answers to these questions will determine how we approach all other aspects of political philosophizing.[3] For instance, if we regard humans as power-hungry and self-centred by nature, as opposed to fundamentally peace-loving and cooperative, this will very much influence our views about what form of government is necessary.

Our thinking about human nature sets the foundation upon which our political theories are constructed. Hobbes assumed that humans are isolated, selfish creatures, driven by their "desires" and "aversions." Two basic postulates about human nature provide the foundation for all his political theory: first, that humans are inescapably engaged in a perpetual struggle for power over others that ends only in death; and second, that our strongest aversion is to violent death, which we will seek to avoid at all costs. Hobbes comes to these conclusions about human nature by imagining what people would be like if they lived in a "state of nature"—that is, in a condition free of any government or rule-making authority. Hobbes concludes that a natural condition without authority or rules would be one of constant war "of every man against every man." Life in the state of nature, as Hobbes famously declares, would be "solitary, poor, nasty, brutish, and short."[4] Thus, the only rational thing for humans to do in order to avoid perpetual violence or the fear of it is to quit the state of nature, agreeing mutually to abdicate to a sovereign power all of one's natural rights to govern oneself. **Civil society**, the result of this covenant between rational human beings, is to Hobbes but an expedient. He says that while it is not natural for humans to live in society, their self-interest will compel them to bind together for the purposes of mutual security and benefit.

Aristotle presents an entirely opposite point of view. For him, it is living in society that is natural—humans are *by nature* social and political animals. Only a beast or a god (the subhuman or the superhuman) could live without being a member of a political community. For us humans, it is in our nature to commune with our fellow citizens. More than that, political life is to Aristotle the highest form of self-actuality. We are most alive, most true to our nature, when we are participating in political activity, especially when we are governing in a good state. Because *polis* life is natural, the best states are ones in which the interests of one person are the same as the interests of all. Hence, a person who acts for his or her own good must also act for the good of all fellow citizens.

But if Aristotle is correct and we are by nature social and political beings, why is it so hard for us to get along? Why is there so much strife and political violence in the world? One need look no further than the daily news to note that there are wars and conflicts everywhere, and that people will murder and lie in order to gain or retain power. And history tells that this is not unique to our own time; it has forever been thus. For Hobbes, this is hardly surprising. Humans are simply avaricious and selfish by nature. Conflict is natural. Hence, the primary political objective cannot be to eradicate conflict entirely, since that is an impossible goal. However, one can hope to control and contain conflict through the imposition of stern order by a leader whose will becomes law. A similar perspective was advanced two thousand years earlier by Xun Zi, who contradicted leading Confucian scholars such as Mencius by insisting that human beings are innately evil, selfish, and corrupt. Left uncurbed, according to Xun Zi, what he calls man's "detestable disposition" would lead to anarchy and the destruction of civil society. Like Hobbes, he argued that law and morality are not natural but are social constructs invented in order to rectify the natural human impulse for doing evil.

An alternative perspective is found in the thought of Rousseau. He believed that humans are essentially decent beings but that they have been gradually led away from their natural, congenial condition toward one that is corrupt, unjust, and divisive. This misfortune occurred, Rousseau theorizes, because humans introduced into their lives private property, which led to inequality, selfishness, distrust, and the concentration of power in the hands of a few. Rousseau's thesis, put very simply, is that humans are basically good but have been corrupted by their sociopolitical environment. That is, bad institutions have distorted the natural goodness of humankind. Rousseau offers us hope that human goodness can be rediscovered if social conditions are put right, specifically if an enlightened leader governs in a manner that reflects the will of all. This reasoning, which goes back at least as far as the philosophy of Mencius in the 4th century BCE, has struck a positive chord with a variety of individuals and groups over the years. Modern liberals believe that by reforming social and political institutions we can free individuals from oppressive rules and regulations. Utopian socialists stress the inherent human capacity for consensus and cooperation and imagine strategies for creating a world of peace and harmony. Marx's doctrine of historical materialism rests on a faith in inexorable historical progress toward the highest phase of communist society, in which there will be no classes and therefore no destructive political conflict.

More will be said in a subsequent section on the concepts of the political left and right, but it can be noted at this stage that Western thinkers on the so-called left (liberals, socialists, communists) are more likely than those on the right (conservatives, fascists) to hold the belief that human nature is good, or inherently perfectible, and that political ills stem from societal influences rather than any essential human flaws. Thus, the goal of leftist or liberal political action is to create the sorts of institutions that would be most likely to provide the necessary positive influences to benefit humanity. Thinkers on the political right tend to share a belief in the imperfection of human nature, seeing in the individual varying degrees of weakness, irrationality, perfidy, and immorality. Indeed, conservatives think that humankind is not only morally imperfect but intellectually imperfect as well. Thus, they hold that humans simply cannot know enough to be sure that their radical social experimentation or tinkering with the institutions of government will actually lead to positive change rather than to more sociopolitical problems.[5]

In the Western world, the conviction that humankind is morally imperfect is rooted in the Christian doctrine of original sin. According to this teaching, human beings are fallen creatures, alienated from the goodness of their Creator and divided against each other by selfishness. Most instructive on this topic is the work of St. Augustine, who regarded humans as invariably corrupt and helpless, driven by their most base passions to commit grievous wrongs and to suffer dearly for doing so. In contrast to the Platonic Socrates, Augustine regarded as naïve the idea that people will do what is right and good if they only know the truth. According to Augustine, human beings are from conception wicked and dangerous creatures driven by lust, including the lust for power. No amount of proper education or wisdom will reverse their fallen state. Not surprisingly, he believed that people need to be coerced and restrained by harsh laws, a strict code of behaviour, and brutal punishment for transgression. Augustine accepted that temporal institutions, as creations of a sinful humanity, would always be inherently flawed and could never bring true happiness. Yet he concluded that secular political institutions, no matter how oppressive, must be respected, since they constitute the only earthly bulwark against disorder.

Feminist scholars have noted that Augustine's view of human nature has also had a profound and negative influence over gender relations, contributing to an ethos in Christianity of sexual repression and misogyny. Himself extraordinarily sexually active in his early days, as we know from his *Confessions* (397–98), Augustine later became obsessed with the sexual nature of original sin, regarding it as deriving from spontaneous male sexual arousal (not for the purpose of procreation), which he blamed on women. From this, say his contemporary interpreters, comes the justification for the domination of women and their confinement to the roles of whore, wife, or mother. According to many feminist critics, Augustine's pessimistic views of human nature, sexuality, and politics dominated Christian teaching for centuries, and continues to have some sociopolitical influence even today.[6]

One should note that this general presumption that humans are flawed creatures is not specifically Christian or even religious, since it is shared by many secular and even atheist thinkers. For instance, Sigmund Freud (1856–1939), the founder of modern psychology, said that humans are aggressive and instinctual beings, driven by unconscious, irrational, and destructive desires and impulses. He disagreed with the humanists and socialists who saw humans as altruistic and able to love all of humanity. Instead, Freud regarded humans as antisocial beings at root, driven by the "pleasure principle" to seek to gratify their instinctive urges. Civilization, in this view, is an unnatural but necessary process whereby human instincts for violence and aggression are repressed and controlled, in part by the construction of social conventions that work only due to an inherent sense of primal guilt. Finally, Freud's social and political thought is also instructive about societal views towards women, which limits their roles to either objects of male sexual desire or mother-figures and nurturers (this has been dubbed the "Madonna/whore complex"). While this sounds similar in many respects to Augustine's view of human nature, Freud came to his conclusions from the point of view of science rather than religion. Indeed, he tended to regard the two as mortal enemies, and famously denounced religion as an illusion. At the same time, unlike many political philosophers, his was not a *normative* theory but was presented as an *empirical* and fully objective account of sociopolitical reality. (See Box 5.3.) As he once said, "our theories are based on experience . . . and not just fabricated out of thin air or thought up on the writing desk."[7]

Normative Versus Empirical Studies   BOX 5.3

Two broad paths of inquiry are normally pursued by political scientists: the *normative* approach and the *empirical* approach. Normative studies tend to focus on values and principles, as opposed to the empirical or quantifiable realm of facts. The most obviously normative subfield of political science is what we call political theory or political philosophy. Along with related fields in the humanities, such as ethics, political theory deals with normative issues in society, such as the nature of good and evil or the proper ends of collective action.

Empirical studies, on the other hand, tend to rely on observation and measurement of actual behaviour rather than on the analysis of speculative theories about norms of behaviour. In this regard, much of the work done by empirical political scientists fits in with other key disciplines in the social sciences, such as sociology or economics. While it might be an oversimplification, it is sometimes said that normative political science deals with what *ought* to be, while empirical political science deals with what *is*.

Yet another point of view on the issue of human nature is found in Islam, which does not presuppose any inherent wickedness of human nature. Instead, the Qur'an teaches that human beings are born in a state of *fitrah*, which denotes the inherent disposition toward goodness and virtue in humankind that is manifest in peaceful submission to the will of Allah. Thus, there is no concept of original sin in Islam. People are not perfect, mind you, and must struggle to remain on the right path. But any deviation from one's original virtuous state is due to external factors, suggests the Qur'an, and true repentance of sin can return a person to the original sinless state. According to Muslim theology, humankind's chief failing is pride and rebellion. In their pride, humans attempt to become equals of Allah, and this runs counter to the primary theological concept of Islam, which is *Tahīd*—the belief that there is only one God. Thus, pride is a cardinal sin. The chief virtue, again, is submission to divine will. In Islam, *sharia* is the expression of divine will and it forms a system of obligations and duties that are incumbent upon all Muslims. Politically, this is at the root of the Islamic adherence to a strict legal framework within which both public and private aspects of life are regulated for those living under sharia law. It is often pointed out that in political Islam, there is no inherent separation between matters for the state and those for the church, as there is in **liberal democracy**.

Equality and Inequality

Along with the larger question about the essence of humankind, political philosophers, especially in the modern era, have been intensely focused on the issue of equality. Again, there are religious roots to the doctrine of **egalitarianism**. The Christian belief that all humans are equally created in the image of God provides the foundation for the more robust moral concept that all human beings are equal in worth and status, which can be found in various forms of Western secular thought. Islam is also based on the fundamental notion that each human being is spiritually equal to every other human being in the eyes of God. As with Christianity, moreover, this spiritual egalitarianism in Islam does not always translate into an ethos of social egalitarianism. Social distinctions, such as the relegation of homosexuals to the realm of unnatural beings, and subordination, such as the subordination of women to men, are seen by many religious thinkers as necessary to the maintenance of society, order, and morality. Politically, therefore, the struggle to achieve a greater measure of social equality for all individuals and groups, which has become almost a hallmark of modernity, is often waged against the well-entrenched interests of religious and societal prejudice.

For political philosophy, the initial question is whether human beings are in essence equal or unequal. Clearly, our modern bias is toward the view that humans are in essence equal (although our societies are still rife with social and economic inequalities). Yet the majority of political thinkers throughout history take the opposite view. Ancient Indian political philosophy gives kingship a central place in political life, which is not uncommon, but it also sets out an elaborate system of social stratification. For ancient philosophers and legislators in this tradition, such as the authors of the *Manu-Smrti* (written between 200 BCE and 200 CE), the king was a key figure in a social order based on a caste system. Caste divided society into distinct classes, with individuals assigned their positions and occupational roles by birth: the *Brahmans* were responsible for education and priestly duties, and were said to have divine powers; the *Ksatriyas* were the rulers and warriors; the *Vaisyas* cultivators, manufacturers, and businesspeople; and the *Sudras* were the lowest rank within society, performing the manual jobs and existing essentially in servitude. Below these groups yet are those with *Dalit* status— often called "untouchables" or "outcastes"—who were regarded as literally outside of society and who served in the most subservient positions. Natural law or *Dharma* depended on the observance of these class divisions. In this system, there is a respect for equality of a sort—but it is a matter of "treating equals equally." That is, members of the same caste or class are to be regarded as equal to one another. Clearly, however, there is no concept of universal equality or of the sociopolitical equality of all citizens in society.

Ancient Greeks also presupposed a rank order of humankind, in this case according to one's capacity for reason. On this basis, Aristotle excluded from citizenship whole categories of humanity—for example, artisans, workers, women, and slaves—because they allegedly lacked the ability to reason for themselves. And Plato designed an elaborate theory to justify the rule of the naturally superior individual, the philosopher-king. Throughout the Middle Ages, and well into the modern era, European political philosophers simply assumed that humans were unequal in essence, and did not even question political arrangements which distributed power and resources unequally. It was not until Thomas Hobbes employed the "state of nature" metaphor in *Leviathan* (1651) that one finds the presumption that in nature all men are indeed equal—at least in their equal ability to do harm to one another in their quest to satisfy their own desires. And even so, this observation led Hobbes to the non-egalitarian conclusion that the best possible arrangement was for the people to hand over all of their sovereign authority to a king who would enjoy unfettered power over all citizens.

More recently, and in contradiction to the growing egalitarianism of his contemporaries, Nietzsche maintained that humans are radically unequal in virtually every way that matters. Nietzsche was frustrated by the fact that philosophers and politicians in the modern age were increasingly promoting what he called the "slave" doctrine of equality and the values of the inferior "herd" over what he dubbed "master morality" and the noble doctrine of aristocracy. Writing near the end of the 19th century, Nietzsche—author of the *Untimely Meditations* (1873–76)—was clearly out of step with the ethos of his society. In his more optimistic moments, however, he looked forward to the rise to power of a new breed of "supermen" who would reflect the highest potential for human creativity and vitality. Nietzsche's ideas about a new master race were subsequently misappropriated by apologists for Nazism and used to justify Hitler's racist and nationalist doctrine (in spite of the fact that Nietzsche specifically denounced racism and nationalism as perverted ideologies).[8]

In Anglo-American and European thought of the past 250 years, attitudes toward equality have been especially instructive of the divide between conservatives and liberals. The traditional conservative position is nicely represented by the English thinker and statesman Edmund Burke (1729–97), who argued that humanity is naturally and hierarchically ordered. Like many conservatives, Burke held that the best government is an **aristocracy**, one in which the privileged orders, the high-born and well-bred, would rule wisely and for the good of the whole. Burke very much feared that the egalitarian ethos arising from the French Revolution would undermine the political basis for order and stability—his favoured political values. In contrast to Burke's aristocratic faith in a natural hierarchy, the liberal opinion is that humans are by nature free and equal creatures, equally in possession of their own natural rights (primarily, the right to preserve oneself, but also the right to individual freedom and the enjoyment of private property). Such a philosophy provided the intellectual foundations for the liberal democratic nation-states epitomized by the republics in France and America. The public philosophies of such places are heavily influenced by thinkers such as Hobbes, Locke, and Montesquieu. The main liberal ideas are nicely summed up by Thomas Jefferson (1743–1826) in the *Declaration of Independence*: "We hold these truths to be self-evident: that all men are created equal; that they are endowed by their Creator with certain inalienable Rights: that among these are Life, Liberty and the pursuit of Happiness."

As a statement of political ideals, the words of the *Declaration* stake out an inspiring egalitarian position that is dutifully revered by patriots as symbolic of America's democratic roots. Yet Jefferson's text also illustrates the huge disparity between the ideals of liberal democracy and the stubborn persistence of social and political inequality. The disconnection between egalitarian ideals and reality is particularly striking in the case of the constitutional history of the United States. When the *Declaration* was penned in 1776, and for almost a century thereafter, slavery was allowed in the country. Indeed, the American Constitution, ratified in 1791, legitimated and codified the institution of slavery. Many signatories of the *Declaration*, including Jefferson himself, and many representatives to the Constitutional Convention, including George Washington (who once denounced slavery as "repugnant"), owned slaves. It was not until the Emancipation Proclamation and the passage of the 13th, 14th, and 15th Amendments in the wake of the Civil War that American constitutional law entrenched racial equality—and even then the courts were largely unwilling to enforce any of its provisions on state governments wishing to continue various forms of racial segregation and discrimination. The idea that it is legitimate to separate people according to race, and to treat them unequally, is deeply engrained in American political culture and it has taken an extraordinary effort to counteract this racist prejudice in popular political thought.

Nor should it escape our attention that the *Declaration* and the rights it presumes are limited to "all men" and not to the female half of the population. American women did not receive equal political rights until the 19th Amendment was passed in 1920, and even today women in America are without the protections that would have been extended to them had the proposed Equal Rights Amendment (ERA) been passed. We know also that the rights that were claimed by the American colonists were not extended to the Indigenous peoples of North America, who were largely regarded as savages unfit for citizenship and equal treatment under the law. Finally, political equal rights were not even enjoyed by all white men in the Thirteen Colonies, since those who did not own sufficient property were excluded. In spite of the Founders' lofty rhetoric, therefore, the notion that all human beings should be regarded as equal and treated so by law was not a reality in America at its inception. Indeed, even the formal achievement of equal rights in America, to the extent that this has been achieved at all, must be regarded as a very recent phenomenon.

But America is by no means alone in this regard. For instance, the history of equality and inclusion in Canada demonstrates that the situation in this country has only improved substantially in the very recent past. The Fathers of Confederation (there were no women founders in Canada) did not even attempt to justify their enterprise in terms of democracy or equality, as had the American Founders a century earlier. If anything, Canada's founding was a testament to the resistance of its elites to the ideals of democratic government and egalitarianism. There was no bill or charter of rights proposed in the *British North America Act* (1867), nor were there many laws in place that could be reasonably construed as protecting the basic rights of the individual against the power of the state. While slavery was not a factor in Canada's racial history, certain groups faced special discrimination. For instance, the case of the Chinese in Canada serves to illustrate the historical role of exclusion and racism in Canadian immigration and settlement policies. Chinese immigrants first came to Canada during the Gold Rush, but most came to work on the construction of the Canadian Pacific Railway. When the railway was completed in 1885, the Canadian government imposed the notorious "head tax" on Chinese seeking to enter the country. In 1923, Chinese became the only people Canada has ever excluded explicitly on the basis of race. For the next 24 years, virtually no Chinese were allowed to immigrate to Canada. At the same time, this group was also excluded from the franchise—Chinese-Canadians did not get to vote in Canadian elections until 1947. Of course, they were not alone. First Nations peoples in Canada have also faced extraordinary exclusion and the denial of the rights. The last of these racial limitations on voting rights was not lifted until 1960. Various other racial and religious minorities suffered discrimination at the hands of both the federal and provincial governments, with no recourse through the courts available to them (unlike, say, the African-Americans who did eventually find support for their struggle for equality at the U.S. Supreme Court). It took the entrenchment of the Charter of Rights and Freedoms in 1982 to remove the final legal barriers to equality in Canada.

Clearly, there has long been a gap between the ideals of egalitarian democracy and the realities of existing liberal democratic states. Still, much progress has been made. Over the past few decades, especially since the end of World War II and the passage of the 1948 United Nations Declaration of Human Rights (which opens with an affirmation of the "inherent dignity and of the equal and inalienable rights of all members of the human family"), most liberal democratic states have formally eradicated any official obstacles to equality before and under the law. But does the adoption of formal rules providing for legal equality create an egalitarian society? Now that virtually all of the formal and legal obstacles to equal participation have been dismantled in places such as the United States and Canada, have women, visible minorities, Indigenous peoples, immigrants, and the poor achieved full equality? And does treating individuals equally, regardless of their skin colour or group identity, really produce the desired effect of an egalitarian society?

To be sure, social inequality persists in many forms even in the most advanced Western societies. Statistics indicate that women and minorities suffer inequalities of income, political power, and social status. Moreover, there are significant disparities along **class** lines in all advanced capitalist societies. How can we justify such inequalities in societies that are avowedly egalitarian? How much inequality is permissible, and of what sort? What, if anything, should society or the state do to address the problem of persistent social inequality? Here one finds diverging views, even among those who all regard themselves as egalitarians. For some, including contemporary conservative thinkers and politicians, the answer is typically that we should guarantee formal or legal equality and then rely on the free market to produce an equilibrium of societal benefits. That is, we should make sure that there is no legal or official discrimination allowed (e.g., there should be no laws banning people of colour from applying for medical school or women from running for office) and then accept that a fair system of competition will eventually produce equitable results. Beyond ensuring impartiality and nondiscrimination, however, the state should not be used to provide specific advantages for historically disadvantaged groups, which is the project typically associated with various forms of **affirmative action** programs. The use of the state's power to intervene in the economic or social arena, even for the laudable goal of reducing societal inequality, is regarded by many critics as a worse crime against equality, since it ends up treating some people differently than others on the basis of race or sex or ethnicity.

For the most part, the proponents of contemporary **liberalism** insist that each individual should be equally free to pursue his or her own goals and desires, without discrimination based on race, sex, religion, or other identifiable characteristics. Moreover, they believe that for freedom and equal rights to become reality everyone must have an equal chance to compete fairly, on a level playing field with all others, for a share of the social and economic benefits that society has to offer. Judged by the results, contemporary liberals say, the playing field would appear still to be tilted very much in favour of certain individuals or groups (such as middle-class white men). So in the name of the equality of opportunity, the state must be used not only to protect individuals against discrimination, but also to provide fair chances for advancement and improvement of living standards for all citizens (e.g., through affirmative action programs for hiring minorities). In this fashion, supporters of interventionist liberalism say, no one will be unduly disadvantaged when engaging in societal competition. Yet liberals fully expect that once equality of opportunity is assured—once there is an even playing field—the most talented or industrious individual should be able to reap the rewards of his or her own competitive efforts. As a result of fair and free competition between individuals, liberals admit, there will be some winners and some losers. Social or conventional inequality will therefore exist in a liberal society, since some individuals will gain more because they will work harder or have more ability than others. However, this conventional inequality is justifiable, from the liberal point of view, so long as no one is denied a meaningful opportunity to compete and to be successful, especially on the basis of attributes or identifiers over which they have no control, such as race or gender.

It is at this point that **socialism** breaks with liberalism and insists that true egalitarianism demands more than equal opportunity or equal social and political rights. Socialists are most concerned with material inequality and the equal access to the resources of the community. It is often said, then, that while liberals are content with an equality of opportunity, socialist justice requires an actual equality of condition. For those on the moderate left (e.g., social democrats), the equality of condition is more of an ideal than a practical goal. That is, the objective is to narrow the gap as much as possible between rich and poor, gradually levelling out society's social and economic inequalities by raising the floor for those at the bottom and lowering the ceiling for those at the top. For instance, socialists tend to be troubled by reports, such as the one by the Canadian Centre for Policy Alternatives (CCPA), that document the huge and increasing gap in earnings between those in the economic elite and others in society. In the case of this study, it was found that the top 100 CEOs in Canada earn on average more than 218 times as much as a Canadian working full time for a full year at the average of weekly employment earnings. Put another way, the top CEOs earn as much in just over nine hours of work as their average employees do in a full year.[9] What makes this a special problem is not just that the top salaries are on the rise, but that the average salary has not grown at all, in spite of claims by proponents of the current neoliberal economic policies that there would be a "trickle-down effect," whereby increased profits for the wealthy would result in better wages for workers. Hence, when social democrats complain about matters such as high CEO remuneration, it is not just a matter of envy of the rich—or what Nietzsche referred to as *ressentiment*, the assigning of blame to one's superiors in order to compensate for one's own inferiority and lack of success. Rather, reports such as the one from the CCPA raise fears that the accumulation of enormous wealth by the very few will come at the expense of average citizens, who will be deprived of adequate income and benefits to meet their needs. To achieve greater equality, therefore, social democrats want the state to intervene in the economy, adjusting the effects of the disparities between winners and losers that inevitably arise from market competition. Hence, social democrats promote a variety of redistributive measures, including steeply graduated income taxes, generous social welfare programs, and full employment policies.

For radical socialists and **communists**, however, these social democratic strategies are insufficient, since they can never provide for an absolute equality of condition. For justice to be achieved, it is argued, the fundamental inequality of classes—most importantly, the gap between the **bourgeoisie** and the workers—must be addressed at its root. Redistributive economic policies and trade unionism will not, in themselves, achieve the overthrow of capitalism required for equality to prevail. Indeed, they may do more harm than good. Vladimir Ilyich Lenin (1870–1924), the leader of the Bolshevik Revolution, argued that social democratic parties and their trade union partners could become so successful at achieving their minimal goals within the capitalist system that they sap the energy needed to produce truly revolutionary change. What is needed, from the communist perspective, is an abolition of the private ownership of property and its replacement with full public ownership of all of the means of production. Communists believe that to ensure that the inequalities resulting from market exchanges do not arise, **capitalism** has to be replaced by a planned economy, one in which central authority decides what is to be produced and to whom it will be distributed. At some later stage, perhaps, the state as a coercive instrument need no longer perform this planning function, and society will naturally organize itself according to the Marxian slogan, "From each according to his ability, to each according to his need." But at least for the intermediary period of post-revolutionary socialism, there would have to be a very strong state to impose class equality.

Socialist republics with just such strong states were established in various places during the last century where communist parties came to rule, establishing economic systems modelled after the theories of Marx and Lenin. These included the Union of Soviet Socialist Republics (USSR) and its various satellite states in central and eastern Europe (the so-called Soviet bloc), as well as the People's Republic of China and smaller communist states in North Korea, Cuba, and in several African countries. The existence of such regimes very much complicated the analysis of the ideas and theories put forward by political thinkers who called themselves communist, since some of these theorists who agreed with the goal of a classless society might not have approved of the policies of actually existing communist governments. The subtlety of the distinction between "communism" as expressed by, say, the French thinker Louis Althusser (1918–1990) and "communism" as practised by the tyrannical Soviet leader Joseph Stalin (1878–1953) is often lost on the lay observer. This was especially so during the Cold War years, when anything even remotely connected to the ethos of communism might be labelled as treasonous by patriotic supporters of the Anglo-American version of capitalist liberalism. Yet in spite of the fact that communism is now regarded by many as a failed social experiment, class inequality is still a major source of injustice in the 21st century, and many theorists legitimately regard the eradication of class distinctions through some form of communism as the highest possible goal for political action. Their theories deserve a fair and careful analysis by serious students of political science.

Although inequalities of wealth and income have been the main targets for egalitarians over the years, one can easily point to many other forms of inequality which give rise to heated philosophical debate. For instance, much of the discussion in America over equality revolves around the issue of race. African-American struggles for greater equality rights have received the most scholarly attention, resulting in several insightful, and often radical, political theories of race from the work of W.E.B. Du Bois (1868–1963) to the explosive ideas of Princeton professor Cornell West.[10] In general, philosophical studies of race tend to concur that race is a "socially constructed" phenomenon with significant political implications. That is, race is not a product of biological characteristics, genetics or physiological determinants, but of historical processes and social relations that reflect the distribution of power, as noted in Chapter 3. It is also becoming much more relevant to consider that America, like so many other societies, is multiracial as well as multiethnic in composition. Thus, various writers have written both in favour of and in opposition to the trend toward "multiculturalism" and the recognition of collective rights based on group identity.[11]

Of course, sex inequality has also received extraordinary attention from theorists of all political stripes in recent years. Mind you, political philosophers in the past did not always spend much time debating the matter, since they assumed that men and women were by nature different and that their dissimilarities justified unequal gender roles. Aristotle epitomized this view when he said that "the relation of male to female is naturally that of the superior to the inferior—of the ruling to the ruled."[12] Women are justifiably excluded from politics, in Aristotle's estimation, since they are naturally unfit for rulership. In various renderings, Aristotle's position held sway among political thinkers for centuries. Mary Astell and Mary Wollstonecraft were among the first female authors who challenged this view, arguing that women and men are equally capable by nature. They both regarded the exclusion of women from proper education as the main source of perceived inequity between the sexes. Another notable early proponent of women's rights was John Stuart Mill (1806–73), who advocated for the full political equality of women and denied that there were any politically relevant differences between men and women. It is not due to nature, he said, but to social convention hardened by centuries of oppression that women are kept inferior to men. *The Subjection of Women*, published in 1869, was thought to be extremely radical in Mill's time but is now seen as a classic statement of democratic and liberal feminism.

Most theorists today, in the West at least, agree that women should have the same legal and political rights as men. There are still theoretical disputes, however, regarding the significance of observable gender differences between men and women. For instance, Carol Gilligan, who became known as the founder of "difference feminism," asserted that women have differing moral and psychological tendencies than men. According to Gilligan, men think in terms of rules and justice and women are more inclined to think in terms of caring and relationships. Unlike those who might wish to denigrate women as a result of gender differences, however, Gilligan insisted that Western liberal democracies must value both sexes equally.[13] This position has not been uncontroversial. Although she denied that sex differences were a matter of biology, and instead located the sources of differing psychological orientations between men and women in the socialization process, Gilligan's work is still often criticized for its political implications. If women are seen as somehow different from men in essence, then this can provide a justification for excluding them from certain roles in society. Moreover, some fear that Gilligan's findings can be used to reinforce the sexist presumption that women are prone to emotional and irrational decision-making, and thus cannot be fully trusted in key political positions. This is a significant matter, given that there are still many fields in which women are underrepresented, even if they are not officially excluded.

In the West, at least, official exclusion of women on the basis of biological sex difference is no longer prevalent. Exceptions persist in some areas, such as female participation in male sports leagues. Another, more fundamental, area of exclusion of females still exists in most societies—namely, women's participation in active combat roles in the military. While women have served in military capacities for literally thousands of years, mainly in supporting roles, most modern armies have not allowed female personnel to serve in active combat positions. As one of the last remaining instances of blatant sex discrimination in the policies of Western states, this matter has come in for some close scrutiny by theorists and practitioners alike. Arguments for and against female combat activity have focused on the physical differences between men and women, but also on their differing psychological dispositions, and on the practical effects on members of each of the sexes in having their opposite sex members present in the battlefield.[14]

Liberty Versus Authority

As the gains in the fields of racial and women's equality rights demonstrate, recent history has witnessed a tremendous expansion in the realm of individual liberty, with people able to expect much higher levels of personal freedom from intrusive authority than ever before. Yet almost all political thinkers agree that there is still a legitimate need for governmental authority of some kind. The exception to the rule would be the proponents of **anarchism**, who believe that human beings are capable of managing their own affairs on the basis of cooperation and mutual respect. But other than them, even those who are the most skeptical about authority, including many classical liberals and those today who are conservative-minded and in favour of small governments, find a need for state authority of some sort.

Liberalism has always harboured a degree of uneasiness with the power of the state or with large social institutions, since they can provide a base for power-hungry individuals. It was a liberal thinker, Lord Acton (1834–1902), who famously said that "Power tends to corrupt, and absolute power corrupts absolutely." But he and other liberals do not conclude from this that there should be no state authority—that each individual should be entirely free to do as he or she pleases. On the contrary, the liberal message is that one needs a properly working constitutional democracy. Arbitrary power and tyranny are the likely consequences of regimes without sufficient constitutional checks and balances. According to this logic, the power of one individual or group needs to be held in check by countervailing powers of other individuals and groups. In addition, individuals need to be protected, as much as possible, from arbitrary authority and from pressures to conform to the majority viewpoint. What liberals tend to assume is that liberty consists essentially in the absence of coercive authority. One is free to the extent that one can live as one chooses, seeking one's own happiness, pursuing one's own self-interest, striving to fulfil one's own goals and aspirations. In economics, this translates into the principle of **laissez-faire**, the idea that the economic system works best when there is no interference from government. The virtues of this doctrine were first elaborated by the Scottish writer Adam Smith, who argued that if government abandoned its regulatory function, leaving individuals to enter or leave economic relations as they see fit, the "invisible hand" of the market would maximize individual well-being and ensure public welfare. This concept of *laissez-faire* became the distinguishing feature of modern capitalism and remains its most sacred principle.

Again, even free-market liberals recognize some need for government authority. There is always a threat that unscrupulous individuals will pursue their selfish interests in ways that impinge upon the freedom of others. Consequently, the very freedoms that liberals hold most dear (i.e., the right to "life, liberty, and property") can survive only when people are defended against the violent, coercive, or fraudulent behaviour of others. Protecting people's lives and possessions by maintaining law and order is therefore a fundamental job of government. But is this all that government should do? For some, the answer is yes. The only legitimate role for the state is to be a guarantor of security and a protector of private property. Anything beyond this limited role for government becomes a threat to liberty. Such a minimalist government is often referred to as the "night-watchman state." It tends to be promoted by libertarians and neoliberals. But others doubt that such a state can serve the interests of all people. For them, freedom requires more than simply being left alone to do as you please, since one needs a certain amount of social and economic power to exercise freedom. As you can see, the issue is not as simple as choosing between liberty *or* authority.

To help us clarify this issue, it is worthwhile to turn to Sir Isaiah Berlin (1909–97), who distinguished between negative and positive concepts of freedom.[15] The former is stressed by classical liberals and was discussed above—namely, freedom consists in the lack of external (usually governmental) restraints imposed on the individual. The greatest threat to personal freedom, from this point of view, comes from the unwanted interference from other people, including governments acting on behalf of the people. Representative writers in this tradition would include Locke and Mill, as well as the more recent theorist Robert Nozick (1938–2002), who took as his first principle that people have natural rights, and that any interference in one's activities on the part of the state is, prima facie, a violation of those rights. The latter, the concept of positive liberty, consists in there being sufficient conditions for each individual to develop to his or her full potential. From this perspective, the greatest threat to personal freedom comes not from other people per se, but from an insufficiency of resources, wealth, or the opportunity to act freely. Representative writers in this tradition include Rousseau and Marx, as well as the more recent theorist John Rawls (1921–2002), who took as his first principle that "justice is fairness," which means that the goods necessary to freedom—resources, wealth, and the opportunity to fulfil one's life plans—should be distributed equally unless an unequal distribution is to the advantage of the least favoured in society.

A common way to express Berlin's distinction is to say that negative liberty is freedom *from*, while positive liberty is freedom *to*. Examples of negative liberty are the "fundamental freedoms" protected in liberal democracies through such measures as the Canadian Charter of Rights and Freedoms. Among others, negative freedoms include the freedom of religion, speech, association, and assembly, as well as such legal rights as the freedom from cruel and unusual punishment or the freedom from unlawful search and seizure. In these cases, we are free *from* the unwanted interventions by external authorities. For instance, we are free *from* government restrictions on what we might be able to write in a newspaper article; we are free *from* rules that instruct us on when and where we must worship; and we are free *from* the unwarranted harassment by police officers as we walk or drive down a public street. On the other hand, positive liberty involves the power *to* develop to the fullest of one's potential, the capacity *to* take charge of one's own life and direct one's actions, and the freedom *to* enjoy all opportunities for self-realization and self-fulfilment that might be available. Positive freedom implies not just the existence of certain opportunities (e.g., freedom to pursue higher education) but also the means necessary to take advantage of them (e.g., the motivation to seek such an education and the funds for tuition). Since the achievement of positive liberty involves the removal of concrete obstacles to individual participation and human development, there is an implication that some persons (or more likely, some social institutions) must take responsibility for providing the conditions necessary for its realization. If one takes seriously the right to positive liberty, therefore, one has to accept that it imposes on the collective the obligation to provide meaningful opportunities for self-determination in concert with others. Perhaps the best articulation of this concept of freedom is Rousseau's vision of a society in which all individuals find their freedom through participation in the process of self-government according to the general will.

Not surprisingly, use of the state in the name of positive freedom is often viewed as a potentially dangerous interference in private affairs. Even Berlin himself was wary of the possibilities for authoritarianism that might flow from attempts to implement a strategy of positive liberty. It may be fine, critics say, to encourage everyone to realize his or her own goals and to achieve self-actualization, but not if this comes at an unreasonable cost to others who might have to give up their freedom or some of their resources in order to provide the means necessary for the realization of someone else's life plans. The obvious concern here is that the pursuit of the equal right to self-realization will come at the expense of traditional individual liberties. In particular, it is likely to come at the expense of the individual right to do what one wants with one's own property, since the public goods necessary to produce adequate conditions for all to enjoy equally the opportunities for self-determination will have to be paid for in some fashion—through either taxation or the collective ownership of key resources. In liberal democratic states, those whom we today call fiscal conservatives will point to the deleterious consequences of high taxes, and will argue that efforts at dramatic income or wealth redistribution are an offence to individual liberty. Indeed, many will also argue that the pursuit of public solutions to what are essentially private problems (lack of self-respect, failure to succeed economically, and so on) is simply wrongheaded. Individuals, the argument goes, must take responsibility for their own choices and the satisfactory pursuit of their own life plans, and should not rely upon social institutions to solve their problems for them. For the most part, this is the view from the contemporary political right, and it stems from the presumption that the individual's liberty to do what he or she desires should almost always prevail over the state's authority to force individuals to do what they do not want to do—even if this activity will benefit the greater good of a majority of the people.

When it comes to noneconomic matters, however, the ideological dividing line over the question of liberty versus authority becomes blurry. While contemporary conservatives tend to favour less government and more individual freedom in economic matters, they do not necessarily promote this *laissez-faire* attitude when it comes to social issues. For instance, the issue of reproductive choice for women could be seen as a simple matter of individual rights, where the state should have no authority. Yet conservative-minded citizens in liberal democracies, who may believe in the freedom of an individual's decisions over property, may still tend to uphold the state's right to restrict an individual's decision to end a pregnancy. Likewise, one might argue that homosexuals should be free from any government regulation of their activity, and should be treated no differently than any other citizens. Yet conservatives often do not agree with this position, arguing that homosexuality is unnatural and therefore wrong, and thus upholding the authority of government or society to pass judgment against homosexual activity. Indeed, it is remarkable just how much these sorts of issues can divide members of contemporary societies along clearly discernible ideological lines. One's attitude to abortion rights, for example, has become almost a litmus test of ideological orientation in contemporary America. For the most part, liberals support a woman's right to choose for herself whether to have an abortion, a right that was constitutionally established by a landmark 1973 U.S. Supreme Court ruling, *Roe v. Wade*. American conservatives, on the contrary, overwhelmingly oppose abortion rights and make it their mission to overturn the Supreme Court's decision. Likewise, North American conservatives are uncomfortable with unbridled freedom involving such matters as premarital sexual conduct, euthanasia, drug use, flag-burning, pornography, civil disobedience, and so on.

When considering these sorts of matters, contemporary liberals are most likely to take their cue, knowingly or not, from John Stuart Mill. In his famous essay "On Liberty," Mill defended the thesis that only self-protection can justify either the state's tampering with the liberty of the individual or any personal interference with another's freedom—particularly with respect to freedom of thought and discussion. According to Mill's famous "harm principle," only conduct that might do harm to others (and not action that might do harm only to oneself) is susceptible to the authority of the state or society. "In the part which merely concerns himself," Mill emphatically stated, "his independence is, of right, absolute. Over himself, over his own body and mind, the individual is sovereign."[16] Mill used as an example the case of liquor prohibition, which he saw as an unwarranted infringement on liberty. In our day, we might use Mill's arguments to advocate for, say, the decriminalization of marijuana possession. Even if smoking marijuana might do harm to oneself, the liberal would say, it is not conduct that is harmful to others. Hence, the state should not legislate against its use. In addition, Mill was a powerful advocate of free speech, arguing that only in rare cases (e.g., libel or incitements to riot) were there sufficient reasons to use the authority of the state to curtail one's right to publicize a thought or opinion in whatever form one chooses. Only when there is evidence that speech constitutes a *direct* harm to others can it be legitimately banned. Therefore, it is safe to assume that Mill would today oppose governmental restrictions on the Internet, no matter how offensive or obnoxious its online content.[17]

Among liberal democratic states, America stands out for taking Mill's views on free speech closest to heart. The United States has a very strong constitutional commitment to free speech, which is entrenched in the 1st Amendment and has been repeatedly strengthened by the Supreme Court. What began as a citizen's right to criticize governments and its officials has come to be invoked to protect even such things as exotic dancing, panhandling, distribution of bomb-making information, flag desecration, Internet pornography, and Ku Klux Klan or Nazi propaganda. Indeed, the support for free speech among American civil libertarians is so strong that it has led to the seemingly perverse situation whereby the American Civil Liberties Union (ACLU) has launched a campaign to protect the rights of racists, sexists, homophobes, and other bigots from restrictions placed on them by college and university codes of conduct prohibiting speech that offends any group on the basis of race, gender, ethnicity, religion, or sexual orientation. Needless to say, not all countries protect the free speech rights of their citizens as strongly as the United States. In many cases government authority to control the freedom of the populace, including its speech, amounts to a culture of repression, as we can see in countless places such as North Korea or Saudi Arabia. In some instances, liberal democracies have found it necessary to limit the free speech of some of its citizens in the name of a greater good. Since 1945, for instance, Germany has banned the swastika and various other representations of Nazi symbols in public. German politicians have recently called for an extension of this ban to the whole European Union, a move that has been challenged by Hindus who argue that it is an ancient symbol of peace that should not be forever tarnished by its associations with Hitler.

Finally, John Stuart Mill also raised an issue that has become increasingly important in the century and a half since he pondered it: the danger of the **tyranny of the majority**. Mill was alarmed that the increasing trend toward democratization was putting too much power in the hands of potentially despotic majorities who might impose their views on the minority (often through the pressure of public opinion rather than through government). The results of this situation, he argued, are a loss of individuality and freedom, a stifling social conformity, and a general levelling to the lowest common denominator. The French writer Alexis de Tocqueville (1805–59), author of the famous study *Democracy in America*, came to similar conclusions. Tocqueville found in America an impressive commitment to equality, but he was troubled by the evidence that individual liberty was often damaged by the suffocating force of public opinion. The dilemma that Mill and Tocqueville highlight is a very real one in contemporary liberal democracies. Citizens are free to pursue their own desires, to develop their own tastes, and to determine their own values and attitudes. Yet there is an amazing social and political conformity in liberal democratic societies. This is most evident in the cultural realm—people all wear the same "name brand" athletic clothing, watch the same television programs, read the same popular magazines—but it is clearly present in our political lives as well, as the great bulk of the population shares a similar set of mainstream values, attitudes, perceptions, and expectations. This conventionality can have unpleasant sociopolitical ramifications if it creates a climate that chokes out any alternative lifestyles and ideologies.

The potential danger of a tyrannical majority—or of politicians acting on behalf of what they believe to be majority opinion—is very real in today's democracies. It is a troubling fact that societies founded upon political tolerance can often become incredibly intolerant of alien or non-mainstream views and values. A popular historical example of this phenomenon comes from the Cold War period in America. Swept up in "Red scare" politics, the public became increasingly fearful of a communist threat to American liberty. Republican Senator Joseph McCarthy capitalized on this fear, becoming famous as the chair of a congressional committee investigating "un-American activities." McCarthy used unscrupulous techniques and questionable evidence to attack anyone he deemed to be a communist sympathizer or a subversive. So notorious was he that the term *McCarthyism* is now used generically to refer to the phenomenon of the political witch hunt. What is important to note about this event is that for the most part the American public acquiesced in the vilification of various left-of-centre politicians, bureaucrats, journalists, writers, and performers on the basis that even if they were not members of any communist organization and had not broken any laws they were, by virtue of their opinions alone, guilty of being "fellow travellers" in an unpatriotic cause.

Today there is no longer any Cold War, but the so-called "war on terror" has produced new concerns for the freedoms of individuals

John Stuart Mill (1806–73), one of the most important philosophers of liberalism.

(Source: Library of Congress/LC-USZ62-2939)

against the authority of the state. As fears grow about the potential dangers of terrorist attacks after 9/11, the majority is increasingly asked to allow its leaders to impose restrictions on long-cherished individual freedoms in the name of preserving democracy or maintaining national security. Various such instances come to mind. For example, President George W. Bush authorized wiretaps on U.S. citizens without the required warrants, citing national security reasons. In addition, hundreds of suspected terrorists captured in Afghanistan and elsewhere were then detained at the Guantanamo Bay Naval Base in Cuba, without charge and without the expectation of facing a fair trial. In the meantime, evidence suggests that abuses have been inflicted upon men and women held by the United States at locations in Iraq, Afghanistan, and elsewhere around the world. Most notorious was the case of prisoners held by the American military at Abu Ghraib detention centre in Baghdad, where detainees were tortured, sodomized, humiliated, and otherwise abused. While government authorities condemned the extreme measures at Abu Ghraib, and members of the military were court-martialed for their parts in these specific crimes, the treatment faced by suspected terrorists continues to raise concerns about the level to which individual rights are being sacrificed to the greater goal of state security. For instance, Bush administration officials continued to defend some extremely coercive interrogation measures, such as the use of the technique known as "waterboarding." This matter became an issue of significant public debate, as demonstrated during the confirmation hearings of U.S. Attorney General Michael Mukasey.

Political philosophers have shown a renewed interest in the question of torture, as well. It had been taken for granted for some time that torture is simply not acceptable in a liberal democratic state. Torture was seen as a hallmark of less enlightened times, and its continued existence as an unjustifiable holdover of evil and brutality. States that still practise torture are generally regarded by liberals as pariahs. Yet there has been some questioning of this approach by leading liberal thinkers in the wake of the September 11, 2001 terror attacks on America. For instance, some have argued that while it is wrong for liberal democratic states to condone torture as a common practice, there may be extreme emergency situations in which information can only be obtained via such methods and where attaining this information would prevent a subsequent terrorist act. Other liberal thinkers, most notably the renowned civil rights lawyer Alan Dershowitz, have made the case that legalized torture might be justified in extreme emergency situations if controlled by appropriate mechanisms, such as the requirement to obtain a torture warrant.[18] Finally, political-philosopher-turned-politician Michael Ignatieff has argued in favour of what he calls the "lesser evil approach" whereby liberal democratic states may be justified in resorting to coercive interrogation techniques, indefinite detention of terror suspects, political assassinations, and other measures in order to counter the greater evil of terrorism.[19] These views have been strongly rejected by philosophers who believe that torture can never be justified and that its acceptance as a means to combat terror does fundamental damage to the liberal democratic ideal.

Indeed, many commentators see the willingness of some politicians and pundits to condone the torture of terror suspects as yet another example of the larger dehumanization of the "other" in contemporary Western societies, especially related to Muslims and Arabs. Gripped by a post–9/11 fear of Islamic fundamentalism, public sentiment in Europe and North America appears to be increasingly fearful of Islam and intolerant toward Muslims. This fear has deep roots in what Edward Said (1935–2003) famously labelled "Orientalism"—a range of mistaken beliefs and false assumptions that constitute the typical Western attitude toward Arabs and their culture. Said argued in general that all cultural assessments of other cultures are imbued with ideology, and in particular that Western analyses of the Islamic world are tainted by a colonial sense of superiority that hinders even the most well-meaning non-Arab interpreters of the politics and culture of Arab states.[20] In Western popular culture and the mainstream media, the view of Islam is even more skewed toward the view that most Muslims are religious fanatics, hate the West, support Islamist terrorism, and reject liberal democratic concepts such as equality, tolerance, democracy, and human rights.

Fear of Islam is openly expressed in right-wing and xenophobic political movements in Europe. And some say that it is also prevalent, in less extreme fashion, in much of the popular discourse on immigration and integration of Muslims in Europe and North America. Among the most heated debates involves the wearing of headscarves by young Muslim women and girls. For some critics, the headscarf is a sign of oppression and subordination of women, imposed on girls by their domineering fathers and other male relatives; as such, it should not be allowed in public spaces. This would appear to be the logic behind the French national ban on conspicuous religious symbols in state-run schools. For critics of this law, the headscarf ban is an example of blatant discrimination against Muslims. The ban applies to Jewish skullcaps and large Christian crosses, but it is clearly aimed at the head coverings worn by Muslim girls and is widely seen as a government response to the rise of Islamic fundamentalism among young immigrants. The French government view, however, supported by a vast majority of French citizens, is that the bill upholds the republic's tradition of secularism, and that it protects girls and women against pressure from religious fundamentalists.[21]

Power: Its Nature, Use, and Abuse

As the case of torture demonstrates most vividly, politics necessarily involves the use of power, usually the power of those in state authority over individual members of the community. Indeed, questions about power and its benefits have always been at the centre of political thinking. For the ancients, power was recognized as indispensable to the good life. Aristotle regarded the active exercise of political power, in common with one's fellow citizens, as the highest human activity. Plato justified power as necessary for justice, which he understood as the establishment of the proper order, both for society and the individual. For Christian thinkers, such as Thomas Aquinas (1225–74), all political authority derives from divine law. Political power is sanctioned by God so that there may be peace and justice on Earth. Humans use natural law (i.e., reason) to establish governments and to rule them according to their own laws. This is why the divine law is eternal and unchanging but human laws can vary and change. Likewise, Islam holds that all power is derived from Allah, whose revelations form the basis for the comprehensive code known as sharia law.

Probably the most celebrated theorist of power is Niccolò Machiavelli, generally regarded as the key spokesperson for a new and distinctively modern approach to questions of civil society and humankind. His best-known work, *The Prince*, explains in delightful detail how a ruler might seize and maintain power, justifying all sorts of misdeeds according to their political ends. The best ruler, in Machiavelli's presentation, is a ruthless yet skilful practitioner of the art of politics, one who is willing to put aside conventional morality for the sake of noble political objectives. Hence, it has become common to use the term *Machiavellianism* as a synonym for amoral political calculation and as a justification of sheer power. However, Machiavelli did not justify power for its own sake. His message was that the power of the talented ruler could serve to elevate the populace as a whole, bringing nobility and glory to the collective political enterprise. Machiavelli was a patriot who thought that bringing glory and honour to one's homeland was a noble end that justified almost any means of achieving it. He was thus an early exponent of the justification of power based on specific national units rather than holy empires. Roughly a half a century later, the French political philosopher Jean Bodin (1530–96) would also argue in favour of a state possessing a single, unified, and absolute power. Bodin was one of the first to develop the doctrine of national sovereignty as the source of all legal legitimacy.

In these two thinkers we can see that the question of power in the modern world involves both the matter of who should rule and in what sort of state. Both are old questions in political science, dating in the West to the works of Plato and Aristotle. Plato, of course, made philosophical wisdom the criterion for political power, and regarded the ideal state as one ruled by a philosopher king. Aristotle was more practically minded, and although he preferred aristocracy—the rule of the best—his work suggests that something he called simply "polity" would be the most practicable form of government. It consists essentially in a constitutional fusion of oligarchy and democracy, seeking to balance the social power of the few who are wealthy with that of the many; the key role in polity is played by a large middle class, which provides moderate values and political stability. Throughout the years, religiously minded philosophers in the West and East have regarded piety as the primary virtue in a leader, and assumed that power in the state should be harnessed for the realization of divine purposes. In this regard, both Christianity and Islam disagree with the notion that political power should be directed entirely toward satisfying the mere material needs of the people. Instead, power should serve a spiritual purpose, power holders should be at the service of God, and politics should follow the direction established in revealed truth. Wise legislators are still needed, of course, since holy books do not explicitly state all the social rules which are necessary for every time and place. Yet good rulers does not have to rely solely upon their art or skill, the way Machiavelli's work suggests, since religious law provides the general framework for the derivation of regulations necessary for changing conditions of time and place. Box 5.4 lists a number of definitions of power as held by different individuals or groups.

Democrats of various stripes hold simply that "the people" should rule, either directly or through their elected representatives. An entire branch of political philosophy focuses on what democracy means and how it is best institutionalized in law and in political practice. Debates rage among democratic theorists about, first, the mechanisms or procedures that are most efficacious for ensuring that the will of the people prevails and, second, what the substance of political life in a society must be in order to be deemed truly democratic. That is, some democratic theorists are concerned primarily with analyzing processes for translating the will of the people into political action. Locke and other early liberal thinkers set the groundwork for the theory that government is legitimate only if the people consent to be ruled. It is now largely assumed that full consent implies majority rule in a system of free and fair elections. Of course, many questions arise about the best systems of election, as well as about the larger questions about representation and responsiveness. These latter issues move us somewhat beyond the

Who Rules? What's in a Name?   BOX 5.4

Rule by one: autocracy
Rule by the few: oligarchy
Rule by the hereditary king or queen: monarchy
Rule by the usurper of legal authority: tyranny
Rule by the best or the elite: aristocracy
Rule by the people: democracy
Rule by the most honourable: timocracy

Rule by the wealthy: plutocracy
Rule by thieves: kleptocracy
Rule by the masses: mobocracy
Rule by the clerics: theocracy
Rule by men: patriarchy
Rule by women: matriarchy
Rule by technical experts: technocracy
Rule by administrators: bureaucracy

strictly procedural conception of democracy and move us into the realm of substance. How representative of all of its constituent parts must a government be before it can be called democratic? How responsive must the legislators be to the wishes of the people, and how will this be manifest? Indeed, these and other questions are taken up in a variety of ways by democratic theorists who examine the substance or content of political life from the normative point of view of democracy.

While liberal theorists laid most of the foundations for democratic theory, non-liberal thinkers have also contributed to the critical conceptualization of popular rule. For instance, followers of Karl Marx offer an alternative view of democracy. They tend to conclude that the self-description of liberal capitalist societies as democracies is a sham, since class inequality renders political competition meaningless. In spite of the introduction of supposedly democratic electoral systems, the same rules prevail in capitalist liberal democracies as they have for centuries: namely, that those who control the wealth of society get to monopolize power. Politics through the ages, Marx observed, have been characterized by the rule of one class over others. In modern liberal democracies, where the bourgeoisie or capitalists own all of the means of production (the factories, mines, and so on), the working class (the proletariat) is necessarily dominated and ruled against its interests. Since the mechanism for historical change of class rule is revolution, there must be a violent overthrow of the bourgeoisie by the proletariat in order to bring about a situation that would be democratic, in the sense that the people will rule in their own interest. An obstacle for some observers who seek to appreciate the democratic intention of Marx is his insistence that the transition to communism would necessarily involve a period which he called the **dictatorship of the proletariat**, whereby a government would rule in a tyrannical fashion in order to implement proletarian rule and guard against the reemergence of bourgeois interests. The notion of dictatorship simply does not fit with most people's views of democracy. Still, the concept has to be understood within the larger whole of Marxist-Leninist thought. Actually, it was Lenin more than Marx who emphasized the practical need for a heavy-handed government during the immediate post-revolutionary period. Lenin feared that the working classes, left to themselves, would never become true agents of **revolution**. Therefore, the communist party, as the "vanguard of the proletariat," must rule autocratically, but in the name of the proletariat as a whole. The legacy of Lenin's theorizing is the one-party communist state, which is today only in operation in China, North Korea, Cuba, Laos, and Vietnam.

Indeed, the fall of communism in the USSR and its satellite states in 1989–91 has forced a dramatic rethinking of communist theory. While some regard this phenomenon as proof that Marx

Brant Parker and Johnny Hart, *The King Is a Fink.*

By permission of Johnny Hart and Creators Syndicate, Inc.

was wrong all along, and that the communist state will be consigned to the "dustbin of history" (a phrase of Trotsky's referring to his opponents), others regard it as a necessary end only to the misguided Soviet form of communism. In Marx's view, in fact, communism was expected to emerge out of the contradictions that became apparent in the most advanced capitalist societies, not out of a society like Tsarist Russia which had yet to even go through the processes of industrialization and capitalist development. Therefore, some theorists suggest, Marx's theories were not fundamentally wrong. Communism is still a legitimate moral philosophy, which promotes classless solidarity over individualistic competition and greed, and it is still a possibly accurate scientific theory that will be demonstrated in due course as global capitalism reaches its zenith and an international proletariat leads a revolution against the forces of capital.

Political Ideologies

The Nature and Function of Ideology

Throughout this chapter we have been discussing ideas about politics and the practical policies that they inspire. It has been impossible to avoid touching upon various ideologies in this discussion. We have seen that Burke is a conservative, Mill a liberal, and Marx a communist. These are all well-known ideologies. But what exactly is ideology as a social scientific concept? What does an ideology do? Put broadly, an **ideology** is a reasonably consistent system of political beliefs that aspires to explain the world, to justify certain power relationships, and to maintain or transform existing institutions. An ideology is a system of thought according to which we can orient ourselves politically and act accordingly. Political ideologies provide a link between the world of ideas and the concrete realm of political action—for example, political parties, interest groups, mass movements, and constitutional systems.

In its philosophical aspects, the function of an ideology is to explain the key problems facing a society and to interpret key events. In this way, an ideology provides meaning for human life and history. In its policy-oriented aspects, ideology shapes the objectives and priorities of political action—it encourages the identification of specific social problems and influences the selection of the most desirable and feasible solutions. An ideology thus operates as a perceptual screen that accepts some alternatives but filters out others. Furthermore, by providing reasons for actions, ideology helps those persons holding power to gain acceptance for their deeds. Of course, ideology is also used by activists and opposition politicians who do not exercise governmental power. Ideology can challenge established authority, criticize existing policies, and offer proposals for change. Indeed, a primary function of an ideology is to mobilize human efforts behind a cause, such as ecological preservation (environmentalism) or freedom from government regulation of individual activity (libertarianism).

Ideologies are espoused by intellectuals concerned with politics—writers, teachers, politicians, journalists, lawyers, and so on. But they are necessarily mass belief systems. An ideology must be accepted by a large number of people in order to be effective. Ideological messages are formulated in a manner that can be readily understood by potential followers who do not have the ability, the interest, or the inclination to become political experts. Ideological discourse therefore seeks to simplify the inherent complexity of the world, imposing on apparent disorder a more or less systematic body of concepts and moral beliefs that can be called upon to help people make sense of the political world. In this way, ideology helps people determine how to act appropriately, and how to distinguish right from wrong in political circumstances.

To a certain extent, ideology is a necessary ingredient of modern political life, since it helps individuals make their way in a complex world. In this regard, many experts follow Freud in emphasizing the psychological function of ideology as a means of equipping individuals with an appropriate set of reactions to social and political demands, allowing them to cope with personal strain or anxiety. This sort of analysis would suggest that ideology is an ever-present element in political life, essential as it is to humankind's social and mental requirements.

Ideological Thought

Ideology can also be understood as a *style* of thought. Persons who think in terms of ideology tend to perceive and interpret events in the light of broad and abstract ideas, such as gender equality (feminism) or faith in the common people (populism). When we say that a particular viewpoint or line of argument is "ideological," we mean to suggest that it is based upon a general or abstract set of political principles or doctrines, rather than unique, specific, or concrete conditions. Used in this fashion, ideology refers to a specific manner or style of thinking. Sometimes this will apply to patterns of thought characteristic of a whole class or group of individuals. We might say, for example, that pride in one's consumer possessions is an attribute of bourgeois ideology, since it is characteristic of the predominant ideas, values, and attitudes of the capitalist middle classes. Conversely, the principled refusal to live a life geared toward the accumulation of material wealth, on the basis that the production of unnecessary consumer goods does ecological harm, is an element of environmentalism as an ideological style.

The word "ideologue" is used in its strictest sense simply to refer to an advocate of a particular ideology, or especially to refer to the official exponent of an ideological party line (e.g., the ideologue for the Communist Party of China). Someone who always appears to be propagandizing in favour of a single sociopolitical program will often be called an ideologue. This term, in our society, has an unmistakably derogatory connotation and is often freely batted back and forth between political opponents. It implies that someone is narrow-minded, unduly attached to a single way of seeing the world, and given to overly simplistic explanations for complex social and political phenomena. The term is also commonly used to refer to those who voice their ideas in an uncompromising, doctrinaire manner. Political activists and people advocating fundamental changes in the existing political situation are often accused of being ideologues. For instance, it is not uncommon to hear people complain that the antiglobalization protesters who gather outside of World Trade Organization (WTO) meetings are impractical ideologues. On the other side, critics of the established order in capitalist societies are equally quick to label their opponents as ideologues, knee-jerk proponents of a system of unequal power relations.

What is often ignored by those who resort to using the term "ideologue" as a rhetorical device to undermine an opponent's intellectual or moral position is that the accusers necessarily base their own political views on grounds that are every bit as "ideological" as those they dislike. Yet so long as our political language attaches a negative connotation to the term, it will be employed as a weapon but seldom as a designation of one's own position. Few people proudly declare themselves ideologues. Yet most people are motivated by ideology when they react, either positively or negatively, to political issues or events. Moreover, the claim that one is nonideological is sometimes advanced in a positive context, as if it is a morally superior position to that of the ideologue. Again, the connotation is most likely that one who is nonideological is more likely to be open and objective about political matters, rather than biased or prejudiced toward one conclusion or the other.

As indicated in the example of the anti-WTO protesters, the charge that one is acting or thinking ideologically, rather than pragmatically, can be used effectively against advocates of radical change, especially when those advocates lack social and economic power. Political

Karl Marx (1818–83), the most famous philosopher of socialism.

language is not unlike other political resources in this regard—those who control it (e.g., those who own and operate major outlets of the mass media) will use this resource to their own advantage, in this case by branding their opponents ideologues and painting themselves and their supporters as nonideological pragmatists. The irony here is that a primary source of ideology's bad name comes from the writings of Karl Marx, the intellectual founder of revolutionary communism. To Marx, ideas and values (including ideologies) are determined by concrete material relations within society, especially class relations. When we study ideologies, we are focusing on the distorted and usually misleading reflections of real class interests. Marx also added to the debate the notion of false consciousness, which occurs when a group or class accepts an ideology that in reality is contrary to its "true" or objective interests. Marxists use this concept to explain the fact that so many working-class individuals reject communism and instead share the ideological views of the capitalists. In this way, the workers are said to be duping themselves and helping to prop up an economic and political system that keeps them subservient.

Many commentators in the West, especially during the Cold War, were prone to regard Marxism and other non-liberal ideologies as nothing more than sources of lies and deception designed by manipulative leaders to exploit the people. There is a tendency, in other words, to identify ideology with systems of social control, political mobilization, and manipulation common in such political systems as the USSR, Nazi Germany, and Afghanistan under the Taliban. Again, the basis for this presumption is the view that ideology is a phenomenon that somehow hinders or obscures our ability to see the truth. Ideology is also associated with mass movements and with the mobilization of large numbers of people, who cannot seem to resist being swept up into an ideological frenzy. The image that might stick in one's mind when thinking about ideology is from the propaganda film, *Triumph of the Will*, showing Adolf Hitler addressing the 1934 Nazi Party Congress in Nuremberg. In this film, produced by Leni Riefenstahl, mass crowd shots are interspersed with footage of party followers, including members of the Nazi Youth, preparing for the big event. These images were meant to demonstrate the power and popularity of the Nazi ideology, but today they reinforce the notion that ideology is a dangerous and illiberal force. According to this critique, ideology encourages people to abandon their reliance on individual judgment and rational choice, and leads to a group mentality that is driven more by emotion than reason. Instead of thinking for themselves, critics suggest, ideologically influenced people turn to a preordained and comprehensive vision of total societal conformity—as presented in Marxist-Leninist doctrine, the fascist leadership principle, or fundamentalist religion.

Indeed, one finds in Western public opinion and political discourse an almost blanket condemnation of states with an "official" ideology, since it is taken for granted that such an ideology must be repugnant to individual rights and freedoms. Officially sanctioned ideologies such as communism, it is said, foster an atmosphere in which individuals are discouraged from thinking freely and acting for themselves because they are indoctrinated into systems of belief rather than provided with the skills and opportunities necessary to choose freely and for themselves. Examples easily come to mind. Chinese youth were "brainwashed" during the Cultural Revolution of 1966–76, when the Maoist government sought to restore ideological purity and combat creeping capitalism. Likewise, as we have seen above, citizens of Islamic states are now portrayed in the Western media as "fanatics" whose passions are whipped up in a frenzy of anti-Western hysteria. As valid as these concerns may be in specific circumstances, it is equally important to note the extent to which Western liberal states can privilege one ideological system over others, rendering marginal any political position that is outside the accepted liberal democratic mainstream. Political scientists refer to **political socialization** as the process by which individuals learn about politics, establishing their individual attitudes, values, and ideals. As discussed in Chapter 4, the agents of socialization include the family, schools, religious institutions, peers, and the media—all of which serve to inculcate in the individual a given worldview or political culture that helps establish the parameters of acceptable political thinking.

The Political Spectrum: Right, Left, and Centre

As our discussion so far has served to demonstrate, there can be many different political views stretching across a wide range of possible ideological positions (see Figure 5.1). At this stage, therefore, it might be useful to clarify some of the key concepts often used in debates about political ideas and ideologies. First, it is conventional to use the terms **right** and **left** to refer to the orientation of a person or group according to a spectrum of political positions. It is important to note, however, that these terms can be used only to designate ideas and ideologies in the modern era; they make little sense when applied to periods prior to the dawn of industrial capitalism and the rise of liberal democratic politics. It is not useful to speak of Plato as being on the right, for example, although it makes perfect sense to refer to Marx as a leftist thinker. And while there is some debate about the issue, many believe that these terms do not have much relevance to the political divisions in many non-Western societies either, especially those with the most traditional economic, social, and political institutions or systems.

Many of the ideological terms we use today are firmly rooted in European political experience and actually date from the time of the French Revolution and immediately thereafter, when people's reaction to the events of 1789 were indicative of their basic political orientation. Conservatives, like Edmund Burke, were generally opposed to the ethos of the revolution, while liberals and socialists, in varying degrees, generally approved of the spirit of the revolutionary movement. In fact, the terms *right* and *left*, in reference to political positions, come to us from the seating arrangements in the French National Assembly of 1789, where members of the nobility, who supported the retention of substantial powers for the monarchy, were seated on the right side of the presiding officer. Seated on the left were those who wished to reduce dramatically or eliminate entirely the powers of the monarch, favouring instead a pure republic in which the elected representatives of the people would be sovereign. Today we still say that the more conservative individuals and groups, or those who desire the least radical change to the status quo, are on the right, in contrast to the progressives or radicals on the left, who seek far-reaching and often revolutionary change.

The virtue of this left–right terminology is that it helps us visualize the relationships between and among ideological perspectives. The notion of a spectrum or a continuum also helps us realize that there are overlapping values and ideals, and that being on the left or the

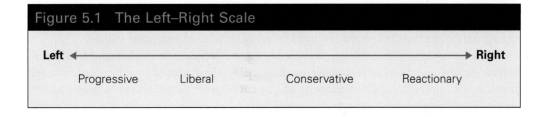

Figure 5.1   The Left–Right Scale

Left ◄—————————————————————————————————————► Right

Progressive   Liberal   Conservative   Reactionary right is very much a matter of degree. While there is more than one set of measures that can be used to place thinkers or parties along the spectrum, a popular measure of placement is attitude toward societal change, including both the degree of change deemed necessary and the direction of the change that is preferred. On the left, progressives (anarchists, communists, socialists) tend to be discontented with the status quo and demand rapid and extensive change. The term *progressive* indicates that the political change desired tends to be forward-looking and inclusive, intended to improve the general lot of all people in society, especially the poor and disadvantaged. Sometimes, these individuals are called "radicals." The word *radical* comes from a word for root, and so in political circumstances what the radicals want to do is to get to the roots of societal injustice and, if need be, to uproot the entire economic and political system in order to remake society along more egalitarian lines. For example, radicals in capitalist societies see the private ownership of the means of production as the root source of injustice. Hence, they wish to eradicate capitalism itself and replace it with some version of communal property ownership. Radicals often believe that only through violent revolutionary upheaval will society be changed in total. But not all progressives are committed to the use of revolutionary tactics, and most do not condone violence as a strategic option for realizing their political goals. There is a range of progressive beliefs, depending on the extent of change desired and the means deemed appropriate to achieve it. Hence, anarchists and communists are considered to be farther to the left than socialists, and social democrats and reform liberals closer to the centre than others in the progressive range. Since the late 1990s *progressive* has become a more popular term to refer to left or liberal positions in American politics. Progressive has replaced "liberal" in campaign literature and political discourse because politicians and activists on the left of the American political spectrum feel that "liberal" has become a negative term.

Nevertheless, it is customary to label as "liberal" the moderate range that covers a wide variety of different political views between the socialist/communist left on the one hand and the conservative/reactionary right on the other. Here again, one must be sensitive to the extent of the subtle range of different viewpoints captured within this middle category. On the left of this range one finds reform-oriented or left-liberals who, like social democrats, favour quite progressive social change. They share the view that government should be used to improve social and political life through various types of social planning and policy experimentation. Reform liberals champion equality of opportunity and are willing to use the state to achieve the goal of improving the lives of the less advantaged. Historically, reform liberalism was associated in the United States with proponents of President Franklin Roosevelt's New Deal legislation in the 1930s and with the civil rights movement and the "war on poverty" in the 1960s. Reform liberalism is also sympathetic to the goals of liberal feminism, which came to prominence in the 1970s. In Canada, and elsewhere outside of the United States, reform liberalism brings to mind the use of a mixed economy (private ownership along with some public corporations), a Keynesian approach to fiscal policy (the use of public funds to "prime the pump" of economic development), and a far-reaching **welfare state** system (characterized by old age pensions, universal medical coverage, unemployment insurance, social assistance programs, and the like). Indeed, one will still find the term *welfare liberal* used to designate these left-of-centre liberals and to distinguish them from more business-oriented liberals. More often, however, they are simply called left-liberals, since they support extensive reforms or changes to existing institutions or practices in a manner similar to social democrats and other leftists.

More to the right within the liberal range are those who might be dubbed classical liberals or business liberals (and now more often as neoliberals). These people are concerned, first and foremost, with the right to private property and with the protection of individual liberty against intrusive government action. As is often noted, there is not much of a difference on economic matters between the classical liberal position and the views of those we would today call conservatives, including members of Conservative parties in the United Kingdom or Canada or the Republican Party in the United States. This overlap between classical liberalism and contemporary conservatism can cause confusion, especially in those places where a liberal is clearly someone on the left of the political spectrum and not one who, like a classical liberal, promotes a limited state and a *laissez-faire* style of capitalism. To make matters even more confusing, the term **neoconservatism** is widely used to refer not just to those who were socially conservative but also to free-market champions of the 1980s. In many ways, the term **neoliberalism** is the much more accurate term to identify the ideology of contemporary political philosophers and politicians who support *laissez-faire* capitalism and global free trade. In terms of global economic policy, in particular, neoliberalism is an important term for those associated with such organizations as the International Monetary Fund (IMF) and the World Bank. And it is a policy stance that has captured the imagination of politicians of various party political stripes in countries from New Zealand to Chile to the United Kingdom.

Conservatism is properly situated on the right of the political spectrum. Yet there are many sorts of conservatives. The traditional conservative position is a rarity in contemporary North American politics, but still has a place in many societies. Conservatives place order and authority above liberty in their hierarchy of values, stressing the duties of citizenship and not just the rights of citizens. Traditional conservatives are not necessarily enamoured of the values of competitive capitalism. Instead, they have faith in the traditional ways, and trust in the notion of *noblesse oblige*—the idea that the elite of society has an obligation to help the less fortunate by ruling in the best interests of all. Today there are few (if any) such conservatives, at least in positions of political prominence. However, conservatism as a predisposition is still very much alive, not only in the West but everywhere in the world. It is sometimes said that the conservative is by nature relatively content with things the way they are (or the way they used to be) and that he or she therefore instinctively defends existing institutions against challenges from reformers. Conservatives are skeptical about the human ability to improve life through social engineering on any grand scale. Hence, they prefer the tried and true to the new and experimental. Conservatism today is especially evident among those who decry the many "progressive" social changes that are associated with such movements as feminism, gay and lesbian rights, multiculturalism, and so on. We often refer to these people as social conservatives, since they are most concerned with preserving traditional cultural values and accepted social virtues. In contrast, fiscal conservatives are worried mainly about the growth of government and rising taxation rates, and they are indistinguishable, as mentioned above, from classical liberals or what are now called neoliberals (see Box 5.5).

Most conservative persons are relative moderates in politics. They realize that some change is inevitable, but they prefer change to be evolutionary and organic rather than revolutionary and experimental. Conservatives are comfortable with existing institutions and want primarily to hold on to those things most valued in society. The political reactionary, on the other hand, is not content with the way things are and wants to return to some bygone day, real or imagined, when things were better. The level of discontent and frustration is very high among reactionaries, and they are usually willing to go to extreme lengths to change things. In this regard, they resemble radicals on the extreme of the political left. But unlike leftists, who regard themselves as progressives, reactionaries seek retrogressive social change. For the most part, the reactionary wants to turn back the tide of egalitarianism and inclusiveness that is characteristic of the contemporary world. Indeed, they believe that many modern problems stem from an excess of democracy, an overabundance of choices and options that lead people away from the proper values of society. Hence, reactionaries often tend to favour stern government by the elite few, preferably by military rulers.

The terms *neoliberalism* and *neoconservatism* are regularly used today to refer to related but slightly different trends within global politics. Neoliberalism is an economic philosophy that holds that a system of free markets, free trade, and the free flow of capital is the best way to ensure the greatest social, political, and economic good. It argues for reduced taxation, reduced government regulation, and minimal state involvement in the economy. Neoliberals support the privatization of health and welfare benefits, the weakening or dismantling of trade unions, and the general opening up of the economy to foreign competition. The term itself is not normally used by proponents of such policies; rather, it is widely employed in a pejorative sense by heterodox university professors and by leftist politicians, such as the Latin American leaders Hugo Chavez and Evo Morales. Neoconservatism, a somewhat older term, is applied to politicians on the political right in Anglo-American democracies who combine neoliberal economic policies (low taxes, smaller government, limited social spending) with conservative social policies (opposition to abortion, gay rights, feminism) and a "hawkish" foreign policy (increased military spending, pro–nuclear weapons, vigilant "war on terror"). While they denote distinct ideological phenomena, the two terms are often used interchangeably, which is especially understandable since the original neoconservatives, U.S. President Ronald Reagan and British Prime Minister Margaret Thatcher, are also widely regarded as among the most prominent and influential neoliberals.

Reaction is the ideology of the far right, and it can be associated with a number of movements and dispositions that might be described as traditionalist, fascist, totalitarian, or ultranationalist. The "religious right" is another term that is sometimes associated with reaction, and is also properly placed beyond conservatism on the traditional left–right ideological scale. In this instance, the goal is to return society to its traditional religious roots and to reverse the global trend toward secularism, modernity, and relativistic morality. Religious reactionaries can be found in Christian-majority contexts as well as in Muslim-majority societies. In the past century, the reactionary politics of the Catholic conservative movement in Europe and elsewhere, which promoted a stronger role for the Church in social and political matters, took a reactionary position on a variety of issues. More recently, fundamentalist Protestants became a powerful reactionary political force, especially within the Republican Party in the United States. While there is much diversity within the movement generally dubbed "the religious right" in America, some generalizations can be made. They oppose many social policies that might contradict what they refer to as "family values," including abortion rights and same-sex marriage; they argue for a return to more traditional gender roles in society, and oppose state funding for daycare; they are generally skeptical about the role of the Supreme Court and object to judicial activism; and they do not believe in the strict separation of church and state, and support prayers and the teaching of Creationism in public schools. Of course, currently much is made also of the role of Islamic fundamentalists who promote an equally reactionary politics in Muslim-dominated societies in the Middle East and North Africa. Here too, the goal is to return to some more "pure" form of social and religious practice, especially by reverting to a strict observance of sharia law. Politically, Islamic fundamentalism is evident most as a repudiation of the values of secular modernism, including the notions of equal rights for men and women and the idea of a separation of church and state. Instead, Islamic fundamentalists pursue the establishment of Islamic states in all Islam-majority societies.

Finally, reactionary politics is particularly evident, especially in Europe, as a highly racist, xenophobic, militaristic, and ultranationalist political movement. The Nazi and fascist movements of the 1920s and 1930s in Germany and Italy were exemplars of this sort of far-right politics. Historically, fascists capitalized on the fear people had of outsiders and aliens, especially at a time of economic crisis, and championing the alleged values of the founding race or of the ancestral nation. In Nazism in particular one finds the extreme philosophy of racial hatred, focused primarily (though not exclusively) on hatred of Jews. This anti-Semitism was combined with a totalitarian ideology intent on controlling all aspects of social life. When the National Socialists came to power in Germany, as is now so well known, they implemented a well-orchestrated confiscation of Jewish rights and property, followed by the most horrific extermination program in history, murdering six million Jews.

Today, shocking as it may seem, there are many explicitly neo-Nazi or neofascist movements, along with various others who take a reactionary position on issues ranging from immigration policy to human rights. Although this is a minority view virtually everywhere, the far right has risen to significant levels in several jurisdictions, and political parties associated with the extreme right have won seats in many liberal democratic countries. Prominent parties of the reactionary right include the National Front, the third-largest party in France; the Freedom Party (and now Jörg Haider's new Alliance for the Future of Austria); Belgium's Flemish Bloc; the Swiss People's Party; and many others. One also finds reactionary political views represented, rather less coherently, among the assorted neofascist or skinhead groups in Germany, as well as in the white supremacist or militia groups in the United States. Political reactionaries are often ultranationalist in political orientation, and they idealize a time when every country was allegedly more pure, racially and culturally. The far-right agenda normally seeks an end to foreign immigration and a denial of citizenship rights to ethnic minorities, especially Arabs and Sinta and Roma peoples.

A popular way to conceive of the differences between left- and right-wing individuals and groups is to place them on a scale according to their attitude toward the use of the state as an instrument for effecting social and political policy (see Figure 5.2). On the whole, representatives of the political right are less comfortable with the use of state power to promote collective political purposes than people on the left. Free-market capitalists would therefore be regarded

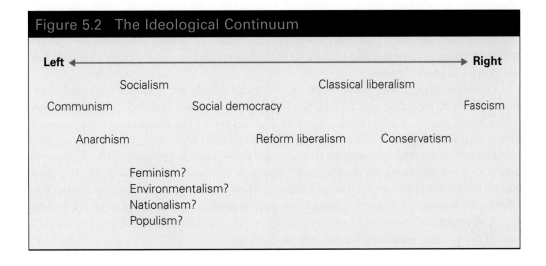

Figure 5.2   The Ideological Continuum

Left ◄————————————————————————————————► Right

Socialism   Classical liberalism

Communism   Social democracy   Fascism

Anarchism   Reform liberalism   Conservatism

Feminism?
Environmentalism?
Nationalism?
Populism?

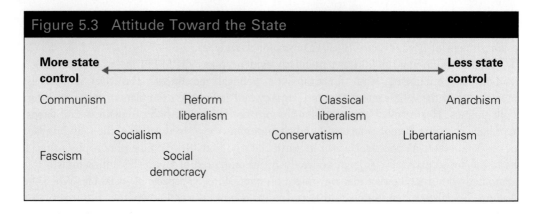

Figure 5.3   Attitude Toward the State

More state control			Less state control
Communism	Reform liberalism	Classical liberalism	Anarchism
Socialism		Conservatism	Libertarianism
Fascism	Social democracy		

as right-wingers, while socialists and communists would be leftists. Still, as we have already seen, there are differences of degree on each end of the spectrum. On the right, more ideologically driven fiscal conservatives will oppose almost all government regulation and intervention, while more traditional conservatives will allow for a considerable degree of state control or direction in order to ensure order and stability for the community as a whole. On the political left, social democrats, with their faith in a mixed economy, will be closer to the moderate centre than those adhering to various brands of hard-line communism, which calls for total public ownership and full state control of the economy.

However, if we use attitude toward the role of the state as the only means of determining the left–right split, we have to deal with certain anomalies (see Figure 5.3). First, **fascists** and communists are both, in principle, willing to use a strong state to impose their philosophical views throughout the entire society. Yet these ideologies are clearly on opposite ends of the spectrum in terms of the goals they wish to achieve. Fascists and communists are mortal enemies. In fact, **fascism** first arose as an extreme reaction against the rise of socialism and communism, and much of the initial fascist violence was directed at trade unions and other progressive organizations in society. Likewise, economic libertarianism and anarchism could appear to fit on the same side of the scale, since they both stand for the maximization of individual freedom and the absence of a coercive state. Yet, if one turns to the motivation for opposing state power, these ideologies clearly belong on the opposite ends of the left–right scale. Libertarianism defends the unfettered individual right to acquire and enjoy personal property without interference from the community. In this regard, it is quite similar to classical liberalism or fiscal conservatism, ideologies of the political right. Anarchism, on the other hand, shares many of the general values of radical socialism and communism. Many leading anarchists, such as Mikhail Bakunin (1814–76) or Emma Goldman (1849–1940), began their political lives as communists and later broke with their comrades over the latter's insistence on the heavy use of state power.

Finally, we should note that there are several "isms" that do not fit comfortably on the left–right spectrum, including nationalism, populism, and environmentalism. Take **nationalism**, which is explored in greater detail in Chapter 3 of this book. The Nazis and their precursors, along with contemporary anti-immigrant political groups, are proponents of a vehement nationalism. That is, they promote the interests and values of their own nation above all others, and regard the autonomy of their national unit as a primary political good. Yet this same conviction is shared by various groups, many of whom see national liberation as a means by which to construct a socialist or communist society organized around the principle of equality for all members of the national community. One version of nationalism is firmly on the right side of the political spectrum; the other is on the left.

Likewise, populism—the faith in the wisdom of the common people—is neither inherently right-wing nor left-wing. In Canada, populism of the political right expressed itself in the Alberta Social Credit Party in the 1930s, and it inspired the founders of the federal Reform Party in the 1990s. At the same time, left-wing populism was a major influence in the first major social democratic party in Canada—the Co-operative Commonwealth Federation (CCF), forerunner to today's New Democratic Party. Populism has been an essential feature of American political culture, playing an explicit role in party politics in the late 19th and early 20th centuries in parties such as the Populist Party and Theodore Roosevelt's Progressive Party. Today, populism is probably most powerful in Latin and South America, where several leaders on both the right and the left have been swept to power on populist waves of support.

One of the fastest-growing and most truly global ideological movements in the 21st century is environmentalism, which holds that the main goal of sociopolitical action should be to preserve the natural environment. It is also difficult to locate environmentalism on the traditional left–right scale, though most observers would put it on the left side due to its generally progressive policy orientation. Proponents of environmentalism, however, often proudly claim to be "neither left nor right, but green." Environmentalists suggest that their ideology is unique in that it is the only one that repudiates the idea that humans should dominate and subdue nature. Although they may disagree about the ways to distribute the goods derived from the human exploitation of the environment, ideological conservatives, liberals, socialists, and communists all encourage the idea of humanity mastering nature for its own purposes. Environmentalists alone challenge this "human-centred" approach and promote an alternative "Earth-centred" philosophy. As we have seen in other ideologies, there is a range of opinion or of political positioning among adherents to environmentalism. On the more moderate wing, one would find proponents of policy change aimed at gradually reducing the effects of pollution, conserving more of our natural resources, and generally lowering the overall harm done to the natural environment by human activity. On the more radical side, one finds those who call for more drastic measures to reverse humankind's damage to the environment, as well as adherents to the animal rights or "Deep Ecology" movements. As we have found in other movements, then, environmentalism includes both a "reformist" brand and a more "revolutionary" version, with many self-described ecological followers fitting in at various locations between these poles.

The ideology of **feminism** is also somewhat independent of the traditional ideologies, although it is by definition a progressive ideology calling for a change to the status quo of male domination. Feminism affirms the equality of the sexes and decries the subjugation of women in all of its forms. Again, there is a continuum of sorts along which one can imagine placing feminist individuals and groups according to their degree of radicalism, especially involving the practical issues of what is to be done to realize greater equality. In its less radical form (often called liberal feminism), the feminist program calls for various concrete measures aimed at producing an equality of opportunity for women—for instance, by advocating affirmative action plans or pay equity legislation. In its more radical variants, feminism regards the systematic oppression of women by men through violent patriarchy as the most fundamental moral problem. From this point of view, all of the traditional ideologies are implicated, since they are inherently male-centred and hence illegitimate. Like other major ideologies, feminism is based on a presumption that its core principles are applicable universally and not just to members of certain societies. Accordingly, feminism comes into conflict with those who argue that each culture or society or religious group should be able to determine its own values, including those regarding the relative status of women. Probably in no case does this matter get greater attention today than in the case of women and Islam. Feminists by and large oppose the social inequality prevalent in Muslim-majority societies, and urge a broadening of women's rights under Islam. Defenders of Islamic tradition complain that Western feminists are imposing an alien ideology on a unique culture, and suggest that there is a systematic misinterpretation in the West of Muslim women and their rights in the Islamic state.

CONCLUSION

As this survey of key political theories and ideologies should have demonstrated, ideas continue to play a large role in politics. Our understanding of political events and our orientation toward the political world are informed by a long tradition of political thinking, stretching back in the West at least as far as the ancient Greeks. The types of laws we live under, and the sorts of governments we support, were developed under the influence of leading political thinkers. By examining the works of the great thinkers of the past, we can better comprehend our own societies as well as equip ourselves to participate as active citizens in our own communities. And ideology plays a continued role in our lives as students and citizens. Even if we do not see ourselves as ideologues, most of us have strongly held political beliefs about who should rule and what should be done by those in positions of political power. Moreover, contemporary political elites—government officials, politicians, media representatives, interest group leaders, and others active in the political process—represent ideological points of view, in spite of their frequent reluctance to be seen to do so. Conflicting ideologies offer us a means of understanding our society, situating ourselves in the political world, and participating in actions intended to advance our interests and those of our communities.

DISCUSSION QUESTIONS

1. Given the nature of human beings, is it possible for all people to be united in a conflict-free society?

2. If human beings are equal in essence, what explains the fact that there are inequalities of rank, status, power, and wealth in virtually every society?

3. Should men and women always and in all ways be treated equally?

4. In what cases are you willing to see the state interfere in society, in particular by limiting the right of individuals to live as they choose? Consider issues such as euthanasia, abortion, and pornography.

5. Are the terms *right* and *left* still relevant today? Do they help explain such ideologies as environmentalism or feminism?

6. How is a traditional conservative, such as Edmund Burke, different from someone we call a conservative today?

7. Define the terms *neoconservative* and *neoliberal* and discuss their significance in contemporary Western liberal democracies.

8. Is it accurate to say that only radical regimes, such as those in Nazi Germany or the communist USSR, govern ideologically?

KEY TERMS

AFFIRMATIVE ACTION: The giving of preferential treatment to targeted groups in such areas as employment, promotion, housing, or education to redress the effects of past discrimination. Affirmative action began in America in the 1960s, focusing mainly on increasing opportunities for African-Americans.

In the 1970s, it began to be used to increase the number of women in professional and managerial positions. Affirmative action is also used to promote hiring of ethnic minorities and Aboriginal people. While the bulk of reform-oriented liberals, feminists, and minorities support it, many contemporary conservatives claim that affirmative action amounts to reverse discrimination. (126)

ARISTOCRACY: Government by an elite or privileged class or by a minority regarded as those best fit to rule. For the Ancients, as seen in the works of Aristotle and Plato, the term is reserved for the rule by the few "best" (*aristos* in Greek). Indeed, aristocracy was regarded by the Ancient philosophers as the very highest form of government, since it implied that the most educated, wise, brave, and selfless people would rule in the interests of the whole society rather than their own. According to this understanding, membership in the aristocracy was based on character and achievement, not just heredity. But during the Middle Ages in Europe the term became associated with a particular social class, otherwise known as the "nobility." Members are born into this class (or are allowed to purchase their way in to it by the monarch), and they can automatically pass on their titles and privileges to their descendants. While some might argue that superiority still inheres with the upper classes, and thus aristocrats deserve a disproportionate role in decision-making, the term aristocracy has generally lost its original positive connotation and it is now common for it to carry a pejorative meaning in liberal democratic societies. (124)

BOURGEOISIE: In Marxist theory, the ruling class in capitalist society consisting of those who own the means of production, such as factories or mines. This capitalist class rules over the proletariat, or working people. In contemporary society, the term "bourgeois" has come to refer simply to the middle classes, those between the very wealthy and the working classes on the social scale. The term is often used in a derogatory fashion to refer to anything conventional and middle-of-the-road, as in "bourgeois values." (127)

CAPITALISM: An economic system in which the means of production (land, factories, technology, etc.) are privately owned and operated according to the profit motive. Decisions about production, investment, and distribution of resources are determined according to market forces (i.e., whether a profit can be made producing and marketing a product), rather than collective or community priorities. In capitalism, workers do not collectively own the means of production and perform their work in exchange for wages or salary. Although it is often called the "free enterprise system," capitalism can exist in certain variants even where the state controls the system and directs the economy according to capitalist principles. (127)

CONSERVATISM: The ideology defending the status quo against major social, economic, and political change. The classic statement of this philosophy can be found in the speeches and writing of the English statesman Edmund Burke. He argued that political order and stability will be maintained only if change is gradual and evolutionary rather than rapid and revolutionary. Today conservatism is often used to label anyone on the political right, especially those who want to conserve the free-market capitalist system against radical demands for progressive reforms. (143)

DICTATORSHIP OF THE PROLETARIAT: A Marxist concept that refers to the interim period immediately after the proletariat (the working class) has triumphed in revolutionary class war over the bourgeoisie (capitalists). Lenin explained that even after taking power in one country, the proletariat will have to remain on guard against the power of the capitalists. He used this concept to justify the class rule of the communists in a one-party state. In theory, the rule of the proletariat was expected to give way to the classless society in the final stage of history, when full communism was realized. (137)

EGALITARIANISM: The doctrine that advocates that people should be treated as equals regardless of differences of wealth, income, class, sex, religion, ethnicity, physical ability, and so on. At minimum, egalitarianism promotes the equality of social and political rights for all citizens. At maximum, egalitarianism calls for a much greater equality of wealth and income for all persons across all divisions in society. Reform-oriented liberals emphasize the former, postulating a need for an equality of opportunity, which guarantees to all the equal chance to compete for the social, economic, and political benefits available in society. Socialists emphasize the latter, interpreting egalitarianism to require an equality of condition, so that all goods and resources in a society would be distributed equally. (123)

FASCISM: The political system of the extreme right, based on the principles of the strong leader (dictator), a one-party state, nationalism, total control of social and economic activity, and arbitrary power, rather than constitutionalism. In 1922 in Italy, Benito Mussolini created the first fascist regime, emulated by Adolf Hitler in Germany. Fascist regimes also held power in Spain and Argentina. Today there are numerous neofascist movements advocating ultranationalist, racist, and anti-immigrant political positions. (146)

LAISSEZ-FAIRE: A French phrase meaning literally "Let do"; this economic theory provides the intellectual foundation for the system of free-market capitalism. Following the principles of Adam Smith, proponents of *laissez-faire* believe that the economy works best when there is no government intervention. Thus, the theory rejects state ownership or control, advocates a free market, values individualism, and promotes free trade. (130)

LIBERAL DEMOCRACY: A form of government common to Western political systems in which there is a combination of the "liberal" right to individual freedom and the "democratic" right to representative government. Hence, in liberal democracies one can expect to find that the ability of the elected representatives to exercise decision-making power is subject to the rule of law as established by a constitutional system that recognizes fundamental rights and freedoms (e.g., free speech, freedom of the press and religion, and the right to free association) along with certain legal rights to property, privacy, equality under the law, and so on. Liberal democracies also include protection for minorities against the possible encroachment on their rights by the majority. At the same time, liberal democracies are characterized by certain institutional structures of representative government: open and free elections with multiple party systems, civilian rule, separation of powers between the executive and legislative branches, an independent judiciary, and a political culture of tolerance and pluralism. (123)

LIBERALISM: The ideology based on the paramount value of individual liberty. Liberals regard the individual as a rational creature who can use his or her intelligence to decide how best to live life and to maximize individual well-being. Liberalism assumes that all humans are free and equal by nature, and that society is a vehicle for the protection and enhancement of our natural rights. In its earlier form, often called classical liberalism, this ideology assumed a limited role for the state. In later years, liberals tended to advocate a larger role for the state to guarantee equality and to help foster the full development of the individual. There are many forms of liberalism, and it has become a widely held political position across the Western world. (126)

SOCIALISM: The doctrine advocating economic equality of the classes and the use of government to serve the collective good of the whole society. Socialists value the collective good over the private interests of individuals, and thus emphasize cooperation over competition. Socialists support a positive role for government in the economy. They advocate public ownership of key industries, regulation of the market, redistribution of resources, and protection of fundamental social rights and freedoms. Although general agreement about the goals of socialism exists, there is a wide variety of opinion on how best to achieve them. Social democrats insist on working within the parliamentary system and achieving socialism through democratic and evolutionary change. Communists and other, more radical socialists believe in the need for total, revolutionary change, often through the violent overthrow of the existing regime. (127)

TYRANNY OF THE MAJORITY: Abuse of the minority by the majority through excessive use of power. Many liberals believe that we have as much to fear from the oppression at the hands of unconstrained majorities as we do from the despotic rule of an all-powerful ruler. Majority tyranny was a special concern for 19th-century liberals, who distrusted the masses and feared that universal suffrage would lead to class rule of the poor over the wealthy and the more refined citizens. Today majority tyranny is evident in the social and cultural realms, where the conformity of popular opinion runs counter to individual freedom and the right to be different. As well, ethnic and other minorities feel oppressed by the actions of majorities, who can rule through the sheer force of superior numbers. (133)

WELFARE STATE: A concept that stresses the role of government as a provider and protector of individual security and well-being through the implementation of interventionist economic policies and social programs. This positive role for government stands in contrast to the minimalist government (or "night-watchman state") that has as its only function the protection of personal property and individual security. The welfare state is regarded as having a positive role in promoting human welfare and in shielding the individual against the economic and social consequences of unemployment, poverty, sickness, old age, disability, and so on. (142)

WEB LINKS w(w)w

The Keele Guide to Political Thought and Ideology on the Internet:
http://www.keele.ac.uk/depts/por/ptbase.htm

Philosophy Resources on the Internet: Electronic Texts in Philosophy:
http://www.epistemelinks.com/Main/MainText.asp

Marxists Internet Archive:
http://www.marxists.org

Peter Suber's Guide to Philosophy on the Internet:
http://www.earlham.edu/~peters/philinks.htm

Anarchy Archives:
http://dwardmac.pitzer.edu/anarchist_archives

Other Interesting Sites Related to Political Philosophy:
http://www.swif.uniba.it/lei/filpol/filpole/sifpwoe.htm

FURTHER READING

Ball, Terrence, and Richard Dagger. *Political Ideologies and the Democratic Idea*. 6th ed. New York: Longman, 2005.

Bird, Colin. *An Introduction to Political Philosophy*. Cambridge: Cambridge University Press, 2006.

Cohen, G.A. *If You're an Egalitarian, Why Are You So Rich?* Cambridge: Harvard University Press, 2001.

Coole, Diana. *Women in Political Theory: From Ancient Misogyny to Contemporary Feminism*. 2nd ed. Boulder, CO: Lynne Rienner Publishers, 1993.

Hallowell, John, and Jene M. Porter. *Political Philosophy: The Search for Humanity and Order*. Scarborough, ON: Prentice-Hall Canada, 1997.

Harvey, David. *A Brief History of Neoliberalism*. New York: Oxford, 2006.

Kymlicka, Will. *Contemporary Political Philosophy: An Introduction*. 2nd ed. Toronto: Oxford University Press, 2003.

Rupert, Mark. *Ideologies of Globalization: Contending Visions of a New World Order*. New York: Routledge, 2001.

Tinder, Glenn. *Political Thinking: The Perennial Questions*. 6th ed. New York: HarperCollins Publishers, 1995.

ENDNOTES

1. Aristotle, *The Politics*, trans. Ernest Barker (London: Oxford University Press, 1958), bk. III, chs. 6–7.

2. This phrase was popularized by Samuel P. Huntington, "The Clash of Civilizations?," *Foreign Affairs*, 72(3) (Summer 1993): 22–49.

3. In formulating the key questions in the history of political thought in the following paragraphs, I owe a debt to Glenn Tinder, whose influential textbook *Political Thinking: The Perennial Questions*, 6th ed. (New York: HarperCollins, 1995) introduces students to political philosophy by examining the great questions underlying the theory and practice of government. Although now a bit dated, the book outlines many of the key issues that have stimulated political thinking over the years. Students interested in exploring the full range of such questions, which is obviously beyond the scope of the present chapter, would do well to read this volume.

4. Hobbes, *Leviathan*, ed. C.B. Macpherson (Harmondsworth: Penguin English Library, 1981), ch. 13, pp. 185–86.

5. See Anthony Quinton, *The Politics of Imperfection: The Religious and Secular Traditions of Conservative Thought in England from Hooker to Oakshott* (London: Faber & Faber, 1978).

6. For example, in *Adam, Eve and the Serpent*, Elaine Pagels argues, "Augustine's theory of original sin not only proved politically expedient, since it persuaded many of his contemporaries that human beings universally need external government . . . but also offered an analysis of human nature that became, for better and worse, the heritage of all subsequent generations of western Christians and the major influence on their psychological and political thinking" (New York: Vintage Books, 1989, p. xxvi). Another lively account of Augustine's influence on Christian attitudes toward women can be found in German theologian Ute Ranke-Heinemann's book *Eunuchs for the Kingdom of Heaven: Women, Sexuality, and the Catholic Church* (New York: Doubleday, 1990). Among other things, Ranke-Heinemann notes the depersonalization of women into whore, wife, or mother may be traced to Augustine, and that he was essentially responsible for the view toward women characterized by what the Germans call the three K's, *Kinder, Küche, Kirche* ("children, kitchen, church").

7. Sigmund Freud, *Psychoanalysis and Faith*, ed. H. Meng and E. Freud (New York: Basic Books, 1963), p. 27.

8. See Jacob Golomb and Robert S. Wistrich, eds., *Nietzsche, Godfather of Fascism? On the Uses and Abuses of Philosophy* (Princeton: Princeton University Press, 2002).

9. Hugh Mackenzie, "The Great CEO Pay Race: Over Before It Begins" (Ottawa: Canadian Centre for Policy Alternatives, December 2007); available at http://growinggap.ca/files/CEO%20Pay%20Study%20FINAL.pdf.

10. For Du Bois, see *Black Reconstruction in America: 1860–1880* (1935; rpt. New York: Atheneum, 1992). For West, see *Race Matters* (New York: Vintage, 1994).

11. For a popular critique of multiculturalism and group rights, see Arthur M. Schlesinger, Jr., *The Disuniting of America: Reflections on a Multicultural Society*, rev. exp. ed. (New York: W.W. Norton & Co., 1998). For an analysis of group rights, see Iris Marion Young, *Justice and the Politics of Difference* (Princeton: Princeton University Press, 1990).

12. Aristotle, *The Politics*, bk. I, ch. 5, para. 6.

13. See Carol Gilligan, *In a Different Voice: Psychological Theory and Women's Development* (Cambridge: Harvard University Press, 1982).

14. For a fascinating exchange of views on this issue, see Lorry M. Fenner and Marie E. deYoung, *Women in Combat: Civic Duty or Military Liability?* (Washington, DC: Georgetown University Press, 2001). Fenner, a U.S. Air Force intelligence officer, calls for opening all aspects of military service to women. She contends that, historically, reasons for banning women from combat have been culturally biased. In contrast, deYoung, a former U.S. Army chaplain, argues that the different physical fitness levels of men and women would, in combat, lower morale for both sexes and put women at risk of casualty. Further, she contends that women have neither the physical nor the emotional strength to endure the overall brutality of the combat experience.

15. Isaiah Berlin, "Two Concepts of Liberty," in *Four Essays on Liberty* (New York: Oxford University Press, 1969).

16. John Stuart Mill, *On Liberty* (New York: Bobbs-Merrill, 1956), p. 13.

17. On the other hand, the American feminist philosopher Andrea Dworkin (1946–2005) mounted a strong argument that harm is caused to women by pornography. If she is correct, pornographic websites might legitimately be banned on the basis of Mill's harm principle. See Andrea Dworkin, *Pornography: Men Possessing Women* (London: Pedigree, 1981).

18. Allan Dershowitz, *Why Terrorism Works: Understanding the Threat, Responding to the Challenge* (New Haven: Yale University Press, 2002), pp. 131–64.

19. Michael Ignatieff, *The Lesser Evil* (Toronto: Penguin Canada, 2004), pp. 136–43.

20. Edward Said, *Orientalism* (New York: Vintage Books, 1978).

21. See John R. Bowen, *Why the French Don't Like Headscarves: Islam, the State, and Public Space* (Princeton: Princeton University Press, 2006).

Part

4

The Structure and Operations of Government

KATHRYN ROYAL

K athryn Royal graduated with an Honours B.A. in political science from the University of Western Ontario in London in 2003. After graduating, she pursued an M.A. in political science at McMaster University in Hamilton, with a particular focus on policy and international relations.

As a student at Western, Kathryn was involved in several clubs, on one of which she sat as an executive member. She also worked on initiatives to raise awareness of environmental issues, and subjects related to poverty in the developing world. Although her major area of study was political science throughout her studies at Western and McMaster, she also took classes in business, economics, statistics, and political economy to focus on the interaction between these areas.

In 2005 Kathryn started her career at the Ontario government as an economist by applying to the Ontario Ministry of Finance in an open competition posted on the Government of Ontario's website. Currently Kathryn works as an economic specialist in the Treasury Board Office at the Ministry of Finance. As part of the Fiscal Strategy and Coordination Division, she works with a team to undertake fiscal and financial policy analysis for the government. The team is responsible for producing and coordinating major portions of the provincial budget and quarterly updates, as well as providing strategic analysis and policy advice to the Minister of Finance and senior government officials.

Chapter Six

DESIGNING AND LIMITING GOVERNMENTS BY CONSTITUTIONS

Stephen Phillips

CHAPTER OBJECTIVES

After you have completed this chapter, you should be able to:

■ identify the main functions of constitutions

■ understand the relationship between the written and unwritten rules of a constitution

■ distinguish between confederal, federal, and unitary constitutions

■ recognize the main mechanisms of constitutional change

Introduction

For much of the past 50 years, constitutions were a neglected topic of study for political scientists, and in most states they rarely figured prominently (if at all) in national political debates. At first blush, this is hardly surprising; after all, while constitutions allocate political power to core institutions of government, such as executives, legislatures, and judiciaries, they do not state with precision the political ends to which such power is to be applied. Thus, while a constitution may assign wide powers of taxation to the national government, it does not specify how the proceeds of such taxation must be spent. Should the government provide free university tuition for qualified students or allocate more funds to municipalities for public transport? Should it spend more money on its armed forces or increase old age pensions? In most states, it is questions such as these, rather than those of constitutional authority, that chiefly engage the attention of governments, political parties, pressure groups, politically attentive citizens, and the media. Moreover, for many years constitutions were thought to have no obvious effect on the policy choices of governments. Rather, such choices were presumed to hinge primarily on socioeconomic factors such as class, political culture and ideology, and the influence of organized interest groups.[1] Consequently, these subjects became the principal focus of political studies, especially in the United States, while the study of constitutions was left to legal scholars.

Today there is a new interest in constitutions among political scientists, generated by two major developments. The first is a growing recognition that the design of state institutions and the allocation of power among them have an important bearing on political outcomes. In other words, what governments do, or fail to do, may be shaped to a considerable extent by their constitutional structure. This insight, developed by political scientists such as James March and Theda Skocpol, is part of an approach to studying politics known as neoinstitutionalism.[2]

The second development sparking interest in the study of constitutions has to do with the drafting of new constitutions in many states in the past two decades, such as the post-communist states of Eastern Europe and post-apartheid South Africa. Established democracies, such as Canada, the United Kingdom, and Australia, have also undergone or debated important constitutional reforms in recent years. In addition, the continuing redesign of the European Union (EU) and its governing institutions is an ongoing exercise in constitution-making. That project, in turn, is shaping the politics of the EU's 27 member states in important ways. In short, there are sound reasons for students of politics to take a closer look at the once-neglected subject of constitutions.

What Is a Constitution?

The term **constitution** has two generally accepted meanings. In its broader sense, the constitution of a state is that body of fundamental laws, rules, and practices that defines the basic structures of government, allocates power among governmental institutions, and regulates the political relationship between citizens and the state.[3] In this sense, all states have an identifiable constitution, whether they be established liberal democracies (such as Canada and the United Kingdom), communist states (such as North Korea and the People's Republic of China), or authoritarian states of various kinds (such as Nigeria, Myanmar, and Iran). In its second, narrower sense, the term *constitution* refers to a specific document or collection of documents that embody the legal rules of the constitution. Examples of such constitutional documents include the *Constitution of the United States*, the *Basic Law* of Germany, and Canada's *Constitution Acts*, 1867 and 1982.

In either case, constitutional rules are binding on political actors, taking precedence over nonconstitutional rules. This is made clear in Section 52 of Canada's *Constitution Act*, 1982, which declares the Constitution to be "the supreme law of Canada" such that any law that is inconsistent with its provisions "is, to the extent of the inconsistency, of no force or effect." Constitutions also embody norms and understandings about the appropriate exercise of political power. For example, if Canada's governor general were to refuse to sign a bill duly passed by Parliament, she would assuredly be accused of acting unconstitutionally, even though, in theory, she possesses the legal authority to withhold assent to bills.

Emergence of Modern Constitutions

The idea that constitutions should limit the exercise of governmental power is relatively new, having been established in England in 1688, when parliament achieved supremacy over the King, an event known as the Glorious Revolution. The principle of **constitutionalism** holds that political leaders, no matter how exalted, are bound to follow the constitution. Constitutional laws, in turn, limit government in several ways. First, by allocating power to various institutions of government, the constitution avoids an undue concentration of power in the hands of a single person or group of officeholders. After 1688, the English Constitution transferred lawmaking authority from the king alone to the "King-in-Parliament," meaning that laws were to be enacted with the advice and consent of the two houses of parliament, the House of Commons, and the House of Lords. Meanwhile, the power to execute laws was left to the king and his ministers, while the power to resolve disputes about the law was to be exercised by an independent judiciary.

England's constitution was lauded by the French political philosopher Montesquieu, who saw in its partial separation of executive, legislative, and judicial powers an effective safeguard against tyranny. His most important work, *The Spirit of the Laws* (1748), elaborated a theory of the separation of powers that profoundly influenced the framers of the U.S. Constitution of 1787.

Constitutions may further limit government by requiring that certain procedures be followed in the making and implementing of decisions. For example, police in Canada may not ordinarily enter a private residence without a judge's warrant. Constitutions may also limit government by imposing restrictions on the content of prospective laws or executive actions through a constitutional bill of rights. Such substantive limits include the First Amendment of the U.S. Constitution, which prohibits Congress from passing laws to establish a state religion or to abridge freedom of speech. Such guarantees are designed to protect the **civil rights and liberties** of citizens.

It must be acknowledged that while all states today have a recognizable constitution, not all of them adhere to the principle of constitutionalism. Here it is useful to distinguish between two kinds that do not: nominal and façade constitutions. A nominal constitution, rather than limiting the power of the state, simply describes and legitimizes "a system of limitless, unchecked power."[4] Such a constitution would not embody the principle of constitutionalism because even the most capricious and oppressive measures of the state would always be in accordance with the constitution. From this point of view, a constitution that vested all executive, legislative, and judicial powers in an elected assembly would violate the principle of constitutionalism no less than one that vested all political power in an absolute monarch. A façade constitution, in contrast, is one whose provisions are routinely ignored. The arbitrary arrest, torture, and extrajudicial execution of civilians carried out by certain regimes professing to respect the rule of law attests to the sham nature of their constitutions. The real purpose of such constitutions is to serve as window dressing for the international community. Nevertheless, even if the constitution of a state does not accurately describe how political power is actually used in all circumstances, it may perform other functions that reveal something about the political character of the state.

Functions of Constitutions

Constitutions perform a variety of functions. The most common of these functions, and the constitutional provisions associated with them, are as follows:

1. *To define the structure of major institutions of government.* Constitutions typically identify the principal offices and institutions of the state, specify who is eligible to hold office, and indicate how officeholders are to be selected—for example, by election or appointment—and for what term.

2. *To divide powers and responsibilities among the various institutions of government.* The constitutions of most states divide powers and responsibilities horizontally among the executive, legislative, and judicial branches of government. The constitutions of federal and confederal states (discussed later) also specify how powers and responsibilities are to be allocated vertically between two levels of government.

3. *To regulate relations between the citizen and the state.* Constitutions often contain rules regulating how power will be exercised by the state in relation to individual citizens or members of minority groups. These rules are usually characterized as rights and codified in a constitutional charter or bill of rights. Such rights fall into two broad categories: negative rights and positive rights. Negative rights are designed to protect the interests of

individuals and minorities by restricting the scope of allowable government action. Many constitutions guarantee freedom of religion, thereby limiting the power of the state to ban or unduly restrict religious worship. Positive rights, in contrast, impose a duty on the state to provide certain benefits to citizens. For example, Canada's constitution requires the federal government to deliver its services to citizens in English and French.

4. *To serve as a political symbol.* A constitution is normally expected to vest legitimacy in the state and may even serve as a focus for the allegiance of its citizens. To this end, many constitutions expressly invoke values and touchstones embedded in the history of a nation or people; other constitutions may seek to effect a break with the past and to proclaim the advent of a new political era. For example, the preamble of the constitution of the Republic of Ireland, adopted in 1937, pays tribute to past generations for "their heroic and unremitting struggle to regain the rightful independence of our nation."[5] The preamble of the 1954 constitution of the People's Republic of China declared that the Communist Revolution of 1949 marked the end of "imperialism, feudalism, and bureaucratic capitalism" and the beginning of a process of social transformation leading "to the attainment of a socialist society."[6] Other constitutions emphasize order and continuity; for example, the Canadian constitution, in its most memorable phrase, authorizes Parliament "to make laws for the Peace, Order, and Good Government of Canada."

5. *To specify a method for amending the constitution.* The procedure for amending most constitutions is more onerous than that for amending ordinary laws. Among other things, the relative difficulty of amending constitutions is designed to maintain the stability and continuity of the political order and to prevent transitory democratic majorities from abolishing too easily the constitutional rights of minorities.

Origins of Constitutions

The introduction of a new constitution or the significant amendment of an existing one usually follows tumultuous and often bloody events. Such events mark the end of one chapter in the political history of a state or people and the beginning of another. Among the circumstances that give rise to new constitutions, we may count the following:

1. *Revolution.* **Revolutions** bring about extensive political, social, and/or economic change. The American Revolution of 1774, the French Revolution of 1789, and the Bolshevik Revolution of 1917 overthrew the existing political order and ultimately produced new constitutions. More recent events include the revolutions in Eastern and Central Europe in 1989 that brought an end to communist rule (see Box 6.1).

2. *Decolonization.* Most of the states in existence today came into being after 1945 as colonies in Asia, Africa, the Caribbean, and elsewhere gained their independence from European powers. In many cases, as in French Algeria and Portuguese Angola, independence was achieved after bloody wars of national liberation.

3. *Aftermath of war.* The defeat of a state in war may so discredit the political regime that the old constitution is scrapped and a new one adopted. In some cases, such action is driven by a new balance of domestic political forces, as occurred in 1870 when France's imminent defeat in the Franco-Prussian War led to the downfall of the Second Empire and the establishment of the Third Republic. Similarly, Germany's defeat in World War I brought an end to the authoritarian Prussian-dominated Second Reich and led to the founding of the Weimar Republic in 1919, based on a liberal democratic constitution. In other cases, such as in Japan and in Germany following World War II, a new constitution is adopted by the defeated state at the behest of foreign military occupiers. The

The Fall of Communism in Romania

BOX 6.1

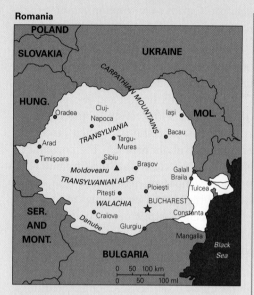

Romania

Source: U.S. Department of State (http://www.state.gov/p/eur/ci/ro)

The days of communist rule in Eastern Europe were numbered when Soviet leader Mikhail Gorbachev announced in the late 1980s that the Soviet Union would not prop up by force of arms communist regimes that lacked popular support. With this announcement, Gorbachev rescinded the Brezhnev Doctrine, according to which the Soviet Union had reserved the right to intervene in the affairs of other communist states in the name of "proletarian internationalism."[7] This dramatic change of policy by the Kremlin emboldened opponents of communist regimes openly to defy their leaders, triggering a wave of popular revolutions across Eastern Europe, from the Baltic to the Black Sea. Remarkably, these developments occurred with little or no bloodshed. A notable exception was Romania, where the communist regime of Nicolae Ceauşescu attempted to hold onto power by force, at a cost of some 1,100 lives.

Ceauşescu's regime was particularly repressive, even by East Bloc standards. By the 1980s, the regime was marked by a deepening economic crisis (resulting in frequent shortages of fuel and food), growing intolerance toward the country's Hungarian and other ethnic minorities, and an increasingly bizarre cult of personality built around Ceauşescu. Unlike other East Bloc countries, such as Poland and East Germany, where organized dissidence movements had emerged, Romania kept a tight lid on political dissent through the feared *Securitate* (secret police).

In December 1989 in the Transylvanian city of Timişoara, the army opened fire on a crowd of demonstrators. As the news spread, protests soon broke out in other cities. Ceauşescu was greeted with jeers at a mass rally in Bucharest as he delivered a speech from the Central Committee building. By this time, fighting had broken out between rebel elements of the army and members of the *Securitate*. In the midst of this disorder, Ceauşescu attempted to flee the country, but was captured by supporters of the self-styled National Salvation Front (NSF), a shadowy organization that had emerged as the protests spread. On Christmas Day, after a hasty trial, Ceauşescu and his wife were sentenced to death and summarily executed.

The very next day, Ion Iliescu, chair of the NSF, appointed Petre Roman as prime minister to head a provisional government pending the calling of national elections to be held in the spring of 1990. In the meantime, the government hastily prepared an electoral law and interim constitution. Given its prestige, and the limited time available for other parties to get organized, the NSF swept to power in the elections of May 1990. The task of preparing a new constitution was assigned to a constituent assembly, which comprised the combined membership of the two houses of the Romanian parliament. In November 1991, the Assembly approved a draft constitution by a majority vote of over 80 percent. The constitution was then submitted to the people for ratification in a national referendum. It was approved in December 1991 by a majority of 79 percent on a turnout of about 70 percent of eligible electors.[8]

The new constitution established a bicameral parliament in which members of both houses are directly elected. Executive power was divided between a directly elected president and an appointed prime minister. Loosely modelled on the constitution of France's Fifth Republic, the new Romanian constitution combined elements of presidential and parliamentary systems of government.

partitioning of Germany in 1945 into separate zones of occupation led in 1949 to the founding of two states: the Federal Republic (West Germany), under a liberal democratic constitution, and the German Democratic Republic (East Germany) under a Soviet-style communist constitution. Following the collapse of Soviet power in Eastern Europe in 1989–90, the two Germanys were reunited under the constitution of the Federal Republic.

4. *Secession.* Another occasion for the drafting of new constitutions is the breakup of a state following the secession of one or more of its constituent regions. In 1971, an uprising in East Pakistan against rule by West Pakistan led ultimately to East Pakistan's secession and the founding of the new state of Bangladesh. A more peaceable breakup occurred in Czechoslovakia in 1993, resulting in the establishment of two new states, the Czech Republic and Slovakia. Attempted secessions may also give rise to constitutional change. A case in point is the defeat in the U.S. Civil War of the Confederate States of America, which had attempted to secede from the United States. The postwar (or Reconstruction) period saw passage of the so-called Civil War amendments to the U.S. Constitution, which outlawed slavery and extended to the state governments the provisions of the U.S. Bill of Rights. In Canada, secessionist pressures in Quebec have generated several rounds of intensive constitutional debate. When Quebec voters rejected secession in a referendum held in May 1980, the federal government sought to weaken the appeal of separatism by implementing a controversial package of amendments to the Canadian constitution, key elements of which included the *Charter of Rights and Freedoms* and a domestic amending formula.

Not surprisingly, the circumstances in which new constitutions are adopted have a major influence on their content. The United States Constitution, for example, affirms the ideals of liberal constitutionalism that were beginning to gain ground in Europe in the late 18th century. However, so thorough was their repudiation of monarchy that the drafters went much further in restricting and diffusing governmental power than most other liberal democracies have thought necessary or desirable. As Harold Laski observed, "The American system, in its ultimate foundations, is built on a belief in weak government."[9]

Many national constitutions reflect an intention to remedy the perceived defects of past constitutions. Examples of such reactive constitutions include the West German constitution of 1949 and the French constitution of 1958. West Germany's constitution, known as the *Basic Law*, was drafted with a view to addressing the shortcomings of the Weimar Constitution of 1919 and preventing a recurrence of the political extremism that had preceded the rise to power of the Nazis. It was thought, for example, that one source of political instability in Weimar Germany was the ease with which parliament could defeat a government on a vote of non-confidence. Under the *Basic Law*, therefore, the Bundestag (German Parliament) may remove the chancellor only on a constructive vote of non-confidence. This requires the opposition parties simultaneously to remove the chancellor and to install his or her successor, a more difficult undertaking than merely bringing down the government. The *Basic Law* also authorizes the Federal Constitutional Court to ban political parties that seek to undermine democratic institutions.[10]

France's constitution of 1958 reflects the accumulated experience of the many constitutions adopted and discarded since the French Revolution. The constitution of the Fifth Republic established a mixed presidential–parliamentary system in which executive power is divided between a directly elected president and a prime minister and cabinet (who are responsible to parliament). It is designed to avoid an excessive concentration of executive power in one person (a tendency known in France as "Bonapartism") and an excessive diffusion of power among political parties and factions in the National Assembly.

Types of Constitutions
Written Versus Unwritten Constitutions

A traditional basis of classifying constitutions is to distinguish between **written** and **unwritten constitutions**. A written constitution is one whose fundamental rules have been reduced to a single document or limited set of documents. An unwritten constitution, in contrast, is one whose subject matter is dispersed across a variety of statutes, court rulings, and unwritten political practices known as constitutional conventions. Though widely used, this terminology is unsatisfactory for at least two reasons. First, since the United Kingdom, New Zealand, and Israel are the only states in the world having an unwritten constitution, the overwhelming majority of constitutions cannot usefully be classified under this scheme. Second, the term *unwritten constitution* wrongly implies that most if not all of the constitutional rules of the state exist in the form of conventions. Yet much of the "unwritten" British constitution exists in written form, chiefly in leading common law cases and in various acts of parliament, such as the *Bill of Rights* (1689), the *Act of Settlement* (1701), and the *Parliament Acts* of 1911 and 1949. At the same time, it must be said that many of the constitutional rules of states having a written constitution exist in unwritten form.[11] It is perhaps more appropriate to distinguish between codified and uncodified constitutions. In each case, the constitution consists of both written and unwritten rules.

As noted above, conventions are an important element of all constitutions. A **constitutional convention**, according to K.C. Wheare, is "a binding rule, a rule of behaviour accepted as obligatory by those concerned with the working of the Constitution."[12] Because conventions are not entrenched in a constitutional document or enacted in statutory form, they lack legal status and are not enforceable by the courts. Nevertheless, they are indispensable to the operation of modern constitutions, providing "the flesh which clothes the dry bones of the law."[13] Conventions not only provide guidance where the written constitution is silent, but also specify how the legal powers set out in the written constitution are to be exercised.

For example, many of the principles of parliamentary government in Canada are defined by convention rather than by the *Constitution Act, 1867*. The role of the prime minister and cabinet in Canada is nowhere spelled out in the written constitution. Similarly, the *Act* is silent on one of the central features of parliamentary government: the obligation of the government to resign or to seek a dissolution of Parliament if it is defeated in the House of Commons on a vote of confidence. These institutions and practices were well-established conventions of British parliamentary government by the late 1700s and were well known to the Canadian politicians who drafted the *British North America Act* (later called the *Constitution Act, 1867*) between 1864 and 1866. Accordingly, it was felt sufficient to declare in the preamble of the *BNA Act* Canada's desire to adopt a constitution "similar in principle to that of the United Kingdom." In this way, Canada's written constitution acknowledged and continued in force a large body of British conventions which had been adhered to for at least 20 years by the pre-Confederation governments of Britain's North American colonies.

In addition to filling in gaps in the written constitution, conventions indicate how its legal powers are to be exercised. For example, Section 50 of the *Constitution Act, 1867* refers to the power of the governor general to dissolve the House of Commons for a general election. By convention, however, it is understood that this power is to be exercised only on the advice of the prime minister. In Westminster systems, the power of prime ministers to determine the timing of general elections (within the five-year maximum term of a Parliament) is one of the most formidable powers they have at their disposal.[14] In the case of Canada, this conventional power of the PM was curtailed in 2007 when Parliament passed a law providing for fixed election dates. Under the terms of the new law, general elections are to be held every four years; accordingly, the PM may only request an early dissolution if the government loses a vote of confidence.

It should be noted that not all established political practices constitute *conventions*. Practices that are not generally thought to embody important constitutional principles are known as *usages*. Although neither conventions nor usages are legally enforceable, "there is a stronger moral obligation to follow a convention than a usage," and the breach of a convention is liable to attract louder criticism.[15] For example, in naming a chief justice of the U.S. Supreme Court, it is customary for presidents to appoint someone who has previous judicial experience. When President Eisenhower departed from this practice in 1953 by nominating Earl Warren, former governor of California, the nomination was mildly criticized but ultimately ratified by the Senate.[16] Breach of a convention is viewed more gravely, as proved to be the case when Franklin D. Roosevelt broke a U.S. convention limiting presidents to two terms of office by seeking (and winning) an unprecedented fourth term in 1944. Controversy about Roosevelt's breach of the term-limit convention led to its being entrenched in the U.S. Constitution in 1951 as the Twenty-Second Amendment.

Vertical and Horizontal Divisions of Power

Another way of classifying constitutions turns on the allocation of governmental authority within the state. Constitutions allocate governmental authority both vertically and horizontally among the leading institutions of the state. When referring to the vertical division of power, we are concerned with the allocation of sovereign or supreme lawmaking authority between the national government and various subnational governments. Depending on the way in which sovereignty is divided between different *levels* of government, we may identify three major types of constitution: confederal, federal, and unitary.

Constitutions may also be classified on the basis of the horizontal division of governmental authority, *at the national level*, between the executive and legislative branches. Here we may identify three principal forms of government: parliamentary, presidential, and semi-presidential systems. We will consider these latter forms of government in Chapter 7. For now, we will consider confederal, federal, and unitary systems, as illustrated in Figure 6.1.

Confederal States

A confederal state (or confederation) is one in which sovereignty is retained by numerous existing states that agree to cooperate in order to achieve certain common purposes.[17] Under a confederal constitution, the central government exercises only such powers as are delegated to it by the constituent states. That is to say, any powers transferred to the central government

Figure 6.1 Confederal, Federal, and Unitary Constitutions

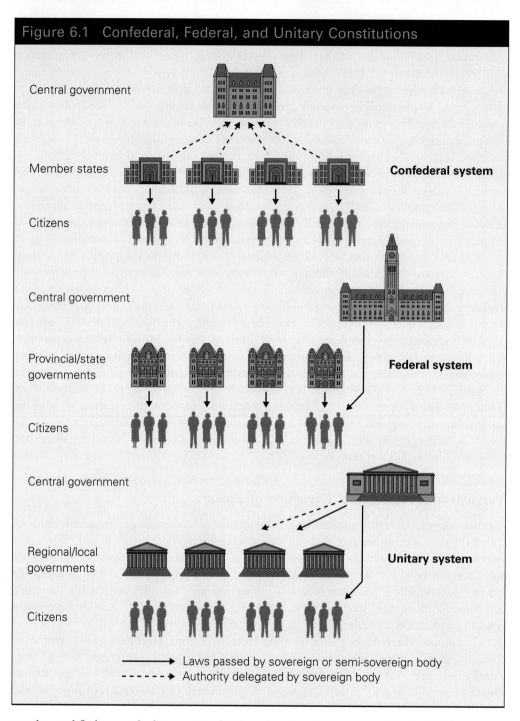

Central government

Member states **Confederal system**

Citizens

Central government

Provincial/state governments **Federal system**

Citizens

Central government

Regional/local governments **Unitary system**

Citizens

→ Laws passed by sovereign or semi-sovereign body
- - -> Authority delegated by sovereign body

may be modified or revoked at any time by the subnational governments. Typically, the powers of the central government are limited in number and scope. For example, the central government usually lacks the power to levy taxes and relies instead on periodic financial contributions from the constituent states. Moreover, the states may exercise a power of veto over certain decisions taken by the central government or else reserve the right to opt out of decisions with which they are unwilling to comply. Finally, states belonging to a confederation retain the right of secession.[18]

Relatively few examples can be cited of functioning confederations today. In North America, the oldest confederal form of government is the Iroquois Confederacy, an association of six Iroquoian First Nations.[19] Some confederations evolve into federations, as in the case of the 13 American states that established a confederal association under the Articles of Confederation in 1781. The chronic inability of the central government to take action in the common interests of the states led to the drafting of a new federal constitution in 1787.

The **European Union**, an association of 27 sovereign states, embodies many of the characteristics of a confederation. So too does the Commonwealth of Independent States, an association of former Soviet republics established in 1991 to promote cooperation in areas of mutual interest. The confederal nature of the EU is reflected in the fact that any member state may opt out of key decisions agreed to by the others. For example, Britain, Sweden, and Denmark chose to retain their national currencies and to refrain from participating in the launching of the common EU currency, the Euro, in 2002. Similarly, in 1989, Britain's Conservative government, alone among the then 12 members of the European Community, chose to opt out of the Social Charter, a set of social and employment rights addressing such matters as the right to social assistance and equitable wages and the right to join a union. Britain reversed its position in 1997 following the election of a Labour Government.[20]

Also consistent with the confederal principle is the fact that the EU does not directly tax the citizens of its member states but relies instead on revenues transferred to it by national governments. The sources and extent of these revenues are determined in multiyear agreements reached by the EU's Council of Ministers, a confederal body on which each member state has one representative.[21]

The structure of the EU and its governing bodies is defined by a series of treaties that have been signed by each of the member states. The earliest treaty, the Treaty of Rome, established the European Economic Community (EEC) in 1957. The Treaty, drafted by the EEC's six founding members,[22] has been supplemented and amended many times over the years, most notably by the Single European Act of 1986, the Treaty on European Union of 1992 (better known as the **Maastricht Treaty**), the Amsterdam Treaty of 1997, and the Treaty of Nice of 2001. Each new treaty must be ratified by every member state before it can take effect.[23]

In order to consolidate and simplify these various treaties into a single document, and to simplify the EU's increasingly cumbersome decision-making rules, the EU resolved in 2002 to draft a unified constitution. The task of writing such a document was given to a committee headed by former French president Valéry Giscard d'Estaing. The final text of the constitution was approved by the European Council in June 2004 and signed by all 25 EU heads of government in October of that year. Among other things, the constitution proposed new powers for the EU executive (the European Commission), the European Parliament, and the European Court of Justice. It also proposed to remove national vetoes in certain areas.

However, the EU constitution was still subject to ratification by each country in accordance with its own laws. While some countries submitted it to their national parliaments, others held national referendums. By early 2005, nine countries had ratified it; however, the process came to a halt in May of that year when voters in France and the Netherlands rejected it in separate referendums. Many opponents of the constitution saw it as a stepping stone to European federalism, a form of association that would entail a transfer of sovereignty from national parliaments to the EU. Others objected to the enshrinement of neoliberal economic doctrines that they felt posed a threat to the future of the European social market model of capitalism.[24]

In 2007, EU leaders resolved to resume the project of institutional reform. But instead of resurrecting the failed constitution, they sought to achieve most of their objectives by amending, rather than replacing, existing EU treaties. To that end, a new "amending treaty"

Former French President Valéry Giscard d'Estaing casts his ballot in the French referendum on the EU Constitution, May 29, 2005.

AP Photo/Patrick Gardin

was signed at Lisbon in December 2007. According to its proponents, the Treaty of Lisbon is not a constitution and thus need not be ratified by politically risky national referendums. In accepting this view, the British and Danish governments announced, amid much controversy, that they would scrap plans for a referendum and proceed instead with parliamentary votes on the new treaty. Other EU countries declared similar intentions, with the exception of the Irish Republic, which held a national referendum on the Lisbon Treaty in June 2008. When the Irish rejected the Treaty, however, EU leaders were forced to consider yet other alternatives.

Federal States

Under a federal constitution, sovereignty is formally divided between two levels of government: a national (or central) government and a number of subnational governments. Both levels of government exercise legislative authority over the territorial units that make up the federation, such that neither level is subordinate to the other. These territories are known variously as provinces, states, *cantons* (in Switzerland), or *Länder* (in Germany).[25]

While unitary constitutions outnumber federal constitutions by a ratio of nine to one, federalism is a significant form of government nonetheless. Approximately one-half of the world's population live in federal states, and **federalism** tends to be the constitutional system of choice for geographically large countries such as Canada, Australia, Brazil, India, Russia, and the United States, as can be seen in Table 6.1.

Federal unions are formed for a variety of purposes. For small states, membership in a federation may offer the advantage of a common military defence against external threats. It may also offer economic advantages in the form of a larger internal market for trade and the building of national economic infrastructure by a central government that has superior financial resources. Both of these factors had a bearing on the decision of several of Britain's North American colonies to establish a federal union in 1867 and on that of the Australian colonies to do likewise in 1901. At the same time, federalism allows the territorial units to retain their separate identity and to continue to exercise decision-making authority over a range of local matters. Canada's adoption of a federal constitution in 1867 was, in large part, a concession made to French-Canadian political leaders anxious to retain authority at the provincial level over matters vital to the preservation of their culture, religion, and language.

Table 6.1 Federations of the World

Argentina	Germany	South Africa
Australia	India	Switzerland
Austria	Malaysia	Tanzania
Belgium	Mexico	United Arab Emirates
Brazil	Nigeria	United States of America
Canada	Pakistan	Venezuela
Comoros	Russia	

Source: Barry Turner, ed., The Statesman's Yearbook 2008 *(New York: Palgrave Macmillan, 2007). Reproduced with permission of Palgrave Macmillan.*

Intergovernmental Division of Powers Under a federal form of government, the written constitution allocates authority to each level of government to pass laws in relation to particular subjects. This division of powers may be effected by enumerating separate heads of authority for the national and subnational governments. For example, the Canadian constitution assigns to the federal parliament the authority to pass laws in relation to such matters as national defence and marriage and divorce. It goes on to assign to the provincial legislatures, in their list of **enumerated powers**, authority over such matters as hospitals and municipal government. Other constitutions, such as those of the United States and Australia, allocate lawmaking power over certain subjects to the national government and declare all non-enumerated subjects to be the responsibility of the subnational governments. In either case, the constitution grants to one level of government or the other the power to deal with matters not clearly assigned to either level of government. These **residual powers** belong to the federal government in Canada and India and to the state governments in Germany and Switzerland.

Most of the fields of legislative authority listed in federal constitutions are to be occupied exclusively by one level of government or the other. In other words, if banking is assigned to the federal government, a provincial government may not pass laws in relation to banks. However, federal constitutions may also grant **concurrent powers**—that is, designate certain areas of jurisdiction in which both levels of government may pass laws. Where there is a conflict between a federal and a provincial law in a jointly occupied field, the constitution specifies which law shall prevail or have paramountcy.

Responsibility for administering, enforcing, and interpreting laws does not necessarily follow the intergovernmental division of legislative powers. For example, most civil servants in Germany are employed by the *Länd* governments and are responsible for implementing both *Länd* and federal laws. In Canada, the power to enact criminal law is a federal responsibility; the provinces, however, are responsible for the administration of justice in their provinces, which includes the provision of police services, the handling of most criminal prosecutions, and the administration of a unitary system of courts that adjudicates disputes falling under provincial and federal jurisdiction. In the United States, in contrast, the federal principle is reflected in a dual system of state and federal courts, each of which is restricted to adjudicating cases of state law and federal law respectively.

Judicial Review As a practical matter, no constitution divides legislative powers between the two levels of government with absolute precision. Inevitably, there is considerable functional overlap between the broad categories of federal and provincial jurisdiction. For example, in Canada, the *Constitution Act*, 1867, assigns responsibility for unemployment insurance to the federal parliament (Section 91[2A]) and responsibility for education to the provincial legislatures (Section 93). Who, then, has jurisdiction to establish job training programs, involving classroom instruction, for recipients of federal Employment Insurance benefits? Similarly, does a province's jurisdiction over health and welfare allow it to apply occupational health and safety standards to industries such as national airlines, railways, and broadcasting, which are otherwise subject to federal regulation under Ottawa's power over interprovincial transportation and communications?

In federal systems, disputes of this kind typically are resolved by the courts, which are armed with the power of **judicial review** over law and executive action. If the courts find a particular law to be in violation of the constitutional division of powers, or in conflict with some other aspect of the written constitution, such as a bill of rights, they have the authority to declare it invalid. Germany's *Basic Law* explicitly establishes a Constitutional Court with the power of judicial review. In other federations, such as Canada and the United States, judicial review is not provided for in the written constitution but has come to be accepted as a legitimate power to be exercised by each country's Supreme Court.[26]

Evolution of Federal Systems As noted above, a literal reading of the written constitution paints an incomplete and often inaccurate portrait of the real constitution of a state. This is especially true of federations, in which power may be considerably more centralized or decentralized than the written constitution would lead one to suppose. How, then, do federal constitutions evolve over time, if not by formal amendment? Three agents of change may be identified.

First, through judicial review, the courts may interpret particular fields of jurisdiction narrowly or expansively. For example, the Judicial Committee of the British Privy Council, which served as Canada's final court of appeal between 1867 and 1949, tended to give a restrictive reading to powers assigned to the federal parliament and a comparatively wide reading to powers assigned to the provinces. In contrast, the United States Supreme Court enlarged many areas of federal jurisdiction, especially in cases decided after 1937. These divergent judicial legacies explain in part why American federalism is decidedly more centralized today than its Canadian counterpart, contrary to the intentions of each country's founders.

A second factor shaping the nature of federalism is the political legitimacy attached to the exercise of certain federal and provincial powers. In other words, is the vigorous use of certain legal powers held by one level of government or the other widely accepted as appropriate? In Canada, strong regional and provincial loyalties, overlaid by a robust defence of provincial autonomy by successive Quebec governments, has inhibited federal governments from exercising the full range of their legal powers. For example, the federal cabinet has the unrestricted legal authority to disallow any provincial law within a year of its passage.[27] However, owing to strenuous objections by the provincial premiers to the use of the disallowance power, it has long since fallen into disuse.[28] In Australia and the United States, in contrast, there is a broader acceptance of political initiatives by the federal government.[29]

A third agent of change in federations has to do with social and economic developments and their impact on financial relations between the national and subnational governments. Federations established in the 19th century tended to assign constitutional responsibility for health and social welfare to the subnational governments. These subjects were not considered to be matters of national importance in an era in which hospitals and welfare services were largely provided by religious and private charitable institutions. By the 20th century, with the rise of the welfare state, governments began to assume responsibility for the provision of a wide array of public services and benefits. In federations, these burgeoning responsibilities often exceeded the revenue-raising capacity of the provincial or state governments, creating a problem of **fiscal imbalance**.

In most federations, the central government's financial resources are superior to those of the subnational governments; the national government, after all, has a broader tax base than that of any single province or state and typically has access to a wider range of tax instruments (such as customs duties, excise taxes, and corporation taxes). As a result, the problem of fiscal imbalance in federations is usually addressed through the transfer of federal funds to the subnational governments (see Table 6.2). Such transfers give the central government the potential to influence the content and administration of laws falling outside its jurisdiction. This is most obviously the case where the central government attaches conditions to funds transferred to the subnational governments. The use of such conditional grants has had the effect of centralizing power in many federations by giving the federal government leverage over the policies and programs of the subnational governments. Such grants are used extensively in

Table 6.2 Conditional Grants as a Percentage of Federal Transfers to Subnational Governments in Selected Federations, 1996–2002

Federation	Percentage
United States	100.0
Switzerland	73.1
Germany	64.5
Australia	47.1
India	40.7
Brazil	25.0
South Africa	11.5
Canada	4.3

Note: Total transfers = share of central taxes plus unconditional grants plus conditional grants.

Source: Ronald L. Watts, "Autonomy or Dependence: Intergovernmental Financial Relations in Eleven Countries," Working Paper 2005 (5) (Kingston, ON: Institute of Intergovernmental Relations, Queen's University), p. 54.

the United States to ensure the compliance of state and local governments with a variety of federal laws, from civil rights legislation to environmental regulations.

Strictly speaking, conditional grants do not impair the constitutional authority of the provinces, because the latter are free to decline them. Politically, however, it is difficult for the government of a province or state to refuse federal largesse; after all, its citizens have contributed to these funds through their federal taxes. Less intrusive federal fiscal transfers include unconditional grants and federal tax abatement agreements, whereby the federal government partially vacates a field of taxation jointly occupied by both levels of government in order to create additional "tax room" for the provincial or state governments. The reliance of subnational governments on fiscal transfers from the federal government is a useful benchmark for measuring the effective degree of centralization of a federation.

Intrastate Federalism So far we have been discussing the intergovernmental division of powers. This aspect of federalism is known as *interstate federalism*. Another feature of federal systems has to do with the representation of the subnational units within the institutions of the central government. This aspect of federalism, known as *intrastate federalism*, is typically reflected in the formal representation of states or provinces in the upper house of the national legislature. For example, in the United States Senate, each of the 50 states has two senators, who are elected to a six-year term. In Germany, the governments of each of the 16 *Länder* appoint between three and six members to the Bundesrat (or Federal Council), who act as delegates of the *Länd* governments. The *Länder* are also represented in Germany's central bank, the Bundesbank.

Other forms of intrastate federalism may form part of the unwritten constitution or of established political practice. For example, in Canada, it is customary for prime ministers to ensure that their cabinet contains members of parliament representing each of the 10 provinces. Similarly, when appointing judges to the Supreme Court of Canada, prime ministers strive to maintain territorial balance.[30]

The Case For and Against Federalism Leading arguments in favour of federalism include the liberal idea that federalism provides an institutional safeguard for individual liberty and minority rights by ensuring that political power is not concentrated exclusively in the hands of the central government. Indeed, by dividing political authority between two levels of government, federalism arguably acts as a second check on the potential abuse of political power, along with the constitutional separation of powers within each level of government. James Madison expressed this idea in *The Federalist Papers* as follows:

> *In the compound republic of America, the power surrendered by the people is first divided between two distinct governments, and then the portion allotted to each subdivided among distinct and separate departments. Hence a double security arises to the rights of the people. The different governments will control each other, at the same time that each will be controlled by itself.*[31]

The interests of a national minority group are best served under a federal constitution where its members are concentrated in a particular region of the country. In that way, they may hope to have effective political influence and may even constitute a majority in the legislature and government of that region. This is the case in Canada with regard to francophones, 85 percent of whom live in the province of Quebec. Likewise, the Sikh and Muslim populations of India constitute majorities in the states of Punjab and Kashmir respectively, while being heavily outnumbered at the national level by the majority Hindu population.

A related strength of federalism is that it permits subnational governments to adopt policies that reflect the preferences of local populations, whereas the central government may tend to reflect the interests of a dominant section of the national electorate. For example, governments of regions of the country in which conservative social values are prevalent might choose to maintain stricter liquor licensing and Sunday trading laws than those of regions in which more liberal values hold sway. Similarly, federalism would allow states or provinces whose populations attach a high priority to the environment to implement more stringent measures to combat pollution and global warming. In the United States, for example, California has long taken the lead in enacting strict controls on automobile emissions.

By allowing for a diversity of policies across the country in areas assigned to the subnational government, federalism may foster policy innovation. As the provinces take different approaches to addressing problems common to them all, they serve as laboratories of policy experimentation. Policies that prove to be successful and popular in one jurisdiction may then be emulated by others. For example, Saskatchewan's CCF–NDP government pioneered Canada's first comprehensive public health insurance program in 1962 in the face of fierce opposition from the province's doctors and the Saskatchewan Liberal Party. Yet the program, once implemented, proved to be such a success that it was soon embraced by the federal government and adopted by every other province.

There are, of course, potential drawbacks to federalism. Federalism does not necessarily serve the interests of minorities that are geographically dispersed. In fact, it may be inimical to their interests by making them vulnerable to hostile local majorities. Despite the abolition of slavery in the United States in 1865, African-Americans remained subject to many forms of discrimination for decades to come. In numerous southern states, this discrimination was institutionalized in the form of racial segregation of schools and other public services and systematic efforts by state officials to thwart the registration of black voters. In these circumstances, African-Americans applied to the national government, including the federal courts, to challenge oppressive measures in their home states.

This aspect of federalism remains contentious today in the United States, where the states have jurisdiction over the conduct of national elections. Both the 2000 and 2004 U.S. presidential elections were marred by charges of political partisanship and racism in several states, including the states of Florida and Ohio, states in which leading Republican Party officials were in charge of the state's electoral process. In Canada, by contrast, responsibility for the conduct of federal elections lies with an independent, nonpartisan national body, Elections Canada.

Federalism may also give rise to intergovernmental conflicts over jurisdiction and may obstruct or delay decisions requiring joint action by both levels of government. In this regard, federalism has been a factor impeding the development of social security programs.[32] On the other hand, federalism may make it equally difficult to curtail programs over which both levels of government have some say. In an era of incessant cuts to public programs in many countries, this feature of federalism is not insignificant.[33] For example, in Canada contributory public pensions are an area of concurrent jurisdiction. As a result, the federal government may not make changes to the Canada Pension Plan without the consent of two-thirds of the provinces representing at least two-thirds of the population.

Finally, as an institutional response to the challenge of governing a large, culturally heterogeneous state, federalism may be a double-edged sword. Rather than merely accommodating existing territorial differences in the country, it may reinforce and even magnify them as provincial governments compete with the central government for power and prestige. "Province-building," in short, may strengthen the parochial identities of citizens at the expense of their attachment to the national political community.[34] In extreme cases, this tendency may give rise to secessionist movements.

Unitary States

Under a unitary form of government, sovereignty is vested in the central government alone. Other levels of government, such as regional, county, or municipal governments, exercise only those powers that have been delegated to them by the national government. Consequently, such powers may be modified or withdrawn as the national government sees fit. Britain, France, Japan, and New Zealand are all examples of unitary states.

By centralizing constitutional authority, a unitary state enables the national government to make decisions on a full range of matters of importance to the nation as a whole, unimpeded by the jurisdictional conflicts to which federations so often are susceptible. This capacity for decision-making at the centre offers the potential for uniformity and consistency in the design of social and economic policies. Over time, the leading role taken by the national government in public affairs may promote national unity by fostering among citizens a stronger sense of allegiance to the national political community. This was a principal aim of the Jacobin leaders of the French Revolution, and their heirs, who set about establishing in Paris a strong central government that would enact laws for all of France. So centralized became the French state that under the Third Republic (1870–1940) it was said that at any minute of any hour of the school day, the French Minister of Education knew the exact page of the national curriculum that a student in any grade should be reading!

On the other hand, an excessive centralization of authority may have undesirable consequences. The national government may be insensitive to regional differences in the country, which arise from diverse local conditions. The imposition of uniform national policies may provoke resentment and undermine the legitimacy of the national government and, ultimately, that of the constitution itself. In practice, all unitary states delegate at least some authority to subnational governments. This delegation of authority, known as **devolution**, may be broad or narrow in scope. Under administrative devolution, local authorities are responsible for delivering services and implementing policies made by the central government. Legislative devolution, sometimes known as home rule, involves a partial transfer of lawmaking authority to regional governments.[35]

Unless the terms of devolution are entrenched in the written constitution, the central government may alter them by ordinary legislation. As a result, the vertical distribution of power in a unitary state may shift back and forth between periods of relative centralization and decentralization, depending on changing political conditions both locally and nationally. This point may be illustrated by reference to the politics of devolution in the United Kingdom in the past 25 years. In the 1980s, the British Conservative government of Margaret Thatcher imposed severe restrictions on local government authorities in furtherance of its program of reducing government expenditure and privatizing public services. For example, local governments were required to offer for sale government-owned council houses to their renter-occupiers and were prohibited from using the proceeds of such sales to build new public housing units. Legal restrictions were also placed on local rate (or property tax) increases in order to prevent local councils from avoiding cuts to public services made necessary by reductions in central government grants. When the Greater London Council (GLC) openly campaigned against the government's policies, the government responded by passing legislation abolishing the GLC itself![36]

At the same time, the Conservative government was steadfastly opposed to devolving power to regional assemblies for Scotland and Wales, a long-standing demand of Scottish and Welsh nationalists and of sections of the British Labour Party. The Conservatives feared that regional devolution would open the door to a "dis-United Kingdom."

In 1997, the Labour Party, led by Tony Blair, was elected to office on a platform that included support for regional devolution and enhanced authority for local governments. After the new government's devolution proposals were approved by voters in separate referendums held in Scotland and Wales in 1997 and in Northern Ireland in 1998, it proceeded to establish regional assemblies, each structured differently to reflect the unique conditions in each of the three regions. The Scottish parliament is an example of home rule, since it has lawmaking powers in designated fields, including a limited power of taxation. The Welsh Assembly exemplifies administrative devolution, since it lacks the authority to pass primary legislation.[37]

The Northern Ireland Assembly was established as part of a larger agreement addressing many aspects of the 30-year political conflict in Ulster. However, continuing conflict between the Protestant Unionist and Roman Catholic Nationalist parties made it impossible to form a stable power-sharing executive. As a result, the Assembly was suspended in late 2002 by the British secretary of state for Northern Ireland and direct rule from London restored. By early 2007, an agreement on outstanding issues was brokered by the British and Irish governments. Following fresh Assembly elections held in March 2007, a new Executive was formed and the Assembly's powers were restored.

Constitutional Change

How does a constitution change over time, short of being replaced by an entirely new constitution? Under conditions of relative political stability, there are three principal mechanisms of constitutional change: evolving usages and conventions, judicial review, and formal amendment.

Usages and Conventions

Since all constitutions consist of both written and unwritten components, changes in the latter may transform a constitution in significant ways. For example, the role and powers of the president under France's Fifth Republic were powerfully shaped by the two longest-serving occupants of the office, Charles de Gaulle (in office from 1958 to 1969) and François Mitterrand (in office from 1981 to 1995). As president, de Gaulle established the preeminence of the presidency, even in areas that the written constitution appeared to assign to the prime minister and government. De Gaulle was able to enlarge the scope of presidential power as long as his political allies in parliament commanded majority support and he was free to appoint prime ministers who would defer to him. In 1986, a Socialist president, François Mitterrand, was forced to appoint a Conservative prime minister and government when the Left lost its majority in the National Assembly. It was unclear whether the constitution could accommodate such a bifurcation of political authority; some even speculated that Mitterrand would resign and force early presidential elections. Instead, a *modus vivendi* was reached between the president and prime minister under which the former retained paramount responsibility for foreign affairs while the latter took responsibility for most aspects of domestic policy. This pattern, once established, guided subsequent "cohabitations" in the 1990s.[38]

Judicial Review

Another means by which constitutions may evolve is judicial review. Through judicial review, the words of the written constitution may be reinterpreted by the courts to reflect changing times and circumstances. This function of judicial review was memorably captured in 1930 by Britain's Lord Chancellor, Viscount Sankey, who described Canada's constitution as "a living tree, capable of growth and expansion within its natural limits."[39] The particular case before the court had to do with whether women were "qualified persons" within the meaning of the *British North America Act* and thereby eligible for appointment to the Canadian Senate. The Supreme Court of Canada had ruled that women were not qualified persons for this purpose since the act, drafted in 1867—decades before women acquired the right to vote—refers to members of parliament in masculine terms only. In overruling that judgment, the Judicial Committee of the British Privy Council said that constitutions should be interpreted in the light of contemporary circumstances rather than being frozen in time. This view is not universally accepted. For example, in the United States some conservative jurists contend that the courts should interpret the constitution strictly in accordance with the "original intent" of its 18th-century drafters.

Constitutional Limits in an Age of Terrorism In recent years governments throughout the world have been invoking the war against terrorism as a justification for the enactment of stringent new security measures, many of which infringe civil liberties and other constitutionally protected interests. For example, special counter-terrorism laws were passed in the United States, Britain,

and Canada following the September 11, 2001 attacks on the United States. Some of these measures restricted or suspended altogether rights of due process for terrorism suspects, including the right of *habeas corpus* and the right to counsel. The surveillance powers of police and security services were also widened at the expense of privacy rights.

In many cases, courts have upheld the constitutionality of such laws and sanctioned restrictions on civil liberties. In other cases, however, the courts have declared such measures to be unlawful, in whole or in part. Examples of the latter include the ruling of the Supreme Court of Canada in February 2007 declaring security certificates to be a violation of certain provisions of the *Charter of Rights and Freedoms*. Such certificates empowered the state to conduct secret trials of noncitizens accused of having ties to terrorism and to impose indefinite prison terms.[40]

Likewise, in June 2006 the Supreme Court of the United States struck down an executive order pursuant to which President Bush had sought to establish special military commissions to try detainees at the notorious facility at Guantanamo Bay, Cuba. Invoking the constitutional principle of the rule of law, the Court found that the commissions were not authorized by federal law and that they violated the Geneva Conventions.[41] The ruling is the subject of the cartoon here. The Court went on to say that the President might put the commissions on a lawful footing by obtaining the necessary authority from Congress.

Constitutional Amendment

If the constitution is a framework of fundamental laws of the state, it follows that it should not be easily amendable. After all, it would be disruptive and upsetting if the rules of a hockey game could be amended by the home team in the middle of the third period, or if the bylaws of a students' council were fundamentally changed every couple of weeks. Nevertheless, there are occasions when a constitutional amendment is thought to be necessary. In most states, the constitution prescribes a special procedure for its own amendment, a procedure that requires a higher threshold of support than is required for amendments to ordinary laws. Even so, not all **amending formulas** are equally onerous; some are relatively flexible while others are relatively rigid.

Not surprisingly, the most **flexible** amending procedures are found in those states that have unwritten constitutions; indeed, Britain's constitution may be amended through ordinary legislation. Unitary states having a written constitution usually specify the need for an extraordinary parliamentary majority for constitutional amendments. For example, Finland's constitution provides that proposed amendments shall be approved by at least two-thirds of the membership of the country's unicameral parliament.

Amending formulas employed in federal systems are among the most **rigid** because of the requirement to secure agreement both at the national level of government and among some combination of the states or provinces. For example, the United States Constitution requires that constitutional amendments be approved by two-thirds majorities of both houses of Congress and ratified by three-quarters of the states. Since the ratification of the first 10 amendments to the U.S. Constitution in 1791 (known collectively as the Bill of Rights), only 17 amendments have been ratified.

Until 1982, the principal component of Canada's written constitution was the *British North America Act*. Since it was a British statute, most parts of it could be amended only by the U.K. parliament; in practice, however, the British willingly enacted amendments requested by the Canadian federal government. Within Canada, a constitutional convention developed to the effect that the consent of a substantial number of provinces was required before the federal government could legitimately request amendments affecting the fundamental interests of the provinces. In 1982, with the patriation of its constitution, Canada acquired a revised constitution, which included a domestic amending formula that codified the requirement for provincial ratification of key amendments (see Box 6.2).

Canada's amending formula is found in Part V of the *Constitution Act*, 1982. Strictly speaking, the amending formula consists of five different formulas. The formula that applies to a particular amendment depends on the subject matter of the amendment.

General Amending Formula

The general amending formula (*Section 38*) applies to most types of constitutional amendments, including the federal–provincial division of powers. It requires that an amendment be approved by Parliament and by the legislatures of at least two-thirds (or 7 out of 10) of the provinces whose combined population is equal to at least 50 percent of the population of all the provinces.

As worded, this means that Ontario or Quebec must give their consent. After all, if neither of them does, then the remaining 8 provinces would only have a combined population of about 38 percent of the population and thus fail the second part of the 7 + 50 requirement.

Note too that Section 38 contains an *opting-out* clause designed to protect the interests of individual provinces. Under subsection (3), if a majority of provinces agree to an amendment transferring a certain category of provincial jurisdiction to Parliament, up to three provinces may opt out of the transfer. Suppose, for example, that all of the provinces except Saskatchewan and Quebec agreed to an amendment transferring to Ottawa responsibility for colleges and universities. By opting out of the amendment, the two dissenting provinces would retain jurisdiction over postsecondary education while Ottawa would assume responsibility for it in the rest of the country.

Unanimity Formula

Certain matters are considered to be so important as to require the unanimous consent of Parliament and all 10 of the provinces. These matters, listed in *Section 41*, include amendments affecting the monarchy and changes to the amending formula itself. Thus, if the federal government resolved to replace the Queen with an elected head of state, such a proposal could be blocked by a single province.

Amendments to Provincial Constitutions

Section 45 gives each provincial legislature the power to amend the constitution of the province. Pursuant to this authority, a province may increase (or decrease) the number of seats in the provincial legislature. It might even use this power to create a bicameral legislature—a legislature consisting of two chambers. Canada's provincial legislatures are unicameral (single-chamber) assemblies, unlike their counterparts in the United States and Australia.

Amendments to Central Government Institutions

Section 44 gives Parliament a parallel power to amend central government institutions that form part of "the Constitution of Canada" (narrowly defined). An earlier version of this formula was used in 1965 to establish a retirement age of 75 for members of the Canadian senate.

Province-Specific Amending Formula

Pursuant to *Section 43*, amendments that would only affect one or two provinces may be made with the consent of Parliament and the province (or provinces) affected. Among the amendments made in the 1990s pursuant to this section were changes to the constitutional basis of the school systems in Newfoundland and Quebec.

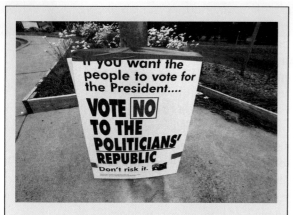

Poster from the 1999 Australian referendum campaign on the Monarchy.

Political banners outside a polling booth for the Republic Referendum, Canberra, 1999 by Loui Seselja, Call Number: PIC NL38605 (B) Frame 25 LOC NL38605 Photographic collection shelves. Reprinted by permission of the National Library of Australia.

A feature of the constitutional amending formula of some states is the requirement that amendments be ratified by citizens in a national referendum. For example, one of the two methods of amendment set out in France's constitution of 1958 states that a proposed amendment, having been approved by both houses of parliament, must be ratified by referendum. This procedure was employed most recently in September 2000 to reduce the term of the president from seven years to five.[42]

Australia's constitution requires amendments that have been approved by parliament to be ratified by a national majority of voters; that national majority, in turn, must consist of majority votes in at least four of the six Australian states. In November 1999, a proposal was submitted to Australian voters to establish a republic by replacing the Queen with an Australian head of state. The amendment was rejected by 55 percent of voters on a national basis and defeated in all six states.[43] Many Australians who favoured a republic nevertheless voted to retain the status quo, because they disapproved of the particular republican model on offer. That model proposed the election of a president by members of the Australian parliament, whereas most supporters of a republic favoured a popularly elected president.

Referendums are sometimes used to establish the **legitimacy** of controversial constitutional proposals, even where there is no constitutional requirement for a referendum. As discussed earlier, the devolution measures implemented in the United Kingdom in 1998 were enacted by parliament only after they had been approved by voters in separate referendums held in Scotland, Wales, and Northern Ireland. Though not legally binding, the national referendum held in Canada in October 1992 on a package of constitutional amendments known as the Charlottetown Accord effectively sealed its fate when the Accord was decisively rejected by voters.

The Politics of Constitutional Amendment

Formal constitutional amendment in most states is not as significant an agent of constitutional change as judicial review or evolving constitutional conventions. In many states this has to do, at least in part, with the rigidity of the amending formula. A mere fraction of the thousands of proposed amendments to the U.S. Constitution has made it past the first hurdle—that of approval by Congress—while less than 20 percent of the amendments approved by the Australian parliament since 1906 have been ratified in national referendums.[44] However, the difficulty of amending a constitution in democratic states also has to do with the fiercely contested nature of constitutional politics. After all, the stakes involved in constitutional change are often higher than those involved in the passage of ordinary legislation. Whereas a controversial law may be repealed, or an unpopular government defeated at the polls, a constitutional amendment, once adopted, is considerably more difficult to undo. Groups opposing an amendment, therefore, have a powerful incentive to campaign vigorously against it, knowing that the threshold of support needed to defeat an amendment is significantly lower than that required to reverse it once it has been ratified.

Constitutional politics also tend to arouse passions when a proposed amendment seeks to enshrine values in the constitution that are not firmly embedded or widely held within the national political culture. This was evident in Canada in the 1980s and early 1990s, when Quebec's desire for constitutional recognition as a "distinct society" was fiercely resisted by many English-speaking Canadians. Antipathy to the "distinct society" clause in the Charlotte-town Accord was one of the factors contributing to the accord's defeat in the 1992 constitutional referendum. Conflicting constitutional visions also doomed the European Union Constitution in the French and Dutch referendums of 2005.

Sometimes governments seek to entrench particular social or economic policies in the constitution so as to put such policies beyond the reach of governments of a different political stripe that may be elected in the future. For example, following the Portuguese Revolution of 1974, the left-wing provisional government proceeded to nationalize key industries and large land holdings. A new constitution, adopted in 1976, declared Portugal to be in "transition to socialism" and referred to the property nationalized since the revolution as "irreversible conquests of the working classes."[45] In the 1980s, a centre-right majority government was elected on a program that included the privatization of some state-owned industries. However, lacking the two-thirds majority in parliament necessary to amend the constitution, the government was unable to implement these promises. It was finally able to act in 1989, when the opposition Socialist Party agreed to the necessary constitutional amendments.

Of course, conservative parties also seek the constitutional entrenchment of elements of their social and economic programs. For example, right-wing Republicans in the United States have long favoured an amendment to the constitution that would require the federal government to maintain a balanced budget. More recently, Republicans have responded to court decisions mandating same-sex marriage by proposing a constitutional amendment that would enshrine the traditional (heterosexual) definition of marriage. In Canada in 1980–81, Progressive Conservative MPs advocated the entrenchment of a property rights provision in the proposed Canadian Charter of Rights and Freedoms (see Box 6.3), to better protect the economic interests of private property owners. The Liberal government ultimately rejected inclusion of such a provision in response to opposition from New Democrat MPs, who feared

The Politics of the Canadian Constitution BOX 6.3

An essential starting point from which to understand the nature of the constitutional debate in Canada today is the tortuous process that led to the patriation of the Constitution in 1982. Prime Minister Pierre Trudeau considered patriation to be the crowning achievement of his term of premiership. Others suggest that the country paid too high a price for it. Whatever history's ultimate verdict, there is no question that Canada is still living with the legacy of patriation.

The Road to Patriation (1968–82)
When Canada effectively acquired its independence from Britain in 1926 it was presumed that the federal and provincial governments would shortly agree on a new constitution with which to replace the *British North America (BNA) Act*, an act of the British parliament. That new constitution would be amendable in Canada by means of a domestic amending formula. However, various attempts to reach agreement between Ottawa and the provinces ended in failure.

By the 1960s, the emergence of a powerful nationalist movement in Quebec raised the constitutional stakes for Canada. Unless relations between English and French Canada could be put on a more stable foundation, it was widely feared that

Quebec's separation from Canada would just be a matter of time. The federal government took a major step toward accommodating the French fact by designating English and French official languages of Canada in 1969.

Trudeau's Liberal government then set out to achieve the constitutional entrenchment of bilingualism, including guarantees of access to minority-language education in the provinces. Despite numerous attempts, however, intergovernmental agreement proved elusive.

The first Parti Québécois (PQ) government was elected to office in 1976. Committed to the founding of a sovereign Quebec state, the PQ called a referendum on independence for May 1980. Toward the end of the referendum campaign, Prime Minister Trudeau pledged that if Quebeckers voted No, his government would seek to renew Canadian federalism. When the ballots were counted, 60 percent of Quebeckers had voted No to independence, as against 40 percent on the Yes side.

The referendum results gave a fresh impetus to Trudeau's quest for constitutional reform. So once again the federal government made overtures to the provinces. In September 1980, the provinces replied by rejecting the federal proposals while insisting on the addition of new items to the reform agenda.

In anticipation of such a stalemate, Trudeau stunned everyone by declaring his government's intention to go to London unilaterally—without the consent of the provinces—in order to request the constitutional changes it deemed necessary. Only two provinces (Ontario and New Brunswick) supported the federal government's position. The other eight provinces were staunchly opposed.

The standoff between Ottawa and the provinces ultimately reached the Supreme Court of Canada. There the provinces argued that in proceeding unilaterally the federal government lacked legal authority or, at the very least, was flouting a constitutional convention requiring provincial consent to major constitutional amendments. Faced with such a politically loaded question, the judges made a ruling that was quite ingenious. In a split decision, they ruled that while the federal government's action was legally valid, it violated a constitutional convention requiring the consent of a "substantial number" of provinces to major constitutional amendments.

The decision enabled both Ottawa and the provinces to claim at least a partial victory; it also allowed both sides to submit to a compromise solution without losing face—always an important consideration in politics.

The major players reassembled in Ottawa in November 1981 in a last-ditch effort to resolve their differences. By the end of the conference, agreement was reached between Mr. Trudeau and nine of the premiers. The provinces would accept the proposed *Charter of Rights and Freedoms*, provided it contained a "notwithstanding clause" that would allow legislatures to override certain sections of it. For its part, the federal government agreed to substitute the provinces' draft amending formula for its own.

Quebec Premier René Lévesque not only refused to sign the agreement but also angrily denounced his fellow premiers for having struck a deal behind his back. In Lévesque's view—and that of many Quebeckers—the new constitution eroded Quebec's jurisdiction over language and education in the province while failing to grant Quebec the right to veto constitutional amendments to which it objected. Lévesque accused English Canada of nothing short of betrayal!

Aftermath of Patriation

By any reckoning, the patriation of the constitution was a historic achievement. With the proclamation of the *Canada Act* on April 17, 1982, the Canadian constitution ceased to be a British statute and became whole with the addition of a domestic amending formula and a *Charter of Rights*.

On the other hand, patriation had been achieved at a high price: Quebec's estrangement from the rest of the country. In the mid-1980s, the Progressive Conservative Government of Brian Mulroney attempted to achieve a *rapprochement* with Quebec in two further rounds of constitutional negotiations. Both the Meech Lake Accord of 1987 and the Charlottetown Accord of 1992 proposed, among other things, to give formal constitutional recognition to Quebec as a "distinct society." However, these proposals aroused considerable opposition across the country, and neither agreement was implemented.

The Meech Lake Accord expired in June 1990 when it failed to secure the unanimous provincial consent required for ratification. Many Quebeckers took the failure of Meech Lake to signify the futility of efforts to achieve a constitutional agreement between Quebec and the rest of Canada. This sentiment produced a dramatic upsurge of support in Quebec for political independence and led to the founding of the separatist Bloc Québécois.

Two years later, at Charlottetown, Prime Minister Mulroney reached agreement with the premiers on a new package of constitutional proposals. The Charlottetown Accord of 1992 largely replicated the Meech Lake proposals, but also embraced a wide range of new issues, from Senate reform to **aboriginal self-government**, in an effort to address many of the criticisms that had been levelled at Meech. Nevertheless, the Charlottetown Accord was soundly defeated in a national referendum held in October 1992. Interestingly, while many Canadians rejected the Accord because they believed that it gave too much power to Quebec, most Quebeckers were of the view that it gave Quebec too little!

The constitutional roller-coaster ride was not yet over. In 1994, the PQ returned to power in Quebec, promising to call another referendum on independence within a year of taking office. The results of the referendum of October 1995 were much closer than before; indeed, only a thin majority of Quebeckers voted against separation—50.6 percent to 49.4 percent.

Following the defeat of the Charlottetown Accord and the uncomfortably close results of the second Quebec referendum, federal politicians were unwilling to reopen the Pandora's Box of constitutional reform. The preferred approach now was to pursue common objectives through political rather than constitutional means. For example, in 1999 Prime Minister Jean Chrétien signed an agreement with the provinces undertaking not to finance new social programs in areas of provincial jurisdiction—such as child care or prescription drugs—without first obtaining the consent of the provinces. In November 2006, acting in a similar nonconstitutional vein, Prime Minister Stephen Harper introduced a resolution into Parliament affirming that "the Québécois form a nation within a united Canada." While the precise meaning of this declaration was far from clear, reaction across the country was remarkably muted. Most critics were evidently reassured by the fact that it did not form part of the Constitution.

that a property rights clause would be used by corporations to challenge legitimate forms of economic regulation.[46]

Nowadays, private property rights increasingly are codified in international trade and investment agreements, such as the **North American Free Trade Agreement (NAFTA)** and the General Agreement on Trade in Services (GATS), and in the rulings of international bodies such as the **World Trade Organization (WTO)**. Through such agreements, states undertake to refrain from enacting laws that may be construed as interfering with international trade and investment. Many observers consider the constraints imposed on governments by these agreements to be analogous to constitutional limitations. However, while modern constitutions are largely concerned with conferring rights on citizens, both as individuals and as members of minority groups, trade agreements confer rights on corporations. Since governments may not infringe the corporate rights enshrined in trade agreements, some observers fear that such agreements may seriously weaken the ability of governments to act in defence of the public interest.[47]

CONCLUSION

This chapter discussed the origins of modern constitutions, outlined their major political functions, and examined the relationship between written and unwritten elements of constitutions. It then described and assessed the principal types of constitutions—confederal, federal, and unitary—that allocate power on a territorial basis. The chapter concluded with an examination of the major processes of constitutional change. It demonstrated that constitutions, as well as the government institutions they authorize, are an indispensable part of the larger subject of politics. In the next three chapters, we take a closer look at the core institutions of government.

DISCUSSION QUESTIONS

1. In what circumstances is federalism likely to preserve the unity of a territorially diverse state? In what circumstances is it likely to exacerbate territorial differences?

2. What is the best method for amending a constitution? Should the method used to amend the constitution of a unitary state differ from that used to amend the constitution of a federal state? Explain.

3. How much detail should a written constitution provide with regard to each of the following matters?

   (a) the structure of government institutions

   (b) the values and principles on which the state is based

   (c) the rights of citizens vis-à-vis the state

   (d) social and economic policies

4. Are the interests of minorities better protected under federalism (or a decentralized unitary system) than under a centralized unitary state? Does the existence of a constitutionally entrenched bill of rights make a difference to your answer?

5. Which pose a greater threat to the freedom, security, and well-being of citizens today: governments or global corporations? Should constitutions in the 21st century be as preoccupied as those of the 19th and 20th centuries with restricting the power of governments?

KEY TERMS

CONSTITUTION: The body of fundamental laws, rules, and practices that defines the basic structures of government, allocates power among governmental institutions, and regulates the relationship between citizens and the state. (157)

CONSTITUTIONAL CONVENTION: An unwritten rule of constitutional behaviour that fills in gaps in the written constitution and conditions the exercise of legal powers under the constitution. While considered obligatory, such rules are not legally enforceable. (162)

CONSTITUTIONALISM: The idea that the constitution should limit the state by separating powers among different branches and levels of government and protecting the rights of individuals and minorities through a bill of rights. (157)

FEDERALISM: A form of government in which the sovereign powers of the state are formally divided under a constitution between two levels of government, neither of which is subordinate to the other. (166)

FISCAL IMBALANCE: In federal states, the constitutional responsibilities of the provincial or state governments to deliver a wide range of public services often greatly exceed the financial capacity of such governments. This gulf between public expenditures and public finances usually requires the central government to provide cash and other transfers to the provinces. (168)

UNWRITTEN CONSTITUTION: A constitution whose subject matter is dispersed across a variety of statutes, court rulings, and unwritten political practices known as constitutional conventions. (162)

WRITTEN CONSTITUTION: A constitution whose fundamental provisions have been reduced to a single document or set of documents. (162)

WEB LINKS

International Constitutional Law Project:
http://www.oefre.unibe.ch/law/icl

Europa, Gateway to the European Union:
http://europa.eu/index_en.htm

Privy Council Office, Intergovernmental Affairs:
http://www.pco-bcp.gc.ca/aia

Institute of Intergovernmental Relations, Queen's University:
http://www.queensu.ca/iigr

Centre for Constitutional Studies, University of Alberta:
http://www.law.ualberta.ca/centres/ccs

The Constitution Unit, School of Public Policy, University College London:
http://www.ucl.ac.uk/constitution-unit

FURTHER READING

Bagehot, Walter. *The English Constitution.* Cornell: Cornell University Press, 1966.

Banting, Keith G., and Richard Simeon. *Redesigning the State: The Politics of Constitutional Change in Industrial Nations.* Toronto: University of Toronto Press, 1985.

Bogdanor, Vernon, ed. *Constitutions in Democratic Politics*. Aldershot: Gower, 1988.

Elster, Jon, et al. *Institutional Design in Post-Communist Societies: Rebuilding the Ship at Sea*. Cambridge: Cambridge University Press, 1998.

Heard, Andrew. *Canadian Constitutional Conventions: The Marriage of Law and Politics*. Toronto: Oxford University Press, 1991.

Hyden, Goran, and Denis Venter. *Constitution-Making and Democratisation in Africa*. Pretoria: Africa Institute of South Africa, 2001.

Vile, M.J.C. *Constitutionalism and the Separation of Powers*. Oxford: Clarendon Press, 1967.

Watts, Ronald L. *Comparing Federal Systems*. 2nd ed. Montreal and Kingston: McGill-Queen's University Press, 1999.

ENDNOTES

1. Vernon Bogdanor, "Introduction," in Vernon Bogdanor, ed., *Constitutions in Democratic Politics* (Aldershot: Gower, 1988).

2. See Peter B. Evans, Dietrich Rueschmeyer, and Theda Skocpol, eds., *Bringing the State Back In* (Cambridge: Cambridge University Press, 1985); James G. March and Johan P. Olsen, *Rediscovering Institutions* (New York: Free Press, 1989); and R. Kent Weaver and Bert A. Rockman, *Do Institutions Matter? Government Capabilities in the United States and Abroad* (Washington, DC: Brookings Institution, 1993).

3. S.E. Finer, ed., *Five Constitutions* (Harmondsworth: Penguin, 1979), p. 15.

4. Giovanni Sartori, "Constitutionalism: A Preliminary Discussion," *American Political Science Review* 56 (December 1962): 853–64.

5. Quoted in Ivo D. Duchacek, *Power Maps: Comparative Politics of Constitutions* (Santa Barbara: American Bibliographical Center, 1973), p. 18.

6. *Ibid.*, p. 23.

7. It was under this pretext that Soviet forces had invaded Czechoslovakia in the infamous Prague Spring of 1968, replacing the reform Communist government of Alexander Dubček with Czech leaders who were faithful to the Soviet model of communism. Ironically, Ceaușescu had criticized the Soviet invasion as an unwarranted breach of national autonomy.

8. Tom Gallagher, *Romania After Ceaușescu: The Politics of Intolerance* (Edinburgh: Edinburgh University Press, 1995); and Karen Henderson and Neil Robinson, *Post-Communist Politics: An Introduction* (Hemel Hempstead: Prentice-Hall, 1997).

9. Harold Laski, *The American Presidency: An Interpretation* (New York and London: Harper and Brothers, 1940).

10. This power was used in the 1950s to ban a neo-Nazi party and the West German Communist Party.

11. K.C. Wheare, *Modern Constitutions*, 2nd ed. (London: Oxford University Press, 1966), p. 15.

12. *Ibid.*, p. 122.

13. W. Ivor Jennings, *The Law and the Constitution*, 5th ed. (London: University of London Press, 1959), p. 81.

14. Ordinarily, the governor general may not refuse a prime minister's request for a dissolution. This is not to say that in appropriate circumstances the governor general would not be justified in exercising his or her prerogative to deny such a request or even to dismiss the prime minister. See Eugene Forsey, *Freedom and Order: Collected Essays* (Toronto: McClelland and Stewart, 1974).

15. Peter W. Hogg, *Constitutional Law of Canada*, Student Edition (Scarborough: Thomson Carswell, 2006), p. 25.

16. The most sustained criticism of the appointment in the Senate Judiciary Committee came from southern Democrats displeased with what they took to be Warren's excessively liberal views and from a North Dakota senator who insisted that the appointment be filled by someone from his home state. Henry J. Abraham, *Justices and Presidents* (New York: Oxford University Press, 1992), pp. 257–58.

17. While Canada styles itself as a confederation, it is more accurately classified as a federation. The error stems from the fact that in the 19th century the terms *confederation* and *federation* were often used interchangeably. For example, Switzerland continued to style itself as a confederation after adopting a federal constitution in 1848.

18. Karl W. Deutsch, *Politics and Government: How People Decide Their Fate* (Boston: Houghton Mifflin, 1970), pp. 181–82.

19. Donald S. Lutz, "The Iroquois Confederation Constitution: An Analysis," *Publius* 28 (1998): 99–127.

20. Duncan Watts and Colin Pilkington, *Britain in the European Union Today*, 3rd ed. (Manchester: Manchester University Press, 2005), pp. 179–182.

21. Ronald L. Watts, *The Spending Power in Federal Systems: A Comparative Study* (Kingston: Institute of Intergovernmental Relations, Queen's University, 1999), pp. 40–46.

22. France, the Federal Republic of Germany, Italy, Belgium, the Netherlands, and Luxembourg.

23. Neill Nugent, *The Government and Politics of the European Union*, 6th ed. (Durham, NC: Duke University Press, 2006).

24. For the full text of the constitution, see the EU's official website: http://europa.eu/scadplus/constitution/introduction_en.htm; accessed May 10, 2008. For later developments, see "MPs Consider Fallout from EU Vote," *BBC News*, March 5, 2008 at http://news.bbc.co.uk/go/pr/fr/-/2/hi/europe/6901353.stm.

25. Part of the land base of the federation may be under the exclusive authority of the central government. Examples include the Canadian federal government's authority over the country's three northern territories (Yukon, the Northwest Territories, and Nunavut) and the Australian Commonwealth government's authority over the Northern Territory, the Australian Capital Territory of Canberra, and the various island territories.

26. The U.S. Supreme Court asserted its authority to review the constitutionality of acts of the federal executive in 1800 in the case of *Marbury* v. *Madison*, [1805] 5 U.S. 137 (1 Cranch). On the origins of judicial review in Canada, see B.L. Strayer, *The Canadian Constitution and the Courts*, 3rd ed. (Toronto: Butterworths, 1988).

27. See Sections 56 and 90 of the *Constitution Act*, 1867.

28. The last time the disallowance power was used was in 1943, when the federal cabinet disallowed legislation relating to banking and currency passed by the Social Credit government of Alberta.

29. See Peter H. Russell, "The Supreme Court and Federal–Provincial Relations: The Political Use of Legal Resources," in R.D. Olling and M.W. Westmacott, eds., *Perspectives on Canadian Federalism* (Scarborough: Prentice-Hall, 1988).

30. The Supreme Court Act stipulates that at least one-third of the nine-person Court must be members of the Bar of Quebec. This requirement ensures that there is a sufficient number of judges who are qualified to hear appeals arising from Quebec's Civil Code, a system of private law that differs materially from the common law legal system in force in the other provinces and territories. In practice, the remaining seats are allocated as follows: three to Ontario, two to the Western provinces, and one to the Atlantic provinces.

31. Clinton Rossiter, ed., *The Federalist Papers* (New York: Mentor, 1961), p. 323.

32. Keith G. Banting, *The Welfare State and Canadian Federalism*, 2nd ed. (Montreal and Kingston: McGill-Queen's University Press, 1987), p. 41.

33. For example, in the 1990s, the Christian Democrat government of Helmut Kohl was stymied in its efforts to curtail pension benefits because of opposition from state governments represented in the upper house of the German parliament.

34. The term *province-building* was coined by Edwin R. Black and Alan C. Cairns in "A Different Perspective on Canadian Federalism," *Canadian Public Administration* 9 (March 1966): 27–44.

35. Andrew Heywood, *Politics*, 2nd ed. (Basingstoke, UK: Palgrave, 2002), p. 167.

36. Eric J. Evans, *Thatcher and Thatcherism*, 2nd ed. (London: Routledge, 2004), pp. 58–64.

37. Bill Jones, "Devolution," in Bill Jones et al., *Politics UK*, 4th ed. (Harlow: Pearson Education, 2001). See also Matthew Leeke, Chris Sear, and Oonagh Gay, "An Introduction to Devolution in the UK," *Research Paper 03/84* (London, Eng.: House of Commons Library, Parliament and Constitution Centre, November 17, 2003).

38. David S. Bell, *Presidential Power in Fifth Republic France* (Oxford: Berg, 2000).

39. *Edwards v. A.-G. Can.*, [1930] A.C. 114.

40. Kirk Makin, "A Big Thumbs-Up for Civil Libertarians," *Globe and Mail*, February 24, 2007, p. A-4.

41. Charles Lane, "High Court Rejects Detainee Tribunals," *The Washington Post*, June 30, 2006, p. A01.

42. The reduced term took effect at the beginning of the presidential mandate in 2002.

43. John Warnhurst and Malcolm Mackerras, eds., *Constitutional Politics: The Republic Referendum and the Future* (St. Lucia: University of Queensland Press, 2002); Ian McAllister, "Elections Without a Cue: The 1999 Australian Republic Referendum," *Australian Journal of Political Science* 36(2) (July 2001): 247–69.

44. Gwyneth Singleton et al., *Australian Political Institutions*, 8th ed. (Frenchs Forest, NSW: Pearson Education Australia, 2006), p. 57.

45. Kenneth Maxwell, *The Making of Portuguese Democracy* (Cambridge: Cambridge University Press, 1995), p. 159.

46. The proposed property rights clause was also opposed by a majority of the premiers, who feared it would encroach on the legislative authority of the provinces. Alexander Alvaro, "Why Property Rights Were Excluded from the Canadian Charter of Rights and Freedoms," *Canadian Journal of Political Science* 24(2) (June 1991): 309–29.

47. Stephen McBride, Paradigm Shift: Globalization and the Canadian State, 2nd ed. (Halifax: Fernwood, 2005); Stephen Clarkson, *Uncle Sam and Us: Globalization, Neo-conservatism, and the Canadian State* (Toronto: University of Toronto Press, 2002).

Chapter Seven

THE POLITICAL EXECUTIVE AND BUREAUCRACY: On Top and on Tap

Stephen Phillips

CHAPTER OBJECTIVES

After you have completed this chapter, you should be able to:

- identify the main functions of the executive branch

- distinguish the role of head of state from head of government

- compare parliamentary, presidential, and semi-presidential executives

- describe the political role of the bureaucracy

- recognize the various means by which the executive is held accountable

Introduction

The main functions of modern states are carried out by the three great branches of government: the executive, the legislature, and the judiciary. The executive is most certainly the least specialized of the three. In fact, the broad range, and sheer number, of tasks to which the executive sets its hand is truly remarkable. Consider the many instances that routinely bring citizens into direct contact with the state. Every year, millions of Canadians post (or send electronically) their income tax returns to the Canada Revenue Agency. If they are lucky enough to qualify for a refund, it will be delivered to them by an employee of Canada Post. Workers who lose their jobs must pay a visit to the local office of Human Resources and Skills Development to apply for unemployment benefits. Business owners must file a host of bureaucratic forms with various government agencies; at the same time, they may have to consult various government agencies to ensure their compliance with regulations having to do with land use, employment standards, or other matters. In each of these cases, citizens interact directly with the executive branch of government.

By way of contrast, citizens rarely, if ever, come into contact with the judiciary. Few citizens have occasion to attend the local courthouse, to appear before a judge, or to be called upon to do jury duty. A larger number of citizens—albeit still a minority—may have direct dealings with their member of parliament or their member of the provincial legislature. Citizens may write to their MP to seek assistance with a local problem or to convey their views on a cabinet came to dominate parliament. Crossman and others went on to describe a significant centralization of power within the executive branch itself since the end of World War II. On this view, prime ministers and senior bureaucrats exercise such wide-ranging powers nowadays that, in many respects, the cabinet has joined parliament and the Crown in forming part of the dignified (or decorative) part of the constitution.

Functions of the Executive

Today the main functions of the executive may be stated as follows:

- *To provide political leadership to the nation.* It is to the executive branch that citizens look to take the initiative to address political problems. Most of those problems are of a routine, ongoing nature, but citizens also expect the political executive to respond swiftly, decisively, and competently to national crises, both domestic and foreign. Note that while the approval of parliament (or the legislature) is often required in order to give formal, legal effect to the policies of the government, the initiative for most legislation lies with the executive.
- *To implement laws formally approved by the legislature.* The political executive dominates the early stages of the policy process, at which policy is formulated, as well as the latter stages, at which policy is implemented. In regard to the latter function, executive agencies of the state (chiefly, the bureaucracy) are responsible for ensuring that taxes are collected, that public services are delivered, and that a host of regulatory laws are enforced. In Canada, the prime minister and his or her government have ultimate political responsibility for the efficiency, effectiveness, and fairness with which such functions of the state are carried out.
- *To make rules and regulations.* In modern democratic states, the government needs legal authority from the legislature to carry out most of its operations. Legislative grants of authority to the executive tend to vest wide powers in the government to draw up detailed regulations that flesh out the often skeletal framework of legislation. In Canada, for example, the *Firearms Act* authorized the federal government to establish a national registry for firearms and to determine the procedures to be followed (and the fees to be paid) to register a gun. Other statutes give the Minister of Immigration the authority to establish a procedure to process claims for refugee status and the Minister of Agriculture—or agencies that the ministry sets up—wide powers to set production quotas for dairy and poultry farmers.
- *To administer government departments and other agencies.* As in any large organization, governments need to be organized into specialized units that are responsible for performing particular functions. A key task of the political executive is to organize the apparatus of the state, including its personnel, which may number in the hundreds of thousands. In carrying out this managerial role, the political executive relies heavily on the advice of high-ranking public officials within the bureaucracy.

Head of State Versus Head of Government

The political executive sits at the apex of the executive branch. On closer examination, we may distinguish between two leading offices of state: the **head of state** and the **head of government**. In parliamentary and semi-parliamentary systems, these posts are filled by separate officeholders. This arrangement is known as a **dual executive**. In presidential systems, the two positions are combined and held by a single office-holder, an arrangement known as a **single executive**. For now, let us take a closer look at the respective roles of the head of state and the head of government under a parliamentary system of government.

German Chancellor Angela Merkel confers with the Federal President, Dr. Horst Koehler.

AFP/Getty Images

In parliamentary systems, the office of head of state is held either by a constitutional monarch or an elected president. Spain, Japan, and the Netherlands are examples of parliamentary democracies having a monarchical head of state. Heredity is the principle governing succession to the throne, although the rules of succession vary somewhat among national monarchies. For example, in Norway the eldest child of the reigning monarch is deemed the heir apparent, whether male or female, whereas in Japan only males may accede to the throne.[4] In Britain, the line of succession privileges male heirs; under the law of primogeniture, women may accede to the throne only in the absence of a male heir. Moreover, the 1701 *Act of Settlement* bars Roman Catholics from acceding to the British throne. Not surprisingly, there has been much debate about repealing these laws, neither of which can easily be reconciled with contemporary views about equality.

Interestingly, Queen Elizabeth II is head of state of not only the United Kingdom but also some 15 other countries belonging to the Commonwealth, including Canada, New Zealand, and Jamaica (see Box 7.1).[5] However, with the exception of the United Kingdom, the Queen's duties in each of these countries are carried out by her representative, known as the Governor General (GG). In federal states, such as Australia and Canada, the Queen also has representatives at the state or provincial level of government. They are known as Governors or Lieutenant Governors. These officials are appointed by the Queen, on the advice of the Prime Minister—or the State Premier, as the case may be—and usually serve a five-year term.[6]

A parliamentary republic is headed by an elected president, but despite the use of this latter title, we should not confuse it with a presidential system such as that of the United States. In a parliamentary republic, the president may be directly elected by the people, as in Portugal, Austria, and the Republic of Ireland. In other states, including Greece and Italy, the president is chosen by members of the national parliament or, as in Germany, by an electoral college comprising members of the federal and state parliaments.

The second part of the parliamentary dual executive is headed by a prime minister or premier (known in Austria and Germany as the chancellor). The prime minister (PM) is appointed by the head of state, usually following a general election, and is invited to form a government by naming a cabinet. In most cases, the prime minister is the leader of the party having the largest number of seats in parliament. As head of government, the prime minister advises the head of state on the exercise of the legal powers held by the latter, and, except in highly unusual circumstances, the head of state is obliged to comply with the prime minister's advice.

What then is the point of having a head of state separate from the head of government? There are three generally accepted roles for the head of state.

1. *To carry out ceremonial duties.* Part of the role of a head of state consists in dedicating new bridges and hospital wings; conferring awards and other honours; formally receiving and accrediting new ambassadors to the country; and hosting state banquets for visiting heads

The Multiple Crowns Worn by Elizabeth II BOX 7.1

Canada is a constitutional monarchy and Queen Elizabeth II is Canada's head of state. However, that does not mean that Canada is still a colony of Great Britain. Along with other self-governing Dominions of the British Empire, Canada gained full political independence as a result of decisions taken at the Imperial Conference of 1926, and later codified in the Statute of Westminster of 1931.[7] In order to give effect to Canadian independence, it was necessary to transform the status and role of the monarchy. Before 1926, the British monarch was the indivisible head of the Empire. Thus, Britain's declaration of war against Germany in August 1914 meant that Canada and the rest of the Empire were automatically at war.

After 1926, the Crown was deemed to be divided into a series of national crowns, one for each of the Dominions that had achieved full powers of self-government. As Vernon Bogdanor puts it: "the concept of a single Crown uniting the members of the Commonwealth [was] replaced by that of several crowns linked by the person of the sovereign."[8] After 1926, the monarch was to take advice solely from his or her Canadian ministers on all matters concerning Canada. Likewise, the monarch was to take advice solely from his or her Australian ministers on matters concerning Australia, and so on.

As a practical matter, the governor general, in Canada as in other Commonwealth countries, exercises almost all of the powers of the monarch. For that reason, the governor general is head of state in all but name—a point that leads some observers to describe countries like Canada and Australia as "crowned republics."[9]

of state. By performing these duties, the head of state lightens the burden of the PM, allowing him or her to concentrate on government business.

2. *To serve as the nonpartisan representative of the state.* Unlike the prime minister, the head of state is expected to represent the nation as a whole, even if, as in many parliamentary republics, he or she was elected to office as the official candidate of a political party. Being above the partisan fray, the head of state has the potential to represent all shades of political opinion and to serve as a focus for national unity. To this end the head of state, in public pronouncements, tends to address broad, unifying themes and can even act as a kind of moral compass for the nation. As president of the Federal Republic of Germany from 1999 to 2004, Johannes Rau made a series of speeches reflecting on the nation's Nazi past and warning of a recurrence of political extremism in Germany.

3. *To act as guardian of the constitution.* There are two major aspects to this function. First, if the PM seeks to undermine the constitution, the head of state may take corrective action by using the wide legal powers at his or her disposal. This is the so-called "fire extinguisher" function of the head of state.[10] For example, if the PM were to ignore a parliamentary vote of non-confidence, the head of state would be within his or her rights to dismiss the PM. Second, if there is a temporary vacuum of governmental authority—for example, if the PM and cabinet were killed in a terrorist attack—the head of state could assume effective control of the state pending the formation of a new government. Such an event occurred in the Caribbean island nation of Grenada in 1983 when the governor general, Sir Paul Scoon, assumed the reins of government following the murder of Prime Minister Maurice Bishop in an attempted *coup d'état.* The coup was thwarted, controversially, by a U.S. military invasion of the island.[11]

In the normal course of events, the head of state exercises his or her formal powers only on the advice of the prime minister or the cabinet as a whole. Nevertheless, there are certain situations in which the head of state has some discretion and is not bound to follow the advice of the ministry. In such cases, the head of state may exercise what are known as reserve or prerogative powers. These are residual powers of the crown that have not been abolished by parliament or the written constitution. However, the head of state does not have an entirely free hand in exercising such powers; rather, he or she is expected to follow any applicable constitutional conventions. In many states that adopted new constitutions after 1945, some of these conventions have been spelled out in the constitution.

Two of the main prerogative powers held by the head of state in a parliamentary system are the power to appoint or dismiss the prime minister and the power to dissolve parliament for a general election.

Appointment and Dismissal of the PM

In appointing a prime minister, the head of state is guided in most cases by well-known constitutional conventions. For example, if an incumbent government is reelected in a general election, the current PM stays on and is invited to form a new government. If the ruling party is decisively defeated, the outgoing PM tenders his or her resignation to the head of state, who then appoints as the new PM the leader of the party that won a majority of parliamentary seats. Sometimes, however, it may not be immediately apparent which party leader is in a position to form a government following a general election. In such cases, the head of state may have to conduct extensive discussions with parliamentary leaders and to exercise his or her own judgment in naming a prime minister, subject to any applicable conventions. Situations of this kind arise in European democracies from time to time, in which multiple parties are represented in parliament and coalition governments are the norm.

Another well-established convention arises when a prime minister chooses to resign before the government is obliged to go to the polls. Given the reality of party government, prime ministers who wish to retire before the next election will usually announce that their resignation is to take effect as soon as the party has elected a successor—a process that may take days or months, depending on the procedure by which the governing party selects its leader. In Canada, governing parties elect their leaders in large national leadership conventions or by way of a balloting of the entire membership of the party. By either of these methods it can take months to select the successor to a retiring PM; in the meantime, the incumbent remains in office until the party has made its choice.[12]

A more controversial power of the head of state is the power to dismiss the head of government. This power is to be used only in the most extraordinary circumstances, if at all, because in democratic states the general rule is that a prime minister and cabinet are responsible to parliament and ultimately accountable to the electorate. In 1975, however, the governor general of Australia created a firestorm of controversy when he dismissed the prime minister, who headed a majority government at the time (see Box 7.2).

The Dissolution Power

The other main prerogative power is the power of dissolution—the power to dissolve parliament and call a general election. As a general rule, the head of state exercises this power on the advice of the prime minister in one of two circumstances: when the prime minister (still having the confidence of parliament) sees the need for an early election or when the government has been defeated in parliament on a confidence motion. However, the head of state is not bound to dissolve parliament in either of these cases: he or she retains some

The Day a Governor General Fired a Prime Minister

BOX 7.2

On November 11, 1975 Australians were shocked to learn that the Governor General, Sir John Kerr, had fired the Prime Minister, Mr. Gough Whitlam, despite the fact that Whitlam's Labor Government held a majority of seats in the House of Representatives, the lower house of the Australian parliament. The ostensible reason for this unprecedented use of the reserve powers of the Crown was the government's inability to secure passage in the Senate of its supply bills—bills giving the government legal authority to spend public money. For three weeks, the Liberal and National Country parties in the Senate had refused to approve supply unless Whitlam agreed to call early elections for the House of Representatives. This Whitlam refused to do on the grounds that in blocking supply the Senate was violating a long-standing convention of British parliamentary government. Adding fuel to the fire was the fact that the Opposition parties had recently gained control of the Senate by flouting another constitutional convention.[1]

Whitlam resolved to break the deadlock between the two houses by advising the Governor General to call early Senate elections. When the Prime Minister arrived at Government House, the Governor General's official residence, he was unaware that Sir John had already summoned the Opposition leader, Mr. Malcolm Fraser. While Fraser waited in an adjacent room, out of view of the Prime Minister, Sir John abruptly informed Whitlam of his dismissal from office. He then invited Fraser to form a new government on condition that Fraser ensure the immediate passage of supply and that he advise a double dissolution of Parliament—the simultaneous election of both houses. Fraser agreed to these terms.

Later that afternoon, Fraser entered the House of Representatives to inform members that the Governor General had just appointed him the new Prime Minister. In response, Labor members, who were still in the majority, passed a motion of non-confidence in Fraser and called on the Governor General to reappoint Whitlam! By this time, the Governor General had already despatched his secretary to the steps of Parliament House to read the proclamation dissolving Parliament and fixing the date of the general election (December 13, 1975). The proclamation ended with the words, "God Save the Queen." Taking his cue from those words, an indignant Gough Whitlam famously declared: "Well may we say God save the Queen because nothing will save the Governor General!"

Most Australians had disapproved of the Opposition's obstructionist tactics and were stunned by Kerr's response. Some even accused him of staging a *coup d'état*. Indeed, as news of Whitlam's dismissal spread, thousands of workers walked off the job in protest. Nevertheless, once the election campaign was under way public attention began to focus on other issues—notably the parlous state of the economy—and on polling day Fraser's Liberals won sizable majorities in both Houses.

Kerr considered the election results to be a vindication of his actions. However, most political analysts fault the Governor General for having resorted to such a drastic measure as the dismissal of an elected government. On this view, Kerr should have confided in his prime minister and helped to broker a political solution to the impasse. Others, however, applaud Kerr's conduct, including Sir Garfield Barwick, then Chief Justice of the Australian High Court and a former (Liberal Party) Attorney General.[13]

The events of 1975 left a bitter legacy and remain a *cause célèbre* to this day, more than 30 years later. In Australia, November 11 is a day of remembrance in more than one respect! Today "the Crisis" serves as a reminder of the vast reserve powers of the Crown in many parliamentary democracies. It also underscores the importance of conventions that preclude the use of such powers in all but the most extraordinary circumstances. Finally, it sounds a cautionary note about the difficulty, if not impossibility, of combining an all-powerful elected senate—one capable of blocking a budget—with a parliamentary system of responsible government.

1 When two Labor-held seats in the Senate had become vacant several months earlier, convention dictated that the vacancies be filled by nominees of the Labor Party; that way, party standings in the Senate, as of the previous Senate election, would be maintained. Instead, the state governments of New South Wales and Queensland, both ruled by opposition parties, chose to fill the seats with their own supporters. As a result of these breaches of constitutional convention, the Opposition gained effective control of the Senate.

discretion. In 1926, Canada's governor general, Lord Byng, did refuse to grant a dissolution requested by the prime minister, William Lyon Mackenzie King, creating a political uproar that came to be known as the King–Byng Affair.

Some believe that the lesson of the King–Byng Affair is that the Governor General may never again refuse the request of a PM for a dissolution. That view is certainly wrong. Constitutional experts agree that there are still circumstances in which the GG would be perfectly entitled to refuse a dissolution request.[14] What if a PM insisted on calling a series of elections merely because he was dissatisfied with the results? While such a scenario might seem unlikely, it is a possibility.[15]

Parliamentary, Presidential, and Semi-presidential Systems

As discussed in Chapter 6, the distinction between confederal, federal, and unitary states has to do with the vertical distribution of power between national and subnational governments. But what about the horizontal distribution of power within one level of government or the other? Here we may distinguish between parliamentary, presidential, and semi-presidential systems.

Parliamentary Systems

The parliamentary form of government, in its modern form, originated in Great Britain in the 18th century and has been widely imitated throughout the world. Countries having a parliamentary system include Canada, Australia, Germany, Japan, and Sweden. While there are important national variations in the form and function of parliamentary systems, certain essential features may be identified. First, parliamentary systems have a dual executive consisting of a separate head of state and head of government. A second feature of parliamentary systems has to do with the relationship between the executive and the legislative branches of government. In parliamentary systems based on the British ("Westminster") model, there is an overlapping of powers and personnel between the two branches, which arises from the fact that the PM and members of the cabinet simultaneously hold office in both. As elected members of the legislature, the PM and cabinet (usually referred to more simply as "the government") are intimately involved in parliamentary affairs, from introducing government bills to responding to questions from opposition MPs. Indeed, the prime minister and cabinet dominate the parliamentary agenda, starting with the **Speech from the Throne**, an outline of what the government hopes to achieve in any given session of parliament. At the same time, the PM and cabinet are responsible for discharging the executive functions of the state. As such, their duties include administering the daily operations of government departments and exercising a host of executive powers, from conducting foreign relations with other states to appointing hundreds of public officeholders, such as judges, ambassadors, senior civil servants, and the heads of various agencies, boards, and commissions. This intersection of the two branches of government in the PM and cabinet is known as the **fusion of powers**.

A third feature of parliamentary systems is the doctrine of **responsible government**, according to which the government may hold office only as long as it maintains majority support in the legislature. If the government is defeated on a vote of confidence, it must resign or seek early elections. In Westminster systems, the prime minister also has the discretion to call an early general election, even if the government retains the confidence of parliament. This point is discussed further below.

Parliamentary systems based on the Westminster model entail an enormous concentration of power in the hands of the PM and cabinet. This is especially so in cases where the governing party has an absolute majority of seats in parliament; that is, a **majority government**. Moreover, political parties tend to be highly disciplined and cohesive in parliament; after all, the governing party cannot afford to lose a vote of confidence. As a result, it is customary for MPs belonging to the same party to vote as a bloc on bills and resolutions before parliament.

Advantages of Parliamentary Government Parliamentary constitutions have many advantages. First, a government with a stable parliamentary majority is able to act decisively to implement its legislative program. This is equally true whether the government is formed by a single party or by a durable multiparty coalition. More specifically, parliamentary governments are well equipped to adopt measures designed to serve the national interest, even if such measures be opposed by powerful sectional groups in the country. Indeed, disciplined parties, while disparaged by many Canadians, provide individual MPs with some degree of protection against the efforts of powerful lobby groups to influence the votes they cast in parliament.[16] Second, by concentrating political power in the PM and cabinet, parliamentary systems clarify political responsibility. The opposition parties in parliament hold the government to account both for its policies and its administrative competence. Equally, general elections in parliamentary systems tend to offer electors a choice between parties campaigning on national issues, rather than being a series of contests among individual candidates on local issues.

Third, the mechanism of the **non-confidence vote** allows for the removal of a government that has lost support in parliament. Such was the case in Britain in March 1979, when the Labour government of James Callaghan was defeated in the House of Commons—by a single vote—and was obliged to call an early election. In Canada a similar fate befell the Liberal Government of Paul Martin in November 2005.

Disadvantages of Parliamentary Government A leading criticism of parliamentary systems is that they vest excessive power in the hands of the government. According to Lord Hailsham, a former British politician, a majority government constitutes an "elective dictatorship," since it faces no effective check on its power in parliament. This is especially true of parliamentary systems such as those of Canada and Great Britain, in which the electoral system tends to give one party an absolute majority of seats and in which the upper house of parliament lacks effective power.

Another criticism of parliamentary systems is that by engendering disciplined national parties, they leave MPs less free to represent local interests, particularly where those interests conflict with the policy of the party to which an MP belongs. MPs affiliated with the governing party are especially constrained in this regard.

Finally, parliamentary government can be unstable if no party is able to secure majority support in parliament. This has been the experience of Italy, where there have been over 50 changes of government since 1945. Governments in France under the Fourth Republic (1946–58) were also notoriously short-lived. On the other hand, as many commentators have noted, postwar governments in Italy and Fourth-Republic France were less unstable than they appeared. Typically, the same coalition partners remained in office following a change of government, key ministers were reappointed to the same portfolios, and major government policies continued in force.

Presidential Systems

The presidential (or congressional) form of government originated in the United States in the 1780s. Although not as widely practised as its parliamentary counterpart, it has been adopted by most Central and South American states. The U.S. presidential system was designed with a view to avoiding an undue concentration of political power in any single branch of government. Consequently, there is a strict **separation of powers** among the executive, the legislature, and the judiciary.

Under a presidential system, executive functions are consolidated in the president, who is both head of state and head of government (known as the *administration*). Legislative powers are assigned to the bicameral Congress, which comprises the Senate and the House of Representatives. On the relationship between the legislature and the executive, it is more accurate to say that there is a separation of personnel and a sharing, rather than a separation, of powers. For one, the president and all members of the cabinet are barred from sitting in Congress while holding executive office.[17] In addition, presidential elections are held independently from congressional elections. Thus, while the president is elected every four years, elections for the House of Representatives are held every two years; senators, meanwhile, serve six-year terms, one-third of the Senate being up for election every two years.

The exercise of executive and legislative powers is subject to a complex system of **checks and balances**. Bills passed by both houses of Congress may be vetoed by the president. Congress, in turn, may override a presidential **veto** by a two-thirds majority vote of both houses. This sharing of legislative power by the two branches is also reflected in the joint exercise of certain executive powers. For example, key presidential appointments, from cabinet secretaries to federal judges to the heads of key executive agencies, must be formally confirmed by the Senate. Similarly, treaties negotiated by the president must be ratified by a minimum two-thirds majority vote of the Senate.

Since both branches have fixed terms of office, the president may not dissolve Congress to hold early elections; by the same token, Congress may not remove a president in whom it no longer has confidence, except by the extraordinary procedure of impeachment. Under Article II (Section 4) of the U.S. Constitution, the president may be impeached for "Treason, Bribery, or other high Crimes and Misdemeanours." If articles of impeachment are approved by the House of Representatives, the matter proceeds to the Senate, where the president can be removed from office on a two-thirds majority vote. No U.S. president has been successfully impeached, although Richard Nixon resigned the presidency in 1974 after articles of impeachment were passed by the House Judiciary Committee.[18]

The Case For and Against Presidential Government Proponents of presidentialism cite various points in its favour. Among other things, it is argued that presidential executives are stable owing to their constitutionally fixed terms and to the provision made for the automatic installation of the vice-president in case the president is unable to complete his or her term. At minimum, these features of presidentialism help to avoid the frequent changes of government to which parliamentary systems may be susceptible. It has also been observed that presidents have a larger pool of talent from which to make cabinet appointments than do prime ministers in Westminster systems. Not being restricted to persons who have been elected to parliament, presidents may appoint cabinet secretaries from the ranks of business, academia, or other institutions.

Presidentialism also gives the legislature a more meaningful role as a lawmaking body by allowing members of the congress to defeat, or substantially amend, a bill sponsored by the president without automatically removing the president from office. Parliamentary executives, in contrast, too often hold the latter prospect like a hammer over the heads of MPs to cow them into supporting the government's measures. Congressional legislators therefore enjoy greater freedom from party discipline and have more scope to represent local interests. But the leading argument made in support of presidentialism is that the diffusion of political authority safeguards individual liberty against unreasonable encroachment by the state.[19]

Critics of presidentialism deplore its tendency to produce deadlock between the two branches of government. This feature of presidential systems arises from the diffusion of decision-making authority and the reciprocal vetoes held by the executive and legislative branches. Moreover, being separately elected, each branch can claim to have a mandate from the people and, for that reason, may be unwilling to reach a compromise with the other branch. And since the president lacks the power to dissolve congress, there is no effective means to end the impasse. In the United States, the fragmentation of political authority arguably has helped well-funded lobby groups to block the adoption of such measures as effective gun control and universal health insurance. A related shortcoming of presidentialism is the difficulty that voters face in assigning responsibility for political decisions (or political inaction) under a system of dispersed decision-making authority. This difficulty is compounded by the organizational looseness of national parties and by the tendency for congressional candidates to campaign for election on local rather than national issues.[20]

Proponents of presidential government reply to these points by noting the capacity of a strong president to unify the nation and to command considerable political authority. As the only officeholder to be elected by the nation as a whole, the president can claim to have a truly national mandate. In addition, presidents derive considerable authority from their dual status as head of state and head of government, not to mention their role as commander-in-chief of the armed forces. Indeed, the prestige of the office can transform even a mediocre politician into a statesman in the eyes of many ordinary citizens. In times of national crisis, this symbolic resource can be a considerable asset for presidents as they seek to mobilize support from Congress and the nation. On the other hand, critics are quick to note the vulnerability of presidential systems when the chief executive brings the office into disrepute. When U.S. President Richard Nixon was implicated in criminal behaviour in the Watergate affair of 1972–1974, his status as head of state created a crisis of legitimacy in the institution of the presidency. Presidentialism can also exhibit antidemocratic features, as when presidents (and their supporters) equate legitimate political opposition to the head of state with disloyalty to the state itself.[21] To critics of presidentialism, such as Juan Linz, it is no coincidence "that most of the countries with presidential constitutions have been unstable democracies or authoritarian regimes."[22]

Another point of contention between advocates of parliamentary and presidential government concerns the question of prior political experience. In parliamentary systems, prime ministers usually come into office after many years of service in parliament and in senior cabinet positions. As such, they bring to the office direct knowledge of national politics and the inner workings of cabinet government. In presidential systems, the chief executive is more likely to take office with little or no prior experience in national government. In the U.S. four of the five most recent presidents were state governors prior to their election to the White House. While presidential candidates often seek to make a virtue of their status as Washington "outsiders," it is debatable whether inexperience in national government is a desirable quality for the leader of a major democracy, let alone a world superpower.

Semi-presidential Systems

A halfway house between parliamentary and presidential systems is the so-called semi-presidential form of government. Semi-presidential systems combine elements of parliamentary and presidential government; in a broad definition, they combine a popularly elected president with a parliamentary prime minister.[23] Unlike the head of state of a parliamentary republic, the president has real power and the authority to use it. The quintessential example of a semi-presidential system is France under the Fifth Republic, especially since 1962 when the presidency became a popularly elected office. Other examples of semi-presidential systems include Finland, Russia, and several of the new democracies of Eastern Europe, including Poland, Romania, and Bulgaria (see Table 7.1).[24]

Sometimes the label "semi-presidential" is applied to any parliamentary system having a directly elected president. By this broad definition, countries such as Austria and the Republic of Ireland would be classified as semi-presidential systems. But as Lijphart points out, the real test of a semi-presidential system is whether the president, rather than the prime minister, is the preeminent head of government.[25] In states such as Russia and France, the president is usually in charge. While leaving the day-to-day business of government in the hands of the prime minister, the president reserves the right to intervene in matters of policy and administration. The president may even sack a prime minister who still has the confidence of parliament.[26]

France is an interesting case because the president's wide powers, which are largely unwritten, are significantly curtailed when parties opposed to the president win control of the National Assembly. In that case, the president is obliged to appoint a prime minister acceptable to the new parliament. In such periods of cohabitation, France functions much like a parliamentary republic, with the notable exception that the president retains responsibility for foreign affairs and can dissolve the National Assembly on his own initiative before the expiration of its five-year term.

Table 7.1 Selected Parliamentary, Presidential, and Semi-presidential States

Parliamentary	Presidential	Semi-presidential
Australia	Argentina	Belarus
Belgium	Brazil	Bulgaria
Canada	Chile	Finland
India	Costa Rica	France
Italy	Indonesia	Lithuania
Jamaica	Mexico	Poland
Japan	Nigeria	Romania
Norway	Philippines	Russia
Spain	United States	South Korea
United Kingdom	Venezuela	Ukraine

Source: Based, inter alia, on Robert Elgie, "The Classification of Democratic Regime Types: Conceptual Ambiguity and Contestable Assumptions," European Journal of Political Research *33(2) (1998): 228.*

The Chief Executive: Prime Ministers Versus Presidents

Prime ministers and presidents sit at the apex of power in parliamentary and presidential systems of government. As chief executives, they are widely seen to have ultimate responsibility for the executive branch as a whole, even though much of their decision-making authority is formally shared with other political actors. This point was famously made by U.S. President Harry S. Truman: a sign on Truman's desk proclaimed, "The buck stops here." Let us examine the vastly different institutional settings in which prime ministers and presidents operate, their status and powers, and the political institutions that enhance and constrain the exercise of power.

The Prime Minister

In parliamentary systems, the political executive consists of the **prime minister** and **cabinet**. In fact, parliamentary government is sometimes called **cabinet government**, a phrase that denotes the fact that the cabinet is the decision-making centre. More specifically, government policy is formally set by the cabinet through a collective and collegial process of decision-making. According to this theory of cabinet government, the prime minister is *primus inter pares* (first among equals) at the cabinet table.

The office of prime minister originated in Great Britain in the 18th century. Sir Robert Walpole is generally considered Britain's first prime minister. During Walpole's long premiership (1721–42) certain conventions of cabinet government began to take form. Nevertheless, well into the 19th century, monarchs continued to exert personal influence over affairs of state because of their capacity to buy the allegiance of members of parliament elected from "pocket boroughs" (parliamentary districts containing small numbers of eligible voters). The *Reform Act* of 1832 abolished most of the pocket boroughs, thereby requiring MPs to reflect more faithfully the views of their constituents. Henceforth, the king would be obliged to appoint a prime minister who was Parliament's first choice, if not necessarily the king's.[27] As a result of these developments, the prime minister emerged as the effective head of government. According to Bagehot, the rights of the monarch in relation to the prime minister could now be summed up as follows: "the right to be consulted, the right to encourage, and the right to warn."[28] The monarch no longer had the right to refuse the advice of a prime minister having the confidence of the cabinet and of parliament.[29]

If the 19th century saw political power shift decisively from the crown to parliament, the 20th century saw a comparable power shift from parliament to the political executive. Meanwhile, within the executive itself in recent years, more and more power has become concentrated in the hands of the prime minister at the expense of the cabinet as a whole. Before exploring this question, let us identify the principles of cabinet government and discuss the formal role of the PM.

Principles of Cabinet Government The following are three core principles of cabinet government in Westminster systems such as Canada's:

- **Collective responsibility**. This term means that all members of the government ("the ministry") are collectively responsible to parliament for government policy and for the overall performance of the government. Thus, when a minister introduces a bill into parliament on behalf of his or her ministry, that bill is taken to be a statement of government policy. The defeat in parliament of a bill introduced by a particular minister is therefore treated as a repudiation of the policy of the government as a whole. As noted earlier, the defeat of an important government bill is treated as a vote of non-confidence and has the effect of bringing down the government.

- **Cabinet solidarity**. This term refers to the constitutional obligation of all ministers to publicly support the policy of the government. Cabinet meetings are held behind closed doors and are subject to strict rules of cabinet secrecy. Ministers can feel free to speak candidly about proposed government policies and actions; however, once cabinet has reached a decision, all ministers are obliged to explain and defend it in public. This practice enables parliament to identify the policy of the government and thus to hold the cabinet collectively responsible for it.

Any minister who is unable to support the decisions of his or her colleagues must resign from the cabinet. In Britain, it is not uncommon for ministers to resign from the cabinet on matters of principle. For example, in 2003, Robin Cook and Clare Short, two members of Tony Blair's government, resigned from the ministry to protest the government's decision to participate in the U.S.-led invasion of Iraq. In 1990, Geoffrey Howe, a senior minister in Margaret Thatcher's government, resigned in protest against the Prime Minister's policy toward Europe and her autocratic style of leadership. In Britain, resigning ministers tend to make a big splash when they depart the government by giving a resignation speech in the House of Commons—delivered while the PM sits a few yards away trying to look nonchalant!

In Canada, it is relatively rare for ministers to resign because of philosophical or policy differences with their colleagues. A recent exception to that rule occurred in November 2006 when Michael Chong resigned from the Cabinet of Stephen Harper to protest the Government's decision to designate the Québécois as a nation (see Chapter 6). However, it is more common for ministers to resign as a result of their being caught up in political scandals.

- **Ministerial responsibility**. This term refers to the responsibility of individual ministers to parliament. Ministers have political responsibility for the administration of their departments and for the actions of all the officials who work in those departments. In other words, the minister must answer to parliament for the efficiency (or inefficiency) with which his or her department is run. Under this doctrine, a minister is responsible not only for his or her own actions and decisions, but also for the actions and decisions taken by officials in the department—whether or not the minister was aware of them. In other words, the minister is the public face of the department and must take *political* responsibility for it.

Holding Government to Account In formal terms, there are various mechanisms for holding the executive accountable for its conduct in parliamentary systems. The oldest form of parliamentary control of the executive is the power of the purse—that is to say, the requirement that parliament authorize public spending and the imposition of new taxes by the executive. Parliament also has the opportunity to scrutinize public expenditures after the fact when ministries prepare detailed public accounts; in Canada, these records are examined by an independent officer, the Auditor General, whose annual report is then submitted to Parliament. Shortly before Jean Chrétien stepped down as prime minister in 2003, Auditor General Sheila Fraser delivered a scathing indictment of the way in which federal advertising and sponsorship contracts had been tendered by the Department of Public Works in the years following the 1995 Quebec referendum on independence. The political outcry that ensued led Chrétien's successor, Paul Martin, to appoint a judicial enquiry into the so-called sponsorship scandal.

On a day-to-day basis, ministers are obliged to explain and defend government policy and executive actions through the oral question period as well as through routine debates in parliament. Ministers and senior civil servants are also expected to appear before parliamentary committees.

From time to time, opposition parties demand the resignation of a minister for maladministration. While such demands are rarely complied with, ministers are more likely to resign if they are deemed to be personally responsible for a questionable action than if the fault lies with subordinates in the minister's department. In either case, the minister is obliged to answer to parliament. This dilution of the doctrine of ministerial responsibility has led some to identify a new doctrine of ministerial answerability.[30] The general rule nowadays appears to be that the prime minister decides whether to request the minister's resignation, on the basis of an assessment of the minister's overall usefulness to the government.

Beyond the formal institutions of parliament, the news media can act as an important agent of government accountability. While the media are usually drawn to the more sensational and melodramatic aspects of political life, investigative journalists nevertheless can expose serious cases of executive misconduct or bring to light the consequences of ill-conceived government policies. Adverse news coverage, in turn, can act as a spur to corrective action. On the other hand, the fear of politically damaging media reports may deter government officials from pursuing bold and necessary reforms.

Prime Ministerial Government The prime minister occupies a position of preeminent power in Westminster systems. As noted above, many observers have detected a long-term trend toward the growing concentration of decision-making power in the hands of the PM at the expense of the cabinet. On this view, cabinet government has been superseded by **prime ministerial government**.[31] An early cartoon depicting this phenomenon is reproduced here.

'And now that we're reshuffled — onwards and upwards!'

This 1967 cartoon depicts the governing style of British Prime Minister Harold Wilson.

William Papas, "And now that we're reshuffled - onwards and upwards!", The Guardian, 7 January 1967 ; The British Cartoon Archive, University of Kent, catalogue record 10434 at http://www.kent.ac.uk/cartoons/

Others dispute this dire assessment; in their view, there remain significant checks on the powers of prime ministers. Nevertheless, it cannot be doubted that prime ministers have wide decision-making powers. Some of these powers are based on written or unwritten rules of the constitution. Other powers have a legal basis in collective decisions of the cabinet to delegate certain heads of authority directly to the PM. Among the most important powers that are wielded by the prime minister, we may count the following:

- *To make appointments to cabinet.* The prime minister names the members of the cabinet, who are then sworn into office by the head of state. In Westminster systems, the only constitutional requirement to be met is the need for ministers to have a seat in parliament (normally the lower house of a bicameral legislature). The prime minister also has the power to remove ministers from the cabinet or to reassign them to other portfolios (called a cabinet shuffle).

- *To determine the organization of cabinet and of government departments.* Every prime minister has the discretion to determine how large the cabinet shall be. In a small cabinet, some ministers will have responsibility for two or more departments of government. Alternatively, the PM may choose to merge separate departments into a smaller number of large departments. When he took office in 1984, Prime Minister Brian Mulroney formed a cabinet of 40, while in 1993, Jean Chrétien formed a cabinet that was barely half as large. But Chrétien created a second tier of junior ministers, called secretaries of state, modelled on British practice. Not having cabinet rank, junior ministers played no formal role in formulating government policy; their role was to assist cabinet ministers in the performance of certain administrative and parliamentary duties.

- *To call a general election.* By convention, the prime minister has sole authority to advise the head of state on the timing of a general election, within the normal lifespan of a parliament. As noted, this advice is usually followed. Armed with this power, the PM may choose an election date that maximizes the governing party's chances of reelection. As the opposition parties are not privy to the PM's intentions, it is difficult for them to prepare their election campaigns with certainty.

  Some have argued that the PM should not be able to play games with election timing in this way. They contend that elections should be held at fixed intervals, as in the United States. In Canada, several provinces have passed laws establishing fixed election dates. As noted in Chapter 6, a similar law governing federal elections was adopted by Parliament in 2007. In all of these cases, an early election may still be triggered by the defeat of the government on a confidence vote.

- *To make appointments to various posts within the government.* In addition to appointing cabinet ministers, the prime minister also chooses a host of other public officials, such as high-ranking civil servants, senior members of the judiciary, ambassadors, and the heads of state-owned enterprises. Some of these appointments are made on the basis of patronage—i.e., the appointee's main qualification being his or her past political services to the governing party. Ex–cabinet ministers and former members of parliament are often rewarded with government appointments, such as when Prime Minister Stephen Harper appointed former Conservative Finance Minister Michael Wilson as Canada's Ambassador to the United States, rather than appointing a career diplomat.

- *To convene and chair cabinet meetings.* The prime minister can call cabinet meetings at any time, and has various means of influencing its decisions. First, through control of the agenda, prime ministers can ensure that no item of business can come before cabinet without their approval. Thus, if prime ministers are unsure that an important issue will go their way in cabinet, they can keep it off the agenda until they have mobilized sufficient support for their preferred outcome. Second, the prime minister controls the establishment of cabinet committees and determines their membership. The recommendations of these committees go to the full cabinet, where they are usually ratified. Third, instead of calling a vote within cabinet—where the PM might not prevail—the prime minister sums up discussion by articulating the predominant mood of cabinet—as the PM sees it. Even if the prime minister's definition of consensus does not reflect the majority view, the PM's summation becomes the official position of the government and is recorded as such in the minutes. At that point, the doctrine of cabinet solidarity obliges all ministers to defend the policy of the government or to resign from cabinet.

- *To act as chief spokesperson for the government.* Occasionally, when journalists pose questions to ministers about the pressing issues of the day, a minister will go out on a limb and state a position that is inconsistent with government policy as the PM sees it. In that case, the PM will usually make a statement purporting to explain what the errant minister really intended to say! In such cases, the minister invariably endorses the PM's view; as a result, all members of the government are once again in the happy position of singing from the same hymnbook. In the case of a fundamental disagreement between the prime minister and a senior minister, it is understood that the minister must give way. Shortly after the election of the Socialist–Green coalition government in Germany in 1998, a serious disagreement about economic policy broke out between Chancellor Gerhard Schroeder and his finance minister, Oskar Lafontaine. When Lafontaine refused to back down, he was obliged to resign.

Limits on Prime Ministerial Power Despite their undoubted power, prime ministers cannot act with impunity. To be a successful leader, the prime minister needs to be aware of important political constraints and to exercise power with discretion. The nature of such constraints varies from one state to another and can even vary over time within a single state.

In the matter of cabinet formation, the PM may wish to appoint all of his or her closest political allies, but there are other considerations that cannot be ignored. For example, in most European countries national elections are conducted using some form of proportional representation (PR). One of the characteristics of PR-based elections is that single-party majority governments are rarely formed; instead, one of the major parties is obliged to enter into a coalition with one or more of the other parties represented in parliament. In such cases, prime ministers must reach agreement with their coalition partners on the allocation of cabinet posts. Even if the government is formed by a single party, the prime minister must be mindful of certain political realities. If the governing party contains distinctive ideological camps, party unity may demand that major currents of opinion be adequately represented in cabinet.

In other countries, the importance of ideology may be overshadowed by the need to ensure that major social groups and regional populations are represented in the cabinet. In Canada, the prime minister is expected to ensure that at least one MP from each province has a seat at the cabinet table. Canadian prime ministers must also maintain an appropriate balance of anglophone and francophone ministers. It should be added that in all Western democracies today, prime ministers are expected to provide at least some representation for women in the cabinet (see Box 7.3).

To the extent that ministers need to acquire specialized knowledge of their department, they rely on the expertise of permanent officials in the department. Critics contend that this reliance on senior bureaucrats is a recipe for ministers to become captive to the interests of their departments.

Interestingly, the internal rules of the governing party may also curtail the power of the prime minister. For example, under the constitution of the Australian Labor Party (ALP), members of the cabinet are to be elected by members of the Labor caucus in parliament. A Labor prime minister may, however, assign cabinet members to specific portfolios. Party constitutions also determine the procedure by which a party leader may be removed. If the party is in power, removal of the leader

Odd as it may seem, prime ministers are not unduly concerned, when forming a cabinet, that a minister possess expertise in the subject matter of his or her portfolio. Thus, it is not thought necessary to appoint a physician minister of health or a retired general minister of defence. The role of the minister is to act as political head of the department; accordingly, he or she is expected to defend its interests at the cabinet table, to explain and promote government policy in parliament and the country, and to ensure that the department is soundly administered. To fulfil these functions, the minister requires *political* skills, which are usually honed as a result of years of parliamentary experience.

entails a change of prime minister. In some parties, the leader can be removed by his or her parliamentary colleagues with remarkable dispatch. In this way, Margaret Thatcher was forced to step down as British Conservative Party leader and prime minister in 1990. Likewise, the National Party prime minister of New Zealand, Jim Bolger, was ousted by his colleagues in 1997. In other parties, the leader is elected by a vote of the party's rank-and-file or by a vote of elected delegates at a party convention. These extraparliamentary methods of selecting and deselecting leaders are said to promote internal party democracy and to make party leaders more accountable to their members. Paradoxically, leaders who are elected outside parliament appear to have a more secure grip on power.[32]

While there has undoubtedly been a long-term trend toward the concentration of power in the hands of prime ministers, not all first ministers are able or even willing to centralize power to the same degree. The balance of power between the prime minister and the cabinet is conditioned by such factors as the PM's personality and governing style. While some prime ministers choose to centralize power in their office, others prefer a more collegial style of governance in which the advice of cabinet is both sought and heeded. The prime minister's ability to dominate cabinet is also conditioned by the calibre of the ministers. If there are strong personalities around the table, prime ministers are less likely to be successful in bending the cabinet to their will. The PM's authority also hinges on the government's position in parliament. Other things being equal, a prime minister must be more conciliatory toward cabinet (and caucus) colleagues when the government is in a minority position in parliament; in such cases, the PM must also exercise more tact in dealing with the opposition parties. On the other hand, prime ministers who have just led their party to a resounding election victory are in a strong position to assert their authority in cabinet, in caucus, and in parliament.

The President

In certain respects, presidents command wider authority than prime ministers. Article II of the U.S. Constitution vests executive power in the president alone. Accordingly, "[t]he president is not first among equals; he is explicitly 'number one,' the person in charge."[33] The cabinet is not, therefore, a body for collective decision-making. While the president may consult individual members of the cabinet (called "cabinet secretaries" in the U.S.), he is under no obligation to do so. In other words, the policy of the administration on all matters is ultimately that of the president. The president also derives considerable political authority from the fact that he is directly elected by the people, unlike a prime minister.[34]

On the other hand, as noted earlier, presidents are subject to a host of formal checks and balances. For example, in the U.S. only Congress can create new departments and agencies and authorize the funds necessary to run them. Moreover, the president must formally submit cabinet nominees to the senate for confirmation. This requirement also applies to other senior executive appointments, including ambassadorships and the heads of major federal agencies such as the FBI, the CIA, and the Federal Communications Commission, as well as the Supreme Court bench. Senate confirmation hearings are not a mere formality; indeed, it is not unheard of for the senate to reject presidential nominees. In 2005, President George W. Bush was forced to withdraw his nomination of Harriet Miers for the Supreme Court in the face of strong opposition from members of the Senate Judiciary Committee. The President's substitute nominee, Samuel Alito, met with the approval of most senators and was duly confirmed.

One striking difference between presidential and parliamentary executives lies in the field of foreign affairs. In Westminster parliamentary systems, the political executive has exclusive authority over foreign relations, including the power to conclude treaties, to commit troops overseas, and even to declare war. The formal approval of parliament is not required in these cases; it must be said, however, that governments will often allow parliament to vote on such matters in order to lend greater legitimacy to the decisions taken by the prime minister and cabinet. For example, the parliament of Canada formally approved a resolution declaring war on Germany in September 1939. In 2003, British Prime Minister Tony Blair yielded to pressure from backbench members of his own party to hold a debate in parliament on the deployment of British troops in Iraq.

In presidential systems, the president must submit treaties to the legislature for ratification, and in the United States, they must be approved by at least two-thirds of the senate. Ratification is not guaranteed in all cases, and in 1979 President Carter withdrew a major arms control treaty (SALT II) he had negotiated with the Soviet Union because it lacked sufficient support in the senate. Article I (Section 8) of the U.S. Constitution gives Congress, not the president, the power to declare war. In practice, this formal limitation has not significantly hampered the ability of presidents to send troops into combat. During the Vietnam War, the Johnson and Nixon administrations committed tens of thousands of troops to Indochina without a formal declaration of war. Instead, following an attack on U.S. ships in the Gulf of Tonkin in 1964, Johnson sought, and obtained, broad congressional approval for combat operations in Southeast Asia. The Gulf of Tonkin resolution authorized the president "to take all necessary measures to repel any armed attack against the forces of the United States and to prevent further aggression."[35]

In 1973, Congress attempted to curtail the president's power to send U.S. troops into combat with the passage of the War Powers Resolution. It requires the president to consult with Congress prior to the start of hostilities and to remove U.S. troops from theatres of combat within 60 days if Congress has not declared war or passed a resolution authorizing the use of force. In practice, this limitation on the power of presidents to wage war has proven to be ineffective. As chief executive and commander-in-chief of the armed forces, the president is in a powerful position to define threats to the security interests of the state. Among other things, the president has access to intelligence information to which most members of Congress are not privy. Moreover, the president in most cases can appeal successfully to the patriotism (if not jingoism) of citizens when embarking on military operations abroad. This point is illustrated by the U.S. Senate's 77–23 vote in October 2002 authorizing the president to use military force against the regime of Saddam Hussein. At that time, the White House insisted that Iraq possessed "weapons of mass destruction" and thereby posed a clear and present danger to the stability of the Middle East, a claim later proven false.[36] Equally unfounded were administration claims that Iraq was behind the September 11 attacks on the World Trade Center and the Pentagon. Figure 7.2 is an organization chart of the whole U.S. government apparatus.

Figure 7.2 Organization of the U.S. Government

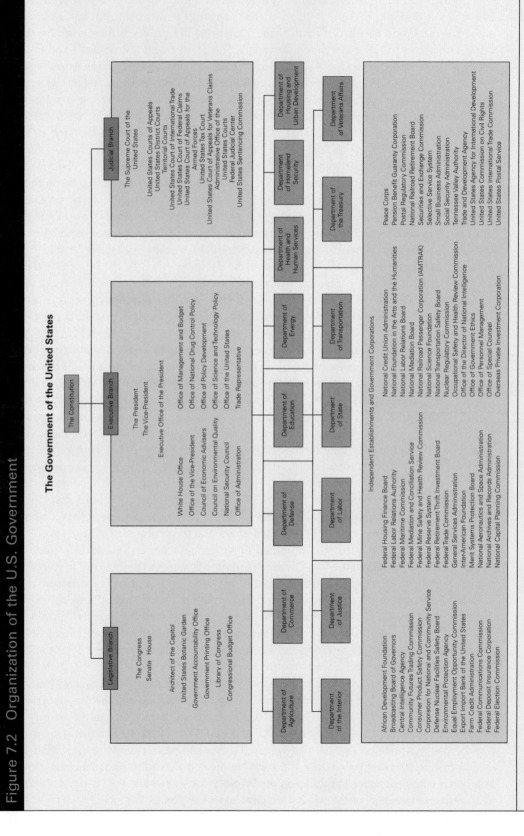

The Government of the United States

The Constitution

Legislative Branch

The Congress
Senate   House

Architect of the Capitol
United States Botanic Garden
Government Accountability Office
Government Printing Office
Library of Congress
Congressional Budget Office

Executive Branch

The President
The Vice-President

Executive Office of the President

White House Office
Office of the Vice-President
Council of Economic Advisers
Council on Environmental Quality
National Security Council
Office of Administration

Office of Management and Budget
Office of National Drug Control Policy
Office of Policy Development
Office of Science and Technology Policy
Office of the United States
Trade Representative

Judicial Branch

The Supreme Court of the
United States

United States Courts of Appeals
United States District Courts
Territorial Courts
United States Court of International Trade
United States Court of Federal Claims
United States Court of Appeals for the
Armed Forces
United States Tax Court
United States Court of Appeals for Veterans Claims
Administrative Office of the
United States Courts
Federal Judicial Center
United States Sentencing Commission

Department of
Agriculture

Department of
the Interior

Department of
Commerce

Department
of Justice

Department of
Defense

Department of
Labor

Department of
Education

Department
of State

Department of
Energy

Department of
Transportation

Department of
Health and
Human Services

Department of
the Treasury

Department
of Homeland
Security

Department of
Housing and
Urban Development

Department
of Veterans Affairs

Independent Establishments and Government Corporations

African Development Foundation
Broadcasting Board of Governors
Central Intelligence Agency
Community Futures Trading Commission
Consumer Product Safety Commission
Corporation for National and Community Service
Defense Nuclear Facilities Safety Board
Environmental Protection Agency
Equal Employment Opportunity Commission
Export-Import Bank of the United States
Farm Credit Administration
Federal Communications Commission
Federal Deposit Insurance Corporation
Federal Election Commission

Federal Housing Finance Authority
Federal Labor Relations Authority
Federal Maritime Commission
Federal Mediation and Conciliation Service
Federal Mine Safety and Health Review Commission
Federal Reserve System
Federal Retirement Thrift Investment Board
Federal Trade Commission
General Services Administration
Inter-American Foundation
Merit Systems Protection Board
National Aeronautics and Space Administration
National Archives and Records Administration
National Capital Planning Commission

National Credit Union Administration
National Foundation in the Arts and the Humanities
National Labor Relations Board
National Mediation Board
National Railroad Passenger Corporation (AMTRAK)
National Science Foundation
National Transportation Safety Board
Nuclear Regulatory Commission
Occupational Safety and Health Review Commission
Office of the Director of National Intelligence
Office of Government Ethics
Office of Personnel Management
Office of Special Counsel
Overseas Private Investment Corporation

Peace Corps
Pension Benefit Guaranty Corporation
Postal Regulatory Commission
National Railroad Retirement Board
Securities and Exchange Commission
Selective Service System
Small Business Administration
Social Security Administration
Tennessee Valley Authority
Trade and Development Agency
United States Agency for International Development
United States Commission on Civil Rights
United States International Trade Commission
United States Postal Service

Source: *The United States Government Manual, 2007–08* (Washington, DC: United States Government Printing Office, 2007).

Central Agencies

Political executives face a formidable challenge in developing public policy and managing the multifaceted operations of the modern state. In an attempt to establish a more efficient and rational system of decision-making, governments have increasingly come to rely on **central agencies**. Unlike government departments, central agencies do not, in the main, have regulatory or program responsibilities. Rather, their mandate is to support the work of the political executive. Three key functions of central agencies are to prepare strategic plans for government; to develop and integrate economic and budgetary policies; and to allocate and manage the human and other resources of government.[37] Central agencies assumed a larger role in Canada and other Western democracies beginning in the 1970s as governments sought to fashion a more coordinated approach to policy-making and to exert more effective control over public spending.

In Canada three key central agencies are the **Prime Minister's Office**, the **Privy Council Office**, and the **Department of Finance**.[38] The Prime Minister's Office (PMO) is staffed by political appointees of the prime minister. Its task is to provide partisan political advice to the PM—advice that civil servants are precluded from giving. Among other things, it assists the PM in developing overarching goals for the government as well as writing speeches and organizing the PM's busy schedule. Not surprisingly, members of the PMO can expect to be replaced when a new prime minister is sworn into office.

The Privy Council Office (PCO) is staffed by civil servants seconded from various government departments. The PCO is headed by the Clerk of the Privy Council and Secretary to the Cabinet, who is the highest-ranking civil servant in Ottawa. Being a nonpartisan agency, the PCO serves the government of the day, regardless of its political stripe. The main roles of the PCO are to coordinate the flow of information to the PM and cabinet and to provide analysis of major policy proposals. The PCO also advises the PM on the organization of government and on the appointment of senior civil servants in government departments and of officials who serve on various agencies, boards, and commissions.

The Department of Finance provides economic expertise to the government. It is responsible for managing the national economy, raising revenue through taxation and other measures, fixing public expenditures, and making economic forecasts. In the 1990s, the Department of Finance had a large say in determining the fate of a wide range of public programs as governments sought to reduce the federal budget deficit through public spending cuts.

In the United States, the president relies on a myriad of central agencies. These include the **Executive Office of the President** (EOP), which employs over 2,000 officials and serves as the functional equivalent of the PMO. Other executive agencies that report directly to the president include the Office of Management and Budget, the National Security Council, and the Council of Economic Advisers. Given the unitary nature of the U.S. political executive, cabinet secretaries, advisors, and other officials constantly seek the ear of the president. The president's Chief of Staff therefore occupies a position of great importance since it is his or her role to act as gatekeeper to the president. Ideally, the Chief of Staff and other key officials in the White House Office keep the president's workload to manageable proportions while ensuring that he or she keeps abreast of crucial issues across the full range of government operations.

The Bureaucracy: The Administrative Arm of Government

So far, we have looked at the upper echelons of the executive branch—the formal executive, the political executive, and the central agencies that support the work of the latter. In numerical terms, these institutions make up but a small fraction of the total membership of the executive branch of government. On a day-to-day basis, the functions of government are carried out by thousands of public servants, commonly called bureaucrats (or functionaries). In this section, we consider some of the functions carried out by bureaucrats and distinguish the role of senior officials from that of line officials. We also identify the organizing principles of the public service and the main structural forms through which bureaucratic authority is exercised. Finally, we address the question of political control of the bureaucracy.

To many people, the term **bureaucracy** carries a negative connotation. It is popularly associated with a rigid adherence to routine, a lack of imagination and compassion in dealing with ordinary citizens, and an obsessive preoccupation with arcane rules and procedures ("red tape"). In North America in particular, disparaging references to the public service are regularly featured in the popular press, where examples of bureaucratic rigidity or incompetence are portrayed as the norm rather than the exception. The rise of neoconservative parties in Western democracies in the 1980s gave added momentum to this unflattering view of the public service.[39] As part of their larger critique of Big Government, neoconservatives routinely denounce the inefficiency of the public sector while extolling what they take to be the inherent superiority of private enterprise. Building on these assumptions, many critics of the public sector insist that government should be run like a business. To others, it is far from clear that the application of business principles to government is either appropriate or desirable.

The German sociologist Max Weber considered bureaucracy to be the most rational form of organization for modern states. He identified the following essential characteristics of a well-ordered bureaucracy:[40]

- hierarchical organization of public offices
- specialization of labour
- decisions based on the application of impersonal rules
- a clear demarcation of legal authority between public offices
- recruitment to the public service on the basis of technical qualifications
- promotion based on seniority or achievement (or both)

In regard to the relationship between bureaucrats and political leaders, Weber did not doubt that the former should be subordinate to the latter. In that respect, he agreed with Woodrow Wilson, a professional political scientist prior to becoming president of the United States. Wilson contended that there should be a clear division between politics and administration—politics being the concern of elected politicians and administration the purview of bureaucrats.[41] In practice, the line between politics and administration is not so clear. Politicians rely heavily on the expertise and advice of senior bureaucrats in formulating public policy. At the same time, lower level bureaucrats must exercise discretion in executing their duties.

Senior Bureaucrats Versus Line Officials

It is useful to distinguish the role of senior bureaucrats from that of subordinate officials. In Canada, the highest-ranking officials in government departments are called **deputy ministers**. In Britain, such officials are called permanent secretaries. They, along with a cadre of senior administrators, have a dual role—they are responsible both for developing policy advice for ministers and for overseeing the administration of government departments. Such officials are sometimes called **mandarins**, a term originally used to denote the senior bureaucrats of Imperial China. Line officials, on the other hand, are concerned with the delivery of government programs and the enforcement of regulations.

Deputy Ministers In Westminster systems, deputy ministers are appointed directly by the prime minister. While they are usually career public servants with a wealth of experience in government service, they may, on occasion, be recruited from outside the public service, usually from academia, nongovernmental organizations, or the corporate world. Some of the leading functions of senior officials include the following:[42]

- *Policy initiation.* A key role of deputy ministers is to advise the political head of the department (the minister) on policy matters. Having expertise in the subject matter of their respective departments, deputy ministers identify issues that need to be addressed and then present their minister with various options for addressing those issues. In cases where the minister himself or herself takes an active interest in policy, it is the responsibility of the deputy minister to provide expert advice on the ways and means by which the minister's goals can be realized.
- *Channel for inputs.* Senior officials serve as a channel for transmitting information, advice, and political demands from pressure groups (and civil society in general) to the minister. Since most government policy originates in departments, it makes sense for organized groups wishing to influence public policy to seek access to senior departmental personnel. In fact, it is usually more fruitful for pressure groups to intervene at this pre-legislative stage of the policy process than to lobby for legislative changes at the parliamentary stage.
- *Rule-making.* After a law has been enacted by parliament, it falls to senior bureaucrats to draft detailed rules and regulations to flesh out the broad strokes of legislation. This post-legislative function is highly significant and is often conducted in close consultation with interested groups. While the minister has final authority to give legal effect to draft regulations, he or she relies heavily on the advice of departmental officials.
- *Management.* Deputy ministers—not ministers—assume the task of managing government departments on a day-to-day basis. While the minister has political responsibility for the department, it is the deputy minister who manages departmental budgets and personnel and ensures the efficient delivery of public programs and services.

Line Officials Line officials are those bureaucrats who interact with the public in the course of delivering government services and enforcing rules and regulations. Two of their leading functions include:

- *Implementation and enforcement.* Most public servants are engaged, directly or indirectly, in the delivery of public programs and services and in the implementation and enforcement of rules and regulations. This is true of tax collectors, customs officers, food safety inspectors, and a host of other functionaries.
- *Interpretation and adjudication.* In the process of implementing public policies and enforcing regulations, bureaucrats necessarily must exercise some discretion. Does a claimed expense qualify for a tax deduction? Does a disability pension application meet the eligibility criteria? Has a prison inmate satisfied the conditions for parole? In all of these cases, bureaucrats must exercise their judgment in applying rules of general application to specific fact situations.

Organizing Principles

As with other aspects of its parliamentary system of government, bureaucracy in Canada is closely modelled on the British civil service. Key defining principles of the Anglo-Canadian administrative state are set out below.

Merit The **merit principle** governs recruitment to, and promotion within, the bureaucracy. It stipulates that positions within the public service should be filled by the best-qualified persons on the basis of competitive entry requirements. This principle is to be distinguished from the earlier spoils system, under which most public offices were filled by **political patronage** appointments. Political patronage worked reasonably well as long as the role of government was fairly limited. However, by the early 20th century, the nature and scope of governmental activity in many countries began to undergo a radical change, with the development of public health measures, the establishment of government-run research labs, the introduction of social security programs, and the growing need for government regulation of various kinds. These new responsibilities required the state to recruit public officials with specialized knowledge and expertise. Competence, not party affiliation, became the new imperative for recruitment.

In Canada, the merit principle was formally enshrined in legislation with the establishment of the Civil Service Commission (CSC) in 1918. In the decades that followed, well-defined procedures were laid down for recruitment to the civil service and for promotion within its ranks. Senior managers are responsible for hiring and promotion within the public service, subject to the procedures laid down by the Public Service Commission, or PSC (successor to the CSC). Any breach of the rules can be appealed to the PSC.

This is not to say that patronage has been, or arguably should be, banished entirely from government service. There remain a number of exempt positions within government departments that may be filled at the discretion of ministers.

Security of Tenure Public servants are protected from arbitrary dismissal by governments. The principle of security of tenure reinforces the idea that the public service is a professional corps of men and women pledged to faithfully execute the functions of the state. In this context, security of tenure does not mean that public servants can never be dismissed. On the contrary, public servants who are found to be negligent, incompetent, or corrupt are subject to a range of disciplinary sanctions, including dismissal. However, discipline is meted out not by the minister but by disciplinary bodies within the public service that operate at arm's length from government in order to ensure their impartiality.

It should also be noted that governments have wide powers to lay off public servants for budgetary reasons or as part of a reorganization of government departments. Indeed, there was a major downsizing of government personnel in Canada and other countries in the 1990s. However, in reducing the number of public servants, the government may not single out a particular individual for dismissal in a deliberate and punitive way.

Political Neutrality The modern era demands strict political neutrality on the part of public servants. This principle goes hand in hand with the previous points about merit and security of tenure. That is to say, public servants are expected to serve the government of the day, whether or not they personally support the party in power or are in accord with its policies. It is the politicians, after all, who must answer for the wisdom and effectiveness, or lack thereof, of the government's policies.

Anonymity Public servants work in relative obscurity. Indeed, when political controversy envelops a government department, it is the minister who answers for the department, pursuant to the doctrine of ministerial responsibility. In such cases, the identity of public servants is generally not disclosed. The reason for maintaining the anonymity of public servants is to prevent them from being drawn into the political crossfire in parliament and the press. If ministers could publicly point the finger of blame at their officials, then ministers would cease to carry political responsibility. Such accusations would also tend to prejudice any internal disciplinary proceeding against the officials in question. All the same, the veil of anonymity is lifted from time to time. This chiefly occurs when public officials are called to testify before parliamentary committees and public inquiries.

Representative Bureaucracy While merit remains the paramount guiding principle of the public service, it has been complemented in recent years by the goal of creating a more representative bureaucracy. The idea here is to foster the development of a public service that more accurately reflects the demographic composition of society. In Canada, the Official Languages Act (1969) was designed in part to promote the recruitment of francophones into the federal public service at a time when its higher levels were almost exclusively populated by anglophones. In more recent years, the federal government has striven to promote the recruitment of various groups that are underrepresented in the public service, particularly at managerial levels. Four groups have been targeted since the mid-1980s: women, Aboriginals, people with disabilities, and visible minorities.[43]

Bureaucratic Structures

Government bureaucracies are organized into a bewildering variety of institutions. Three of the organizational forms through which bureaucratic authority is exercised are government departments, regulatory agencies, and state-owned corporations. A key distinction among them has to do with the extent to which each of them is subject to ministerial control and direction. The extent of ministerial direction runs along a continuum; it is highest in the case of departments and lowest in the case of state-owned industries.

Government departments are formally headed by a minister, who is responsible both for policy and administration. In reality, ministers rely heavily on their deputy minister in discharging both functions. As political head of the department, the minister takes the department's policy proposals to cabinet while explaining and defending its existing policies in parliament and the country. The deputy minister assumes responsibility for the day-to-day administration of the department, for most ministers have neither the time nor the skill to micromanage their departments.

In Westminster systems departments are subject to scrutiny in parliament through the Estimates system. That is to say, every department is required to draw up detailed spending plans for the year, which are tabled in parliament. The Estimates are then sent to parliamentary committees, where MPs have an opportunity to grill the minister, and sometimes the deputy minister, not only on the department's spending plans but also on the operations of programs and services delivered by the department. The Estimates must be formally voted on and approved by parliament before the government may seek authority to appropriate public money to fund its spending plans. At the end of the financial year, departments prepare reports on how they have spent their budgets. They are audited by the auditor general, whose report is reviewed by the public accounts committee of parliament.

Because the minister is political head of the department, departmental affairs frequently become the target of opposition party attacks in parliament. For example, in the years when the post office was a government department, the Postmaster General would always be bombarded by opposition questions during a national postal strike. In the late 1970s, the post office was converted into a Crown corporation. This change of organizational form gave the managers of Canada Post more freedom from ministerial control to manage the postal service. At the same time, by establishing a more arm's-length relationship between the government and the post office, the government became somewhat more insulated from the political flak that greeted unpopular decisions taken by Canada Post—such as the closure of rural post offices and continual increases in the price of stamps!

Regulatory Agencies The term *regulatory agency* embraces a wide range of agencies, boards, and commissions. A task common to all of them is the interpretation and application of regulations under various statutes (acts of parliament). To the extent that this role involves court-like functions, certain regulatory agencies are referred to as "quasi-judicial" bodies. For example, the Immigration and Refugee Board acts like a court in determining whether an applicant for landed immigrant status or refugee protection has met the relevant statutory and regulatory requirements and has been dealt with properly by the bureaucracy.

Members of regulatory agencies are appointed by the PM, the relevant minister, or the cabinet as a whole under the authority of enabling legislation. Given the quasi-judicial nature of many regulatory bodies, however, they must be free from ministerial interference to decide individual cases. It is improper, therefore, for a minister to direct, or even to lobby, a regulatory agency as to how it should decide a particular application that is before it. On the other hand, it is permissible for the cabinet to issue policy directives to regulatory agencies. The purpose of such directives is to clarify the policy purposes underpinning a particular body of regulations. For example, if the CRTC were consistently lenient toward broadcasters that failed to meet Canadian-content requirements, it would be permissible for the Cabinet to issue a directive requiring the commissioners to interpret the relevant regulations more stringently. Regulatory agencies are subject to less searching scrutiny by parliament than government departments.

State-Owned Corporations State-owned corporations (known in Canada as **Crown corporations**) are established by government to fulfil a variety of public policy purposes, such as the promotion of regional economic development, the advancement of arts and culture, or the provision of transportation services. Such corporations are subject to the least ministerial control. The cabinet appoints a board of directors, which in turn appoints a president and other senior executives to manage the corporation. Unlike a publicly traded company owned by shareholders, a crown corporation is wholly owned by the government.

However, unlike deputy ministers in government departments, who must comply with the rules of the Public Service Commission when making decisions on hiring and promotion, the managers of crown corporations have a freer hand in personnel matters. While some crown corporations are directed to act like a commercial corporation and to turn a profit, many of them require subsidies from the public treasury. For example, every year the CBC receives a subsidy, formally approved by Parliament, to carry out its mandate.

Political Control of the Bureaucracy

Strictly speaking, the government makes policy and the bureaucracy executes it. However, as noted above, the lines between policy and administration are not so clear-cut. In particular, senior bureaucrats play a large role in the development of government policy; likewise, to the extent that implementation requires the use of judgment and discretion, even lower-level bureaucrats can shape the content of public policy. According to constitutional theory, the bureaucracy is subject to control by the government, which in turn is responsible to parliament. Many observers contend that this theory does not always correspond to reality. In particular, it underestimates the inherent power of the bureaucracy. Table 7.2 sets out some of the characteristics of senior bureaucrats and the corresponding ones of ministers.

Table 7.2 Comparison of Characteristics of Bureaucrats and Ministers

Bureaucrats	Ministers
Expert knowledge	General knowledge
Long tenure	Short tenure
Anonymity	Political responsibility

The relationship between senior bureaucrats and their ministers can sometimes be highly unequal. Ministers come to office knowing little or nothing about the workings of their department or the subject matter of their portfolio. Being novices, they must rely on the experience and expertise of their officials. Moreover, because of their relatively short tenure, most ministers are not in a position to pursue far-reaching policy changes—or, at least, not more than one at a time. There are also political risks that innovative ministers must take into account. After all, ministers who put their weight behind a particular initiative within the department know that they will carry full responsibility for any teething problems that it may experience in its early stages. At the same time, a reform-minded minister may not reap the rewards of a successful policy, since it may take years for a new program or policy to bear fruit. By that time, the minister will likely be in another portfolio or perhaps back on the opposition benches.

Winston Churchill once remarked that experts should be "on tap, not on top." Yet many students of bureaucracy—and some former politicians—contend that it is all too easy for ministers to be captured by their senior officials.

Countervailing Power Recognizing the danger that ministers, and the government as a whole, may become unduly influenced by the interests and preferences of the bureaucracy, governments have attempted to enhance their political control of the bureaucracy. Steps toward this end include the following:

- *Turnover of senior officials by a new government.* A new prime minister—particularly one who has just led his or her party to victory at the polls after a long spell in opposition— can signal an intention to pursue a new agenda by replacing some of the top-ranking bureaucrats. While it is inadvisable for a new government to dispense with too many experienced hands at the top, a certain amount of turnover can reinvigorate the bureaucracy as a whole. This practice is more characteristic of changes in administrations in the United States than at the federal level in Canada.
- *Use of political staff.* Nowadays, all governments make use of political advisors to provide them with advice that is independent of the advice generated by the bureaucracy. Such advisors are called "exempt staff" because they are hired outside the normal rules that govern recruitment to the public service. This practice is highly developed in France, where ministers have their own "ministerial cabinet," a body of appointed advisors who serve the minister's political interests and monitor the activities of departmental officials.[44]
- *Enhanced role of central agencies.* One of the functions of central agencies is to counteract the influence of individual departments on the formulation of government policy. In Canada, the enlarged role of the PCO, the Department of Finance, and other central agencies reflects, in part, a strategy of using bureaucrats to check the power of other bureaucrats.
- *Election of a party with clear policy aims.* Other things being equal, a government will be better able to overcome bureaucratic inertia if it comes to office with a clear idea of what it intends to accomplish. This point is well illustrated by the records of reform-minded governments across Canada over the years. Provincial examples include the Saskatch- ewan government of T.C. Douglas (1944–61), the Quebec government of Jean Lesage

(1960–66), and the Ontario government of Mike Harris (1995–2002). Likewise, the British governments of Clement Attlee (1945–51) and Margaret Thatcher (1979–90) and the New Zealand government of David Lange (1984–89) instituted sweeping (and controversial) changes in economic policy and the delivery of government services.

New Public Management: Running Government as a Business

The downsizing of government in many countries in the 1990s did much to mitigate concerns about all-powerful bureaucracies. This development formed part of a larger reconfiguration of the role of government that saw the dismantling of certain elements of the postwar **welfare state**, the **privatization** of many state-owned industries, and the diffusion of **neoliberal**, anti-statist norms embodied in global trade agreements. In Western democracies, a renewed faith in the efficacy of the capitalist marketplace has had important effects on the organization and functioning of the executive branch of government. Increasingly, government services are being outsourced to private contractors, public–private partnerships, or other forms of alternative service delivery. The expectation is that public services can be delivered more efficiently by the private sector or by the application of business principles. The advent of this philosophy, known loosely as the **New Public Management**, has brought in its train a new emphasis on the use of quantifiable measures of performance, the expansion of public choice, and the achievement of efficiency gains, usually expressed in terms of financial cost savings.[45]

The New Public Management (NPM) is still in its formative stages and it is far from clear whether it represents an inexorable trend.[46] It is more advanced in some countries, such as Britain and Australia, than in others, including Canada. Proponents of NPM point out that the goal of using public resources with maximum efficiency is shared by conservative and social democratic governments alike. They also reassert the view that politics should be separated from the technical business of administration.[47]

Critics reply that politics and administration cannot be neatly compartmentalized. Democratic governments must accommodate many different, and often conflicting, political demands. Such demands have to do not only with the ends of public policy but also with the means of realizing them. In choosing among alternative courses of action, efficiency is just one of many considerations.[48] As one observer aptly put it, "one person's red tape is another's due process."[49]

In any case, it may be difficult to measure quantitatively the performance of public bodies. For example, the benefit of health and safety regulations lies in the harm that is avoided, even if the financial costs of regulation can easily be measured. Conversely, the costs of deregulation may only become evident in the long run.

CONCLUSION

The executive branch of government is powerful and pervasive. It provides political leadership for the nation while also having responsibility for the day-to-day administration of government operations. The executive assumes a wide variety of institutional forms, even among states having a shared commitment to democratic values. In this chapter, we considered three main types of executive: parliamentary, presidential, and semi-presidential. In evaluating these different forms of government, it is useful to consider the relative weight each assigns to the goal of firm and effective government and the need for the legislature to hold the executive to account. We should also be mindful of the capacity of the political executive to assert control over the administrative executive.

DISCUSSION QUESTIONS

1. Where does power lie in a parliamentary system?

2. Where does power lie in a presidential system?

3. Discuss the advantages and disadvantages of separating the head of state from the head of government.

4. Are prime ministers too powerful? If so, how should their powers be curtailed?

5. Are the traditional governing principles of Anglo-Canadian bureaucracy still relevant today?

6. Should governments be run like a business?

KEY TERMS

CABINET SOLIDARITY: The constitutional duty of ministers to publicly support the policy of the government. Ministers who openly dissent from government policy must resign from the government. (200)

CENTRAL AGENCIES: Those agencies of the state that assist the political executive to coordinate and control overall government operations. They provide both policy advice and administrative support. (207)

COLLECTIVE RESPONSIBILITY: In Westminster parliamentary systems, members of the political executive are collectively responsible to parliament for government policy and for the overall administrative performance of the government. (199)

DUAL EXECUTIVE: A form of executive in which the posts of head of state and head of government are divided, and each is held by a separate officeholder. In parliamentary systems, the head of state is a constitutional monarch or an elected president and the head of government is the prime minister. (189)

EXECUTIVE: The branch of government concerned with the implementation and enforcement of laws and other authoritative decisions of the state. The executive also formulates public policy and provides political leadership. (187)

FUSION OF POWERS: In parliamentary systems, the joint exercise of legislative and executive powers by the prime minister and members of the cabinet, who simultaneously hold office in the legislative and executive branches of government. (195)

MINISTERIAL RESPONSIBILITY: The responsibility of individual ministers to answer to parliament for the administration of their departments, including the actions of public officials employed in such departments. (200)

RESPONSIBLE GOVERNMENT: A defining principle of Westminster-style parliamentary government, which states that the cabinet may only hold office as long as it has majority support in the legislature (or lower house in a bicameral parliament) on votes of confidence. (195)

SEPARATION OF POWERS: A principle of constitutional government that is usually taken to mean that the legislative, executive, and judicial functions of the state should be carried out by separate branches of government. No one may hold office in more than one branch at the same time. (196)

SINGLE EXECUTIVE: A form of executive in which the posts of head of state and head of government are combined and held by a single officeholder. This arrangement is characteristic of presidential systems, such as those of Argentina, Mexico, and the United States. (189)

WEB LINKS www

Prime Minister's Office:
http://www.pm.gc.ca

Privy Council Office:
http://www.pco-bcp.gc.ca

American Presidency:
http://www.whitehouse.gov
http://www.americanpresidents.org

United Kingdom Prime Minister:
http://www.number-10.gov.uk

Martin Stanley, "How to be a Civil Servant":
http://www.civilservant.org.uk

FURTHER READING

Jones, Charles O. *The Presidency in a Separated System*. 2nd ed. Washington, DC: The Brookings Institution, 2005.

Kelly, Paul. *November 1975: The Inside Story of Australia's Greatest Political Crisis*. St. Leonard's, NSW: Allen and Unwin, 1995.

Lijphart, Arend, ed. *Parliamentary Versus Presidential Government*. Oxford: Oxford University Press, 1992.

Linz, Juan J., and Arturo Valenzuela, eds. *The Failure of Presidential Democracy: Comparative Perspectives*. Vol. 2. Baltimore: Johns Hopkins University Press, 1994.

Peters, B. Guy. *The Politics of Bureaucracy*. White Plains, NY: Longman, 1995.

Pika, Joseph A., and John Anthony Maltese. *The Politics of the Presidency*. 6th ed. Washington, DC: Congressional Quarterly Press, 2004.

Savoie, Donald J. *Court Government and the Collapse of Accountability in Canada and the United Kingdom*. Toronto: University of Toronto Press, 2008.

———. *Governing from the Centre: The Concentration of Power in Canadian Politics*. Toronto: University of Toronto Press, 1999.

ENDNOTES

1. Andrew Heywood, *Politics*, 2nd ed. (Basingstoke, UK: Palgrave, 2002), p. 334.

2. J.H. Baker, *An Introduction to English Legal History*, 4th ed. (London: Butterworths, 2002), chs. 1–2.

3. Walter Bagehot, *The English Constitution*, Introduction by R.H.S. Crossman (Ithaca, NY: Cornell University Press, 1966), pp. 67–68. Originally published in 1867.

4. This rule has been the subject of growing debate in Japan in recent years both because of changing social mores and because the heir apparent to the throne, Crown Prince Naruhito, has yet to produce a male heir. In 2005 a government-appointed commission recommended that the law of succession be changed to allow females to accede to the throne. However, the impetus for change largely dissipated with the news in 2006 that the wife of Crown Prince Naruhito's brother had given birth to a boy, Hisahito, who now stands third in line to the throne.

5. The Commonwealth is a voluntary association of 53 states that were once colonies of the United Kingdom. After achieving political independence, many chose to retain the Queen as their head of state, although the majority, including India and all of the African members, chose to become republics.

6. In Canada, Lieutenant Governors are appointed by the Governor General on the advice of the Prime Minister. In Australia, Governors are appointed by the Queen on the advice of the state premier. See David Butler and D.A. Low, eds., *Sovereigns and Surrogates: Constitutional Heads of State in the Commonwealth* (Basingstoke, U.K.: Macmillan, 1991).

7. Despite the passage of the *Statute of Westminster*, Canada's constitution until 1982 remained a British statute, amendable only by the U.K. parliament. See the discussion in Chapter 6 on the patriation of Canada's constitution.

8. Vernon Bogdanor, *The Monarchy and the Constitution* (Oxford: Clarendon Press, 1995), p. 252.

9. Brian Galligan, *A Federal Republic: Australia's Constitutional System of Government* (Melbourne: Cambridge University Press, 1995), and David E. Smith, *The Invisible Crown: The First Principle of Canadian Government* (Toronto: University of Toronto Press, 1995).

10. Frank MacKinnon, *The Crown in Canada* (Calgary: McClelland and Stewart, 1976).

11. Peter Fraser, "A Revolutionary Governor General? The Grenada Crisis of 1983," in D.A. Low, ed., *Constitutional Heads and Political Crises: Commonwealth Episodes, 1945–1985* (New York: St. Martin's Press, 1988).

12. On the other hand, if the PM is in a hurry to step down, the government caucus may select an interim leader to hold the reins of office pending the holding of a leadership convention.

13. Paul Kelly, *November 1975: The Inside Story of Australia's Greatest Political Crisis*. St. Leonards, NSW: Allen and Unwin, 1995; Colin Howard and Cheryl Saunders, "The Blocking of the Budget and Dismissal of the Government," in Gareth Evans, ed., *Labor and the Constitution, 1972–1975: Essays and Commentaries on the Constitutional Controversies of the Whitlam Years in Australian Government*. Melbourne: Heinemann, 1977; Garfield Barwick, *Sir John Did His Duty*. Wahroonga, NSW: Serendip, 1983.

14. Peter W. Hogg, *Constitutional Law of Canada*, Student Edition (Scarborough: Thomson Carswell, 2006), pp. 290–91.

15. J.R. Mallory, "Crises That Didn't Happen: Canada 1945–1985," in D.A. Low, ed., *Constitutional Heads and Political Crises*, pp. 229–31. The situation in Ontario after the 1985 provincial election is a good example.

16. C.E.S. Franks, *The Parliament of Canada* (Toronto: University of Toronto Press, 1987), p. 96.

17. An exception to that rule in the U.S. concerns the Vice-President, who presides over the Senate and casts the deciding vote in case of a tie.

18. In 1868, impeachment proceedings against President Andrew Johnson failed by a single vote to meet the two-thirds threshold in the Senate. In more recent times, the Senate voted in 1999 to acquit President Bill Clinton in the Monica Lewinsky affair.

19. See Matthew Soberg Shugart and John M. Carey, *Presidents and Assemblies: Constitutional Design and Electoral Dynamics* (Cambridge: Cambridge University Press, 1992).

20. See Juan J. Linz, "Presidential or Parliamentary Democracy: Does It Make a Difference?," in Juan J. Linz and Arturo Valenzuela, eds., *The Failure of Presidential Democracy: Comparative Perspectives*, vol. 2 (Baltimore: Johns Hopkins University Press, 1994).

21. U.S. President George W. Bush arguably strode down this path in his address to a joint session of Congress on September 20, 2001 when he said: "Every nation, in every region, now has a decision to make. Either you are with us, or you are with the terrorists."

22. Juan J. Linz, "Presidential or Parliamentary Democracy," *op. cit.*, p. 4; Alfred Stepan and Cindy Skach, "Constitutional Frameworks and Democratic Consolidation: Parliamentarism Versus Presidentialism," *World Politics* 46(1) (October 1993): 1–22.

23. Maurice Duverger, "A New Political System Model: Semi-presidential Government," *European Journal of Political Research* 8 (June 1980).

24. Karen Henderson and Neil Robinson, *Post-communist Politics: An Introduction* (Hemel Hempstead: Prentice Hall, 1997), p. 168.

25. Arend Lijphart, Patterns of Democracy: Government Forms and Performance in Thirty-Six Countries (New Haven, CT: Yale University Press, 1999), p. 121.

26. Robert Elgie, ed., *Semi-presidentialism in Europe* (Oxford: Oxford University Press, 1999).

27. John P. Mackintosh, *The British Cabinet*, 2nd ed. (London: Methuen, 1968), ch. 3.

28. Walter Bagehot, *The English Constitution*, p. 111.

29. Mackintosh, *The British Cabinet*, p. 118.

30. Paul G. Thomas, "The Changing Nature of Accountability," in B. Guy Peters and Donald J. Savoie, eds., *Taking Stock: Assessing Public Sector Reforms* (Montreal and Kingston: McGill-Queen's University Press), 1998. See also Donald J. Savoie, *Court Government and the Collapse of Accountability in Canada and the United Kingdom* (Toronto: University of Toronto Press, 2008).

31. For a good overview of this debate, see Patrick Weller, *First Among Equals: Prime Ministers in Westminster Systems* (London: Allen and Unwin, 1985). For a Canadian perspective, see Donald J. Savoie, *Governing from the Centre: The Concentration of Power in Canadian Politics* (Toronto: University of Toronto Press, 1999), ch. 4.

32. Thomas M.J. Bateman, "Party Democracy Increases the Leader's Power," *Policy Options* (September 2001): 20–23; and Christopher Moore, "Backbenchers Fight Back," *National Post*, February 13, 2001, p. A16.

33. Norman C. Thomas and Joseph A. Pika, *The Politics of the Presidency*, 4th ed. (Washington, DC: Congressional Quarterly Press, 1997), p. 259.

34. Strictly speaking, U.S. presidents are indirectly elected by the Electoral College, a body of men and women, elected in each state, who are pledged to cast their votes for the presidential candidate who wins the most votes in their state. Ordinarily, the candidate who wins the most votes nationwide also wins a majority of Electoral College votes. However, this was not the case in the presidential election of 2000, when Democratic candidate Al Gore won half a million more votes than Republican candidate George W. Bush. Bush nevertheless won a majority of votes in the Electoral College. See Chapter 10.

35. Walter LaFeber, *America, Russia, and the Cold War, 1945–2006*, 10th ed. (New York: McGraw-Hill, 2008), pp. 250–52.

36. Neither UN nor subsequent U.S. weapons inspectors were able to find evidence of WMDs in Iraq.

37. Colin Campbell, *Governments Under Stress* (Toronto: University of Toronto Press, 1983).

38. Kenneth Kernaghan and David Siegel, *Public Administration in Canada*, 4th ed. (Scarborough: ITP Nelson, 1999), pp. 215–19.

39. Donald J. Savoie, *Thatcher, Reagan, Mulroney: In Search of a New Bureaucracy* (Toronto: University of Toronto Press, 1994), pp. 88–94.

40. Max Weber, *The Theory of Social and Economic Organization* (New York: Oxford University Press, 1947). Originally published in 1922.

41. Woodrow Wilson, "The Study of Administration," *Political Science Quarterly* 2(2) (June 1887).

42. Kernaghan and Siegel, *Public Administration in Canada, loc. cit.*

43. *Ibid.*, ch. 24.

44. Alistair Cole, *French Politics and Society* (London: Prentice-Hall, 1998), pp. 110–11.

45. Allan Tupper, "New Public Management and Canadian Politics," in Janine Brodie and Linda Trimble, eds., *Reinventing Canada: Politics of the 21st Century* (Toronto: Pearson Education, 2003).

46. See Peters and Savoie, *Taking Stock, loc. cit.*

47. David Osborne and Ted Gaebler, *Reinventing Government* (Reading, MA: Addison-Wesley, 1992).

48. Janice Gross Stein, *The Cult of Efficiency* (Toronto: Anansi, 2001).

49. Donald J. Savoie, "What Is Wrong with the New Public Management?," *Canadian Public Administration* 38:1 (Spring 1995): 112–21 at 116.

Chapter Eight

LEGISLATURES: Centre Stage but Not Top Billing

Andrew Heard

CHAPTER OBJECTIVES

After you have completed this chapter, you should be able to:

■ understand the potential roles of a legislature in a political system

■ discuss the range of actors that undermine the effectiveness of legislatures

■ outline how laws are made

■ differentiate among the different kinds of representation that legislators can undertake

■ discuss ideas for the reform of legislatures

What Are Legislatures?

Legislatures are at once the centrepiece of democratic countries and yet at the same time are often viewed as the most visible failures of those very democracies. An elected legislature holds the promise of the people's representatives assembling together to debate, deliberate, and decide upon the nation's business. In a multiparty democracy, one would expect that significant differences of opinion would be expressed as members of the different parties listen to and weigh competing views of how best to deal with the issues of **public policy** under consideration. Perhaps even some visible compromises and changes of heart might be made among the parties as they try to forge a consensus on what is best for their society. The members of the legislature would be able to identify the most serious weaknesses in a proposed law, make the necessary changes, and reject any measures that proved to be profoundly unpopular with the people they represent. Unfortunately, reality often falls disappointingly short of these expectations.

This chapter explores the potential roles that legislatures might fill in any political system and then examines the practical factors that can limit that potential. The emphasis here is on balancing idealism with a fuller understanding of the limitations under which legislators do their work. It is equally important to resist the temptation to slip into cynicism and view legislatures as simply rubber stamps that blindly approve policies proposed by the executive. There are indeed a number of important and substantive functions that legislatures can undertake, and an appreciation of these can lead to useful suggestions for legislative reform. This chapter reviews legislatures generically, but also provides an opportunity to understand Canadian and other legislatures around the world. In order to assess our own legislatures, it is essential that we have a global view that allows us to appreciate what can and does occur elsewhere; with a comparative perspective, we can better understand what might be done to improve our own political institutions (see Box 8.1).

The first task is to identify just what a legislature is. For a political institution to be called a legislature, that institution must be centrally involved in the lawmaking process. Moreover, the legislature must actually make law; it is not simply a consultative body that provides advice to another lawmaking official or institution. For example, the Shura Council in Saudi Arabia cannot be described as a legislature, since its only formal power is to offer advice on public policy to the council of ministers. However, legislatures are not the only institutions or political actors in a political system that make law. It is important to distinguish between the legislative power and the legislative branch of government—the power to make law is not restricted to just the legislative branch.

All political systems provide some legislative power to the executive branch of government; there are several possible forms this power might take. First, the constitution of a state may explicitly provide some lawmaking powers to the executive. For example, the president of the country may be able to make some laws by decree. Every political system also provides in some fashion that laws may be made by the ministers or cabinet who head up the executive departments of government; these laws can be called various things in different countries, such as regulations, ordinances, or orders in council. The lawmaking power of the executive is often actually power that is delegated to the executive by the legislature. In every political system, the judiciary also exercises some lawmaking power in the course of interpreting and enforcing the legal rules enacted by the legislature or executive. So we find that the legislative power can be spread across all three branches of government.

However, the exercise of lawmaking by other institutions or officials in the political system does not mean that they constitute legislatures. Constitutions usually vest the prime lawmaking power in one particular institution, the legislature, while only limited lawmaking power belongs to the executive. And the lawmaking power of the judiciary is only an implicit power that is exercised in the course of its principal task, which is interpreting and enforcing the law.

Legislatures appear to have important symbolic cachet, judging by their proliferation over the 20th century. The vast majority of states today have a formal legislative body: 189 all told in

---

The Structure of Legislatures   BOX 8.1

A **unicameral legislature** has only one chamber, and all members of the legislature belong to and participate in that chamber.

Example of a unicameral legislature: Israel

Knesset: 120 members

A **bicameral legislature** has two separate chambers (often called houses), and members of the legislature belong only to

one of those chambers and have a right to participate in only their chamber's proceedings.

Example of a bicameral legislature: Canada

Upper house: Senate 105 appointed members

Lower house: House of Commons 308 elected members

2007.[1] Many authoritarian regimes have legislatures in order to create a façade of democracy by holding elections and letting the people's "representatives" pass laws. In these instances, legislatures are truly rubber stamps, and any laws proposed by the rulers are dutifully passed with no criticism of the government. Only a few countries do without a legislature, reserving principal lawmaking power for the executive.[2] In a few of these countries, an absolute monarch still exercises the lawmaking power; in Saudi Arabia, for example, the king is the sole source of formal legislative power. However, most of the states without legislatures are ones ruled by a dictator, who issues laws by personal decree.

Potential Functions of Legislatures

In studying legislatures, political scientists have a number of concerns and interests. First and foremost, we are concerned with identifying what specific roles legislatures may fill in a political system and what factors have an impact on how effectively the legislatures carry them out. Legislatures can play vital informal roles in a political system, on top of the formal ones detailed in their countries' constitutions, and a deeper understanding of the functioning of any particular legislature may well arise from an appreciation of the broader contexts in which all legislatures operate in general.

One can easily identify a few key roles that legislatures perform, such as making laws, representing the people, and debating public issues. A simple reason for most legislatures' failure to fill these roles can be just as readily identified: many legislatures are effectively controlled by the executive or by the leaders of a dominating party or coalition of parties. In

Graeme MacKay/Artizans

either case, strict discipline of the members of the legislature prevents them from taking independent positions on matters under debate and consideration. Examined in such stark terms, most legislatures around the world, whether they are part of democratic or authoritarian systems, would have to be written off as failures; they would be nothing better than symbolic ornaments in contrast to the executive's total control of the policy process. One could also argue that even in legislatures where individual members have considerable personal discretion to decide what position to take on a matter under debate, such as in the U.S. Congress, the realities are that the legislators simply choose the positions demanded by those who provide them with the financial support needed to get reelected. On closer examination, however, such views of legislatures may prove to be more cynical than accurate.

Perhaps the best starting point for examining legislatures is to review briefly all the possible roles that legislatures can play in a political system. The great variety of functions can be surprising to many, and they give a clue to the potential value of a legislature that works well. The lawmaking role of legislatures is the most visible (and will be dealt with in detail below), but there are many other functions that are equally important—and sometimes even more so.

The following are the potential roles of legislatures:

- to legislate
- to represent
- to debate
- to educate
- to institutionalize opposition
- to investigate issues and events
- to suggest or initiate new policies
- to scrutinize executive activities
- to legitimate the policies of the executive
- to ratify or veto executive decisions and actions
- to refine and improve policies suggested by the executive
- to decide who holds executive offices (in parliamentary systems)
- to provide alternative governments or political leaders
- to provide an ombudsman service for citizens
- to adjudicate in a judicial or quasi-judicial role.

In the process of passing new laws, legislators can actively engage in several other general functions as well. In a fully democratic system, members of the legislature debate the wisdom of any proposed law (or **bill**) and consider a variety of suggested improvements. Inevitably, such debates over the preferred policy and form in which to enact it involve a subtle but important educational role. Through listening to these debates, it is possible for those in power to learn about different perspectives on their policy proposals, and at the same time others may see the weaknesses in their own initial positions. Perhaps the most crucial part of this educational function occurs when the media effectively report on events in the legislature and influence the views held by the general public.

In the course of these debates, members also engage in representing the interests of a wide range of groups in the general population. Depending upon the number of political parties present in the legislature and the discipline imposed on members of those parties, quite a wide range of views may be raised. This can have an important symbolic function in providing citizens with a direct and visible display of views they personally support being expressed in the legislature. As a result of these "talking" functions, legislative assemblies serve as a crucial institutional channel through which disputes get aired publicly and settled in an authoritative fashion by a majority vote.

The Nova Scotia House of Assembly is the oldest legislative building in Canada, with deliberations held here since 1819. In 1848, it was the site of the first successful passage of a non-confidence motion in any colonial legislature in the British Empire. This marked the start of responsible government in Canada.

Chris Reardon/Courtesy of Nova Scotia House of Assembly

One of the important functions of legislatures can be to institutionalize **opposition**. While we may take this for granted in a democratic society, we would soon miss the opposition if it were to be suppressed. On a broad level, people are less likely to take to the streets in violent demonstrations or start a civil war if they believe that opposition to the ruling party's policies plays some role in the legislature. Indeed, a hallmark of how democratic a country is can be seen in how free members of the legislature feel to openly criticize the government. An illustration of the importance of institutionalizing opposition came after the Liberal Party won every seat in New Brunswick's 1987 elections for the provincial legislature. Although they had no obligation to do so, the Liberals invited the leader of the Progressive Conservative Party to appear in the assembly on a regular basis to participate in Question Period, when cabinet ministers are questioned about their conduct of public affairs.

Legislatures also have the potential to conduct investigations into issues and events of political importance. Committees most effectively carry out these investigations, but sometimes a series of questions on the main floor of the legislature can reveal the facts of some controversial happening. When an inquiry is held into an event, it is usually conducted as part of the legislature's role of overseeing the work of the executive branch of government, essentially to discover what government officials did or did not know or do. A committee can also hold hearings on a matter of public policy in order to make suggestions about how the policy can be improved; these can range from very focused issues, such as policies dealing with juvenile offenders, to much broader questions, such as the nation's basic foreign or defence policy. Hearings into matters of public policy are also often held as part of the process of considering legislation.

Many important functions of legislatures relate to their relationship with the executive branch of government. Briefly stated, the legislature has two sorts of functions to perform with respect to the executive. The first relates to processing and legitimating the executive's decisions concerning new policies it wants enacted into law, and the second involves performing an overseeing function to scrutinize how the executive has carried out its responsibilities. Particularly in parliamentary systems, where the cabinet controls most of the policy process and proposes virtually all the bills that eventually become laws, the legislature has an important symbolic role in performing at least a ritual public debate and examination of these proposals.

Many legislatures perform a role not found in Canada, with the requirement that the legislature review and ratify any international agreements the executive has signed; for example, the U.S. Senate must ratify treaties. Some legislatures allow individuals and groups from the public to make presentations to the committees that study the cabinet's proposed laws and international treaties, and this public input adds another layer of democratic legitimation to the legislation. But in order for this legitimation to have substance, the scrutiny of bills must be more than just a ritual. If legislation is to be legitimate, there must be a meaningful debate of the merits and flaws of the proposals and a real possibility of amending the bills and forcing the government to withdraw the most unpopular proposals.

Similarly, legislatures can have a significant function to perform when they oversee the executive. This oversight can involve two types of activity: one is to ensure that the government is acting acceptably and properly, in the legislature's view; the other is to ensure that the executive complies with the policies previously approved by the legislature. These oversight functions, when done well, can provide a significant check on a government that might otherwise try to cover up its misdeeds and abuses. In parliamentary systems, the legislature wields an ultimate threat over the executive: the power to cast a vote of **non-confidence** in the cabinet and force it to either resign or call an election. This is a powerful sanction that may be rarely exercised in countries such as Canada, where the party forming the cabinet usually controls a majority of the legislature's members in a **majority government** situation. But it is a real sanction that has brought down governments in Canada and in many other countries as well; five Canadian federal governments have either resigned or called an election as a result of a vote of non-confidence, but they were all instances of **minority governments**. The Americans' presidential system does not provide their legislatures with the power to vote non-confidence in the political executive, but Congress still has the capacity to expose and informally censure executive wrongdoing and mismanagement. Semi-presidential systems such as those in France and Russia put the president out of normal reach, but the prime minister and cabinet can be subject to non-confidence motions.

The most visible difference in executive oversight between the U.S. system and parliamentary government lies in the **Question Period** that just about every parliament holds. On regular occasions, members of the legislature may put direct questions to the prime minister and other cabinet ministers about their policies and the actions of their officials. While substantive answers are rare indeed, Question Periods do provide the opportunity to highlight government bungling and misdeeds, which every now and again can blow up into real political crises that eventually force the resignation of a cabinet minister or the downfall of the whole cabinet. Question Period also forces individual cabinet ministers to account publicly for their actions. The media play a crucial role in this regard by publicizing and focusing attention among the electorate on the events in the legislature; indeed, media coverage is important to many dimensions of the legislature's effectiveness.

An important function for legislatures in many countries involves selecting or confirming senior executive officials. One review of constitutions found at least 19 states where members of the legislature directly choose the head of state.[3] In some cases, such as India and Germany, members of the lower house meet in a joint session with representatives of the state legislatures and collectively elect the president. In the United States and the Philippines, the legislature selects the president in the event of a tie after the general population has voted. This role is only a formal one for the U.S. House of Representatives, whose members vote to choose the president if no candidate wins a majority of votes in the electoral college convened after the general election; in almost all circumstances, the House vote simply confirms the candidate who won the most electoral college votes.

Legislatures in parliamentary systems have several roles that are not applicable to the U.S. congressional system because of the principle of **responsible government** that gives parliamentary systems their essential character. A cabinet must have the formal confidence of a majority in the legislature in order to govern; in legislatures with two houses, this principle usually applies just to a majority in the lower house. In a broad sense, a parliament ultimately decides whether a cabinet can stay in office; the head of state may appoint a new prime minister and cabinet, but they

Michael de Adder/Artizans

have to obtain and maintain the confidence of the legislature in order to govern for any period of time. Parliaments are usually organized in an adversarial fashion, in which government MPs square off against the opposition. One theoretical role of the opposition is to provide an alternative government. Should the legislature force the resignation of the government, the head of state must be able to count on the opposition to step in and act as the new government, at least until new elections are held. But in a broader political sense, the opposition party or parties continuously act in the legislature to portray themselves to the public as an alternative to the ruling party or **coalition government**.

The U.S. system, however, gives the legislature another role in deciding who holds executive positions. The senate must approve the president's nomination of individuals to the cabinet, senior levels of the civil service, the judiciary, and the armed forces. In the 109th Congress, which sat in 2005–06, the Senate considered a total of 55,855 nominations, out of which 310 were either withdrawn or not approved for one reason or another.[4] The most visible of these nomination reviews involve hearings to scrutinize individuals who have been nominated to sit on the Supreme Court, a task sometimes suggested as a useful innovation for the Canadian parliament to consider.

Loosely related to the executive oversight function, and an important part of many legislatures, is an ombudsman role. In this role, a legislator acts on behalf of citizens and tries to sort out troubles they may be having with the bureaucracy. This is usually known as **constituency** work (or service), and the vast bulk of it occurs outside the legislative chamber, with legislators or their staff phoning or writing to civil servants or cabinet ministers on behalf of the person involved. In a parliamentary system, MPs can raise questions during Question Period or in committee hearings about specific cases they are handling, but the sheer volume of constituency work means that only a fraction of cases are dealt with in a public forum in this manner. Despite the "invisible" nature of constituency work, it has come to be the most time-consuming task of legislators in many countries.

Two studies in the 1990s revealed that Canadian MPs devote on average over 42 percent of their time to constituency work.[5] A 1996 survey of British MPs found they spent a similar amount of time on constituency work, about 40 percent.[6] However, there is a great disparity between the Canadian public's general perception of the importance of this function compared to that of their MPs. In a 1993 Gallup poll, the public rated this the least important part of an MP's work, but when MPs were asked the same question, they rated it as their number one priority.[7] The difference might be explained by the personal satisfaction MPs feel in helping individuals, in a job that has few direct personal rewards; on the other hand, only a very small segment of the population ever turn to their MP for help, and so this work is of little consequence to most of the general public.

A limited exercise of judicial power can also be one of the functions that legislatures are expected to fill. The most important examples involve the impeachment of senior public officials. When the U.S. House of Representatives charged President Clinton in impeachment proceedings in 1998, the Senate acted as a jury of a court chaired by the chief justice—and found Clinton not guilty. Brazil, India, and the Philippines are other countries whose legislatures conduct impeachment hearings of not just the president but of senior judges and other officials. In 2001, the Indonesian parliament impeached President Abdurrahman Wahid on charges of extensive corruption. Another quite common exercise of judicial power is seen in the 24 countries whose legislatures act as courts to hear charges of disputed or corrupt elections; this function is a power of parliaments historically descended from the British model, but most are like Canada in delegating this function to the courts.

The British parliament appears unique in the world because the highest court in the land has for centuries been a committee of the House of Lords, the Appellate Committee. The specially appointed Law Lords heard cases in five-judge panels; when they pronounced judgment, they delivered a report to a full meeting of the House of Lords. However, the *Constitutional Reform Act*, passed in 2005, will replace the Law Lords with an independent Supreme Court in 2009.

The historic British model involved the principle of the High Court of Parliament, reflecting its early origins as a council that dispensed justice. However, Westminster-model legislatures today continue to retain one aspect of this principle, in acting as a court to try charges of "contempt of Parliament" that can still result in imprisonment for the guilty. In 1992, for example, the Quebec National Assembly ordered imprisonment for someone who was found to be in contempt.[8]

Factors Limiting the Effectiveness of Legislatures

Legislatures have many functions, but just how effectively these are performed depends upon a wide range of factors. Many of them are interrelated, and attempts to reform the legislature by trying to deal with one factor may not succeed; they may even exacerbate the situation, since other limiting factors are at play.

Two factors that go hand in hand in limiting a legislature's ability to fulfil its functions effectively are party discipline and the domination of the legislature by the executive. These are almost inherent problems in modern parliamentary systems, but they can play a key role in presidential systems as well. Fairly strict party discipline is needed in a parliamentary system for a variety of reasons: the cabinet must have the support of a majority in the legislature in order to remain in office; the cabinet is supposed to be the focus of the policy process and secure the passage of most of its legislation; and cohesive party blocs are the organizational foundation of most of parliament's daily work. Indeed, parliamentary government in the modern context is really *party* government.

The following are the factors limiting the effectiveness of legislatures:

- executive dominance
- party discipline
- size
- frequency of meetings
- amount and complexity of legislation
- number, size, and membership of committees
- research and support staff
- legislators' pay
- procedural rules
- informal rewards and penalties
- electoral system
- media attention
- political culture

Canada is typical of other parliamentary systems, with the prime minister and cabinet managing to direct almost everything that transpires. The cabinet is able to do this because of strict **party discipline**, which is the requirement that all members of a legislature belonging to the same party should normally vote according to the party's position on an issue. Each party selects one of its members of the legislature to act as an official called a *whip*, whose primary functions are to assign members to particular duties in the legislature and to make sure that they vote the way the party requires them to. Whips rely mainly on peer pressure and persuasion, but they also have a range of informal rewards and punishments at their disposal. In addition to the whip's rewards and penalties, the parliamentary party as a whole known as the *caucus* (see Box 8.2) can impose even more severe punishments, such as temporary exile or

Some of the most tangible work of legislatures occurs behind closed doors in caucus meetings. A **caucus** is a group of legislators united in a common cause. The most common kind of caucus is the party caucus, in which the members of a legislature who belong to the same party gather on a regular basis to discuss party affairs, in particular, what position the party should take on issues coming up in the legislature. These meetings are invariably confidential, although leaks to the media often occur. Some of the most heated debates in Canadian legislatures occur not in the public arena of the formal chamber itself but in the party caucuses. Here, legislators can make their most forceful arguments on behalf of the interests and constituents they represent. Once the caucus debate is over and the party's position is established, however, members are supposed to fall into line and defend that position publicly. As a result, much of the real representational function of the legislature occurs out of the public eye and usually goes unreported in the media.

Government caucuses in parliamentary systems can also serve an important function in the legislative process. In many party caucuses, committees are established to look at policy issues and suggest new laws or even changes to bills already before the legislature. Some but not all of these suggestions are taken up by the cabinet and included in the measures that are presented publicly in the legislature. In addition, many government caucuses allow the ordinary members to question cabinet ministers about their policies and conduct. Again, some of these exchanges are extremely frank and are important parts of actual oversight of the executive.

Other types of caucus meetings are organized for the members of parties from particular regions of the country or even for members of different parties who share a common interest. Each party in the Canadian parliament has regional or provincial caucus meetings prior to its general caucus meeting, for example, while the U.S. Congress also has bipartisan caucuses that include members from all the parties; examples include the Congressional Caucus for Women's Issues, the Congressional Black Caucus, and the Congressional Corn Caucus.

permanent expulsion from that caucus. Expulsion is the ultimate punishment, since most Canadian voters—like many voters elsewhere—decide for whom to vote on the basis of a candidate's party or the party's leader. Surveys of the past eight federal elections show that few Canadian voters make their voting choice primarily on the basis of the individual candidates. In the 2000 election, for example, less than half of Canadian voters had any preference for individual candidates, and the individual candidate was decisive in the voting decision for only 5 percent of voters.[9] Members expelled from their party may sit as an independent or "cross the floor" to join another party.

Party discipline is something of a mixed blessing in legislatures. While disciplined party blocs make the legislative process more efficient and clarify voters' choices, party discipline also seriously impedes the legislature's ability to perform many of its functions. In particular, the ruling party or coalition of parties is able to keep tight control over the outcome of most decisions in the legislative chamber and in committees. At both the federal and provincial levels in Canada, party discipline is very strict. This means that the Cabinet will almost never lose a vote on a bill or have to face a committee report criticizing the government's policies. So long as discipline holds for a Cabinet with a majority of seats, the legislature will not cast a vote of non-confidence in the government.[10] Party discipline is taken to its extreme in the Labor parties in Australia and New Zealand, which both require their MPs to sign a pledge that they will always vote according to the party position.[11] In contrast, parties in the British parliament display a much looser discipline; one study of voting patterns in the British house of commons found dissident votes in 20 to 28 percent of recorded votes in the three parliaments that sat in the 1970s.[12]

The American presidential system is a very different type of government, and members of Congress demonstrate a freedom to vote as they choose that would be the envy of many legislature members in parliamentary systems. However, it is a mistake to equate the relative freedom in the United States with a lack of party cohesion. There has, in fact, been a trend to much stronger caucus unity and more votes split down party lines. In the House of Representatives, the Republicans on average voted with a majority of their caucus in 91 percent of major votes in 2003, while Democrats did so 87 percent of the time; these numbers contrast with 60 percent and 58 percent respectively in 1970. Even the Senate, which has traditionally been a bastion of independent-minded members, has seen a similar change. In 2003, Republican senators voted with the majority of their caucus in 94 percent of votes and Democrats did so 85 percent of the time; the same figures for 1970 were 56 percent and 55 percent.[13]

The combination of party discipline and executive dominance has a significant effect on a legislature's ability to perform a range of its potential functions. Lawmaking may get boiled down simply to a public debate prior to approving most of whatever the cabinet has proposed. Figure 8.1 shows that even during the two minority governments headed by Paul Martin and Stephen Harper, bills sponsored by cabinet ministers have been much more likely to pass than

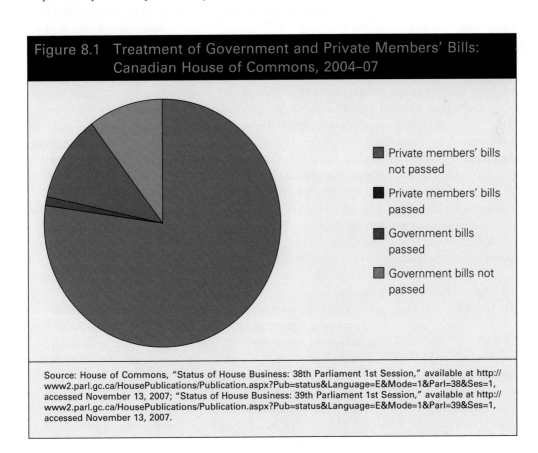

Figure 8.1 Treatment of Government and Private Members' Bills: Canadian House of Commons, 2004–07

- Private members' bills not passed
- Private members' bills passed
- Government bills passed
- Government bills not passed

Source: House of Commons, "Status of House Business: 38th Parliament 1st Session," available at http://www2.parl.gc.ca/HousePublications/Publication.aspx?Pub=status&Language=E&Mode=1&Parl=38&Ses=1, accessed November 13, 2007; "Status of House Business: 39th Parliament 1st Session," available at http://www2.parl.gc.ca/HousePublications/Publication.aspx?Pub=status&Language=E&Mode=1&Parl=39&Ses=1, accessed November 13, 2007.

those proposed by private members; during minority governments, opposition parties could combine to pass bills introduced by private members but in practice do not often do so. When a government has a majority in the legislature, party discipline usually can seriously weaken the examination of cabinet proposals and oversight of executive, and committees are often unable to produce innovative policy suggestions that run counter to the cabinet's policy agenda.

Other variables can also limit a legislature's effectiveness. Factors as basic as the size of the legislature, the number of days in the year it sits to conduct business, the research and support staff working for individual legislators, and the internal procedural rules of the legislature all can leave a legislature quite hamstrung. Canadian provinces have legislatures ranging in size from 27 to 125 members, with an average size of 69 and a cabinet of about 20 ministers. Provincial cabinets, therefore, form a significant portion of the legislature's total membership and an even higher proportion of the governing party's caucus. In 2005, provincial cabinets filled, on average, 30 percent of the legislature's seats, and 47 percent of the ruling party's membership in the legislature. Just this simple fact of size provides a significant explanation for the high level of executive dominance of the legislative process in Canadian provincial government and weakens the legislature's ability to effectively fill several others of its potential roles. In comparison, the House of Commons in Ottawa has 308 members, and the Harper cabinet in 2007 constituted only about 10 percent of the total membership of the House. With the cabinet's presence diluted by the size of the chamber, the federal parliament is not as strongly controlled by the cabinet as are provincial legislatures. Even the size of the Canadian House of Commons stands in stark contrast to the lower houses of Britain, with 646 members; France, with 577; Germany, with 614; and the United States, with 435.

The differences in size between the provincial legislatures and the federal House of Commons also mean that, in comparison to most provincial legislatures, the House of Commons can have many more functioning committees at work, because there are more than enough MPs to sit on them. Those Commons committees can be free of Cabinet ministers, while many provincial legislatures may need to have Cabinet ministers sitting on committees, if only because there are not enough competent government **backbenchers** to do the work. As a result, committees in Ottawa can have relatively more independence from the executive than most provincial committees.

Another quite practical consideration is how much business a legislature is expected to do in a certain period of time. For example, in 1998–99 the New Brunswick legislature had to consider 61 government bills in just 40 days, while performing many other tasks at the same time. In contrast, the British Columbia legislature sat for 162 days during that same period and had 99 government bills to consider. The New Brunswick legislature could devote only a fraction of the time to each bill compared to that available to the British Columbian MLAs. Little wonder, then, that the New Brunswick legislature amended only 23 percent of the government bills while the British Columbians were able to consider and pass amendments to 37 percent of their bills.

A related issue is how much legislators get paid. If they are paid a relatively low wage, then one cannot expect the legislature to sit year-round, as many members will need to supplement their income. Furthermore, many competent professional people will not want to take a significant cut in pay in order to leave their normal jobs and run for political office. Canadian reluctance to pay much for politicians was plainly evident when the Saskatchewan government decided in 1993 to reduce the size of the provincial legislature by eight members, and Ontario in 1995 by 27 members, as part of a general cost-cutting drive. Savings continue with the research and support staff available to Canadian legislators. Many provincial legislators make do with just one or two staff members, and even MPs in Ottawa have allowances for only four staff members to serve them in Parliament and in their constituency offices. Their U.S. counterparts in Washington have dozens of staffers, and committee chairs can have over a hundred working for them. This is not just a matter of stinginess; it has a direct impact on the kind of job legislators can do. They are simply not able to perform serious reviews of public policy without sufficient staff to provide the technical expertise needed to formulate independent policy appraisals and initiatives.

The procedural rules of a legislature can also limit its effectiveness. Whoever controls the timetable in the legislature controls what business will be considered and how much time is to be devoted to any particular measure. In most parliamentary systems, the government is able to exercise this level of control through a cabinet minister known as the House Leader. **Closure**, or time allocation, is one procedural tool available to control the amount of time spent debating any particular item on parliament's agenda. With closure, the government can cut off debate and force a vote to be held. Between 1993 and early 2002, the Chrétien government used closure or time allocation in the House of Commons 75 times. It is the counterpart to the opposition's use of extended debates, or a **filibuster**.

While one theory of parliamentary government is that the cabinet is held "continuously" accountable to the legislature, the procedural rules may allow only limited opportunities for this to occur. In the Canadian House of Commons, there is a 45-minute Question Period every day, but British Columbia has Question Periods that last only 15 minutes. In the United Kingdom, members can ask the prime minister questions only once a week. Just with these differences in the rules, one sees a significant difference in the ability of legislators to hold cabinet ministers to account.

No legislature allows business to unfold in a haphazard fashion, and someone has to decide what will be considered when. In Canadian legislatures, the government house leaders are in total control. They consult with house leaders from the opposition parties, but this consultation may not have any influence on what the government decides to do. Other jurisdictions avoid this problem by providing in their rules that the Speaker of the assembly can decide whether important measures should be brought forward for a vote; the Speaker of the British House of Commons, for example, has broad personal discretion to select the issues that are debated and voted upon.

Other crucial procedural rules deal with who can introduce what. In presidential systems, a great deal can change in the functioning of the legislature if the president is able to directly introduce bills into the legislature, as is the case in Mexico. In the United States, on the other hand, the president is unable to introduce bills and must negotiate with individual members of Congress to find someone who will "sponsor" the bill and introduce it.

The number, size, and membership of committees can also influence a legislature's ability to perform its roles effectively in assessing and amending bills, as well as in conducting investigations into events and issues. Small legislatures, such as most Canadian provincial legislatures, have few committees and make little use of even those they have. Some legislatures funnel most proposed legislation through Committee of the Whole, which is all the members of the legislature simply sitting as one large committee. This is a highly inefficient process, since bills can be dealt with only one at a time, and no other business can be conducted in the legislative chamber while this goes on. Legislatures that have a well-developed committee system are able to process much more business and do so in greater depth. Greater efficiency and scrutiny can occur because work can proceed in parallel in many committees at the same time, and the members of these committees can develop more expertise if these are set up to deal with specific policy areas such as transportation, health, or banking. Another, related factor is whether committees are created on an ad hoc basis or standing basis. A permanent committee with stable membership is able to consider issues with considerably more expertise.

An important question is whether cabinet ministers should sit on or chair parliamentary committees. Nova Scotia and Quebec are two provinces that regularly allow both, but such a suggestion would cause outrage in the Canadian and British parliaments. As mentioned earlier in this chapter, the presence of cabinet ministers undermines the legislature's ability to form independent judgments of the policies proposed by the executive and reduces its capacity to act as a check against the executive's power. However, the active participation of cabinet ministers in parliamentary committees can have positive effects. Since cabinet is usually the ultimate body that decides whether its caucus members should vote for an amendment, there is something to be said for cabinet ministers being present and engaged in the committee discussions so they can learn at first hand about the merits of proposed amendments.

Several sets of factors external to legislatures can also have an impact on their effectiveness. The first is the electoral system, which may produce legislative assemblies that bear little resemblance to the choices made by the voters. This is a particular problem in countries such as Canada with the **first-past-the-post** system. In this system, the person who gets the most votes in a riding wins the seat; as a result, candidates who have wide support but do not manage to come in first place do not get to represent the people who voted for them. The worst example of this system's potential to distort the citizens' choices was seen in the 1987 New Brunswick election, where the Liberals won about 60 percent of the votes but gained every seat in the legislature; this meant that the 40 percent of the electorate who voted for other parties were left with no one to represent them. The B.C. Liberal Party won 97.5 percent of the legislature's seats in 2000 with only 58 percent of the overall vote. Some countries have electoral laws that ban certain parties, or ensure that there is only one official party for all elections; again, this limits the legislature's ability to represent the people and assess policy proposals. For example, legislatures in communist countries are usually filled in uncompetitive elections in which only communist party candidates are allowed to run. Informal domination by a single ruling party can also stifle effective opposition in some apparently democratic countries. Singapore may have a capitalist economy and the framework of Western democracy, but it has been tightly ruled by the People's Action through largely uncompetitive elections; 55 of the 84 elected seats in Singapore's parliament were filled by acclamation in the 2001 elections. With few opposition members in a legislature, the executive is able to command at will, and the representative and executive oversight functions of the legislature are very poorly fulfilled.

Another external factor is the role of the media in conveying to the public what transpires in the legislature and in covering the public's reaction. The media are known as the "Fourth Estate" precisely because of their crucial role as a link between political institutions and actors on the one hand and the general public on the other. In countries that control the media or where media are concentrated in a few hands, the coverage of both legislative events and public reaction can be distorted, to say the least. Even in societies with a vibrant media, there are problems, with only a few items being selected for coverage because of space and time constraints, the policy preferences of the media owners, or the public's lack of interest. Furthermore, effective coverage of legislatures requires considerable knowledge of the political system and issues, and poor coverage can often result from reporters' inexperience. Ironically, the success of legislatures that work effectively and efficiently through an extensive committee system may become a barrier to full media coverage. The U.S. Congress, for instance, has about 300 committees and subcommittees, and it is impossible for the media to cover the work of any but a select few.

The largest and most intangible of the external factors is the general political culture of a society. The most visible manifestation of this factor is the poor representation of women in all legislatures, since political cultures around the world continue to favour males in many subtle and not-so-subtle ways. The same absence from the legislature applies to minority groups in many societies. This underrepresentation of groups in the legislature not only undermines the representation function, but can also have an impact on the specific policies considered and on how they are treated. Other general cultural values come into play in the legislature as well. Whether the general public wants or tolerates very strong leadership by the executive or prefers individual members of the legislature who act independently will have an effect in the long run on the strength of party discipline in the legislature. Dozens of national parliaments across the globe are modelled on the British system, yet each performs its potential functions to varying degrees.

Several countries have presidential systems modelled on that of the United States, but in practice none is very similar to the U.S. system. Certain differences among parliamentary and congressional legislatures can be explained by procedural rules or other specific details of the legislature, but unique political cultures remain the most important cause. The impact of political culture, at least at the elite level, is seen in quite another context in Mexico. The legal framework of its constitution is fairly similar to that of the American, with a presidential system of government. But a range of cultural factors have led to a much tighter party discipline in the ruling party, which allows the president to direct the work of the legislature to such an extent that the practical workings of the Mexican legislative process bear little resemblance to those of its U.S. counterpart.

Lawmaking

Lawmaking is one of the most important roles of legislatures, and it is this function that sets them apart from the other branches of government. The process through which proposals must pass before they become law can give ample opportunity for them to be amended or even scrapped entirely. There is definitely the potential for new public policy proposals to be significantly improved and for unpopular or impractical ones to be abandoned as a result of scrutiny in the legislature and subsequent public reaction. In authoritarian regimes, the legislature plays little more than a formal, ritual role in enacting into law the policies already decided upon by the political executive or ruling party. In democratic parliamentary systems, the legislature has a substantive role to play in making laws, even if the cabinet is the main source of legislative initiatives and directs much of the process in the legislature. For the most part, however, MPs focus on reviewing the cabinet's proposals rather than developing new initiatives of their own. In democratic presidential systems, the legislature can have a truly independent role to play in developing and initiating new legislation, as well as in scrutinizing proposals developed by the executive.

The lawmaking procedure in the legislature is only part of the whole ongoing public-policy process. Ideas for new laws are generated throughout the political system by individuals, groups, and corporations, as well as by political parties, civil servants, the cabinet, individual members of the legislature, and committees of the legislature. The ideas are then reviewed and drafted into legal language suitable for a future law; at this point, they are ready to be introduced into the legislature. The legislature considers the proposed laws, makes any changes that the majority thinks necessary, and decides whether to enact these proposals into law. Most modern statutes passed by the legislature cannot contain all the detail necessary for their implementation, so they delegate to the executive branch the power to pass regulations filling in the details; this is known as delegated or subordinate legislation. The law and its regulations are then ready to be implemented and administered by the executive. It is at this point that the ideas for new public policies become reality. The new policies, in turn, generate a reaction among those in the public who are affected, which can eventually lead to ideas and demands for yet new laws. In this whole process, the legislature can potentially provide the most important public stage for formal debate and improvement of public policies.

In parliamentary systems such as Canada's, cabinet ministers propose most of the measures that are eventually enacted into law. When cabinet ministers decide to propose a change to public policy that needs to be achieved through legislation, they consult the civil servants in their department for advice on the best means to achieve that policy. The ideas are then presented to the cabinet or a cabinet committee and, if approved, are drafted into a legal document. The cabinet then reviews the matter again and makes a final decision on whether to present the measure to the legislature. When there is an opening in the work schedule in the legislature, the sponsoring cabinet minister introduces the measure as a bill.

The Canadian parliament follows a legislative process that is similar to that in most legislatures patterned after the British model, although each legislature has its own particular variations in detail. In Canada, as illustrated in Figure 8.2, the bill goes through three readings, or particular stages, each of which serves a specific purpose. The First Reading occurs when the bill is first introduced. It is only a formality, in that it gives everyone notice that the bill has entered the pipeline; no debate occurs at this time. The next stage, Second Reading, is the consideration of the main principles of the bill; considerable debate can occur at this time. After Second Reading, the bill usually enters the committee stage, where detailed examination occurs. In the Canadian parliament, the committee usually invites interested members of the public to present their views of how the bill can be improved. While there is great potential for this public input, the sheer volume of people wanting to have their say on controversial bills means that a very deliberate and partisan process occurs within the committee to decide who will actually be allowed to give testimony. Depending on the controversy engendered by the bill and on subsequent media coverage, significant changes can be made when the governing party's members of the committee believe that it is in their best interests to do so. Often, they check informally with the minister who sponsored the bill to see if he or she agrees to the changes, but sometimes the minister appears as a formal witness to defend the proposal and discuss potential amendments. The committee then reports back to the legislature, and all the members can debate and vote on any changes the committee proposed. After that, a debate on Third Reading is held, and members have a final opportunity to consider the bill as a whole.

Once a bill has passed Third Reading, it is sent to the other house and goes through the same stages all over again. The Canadian parliament contains two chambers or houses, the House of Commons and the Senate, and a bill must be approved in identical form by both before it can become a law. The vast majority of bills are introduced first in the House of Commons, because the lower house is elected, while the Senate is appointed. The Senate does sometimes make changes to bills that have already been passed by the House of Commons, and then the Commons must decide whether to accept the Senate amendments or reject them. Occasionally, a bill goes back and forth several times between the Senate and House of Commons before one of them compromises, but since the Senate is an appointed body, it normally should be the one that eventually gives way.[14] Only on rare occasions does the Senate actually defeat a bill.

Once a bill has been agreed to by both the House of Commons and the Senate, it is ready for Royal Assent by the Governor General and it becomes an act of Parliament. No Canadian provincial legislature has the equivalent of the Senate, so a bill goes through the three readings in the assembly and then gets Royal Assent from the Lieutenant Governor. The whole process of considering and passing legislation in Parliament usually takes several months, but can often go on for a year or more; public reaction to the bill becomes crucial during such an extended period and often induces the cabinet minister responsible for the bill to accept or propose important amendments. On rare occasions, however, a bill can go through all stages in the House of Commons in a day; such speedy consideration usually occurs only if all the political parties represented in the House agree.

Perhaps the most important question that emerges from a review of the legislative process is how effective the legislature actually is. Table 8.1 gives a summary of the treatment of government bills in several Canadian legislatures, as well as in the Australian parliament, for comparison, and demonstrates that legislatures do have a substantial role to play in reviewing

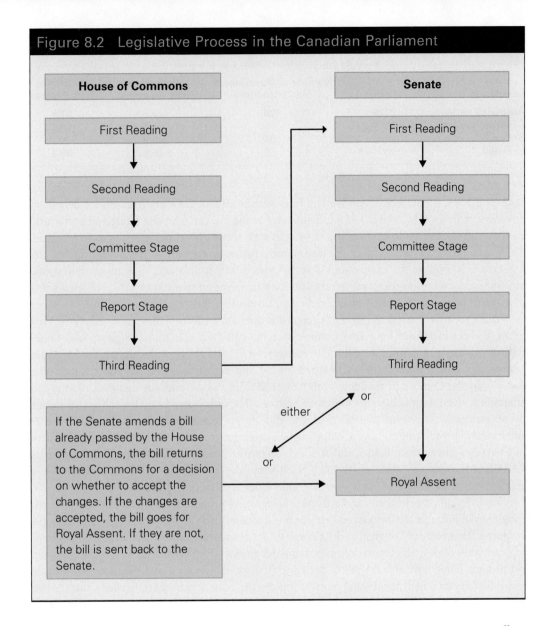

Figure 8.2 Legislative Process in the Canadian Parliament

House of Commons	Senate
First Reading	First Reading
Second Reading	Second Reading
Committee Stage	Committee Stage
Report Stage	Report Stage
Third Reading	Third Reading

If the Senate amends a bill already passed by the House of Commons, the bill returns to the Commons for a decision on whether to accept the changes. If the changes are accepted, the bill goes for Royal Assent. If they are not, the bill is sent back to the Senate.

either

or

or

Royal Assent

the bills proposed by the cabinet. One obvious measure is that the government never gets all its bills through the legislature. Although some provincial governments come very close to complete adoption on occasion, many government bills fail to pass the legislature simply because the members run out of time before the end of the session.[15] A more useful measure of the practical importance of legislatures is the percentage of government bills that get amended. Table 8.1 reveals that a significant number do. Despite the tight party discipline, governments often accept significant changes to their proposals once these are considered by their legislatures. For example, in Ontario, the governing Liberals controlled about 70 percent of the seats, but saw almost three-quarters of their government bills amended in 2006/07. However, the dynamics of a legislature not only vary greatly from one jurisdiction to another but also from one period of time to another. In British Columbia, the governing Liberals controlled just under 60 percent of the seats but managed to limit amendments to only 9 percent of their bills; curiously, when the same party held over 95 percent of the members of the legislature between

Table 8.1 Success of Government Bills in Selected Parliamentary Systems

Legislature	Period	Number of Government Bills Introduced	Percent of Bills Amended	Percent of Bills Enacted
Australian parliament	2006	188	20.7	91.5
Canadian parliament	2006–07	69	31.9	58.0
British Columbia	2006	34	8.9	94.1
Ontario	2005–07	58	75.4	98.3

Note: These figures include only government public bills.

2000 and 2004, 35 percent of government bills were amended. The opportunities for debate on government proposals, both in the legislature and in the media, allow the interested public and the government caucus to think about the issues and to exert pressure for changes to be made. There certainly are times when a government manages to ram a measure through the legislature, whipping its troops into line to pass a bill untouched. But most democratic governments cannot do this consistently and have to relent on many occasions, allowing some changes to be made to its bills and deciding to drop other bills altogether.

The legislative process in the U.S. Congress is quite different from that described above. First of all, the president and his cabinet cannot directly introduce bills into Congress; as a result, individual members sponsor all bills. The executive still has a strong influence on the legislative process, but this is done entirely through lobbying and negotiating with members of both the Republican and Democratic parties in both houses of Congress. Second, the vast bulk of time and attention is given to legislation in committee hearings. The only opportunity for substantial debate by all members of a house comes up at the end of the process. Third, virtually every bill is significantly altered along the way. Competing bills dealing with similar issues can be introduced by different members of both houses and are often eventually consolidated into one. Because there is much looser party discipline in the U.S. Congress, the passage of a bill depends upon a tremendous amount of negotiating among individual legislators and their staff.

Table 8.2 illustrates the enormous filtering of legislative proposals that occurs in Congress, with thousands of bills that are introduced being reduced to a few hundred that pass into law; this table compares the activity of Congress under George W. Bush and Bill Clinton. An individual senator or representative often gives support only in exchange for an amendment that deals with one of his or her pet projects. Thus, a bill that ostensibly deals with transportation can include sections that provide meal vouchers for schoolchildren and money for pig farmers. Another major difference is that the two houses of Congress are both elected and have equal political power. As a result, an important part of the legislative process is securing eventual agreement between the two houses on identical terms for a bill; there is a joint conference committee specially charged with reconciling two versions of the same bill.

The other important difference between the U.S. and parliamentary systems arises because the president has a real **veto** over measures passed by Congress, while the official sanction by the head of state in a parliamentary system is always automatic. If a president opposes a bill passed by Congress, he or she can veto the legislation. Between 1789 and 2007, presidents vetoed 1489 bills passed by Congress. Between 2000 and 2004, George W. Bush became the first president not to veto a single measure passed by Congress since James Garfield, in 1881. Bush may have avoided vetoing for several reasons during his first term in office, including Republican control of both houses, strong party cohesion in Congress, and the backdrop of the "war on terror" freezing out opposition to many measures. After the Democrats gained control of both houses of Congress in the 2006 elections, Bush resorted to vetoing 10 bills by mid-2008; two of those vetoes were overridden by Congress. The Constitution gives Congress the ability to override a formal presidential veto, but an override requires a two-thirds vote in both

Table 8.2 Passage of Legislation in the 106th and 109th U.S. Congresses, 1999–2000 and 2005–06

	HOUSE OF REPRESENTATIVES		SENATE	
	2005–2006	1999–2000	2005–2006	1999–2000
Bills introduced	6,438	4,872	4,122	2,658
Senate bills passed	61	198	336	363
House bills passed	501	708	328	402
Bills vetoed by President	1	12*	—	—
Vetoes overridden by Congress	0	1*	—	—
Bills enacted into law	418	604	—	—

* The categories bills vetoed, vetoes overridden, and bills enacted apply jointly to both houses, since bills have been approved in identical form by both.

Source: "*Résumé of Congressional Activity: 109th Congress, 2nd Session,*" available at http://senate.gov/reference/resources/pdf/109_2.pdf, accessed June 2, 2008; "*Résumé of Congressional Activity, 109th Congress, 1st Session,*" available at http://www.senate.gov/reference/resources/pdf/109-1res.pdf, accessed June 2, 2008; "*Résumé of Congressional Activity: 106th Congress,*" available at http://thomas.loc.gov/home/resume/106res.html, accessed May 1, 2005.

houses; as a result, only 106 vetoes have been overridden. Another technique is known as the "pocket veto," in which the bill dies if the president does not sign it within 10 days of the adjournment of Congress. The pocket veto has been a favourite of many presidents, with 1066 such vetoes recorded.[16] Many of the presidential vetoes came not because the president objected to the whole bill, but because he wanted to reject one of the particular items unrelated to the main purpose that had been added into a bill to secure its passage in Congress. In order to prevent so many "babies being thrown out with the bathwater," an act of Congress was passed in 1996 to give the president what is called a *line-item veto*. This procedure allowed the President to sign a bill into law while vetoing particular items within the bill. However, the U.S. Supreme Court struck down the line-item veto as unconstitutional in 1998.[17]

Representation

A very important function of all democratic legislatures is to represent the citizenry in the heart of government institutions. Representation lies at the core of the democratic mandate of a legislature to manage the affairs of a society; because of it, members of the legislature are able to perform all the other functions of the legislature. While it is easy to state this as a vital role, it is surprisingly difficult to define what representation actually entails. The difficulties emerge because there are crosscutting views about *whom* members of the legislature should represent and *how* they should represent them. Unfortunately, no legislature is ever a mirror reflection of all the diverse segments and groups in society; in countries that use the first-past-the-post electoral system, the members of the legislature are seldom even a proper reflection of the electorate's support for the different political parties.

Someone recently elected to a seat in the legislature soon finds himself or herself torn in different directions by a wide range of groups and interests demanding that the legislator act or speak on their behalf. First, there are territorial community interests, which can be as large as the whole constituency in which the legislator ran for election or as small as a town, village, or neighbourhood. In this role, a legislator is representing all the members of the community as a collective whole. Second, there are non-territorial sectional interests or groups that may be represented. One of the first tugs on legislators' attention is the call for special attention to be paid to those people who actually voted for them. This is a reasonable demand, since these people chose the candidate because of the policies he or she promised to pursue. However, legislators can quickly realize that the demands of the whole community can often run counter to the demands of the segment of that community who voted for them. This tension is heightened in the many constituencies where someone is declared elected with less than a majority of votes; such legislators start from a position where a majority of their constituents are opposed to their policy positions.

Members of an elected legislature also wrestle with a separate responsibility to represent the political party on whose platform they ran and got elected. Another non-territorial set of interests that legislators can represent are those relating to economic sectors or enterprises that are particularly important in the region they represent; thus, MPs can work hard on behalf of grain growers, vehicle manufacturers, a paper mill, fishers, or the high-tech service sector in their region. Finally, legislators can represent the particular social groups to which they personally belong, be they gender, linguistic, religious, ethnic, and so on. This can be an important form of representation, given the domination of most legislatures by only one social group: males from a narrow range of professional backgrounds. The ultimate goal of this aspect of representation is that the legislature should be a microcosm or mirror of society, with members of all the significant groups present in roughly proportional numbers. When we take all these potential subjects of representation together, it should be evident that a legislator often faces competing expectations to represent groups with very different (and even opposing) interests when it comes to any specific matter of public policy under consideration.

Even if it becomes clear whom a legislator should try to represent on a particular issue, there is still controversy about how that representation should be practised. Two basic approaches can be distinguished: the delegate and the trustee. The delegate perspective requires a legislator to discern the will of the group to be represented and then to voice and pursue those interests; the delegate essentially acts in the place of those he or she represents. The delegate's own views are supposed to be set aside in favour of representing the views of the group. This perspective is based on powerful arguments of democratic theory, coming from classical liberalism, that legislative activity should always reflect the will of the people and particularly of the specific group to be affected by a piece of legislation. The difficulties with this view arise both from democratic theory and from the complicated nature of society and public policy.

Modern liberal democratic theory does not support the unflinching reign of the majority—indeed, this is sometimes called the **tyranny of the majority**. Political decision-makers are supposed to accommodate and protect minority interests as well as those of the majority. So which group's delegate should the legislator be? Should it be the community's majority or the minority group whose interests may be significantly compromised? Furthermore, do all groups affected by legislation deserve to be represented equally? After all, a change to the criminal law involves the interests of both the victims of crime and the alleged criminals themselves. Even if a legislator decides which particular group he or she should speak for, it can still be difficult to discover what the preponderant view of that group really is—short of conducting ongoing opinion polls. Legislators do rely heavily on the letters and phone calls they receive, but these are always from a tiny, self-selecting group among their constituents. Sometimes petitions that are circulated in a community garner thousands of signatures, but these are not necessarily definitive of the group's position either.

The trustee view of representation suggests a very different role for legislators in acting on behalf of the groups they represent. In this view, legislators should understand the opinions and wishes of those they represent, but in the end they must use their own best judgment of what position to take on an issue. The earliest proponent of this view was Edmund Burke, a Whig politician in 18th-century Britain, but his views on this subject in particular are regarded as typical of classical Tory conservatism. An excerpt from Burke's famous speech to his voters in 1774 is reproduced in Box 8.3. An interesting footnote to this speech is that Burke lost the election in which he made it!

BOX 8.3

Certainly, gentlemen, it ought to be the happiness and glory of a representative to live in the strictest union, the closest correspondence, and the most unreserved communication with his constituents. Their wishes ought to have great weight with him; their opinion, high respect; their business, unremitted attention. . . . But his unbiassed opinion, his mature judgment, his enlightened conscience, he ought not to sacrifice to you, to any man, or to any set of men living. These he does not derive from your pleasure; no, nor from the law and the constitution. They are a trust from Providence, for the abuse of which he is deeply answerable. Your representative owes you, not his industry only, but his judgment; and he betrays, instead of serving you, if he sacrifices it to your opinion.

There are several justifications for this approach, and they reveal a different notion of the role of the representative and of public policy than that found in arguments for the delegate model. The first principle is that people entrust their representative to act in the best interests of their overall welfare. Just what specific measures may favour their long-term welfare may not be immediately clear to the people, who can be motivated by individual self-interest and by the passions of the moment. It is the job of the elected representative, in this view, to ascertain all the facts and listen to the range of opinions expressed during debates in the legislature, and then come to his or her own conclusion about what should be done. In all of this, too, the legislator is viewed not simply as a representative of a particular group or community who pursues nothing but their parochial interests. The legislator is also a national (or provincial) decision-maker who must also be concerned with the welfare and interests of the whole society. Legislators have to find a balance in the conflicts of interest between what may be good for the whole nation or province against the welfare of their own constituency. Box 8.4 discusses the question of a representative facing the even more difficult question of changing parties.

Representation is an abstract concept that carries enormous moral and philosophical weight. However, it is also something that has to operate within the real world of everyday politics. In fact, legislators usually end up living out all the different types of representation reviewed above at different times and on different issues. The real-world setting of modern legislatures also means that the fundamental principle guiding a legislator's public actions is that of party discipline. Usually the most vociferous representation of community or group interests occurs in parliamentary settings within a party's caucus, where individual legislators try to convince their colleagues that the party's policy should reflect these interests. Despite party discipline, however, individual legislators speak out in public from time to time in order to fully represent interests that are even more important to them than party loyalty. Breaking party ranks can occur for two reasons: legislators realize that the local groups feel so strongly about an issue that they may well face defeat in the next election if they do not speak out publicly, and individual legislators do from time to time simply hold extremely strong personal beliefs that a group's interests must be represented publicly regardless of the consequences.

A serious representational issue in many countries is the fact that their legislatures are so dominated by males and members of the largest ethnic group (see Figure 8.3 and Table 8.3). One of the issues that emerges from the microcosm or mirror view of representation is that

BOX 8.4

When representatives have been elected to a legislature as candidates for a particular party, should they be able to change their party whenever they want, or should they have to resign their seat and face an election as a candidate for the new party? The problem of "floor-crossing" is an ongoing controversy in many countries. The most recent storm of debate in Canada arose after the 2006 federal election when David Emerson agreed to sit as a Conservative MP and member of Stephen Harper's cabinet, only days after he had been elected in the Vancouver-Kingsway riding as a Liberal candidate. Great howls of protest erupted in his riding, with many people arguing that Emerson had betrayed the citizens' electoral choice in Vancouver-Kingsway. The voters there had relegated the Conservative candidate to third place in the election Emerson had won as a Liberal. The Ethics Commissioner of the House of Commons conducted a brief inquiry and concluded that the current code of conduct had not been breached by Mr. Emerson. Another famous instance of floor-crossing happened when Belinda Stronach switched from the Conservatives to the Liberals shortly before a confidence vote in May

2005; without her move, Paul Martin's Liberal government would have otherwise lost the vote and had to either resign or call an election.

There are two sides to the debate, with those influenced by Edmund Burke's view of representation arguing that elected members of the legislature should be able to take any course of action they believe best serves the interests of their constituency, including a change of party. Others, however, assert that modern voters essentially decide to vote on the basis of their choice of parties, and that their votes are undermined if their elected representative switches to a different party. Both South Africa and New Zealand have enacted legislation to require those who switch parties to resign and face an election if they wish to belong to a new party. These laws were subsequently challenged in court with quite different results. The South African Constitutional Court struck down the law in 2002, on the grounds that it interfered with a representative's freedom of action, while the New Zealand Supreme Court upheld the law in 2004, noting the centrality of political parties to elections and to the work of parliament.

legislatures do not currently reflect the composition of their societies as a whole. There are important practical and symbolic problems with systemic underrepresentation, and these are compounded when important social groups are completely lacking from the legislature. Not only may groups feel excluded from the political process if they are not visible participants in the main political institutions, but their interests may be only weakly represented by the others present—if represented at all. A continued lack of participation in the legislature, and continued losing out in the decisions made there, can contribute to political alienation and eventually lead to political violence. There are many socioeconomic reasons deeply embedded in a society's political culture that combine to create conditions where women and members of minority groups do not or cannot run for office and get elected. The social groups that do participate in the legislature can make a practical difference in the legislative process. A number of studies of the American Congress and Canadian legislatures have suggested that there may be slight but discernible differences in the way members of different ethnic groups and genders

Figure 8.3 Women in World Legislatures, Regional Averages

In an Inter-Parliamentary Union survey of 189 national legislatures, out of a total of 43,374 legislators whose gender was known, women constituted only 17.4 percent as of August 31, 2007.

Source: Inter-Parliamentary Union, "Women in Parliaments: World and Regional Averages"; available at http://www.ipu.org/wmn-e/world.htm; accessed November 13, 2007.

Table 8.3 Women in Selected National Legislatures Around the World

The 184 countries with legislatures are ranked 1 to 125 (because of a number of ties) according to the percentage of women members they included (in lower houses only for bicameral legislatures).

Rank	Country	Percent Women
1	Rwanda	48.8
2	Sweden	47.3
3	Finland	42.0
8	Cuba	36.0
10	Mozambique	34.8
13	New Zealand	32.2
13	Germany	31.6
48	Canada	20.8
52	United Kingdom	19.7
57	France	18.5
63	Italy	17.3
67	United States	16.3
97	Russia	9.4
98	Japan	7.1
106	India	8.3
113	Nigeria	7.0
131	Egypt	2.0
134	Saudi Arabia	0.0

Source: Inter-Parliamentary Union, "Women in Parliaments: World and Regional Averages"; available at http://www.ipu.org/wmn-e/classif.htm; accessed November 13, 2007.

vote on issues—even when other factors such as party affiliation and ideological leanings are accounted for.[18] Some researchers have even argued that women should be represented by women and ethnic minorities represented by members of their own groups, but this is a highly contested idea.[19]

Upper Houses

Although a majority of the world's legislatures are unicameral, some 63 national legislatures are bicameral. In Canada, all the provincial and territorial legislatures have a single chamber, while the national Parliament in Ottawa has two. Since unicameral legislatures are inherently more efficient, with all business conducted in a single process, it may seem strange that so many countries would set up bicameral legislatures. Indeed, many Canadians have become cynical about our upper house, the Senate, and would rather scrap it than reform it. A 2007 opinion poll found that 52 percent of Canadians favoured reforming the Senate, 24 percent preferred to abolish it, and only 16 percent wanted to keep it as it is.[20] The view that favours abolition, however, is probably based partly on a lack of appreciation of both what the Senate actually does and the significant roles that it might play in the political system. There are two main functions for upper houses that are appealing: these houses can act as an additional check and balance in the political process, and they may provide a forum for special representation of sectional (usually based on geographic regions) interests in the country.

Perhaps the most common function is to provide "sober second thought" about measures passed without proper consideration in the lower house. This can be a very useful process in states where one party or a coalition controls a majority of members in the lower house and where party discipline can ensure that this majority approves measures without much debate or against the wishes of the general public. A second chamber can act as a brake on the legislative process, give bills closer scrutiny, and hold up approval while public reaction is gauged. The Fathers of Confederation, who designed Canada's national political institutions, reflected 19th-century British thought in choosing an appointed second chamber to act as a restraint on the "passions of the moment" to which the elected MPs in the lower house could be susceptible. Our Senate, whose members are appointed and now sit until the age of 75, was modelled on the House of Lords in Britain, whose members were hereditary and appointed aristocrats. Box 8.5 addresses the different ways in which members of an upper house can be selected.

Just how effective a second chamber can be depends entirely upon its powers in the legislative process and how it uses them. Essentially, it depends upon whether the consent of the upper house is actually needed before a proposal can become law or whether the upper house can merely delay the approval process. A number of upper houses possess a "suspensive veto" only. This means that if the members of the upper house vote down a measure already approved by the lower house or fail to approve it within a set period of time, the members of the lower house can pass a motion restating their approval of the bill; the bill then becomes law, regardless of its treatment in the upper house. The House of Lords in Britain has only a suspensive veto, but it serves as a useful check and balance by forcing the government to slow down and gauge public opinion before the proposals are finally enacted into law. If the House of Lords rejects a bill, the government can reintroduce it into the House of Commons a year later and pass it without the need of sending it to the House of Lords again. The waiting period forces the government to reconsider the original measure, and the government often decides to compromise by making important changes to the bill or even to scrap it entirely.

An upper house can be even more effective if the constitution provides it with an absolute veto. In that case, the upper house has the power to defeat a bill, and both houses must pass a bill in identical form before it can become law. In countries such as Canada, the United States,

Members of upper chambers acquire the right to sit in the house in a variety of ways, and some chambers use more than one method. In Canada, all senators are chosen by the prime minister and appointed by the governor general, and they serve until the age of 75. In the United States and Australia, all senators are directly elected by the people. In India, most members of the upper house are indirectly elected, which means they are chosen by the legislatures of each state. In Russia, each state's governor and the speaker of the state legislature are ex-officio members of the country's upper house. Britain's House of Lords is composed of about 750 members, with 594 appointed for life, 92 hereditary peers chosen either by their fellow life peers or by their political parties, 26 bishops of the Church of England, and (until 2009) 28 Law Lords who are current and former members of Britain's final court of appeal, the House of Lords Appellate Committee.

Australia, India, and Japan, the upper house has an absolute veto over all legislation.[21] In other countries, the upper house has a veto only over certain types of legislation. In Germany, for example, the upper house can veto only legislation that would affect the equivalent of provincial governments. Armed with an absolute veto, the sober second thought offered by the upper house can indeed force the government or lower house to reflect seriously on its proposals. This absolute veto is seen as an important part of the checks and balances involved in some political systems' legislative process. For this reason, almost all the American and Australian states have a bicameral legislature. An upper house may also simply amend the bill rather than veto it outright; in that case, the two houses eventually have to reach an agreement on the final form of the bill. Even in countries where the upper house has only a suspensive veto, amendments made to legislation are often voluntarily adopted by the lower house; this may be done out of expediency to pass the bill as quickly as possible or because the amendments relate to some uncontroversial technical improvements.

An important consideration, however, is whether informal constitutional principles prevent an upper house from freely exercising its absolute veto or even from amending legislation. The Canadian senate, for instance, is constrained by constitutional conventions from using its powers to their full extent. Still, the senate plays a role of some substance in the legislative process in amending legislation and forcing the government to reconsider its proposals before asking the House of Commons to reaffirm its policies; occasionally, the government even agrees to amendments proposed by the senate.[22]

The other principal function of an upper house is to provide special representation in the legislature for territorial or non-territorial populations and interests that would otherwise go underrepresented or completely unrepresented. Territorial representation is very common in upper houses; for example, the French senate's members are chosen by the city, town, and county (*département*) councils. All federal countries have bicameral legislatures in order to provide the provinces or states with a more equal or more effective representation than they have in the lower houses; this increased representation can come either through a more equitable distribution of seats among the regions or provinces or by having representatives of the state or provincial governments sit as members of the upper house. Seats in the lower house are usually distributed roughly according to population, which allows large provinces or states to swamp the smaller ones; in the United States, for example, California has 52 members in the House of Representatives, while a small state such as Rhode Island has only two. A great imbalance like this is rectified in some countries by providing each state or province equal representation in the upper house; in the United States, each state has two seats in the senate regardless of size, and in Australia each state has 12.

Other federations do not have strict equality in the share of seats the states or provinces have in the upper house, but they do provide a more equitable distribution of seats. For instance, each of Germany's 16 states has between three and six seats in the Bundesrat, depending on its size. A few federations still have very significant disparities. Eight of India's states have only one seat in the upper house, the Rajya Sabha, while Uttar Pradesh has 34. Canada is rather odd, with a senate that was originally designed to provide equal shares of seats for regions, not the provinces per se. The Maritime provinces, Quebec, Ontario, and the four Western provinces count as regions, each having 24 seats.[23]

But the question remains: Is the representation of territorial interests in an upper house aimed at representing the population of the provinces or states, or is it meant to provide representation for the interests of their governments? Some countries choose to elect their upper-house representatives in order to give the citizens a direct voice; Australia and the United States are examples. Others choose to provide representation for the state or provincial governments rather than the people; for example, in Germany, Russia, and South Africa, political leaders from the state or provincial governments are members of the nation's upper house, and, in a sense, these chambers function like a permanent federal–provincial conference. Canada is an oddity in providing neither form of representation, since the federal government appoints all the members of the senate; as a result, neither the provincial population nor provincial governments are directly represented.

Upper houses can also provide representation of non-territorial sections of the population. Several countries allocate some of the seats in the upper house to representatives of particular professions. In Ireland, for instance, two universities each elect three senators, and 43 other senators are elected from five occupational groups.[24] And in Pakistan, five members of each delegation chosen by the provincial legislatures to represent them in the national senate must be members of certain religious or occupational groups.

Reform of Legislatures

There are as many ways to reform legislatures as there are limitations on their effectiveness. Some reforms involve the internal structure and procedures of the legislature, while other changes might occur if only factors external to the legislature change, such as the electoral system, media coverage, or something as amorphous as the society's political culture. In parliamentary systems, most reforms centre on finding ways to reduce the cabinet's dominance of the legislature and on loosening party discipline. One of the most frequent suggestions is that legislatures make greater use of "free votes." Occasionally, votes in a legislature are held where the parties agree that they will not formally require their members to maintain party loyalty; the members are free to vote according to their own personal judgment. These votes usually involve matters of deep personal conscience, such as capital punishment or abortion, and the suggestion is that free votes could also be extended to matters that do not imply a vote of confidence in the government.

Another suggestion in Canada is that the political parties could adopt the British practice of notifying members of where a vote fits on a sliding scale of the degree of party cohesion expected. For example, a "three-line whip" means "You'd better get out of your hospital bed and vote for the party's position"; such votes are normally matters of confidence. This scale for votes also includes two-line and one-line whips, with decreasing requirements for party cohesion. In fact, Paul Martin introduced a form of this procedure in 2004 after he became prime minister, and was fairly lenient on some measures, such as the same-sex marriage bill. But in the 2005 minority government position, the budget would not have passed without a three-line vote for Liberal MPs, the support of the NDP, the postponement of Independent MP Chuck Cadman's cancer treatments, the crossing of the floor by Belinda Stronach, and the tie-breaking vote of the Speaker. Extensive use of free votes, however, would mean that MPs need to use their own personal judgment more often; in the long run, more free votes require a much greater support and research staff for individual MPs, so that they can hold an informed assessment of the issues involved.

Other suggestions for parliaments centre on the degree of independence that legislative committees have to investigate policy issues on their own initiative, rather than requiring a cabinet-sanctioned motion in the legislature to begin the hearings. Considerable attention has also been focused in many parliamentary systems on changing the procedural rules dealing with bills introduced by private (non-cabinet) members, in order to give them a better chance of getting passed into law. Another reform that has significant potential—but a very low political profile—is to strengthen a legislature's ability to review delegated legislation and annul the regulations passed by the executive that go beyond the policies originally envisaged by the legislature when it passed the act authorizing the delegated legislation in the first place.

The upper houses of parliament in both Canada and the United Kingdom have come under increasing criticism for their non-elected membership; critics argue that legislatures must be elected to enjoy basic legitimacy in modern democracies. The British government has embarked on a series of reforms to transform the House of Lords over the past 20 years, but the government's latest proposals in 2007 fell short of proposing an entirely elected body. Instead the government's report noted the broad support in cross-party proposals for retaining an appointed element of experts and decided it would ultimately prefer to see the House of Lords as a hybrid body, with one half elected and one half appointed by an independent commission.[25] In Canada, the most vocal proponents of Senate reform argue that the body should be completely elected. This proposal was embodied in the "Triple-E" model first proposed in the 1980s in Alberta. These senators would be elected on a province-wide basis, and the Senate would fully exercise its legislative powers to amend or defeat legislation. The scheme would also see an equal number of senators for each province, as there are in Australia and the United States. The difficulty with this proposal is twofold. First, Ontario and Quebec reject the suggestion because their level of representation would be severely reduced. Second, the result of electing senators could possibly import into that house all the problems of tight party discipline that lie at the root of many of the problems in the House of Commons, leading to deadlock between the two chambers. The Harper government made two proposals in 2006 and 2007 to reform the Senate by limiting new senators to an eight-year term and also to allow general elections for any future vacancies. While there is strong support for reform, there are serious constitutional limits to what the federal government can achieve without formal amendments to the Constitution; formal amendments seem unlikely because of strong resistance by the Quebec and Ontario governments.

Several countries have seen debates over redressing the underrepresentation or exclusion of women and Indigenous peoples. One shortcut solution that is sometimes discussed is to set aside a certain number of seats in the legislature to ensure that at least some groups have a physical presence. For example, New Zealand has long had separate seats for the Indigenous Maori population, and a Royal Commission on Electoral Reform proposed in 1991 that Canada set aside some seats in Parliament for Aboriginal representatives.[26] So far, such ideas have not met with widespread support. In some countries, the idea of setting aside a specific number of seats for a group results in fierce controversy. For instance, fist fights broke out in the Indian parliament in 1998 when it debated an amendment to the constitution that would have required that one-third of the seats be reserved for women in the lower house of parliament and in all the state legislatures.[27] In Canada, residents of what was to become Nunavut voted down a 1998 referendum proposal to require equal representation for women and men in the new territorial legislature. Other ways to remedy these problems of underrepresentation within the legislature involve reforms outside of the legislature itself. For example, some political parties around the world voluntarily adopt policies requiring an equal number of male and female candidates and a certain number of candidates from particular ethnic groups. Other suggestions include adopting a proportional representation system, with party lists that can be deliberately constructed to provide representatives from the social groups in question.

CONCLUSION

This chapter has provided a brief examination of a range of issues related to the legislative branch of government. Legislatures are institutions with complex structures and processes, and their relationship with the rest of the political system involves many interconnected threads. Their many possible functions are all limited by a range of real-world constraints, some of which are integral to a particular system of government; executive dominance and party discipline remain both cornerstones and millstones of parliamentary government, for instance. However, this review of legislatures should open your horizons to the important contributions that most democratic legislatures do make to their political systems. These contributions can indeed be improved, but the interrelation between the structure and procedural rules on the one hand and political culture on the other mean that there are few quick fixes.

DISCUSSION QUESTIONS

1. Which form of representation do you find yourself favouring: the delegate or the trustee approach?

2. What range of social groups do you feel you belong to? If you were an MP, on what sorts of issues would you believe that you should "represent" one of those groups rather than the others?

3. Imagine that you are a member of the governing party's caucus in the Canadian House of Commons who is not in Cabinet. Think of what you would say in a caucus meeting about the need to loosen party discipline. Then picture yourself as the Prime Minister and think of what you would say in response.

4. What do you think is the single most important constraint on Canadian legislatures that stems from our political culture? Can you see any way in which the cultural values involved may change?

KEY TERMS

BILL: The formal text of a proposed law before it has been enacted into law. Prior to being introduced into the legislature, it is known as a draft bill. Once it has been introduced, it is known as a bill. When the bill has completed all stages of the legislative process, it becomes law and is known as a statute or an act. (223)

CLOSURE: A term used to describe procedural rules that permit the majority to put an end to debate on a motion and require that a vote on the matter be held; also known as cloture, the guillotine, and time allocation in various countries. (231)

COALITION GOVERNMENT: A government that occurs when two or more parties hold seats in cabinet supported by a combination of parties that forms a majority in the legislature. (226)

CONFIDENCE (OR NON-CONFIDENCE) VOTE: There are three types of such a vote. It may be an explicitly worded motion indicating that the legislature either has or does not have confidence in the government; a vote on a matter that the government has previously declared to be a matter of confidence; or a vote on important measures that are central to the government's plans, such as the budget. (225)

FILIBUSTER: A device used by a member or group of members who take advantage of the procedural rules of a legislature that allow members to speak for extended periods of time in order to stall proceedings. (231)

LEGISLATURE: An institution with primary responsibility to enact laws. (220)

MAJORITY GOVERNMENT: A government in which one party holds all the seats in the cabinet as well as the majority of seats in the legislature (or lower house in bicameral legislatures). (225)

MINORITY GOVERNMENT: A government in which one party holds all the seats in the cabinet but has less than 50 percent of the members in the legislature. (225)

PARTY DISCIPLINE: The practice that all members in a legislature belonging to the same political party should normally vote the same way, in accordance with their party's stand on the issue at hand. (227)

RESPONSIBLE GOVERNMENT: A defining principle of Westminster-style parliamentary governments, which states that the cabinet may only hold office as long as it has majority support in the legislature (or lower house in a bicameral parliament) for votes of confidence. (225)

WEB LINKS

Nelson Education: Introduction to Legislatures (World):
http://polisci.nelson.com/introlegs.html

Nelson Education: Legislatures (Canadian):
http://polisci.nelson.com/legislatures.html

Library of Parliament: The Opposition in a Parliamentary System:
http://www.parl.gc.ca/information/library/PRBpubs/bp47-e.htm

Inter-Parliamentary Union:
http://www.ipu.org

FURTHER READING

Docherty, David C. *Legislatures*. Vancouver: UBC Press, 2005.

———. *Mr. Smith Goes to Ottawa*. Vancouver: UBC Press, 1997.

Franks, C.E.S. *The Parliament of Canada*. Toronto: University of Toronto Press, 1987.

Heard, Andrew. *Canadian Constitutional Conventions: The Marriage of Law and Politics*. Toronto: Oxford University Press, 1991.

Inter-Parliamentary Union. *World Directory of Parliaments*. Geneva: IPU, 1998.

ENDNOTES

1. Inter-Parliamentary Union, "Women in Parliaments: World Classification"; available at: http://www.ipu.org/wmn-e/classif.htm; accessed November 12, 2007.

2. It should be noted that even in countries without a legislature, the judiciary still exercises a certain amount of legislative power by interpreting and enforcing the laws passed by the executive.

3. Inter-Parliamentary Union, *Parliaments of the World: A Comparative Reference Compendium*, 3rd ed., vol. 2 (Aldershot: IPU, 1986), p. 1125.

4. Calculated from: "Résumé of Congressional Activity: 1st Session of the 109th Congress," available at http://www.senate.gov/reference/resources/pdf/109-1res.pdf, accessed June 2, 2008; and from "Résumé of Congressional Activity: 2nd Session of the 109th Congress," available at http://www.senate.gov/reference/resources/pdf/109-1res.pdf, accessed November 12, 2007.

5. David C. Docherty, *Mr. Smith Goes to Ottawa* (Vancouver: UBC Press, 1997), p. 129.

6. Philip Norton, "The United Kingdom: Restoring Confidence," *Parliamentary Affairs* 50 (1997): 360.

7. Docherty, *op. cit.*, pp. 190–91.

8. J.P. Joseph Maignot, *Parliamentary Privilege in Canada*, 2nd ed. (Montreal and Kingston: McGill-Queen's University Press, 1997), p. 335.

9. André Blais et al., "Does the Local Candidate Matter?"; available at http://ces-eec.mcgill.ca/publications2000.html#10; accessed June 2, 2008.

10. Louis Massicotte, "Party Cohesion in the Ontario Legislative Assembly, 1867–1990," paper presented at the annual meeting of the Canadian Political Science Association, Calgary, June 1994.

11. Keith Jackson, "Caucus: The Anti-Parliament System?," *Parliamentarian* 59(3) (July 1978): 160.

12. Philip Norton, *The Commons in Perspective* (Oxford: Martin Robertson, 1981), p. 227.

13. *Congressional Quarterly Almanac Plus 2003* (Washington, DC: CQ Press, 2004), p. B14.

14. Andrew Heard, *Canadian Constitutional Conventions: The Marriage of Law and Politics* (Toronto: Oxford University Press, 1991), pp. 87–98.

15. Ontario Legislative Library Legislative Research Service, "The Ontario Legislature: An Overview"; available at http://www.lirico.ca/ipac20/ipac.jsp?session=U20935105W592.96415&profile=lirico-eng&uri=link=3100007~!429006~!3100001~!3100002&aspect=subtab101&menu=search&ri=1&source=~!horizon&term=Ontario.+Legislative+Library.+Legislative+Research+Service.&index=#focus; accessed June 2, 2008.

16. These figures are calculated from information at "Presidential Vetoes, 1798–2008," available at http://www.infoplease.com/ipa/A0801767.html, accessed May 21, 2008;

and "House Overrides Bush Veto of Farm Bill," available at http://news.yahoo.com/s/nm/20080522/pl_nm/bush_farmbill_dc_7, accessed May 21, 2008.

17. *Clinton v. City of New York*, [1998] 118 S. Ct. 2091.

18. For example, see Jane Arscott and Linda Trimble, eds., *In the Presence of Women* (Toronto: Harcourt Brace, 1997); and Julie Dolan, "Support for Women's Interests in the 103rd Congress: The Distinct Impact of Congressional Women," *Women in Politics* 18(4) (1997): 88. Note, however, that contrary conclusions have been found with respect to African-American members of the American Congress; see Carol M. Swain, *Black Faces, Black Interests: The Representation of African Americans in Congress* (Cambridge: Harvard University Press, 1993).

19. Jane Mansbridge, "Should Blacks Represent Blacks and Women Represent Women? A Contingent 'Yes,'" *Journal of Politics* 61 (1999): 628. This article contains a good review of the arguments for and against mirror or descriptive representation.

20. Ipsos Reid, "The Future of the Senate"; available at http://www.ipsos-na.com/news/pressrelease.cfm?id=3717; accessed June 2, 2008.

21. Except that the Canadian Senate does not have an absolute veto over constitutional amendments, as mentioned in Chapter 6.

22. Heard, *op. cit.*, pp. 87–98.

23. Quebec and Ontario each have 24 seats. The Maritime provinces' 24 seats are divided into 10 seats each for Nova Scotia and New Brunswick and four seats for PEI. The four Western provinces each have six seats. When Newfoundland entered Confederation, it was given six seats. Each of the three territories has one senator, for a grand total of 105.

24. These five occupational groups are Culture and Education, Agriculture, Labour, Industry and Commerce, and Public Administration.

25. Royal Commission on Electoral Reform and Party Financing, *Final Report*, vol. 1 (Ottawa: 1991).

26. "The House of Lords: Reform," February 2007; available at: http://www.official-documents.gov.uk/document/cm70/7027/7027.pdf; accessed November 13, 2007.

27. Shri G.C. Malhotra, "Parliamentary Pandemonium: Taking Opposition Too Far," *Parliamentarian* 80(2) (April 1999).

Chapter Nine

THE JUDICIARY: Politics, Law, and the Courts

Andrew Heard

CHAPTER OBJECTIVES

After you have completed this chapter, you should be able to:

■ understand the role of law and the courts in a political system

■ evaluate the strengths and weaknesses of different methods of appointing judges

■ discuss the issues involved in judicial independence and impartiality

■ outline how access to the courts is restricted

The Role of Law and the Judicial Function

In stable societies, law and judges play crucial roles that are not always seen or widely appreciated. Law sets the most basic rules of behaviour for all citizens and can impose fundamental limits on the power of government officials. The judicial power is an essential part of the power of governments, and through it authoritative decisions are made on disputes covering a wide range of matters. The courts have become so much a part of the fabric of our political system that they are often simply taken for granted. Yet they are in some ways "the power behind the throne." The courts perform many vital functions and have an enormous cumulative impact, not only through the policies they enforce on behalf of the elected government but also through those they develop and implement themselves. Perhaps ironically, the power of the judiciary may be most appreciated in countries where the courts are weak, corrupt, or simply subservient to the whims of the political or military leaders of the day. There, many people long for the day when the courts will become independent developers and protectors of constitutional limits on the rulers and provide effective punishments for those who undermine basic law and order or openly terrorize people through brute force.

If you stop to think about your life, you will find that much of it depends upon laws that tell you what to do and not do, help you have what you are entitled to, protect you from false accusations, and provide you with a peaceful way to resolve disputes that arise. You also probably do many things the law requires you to do, whether you like it or not, because you believe that, in general, it is right and proper to obey the law. While we all probably break some laws some of the time, most of us still believe that we should obey most laws most of the time. In democratic countries such as Canada, obedience to the law and respect for the courts are ingrained in the general political culture (see Figure 9.1).

The existence of courts to adjudicate disputes ensures that conflicts are decided by rules of law and not through the rule of might. If you have a dispute with your neighbour or a store clerk, you do not have to resort to rounding up the biggest of your friends to go and sort it out. Moreover, the courts ensure that a mere accusation is not sufficient for someone to be punished—guilt or innocence must be carefully and objectively determined. Finally, the courts can ensure that the rule of law is observed and that the government does not act outside its powers or fail to perform duties required under law.

Unfortunately, the costs of judicial proceedings raise serious questions about the equal access of all to the courts. There are also deep controversies over the extent to which judges can, or should, exercise their own discretion in interpreting the law to reflect their own personal values. Furthermore, there are important questions about how judges are appointed and removed from office, as well as the extent to which elected politicians should be involved in those decisions.

Connections Between Law, Morality, and Politics

Law is not an independent force in a society, nor is it simply a set of rules of procedure. Law gives life to the policies of the government. Law may be either an instrument of justice, as is the ideal in a democratic society, or an instrument of oppression. What matters in the end is the content of the law and how it is applied and enforced. Law may be the embodiment of the noblest principles of a free democracy, or it may be the instrument used to implement torture and mass murder. Canada's legal history provides examples of the best and worst of the content of law. The law provides Canadians with free schooling, minimum wages, workplace

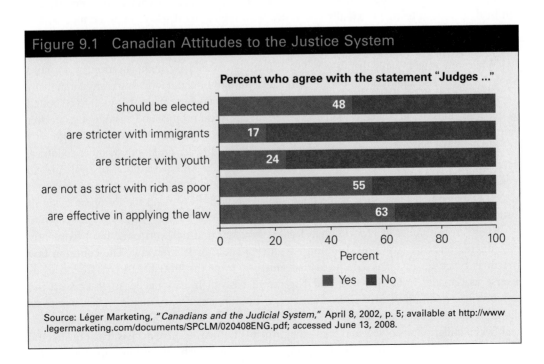

Figure 9.1 Canadian Attitudes to the Justice System

Percent who agree with the statement "Judges ..."

should be elected	48
are stricter with immigrants	17
are stricter with youth	24
are not as strict with rich as poor	55
are effective in applying the law	63

Yes ■ No

Source: Léger Marketing, "*Canadians and the Judicial System*," April 8, 2002, p. 5; available at http://www .legermarketing.com/documents/SPCLM/020408ENG.pdf; accessed June 13, 2008.

safety, universal health care, and unemployment insurance; the *Charter of Rights* protects many rights, such as our freedom of speech and the right to vote. However, Canadian laws have also prohibited women, Chinese Canadians, and Aboriginal people from voting. Canadian laws also provided the basis for interning Canadian citizens of Japanese descent during World War II and for the complete seizure of their property and businesses.[1] There were even laws in British Columbia, Saskatchewan, Manitoba, and Ontario that prohibited white women from working for Chinese or Japanese males.

The content of law is very much a reflection of the prevailing mores and values of a society at any given time. More to the point, the law in any society embodies the prevailing moral values of the dominant elite. As times and attitudes change, so do the moral beliefs enacted into law and enforced by the courts. In Canada, homosexual activity was once illegal, but recently the courts have required Canadian governments to extend spousal benefits to same-sex couples. Indeed, marriage itself has been extended to same-sex couples after a series of court rulings. Thus, the content of the law and the morality enforced by the law change over time and vary from one country to another. While adultery was once illegal in the United States, it is no longer a crime enforced by the courts; on the other hand, it is still an offence for which people are executed in Saudi Arabia and Iran. Given the intimate connection between law and politics, intense political conflicts are involved in what gets written into law and how that law is interpreted.

Different Types of Law

There are different types of law to regulate different types of activity and disputes. The major division in law is public versus private. **Public law** includes constitutional law, criminal law, and many aspects of international law. Public law involves the rules of how government is structured and the powers and relations between various government bodies and officials and between the government and the public. Criminal law, part of public law, is largely concerned with matters of public safety, health, and morality. Thus, it is a crime to beat or murder somebody; it is a crime to sell dangerous drugs; and it is a crime for an adult to have sex with a child. **Private law** can be described as being principally concerned with regulating disputes between members of the public, be they individuals, groups of people, or corporations. The many different areas of private law govern contracts, corporations, inheritance, real estate, and employment.

While one might think that law is just something created by each government within a country, there is also an important body of **international law**. International law is created in many ways: formal treaties or conventions signed by the governments of the states that wish to be bound by it, declarations of the United Nations, and even the historical practice and custom of states over time. International law covers not only how the governments of different countries deal with each other, but also how businesses and individuals from one country are dealt with by other countries. International trade could not exist at today's levels without a strong collection of legal rules to regulate trade and settle disputes. There are even some international courts set up to deal with aspects of international law, such as the International Court of Justice and the European Court of Justice. See Chapter 15 for more on this aspect of law.

There are a number of very different legal systems around the world; the most frequently encountered ones are based on common law, a civil code, or Islamic law. The **common law** system is practised in many countries that emerged from the British Empire. Countries as diverse as Canada, India, Jamaica, and Nigeria all base their national legal systems on the common law tradition of Britain. In this system, the fundamental principle is that like cases should be decided alike and that courts are bound by the precedents of previous decisions that dealt with similar points of law and fact—the principle known as *stare decisis*. Historically, the common law also described a set of judge-made rules that British judges developed in the late

Middle Ages in the absence of extensive formal legislation by parliament. Only a small subset of these common law rules survive today; in Canada and Britain, they relate mainly to private law and some aspects of the power of the executive branch of government.

The civil code systems of law are found mainly in Western Europe and in newer states that emerged from the French Empire. In this system, the law is organized as a set of principles that, in theory, are applied freshly to each case. In practice, however, judges pay close attention to past decisions on the particular sections of the code involved in a case. This family of legal systems has an ancient lineage. While there are separate French, German, Dutch, and Swiss origins of the modern systems, in the French case dating from a code enacted under Napoleon Bonaparte in 1804, many principles can be traced back to the laws of the Roman Empire. It should be noted that Quebec has continued to use an updated version of the Napoleonic Code for private law matters, while the other provinces have systems based on British common law.

The most strikingly different system of law in fairly wide use today is the Islamic system of law, known as the *sharia*. This system is based on a collection of ancient Islamic teachings on how people should behave and what punishments are appropriate for particular transgressions. Essentially, the Islamic holy scriptures, the Qur'an, and the later writings of scholars form the basis of the sharia. Because the sharia is based on a collection of writings, it can operate in somewhat different ways in the countries that use it, as different aspects are emphasized. Its strictest implementation is found in states such as Saudi Arabia and Iran, where punishments that seem cruel by Western standards are meted out: floggings, the severing of a hand for theft, and execution for adultery, either by beheading or stoning. The sharia also entrenches different standards for the sexes, with a prohibition against convicting a man on the evidence of one woman while a woman may be convicted on the word of one man. The adoption of Islamic law in the late 1990s by several of Nigeria's states caused significant controversy in that country, and a constitutional challenge to its use was started in early 2002 by activists who claim that it violates Nigeria's constitutional guarantees of equality by subjecting citizens in some parts of the country to significantly harsher penalties. Other states, such as Egypt, have adapted Islamic law and implemented more moderate aspects of the code. In general, Islamic marital law is patriarchal, with significantly more rights for men than women, especially with respect to matrimonial property. Canadian courts have at times refused to apply foreign court judgments that enforced Islamic matrimonial law. For example, Justice Burchell of the Nova Scotia Supreme Court said in 1987: "To put it simply, I will not give effect to Iranian matrimonial law because it is archaic and repugnant to ideas of substantial justice in this province."[2] This backdrop highlights the controversy in recent years in Ontario, where the provincial government considered permitting family law cases to be settled through alternative dispute resolution settings, including a couple's religious institutions. This would have meant that disputes between Islamic spouses in Ontario could be settled according to Islamic law if both parties agreed; critics argued, however, that this meant Islamic women would be pressured into using a system inherently unfair to women. The government later abandoned this policy proposal.

The Judicial Function

With laws comes a need to interpret and enforce them. Judicial power is exercised by those institutions and officials authorized to interpret and enforce the law. Here it is important to distinguish between judicial power and the courts. Although courts are usually the primary focus of judicial power, most political systems also include other officials or institutions who have an important role to play in interpreting and enforcing laws. Where judicial power is exercised by officials or bodies other than judges and the courts, it is usually known as quasi-judicial power. In all industrialized democracies and in most other states, the executive branch of government exercises a considerable amount of such power. For example, if you had a dispute with your landlord, you would go to a residential tenancies tribunal, where it would be heard and settled according to the laws governing apartment and house rentals. Or if you felt you had been unfairly denied unemployment insurance or welfare benefits, you would first argue your case before tribunals composed of civil servants. Refugees in Canada have their cases initially decided by a panel of officials whose job it is to determine whether someone qualifies as a refugee and may remain in the country. Thus, important issues about whether people can stay in their apartments, have enough money to live on, or remain in the country are decided according to the relevant laws by **administrative tribunals**, which are not actual courts. However, the decisions of these tribunals can usually be appealed to the courts for a final decision.

The judicial function can also be carried out by very different types of courts, and the legitimacy or effectiveness of judicial powers may depend on which courts deal with which matters. When political scientists and lawyers refer to "the courts," we normally mean what are properly called civil courts, which are presided over by civilian judges with some degree of independence from the other branches of government and political authorities. Military courts, in contrast, are presided over by serving members of the military; depending upon the country, the presiding officers may or may not have legal training. In Canada and Britain, for example, the lowest level of military tribunals, known as *summary trials*, are presided over by the normal officer commanding the unit, who might be an engineer, a pilot, or an infantry officer. Nevertheless, some courts-martial have presiding officers who are trained lawyers.

Military courts are usually characterized by expedited processes, fewer legal protections for the accused, and harsher penalties. While most democracies restrict the jurisdiction of military courts to members of the armed forces, some countries may try the most serious offences against the state in military courts and leave more minor cases to the civil courts. And, of course, countries run by military dictators may rely exclusively on military tribunals. The use of military courts has become a political issue in the United States, as President Bush announced in 2001 that alleged terrorists captured during the war in Afghanistan would be held at a U.S. naval base in Cuba and tried before military commissions. The concern of many is that those to be tried by these tribunals lack the constitutional rights that they would normally have if tried before the civil courts within American territory.

Some countries also have religious courts that may operate alongside civil courts or instead of them. Countries that fully implement the Islamic sharia, such as Saudi Arabia and Iran, are most likely to empower religious courts to try cases dealing with public offences. Religious courts usually provide few if any opportunities for an accused to be properly represented by legal counsel, and the laws they enforce are interpretations of religious doctrines and decrees by religious authorities rather than individual laws passed by the legislature. Perhaps the most famous example in recent times were the religious courts that dished out a brutal justice under the Taliban rule of Afghanistan in the 1990s. However, much of Western Europe also experienced religious courts in the Middle Ages, when tribunals of the Roman Catholic church exercised considerable authority; the trials of the Inquisition are the most notorious examples, with thousands put to death.

The Role of Courts

The primary function that is part of everything else performed by the **judiciary** is the interpretation and enforcement of the law. Laws are necessarily worded in ambiguous ways and cannot foresee all the future circumstances to which they must be applied. Thus, the judges must fill in the blanks and flesh out the wording of legal rules; they interpret what the laws mean. The judiciary also enforces the law by determining the guilt or innocence of those charged with an offence and by punishing those who do not obey the law. The courts do not go out and look for wrongdoers; they deal only with those who are brought before them. This role of enforcing the law ensures that there is general obedience to the rules of society and that peaceful people can be protected from wrongdoers.

In the criminal context, the judiciary comes into play after the police or some other executive agency has discovered evidence of wrongdoing. The courts also have an important role in helping to settle private disputes (often called civil disputes) between individuals, groups, or companies. When we have a dispute over what someone has done to our property and want compensation to pay for the damages, we can go to the courts. In business, if a company does not live up to its contractual agreements or provides faulty or damaged goods, the dispute can be settled in the courts. Many disputes in our private lives can be settled in courts, according to laws that apply to everybody. Judges decide who is to blame and who violated the law; they then determine what penalty is appropriate and what compensation is due to the person or group that was wronged. Because of this, we do not have to rely on violence or vengeance to get what is owed to us. This function of the judiciary allows us to live in a peaceful society.

The courts can also act as referees that decide whether government officials are acting within their powers. The power of judicial review is the power of the courts to decide whether law authorized an action taken by a government official or body and whether a law is actually constitutional.

Courts settle disputes primarily through adjudication, which is the settling of a dispute by applying rules (laws) to the facts of a case. Adjudication is quite different from arbitration and mediation, in which one tries to find an equitable resolution to a dispute that ideally provides the best possible solution for all parties involved. Courts face a conundrum in adjudicating disputes. Although judges are supposed to apply the law to the facts of the case, the law is often ambiguous or even plagued by gaps and loopholes; there is not always a clear, existing law to apply. As a result, judges have an important role to play in interpreting the existing law. In the process of interpreting the law, judges sometimes have to make new law. Furthermore, in the process of interpreting and making new law, judges are often involved in a substantial way in policymaking, a role that is seen most clearly in interpreting constitutional rights but is involved in virtually all aspects of judicial interpretation.

The courts also have an important role to play in enforcing legal limits on the powers of politicians. While this role is almost taken for granted in established democracies, it is vital in transitional democracies, where political leaders are tempted to ignore constitutional limits in trying to implement their policies. For example, judges in Zimbabwe tried for many years to restrain President Mugabe's tightening grip on that country and steer his government into respecting the country's constitution. However, they lost their fight in 2001, when the majority of the top court resigned after the chief justice decided that he could no longer guarantee the safety of the members of that court who had stood up to Mugabe. After their resignations, Mugabe appointed new judges loyal to his policies, and they quickly went about giving the court's stamp of approval to his government's actions.[3] President Musharraf managed a similar purge of the Pakistani judiciary in 2007, as he attempted to sustain his military rule (see Box 9.1). At least the Zimbabwean and Pakistani judges fared better than those in Uganda in the 1970s, some of whom were assassinated by President Idi Amin's security forces.

In enforcing limits on the powers of politicians, the courts are enforcing the principle of the rule of law. Although this principle is open to many interpretations, key aspects can be identified to reinforce the idea that law should govern all actions of governments. Laws must emanate from a known, formal institution authorized by the constitution to exercise legislative power. Citizens must be able to find out what the laws are that they are bound to obey. The law

Musharraf's Crackdown on the Courts

BOX 9.1

KARACHI—In the current upheavals in Pakistan, one thing appears certain. Military ruler Gen Pervez Musharraf will not entertain letting former Supreme Court Chief Justice Iftikhar Chaudhry back into his job. On Sunday he lashed out at Mr Chaudhry again, calling him corrupt and a hurdle in the way of the smooth working of the government. He told journalists in Islamabad that the entire problem of the judiciary boiled down to one individual, Mr Chaudhry, who he sacked as part of the state of emergency introduced on 3 November [2007]. If that is the case, then why have so many other judges also been sacked, Mr Chaudhry asks?

The Supreme Court had, in recent weeks, set itself two pivotal tasks. The first, to decide if Gen Musharraf is eligible to stand for another term as president when his current term expires this week. The second, to decide if an amnesty he had signed that clears Benazir Bhutto and others from corruption cases is legal. In other words, the Supreme Court had set itself the task of deciding if the whole delicate framework of a future power-sharing deal should be allowed to proceed.

Gen Musharraf introduced the emergency in a way that meant judges could stay in their jobs only if the government invited them to swear a new oath of office. Mr Chaudhry was only one of many judges not to receive that invitation—hence the widespread belief that the main purpose of the state of emergency was to subdue once and for all an increasingly troublesome judiciary.

The imposition of emergency rule has led to a virtual collapse of the higher judiciary in Pakistan—that is the Supreme Court and the High Courts of the country's four provinces. Nearly 60% of the judges have been ousted from office either because they were not invited to take a new oath of office, or because they refused the offer. . . .

While the judicial system is thus paralysed, a little-noticed amendment to the Army Act has created further problems for the judicial system. Since 2003 military intelligence outfits that have no legal powers of arrest have picked up hundreds of people from various parts of the country and kept them in undeclared custody for months, even years. There is widespread evidence that most of these "missing persons" are non-violent supporters of nationalist groups from Balochistan and Sindh provinces. Those who have been released have talked of being kept in solitary confinement and being tortured. There are also reports of people dying, or being permanently incapacitated, while in illegal detention.

In no case yet have the intelligence agencies been prepared to stand up in court and defend themselves. This was evident when the agencies concerned were forced by the Supreme Court to produce more than 160 such persons before it this year. All of them had to be released due to lack of evidence against them. The government now hopes that such detainees will be dealt with through summary trials in military courts.

SOURCE: M. Ilyas Khan, "Musharraf's Crackdown on the Courts," BBC News website, November 14, 2007; available at http://news.bbc.co.uk/2/hi/south_asia/7094523.stm; accessed June 13, 2008.

should apply to everyone in the society, including all government officials. This does not mean that the law cannot make distinctions or exceptions, just that those exceptions must be included in the law itself. And finally, the law must ultimately be enforced by proper courts of law. These aspects of the rule of law do not in themselves mean that a government is going to be democratic or benevolent; after all, even the apartheid regime in South Africa used proper laws and courts to enforce white supremacy and the brutal oppression of the non-white majority. However, one can say that no democratic government can function without respecting the rule of law. Thus the rule of law is a necessary but not sufficient condition for democracy.

In fulfilling their general roles, the courts may at times play a very active role in highly charged political disputes. For example, the Canadian Supreme Court has twice been asked to settle high-profile political controversies. In 1981, it had to rule on the constitutionality of Prime Minister Trudeau's plans to patriate the Canadian constitution and introduce the *Charter of Rights* without gaining the consent of the provincial governments. In the *Patriation Reference* case, the Supreme Court ruled that the federal government's proposed unilateral actions were legal but contravened the informal constitutional conventions that required substantial provincial consent to changes to provincial powers. Then in the 1998 *Quebec Secession Reference* case, the Court was asked to declare whether Quebec had a right to secede from Canada under either domestic constitutional law or international law. It ruled that Quebec did not have this right at all, but that the rest of Canada would be under a moral obligation to negotiate the terms of separation if a clear majority voted in favour on a clear question to pursue independence. In both the *Patriation Reference* case and the *Quebec Secession Reference*, the court appeared to carefully craft a decision that went beyond the strict law and to provide answers that played to both sides of the political disputes at hand.[4] The structure of the Canadian court system is outlined in Figure 9.2.

Decades earlier, the U.S. Supreme Court catalyzed profound social and political changes in ordering that the racially segregated school systems be integrated, leading to a system of court-monitored busing of millions of school children.[5] In December 2000, the U.S. Supreme Court

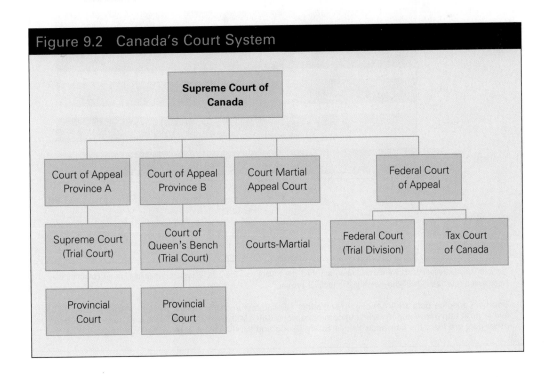

Figure 9.2   Canada's Court System

became embroiled in the fallout from the unclear presidential election results that depended entirely on the outcome of voting in Florida. In a decision that generated much heated debate in the United States, the Court ruled that recounts of the votes cast in certain counties of Florida should not proceed—effectively declaring George Bush the winner and new president.[6] This decision was one of the most controversial made by the Supreme Court in years, with many critics declaring that the court's split along partisan lines showed that Republican-appointed judges came to the rescue of their party's presidential candidate.[7] The Ukraine Supreme Court played a pivotal role in 2004 and 2005 by annulling corrupted presidential elections, ordering a new round of voting, and upholding the results of the later ballot. The court's decisions ended the authoritarian rule of President Leonid Kuchma and his intended successor Viktor Yanukovych. It came as a relief or surprise to many—considering how little confidence Ukrainians have had in their judicial system (see Figure 9.3).

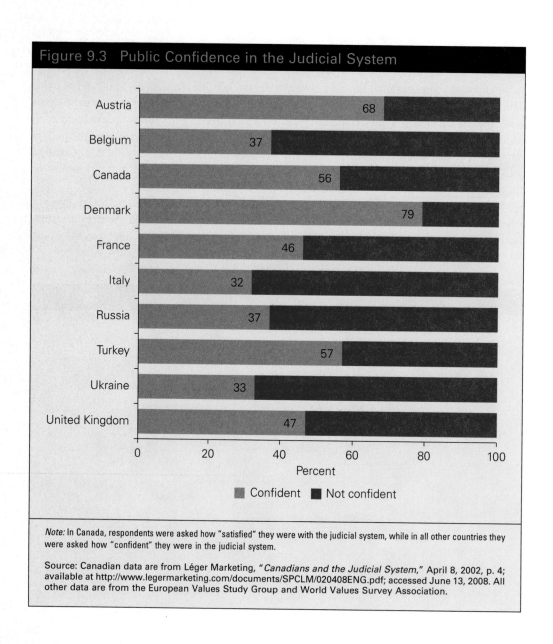

Figure 9.3 Public Confidence in the Judicial System

Note: In Canada, respondents were asked how "satisfied" they were with the judicial system, while in all other countries they were asked how "confident" they were in the judicial system.

Source: Canadian data are from Léger Marketing, *"Canadians and the Judicial System,"* April 8, 2002, p. 4; available at http://www.legermarketing.com/documents/SPCLM/020408ENG.pdf; accessed June 13, 2008. All other data are from the European Values Study Group and World Values Survey Association.

Judicial Review

In democratic countries, as discussed in Chapter 6, the court's powers of **judicial review** are very important to ensuring that the principles of limited government and the rule of law are respected by government actors. If there are to be legal limits on the powers of state actors, then somebody has to review their actions to ensure that they are legal. The courts conduct several different types of judicial review with varying degrees of controversy (see Figure 9.4), but they all involve the same basic role: the review of other state actors to ensure they fulfil their duties and do not act beyond their powers.

One type of judicial review is without controversy in countries that practise the rule of law: to make sure that government officials respect the ordinary statutory provisions that govern their powers. Officials can do only what the law empowers them to do, and they must perform what the law requires them to do. Thus, teachers cannot wear army uniforms and carry guns in the classroom. School board officials must allow parents to register their children to attend school if they meet the normal requirements of age and residency. And no one can be refused a new driver's licence just because he or she has red hair; everyone must be issued a licence having completed all the forms, passed the test, and paid the fee. One example of judges conducting this type of judicial review is the writ of *habeas corpus*; in this process, lawyers can ask the court to determine whether their client is being lawfully held in custody. The police have to establish that the detention is justified under the law.

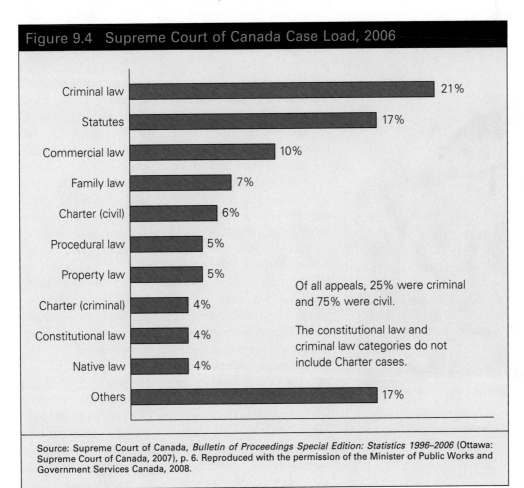

Figure 9.4   Supreme Court of Canada Case Load, 2006

Category	Percentage
Criminal law	21%
Statutes	17%
Commercial law	10%
Family law	7%
Charter (civil)	6%
Procedural law	5%
Property law	5%
Charter (criminal)	4%
Constitutional law	4%
Native law	4%
Others	17%

Of all appeals, 25% were criminal and 75% were civil.

The constitutional law and criminal law categories do not include Charter cases.

Source: Supreme Court of Canada, *Bulletin of Proceedings Special Edition: Statistics 1996–2006* (Ottawa: Supreme Court of Canada, 2007), p. 6. Reproduced with the permission of the Minister of Public Works and Government Services Canada, 2008.

The second broad type of judicial review involves the courts' scrutiny of the other branches of government to ensure that their actions are within the constitution. As mentioned in Chapter 6, constitutions can limit government powers either by dividing power between different levels of government or by protecting citizens' rights. Judicial review on these grounds involves the scrutiny of the actions of specific officials, such as police and customs officers, and may also involve the review of legislation passed by municipal, provincial, or national legislatures. It should be noted that this type of judicial review can occur only in countries having formal constitutional documents that set limits on government bodies and officials. In addition to the court-enforceable *Charter of Rights*, Canada's constitution also sets limits on the powers of parliament and provincial legislatures because of the federal–provincial division of powers. Some countries have no equivalent of the *Charter of Rights* or a federal system, so there is little basis for this form of judicial review.

The review of legislation on the basis of a division of powers is not inherently controversial. If there is to be a real federal system in which the national and regional governments are each given jurisdiction over specific areas of public policy, the courts have to play the role of referee. Someone has to make sure that one level of government does not try to pass laws on matters that are really in the jurisdiction of the other level of government, and the courts have that job.

The Supreme Court of Canada building in Ottawa, a site of increasing significance in the Canadian political system.

CP Photo/Tom Hanson

Controversy can occur, however, if suspicions are aroused that the courts are somehow biased in favour of one level of government. For example, Quebec nationalists have long argued that the Supreme Court of Canada has been biased because the federal government appoints all its members, although academic studies have not found any actual bias in the Court's decisions.

In the process of interpreting the division of powers, the courts can profoundly transform the character of the federal system by either centralizing power in the national government or decentralizing power in the regional governments. For example, Canada's federal system has been significantly decentralized since 1867, thanks in large part to key decisions of the **Judicial Committee of the Privy Council (JCPC)**, a British body that served as Canada's final court of appeal until 1949, when the **Supreme Court of Canada** finally did become "supreme." As noted in Chapter 6, several key decisions of the JCPC limited the federal government's power on the one hand and expanded the authority of the provinces on the other. For one, the federal government's jurisdiction over trade and commerce has been restricted to interprovincial and international trade, while the provinces' power over property and civil rights has been interpreted to give them powers over trade within the province.

Judicial review based on a constitutionally protected set of rights can be even more controversial because of the social and economic policies that judges get to decide (see Box 9.2). The first instance of judges conducting such constitutional review came in the 1803 case *Marbury v. Madison*, when the U.S. Supreme Court under Chief Justice Marshall declared a law unconstitutional.[8] This case marked a watershed in judicial power, as it was the first time a court anywhere successfully

Big M Drug Mart [1985] struck down Sunday closing mandated under the *Lord's Day Act*.

R. v. Oakes [1986] set out the guidelines for interpreting Section 1 and determining the "reasonable limits" that may be placed on the *Charter*'s rights.

Labour Trilogy [1987] decided that freedom of association does not include a right for unions to strike.

Ford v. Quebec [1988] ruled that aspects of the Quebec laws related to language used on signs were unconstitutional.

R. v. Morgentaler [1988] struck down the Criminal Code restrictions on abortions.

Andrews v. Law Society of B.C. [1989] ruled that equality should be determined among groups that are "similarly situated" and that prohibited discrimination may involve unintentional, systemic discrimination.

McKinney v. University of Guelph [1990] ruled that mandatory retirement was acceptable age discrimination.

R. v. Askov [1990] gave some limits to the "reasonable delay" allowed in bringing a matter to trial. This decision led to thousands of charges being dropped. The Court revisited the issue and gave more flexible guidelines in *R. v. Morin* [1992].

R. v. Sparrow [1990] set out important principles about the constitutional status of Aboriginal treaty rights.

Electoral Boundaries Reference [1991] decided that "the right to vote" included the right to "effective representation," and so constituencies could vary in size only according to set limits.

Delgamuukw v. British Columbia [1997] laid down principles about the nature of Aboriginal title to land, particularly in the absence of a treaty.

Vriend v. Alberta [1998] declared that the Alberta *Individual Rights Protection Act* must be read to extend protection against discrimination to cover sexual orientation.

M. v. H. [1999] ruled that the statutory definition of "spouse" must allow for same-sex couples.

R. v. Sharpe [2001] ruled that while possession of child pornography is a crime, it could in some cases be allowed under the defence of "artistic merit."

Same-Sex Marriage Reference [2004] upheld the federal government's proposed law to allow same-sex marriage while refusing to answer whether the *Charter* required it.

Chaoulli v. Quebec [2005] declared that Quebec's prohibition against private health insurance violated the right to security of the person in Section 7 of the *Charter*.

Health Services and Support-Facilities Subsector Bargaining Association v. British Columbia [2007] overturned the Labour Trilogy and ruled that collective bargaining is indeed part of the freedom of association.

claimed the power to invalidate laws passed by the legislature; it is all the more remarkable since this power is found nowhere in the text of the American constitution. This vision of judicial review had been presaged by Lord Coke, chief justice of England's Court of Common Pleas, as early as 1610. In the famous *Dr. Bonham's Case*, Coke argued that the parliament's lawmaking power should be governed by the common law to be enforced by judges: "when an act of parliament is against common right and reason, or repugnant, or impossible to be performed, the common law will controul it, and adjudge such act to be void."[9] While this task of the courts seems logical and necessary if constitutional rights are to have practical substance, critics argue that judges end up acting as policymakers. This debate is worth looking at, since important issues are raised about the powers of the different branches of government and the rights of citizens. The task of constitutional review is viewed as sufficiently specialized in some countries (e.g., France and Germany) that they have a separate constitutional court to rule on the constitutionality of laws.

Those who defend judicial review on the grounds of protecting constitutional rights raise strong arguments. Just as judges must act as the referees of a federal–provincial division of powers, they also have to act as referees to sort out citizens' complaints that the government has infringed their rights in some fashion. While democratic governments do respect their citizens' rights most of the time through self-restraint, many people argue that the courts are still needed to protect the rights of individuals and minority groups which might be sacrificed by the will of the majority. To find a Canadian example of a group who suffered at the hands of the majority, one has only to think of the thousands of Japanese-Canadians rounded up during World War II and stripped of all their businesses and property. Little to no evidence has ever surfaced to show that any of these individuals would have posed any danger to Canada by siding with Japan during the war; indeed, the vast majority were people who had lived in Canada for years, for generations in many cases, and were ready to help Canada's war effort.

The courts provide impartial referees to determine the limits of government power and to protect rights. Judges are free from the electoral pressures that politicians face to placate their supporters and can therefore act as a brake upon hasty or oppressive actions by the government. The courtroom provides a forum for the different arguments to be made and weighed and for reasoned judgments to be delivered—judgments that either uphold the government's actions or strike them down in order to defend the rights of citizens. Surveys noted below have shown that Canadians would much rather have the courts than elected politicians decide on their rights.

Those who oppose judicial review of constitutional rights, however, also have substantial arguments on their side. First of all, some people have argued that a measure of a truly free society is that the people do not need to be protected from their government. Democracy means not just the rule of the majority, but also an accommodation of minority and individual interests along with those of the majority. The balance between the powers of government and the liberties of citizens swings over the course of time as circumstances and public opinion change. Ideally, the politicians who make the choice of this balance are not only elected but are accountable at future elections for their actions. A mature, established democracy such as Canada's learns from its experience and will draw a better balance over time.

But perhaps the most telling argument is that judges are simply not the impartial referees that the public believes them to be. Moreover, their judgments do not merely set the limits of government power—they legislate on crucial areas of such public policy as abortion, mandatory retirement, sexual behaviour, pornography, and union rights. Worse still, in this view, unelected judges sit in judgment on the decisions of the elected government, and those judges enforce their own personal policy preferences in ways for which the public can never hold them accountable. Several studies have shown that individual judges develop very different patterns of support for constitutional rights, with some judges characterized as more liberal (more likely to accept rights claims) and others more conservative (less likely to accept rights claims).[10] Indeed, one study of the Supreme Court of Canada in the 1980s found that the most liberal judge, Bertha Wilson, was more than twice as likely to accept a rights claim than the most conservative judge, William McIntyre. Furthermore, the outcomes of cases in which someone claimed their rights had been infringed were directly related to which group of judges heard the case.[11] When the personal dispositions of judges come to bear in decisions on important social questions, it is argued, judges clearly are no longer simply interpreters of constitutional texts but active policymakers substituting their policy preferences for those of elected politicians.

In the end, the debate may really be one about the degree to which judges make social policy framed by their personal views rather than over whether it should be done. Indeed, a policymaking role is essentially unavoidable in interpreting constitutional rights. In order to define the practical application of the constitutional right to the freedom of expression, for example, judges have to decide whether sexually explicit material is protected in general and whether certain kinds (such as violent pornography or material involving children) can be prohibited. In deciding those kinds of questions, judges have to set the bounds of social policy. However, the question is how "activist" judges become in imposing their own preferences, as opposed to deferring to some degree to the policy choices made by elected politicians. The debate over **judicial activism** is not just an academic one; it gets to the heart of the relative powers of the judiciary, the legislature, and the executive. It is an issue of who sets limits on the powers of government and how accountable to the electorate those with political power should be in a democracy. One perspective on the matter is to view the relationship as a dialogue between the legislature and courts, with each taking turns to express their views on the proper balance of policy goals and civil rights.

Overall, Canadians seem quite aware of the power of the judiciary to set public policy priorities for the country. Most are content with the work of the courts, although their attitudes have evolved over recent years. An Ipsos-Reid poll in 2001 found that 60 percent of Canadians could name a particular Supreme Court case in the past year that stuck in their mind, and 70 percent approved of the court's work.[12] However, the Court has raised some controversies, which were revealed in a COMPAS poll in 2000. In that survey of public opinion, 43 percent of Canadians said they felt that the courts had taken too little power away from the elected politicians, while 28 percent said the courts had taken too much power.[13] These results are not surprising, given the high levels of trust that Canadians have in the judiciary. In a 2007 Léger poll, 74 percent of those surveyed said that they trust judges, while only 15 percent felt the same way about politicians.[14] Such a wide disparity in reported levels of trust, however, may depend on the actual questions asked in the survey. When Canadians were asked a different question in another 2007 poll by Strategic Counsel, only 47 percent said they trusted the courts more than Parliament to serve their interests, while 37 percent trusted Parliament more.[15]

Judicial Appointments

Individuals come to judicial office in very different ways across the world. Judges can be appointed by the executive, nominated by the executive and confirmed by the legislature, chosen by other judges, or even elected (see Box 9.3).

In Canada, the provincial and federal governments appoint judges. Traditionally, **political patronage** played an enormous role in the choice of new judges. A government was most likely to appoint lawyers who were known supporters of the political party in power. The next largest pool of candidates was drawn from lawyers who worked for the government. Lawyers who were known to be active supporters of other political parties were almost never appointed. Patronage had several negative effects because it sometimes resulted in unsuitable or even incompetent individuals being appointed simply because the party in power owed them a favour. Highly qualified candidates might be completely overlooked simply because they supported opposition parties. Furthermore, there is the worry that candidates appointed because of their political connections might rule in favour of the ruling party in later cases that come before them.

Increasing resistance to political patronage grew in the early 1980s, and most governments in Canada have since revised their methods of selecting judges. While political patronage continues to a certain extent, it has been considerably reduced. Governments have been more

A brief look around the world reveals many different ways to appoint judges to a country's highest court. A few are listed below with some examples of states that use the process.

- Some judges are appointed by the head of state and remain "at their pleasure," meaning judges can be fired for any reason: Guinea-Bissau.

- A number of states share the British process of appointment by the head of state, with the actual choice being made by the cabinet: Australia, Canada, Jamaica, New Zealand.

- Judges may also be appointed by the head of state (usually the president) from a list of nominees approved by the national legislature: Indonesia.

- Some countries follow the American process where a legislative committee must approve the president's choice: Argentina, Brazil, Mexico.

- The national legislature elects judges in some countries: Cuba, Nicaragua, Switzerland.

- The judiciary can be responsible for selecting new judges, although the formal appointment may be by the head of state: France, Namibia, Philippines, Romania.

focused on trying to appoint women and people from underrepresented ethnic or cultural groups, as support has grown for a more socially diverse judiciary. In many provinces, independent committees interview candidates and present the government with a ranked shortlist of candidates from which the government makes the appointment. In some cases, the Cabinet routinely selects only the top choice from that short list.

Although the federal government was one of the first in Canada to institute independent committees to screen candidates, it has stopped far short of the provincial reforms. The committees can only classify potential candidates into three broad groups: highly recommended, recommended, and "unable to recommend." The government uses the results of the committee work as guidance, but it is free to select individuals from any of these groups. As a result, patronage continues to flourish in federal judicial appointments. For example, among the first 30 individuals federal Justice Minister Irwin Cotler chose to appoint to the bench in 2004–05, one-third had contributed to the Liberal Party or its candidates in the two years before their appointments. This number is more alarming when one considers that a third of those appointed were in professions where political donations could not normally be made (judges and senior civil servants). Thus, one-half of those eligible to make donations had donated to the Liberals, while none had donated to any other party.[16] The Conservative government was also accused of making patronage appointments after taking office in 2006. They also changed the composition of regional judicial appointment committees to include police representatives, which opponents argue is meant to inject a law-and-order bias into the screening process that would help propel conservatively minded candidates to the top. Since executive discretion still leads to patronage in federal judicial appointments, it is highly desirable to adopt a merit-based system like those in place in many Canadian provinces.

Supreme Court of Canada judges are singular exceptions in the federal government's patronage appointments. While known partisans have been appointed, they have been the exception over the past 50 years. The federal government consults widely with bar societies and other individuals,

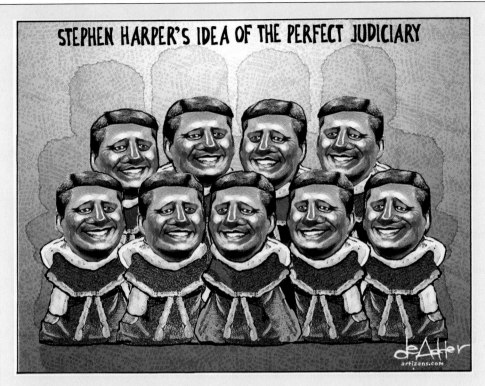

STEPHEN HARPER'S IDEA OF THE PERFECT JUDICIARY

A government can steer the direction of a court by appointing judges with ideological preferences.

Michael de Adder/Artizans

organizations, and governments in the provinces when vacancies for the Supreme Court occur. See Box 9.4 for a discussion of the new appointment system created in 2005.

There are some important differences in the way in which judges come to office in the United States.[17] Federally appointed judges are nominated by the president but have to be approved by the Senate. Potential members of the Supreme Court even have to face days of questioning in a Senate committee before it decides whether to confirm their appointment. In a number of high-profile cases the Senate refused to confirm the President's choice of judges. The general political and legal philosophy of the nominees is one of the prime considerations in the appointment of Supreme Court justices, as Americans use the appointment process to try to steer the policy direction of the Supreme Court. Over a period of time, a court that has been dominated by more liberal judges can be reshaped with the deliberate appointment of more conservative individuals to the court, and vice versa. This process is known as *stacking the court*.

It is important to note that judges are elected in many of the individual U.S. states. Supporters of judicial elections believe modern democracy requires important public decision-makers to be elected, including judges. This method of selecting judges bears some discussion, since an increasing number of Canadians think judges should be elected; 48 percent of Canadians surveyed felt judges should be elected in 2002, but by 2007 judicial elections were supported by 63 percent.[18] Judges in the U.S. usually run under party banners and campaign on their general ideas about how justice should be served. In some jurisdictions, judges cannot run for reelection, but in many they can. The election of judges makes quite explicit the notion discussed earlier in this chapter that judges have to enforce values that reflect the dominant beliefs in their society. While

For decades, political actors have debated ways to reform the way in which judges are appointed to the Supreme Court of Canada. Historically, the federal justice minister and prime minister chose individuals after informal, private consultations. The ill-fated Charlottetown Accord proposals for constitutional change would have been the first substantial reform of the appointment process. The Accord would have required the federal government to choose new appointees from a shortlist of candidates submitted by the provincial governments when a vacancy opened up on the Court. The focus of debate was to include the provincial governments formally in the process of selection.

In recent years, the debate has shifted more to the "democratization" of the appointment process, to include some meaningful role for elected members of parliament to consider potential appointments. With the growing political role of the Supreme Court, many feel that appointments should no longer be made in secret by the executive. Some believe that a parliamentary committee should interview nominees before their appointment, although perhaps not with the veto power of their American counterparts. Others, including sitting and retired supreme court judges, have argued that this invites a political spectacle and would discourage suitable individuals from accepting the position.

In April 2005, federal Justice Minister Irwin Cotler announced a new process that includes formal participation by parliamentarians as well as representatives of the provincial governments, while still retaining the final choice for the federal executive. In the new process, the justice minister would consult privately to produce a list of five to eight nominees whose files would be reviewed by an advisory committee. This committee is to consist of an MP from every official party in the House of Commons, plus a retired judge, a nominee of the provincial governments where a vacancy is occurring, a representative from the local bar society, and two "eminent lay people" chosen by the federal justice minister. The committee would narrow the list of nominees down to three, from whom the federal cabinet would choose the actual appointee. After making the choice, the justice minister would appear before the House of Commons Justice Committee to explain and defend his or her choice of new judge. While this is a departure from past practice, observers have criticized this as cumbersome and as failing to provide a substantive role for the advisory committee.

Shortly after the 2006 federal election, the new Conservative government moved to fill a vacancy on the Supreme Court. On that occasion, the justice minister appeared before an ad hoc committee of parliamentarians to explain his choice of candidate for the court; Parliament was officially dissolved at the time. The chosen candidate, Marshall Rothstein, also appeared before the committee in a nationally televised hearing chaired by Peter Hogg, Professor Emeritus of Osgoode Hall Law School. While unprecedented, this appearance was criticized by many because the ad hoc committee was severely constrained in the kind of questions that could be put to Mr. Rothstein, and the appointment was to proceed regardless of the outcome of the hearing.

elections do provide a direct democratic mandate for judicial power, they present troubling challenges to judicial impartiality. Judges may be tempted to settle cases in a particular way in order to carry out their general election promises, and justice in individual cases may be sacrificed to the judge's determination to demonstrate a consistent pattern of sentencing. Especially where judges can run for reelection, they need to be able to tell the voters that they acted according to the promises they made in the previous election. Furthermore, there is a potential problem with the degree to which individual judges owe favours to those who financed or worked on their election campaigns. Box 9.5 provides a report of the issues that arise when special-interest groups provide election funds to judges competing in an election.

| Judicial Elections and Special-Interest Funding | BOX 9.5 |

NEW YORK, NY—Although pro-business special interest groups outspent progressive interest groups by more than nine to one on television advertising in Supreme Court elections this year, progressive groups had a higher electoral success rate than did their political foes, said two national watchdog groups. All five candidates who benefited from television advertising by progressive groups won election, but only 71 percent of candidates for whom pro-business groups sponsored ads won a seat on the bench.

The highest spending interest group, the Safety and Prosperity Coalition—a Georgia group that received the majority of its funding from the American Justice Partnership, an arm of the National Association of Manufacturers—spent more than $1.3 million on advertisements that supported Mike Wiggins and attacked his opponent, incumbent Justice Carol Hunstein. The Republican Party spent an additional $550,000 to support Mr. Wiggins. Justice Hunstein sponsored her own advertising, spending $960,000. Despite being outspent almost two to one on the air, she defeated her opponent with 63 percent of the vote.

"When special interest groups become so heavily involved in judicial races, citizens conclude that judges answer to constituencies rather than the law," said James Sample, counsel at the Brennan Center for Justice at NYU School of Law. "It is heartening to see, however, that this year many voters were not swayed by special interest advertisements."

In Washington State, where special interest groups sponsored 100% of the 2006 advertising in the state's supreme court races, two pro-business groups outspent the opposition almost four to one, but the candidate they supported, John Groen, lost by almost 10 percentage points to incumbent Chief Justice Gerry Alexander.

Pro-business groups did succeed in helping their chosen candidates win in Michigan, Ohio, and Alabama. In Michigan incumbent Justice Maura Corrigan won with the assistance of an ad sponsored by the Michigan Chamber of Commerce. The Partnership for Ohio's Future—which shares a mailing address and has key overlapping staff members with the Ohio Chamber of Commerce— successfully assisted incumbent Justice Terrence O'Donnell and

Robert Cupp in election to the state's highest court.

In Alabama, the American Taxpayers Alliance—a group that receives at least some of its funding from the U.S. Chamber of Commerce and electric utility companies—spent $721,236 to support incumbent Chief Justice Drayton Nabers and $271,844 to support incumbent Justice Lyn Stuart in their primary battles. Nabers won his primary, but lost to Sue Bell Cobb in the general election, in which he received no special interest assistance with television advertisements.

"As hardball TV ads infect more judicial campaigns around the country, it's time for every state that elects judges to take steps to reduce special interest pressure on the courts," said Bert Brandenburg, executive director of Justice at Stake.

SOURCE: "Despite High Spending, Special Interest Groups Not Entirely Successful in Supreme Court Elections"; available at http://www.justiceatstake.org/contentViewer.asp?breadcrumb=7,55,937; accessed June 13, 2008.

Most countries in Western Europe take quite a different approach to the recruitment of judges. Essentially, being a judge is a professional career. Individuals interested in becoming judges go to special training institutes or universities and take years of courses related to law and the work of judges. The actual selection of new judges from these candidates is done by the judiciary itself. In addition, the judiciary is considered to be a career of advancement, in which people start on the most junior-level tribunal. In theory, the most competent are selected by senior judges to be promoted through levels of increasingly important courts. This model of appointment and promotion certainly avoids the problems of political patronage seen in Canada and the potential for popularity-seeking judges in American judicial elections. However, the European model is criticized for creating an insular and self-perpetuating elite.

Each of the systems has its strengths and weaknesses. A central concern is trying to balance the selection of suitable, competent individuals on the one hand with the means to ensure that judges reflect a society's diversity and prevailing mores on the other. Another issue is the degree to which a country's elected politicians should steer the policymaking function of the courts by deliberately choosing new judges who are sympathetic to the politicians' preferred direction of public policy. Those against such intentional policy steering through appointments argue that it can severely undermine judicial impartiality. In this view, one should simply seek intelligent and competent individuals and leave them to develop their own judicial personalities over time, settling specific cases as they think best. Those who support a more deliberate, ideological selection of new judges argue that the public must recognize the enormous role the judges have in shaping **public policy**. The foundation of democracy is that the will of the people should be the guiding principle of all government power. Thus, the public's elected representatives have a responsibility to choose new judges who reflect the policy directions that the public prefers.

Judicial Independence and Impartiality

An independent and impartial judiciary is essential to the proper functioning of a democracy. Without independence from other branches of government, judges simply become a tool for enforcing the policies of the government of the day. Judges must be impartial in order for the public to have confidence that they will decide cases on the basis of the facts of the case and the relevant law.

Judicial independence refers to the relationship of the judiciary to the legislature and the executive and means that judges can do their work without interference from politicians, bureaucrats, and other government officials, such as the police or the military. Judicial independence in the sense discussed here is unknown in communist political systems, where judges work under the supremacy of the communist party and are "subject to constant party control, supervision, and accountability."[19] Old ways die hard, and some of the post-communist states in Eastern Europe, such as Moldava, have returned to what the International Commission of Jurists calls "telephone justice," with judges routinely expecting and receiving phone calls from cabinet ministers giving directions on how to decide a case of particular interest to the government.[20] The fundamental difficulty is that some governments view the courts as just another government department rather than an independent institution. As such, they expect judges to do what the government wants them to do. Unfortunately, this can mean that judges become active participants in repressing dissent or facilitating corruption.

The Supreme Court of Canada has laid down some important aspects of the relationship between the courts and the other branches of government that underlie judicial independence. In *R. v. Valente*, the court said that judges must have security of tenure, financial independence, and administrative independence.[21] Security of tenure means that judges cannot be removed from office simply because the government does not approve of their decisions; they should hold office until retirement or for a set period of time and should be removed only for major misbehaviour, incompetence, or incapacity. Financial independence ensures that judges need not fear having their pay cut if the government does not like their decisions and that judges have no incentive to try to curry favour by siding with the government in the hopes that their pay will be increased. Administrative independence means that the scheduling of cases and assignment of individual judges to particular cases is done by the judiciary itself; this prevents the government from ensuring a favourable outcome to a case by arranging for a "friendly" judge to hear it. These considerations are not just limited to Canada; the Indian government took an important step in 2004, handing over financial and administrative control of the lower courts to the Supreme Court from the Ministry of Justice and Human Rights.

Judicial impartiality refers to a state of mind in which judges settle cases without applying their preexisting biases in favour of or against the people or issues involved. While impartiality is difficult to define, its essence implies that judges maintain an open mind to arguments about the facts and the proper interpretation of the law before deciding the outcome of the case. It is important to bear in mind that impartiality cannot mean a total absence of preconceived ideas or predispositions, something that is not only humanly impossible but also probably undesirable. There would be little public confidence in the judiciary if judges did not express or act on established biases against the horrors of murder and rape or the outrage of con men who defraud senior citizens of all their savings.

Concerns about judicial independence and impartiality extend well beyond the relationship between the courts and the other branches of government. Judges must also be protected from pressures from the general public, interest groups, unions, and business. If judges bow to pressures not to decide a case the "wrong" way, or anticipate rewards if they decide a case the "right" way, there can be no assurance that judges will act impartially. At the same time, the requirements of judicial impartiality also place restrictions on how judges behave on and off the bench. Canadian judges have been forced to resign because they openly socialized with figures known in organized crime circles, because they have donated money to support the election of particular politicians or political parties, or because they have been convicted of a criminal offence. In these instances, the public could not have confidence that the judges would be free from major biases.

Threats to judicial impartiality and independence come in many forms. Controversy has been stirred several times by cabinet ministers talking to judges about cases the judges have under consideration. For example, Jean Charest resigned from Brian Mulroney's government in 1990 after it became known that he had telephoned a judge. As serious as such direct attempts to influence judges may be in Canada, they pale in comparison to other examples from around the world. Judges in Colombia and Italy live with constant police escorts because of threats to their lives from organized crime. And Italian judges have fought an ongoing battle with Prime Minister Silvio Berlusconi, who was under investigation and convicted on corruption charges several times, only to have his convictions overturned on appeal. Berlusconi has claimed that left-wing judges are persecuting him and declared he would remove police protection for judges. Hundreds of Italy's judges went on a brief strike in late 2001 to protest against a move they believed was intended to bully them into leaving Berlusconi and his associates alone. A more graphic example of intimidation of judges occurred in Indonesia, where former President Suharto's son, Tommy, was sentenced in 2001—a couple of years after his father was forced from office—to 18 months in jail on corruption charges. Shortly afterward, the judge who upheld the sentence was gunned down; unsurprisingly, perhaps, the Indonesian supreme court acquitted Tommy Suharto of the original charges three months after the murder. However, Suharto was charged in early 2002 with contracting the judge's murder, in a move that was widely seen as a test of the success of new President Megawati Sukarnoputri's ability to restore confidence in the country's judicial system.

Judicial impartiality and independence also require judges to distance themselves from becoming involved in political debates and activities outside the courtroom. In a famous case in Canada, the Canadian Judicial Council reprimanded Judge Thomas Berger for having made a public speech criticizing Prime Minister Trudeau's constitutional reform package that led to the *Constitution Act*, 1982. Berger had complained that the constitutional reforms were put together without consultation with the Aboriginal leaders and without any attempt to redress their many grievances. Judges have to walk a fine line in commenting on issues of public interest without compromising the public's perception that they can still rule impartially on related issues, should these end up in their own courtroom.

As important as judicial independence and impartiality are, however, these principles still operate within limits. Although an important aspect of judicial independence and impartiality holds that judges should be able to decide cases without fear that they may lose their jobs, it is also clear that there are limits on what the public and the government will tolerate in judicial decisions. Judge Raymond Bartlett was removed from the Nova Scotia Family Court in 1987 because he frequently quoted the Bible in court and told women appearing before him that they should be subservient to their husbands. Neither of these actions would have been all that remarkable a hundred years ago, but they were considered to be unacceptable in the late 20th century. While judges are supposedly free to behave as they think best, and decide cases as they think best, they cannot simply follow their personal views regardless of how out-of-step they are with prevailing values in their society. In the end, judges may lead or lag behind public opinion to a certain extent, but they will face pressures to resign or be removed if they act too far beyond prevailing mores—even in democratic countries that espouse judicial independence and impartiality.

The Personal Values of Judges Can Shape Their Decisions

While good judges can deliberately set aside many of their personal views in any particular decision, it is all but impossible to set aside all of their basic beliefs on an ongoing basis. As a result, judges tend to develop distinctive patterns in their handling of cases that reflect their own underlying personal values. Like everybody else, judges are products of the socialization processes in their own upbringing. While the settled aspects of the law provide boundaries in many cases, judges have to exercise their personal discretion in many ways as they hear and decide a case before them. Questions of credibility—whose story a judge believes—are entirely discretionary and can be influenced in many subconscious ways by each judge's personal beliefs, likes, and dislikes. Judges often have considerable leeway in deciding what penalty or settlement to impose, and inevitably these decisions hinge to some extent on a judge's personal belief in what is right and appropriate. Box 9.6 provides a hypothetical example and asks you to judge the judge's decision.

Because of the potential for personal background to play a role in judicial decision-making, concern has arisen about the social composition of the judiciary. The historical pattern in all countries has been for males of the dominant social classes and ethnic groups to fill the bench. Academics and social activists have long been concerned that this leads to an institution that embodies and enforces the values of the predominant group or groups. As a result, there have been strong calls in recent decades for the judiciary to become more socially diverse. In established liberal democracies such as Canada, there has been a deliberate policy in the past two decades to try and appoint more women and people of underrepresented social groups to the bench. Even so, critics argue that the underrepresentation of women and ethnic minorities in Canadian courts creates a "democratic deficit."[22]

Social and gender diversity among judges is important at least symbolically in a modern democracy that espouses women's equality and multiculturalism. But does or should this diversity make a practical difference to the kinds of decisions made by the courts and the values they enforce? There are many who say that a socially diverse judiciary does act differently from an exclusively white middle-class one, and they would add that this is a good thing. Modern democratic societies should not have paternalistic and ethnocentric values perpetuated by the courts, as they had in the past. Cultural sensitivity must be embodied in judicial decisions, and what better way for that to occur than to have members from different cultural groups both deciding cases directly and acting as an educational influence on their fellow judges? Furthermore, the diverse groups within a society will have more confidence in the quality of

---

You Judge the Judges   BOX 9.6

What limits would you place on judicial impartiality and the ability of judges to settle cases as they see best? In theory, judges should feel free to express themselves and decide cases without fearing that they will lose their jobs simply because their decisions are unpopular. However, consider the following hypothetical case and ask yourself if you believe the judge should be removed from office.

Judge Smith hears a case in which a person is accused under Canada's *Anti-Terrorism Act* of having plotted to blow up the pipeline carrying oil to the United States; the man was arrested before the attack was carried out. At his trial, the accused states that he was motivated to do this because U.S. corporations are pillaging the environment around the world all for the sake of profits for their shareholders. He wanted to strike a blow against U.S. capitalism by trying to cut off some of their oil.

The judge acquits the man on the grounds that he was exercising his rights under the *Charter* to the freedom of conscience and expression. The judge notes that no actual attack had occurred. And Judge Smith then goes on to say that the accused had been justified in highlighting the fact that the U.S. economy is dripping with the blood of poor people around the world, whose virtual slavery is essential to providing cheap goods for voracious American consumers.

justice delivered by the courts if members of their own groups are judges too. In fact, a number of academic studies reveal measurable differences, although not large ones, between male and female judges, and between African-American and Caucasian judges.

However, the degree to which individual judges may decide cases differently because of their sex and cultural or social background poses a challenge for those who believe that law should be interpreted and enforced as impartially as possible. In theory at least, justice can be properly served only if there is a general uniformity in the ways in which judges apply the law to similar cases.

An important point related to the personal discretion of judges is their fallibility—they can make wrong decisions. In Canada, at least seven people in the past 20 years have been finally exonerated after spending many years in jail for rapes or murders they did not commit. In the United States, 124 people have been freed from death row since 1973, 15 of them after DNA evidence played a crucial role in establishing their innocence.[23] The police occasionally mismanage an investigation, discriminate, lie, or encourage other witnesses to lie, but judges ultimately have to decide for themselves who is telling the truth. Sometimes judges simply believe a liar's testimony.

Discipline and Removal of Judges

The discipline and removal of judges from office raises a number of complex issues. While there can be no independence for judges if they can be fired simply for offending other political actors, there also has to be some way to remove judges who engage in criminal acts or otherwise bring the administration of justice into fundamental disrepute. Both the grounds for removal and the process to be followed can have a profound impact on the independence of the judiciary and the quality of justice in a society.

Who gets to remove judges from office, and for what reasons, varies a great deal around the world. In military regimes, where the military command or president can remove a judge for almost any reason, there is no protection for judges who displease powerful authorities on policy grounds. At the other end of the spectrum is France, where all matters of judicial discipline are handled within the judiciary and there is no role for either the executive or the legislature to play at all. Many countries fall somewhere in the middle, with a mixture of involvement by the three branches of government.

Historically in Britain, the monarchs could remove judges from office whenever they felt offended by what a judge said or did. To protect the judges from such arbitrary removal by the monarch, the British parliament passed the *Act of Settlement* in 1701; after this date, judges could be removed from office only after a parliamentary resolution. The *Act* established the principle, since followed in most common law systems founded on the British model, that judges hold office during "good behaviour," which actually means that judges can be removed for "misbehaviour." It also ensured the supremacy of parliament over the other branches of government and protected judges from being removed on the whim of the executive. The specific grounds for removal, however, are open to considerable interpretation. In general, judges can be removed for failing to perform their duties or behaving in a way that fundamentally undermines the public's confidence in their ability to perform their duties. Those judges who frequently fail to appear for their court sessions or behave completely irrationally in the courtroom can be removed. But there are also wide grounds for removal for behaving in ways that are incompatible with being a judge. For example, Robert Flahiff was forced to resign from the Quebec Superior Court after being convicted of money laundering, and Ronald MacDonald had to resign from the Nova Scotia Provincial Court after being convicted of assaulting his wife.

Canada inherited the British process, and federally appointed judges can be removed from office only by the Governor General after the passage of a joint address by both houses of

Parliament.[24] A trend has emerged in recent decades to distance elected politicians from both the formulation of codes of judicial conduct and the actual removal process. The tendency has been to give judges increasing control over the discipline of their colleagues. This distancing is based on a concern for the independence of judges and the belief that politics should not play a role in the disciplinary process. In all Canadian jurisdictions, complaints about judges are first dealt with either by the normal courts or by an independent judicial council. While this may be viewed as a positive development in general, it does raise the possible problem of a public perception that judges might either "protect their own" or enforce a set of values that are not in step with the prevailing public beliefs. In stark terms, the judges' "old boys' club" might protect its members from the outside world. For this reason, several provinces have included lay members from the public on their judicial councils. However, the Canadian Judicial Council that oversees federally appointed judges is composed entirely of judges.

The United States has moved away from the involvement of the legislature in judicial removal proceedings as well. Although the U.S. Constitution states that Congress can impeach judges, a new process was developed in 1980 to provide for a judicial commission to investigate and rule on judicial misbehaviour. This model is also widespread at the state level in the United States. These judicial commissions have been quite active, with New York's removing 60 of its 3,500 state judges between 1979 and 1985.[25]

While there is no controversy in removing judges who commit criminal offences, much more debate arises when judges make controversial statements that enrage or offend the public. For example, the Canadian Judicial Council recommended the removal of Justice Jean Bienvenue in 1996 when it found that the "judge's remarks about women and his deep-seated ideas behind those remarks legitimately cast doubt on his impartiality in the execution of his judicial office."[26] However, 7 of the 29 members of the council voted against removal on the grounds that Bienvenue's comments were simply reflective of a bygone era and that sensitivity training would be a more appropriate remedy. A central issue is whether judicial independence should protect judges from being removed because they offend contemporary social mores.

In the end, the limits on judicial behaviour are as difficult to define as they are important to a healthy system of government. The crucial role that judges play is founded upon the general authority they have in the public eye, which in turn is based on the belief that judges act impartially to enforce the values of their society. Failure to remove individual judges can erode the public's deference to the courts' authority. In some respects, there is real merit in the elected representatives of the public having a substantive role to play in at least establishing the grounds for removing judges, as the limits on judicial behaviour are then set by people who are both representative of and accountable to the general public. In Canada, a compromise has been reached on the removal process of superior court judges. The Canadian Judicial Council, composed of senior judges across the country, must first investigate complaints about judicial behaviour. If it deems the situation serious enough, it can recommend to Parliament that a judge be removed. As judges play a more visible policymaking role, however, they have come under increasing pressures to be held accountable for their judgments and speeches. There is a danger that the discipline process is used to remove or pressure judges simply because their actions or words are politically unpalatable. And the essence of judicial independence is that judges should be free to make the decision they feel is best without fear of recriminations as a result of its unpopularity.

Access to the Courts

The effectiveness of the courts in their various roles can depend to a large degree on how courts function and who has access to them in practice. Several ongoing weaknesses can be identified in the courts that undermine the potential they have in a society. First and foremost, the courts are essentially passive institutions. As mentioned, judges do not go out and seek legal problems to solve or disputes to settle. Instead, they have to wait for someone to decide to take an issue to the courts. Significant disputes may go unresolved because those involved either cannot or do not want to go to court. This inability or unwillingness to take a dispute to court may arise from the prohibitive costs of a court case, or may be based on a belief that disputes should be settled outside the formal court setting. Just how equal the access to the courts is for all segments of a society has a great bearing on the kind of justice the courts can provide.

The cost barrier is a central weakness of courts as social and political institutions. The legal system and judicial processes are complex, and anyone involved in a court case should really have a professional lawyer to conduct his or her case. In Canada, a relatively short and simple criminal case can cost several hundred to several thousand dollars, so it may cost less to plead guilty than to fight the charges through a full trial. Parties who fail to win their case in the first instance have to decide whether to appeal. But the cost of taking a case before a provincial court of appeal starts at around $25,000 to $50,000. Parties determined to take their case to the Supreme Court of Canada for final resolution can expect to spend at least $150,000 on the simplest case, but more complex cases will cost well over $1 million. Clearly, these are costs that cannot be afforded by the average person. Governments in most liberal democracies have legal aid programs in place to help pay for the cases of the poorest members of their society. However, the limited budgets and personnel available significantly undermine the quality of representation a person can expect. Only some people benefit from paid legal counsel, and a lucky few have their cases appealed to the final court. The rich, of course, can afford to hire the most expensive legal teams and carry their cases up to the top court. In the middle are many people who either have to use up their savings or decide that, while they can finance the first court hearing, they cannot afford to appeal if they lose. A question then arises about how many innocent people are jailed simply because they could not afford a good lawyer or enough of the lawyer's time to mount a proper defence, or because they were not able to appeal an initial verdict that found them guilty.

The problem is even worse outside of the criminal law. Private cases are notorious for lengthy delays and high costs; the time and costs involved in suing a neighbour, a relative, or a business may be prohibitive. This is a particular issue in countries where losers in a private court case have to pay for the legal fees of the person they sued, in addition to their own. The quality of legal services to people of poor and modest incomes is a special concern in family law cases. When couples part or divorce, they need to divide the matrimonial property and decide on their access to and financial obligations for child and spousal support. High-quality legal representation is crucial in these proceedings, as the outcomes of these cases can have repercussions for years. One strong criticism of the cost of court access is that it unfairly affects women in family law disputes. Usually the men involved have higher incomes and more assets at the time of the marital breakup and can therefore afford better lawyers and more of the lawyer's time than women. As a result, men generally have much higher living standards several years after a divorce than do women, who more often than not have to care for their children. In 2002, British Columbia's attorney general, Geoff Plant, was formally censured by the Law Society of British Columbia because of dramatic cutbacks to legal aid services. Earlier in the year, he had announced that legal aid would no longer be available for most family law disputes, including divorce. Legal aid can now be used only if there is a question of physical danger, or in cases wherein children are taken into protective custody.

Justice is supposed to be blind to the participants, and rich and poor are supposed to have equal consideration in the courts. However, the reality of the judicial process is that justice often falls very short of the mark. As legal aid programs are squeezed by government cutbacks and as court costs escalate, many people are left without fully prepared lawyers to argue their cases. Legal aid is seldom available for serious civil cases beyond family matters.

CONCLUSION

All states rely on law to structure their societies, with the policies and mores of the dominant elite groups embodied within them. The courts have a crucial role to play, particularly in democratic countries, in interpreting and enforcing the law. Democratic regimes require independent and impartial courts to act as fair adjudicators of disputes and gain public support and deference. In practice, however, both the institutional independence and personal impartiality of judges are limited. The selection and appointment of judges can be done in several different ways, and a country's choice of a particular process can provide the elected politicians with an opportunity to steer the general policy direction of the courts. Control over the discipline and removal of judges provide firm limits on the behaviour of judges, and there is controversy over the role that politicians should play both in setting the rules for judges and in effecting their removal. Judges inevitably have an important policymaking role to play in interpreting laws and in their exercise of the powers of judicial review.

DISCUSSION QUESTIONS

1. Do you believe that it is important to have all the major social and ethnic groups represented in a country's judiciary? If so, do you believe it is because members of these groups will decide cases differently?

2. Do you trust judges to enforce your rights more than you trust politicians to respect them? What is the basis for your answer—is it just a gut feeling, or do you have specific reasons?

3. What limits, if any, would you place on the independence and impartiality of judges?

4. Do you think judges should be elected, so that they have a democratic mandate to conduct their work?

5. Would you be prepared to sell everything you own in order to afford a lawyer to defend you against a criminal charge that you know you are not guilty of? Does it matter how serious the charge is?

KEY TERMS

ADMINISTRATIVE TRIBUNALS: Boards or commissions established by the government to adjudicate certain disputes by applying laws to the facts; also called quasi-judicial tribunals or regulatory agencies. These tribunals are not proper courts presided over by judges. (254)

COMMON LAW: A system of law in which precedents from relevant cases in the past are applied to current ones. Judges are bound by precedent and should decide like cases alike. (252)

INTERNATIONAL LAW: A complex body of rules, derived principally from the treaties, covenants, and declarations signed by the governments of various countries. The resolutions of international organizations, the writings of academics, and rulings of domestic and international courts can also be sources of international law when the rules are not otherwise clear. (252)

JUDICIAL IMPARTIALITY: A state of mind in which judges preside over and decide cases with an open mind toward the parties and issues involved. (269)

JUDICIAL INDEPENDENCE: A relationship between the courts and the other branches of government that allows judges to function without interference from other government officials. (269)

JUDICIAL REVIEW: A function of the courts in which judges examine actions of the government to determine whether they are authorized by law. This may also include a determination of whether statutes and regulations are contrary to the constitution. (259)

JUDICIARY: The term used to refer to all the judges collectively in a country. It can also mean the whole judicial branch of government, including juries and the courts' administrative staff. (254)

POLITICAL PATRONAGE: The awarding of benefits to individuals or companies based on their support for the governing political party. (263)

STARE DECISIS: A principle of common law systems by which courts are bound to follow prior decisions that involved similar issues of law. A judgment by one member of a court binds other members, and lower courts are bound to follow the decisions of higher courts. (252)

WEB LINKS

Nelson Education: The Canadian Legal System:
http://polisci.nelson.com/legal.html

European Court of Justice:
http://europa.eu.int/cj/en/index.htm

Federal Courts of the United States:
http://www.uscourts.gov

International Court of Justice:
http://www.icj-cij.org

Nelson Education: Introduction to Judicial Systems:
http://polisci.nelson.com/introcourts.html

The Supreme Court of Canada:
http://www.scc-csc.gc.ca

FURTHER READING

Devlin, Patrick. *Judges*. Oxford: Oxford University Press, 1988.

Gall, Gerald L. *The Canadian Legal System*, 4th ed. Toronto: Carswell, 1995.

Green, Ian. *The Courts*. Vancouver: UBC Press, 2006.

Heibert, Janet. *Charter Conflicts: What Is Parliament's Role?* Kingston, ON: McGill-Queen's University Press, 2002.

MacIvor, Heather. *Canadian Politics and Government in the Charter Era*. Toronto: Thomson Nelson, 2006.

Manfredi, Christopher P. *Judicial Power and the Charter: Canada and the Paradox of Liberal Constitutionalism*, 2nd ed. Don Mills: Oxford University Press, 2001.

Morton, F.L. *Law, Politics and the Judicial Process in Canada*, 3rd ed. Calgary: University of Calgary Press, 2002.

Russell, Peter H. *The Judiciary in Canada: The Third Branch of Government*. Toronto: McGraw-Hill Ryerson, 1987.

Waddams, S.M. *Introduction to the Study of Law*, 5th ed. Scarborough: Carswell, 1997.

ENDNOTES

1. During World War II, all Japanese Canadians were interned and had their property disposed of; many German and Italian Canadians were also interned, as were German and Ukrainian Canadians during World War I.

2. *Vladi v. Vladi*, (1987) 79 N.S.R. (2d) 356 at para. 31 (N.S.S.C.T.D.).

3. Peta Thornycroft, "Pro-Mugabe Judges Rule Land Grabs Are Legal," *National Post*, October 2001, p. A15. For more background, see also Angus Shaw, "Zimbabwe Court Allows Seizures of White Farmland," *The Independent*, October 3, 2001, available at http://www.independent.co.uk/news/world/africa/zimbabwe-court-allows-seizures-of-white-farmland-630067.html, accessed June 13, 2008; Andrew Meldrum, "Supreme Court Justice Defies Mugabe Threat," *The Guardian*, February 10, 2001, available at http://www.guardian.co.uk/international/story/0,3604,436086,00.html, accessed June 13, 2008; and British Broadcasting Corporation, "Mugabe Challenges Supreme Court," February 8, 1999, available at http://news.bbc.co.uk/hi/english/world/africa/newsid_274000/274262.stm, accessed June 13, 2008.

4. *Reference re Resolution to Amend the Constitution*, [1981] 1 S.C.R. 753; *Reference re Secession of Quebec*, [1998] 2 S.C.R. 217.

5. *Brown v. Board of Education*, [1954] 347 U.S. 493; *Baker v. Carr*, [1962] 369 U.S. 186.

6. *Bush v. Gore*, [2000] 531 U.S. 98.

7. For example, see Alan M. Dershowitz, *Supreme Injustice: How the High Court Hijacked Election 2000* (New York: Oxford University Press, 2001); David K. Ryden, ed., *The U.S. Supreme Court and the Electoral Process*, 2nd ed. (Washington: Georgetown University Press, 2002).

8. This case is discussed in Henry J. Abraham, *The Judiciary: The Supreme Court in the Governmental Process*, 8th ed. (Dubuque, IA: Wm. C. Brown, 1991), pp. 59–62.

9. 8 Co. Rep. 107a, 114a C.P. 1610; available at http://press-pubs.uchicago.edu/founders/documents/amendV_due_processs1.html; accessed June 13, 2008. Lord Coke's notion was never acted upon by British judges.

10. For example, see F.L. Morton, Peter H. Russell, and Troy Riddell, "The Canadian Charter of Rights and Freedoms: A Descriptive Analysis of the First Decade, 1982–1992," *National Journal of Constitutional Law* 5 (1994): 1.

11. Andrew Heard, "The Charter in the Supreme Court of Canada: The Importance of Which Judges Hear an Appeal," *Canadian Journal of Political Science* 24 (1991): 289.

12. Ipsos-Reid, "Canadian Supreme Decisions: Public's View of the Supreme Court," July 4, 2001; available at http://www.ipsos-na.com/news/pressrelease.cfm?id=1257; accessed June 13, 2008.

13. COMPAS, "The Power of Judges," February 18, 2000; available at http://www.compas.ca/html/archives/powerjudges_surv.html; accessed July 1, 2001.

14. Léger Marketing, "Profession Barometer," May 15, 2007, p. 3; available at http://www.legermarketing.com/documents/spclm/070522ENG.pdf; accessed June 13, 2008.

15. Strategic Counsel, "Canadian Charter of Rights and Freedoms," March 21, 2007, p. 10; available at http://www.thestrategiccounsel.com/our_news/polls/2007-03-21%20GMCTV%20CharterofRights%20Mar%2010-13.pdf; accessed June 13, 2008.

16. Calculated from information available from Elections Canada, "Financial Reports"; available at http://www.elections.ca/scripts/webpep/fin/welcome.aspx?lang=e; accessed June 13, 2008.

17. For a discussion of the American system, see Henry J. Abraham, *Justices and Presidents: A Political History of Appointments to the Supreme Court*, 3rd ed. (New York: Oxford University Press, 1992).

18. Léger Marketing, "Canadians and the Judicial System," April 8, 2002, p. 5, available at http://www.legermarketing.com/documents/SPCLM/020408ENG.pdf, accessed June 13, 2008; Strategic Counsel, "Canadian Charter of Rights and Freedoms," March 21, 2007, p. 12, available at http://www.thestrategiccounsel.com/our_news/polls/2007-03-21% 20GMCTV%20CharterofRights%20Mar%2010-13.pdf, accessed June 13, 2008.

19. Konrad Zweigert and Hien Kotz, *Introduction to Comparative Law*, vol. 1 (Oxford: Clarendon Press, 1987), p. 324.

20. See the Centre for the Independence of Judges and Lawyers, "Moldava: The Rule of Law in 2004," International Commission of Jurists, 2004; available at http://www.icjcanada .org/en/news/news_2004-11-30.pdf; accessed June 13, 2008.

21. *R. v. Valente*, [1985] 2 S.C.R. 673.

22. R. Devlin, A. Wayne MacKay, and Natasha Kim, "Reducing the Democractic Deficit: Representation, Diversity and the Canadian Judiciary, or Towards a 'Triple P' Judiciary," *Alberta Law Review* 38 (2000): 752.

23. Death Penalty Information Center, "Innocence: List of Those Freed from Death Row"; available at http://www.deathpenaltyinfo.org/article.php?scid=6&did=110; accessed June 13, 2008.

24. No judge has actually been removed by a vote of the two houses of Parliament, although several have resigned when it became apparent that removal procedures would have been undertaken.

25. Martin L. Friedland, *A Place Apart: Judicial Independence and Accountability in Canada* (Ottawa: Canadian Judicial Council, 1995), p. 123.

26. Canadian Judicial Council, *Annual Report 1996–1997*, App. G (Ottawa: CJC, 1997), p. 70. This document is also available at http://www.cjc-ccm.gc.ca/english/annual _reports/1996–1997_append.htm; accessed June 13, 2008.

Part 5

Political Participation

KEITH HUTCHINGS, MHA

Keith Hutchings was elected as the Progressive Conservative Member of the Newfoundland and Labrador Assembly for the District of Ferryland in February 2007. In the general election of October that year, he was reelected and then appointed Parliamentary Secretary to the Minister of Human Resources, Labour and Employment. Keith was born the youngest of six children and grew up in the small community of Mobile on the Southern Shore of Newfoundland. He attended Memorial University, graduating with a Bachelor of Arts in Political Science, and later completed a Certificate in Public Administration from Memorial. In later years, Keith continued his education and completed an Occupational Health and Safety Program from Ryerson University in Toronto.

Keith's professional career included 11 years with the Workplace Health Safety and Compensation Commission in various positions including managing various departments within the organization. He then served as Chief of Staff and Executive Assistant to the Leader of the Official Opposition in the Provincial House of Assembly (1996–1998), and also ran his own successful consulting business for the next three years.

Keith participated in many sports, including hockey, running, ball hockey and golf, and has also been involved in coaching minor softball, soccer, and hockey. In addition, he has been active as a volunteer, including Big Brothers/Big Sisters of Eastern NL, as a board member, serving on various sporting executives, and chairing various fundraising events. Keith is married to Lynn Croft and they have two children, Jane and Eric.

Keith's career trajectory reveals in how many directions a degree in political science can lead. He found fulfilling employment in the public sector, obtained additional professional qualifications, established his own business, and then entered the world of partisan politics working for a party leader. His efforts culminated in finding electoral success in his own right, and are likely to lead to even higher office in the future.

Chapter Ten

DEMOCRACY IN ACTION: Elections, Political Participation, and Citizens' Power

Brenda O'Neill

CHAPTER OBJECTIVES

After you have completed this chapter, you should be able to:

- describe the difference between direct democracy and representative democracy

- describe the functions of elections

- compare the plurality, majoritarian, and proportional representation electoral systems

- understand why voters vote the way they do

- describe the many forms of political participation and explain what influences the decision to participate in politics

- explain the use of tools of direct democracy for increasing citizens' political power

Popular Perceptions of Democracy

In the fall of 2007 two events made dramatic headlines: the protests in Myanmar (also known as Burma) and the imposition of emergency rule and suspension of the constitution in Pakistan. Both underscore the importance assigned to democracy and democratic practices around the world. In Myanmar, thousands of monks in red vestments engaged in a silent and peaceful pro-democracy protest against the long-standing military dictatorship, only to be met with curfews, attempted crackdowns on news links to the outside world, riot police, arrests, and deaths. In Pakistan, the imposition of emergency rule was loudly condemned as it allowed for the suspension of political and civil rights and restrictions on the press. So, too, was the arrest and removal of the chief justice of the supreme court following the court's ruling on the illegality of President Musharraf's decision to run for office without stepping down from his military position.

Elections are often seen as the key mechanism for granting citizens a measure of power in democracies, but democracies require far more than elections to be considered legitimate. What additional criteria make for democracies that are acceptable to the international community? Why is judicial independence so important for the democratic legitimacy? What is it about democracy that would lead Buddhist monks to defy government restrictions on protest? Why is democracy valued so highly?

This chapter hopes to help answer these questions and more. Many of us employ the word *democracy* in everyday conversation, but the term is often ill defined or misunderstood. Few citizens in Western states are fully aware of the underlying assumptions, goals, and mechanisms required for the successful adoption and implementation of democracy.

Although there exist many academic definitions of the term, most agree that democracy is something close to "the rule of the people." The main principle is that political power should originate with the people rather than with those who rule. Modern democracy argues that the government's authority rests on the free and fair participation of all who are subject to its rule. Respect for the rule of law also ensures that political leaders do not govern arbitrarily, but rather follow the rules as laid out in the laws and the constitution. An independent judiciary ensures that governments respect the rule of law.

Western states and their citizens rarely challenge the normative superiority of democracies. Democracy is without question the *best* form of government. Unlike authoritarian systems, democracies provide opportunities for citizens to make decisions about the state, its citizens, and its relationship with other states, because ultimately those very citizens will have to live with the consequences of those decisions. In other words, citizens are politically powerful. Citizen participation is assumed to lead to *better* decisions than any alternative system.

The study of politics requires us to challenge popular perceptions in an effort to better understand the use and distribution of political power. Important questions include: What are the requirements of a democratic political system? Do democracies actually provide citizens with such opportunities? Are modern democracies successful? Answering such questions requires a basic

Buddhist monks march on a street in protest against the military government in Myanmar (Burma), September 2007.

AP Photo

understanding of the structures, procedures, and requirements adopted by modern democratic states in an attempt to meet the "democratic ideal." It is not an ideal easily met by regimes—sometimes called *fledgling democracies*—that have only recently adopted the democratic system. But established democracies, while undoubtedly more successful at the democratic challenge, are not without their own weaknesses. Few offer many opportunities for direct rule. Citizens get to vote in regular elections to select representatives in a number of legislative and executive bodies. Citizens might have an opportunity to vote in referendums on whether they support specific pieces of legislation or constitutional changes. They may also be given the opportunity to initiate their own pieces of legislation. But most democratic opportunities provide little by way of direct control over the day-to-day workings of the state. Instead of citizen rule, we have something closer to citizen choice over who will rule. For some, this is an unacceptable alternative; for others, the opportunities afforded by democracies for citizen decision-making are quite sufficient. One goal in this chapter is to explore the basis for such contradictory conclusions.

Citizen Power

In a majority of the world's states, citizens are granted a measure of power to make public decisions. The ideal of democratic governance is to ensure that citizens "enjoy an equal ability to participate meaningfully in the decisions that closely affect their common lives as individuals in communities."[1] In other words, democracy advocates that the ultimate source of political power is the people, and that the best method for deciding upon questions that affect the community is to allow its members to debate alternatives freely and openly and to select the option that receives support from more than half of those affected.

The ideal of democratic governance, however, is rarely met. Modern democracies provide citizens with only an indirect ability to influence public decisions, and not all citizens enjoy equal ability to participate effectively in politics. The lack of formal restrictions on participation is very different from the existence of equal means and skills for participation purposes. What sets democracies apart is the belief that vesting political power in citizens is a laudable goal.

In the 5th century BCE in the city-state of Athens in ancient Greece, citizens were more intimately involved in the day-to-day decision-making required for the community.[2] Given a marked commitment to civic virtue, politics played a part in everyday life. In this version of democracy, called **direct democracy**, citizen power came from participation in popular assemblies—the equivalent of modern-day legislatures. Citizens, not politicians, were responsible for making key political decisions. Consensus was preferred, but the support of a majority of those assembled could also decide on the alternatives. A key difference from today's legislatures is that *all* citizens were meant to participate in these assemblies, not only a smaller number of elected representatives. Democracy, rule of the people, was direct: the people sitting in the assemblies debated and ruled on community questions. And the debate that took place in these assemblies was crucial: if citizens were made aware of alternatives, were allowed to voice their own concerns, and could hear the concerns of others, the outcome of the deliberation was believed to be *better* than that offered by some smaller, select group of individuals. Moreover, in the Athenian system, appointment to offices and executives occurred by lot, in an effort to avoid the problems that accompanied direct election.

Before concluding that this is a system on which to pattern modern democracy, take note of the fact that the ability to meet in assembly requires a limited number of citizens. Gathering thousands of people together anywhere to debate and render decisions is unlikely to be easy or successful; indeed, think about how hard it is to get even a small group of friends to agree on which restaurant to choose for a dinner out. Direct democracy in ancient Greece worked because the city-state was small (an average of 2,000 to 3,000 of the approximately 50,000 citizens would attend an assembly) and citizenship was not extended to slaves, women, and children. These exclusions meant that the men sitting in these assemblies constituted a minority of the population. This minority imposed its will on the majority, an outcome that would be unacceptable in modern democracy. It also worked because slavery provided Athenian citizens with plenty of free time. While this application of direct democracy is likely to leave us uncomfortable, the ideal of all citizens having an equal and direct say in public decisions remains an important standard by which to judge modern democracies.

Few modern democracies are able to employ the model of direct democracy of ancient Greece. Indeed, even among ancient political systems, the Athenian model was atypical. Democracy has evolved in response to the requirements of modern living, and representative assemblies have replaced Athenian popular assemblies. Instead of making public decisions directly on a regular basis, citizens vote for individuals who will act as their representatives in these assemblies. In some modern systems, elements of direct democracy are nonetheless incorporated into the system in an effort to increase citizen participation in decision-making, as we will see later.

Representative democracies retain the important deliberative element of earlier assemblies—decision-makers must be able to gather and debate options before coming to any conclusions—but not the popular basis for filling these assemblies. The considerable time requirement imposed by politics on Athenian citizens is made today only of citizens who choose to stand for public office. The compromise works, however, only if representatives are conscious of the needs, desires, and concerns of the people they are elected to represent; that is, citizens are powerful only if their representatives act in ways that correspond with the desires of the represented. Most modern democracies attempt to ensure this consciousness by requiring periodic elections. Elections mean that representatives must present themselves regularly before those who selected them to defend their actions and to receive the privilege of continuing on in their role. What is often overlooked in this process is each citizen's personal responsibility. To keep modern democracies from degenerating into **elite** rule, citizens must stay informed, active, and committed to the public project to ensure the accountability of elected representatives. Thus elections assume a crucial role in the maintenance of modern democracies. According to Joseph Schumpeter, democracy is the "competitive struggle for the people's vote."[3] Because elections have degenerated to some extent into negative ad campaigns, leader image contests, and fundraising competitions, many challenge the degree to which the democratic ideal is currently being met in modern democracies.

Technology and Democracy

Technological innovation provides the potential for allowing modern democracies to incorporate the popular participation found in direct democracy and perhaps to counter the excesses of elections. E-democracy and **digital democracy** have been championed by many who consider communications technology the perfect vehicle for allowing citizens to regain some of the direct political power lost under representative systems. One estimate suggests that, as of 2007, over 1.2 billion users around the world were connected to the Internet: approximately 19 percent of the world's population.[4] Given the ease of access to and the wealth of information available on the Internet, this medium provides the potential for citizens to become proactive democratic participants. Citizens can be tremendously empowered by communicating directly and instantly with each other, with elected representatives, and with the government. Local government in Bristol, England, for example, launched a website designed specifically to allow young people to upload text, MP3 files, and images in an effort to encourage them to participate more in local politics. The site includes a number of e-petitions launched by youth on such issues as the funding of school kitchens and public swimming pools.[5] Another option rests in the possibility for completing political transactions online, for example by e-voting. Experiments with tele-voting have been conducted in a number of party leadership races in Canada.[6] Information communication technologies (ICTs) offer a whole range of options for increased citizen political participation: text messaging, blogs, websites (including YouTube and Facebook), and e-mail provide opportunities and tools for participation that were unknown even 20 years ago. In July 2007, for example, Democratic presidential candidates squared off in a debate with a twist: questions were submitted online via YouTube.[7] Technological innovation provides the potential for getting many more citizens to discuss, get information about, and participate in politics.

The potential that exists in digital democracy is mitigated, however, by a number of difficulties. Tele-voting experiments have had their share of technological problems: lost PINs (personal identification numbers), computer incompatibilities, site crashes, software glitches, and security breaches. Such concerns are at least as troubling as the problems encountered with the traditional technology of the "butterfly ballot" employed in the 2000 American elections. The ballot used in Palm Beach, Florida, had two vertical columns listing candidates and parties (resembling the wings of the butterfly), and voters punched a hole in the centre to indicate their preference. Unfortunately, the holes were not well aligned with the party and candidate names, and the resulting confusion probably cost the Democrats enough votes to lose the presidency.

Yet there are bigger issues than simply getting the systems to work properly and securely. There is a "digital divide"—that is, a vast gulf separating the rich and the poor with respect to accessing this technology. Remember for a moment that the democratic ideal is to allow citizens *equal ability* to participate meaningfully in public decision-making. There is little doubt that if democracy embraces technology, a number of citizens will be left behind. Democracies such as Denmark, the United States, Sweden, and Canada boast that over 65 percent of their populations have Internet access.[8] Read differently, that means that about 35 percent do not. And those without access are disproportionately made up of the poor, the uneducated and illiterate, and ethnic minorities. Estimates suggest that less than 20 percent of the population in the Middle East and less than 5 percent in Africa have access to the Internet.[9] Unequal access translates into unequal ability. Greater access, however, is not enough to breach the divide. Broadband access in every city may help, but it cannot guarantee ability—citizens must possess the requisite skills to employ this technology successfully. If this fact is overlooked, our democracies might eventually consist of two groups: the powerful and the increasingly powerless.[10] As some point out, however, this would not be very different from the current state of affairs.

One difficulty with which modern democracies grapple is the conflicting desire to increase citizen power while at the same time ensuring that those very citizens respect the rights and obligations of others.[11] Historically, majorities have sometimes voted to remove the freedoms of minorities. While citizens in modern democracies are quick to assert the rights owed them by virtue of their citizenship, fewer acknowledge the obligations involved for greater responsibility for public decision-making. Increasing citizens' political power might result in greater rates of participation, but only if the citizens have both the capacity and the desire to participate. Creating civic capacity by increasing skills and means is partly the responsibility of government, and governments might increase the desire to participate if political systems, structures, and processes were modified to create more effective citizen power. Technology may well provide one potential mechanism for increasing this power.

A further challenge for modern democracy is **globalization**,[12] which has served to erode state sovereignty in such a way that modern democratic institutions may no longer be effective. If important political decisions are being made by nongovernmental organizations (NGOs) or by international political organizations, rather than by democratically elected governments, then increasing citizen political power might ultimately be in vain. Democracy is meant to provide a mechanism by which a community can render decisions on how it will be governed. If institutions and groups outside the community are making such decisions, existing democratic structures are inadequate, as discussed in Chapter 16.

Elections

One of the key democratic instruments is the **election**. Elections are the primary mechanism through which citizens in democratic states participate in the political system. And in terms of citizen power, citizen political decision-making takes place mainly through elections. Elections can provide much information about the condition of democracy in a country. When Canadians went to the polls in the 2006 general election, only 64.7 percent of registered voters bothered to take advantage of their civic right (see Figure 10.1).[13] The turnout rate has been declining in Canada, although it did rebound slightly in 2006, and many take this to indicate that Canadians are dissatisfied with—rather than merely apathetic about—their governments, politics, and democracy.

Elections provide the prime mechanism in representative democracies for holding governments accountable. Governments are made up of representatives belonging to various political parties who are often selected on the basis of territory. Voters are provided an opportunity for retrospective evaluation—they can render a decision on whether they believe the government has done a good job while in office and whether it should be returned to power. At the same time, voters have an opportunity to assess the alternative parties and their promises to see whether another party might deserve a shot at governing on the basis of the platform it puts forward. Elections should occur on a regular basis to ensure that representatives and governments are aware of the need to "face the voters." Competitive or effective elections, then, determine—either directly or indirectly—the composition of the government and attempt to ensure government accountability to citizens.[14] Competitive elections have a number of requirements.[15] Elections should not unnecessarily restrict citizens' right to vote—called the **franchise**—and most modern democracies have relatively

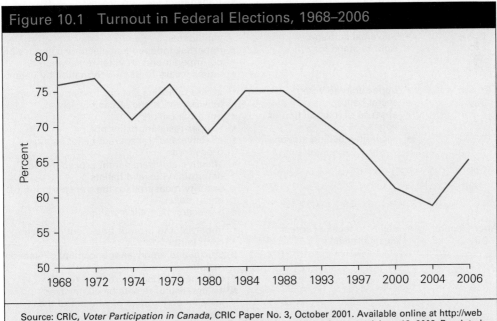

Figure 10.1   Turnout in Federal Elections, 1968–2006

Source: CRIC, *Voter Participation in Canada*, CRIC Paper No. 3, October 2001. Available online at http://web.mala.ca/livingstd/documents/Poli100%20Spring06/cricpapers_nov2001.pdf; accessed June 13, 2008. Reprinted by permission of the Centre for Research and Information on Canada (CRIC); 2004 and 2006 election turnout data obtained from http://www.electionscanada.ca

few limitations on this right. The removal of property qualifications, the extension of the right to vote to women and Aboriginal people, and the lowering of the voting age greatly increased the number of voters in Canada. Free and fair elections require at the very least that political parties be relatively free to assemble and put forward candidates, as noted in Table 10.1. Citizens must be presented with alternatives at elections; if they are not, the process is devoid of meaning. Not all groups, however, are given the freedom to associate and contest elections. In the Federal Republic of Germany, for example, "parties which, by reason of their aims or the behaviour of their adherents, seek to impair or destroy the free democratic basic order or to endanger the existence of the Federal Republic of Germany" are deemed unconstitutional, with the Federal Constitutional Court having the ultimate authority to decide on the question of unconstitutionality.[16] German history helps us to understand why such restrictions are in place.

Intimidation, violence, threats, and bribes should occur neither during election campaigns nor at the polls. The use of the secret ballot was adopted in part to curtail such practices. Finally, the administration of elections should be fair; the counting and reporting of votes cast, for example, should occur in an honest and consistent manner. The recent election ballot reform adopted in Florida came in response to the difficulties encountered in the 2000 presidential election. Optical scan ballots have replaced the butterfly ballot punch card system in the hope of preventing a repeat of that fiasco; counting votes fairly should not require that individual vote counters attempt to "guess" voter intent according to the depth of a dimpled chad on a punch card. More recently, 13 centres served as pilot projects in e-voting during local elections in Britain in May 2007, but the results suggested that security concerns and vote-counting problems continue to plague this modern twist on an ancient act.[17]

Table 10.1 Criteria of Free and Fair Elections

	Free	Fair
Campaign Period	• freedom of expression • freedom of assembly • freedom of association • universal suffrage • right to stand for office	• transparent election process • equality of political parties and groups • equal access to public media by parties and candidates • impartial, independent electoral commission • no impediments to voter registration • equal access to party information by voters
Election Day	• opportunity to vote • secret ballot • absence of intimidation of voters • accessible polling stations	• access to polling stations for party representatives, media, and election observers • impartial ballots • tamper-resistant ballot boxes • effective and transparent ballot counting procedures • effective and transparent procedures for determining invalid ballots • security measures for the transportation of ballot boxes • protection of polling stations
After Election Day	• ability to legally contest election results	• impartial and prompt treatment of election complaints • official and timely announcement of election results • unbiased media reporting of results • acceptance of results by all involved • installation in office of winners of the election

Source: Adapted from Richard Rose, ed., *The International Encyclopaedia of Elections* (Washington, DC: CQ Press, 2000), p. 133. © 2000 Congressional Quarterly Inc.

Function of Elections

What are the effects of competitive elections, and what exactly do elections do?[18] There are two contradictory views on the main function of elections in competitive democracies. The first, called the bottom-up view, suggests that elections are mechanisms for allowing citizens to select their governments, to influence public policies, and to be represented. The alternative, top-down view emphasizes the controlling elements of elections. Competitive elections provide mechanisms for governments to control the democratic process—by focusing dissent, by limiting political participation primarily to elections, and by legitimizing a system in which citizens have little effective power. Most people accept a middle ground between these two positions: elections provide opportunities for exchange between governments and citizens. This conclusion sets the stage for assessing how well elections perform their purported functions.

Choosing a Government

A key function of elections is to decide who will govern. In many liberal democracies, however, this is true only to a degree. Elections normally allow citizens to choose members of the legislature, but legislatures rarely govern, the American

A demonstrator dressed as Uncle Sam holds up a sign rejecting Governor George W. Bush as president during a rally in support of Vice-President Al Gore in Tallahassee, Florida, in December 2000.

CP Photo/Dave Martin

Congress being an exception (see Chapters 7 and 8). Moreover, the formation of a government in parliamentary systems often results from bargaining among the parties represented in the legislature (known as coalition governments) or from some long-standing convention, rather than from direct election. When one party wins a majority of seats in the legislature, it is normally asked to form government (known as a *majority government*). If, on the other hand, a party with the greatest number of seats in the legislature holds only a plurality but is deemed capable of governing, it can nonetheless be asked to form government (known as a *minority government*). It is also the case that parliamentary governments can change between elections. A majority of presidential systems, on the other hand, allow for direct election of the president.[19] Yet the American president, contrary to popular belief, is not directly elected. When American voters cast a vote for president, they are actually voting for a slate of electors called the Electoral College; these electors pledge to vote for the winning candidate in their state when they formally elect the president roughly a month later. Electoral College votes are distributed on a state-by-state basis, equal to the number of members sent from the state to the two houses of Congress, making them roughly proportional to each state's population. Because most states' college electors vote as a block, it is possible for the college to elect a candidate who lost the nationwide popular vote, as was the case in the 2000 American presidential election: Al Gore won 48.4 percent of the popular vote but only 267 of the 537 Electoral College votes. George W. Bush, on the other hand, won only 47.9 percent of the popular vote but captured 271 Electoral College votes to win the presidency.[20] Finally, the public service, courts, and military play an important role in helping the executive to govern, although executive appointment rather than election is normally the rule employed to fill the vast majority of these positions. Accordingly, "competitive elections play an important part in government formation but the relationship is less tight, less strict, than many people imagine."[21]

Mechanism of Accountability

Elections are also mechanisms designed to ensure government accountability. This claim may seem suspect, given the fact that elections do not always directly determine the government. They can, however, force a change in government, particularly if the people are especially unhappy with decisions made during the government's tenure and if a clear alternative party exists. Democratic governments understand that at some point they must face the electorate, a knowledge that can constrain their behaviour to some degree. It cannot guarantee, however, that all government decisions will be popular: the Mulroney government, for example, imposed the Goods and Services Tax (GST) on Canada despite widespread public hostility.

Selection of Representatives

Elections allow citizens to choose their political representatives; they necessarily determine who serves as the representative or representatives of individual territorial districts. But the concept of representation is a difficult one to pin down, as mentioned in Chapter 8. What does it mean to represent others politically? One common interpretation proposes three styles of electoral representation: trustee, party, and constituency.[22] The trustee model emphasizes that although representatives take the interests and concerns of their electors into account, decisions are ultimately made according to the representatives' own judgment. Citizens should, the argument goes, trust their judgment. Such an argument might seem immediately unacceptable, but democracy does value the importance of debate and the articulation of alternative viewpoints for political decision-making—and this is exactly what is supposed to take place in the legislature. Only a minority of ordinary citizens have the information, expertise, and awareness of consequences that would allow them to render equally valid judgments on many current political questions.

The party model, on the other hand, emphasizes that legislators are chosen on the basis of their party membership—very few independents ever get elected—and as a result their responsibility is to support the party position in the legislature. This argument focuses on the fact that many people vote according to party rather than individual candidate; once elected, legislators should be bound to support that party's platform. Such an argument is often heard in Canada to criticize MPs who "cross the floor" to join another political party, a recent example being that of Belinda Stronach, who left the Conservative Party to become a Liberal Party cabinet minister in May 2005.

Finally, the constituency model emphasizes the role that representatives play in supporting the interests of their constituents by helping them to deal with the large government bureaucracy, promoting government spending in the constituency and, in some cases, generating employment opportunities. For many Canadian backbench MPs, this casework can take up a significant portion of their time.

Political representation is particularly important in democracies given that legislators are elected to "represent" the interests of citizens. Political scientists have engaged in a continuing debate on the nature of the concept, making a distinction between substantive and descriptive representation. Is it more important to have political representatives, regardless of who they are, who will make decisions that are in the best interests of a particular constituency (substantive), or to have political representatives whose physical characteristics, such as gender, ethnicity, and age, mirror those of their constituency (descriptive)? In the latter argument, it is often assumed that if a group of legislators physically resemble those they are meant to represent then their decisions are likely to mirror the decisions that would have been made by the very people they represent. Although the descriptive versus substantive representation dichotomy is to some extent a false one, it has nevertheless generated significant discussion in some areas, such as **feminist** political theory where the question of who can "best" represent the interests of women has been raised (see Box 10.1).[23]

How the Canadian Electoral System Discourages Women's Participation BOX 10.1

The Royal Commission on Electoral Reform and Party Financing reported in 1991 its findings concerning the principles and processes governing elections to the House of Commons. In setting out the objectives of Canadian electoral democracy, the study suggested the importance of ensuring equitable access to candidacy. And while few formal restrictions exist, the commission noted that women have been greatly underrepresented among those running as candidates for and those elected to the House. For example, in 1988 women made up only 19 percent of candidates and only 13 percent of those elected. This virtual exclusion of women, it argued, was no longer acceptable. According to the report, "It is not merely a matter of political symbolism; elected representatives will not and cannot effectively represent the full range of Canada's interests if they do not reasonably reflect its society. To this extent, the electoral system fails to secure the best persons to sit in the House of Commons" (p. 8).

Two of the key barriers for women's entry into the House of Commons are the nomination process and the inattention of political parties. The nomination process presents a particular financial barrier to women, whose earnings continue to be less than those of men. First, women are more likely to find themselves in expensive contested nominations rather than in acclamations to run as the party's candidate. And second, they receive fewer and smaller donations than men, in part due to their different social and professional contacts.

To deal with these problems, the report recommended the imposition of spending limits on nomination contest campaigns and the issuing of tax receipts to those who donate money toward nomination contests. The report also highlighted the role played by political parties in increasing the representation of women in the House. Although it noted that the major parties at the federal level had measures designed to assist prospective women candidates (especially the New Democratic Party), progress had been slow. Women continued to be underrepresented in "safe" ridings, which decreased their chances of getting elected. They also continued to work in "pink-collar" positions within party hierarchies (e.g., as constituency association secretaries), rarely stepping stones to political office. The report recommended that "the by-laws and constitutions of registered political parties require the establishment of formal search committees and commit the parties to processes that demonstrably promote the identification and nomination of broadly representative candidates" (p. 121).

Have we made any progress in the years since the report came out? In the 2006 federal election, women made up 23 percent of all candidates and 21 percent of those elected to the House of Commons. Should there have been greater progress than this since 1988? Does it matter whether more women get elected? What do you think?

SOURCE: Royal Commission on Electoral Reform and Party Financing, *Final Report, Vol. 1*, pp. 8 and 121, 1991. Reproduced with the permission of the Minister of Public Works and Government Services, 2008, and courtesy of the Privy Council Office.

Conferral of Legitimacy

Elections are also the mechanism through which governments are granted a measure of **legitimacy**. As a key element of democratic systems, fair and free elections provide a chance for citizens to participate in politics and to decide who will hold political power. With this opportunity, however, comes the expectation that the people will comply with government decisions. The opportunity to choose the rulers in a fair and legitimate manner obliges citizens to obey the decisions of that popularly elected government. The legitimacy of the electoral process provides the government with political authority, but an obligation to obey does not remove the right of political dissent and the opportunity to change such policies.

Establishing a Policy Mandate

Elections are also meant to supply governments with a specific policy mandate for their tenure in office. Understanding the nature of elections provides insight into why this function is rarely fulfilled. Political parties offer specific campaign platforms, filled with a number of policy prescriptions. One might, then, conclude that the winning party has been given a vote of support for its specific policy proposals. In order for this to occur, however, voters must be voting for the party *because* of its policy positions and for no other reason, which is not often the case. A majority of the electorate must also support the party and its platform, which is not always true either. Although Brian Mulroney claimed that the election of the Progressive Conservative Party in 1988 indicated that Canadians wished to go forward with the Canada–U.S. Free Trade Agreement, he failed to mention that the party had won only 43 percent of the popular vote. One cannot make the claim that elections determine public policy if more people vote against than for the positions ultimately adopted. In addition, once parties have formed the government, they can drop key elements of their electoral platforms without major repercussions. This seriously weakens the argument that elections shape public policy. In 2003, for example, Ontario Premier Dalton McGuinty broke an election promise not to raise taxes while in government. The need for the increased taxes notwithstanding, such reversals make it difficult to claim that elections constrain policy choices in government.

Mechanism for Political Education, Mobilization, and Socialization

Finally, elections provide opportunities for political education, mobilization, and socialization. Elections allow for the political education of both voters and members of political parties. Voters can learn about political campaigns, candidates, and party leaders, and the major issues facing the government. Parties and candidates have an opportunity to find out what the people are thinking and also to shape their opinions. Such education can provide an incentive for people to get out and vote and possibly become politically involved in additional ways. Elections can also socialize citizens regarding the requirements of democracy and the importance assigned to politics within a particular country. If such learning is to occur, however, citizens must already be interested enough in politics to pay attention to the media coverage of campaigns. The most recent Canadian election study reveals that on a scale of 0 (not at all interested) to 10 (extremely interested), Canadians possess an average interest of 5.3 for politics in general. This average jumps to 5.9, however, when people are asked more specifically about their interest in the federal election.[24]

Elections and the Media

Any discussion of elections in modern democracies must address the role played by the **mass media**. Television, radio, and newspapers provide an important source of information for voters, a point not lost on politicians and campaign managers. More often than not, the media present the electoral contest as a "horse race." The focus is on which party and leader are ahead on any particular day, rather than on more substantive policy issues or the parties' platforms. This sensational treatment makes for entertaining viewing, listening, or reading; it does little, however, to advance the political education of voters or the message that politics and elections are more than games. Party leaders and candidates have also had to learn to speak in sound bites, since the media like answers in the form of 10-second clips. Not all political questions, however, can be reasonably answered in so short a time.

Style over Substance?

This focus on style, often over substance, leads politicians to hire professional image consultants and speech specialists. The transformation of Preston Manning during his tenure as leader of the Reform Party in Canada suggests the importance assigned to image: a change from glasses to contact lenses, a change in hairstyle (and colour?), a serious overhaul of his wardrobe, and voice lessons. Selecting the proper media image is not always easy. Prime Minister Stephen Harper has suffered his own image problems. He appeared in 2005 at the Calgary Stampede in a too-small leather vest and odd-looking cowboy hat; in 2006 he was criticized on an official visit to Mexico for wearing what appeared to be a fishing vest compared to the starched crisp white shirts worn by Presidents Fox and Bush; and the news media have often remarked on the size of his

Conservative leader Stephen Harper attending the Calgary Stampede in a cowboy outfit.

Stephen Harper photo taken by Mikael Kjellstrom, July 7, 2007. Reprinted with permission of the *Calgary Herald*.

stomach. And although none of this ought to matter for the quality of governance in democracies, the prominence of media coverage has increased the degree to which it does. Citizens need to feel that their leaders are competent, honest, able, and trustworthy. The image that they portray through the media directly determines these attitudes.

Tighter regulation might be the solution to ensuring more realistic, informative, and substance-driven media coverage of politics, but the media's portrayal of politics and politicians would be extremely difficult to control. Although public broadcasters exist (CBC Radio and Television in Canada, for example), much of the industry is dominated by commercial (private) broadcasters and publishers, whose bottom line is either circulation numbers or size of the audience. Maximizing paper sales and viewing audience would prove difficult if the media were forced to provide in-depth and substantial coverage of politics and elections (especially given the low level of interest that Canadians have in politics and elections as noted above). And while regulation might prove successful in altering coverage, the cost to political freedom, namely freedom of expression, would certainly prove too high.

Media Concentration

A further concern is the growing concentration of mass media ownership and its increased commercialization. In the United States, giants such as AOL/Time Warner and Viacom increasingly dominate all forms of mass communication, driven by a set of values not always in line with journalistic ones.[25] The rise in commercialization has meant a simultaneous decrease in the importance of public broadcasting based on a greater sense of public purpose and responsibility. Public broadcasters offer more current affairs and political news programs than commercial broadcasters, and help to produce a politically informed and aware citizenry. Increased concentration also raises concerns about the responsiveness of media empires to local political issues, as exemplified by CanWest Global's decisions to adopt common editorials for various newspapers across the country and to refocus journalists' stories that were at odds with the views of the owners (see Chapter 4). A challenge to media ownership concentration comes from citizen journalism, made possible by the expansion of the Internet. Blogs, wikis, and websites provide almost unlimited alternative sources of information.

Electoral Rules

In each country, the conduct of elections is governed by a set of rules and regulations, which detail the offices that will be filled by the election; financial, nomination, and reporting requirements for candidates and parties that wish to run in the contest; voting eligibility requirements; regulations concerning the drawing of electoral boundaries; and even the requirements for the ballot, such as the order of candidates' names.

Campaign Finance

Key among these rules are those concerning matters of party and election finance: for example, the amount and sources of party funds, party and candidate spending, and *third-party advertising*—a term encompassing spending by organizations other than political parties during elections.[26] The need for financial regulation stems from a concern for equity and fairness among those contesting elections; the control of how money is raised and spent can help "level the playing field" and limit the degree to which money influences electoral outcomes and ultimately government decisions. Restricting how parties can spend during campaigns diminishes their need for raising funds, makes elections more equitable, and reduces candidates' and parties' obligations to those donating the funds.

In 2000, the government of Manitoba adopted legislation designed to address concerns regarding the perception that money unduly influences politics and elections. This legislation bans contributions from corporations and unions to political parties, limits individual contributions to $3,000 per year, limits third-party spending during election periods to $5,000, and reinstates limits on political party advertising during elections. Similar legislation has existed in Quebec since 1977. The National Citizens' Coalition, a right-wing nonprofit organization in Canada, has fought hard against restrictions on third-party election advertising, which it calls "gag laws." On three separate occasions, Alberta courts agreed with the organization's argument that the rules represent an unreasonable violation of the right of freedom of expression. The Supreme Court, however, ruled in favour of the restrictions imposed on third-party spending in the Canada Elections Act in *Harper v. Canada* in 2004. The challenge is to balance the desire for a level playing field with the desire for ensuring free and open debate during elections.

Similar campaign finance legislation was adopted for Canadian general elections by the Chrétien Liberal government in 2003. Designed to enhance the fairness and transparency of the electoral system, Bill C-24 brought the *Canada Elections Act* in line with elections regulation in Manitoba and Quebec by restricting contributions, imposing spending limits on parties and candidates, enhancing financial reporting requirements, and increasing the regulation of political broadcasting. In an effort to level the political playing field and to reduce the perception of undue influence in politics, the system of public financing of election expenses was also further enhanced.[27] Although the 2004 election took place under the new regulatory framework, its overall impact on parties, elections, and participation remains unclear.[28] The Harper government's *Federal Accountability Act* attempted to plug the last loopholes in this field.

Similar legislation was adopted in 2002 at the federal level in the United States. The key element of the *Bipartisan Campaign Reform Act* was the regulation of "soft money" and "issue advocacy," the former involving donations to parties not specifically directed toward the support or opposition of a candidate and the latter involving campaign communications that do not expressly advocate for the election or defeat of candidates. Spending in both has skyrocketed given dramatic increases in the costs of campaigns (mass media and technology costs) and the need to overcome the limits on "hard money" and "express advocacy."[29] Unlike in Canada, however, the U.S. Supreme Court has been less willing to accept that campaign finance regulation be employed to "level the playing field" across political parties (see Chapter 12).

Electoral Districting and Apportionment

Another key set of electoral rules governs electoral districting and apportionment, particularly in electoral systems based on territorial representation, such as those of Canada and the United States. *Districting* (or *redistribution*, as it is called in Canada) refers to the drawing of electoral boundaries in order to establish territorial districts or constituencies from which one or more representatives will be sent to the legislature. The manipulation of district boundary lines to advantage a particular group (or to disadvantage another) is referred to as *gerrymandering*. In an effort to reduce the likelihood of such manipulation, the responsibility for the drawing of electoral boundaries has been placed in the hands of independent bodies, rather than those of the sitting government.

The principle of **representation by population** ("rep by pop") advocates that electoral districts should be roughly equal in population in order to ensure that individuals receive a proportionate share of representation in government, so that each vote is of equal weight. *Apportionment*—the determination of representative seats according to population—should occur regularly, normally after a census, to account for shifting population bases. The rep by pop principle, however, recognizes that other considerations can come into play in drawing boundaries, including a desire to keep the geographic expanse of a district to a manageable size and to ensure minority groups are not scattered across several districts, which would minimize their electoral influence. In federal states, such as Canada and the United States, rep by pop is adopted for the lower house at the national level but not for the upper house. In the United States, representation in the senate occurs on a state basis (two representatives per state). In Canada's senate, representation occurs on a more complicated regional basis. In both instances, however, population size is not a consideration in apportioning seats to the upper house.

Electoral Systems

The rules employed to translate votes into seats have been the subject of great debate in many countries.[30] New Zealand, Japan, and Italy have recently changed their electoral systems in an attempt to address various concerns. Such changes reflect the importance of electoral systems— systems that set the rules for determining how individual votes are translated into legislative seats. To better understand the importance of rules for outcomes, let us employ an academic analogy. Imagine your response if a professor decided to change the format of an exam from multiple-choice to essay questions one day before you were scheduled to write it. Rules (in this example, the format of the exam—multiple choice or essay questions) determine how you will study for the exam and possibly the grade you will receive. Electoral systems are no different—they shape electoral strategies, electoral outcomes, and voter behaviour. Because of this, students of politics require a basic understanding of the various electoral systems in use in today's democracies.

One common method for distinguishing electoral systems focuses on the electoral formula employed—that is, the rule for determining how many votes are required to earn a seat. Two main types of electoral systems are proportional and nonproportional systems (see Table 10.2). Nonproportional systems (such as in Canada, the United States, and Britain) are defended for their tendency to produce majority governments, for encouraging the development of two-party systems, and for encouraging strong territorially defined links between representatives and their constituents. Proportional systems, on the other hand, are defended for the greater fairness in awarding seats that are roughly proportional to the share of votes obtained by each party.

Table 10.2   Electoral Systems

Nonproportional Systems

(a) Plurality (first-past-the-post)

Candidate who wins more votes than any other (i.e., wins the plurality of votes) is awarded the seat. This method is used most often in combination with single-member districts. *Examples:* Canada (House of Commons); United States (House of Representatives).

(b) Majority

Candidate must win a majority of votes (50% + 1) in order to win the seat. Majority is achieved by employing one of three methods:

- *Runoff:* The second ballot lists only the top two candidates from the first ballot round. This method is used most often in combination with single-member districts. *Example:* French presidential elections.

- *Plurality:* A second ballot is also employed, but the winner needs to obtain only a plurality of votes. There is no significant reduction in the number of candidates on the second ballot, although a threshold may be imposed. *Example:* French legislative elections.

- *Alternative:* A single election occurs, but voters rank the candidates in order of preference. Winner must obtain a majority of first preferences. If no candidate earns a majority of first preferences, the second preferences of the last-place candidate are transferred to the remaining candidates until one candidate achieves a majority. *Example:* Australia (House of Representatives).

Proportional Systems
(all in multimember districts)

(a) List System

Seats are awarded to parties that meet or exceed an electoral quota. In a closed-list system, voters cast a single ballot for a party, and candidates from that party's list are elected in the order in which they appear on the list. In the more common open-list system, in addition to choosing to award their votes to a single party, voters can instead choose to award their votes individually to specific candidates on the party lists. *Examples:* Israel; Switzerland.

(b) Single Transferable Vote (STV)

Voters rank their candidate choices across parties. Candidates meeting a quota are awarded a seat. Initial counting looks at first preferences only; any candidate meeting the quota is elected. Second preferences of any surplus votes (in excess of the quota) are then transferred to any remaining candidates. Again, the candidates who meet the quota after the second preferences have been transferred are elected. If seats are still vacant, the weakest candidate is eliminated and the second preferences from those ballots are allocated to the remaining candidates until the quota is met and all seats are allocated. *Examples:* Ireland; Australia (Senate).

MIXED SYSTEMS

Such systems combine elements of nonproportional and proportional electoral systems. The mixed member proportional (MPP) system is an example. Voters have two votes: one for the constituency representative and a second for a party. A share of seats is allocated through single-member districts, while the remaining seats are allocated in order to bring each party's seat share in line with the party's popular vote share. Examples: Germany (Bundestag); New Zealand.

Source: Adapted from André Blais and Louis Massicotte, "*Electoral Systems,*" in Lawrence LeDuc, Richard G. Niemi, and Pippa Norris, eds., *Comparing Democracies: Elections and Voting in Global Perspective* (Thousand Oaks, CA: Sage, 1996). Reprinted by permission of Sage Publications, Inc.

Electoral systems are not merely of academic concern; by the end of 2007, three Canadian provinces (British Columbia, Ontario, and Prince Edward Island) had held referendums on the question of reforming the electoral system.

Nonproportional Systems

Nonproportional type electoral systems are constituency-based (the country is divided into geographically defined constituencies represented by one elected representative) and voters select a candidate on the ballot rather than a party. This group of electoral systems includes the one most familiar to North Americans: the plurality system. The requirement for winning in a plurality system is *to earn more votes than any other candidate but not necessarily a majority*—hence its more common name, **first-past-the-post (FPTP)**. In elections to the Canadian House of Commons, for example, the country is divided into single-member districts: one representative is selected from each territorially defined district. Since a number of political parties nominate a single candidate to run in each district, the winner rarely earns a majority of the votes cast. The cumulative effect of this "wasting of votes" can lead to serious distortions in the vote-share-to-seat-share ratio at the national level (see Table 10.3 for the distortion in Canada's 2006 federal election).[31] Such distortions have fuelled efforts to change Canada's electoral system at both the federal and provincial levels. Since the governing parties often achieve power as a direct result of this distortion, however, one can understand why they might be hesitant to change the system.

An additional but less common nonproportional electoral system is the **majoritarian system**. The distinction between such systems and FPTP is that the winning candidate is required to earn a majority of votes in order to be declared the winner (a majority being 50% + 1). This requirement means that one election will often not produce a winner, since elections normally involve more than two candidates. As a result, majoritarian systems employ one of three mechanisms for producing a winner. Two of these systems require a second election in the event that no candidate earns a majority of votes in the first. The majority runoff systems include only the top two finishers from the first race in the second election. Limiting the subsequent election to only two candidates virtually ensures that a majority winner will be produced. In majority plurality systems, on the other hand, a second election is held without any reduction in the number of candidates (although some countries adopt a threshold to eliminate candidates who earned a small share of the vote). The winner in the second election is the candidate who obtains a plurality of votes—that is, more votes than any other candidate.

The third mechanism, the alternative vote, requires only one election, which many see as its advantage: voters are asked to rank the candidates listed on the ballot in order of preference (e.g., putting a "1" next to the candidate who is their first choice, a "2" next to their second choice, and so on). The winner is the candidate earning a majority of first preferences, or "1"s. If no such

Table 10.3 Distorting Effects of the Canadian Electoral System, 2006

Party	Seats	Seat Share (percent)	Vote Share (percent)	Seat-to-Vote (ratio)
Conservative Party	124	40.3	36.3	1.11
Liberal Party	103	33.4	30.2	1.11
Bloc Québécois	51	16.6	10.5	1.58
New Democratic Party	29	9.4	17.5	0.54
Total seats	**308***			

Note: If the seat-to-vote ratio is greater than one, the party has been awarded more seats than it deserved on the basis of its vote share. If the ratio is less than one, the party has been underrewarded. *One seat was won by a candidate running as an independent.

Source: Elections Canada, "Percentage of Valid Votes, by Political Affiliation" and "Distribution of Seats, by Political Affiliation and Sex"; available at http://www.elections.ca/scripts/OVR2006/25/table7.html and http://www.elections.ca/scripts/OVR2006/25/table9.html; accessed June 13, 2008.

majority is achieved, the second preferences of the candidate with the fewest number of first preferences are then transferred to the remaining candidates. If a majority is still not achieved, the process continues until transferred preferences provide a majority of votes to a candidate.

Proportional Systems

In **proportional representation (PR)** systems, the priority lies in awarding seats to parties in rough proportion to the share of votes earned rather than in awarding the seat to a single candidate from each district. One key to understanding PR systems is that they use multimember districts rather than single-member districts; the allocation of seats according to the proportion of votes earned is only possible if there is more than one seat available. The higher the number of members to be elected per district, the more proportional the system is likely to be. In Israel, the entire country serves as a single constituency, allowing for a large degree of proportionality in seat allocation. The other key to understanding PR systems is that seats are generally allocated to parties rather than to candidates; although there is significant variation across PR systems, political parties are considered to be more powerful in PR than non-PR systems, in part because they often have a greater say than voters in determining which party members get elected to the legislature.

Two specific PR systems are the list system and the single transferable vote. Most PR systems use the **list system**, which requires voters to choose from among lists of candidates prepared by the parties. In a *closed-list system*, voters are presented with a ballot that lists each of the parties contesting the election and the rank-ordering of the candidates each party has selected as their representatives if they win seats in the legislature. Voters cannot indicate preferences for individual candidates on a party's list, but instead select one party's list as their choice. The share of votes the party receives in the constituency determines the number of candidates who will sit in the legislature. Parties derive tremendous power in this system through their ability to set candidate lists. An *open-list system*, on the other hand, allows voters to choose and rank as many specific candidates from among the different party lists as there are seats to be allocated, thereby weakening the power of party officials to determine who gets elected to the legislature. While the power of parties is stronger in closed-list than open-list systems, the former more easily allow for the adoption of measures by parties for targeting certain demographics for increased representation. For instance, "zippering" party lists—making every second candidate on the closed list a woman—has been shown to be a particularly effective mechanism for increasing their numbers in legislatures.

The procedure employed for allocating seats in proportional systems varies, but it normally involves dividing the number of votes cast for the party or candidate by a quota or divisor. Seats are allocated to the parties according to the resulting figure. As an example, the "droop quota" is calculated in the following manner:

$$\frac{\text{total number of votes}}{\text{number seats to be filled} + 1} + 1$$

Each party's total votes earned are then divided by the quota to determine the number of seats they are awarded; any unallocated seats are awarded to the parties with the highest remainders (i.e., the number of votes "left over" after dividing by the quota). The end result is that the "cost" for each seat (in terms of votes) is roughly equal. Some PR systems also adopt thresholds that deny seats to parties that receive very small shares of the vote, normally around 5 to 6 percent. The argument for adopting thresholds is that it keeps extremist parties from gaining a measure of legitimacy, at least that afforded by a legislative seat. Such thresholds necessarily introduce distortion in the seat-to-vote ratio, however, a criticism often aimed at nonproportional systems.

Israel's electoral system provides a simple example of the application of a PR electoral system. As previously mentioned, Israel consists of a single electoral district with a district magnitude of 120 (the number of seats to be filled in the Knesset, Israel's legislature). A closed-list system is in place; more than a month before election day, political parties are required to submit their ordered candidate lists to the Central Elections Committee and voters are provided with a ballot that allows them to allocate a single vote to one of the party lists (rather than to individual candidates). After all the votes have been counted, parties that do not meet the existing threshold (currently 2 percent of all votes cast) are not awarded a seat in the legislature. The *d'Hondt formula* is then employed to allocate seats among the remaining parties. That is, the total votes earned by each party is divided by a set of numbers (1, 2, 3, 4, 5, etc.) and the result (the quotient or average votes per seat earned) determines the allocation of seats; then the first seat is awarded to the party with the highest quotient or average, the second seat to the party with the next highest average, and so on until all seats are awarded.

An alternative to the list system, the **single transferable vote (STV)**, used in both Australia and Ireland, allows voters to rank their candidate preferences on the ballot. As in the alternative vote system, voters can rank as many candidates as there are seats to be allocated in the constituency. This ballot structure provides voters rather than parties with a greater measure of power than many other PR systems. The increased choice offered to voters, and the associated decrease in the power of parties to choose the representatives to send to the legislature, was one of the rationales offered by B.C.'s Citizens' Assembly in 2004 for their selection of STV as the recommended alternative to FPTP.[32] The procedure for determining which candidates are elected involves the use of the droop quota (explained above). Each candidate's first preference votes are counted, and those whose total number of first preference votes received meets the required quota are each awarded a seat. Any surplus or remaining votes over the quota for these elected candidates are then transferred to the second-preference candidates on the winning candidates' ballots. If a candidate earned 40 percent of the winning candidate's overall second preferences, then that candidate receives 40 percent of the winning candidate's surplus votes. Candidates who meet the quota with the addition of these transferred votes are then awarded a seat. If seats remain unallocated at this point, the candidate with the fewest first preferences is eliminated, and the second preferences listed on those ballots are transferred proportionately to the remaining candidates. The process (which at times can be very lengthy given its complexity) continues until all seats are allocated.

Mixed Systems

Several countries have adopted an electoral system that combines elements of the proportional and nonproportional electoral systems into mixed systems. Japan, for example, elects 300 members of its house of representatives using a first-past-the-post system with single-member constituencies. An additional 200 members are independently elected from 11 regional multimember constituencies through a PR system. New Zealand's system also creates two sets of elected members: those elected under the traditional FPTP system in 65 single-member districts and another 55 elected under a PR closed-list system. The difference, however, is that the 55 PR members are awarded to the parties in order to "top up" the seat shares awarded by the single-member districts to ensure proportionality of all seats with party vote shares cast under the list system. Since FPTP over-rewards larger parties, the PR seat allocation corrects this distortion. Most mixed electoral systems hope to maintain the territorial link between the representative and his or her constituents while injecting greater proportionality between each party's vote and seat shares in the legislature.

Electoral reform has recently become a key issue on the political agenda in Canada in light of growing concerns over citizen disengagement and increased political cynicism. The most common criticism directed at FPTP relates to the system's distorting effects when vote shares are translated into seat shares. Because it is a "winner take all" system, votes for parties with anything less than a plurality are essentially wasted. This distortion leads to overrepresentation for parties that win a plurality of the vote (creating "artificial majorities" in the legislature) and underrepresentation for most other parties, as seen in Table 10.3. This distortion can at times be extreme. In 2001, the Liberals came to power in British Columbia with 97 percent of the seats in the legislature, having earned only 57.6 percent of the popular vote. The New Democratic Party, on the other hand, won only 2 of 79 seats despite having earned 21.6 percent of the provincial vote share.

An additional criticism of FPTP relates to the fact that parties whose support is concentrated in a particular region are likely to be overrepresented in the legislature, while parties with weak but more broadly dispersed support are likely to be underrepresented. In Canada, the Bloc Québécois receives an inflated share of seats in the House of Commons because it receives a plurality of votes in a limited number of regionally concentrated ridings. The NDP, on the other hand, is significantly underrepresented despite receiving a fairly consistent level of support across the country, because it fails to achieve a plurality in many ridings, leading to many votes being effectively wasted. Proponents of electoral reform have argued that this regionalizing effect has exacerbated regional tensions in Canada. The underrepresentation of women and Aboriginal peoples has also been identified as a weakness of FPTP. Alternatively, supporters of FPTP point to its tendency to produce majority governments capable of implementing electoral mandates, its encouragement of a territorial link between elected representative and constituents, and its overall simplicity.[33]

Although several Canadian provinces have examined the question of electoral reform, and in some cases held referendums on the question, FPTP remains in place at both the provincial and federal level in Canada. As noted above, the B.C. Citizens' Assembly on Electoral Reform recommended STV as an alternative to FPTP in 2004; a similar assembly in Ontario recommended MMP as the preferred alternative in 2007. Both recommendations were subsequently defeated in provincial referendums. We can nevertheless identify a number of potential consequences resulting from the move to a more proportional electoral system. First, the incentives for voting (fewer wasted votes) and for voting for smaller parties (because they would be more likely to gain seats in proportion to the votes they earn) would likely increase. Accordingly, turnout would likely improve and the party system might become more fractionalized (see Chapter 11). Second, electoral results would likely become proportional; political parties would likely earn seat shares that more closely reflect the share of votes earned. At the federal level, this might help parties such as the NDP and the Green Party, who have been underrewarded historically in seat shares. Third, the representation of minorities and women in legislatures could improve; a move to an electoral system that allowed political parties to more directly determine which of their candidates earned legislative seats might result in more representative chambers. Fourth, some PR systems would allow voters, rather than parties, more say in determining which candidates get elected. Fifth, greater proportionality would likely translate into fewer majority governments and more coalition governments. Without the representational "boost" afforded to winning parties in FPTP, governments are more likely to be formed from the merger of two or more parties than from only one.

Voting

Elections are the primary mechanism for engaging the people in democracies. The study of voting behaviour and the way voters decide have preoccupied political scientists for quite some time, especially since the advent of public opinion polling in the 1940s. Why do people vote as they do? Three theories can be identified that together provide a fairly complete answer to this rather complex question.[34]

Sociological Model

The first theory, the sociological model, explains voting by identifying the social forces that determine individual values and beliefs. People make their decisions on the basis of such things as

- place of residence
- religious group to which they belong (if any)
- ethnic background
- social class
- age
- gender

These important factors work their influence indirectly. For example, gender might affect how one votes by increasing the value one places on publicly funded child care, which in turn would increase the likelihood of voting for parties that endorse such policies. An explanation like this takes us only so far, however, as people belong to many groups, often with conflicting interests; and although group memberships are fairly stable, voters often switch parties from one election to another.

Sociopsychological Model

The second model, the sociopsychological model, casts a wider net in search of an explanation of vote decisions. The focus in this model is on the psychological process of voting—how people come to make their individual choices. The result is a much more complex model of the various factors. One group of influences mirrors the social group influences identified in the sociological model. Friends and family, ethnic groups, and social cleavages are likely to shape the interests and values that voters bring to their vote decisions. But more important are the personal and political factors that often occur closer in time to the decision itself. Key among these is **party identification**—the long-standing psychological attachment or loyalty to a party that can directly influence where one is likely to put one's X on the ballot. Party identification acts as a filter through which individuals interpret election issues, candidates, parties, and leaders; it can serve as a shortcut in what can be the daunting process of gathering the information necessary to make a rational voting choice. But if the explanation for why a person voted for the Liberal Party, for example, is "because I always vote that way," the result is that we really have not explained very much. Moreover, evidence suggests that the importance of party identification is decreasing; younger and more educated voters are less likely to defer to partisan loyalties at the ballot box.

Rational Voting Model

The third model of voting stresses the actual calculus that voters employ. According to this model, voting is a rational decision rather than one based on social ties or partisan identification. The **rational voting** model assumes that, in deciding how to cast their ballot, voters employ a process of evaluation, involving the important issues in

Like Canadians, the British keep electing people they don't like.

Bruce MacKinnon/Halifax Herald/Artizans

the campaign, their assessment of the candidates and the parties' platforms, and their evaluations of the party leaders. This process might compare the alternatives in the search for the "right" choice or it might simply involve an evaluation of the sitting government in an attempt to determine whether a change is needed. This retrospective approach to voting is assumed in campaign slogans that emphasize "a time for change" and helps to explain why voters often punish governments in periods of economic downturn that are at least partly beyond their control. Research suggests, however, that campaigns and campaign strategies set the stage for or frame the evaluations that individuals undertake in elections.[35] A party's ability to remain in government is not, then, completely outside its control. An opposition party's ability to become the government is similarly dependent on its ability to shape the electoral agenda. The rational model also helps explain the current preoccupation with party image and the attention directed to leaders.

The important part played by **public opinion polling** in modern elections should also not be overlooked.[36] Modern polling techniques allow parties to quickly and accurately gauge public opinion and potential reaction. Such information has implications for the timing of elections, the selection of leaders, and campaign strategies, tactics, and slogans. Published polls can also influence voter behaviour, in deterring them from voting for "lost causes" or in providing them with the information necessary for casting a strategic vote. The importance of polls in elections is underscored by the adoption of restrictions on their publication at certain times during election campaigns. The degree to which such restrictions unnecessarily restrict freedom of expression continues to be debated.

Political Participation

A young mother joins a parent–teacher organization to try to change school policy. A university student jumps on a bus to attend a rally in another city to protest against increasing corporate power. A senior citizen attends a political party's constituency meeting to help select the party's candidate in the next election. Each of these is an example of **political participation**, and each provides a measure of political power to the citizens who employ it. If democracy is supposed to afford political power to the people, one could make the claim that healthy democracies are those with high rates of political participation among their citizens.

The avenues available to citizens in liberal democracies for influencing political decisions are many, ranging from the simple act of voting to more involved acts such as running for political office or organizing a petition-signing campaign. Participation can occur on several different levels: individual (voting or attending a rally), organizational (volunteering time to an interest or community group or donating money to a political candidate's campaign), and professional (working as a paid lobbyist or a political appointee). More often than not, such action is undertaken to bring about some kind of political change (including a return to the status quo), directly by influencing decision-makers, or indirectly by gaining sympathetic media coverage or public support for the cause. Participation can also occur for purely expressive rather than instrumental reasons; that is, one may participate to feel a sense of belonging with the community as much as to influence political decisions.[37]

Most liberal democracies make participation voluntary, except for the few that legally require citizens to vote, such as Australia. Note that while a failure to vote in Australia may be illegal, the penalty is minor: only $20.[38] The objective of such laws is to instil a belief in the importance of political participation, which can result in higher rates of participation than one finds in countries such as Canada and the United States. Some have suggested that a similar law should be adopted in Canada in order to increase the rate of participation in elections—a rate that has been steadily dropping. While the adoption of such a law would no doubt increase the number of Canadians who vote, it would do little to change the underlying causes of low voter turnout.

The vast majority of political acts in liberal democracies are legal, but some actors choose other means to affect political decisions. Civil disobedience—that is, breaking laws in a nonviolent fashion to increase public awareness of their injustice—can often be successful. Recent examples in Canada include blockades of logging roads by environmentalists and of public highways by Native groups. The emphasis on nonviolent protest and on accepting punishment willingly helps to generate support for the cause. **Terrorism**, on the other hand, is a more violent but less effective technique sometimes employed by marginal groups in an effort to dramatically focus attention on their cause. The Front de Libération du Québec (FLQ) kidnapped British trade commissioner James Cross in Montreal in 1970 to pressure the federal government to release 23 members of the group imprisoned for terrorist acts. The group, committed to Quebec independence, resorted to murdering Quebec cabinet minister Pierre Laporte in response to the invoking of the *War Measures Act* by Prime Minister Pierre Trudeau. While dramatic, the events did little to increase public support for the group's cause. The terrorist acts committed on September 11, 2001 in the United States are a vivid reminder that the use of illegal acts for political purposes continues.

Early studies of political participation constructed a hierarchy of political activity in the shape of a triangle, with simple activities such as voting at the base and more demanding activities such as running for office at its peak. The width of the base of the hierarchy meant that a good portion of the population were engaged in the simple activities; the narrowness of the top of the hierarchy meant that relatively few were involved in the more demanding ones. Early researchers also assumed that citizens in democracies naturally progressed from simple activities to more demanding ones—from voting to canvassing for a political party to running for office, for example.[39] Reflecting the traditional domination of male thinking in the study of politics, the most active participants were labelled "gladiators," the less active "spectators," and the uninvolved "apathetics." The general conclusion was that many democracies did not meet the level of participation one would expect.

Early research also suggested that those who could afford to participate and those who had the time to participate made up the largest share of the politically active.[40] This included men and those from historically dominant groups, such as the British and to a lesser extent the French in Canada.[41] More recent studies point to the importance of the definition of politics one employs in determining whether certain groups can be considered to be politically active. Immigrant women, for example, have organized immigrant and ethnocultural associations in response to the lack of attention from the women's movement and minority organizations.[42] Such associations have not traditionally been defined as political, however, and as such, immigrant women's level of political participation has been underestimated. More recent studies have also abandoned the conclusion that citizens progress from simple to more demanding political activities. Data suggests that people's political activity tends to cluster into types, the three most common being voting, campaign activity, and communal activity.[43] People choose political activity partly on the basis of the amount of effort required, the degree of cooperation needed among a number of people, the degree of potential conflict involved, and the nature of the issue addressed.

One of the most striking findings regarding political participation is how few people actually participate in traditional activities. A comparison of average turnout rates between 1961 and 1999 in free elections in 40 democracies suggests that where you live determines in large measure the likelihood that you vote; while only 50 percent of eligible voters cast their ballots in Lithuania, 95 percent do in Australia.[44] The rates of participation are much lower for activities that require greater time commitments and resources. Evidence from Great Britain gives a sense of how dramatically the rates drop as the demands of the activity increase; while voting turnout in the 1990s was 72 percent, only 4 percent of the population belonged to a political party, and only 2 percent had canvassed for a candidate.[45]

The rate of participation in various political activities varies by country depending on whether the culture encourages participation and whether the institutional structure makes it easy. Electoral turnout in the United States is relatively low, partly due to the fact that electoral registration depends on individual effort. Some estimates suggest that the rate could increase by several percentage points if a centralized and less demanding system of registration was adopted.[46]

Participation also varies according to the characteristics of individuals, regardless of geography. If those who participate are not drawn equally from all groups in society, government decision-making may not accurately reflect the desires of the population. If age is an important predictor of political activity (see Box 10.2), so too are gender, class, and attitudes. Women are significantly underrepresented in elite political activity, constituting only 17.4 percent of members of national parliaments around the world.[47] The poor and those of lower social classes are less likely to engage in political activity than those with greater access to resources. Political dissatisfaction, political apathy, and political cynicism are likely to turn people away from the political system.

Another striking finding is the degree of change taking place in the kind of political activity that citizens are willing to engage in. Evidence suggests that there has been a rise in the numbers willing to engage in protest behaviour in democracies, both lawful (signing petitions and joining a boycott)

Why Don't Young Canadians Participate More in Politics? BOX 10.2

How closely do you follow politics? Have you voted every time the opportunity was available to you? You have much in common with your peers if your answers are "not very closely" and "not always." Research tells us that young Canadians are less likely to vote than older Canadians. It also reveals that they are less interested in politics but are also happier with democracy and government (see Table 10.4).

Life cycle explanations for this pattern suggest that young people are not participating at high rates because their interests are such that politics is not a priority. Once they start paying taxes, acquire a mortgage, and think about public school for their children, however, they will naturally become more involved. Evidence from a Canadian poll taken in the spring of 2000 by the Institute for Research on Public Policy suggests that the life cycle explanation can help us understand this pattern in opinion and behaviour. Today's young Canadians will be participating at higher rates in 10 years' time. The study also reveals, however, that if we compare the participation rates of today's young Canadians to those of Canadians of the same group in 1990, youth are now participating at lower levels than they were only 15 years ago. Although they will become more politically active as they age, they are unlikely to catch up to the rates exhibited by the previous generation. Can you think of an explanation for why today's young people are less politically active than in previous generations?

SOURCE: IRPP, *Policy Matters* 2(5) (October 2001). Reprinted by permission of IRPP.

Table 10.4 Generational Patterns in Canadian Political Opinion and Behaviour, 2000

	18–27 (percent)	28–37 (percent)	38–47 (percent)	48–57 (percent)	Over 57 (percent)
Attention to Politics					
Not very closely or not at all	59	41	42	36	32
Voted in the 1997 election	66	69	85	92	91
Very or fairly satisfied with democracy	82	75	74	70	65
Total number of respondents	**271**	**268**	**281**	**224**	**211**

Source: Brenda O'Neill, "Generational Patterns in Political Opinions and Behaviour of Canadians," Policy Matters 2(5) (October 2001), pp. 11–12, 16.

and unlawful (attending unlawful demonstrations and occupying buildings), especially in Canada and among younger citizens.[48] Protest activity can be explained by deprivation—political alienation and frustration with the system can lead individuals to pursue unconventional modes of political activity. Alternatively, the resource model stresses that protest behaviour is merely an alternative mechanism for drawing attention to a cause; those with the political skills and resources are more likely to undertake such activity.

Explanations for the changing nature of political participation in modern democracies point to the changing nature of **civil society** or of overall patterns of social interaction (sometimes called *social capital*) and the increasing dissatisfaction with politics and governments. Robert Putnam suggests that citizens in the United States are less engaged at the civic level than they were previously and that this has important implications for the health of that democracy.[49] Community activities, ranging from bowling leagues to parent–teacher associations, provide opportunities for community members to build the social trust and social capital necessary for democratic government. There is debate, however, over whether social capital has indeed declined, or whether it may simply be manifesting itself in different ways, such as recycling (a community-minded event), and in different forums, such as the Internet (through discussion lists and "zines"—noncommercial publications of small circulation).

Neil Nevitte suggests that participation rates have changed due to increased education, the expansion of mass communications, and the rise of a knowledge-based economy. Today people are smarter and can access information much more easily than previous generations. Combine this with a loss of confidence in traditional political institutions, and the result is a shift from traditional to non-traditional forms of participation, including protest (see Figure 10.2).[50]

Is there such a thing as too much democratic participation?[51] Some argue that effective political decision-making requires that leaders enjoy a degree of freedom from democratic demands. Decision-makers are better informed than ordinary citizens and are more likely to be able to make decisions in the general public interest. Individual citizens are more likely to think about the costs and benefits to their own neighbourhoods and groups, for example, and are less likely to have as much information or expertise as political elites. Besides, the argument goes, people are generally politically apathetic. The participation of apathetic citizens leads to uninformed decision-making. To this way of thinking, too much democracy is definitely a bad thing.

For others, however, full participation by an informed and rational citizenry is a necessary and crucial condition for democracy. Such an argument rests on the assumption that the pursuit of individual truths—a goal of liberalism—can and will lead to conflicting interests. The mechanism for controlling such disputes is to establish laws on the basis of popular consent. Popular consent, the argument continues, can be established only through full political participation, and without it the legitimacy of political authority is in doubt. Participation also helps citizens learn greater tolerance, achieve greater rationality, and develop an appreciation for civic activism.

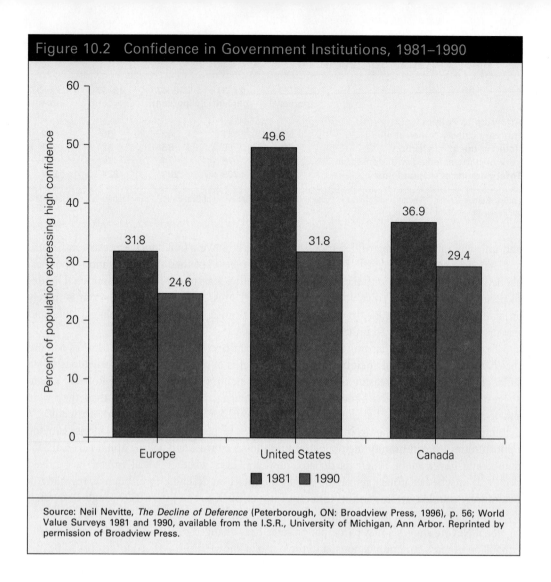

Figure 10.2   Confidence in Government Institutions, 1981–1990

Source: Neil Nevitte, *The Decline of Deference* (Peterborough, ON: Broadview Press, 1996), p. 56; World Value Surveys 1981 and 1990, available from the I.S.R., University of Michigan, Ann Arbor. Reprinted by permission of Broadview Press.

Tools of Direct Democracy

A number of devices have the potential for increasing direct citizen political power in representative democracies. Populist movements and parties in the western United States and Canada have successfully pushed for the adoption of these mechanisms to return a measure of power to citizens to balance that enjoyed by governments. The three most common are the referendum, the initiative, and the recall. Despite their potential, they are not immune from manipulation by governments and powerful groups of citizens alike. The result is that few governments have adopted such mechanisms wholeheartedly; most employ them on occasion, sometimes in an attempt to manipulate the political outcome.

Referendums provide opportunities for citizens to vote directly on pieces of legislation or on constitutional questions. The *binding* referendum requires that the government act on the result of the referendum, and thus provides the greatest potential for citizen power. Such referendums are employed in Australia for constitutional change. *Nonbinding* referendums (sometimes referred to as *plebiscites*) do not tie a government's hands as binding referendums do. In democracies with politically interested, informed, and active populations, however, the reality is that the results of nonbinding referendums would be hard for any government to ignore. In 1992, Canada employed a referendum to determine whether citizens accepted the constitutional changes that the prime minister and premiers had set out in the Charlottetown Accord. The results of that vote were surprising, in that a majority of citizens voted to defeat a constitutional package that had been the result of intense and protracted negotiations between the federal and provincial governments and leaders of Aboriginal communities in Canada. While this was only the third referendum used at the national level, thousands have been used at the municipal level and over 60 at the provincial level, most notably within Quebec regarding secession[52] and in British Columbia, Prince Edward Island, and Ontario on electoral reform.[53] Referendums have both advantages and disadvantages. One advantage is that public decisions are arrived at in a public manner—through free and open public debate.[54] Such debate leads to political education: people are more likely to inform themselves about issues if they have a direct say in the outcome. A second advantage lies in allowing the people to voice their own interests, rather than having those interests filtered through political representatives and political parties. This empowering mechanism provides a potential counter to the increased apathy and growing cynicism occurring in many democratic states; the knowledge that one has an ability to take part in deciding fundamental public questions is likely to increase satisfaction with democracy and the political system. Perhaps most importantly, the use of referendums, especially on divisive issues, can provide a measure of legitimacy to the outcome, since it can be said that "the people have spoken." But such a result is likely only if the public believes that the process was conducted fairly.

The use of referendums can also be problematic. Opponents highlight the fact that referendums can be employed strategically by the political elite for purposes other than to solicit the people's views on the issue. Such concerns were raised in the referendums on sovereignty held in Quebec, for the way the question is phrased can encourage, although rarely guarantee, a particular outcome. Second, referendums do not provide the public with a mechanism for shaping the policy agenda; instead, the people are provided with an opportunity merely to veto a government's proposal.[55] Some observers have also questioned the capacity of the general public to deal with complex issues. Finally, referendums can be highly divisive when the issue is a salient one and if it engenders strong opposing positions in various groups in society.

The **initiative**, on the other hand, is a device that allows registered voters to use petitions to propose the introduction of new laws or change existing ones. Initiatives were meant to complement representative democracy by providing citizens with a populist mechanism for introducing laws the government might be avoiding for whatever reason. One possibility is that a successful petition can force a referendum on the proposed bill, and, if sufficient support is achieved, the bill automatically becomes law. Alternatively, a successful petition can result in the bill being introduced into the legislature, where it follows the normal legislative process.

A successful initiative process should set the requirements fairly high to ensure that minority interests do not hijack the democratic process. In 23 of the 50 U.S. states, on the other hand, initiatives appear on the election ballot if a previously circulated petition receives only a small proportion of the population's signatures; voters then have the opportunity to agree or disagree with the initiative. The process can also be taken over by wealthy interest groups and industries that hire professional signature gatherers to collect the signatures at $1.50 each.[56] Once on the ballot, many of these initiatives pass, even though a majority of the state's population opposes the measure. If only a small proportion of the population actually votes, a minority of dedicated voters can wield tremendous but unrepresentative influence. In some cases, the proposed legislation is even inconsistent with existing laws or constitutional requirements. In others, it dangerously ties the legislature's hands. Proposition 13, for example, which passed in California in 1978, prohibited the state's government from ever increasing property taxes (one imagines it was not too difficult to gather support!). The result, however unintended, is one of the worst public school systems in the nation. Minority interests do not always correspond with those of the greater public good.

The third mechanism of direct democracy employed in representative democracies is the **recall**, which allows registered voters to petition to remove a member of the representative assembly between elections. The mechanism is intended to increase representative accountability by providing a direct means for unhappy electors to "de-elect" their representative without having to wait for the next general election. The same concerns about the initiative exist with the use of the recall. The number of signatures required on the petition to trigger the recall of an elected member should not be so low that the process can be hijacked by a small group of disgruntled voters, for elections are costly affairs in terms of both time and money; but neither should the number be so high as to render the recall process meaningless.

Recall provides an important mechanism for ensuring that representatives keep the interests of their constituents in mind. At the same time, however, the parliamentary system makes it particularly difficult for representatives to always act according to the wishes of constituencies (assuming for the moment that such wishes are easily determined). Party discipline, for instance, requires that the interests of the party determine the actions of each representative, given the constraints of responsible government. In addition, representatives may be provided with information that makes it clear that constituents' interests may be best served in a manner that contradicts their own wishes.

CONCLUSION

Democracy is based on putting a certain measure of political power in the hands of the people. Modern representative democracies provide only a few mechanisms by which citizens are able to influence government policy. Encouraging the use of the referendum, the initiative, and the recall for increasing citizen power rests on the presumption that the citizenry desires to participate more fully in democratic decision-making. Declining voter turnout in Western nations and increased political cynicism suggest that attention should be focused on problems other than simply the lack of opportunity for political participation. Successful democracy requires above all else that citizen participation is effective—citizens must believe that legitimate political action will result in clear and understandable initiatives that respond to that action. The most fundamental of democratic institutions, the election, provides the clearest mechanism for instilling that belief. In too many instances, however, electoral results are ambiguous, do not directly reflect the choices made by the voters, and appear to shut out a number of groups and interests whose chances are directly dependent on achieving electoral success. The democratic ideal will remain an elusive goal until citizens believe they are powerful, regardless of whether they choose to act on that power.

DISCUSSION QUESTIONS

1. What factors do you consciously consider when deciding how to cast a vote in a general election? Can you think of any factors that might affect your decision unconsciously?

2. When should referendums be used? For what issues? Can you think of any occasions or reasons when the use of a referendum might be ill advised?

3. Explain why students' participation in university politics is so low. Does your answer help explain participation in politics more broadly?

4. Should a more proportional electoral system be adopted at the federal and/or provincial level in Canada? Why or why not?

5. What do you consider the greatest challenge facing modern democracies? Why?

KEY TERMS

DIGITAL DEMOCRACY: A broad term meant to encompass the application of technological innovations to politics and political participation; also called *e-democracy* or *e-politics*. (285)

DIRECT DEMOCRACY: A political system in which citizens hold power directly rather than through elected or appointed representatives. (284)

ELECTION: A mechanism by which the expressed preferences of citizens in democratic states are aggregated into a decision regarding who will govern. (287)

FIRST-PAST-THE-POST (FPTP): An electoral system that requires the winning candidate to receive more votes than any other in order to win the seat—that is, to receive a plurality of votes. The majority of first-past-the-post systems employ single-member electoral districts. (297)

FRANCHISE: The right to vote in public elections. (287)

INITIATIVE: A mechanism that allows citizens to petition the government to introduce or adopt specific pieces of legislation or force a referendum on an issue. (307)

LIST SYSTEM: The most commonly adopted form of proportional representation, employing relatively large multimember electoral districts and a ballot that requires voters to choose from among party lists or candidates on party lists. (298)

MAJORITARIAN SYSTEM: An electoral system that requires the winning candidate to receive a majority of votes to win the seat. The majority is normally achieved through a second ballot or by an alternative voting system. (297)

MASS MEDIA: The methods of mass communication, such as television, radio, and newspapers, designed to reach large numbers of people. (292)

POLITICAL PARTICIPATION: Actions taken by individuals and groups in an attempt to influence political decisions and political decision-makers. (302)

PROPORTIONAL REPRESENTATION (PR): An electoral system that attempts to award seats to parties in proportion to the share of votes earned. Such systems must be combined with multimember constituencies. (298)

PUBLIC OPINION POLLING: The use of survey interviews, often conducted over the telephone, with a representative, randomly selected sample of people, providing an accurate description of the attitudes, beliefs, and behaviour of the population from which the sample was drawn. (302)

RATIONAL VOTING: A model that seeks to explain voting decisions by emphasizing the rational evaluation of alternatives (parties and candidates) and the retrospective assessment of the governing party. (301)

RECALL: A mechanism that allows citizens to petition to remove their political representative before the next election period. (308)

REFERENDUM: A mechanism that provides citizens with the ability to vote directly on pieces of legislation or constitutional changes. (306)

REPRESENTATION BY POPULATION: The principle suggesting that the allocation of seats in assemblies should occur in a manner that encourages an equal division of the population across electoral districts, so that each vote is of equal weight. (295)

REPRESENTATIVE DEMOCRACY: A political system in which citizens hold power indirectly by selecting representatives who render public decisions on their behalf in popular assemblies. (285)

SINGLE TRANSFERABLE VOTE (STV): A proportional electoral system that elects candidates in multimember ridings and provides voters with significant freedom by allowing them to rank-order their choices within and across party lists. (299)

WEB LINKS

Elections Canada:
http://www.elections.ca

The U.S. Federal Election Commission:
http://www.fec.gov

Stanford University's Comparative Democratization Project:
http://democracy.stanford.edu

IFES Election Guide:
http://www.electionguide.org

International Institute for Democracy and Electoral Assistance:
http://www.idea.int

Fair Vote Canada:
http://www.fairvotecanada.org

Canadian Election Study:
http://ces-eec.mcgill.ca

FURTHER READING

Butler, David, and Austin Ranney, eds. *Referendums Around the World: The Growing Use of Direct Democracy*. Washington, DC: American Enterprise Institute, 1994.

Courtney, John C. *Elections*. Vancouver: UBC Press, 2004.

Dalton, Russell J. *Citizen Politics: Public Opinion and Political Parties in Advanced Industrial Democracies*. 4th ed. Washington, DC: CQ Press, 2006.

Everitt, Joanna, and Brenda O'Neill, eds. *Citizen Politics: Research and Theory in Canadian Political Behaviour*. Don Mills, ON: Oxford University Press, 2002.

Gidengil, Elisabeth, André Blais, Neil Nevitte, and Richard Nadeau. *Citizens*. Vancouver: UBC Press, 2004.

Harrop, Martin, and William L. Miller. *Elections and Voters: A Comparative Introduction*. Basingstoke, UK: Macmillan, 1987.

LeDuc, Lawrence, Richard G. Niemi, and Pippa Norris, eds. *Comparing Democracies 2: New Challenges in the Study of Elections and Voting*. Thousand Oaks, CA: Sage, 2002.

O'Neill, Brenda. "Indifferent or Just Different? The Political and Civic Engagement of Young People in Canada," prepared for Canadian Policy Research Networks (CPRN) research series *Charting the Course for Youth Democratic and Civic Participation*, September 2007, 48 pp. Available at http://www.cprn.org/doc.cfm?doc=1751&l=en (Document Number 48504); accessed June 13, 2008.

ENDNOTES

1. Darin Barney, *Prometheus Wired: The Hope for Democracy in the Age of Network Technology* (Chicago: University of Chicago Press, 2000), p. 22.

2. This section relies heavily on David Held, *Models of Democracy*, 2nd ed. (Stanford: Stanford University Press, 1996), ch. 1.

3. Joseph Schumpeter, *Capitalism, Socialism and Democracy* (New York: Harper, 1942), p. 265.

4. The percentages vary dramatically around the world, from a high of 70 percent in North America to a low of 4.7 percent in Africa. See Internet World Stats, "Internet Usage Statistics: The Internet Big Picture"; available at http://www.internetworldstats.com/stats.htm; accessed June 13, 2008.

5. See the Ask Bristol website at http://www.viewfinder.public-i.tv/askbristol.php; accessed June 13, 2008.

6. See David Stewart and Keith Archer, *Quasi-Democracy? Parties and Leaders in Alberta* (Vancouver: UBC Press, 2000).

7. Associated Press, "Democratic Presidential Hopefuls Face Off in YouTube Debate," July 24, 2007; available at http://www.foxnews.com/story/0,2933,290514,00.html; accessed June 13, 2008.

8. See Internet World Stats, "Internet Usage Statistics."

9. *Ibid.*

10. For an excellent review of the interplay between democracy and information and communications technology, see Darin Barney, *Communication Technology* (Vancouver: UBC Press, 2005).

11. Held, *Models of Democracy*, p. 317.

12. *Ibid.*, pp. 353–60.

13. See the Elections Canada website at http://www.elections.ca for information on the 2006 and previous general elections.

14. In most parliamentary systems, voters choose the members of the legislature, and the share of seats held by parties within that body determines the government. Hence, voters only indirectly determine which party forms the government.

15. These requirements follow those set out by David Butler, Howard Penniman, and Austin Ranney, eds., *Democracy at the Polls: A Comparative Study of Competitive National Elections* (Washington, DC: American Enterprise Institute, 1981), p. 4.

16. See "The Basic Law for the Federal Republic of Germany," September 23, 1990; available at http://www.psr.keele.ac.uk/docs/german.htm; accessed June 13, 2008.

17. "Halt E-voting Says Election Body," BBC News International online, August 2, 2007; available at http://news.bbc.co.uk/2/hi/uk_news/politics/6926625.stm; accessed June 13, 2008.

18. See Martin Harrop and William L. Miller, *Elections and Voters: A Comparative Introduction* (Basingstoke, UK: Macmillan, 1987), ch. 9.

19. André Blais, Louis Massicotte, and Agnieszka Dobrzynska, "Direct Presidential Elections: A World Summary," *Electoral Studies* 16 (1997): 441–55.

20. See "2000 Presidential Electoral and Popular Vote," U.S. Federal Election Commission; available at http://www.fec.gov/pubrec/fe2000/elecpop.htm; accessed June 13, 2008.

21. Harrop and Miller, *Elections and Voters*, p. 251.

22. Hanna Pitkin, *The Concept of Representation* (Los Angeles: University of California Press, 1967).

23. See, for example, Anne Phillips, "Democracy and Representation: Or, Why Should It Matter Who Our Representatives Are?," in Anne Phillips, ed., *Feminism and Politics* (New York: Oxford, 1998), pp. 161–92.

24. The *2006 Canadian Election Study* is available at http://ces-eec.mcgill.ca/index.html; accessed June 13, 2008. André Blais, Elisabeth Gidengil, Neil Nevitte, Patrick Fournier, and Joanna Everitt were the study's co-investigators. The survey was conducted by the Institute for Social Research at York University and funded by Elections Canada.

25. Peter Dahlgren, "The Transformation of Democracy?," in Barrie Axford and Richard Huggins, eds., *New Media and Politics* (Thousand Oaks, CA: Sage Publications, 2001), pp. 69–70.

26. See Donald Blake, "Electoral Democracy in the Provinces," *Choices: Strengthening Canadian Democracy* 7(2) (2001).

27. James Robertson, "Bill C-24: An Act to Amend the Canada Elections Act and the Income Tax Act," February 5, 2004, Parliamentary Research Branch, Library of Parliament. Available at http://www.parl.gc.ca/37/2/parlbus/chambus/house/bills/summaries/c24-e.pdf; accessed June 13, 2008.

28. See Anthony Sayers and Lisa Young, "Election Campaign and Party Financing in Canada," paper prepared for the Democratic Audit of Australia, September 2004, available at http://www.partyfinance.ca/publications/AustraliaDemAudit.pdf; accessed June 13, 2008.

29. Richard Briffault, "Soft Money, Issue Advocacy and the US Campaign Finance Law," *Electoral Insight* 4(1) (May 2002): 9–14.

30. This section closely follows André Blais and Louis Massicotte, "Electoral Systems," in Lawrence LeDuc, Richard G. Niemi, and Pippa Norris, eds., *Comparing Democracies 2: New Challenges in the Study of Elections and Voting* (Thousand Oaks, CA: Sage, 2002), pp. 40–69.

31. The equivalent distortions in the 2004 election were as follows: Liberal, 1.19; Conservative, 1.08; Bloc Québécois, 1.41; and NDP, 0.39.

32. See http://www.citizensassembly.bc.ca/public, accessed June 13, 2008, for an overview of the mandate of the Assembly, and for its procedures and reports.

33. A number of the arguments for and against the FPTP can be found in Law Commission of Canada, *Voting Counts: Electoral Reform for Canada* (Ottawa: Public Works and Government Services, 2004) and in Louis Massicotte, "Changing the Canadian Electoral System," in Paul Howe, Richard Johnston and André Blais, eds., *Strengthening Canadian Democracy* (Montreal: IRPP, 2005), pp. 65–98.

34. See Mebs Kanji and Keith Archer, "The Theories of Voting and Their Applicability in Canada," in Joanna Everitt and Brenda O'Neill, eds., *Citizen Politics: Research and Theory in Canadian Political Behaviour* (Don Mills, ON: Oxford University Press, 2002), pp. 160–83.

35. Richard Johnston, André Blais, Henry Brady, and Jean Crête, *Letting the People Decide: Dynamics of a Canadian Election* (Montreal and Kingston, ON: McGill-Queen's University Press, 1992).

36. See David Butler, "Polls and Elections," in LeDuc, Niemi, and Norris, *Comparing Democracies 2*, pp. 236–53.

37. Sandra Burt, "The Concept of Political Participation," in Everitt and O'Neill, *Citizen Politics*, pp. 232–46.

38. Australian Electoral Commission; available at http://www.aec.gov.au/Elections/ australian_electoral_system/electoral_procedures/Electoral_Offences.htm; accessed June 13, 2008.

39. Lester Milbraith, *Political Participation: How and Why Do People Get Involved in Politics?* (Chicago: Rand McNally, 1965).

40. Sidney Verba and Norman H. Nie, *Participation in America: Democracy and Social Equality* (New York: Harper & Row, 1972).

41. John Porter, *The Vertical Mosaic: An Analysis of Class and Power in Canada* (Toronto: University of Toronto Press, 1965).

42. Yasmeen Abu-Laban, "Challenging the Gendered Vertical Mosaic: Immigrants, Ethnic Minorities, Gender and Political Participation," in Everitt and O'Neill, *Citizen Politics*, pp. 268–83.

43. Russell J. Dalton, *Citizen Politics: Public Opinion and Political Parties in Advanced Industrial Democracies*, 4th ed. (Washington, DC: CQ Press, 2006), p. 38.

44. Mark Franklin, "Electoral Participation," in LeDuc, Niemi, and Norris, *Comparing Democracies 2*, 148–68.

45. Dalton, *Citizen Politics*, ch. 3.

46. *Ibid.*, p. 41.

47. Inter-Parliamentary Union, "Women in National Parliaments"; available at http://www .ipu.org/wmn-e/world.htm; accessed June 13, 2008.

48. Neil Nevitte, *The Decline of Deference* (Peterborough, ON: Broadview Press, 1996).

49. Robert Putnam, "Bowling Alone: America's Declining Social Capital," *Journal of Democracy* 6 (1995): 65–78.

50. Nevitte, *The Decline of Deference*.

51. See the discussion in William Mishler, *Participation in Canada* (Toronto: Macmillan, 1979).

52. Patrick Boyer, *Direct Democracy in Canada: The History and Future of Referendums* (Toronto: Dundurn Press, 1992).

53. See Elections BC at http://www.elections.bc.ca/elections/ge2005/referendum.htm; accessed June 13, 2008.

54. This section relies heavily on David Butler and Austin Ranney, eds., *Referendums: A Comparative Study of Practice and Theory* (Washington, DC: American Enterprise Institute for Public Policy Research, 1978) and Patrick Boyer, *The People's Mandate: Referendums and a More Democratic Canada* (Toronto: Dundurn Press, 1992).

55. Mendelsohn and Parkin, "Introducing Direct Democracy in Canada," *Choices: Strengthening Canadian Democracy* 7(5) 2001: 7.

56. Doug Sanders, "Practical Pitfalls of the Plebiscite," *The Globe and Mail*, October 24, 2000, p. A3.

Chapter Eleven

POLITICAL PARTIES:
Imperfect but Essential

Heather MacIvor

CHAPTER OBJECTIVES

After you have completed this chapter, you should be able to:

- define the key terms in your own words, providing examples to illustrate your definitions

- name and describe the party types discussed in the chapter

- describe and explain recent trends in party membership numbers and voter turnout

- identify and describe the three major elements within party organizations

- identify the institutional factors that shape party structures, and explain how they operate

- identify the major functions of parties in democratic states

- explain why party systems vary in different countries

Introduction

Do political parties still matter? Early in the 21st century, many citizens of Western democracies would have said no. As evidence, they might have cited the growing influence of nongovernmental organizations (NGOs), the shift of political discussion from party meetings to cable news networks and the Internet, or the widespread and significant declines in party membership and voter turnout. Yet these phenomena, real as they are, do not herald the death or irrelevance of political parties. If we look beyond the established democracies of North America, Western Europe, and Oceania, we find compelling evidence that parties still matter. New and reestablished democracies all over the world display considerable enthusiasm for free electoral competition among a plurality of organized political groups—in a word, for parties.[1] For example, the January 2005 election in Iraq offered voters a choice among 111 individual parties and coalitions of parties.[2] How many of those parties survive the first few years of electoral competition, and the forms that the survivors will take in the future, depend on several factors which we will discuss in this chapter.

This enthusiasm for party competition highlights a fact sometimes forgotten in established democracies: responsive and accountable government cannot exist without political parties. The Institute for Democracy and Electoral Assistance (IDEA), an international organization dedicated to building sustainable democracies around the world, devotes much of its energy to promoting the development of stable party systems in new democracies. It does so because "sustainable democracy is party democracy."[3]

While this chapter accepts IDEA's emphasis on the importance of parties, it argues that parties and party systems are no longer performing their functions as well as they should. In particular, the links between civil society and political parties in Western democracies are weakening. Party organizations are increasingly dominated by their leaders, their elected representatives, and the paid staff at their headquarters, to the detriment of the local volunteers who used to link parties to the wider electorate. Instead of cultivating strong community-based organizations to mobilize party members and voters during and between elections, "electoralist" parties focus almost exclusively on the goal of winning enough seats in the legislature to form governments. In so doing, they are responding to the incentives set by the political institutions within which they operate, particularly the electoral system (see Chapter 10) and the laws that regulate parties and elections.

Established political parties are also adapting to the social and political environments within which they operate. There may be a vicious circle at work: as citizens in Western democracies have turned away from political parties over the past half-century or so, the parties have been forced to adopt new internal structures and methods for communicating with the electorate. Those new structures and methods, in turn, have hampered the parties' ability to mobilize voters and reduced the attractiveness of political engagement through the party system. The result is an ever-widening distance between parties and civil society.

Growing disaffection with political parties is partly attributed to the growing salience of post-materialist values in Western democracies.[4] Post-materialists emphasize direct political action and quality-of-life issues (e.g., the environment and human rights). They reject parties as relics of "old politics," in which voters choose representatives to make decisions for them; the "old" parties' hierarchical, elite-dominated structures compound the alienation.[5] Post-materialism is particularly appealing to young citizens, which helps to explain why voters under the age of 30 are by far the least likely to join parties or to vote in elections. Instead, they participate in public protests (e.g., demonstrations against globalization) and social movements (see Chapter 12).

For much of the 20th century, the major political parties in Western Europe were securely anchored in **subcultures** based on class, religion, and (in a few countries) language. Since the 1970s, these social distinctions have lost much of their power.[6] Labour parties have been diminished by waning working-class consciousness, as the service and public sectors of the economy grew at the expense of manufacturing.[7] Catholic, Protestant, and Christian Democratic parties have suffered from the decline of religious observance in industrial democracies. These social changes have "attenuated the long-term bonds between the public and the parties."[8] As the process of de-alignment accelerated toward the end of the 20th century, parties that were originally created to represent a particular subculture in national politics were forced to adopt new structures and electoral strategies in order to survive. As we will see in Table 11.1, many of these "mass-based" parties have evolved into purely electoral machines.[9]

As long-standing party members died or drifted into other activities, they were not replaced by younger activists. Over time, party memberships in all Western democracies have shrunk significantly. Between 1980 and 2000, parties in Western Europe lost almost half their members.[10] As their volunteer base declined, parties lost much of their capacity to mobilize voters. This labour shortage combined with the social changes discussed earlier to depress voter turnout. A 2002 survey of Canadian non-voters found that people who had been contacted by one or more political parties during an election campaign were significantly more likely to vote than those who had not.[11] Although the growing frequency of non-voting can be attributed to a host of factors,[12] the fact that parties can no longer conduct intensive face-to-face campaigns is clearly significant.

Volunteer labour is not the only party resource threatened by shrinking social bases and weakening public support. Political parties cannot operate without substantial financial resources, especially during election campaigns. Over the past forty years, the cost of mounting a national campaign has grown exponentially. Techniques once reserved for the wealthiest parties, such as daily polling and flashy television advertising, have become standard weapons in the campaign arsenal. To cover the shortfall in their finances caused by their weakening ties to the electorate, and to enable them to take advantage of the new technologies, political parties turned to the public purse. The percentage of party resources derived from state subsidies has grown substantially in recent years, first in Western Europe[13] and more recently in Canada.[14] The growing financial dependence of party organizations on the state may have reduced the incentives for parties to engage directly with groups and individuals in civil society.

As this chapter explains, the weakening ties between parties and electorates are both cause and consequence of recent changes in democratic party systems. Today, most of the major parties in Western states are electoralist in structure and orientation. They continue to perform many of the traditional functions of parties—those directly associated with elections and governing—but they neither mobilize nor represent the electorate as effectively as they once did. Nonetheless, parties are still the only vehicles for which voters can hold their governments accountable, or change the personnel in the legislative and executive branches of government. To that extent, they remain a central focus for students of democratic politics.

This chapter is structured around the four questions: What is a **political party**? How are parties organized? What do parties do? and How do the parties in each country interact with each other? The answers to these questions take up the rest of the chapter.

What Is a Political Party?

A political party is an organization of volunteers and paid professionals who work together to achieve shared political goals, one of which is the election of candidates to public office. The nomination of candidates is the defining characteristic of a political party—as distinct from an interest group. For many parties, the primary goal is to elect enough candidates to the legislature to form a government. Other parties are more concerned with the advocacy of particular ideas or policies.[15] This definition applies to all political parties, regardless of structure, ideology, or social base. To fully understand what parties are and what they do, we must examine the wide variety of party types in new and established democracies. Until recently, most experts categorized parties according to one or two characteristics, such as structure or ideology.[16] These categories were strictly limited by time and space. In other words, they may have been accurate when applied to a handful of countries at a particular moment in history. But they do not provide an accurate picture of the new democracies in Europe, Asia, Latin America, the Middle East, and Africa; nor do they capture the effects of rapid social and political change in established democracies.

Richard Gunther and Larry Diamond have recently proposed a more comprehensive typology of parties.[17] They identify 15 distinct types of party, organized into five broad categories (Table 11.1). Before we turn to the specific types, it is important to understand the broad categories. These are derived from the history and evolution of parties and party systems across a wide spectrum, from the beginnings of democratic politics in 17th-century Britain to the emerging political organizations in 21st-century Asia, Africa, and Latin America.

The first category is the *elite-based party*. These are weakly organized parties "based upon established **elites** and related interpersonal structures within a specific geographic area."[18] They

Table 11.1 Categories and Types of Political Parties

Category	Type	Brief Description	Example(s)
Elite-based	Traditional local notable	Small membership, weak organization; created and dominated by "established elites and related interpersonal networks within a specific geographic area".[19] emerges at an early stage of democratic development, with limited suffrage	British Conservative Party (17th–19th centuries)
	Clientelistic	As above, but with a larger electorate; relationships based less on deference to traditional authority and more on the delivery of tangible rewards to supporters (patronage)	Canadian Liberal and Conservative Parties (1850s–1920s)
Mass-based	Socialist: class-mass	Large membership, tightly organized (often affiliated to outside bodies, e.g., labour unions or social clubs); seeks to redistribute economic power from the upper class to the working class; willing to compete for and exercise power within the existing democratic system; primary goal to win votes and form governments; relies on highly mobilized volunteer membership	British Labour Party (1900–1990s), German Social Democrats (pre-1957)
	Socialist: Leninist	Structure and policy goals similar to the above, but less committed (if at all) to the existing democratic system; smaller membership, more emphasis on ideological indoctrination, less tolerant of competing views	Communist parties in Western Europe (pre-1989)
	Nationalist: pluralist-nationalist	Defined by the shared goal of enhanced territorial autonomy for a particular ethnic or linguistic minority group; seeks to attract as many members and voters as possible from that group; accepts the existing democratic system, although it may seek to create a separate state for its "nation"	Bloc Québécois (Canada); Vlaams Blok (Belgium), Scottish National Party (U.K.)
	Nationalist: ultra-nationalist	Same goal as above, but less committed (if at all) to the existing democratic system; may be willing to achieve its goals through violence; usually dominated by a charismatic leader	National Socialist German Workers' Party (Nazis), 1922–1945; Croatian Democratic Union (1990s)
	Religious: denomi-national	Seeks to represent, and promote the policy preferences of, a particular religious denomination in national politics; accepts the existing democratic system; ideologically moderate; primary goal is to win votes and participate in government	Christian Democratic Party (Germany); Bharatiya Janata Party (India); Justice and Development Party (Turkey)

Continued

Category	Subtype	Description	Examples
	Religious: fundamentalist	Intolerant of competing religious (and nonreligious) viewpoints; creates or reflects a distinct faith-based subculture within the electorate; less committed (if at all) to the existing democratic system	Islamic Salvation Front (Algeria), Welfare Party (Turkey)[20]
Ethnicity-based	Congress	Tries to build coalitions among ethnic subcultures in the wider electorate, both to promote political stability and to ensure that every member group receives its share of state resources	Congress Party (India), 1947–1970s; Barisan Nasional (Malaysia), comprising three ethnic parties (Malay, Chinese, and Indian)
	Ethnic	Tries to secure state benefits for its own ethnic "base" in the electorate; emphasizes the distinctiveness of "its" ethnicity instead of building coalitions with other groups	Inkatha Freedom Party (South Africa), Akali Dal (India)
Electoralist	Catchall	Small membership; weak organization between elections; "superficial and vague ideology and overwhelmingly electoral orientation",[21] appeal to voters based on leader and candidates, not specific policy pledges	Liberal Party of Canada (1920s–present), Progressive Conservative Party of Canada (1920s–2003), Conservative Party of Canada (2003–present), British Labour Party (1990s–present)
	Programmatic	Same structure and electoral orientation as above, but has a more "distinct, consistent and coherent programmatic or ideological agenda"[22]	New Democratic Party of Canada, Reform Party of Canada (1988–2000)
	Personalistic	Founded by a charismatic leader as a vehicle "to win an election and exercise power",[23] commitment to existing democratic system depends on personal ambitions of the founder	Reform Party (United States, 1990s), founded by Ross Perot; Forza Italia (1992–2007), founded by Silvio Berlusconi
Movement/parties	Left-libertarian	Post-materialist in policy (e.g., environmentalist) and political style (often nonhierarchical); usually more concerned with ideas than with power	Green Parties (most Western countries, including Canada)
	Postindustrial extreme right	Small membership, usually dominated by a charismatic leader; hostile to welfare state, immigration, and domestic political/economic elites	Front National (France), Freedom Party (Austria), Swiss Peoples' Party

emerge in the early stages of democratization, when electoral appeals are based on personal contacts and traditional social hierarchies; they generally precede the development of sophisticated electioneering and a national political consciousness. Their tendency to advance the political interests of the wealthy and powerful few has provoked other social groups to establish **mass-based parties**—parties that have deep roots in their respective subcultures, often strengthened by the creation of or affiliation with other organizations, e.g., a specific religious denomination or trade union. The prototypical mass-based parties were established in Western Europe in the 19th and early 20th centuries. They were united by clearly defined ideologies or dogmas; while most sought to attain political power by mobilizing "their" voters, they regarded electoral victory as a means to the end of transforming society to conform to their principles.

In some respects, *ethnicity-based parties* resemble mass-based parties: both types exist to promote the political interests of a specific subculture. The major difference is that mass-based parties promote a vision for society as a whole, whereas ethnic parties are concerned only with their particular segment of that society. Put another way, mass-based parties believe wealth should be generated and distributed in certain ways; ethnic parties just want to get "their" piece of the pie. They are characteristic of new democracies with heterogeneous societies, many of which have been established in the developing world in recent decades.

The fourth type, **electoralist parties**, began to appear in the mid-20th century. Between elections, their memberships are small and inactive; even in the midst of a campaign, the *raison d'être* of an electoralist party, the membership is downplayed in favour of sophisticated media appeals. Electoralist parties emphasize "the personal attractiveness of their candidates,"[24] particularly their leaders, rather than a clear and coherent set of ideological principles—although the programmatic electoralist party is a partial exception, as we will see. Electoralist parties have one overriding goal: to attract as many voters as possible, and thereby to form governments. Exercising power is an end in itself. Most of the major parties in Western democracies belong to this category; they are primarily electoral machines, and only secondarily engaged in linking **civil society** to the state.

The final and most recent category is the *movement party*, which often arises as a reaction against the electoralist domination of politics. The post-materialist parties founded since the 1960s, such as the Green Parties in many Western states, belong to this category. These are weakly organized parties, either because they revolve around a single charismatic leader or because their members reject the very concept of hierarchical structures.

Within these broader categories, Gunther and Diamond devised 15 specific "species" of party. They are differentiated by three characteristics:

1. *Structure.* The size of the membership, the extent and intensity of its organization, and the locus of effective power

2. *Program.* The ideology or subculture that spawned the party, and the emphasis given to the party's stated principles in its electoral appeals

3. *Tolerance.* The strength of the party's attachment to (or rejection of) the existing democratic system, and the level of its tolerance toward other ideologies or subcultures[25]

The examples in Table 11.1, and the discussion of Canada's major parties in Box 11.1, show that parties can morph from one type to another as their social and political environments change over time. Many mass-based parties have also become electoralist in recent years. In the 1990s, Tony Blair "re-branded" Britain's social-democratic Labour Party as the moderate, centrist "New Labour." While the apparent abandonment of the party's long-standing commitment to the working class alienated many members, Blair's "New Labour" won large majorities in three consecutive elections between 1997 and 2005.

At the time of writing, four political parties were represented in the Canadian House of Commons: the Conservatives, the Liberals, the Bloc Québécois (BQ), and the New Democratic Party (NDP). The Conservatives and Liberals were founded in the 19th century as classic elite-based parties. The party in public office (Box 11.3) was completely dominant; there was no central office and little organization on the ground. As the electorate grew and changed, and televised national campaigns replaced local face-to-face exchanges of votes for patronage, the Liberal and Progressive Conservative (PC) parties gradually became electoralist catchall parties. (The establishment of the Conservative Party of Canada is discussed in Box 11.2.)

The NDP is the successor to the Co-operative Commonwealth Federation (CCF), which was founded in 1933 in Regina. The CCF was intended to be a class-mass party representing both urban workers and farmers; its attempts to forge a relationship with organized labour, analogous to those in European Labour and Social Democratic parties, did not succeed. In 1961, following a catastrophic election, the CCF was relaunched as the New Democratic Party. Unlike its predecessor, the NDP was formally allied to the Canadian Labour Congress. However, it has never been a true "class-mass" party; the NDP has never captured even a plurality of votes from organized workers. It is more accurately described as a programmatic party, which seeks to elect as many MPs as possible (although it has yet to account for more than 10 percent of the House of Commons) on the basis of a clearer and more consistent ideology than those advanced by the two catchall parties.

The BQ is the newest of the major parties. It was founded in 1990 by Lucien Bouchard, a former Minister in the PC cabinet of Brian Mulroney. Bouchard was infuriated by the failure of an attempt to renegotiate the Constitution in order to accommodate Quebec's demands. He left the PC caucus to sit as an independent, and announced the creation of the BQ shortly afterward. The new party quickly acquired a ground organization by cooperating with the provincial Parti Québécois. Both are "pluralist-nationalist" parties, whose ultimate goal is the separation of Quebec from Canada. In the 1993 election the BQ won 54 seats and formed the Official Opposition to the Liberals. In subsequent elections, the party placed third; although it only runs candidates in Quebec, the geographic concentration of its support guarantees it considerably more seats in the Commons than its share of the national vote would suggest (see the discussion of electoral system effects, below and in Chapter 10).

In addition to the four parties in the Commons, there are several smaller parties on the register maintained by the Chief Electoral Officer of Canada. The largest of these is the Green Party of Canada, which won almost 5 percent of the national vote in the 2004 and 2006 elections (as against less than 1 percent for the other small parties). Since their foundation in the early 1980s, the Greens had been a typical left-libertarian party. When businessman Jim Harris was elected leader in 2001, he began a concerted effort to transform it into a programmatic party. His professional approach to party structure and campaigning provoked intense internal conflict, which eventually led to his resignation after the 2006 election.[27]

This discussion of party change should not be taken to mean that the adoption of an electoralist model is either inevitable or easy. The extent to which a party can adapt to political and social change is limited by its "genetic code."[28] In other words, the goal for which a party was originally created usually remains intact, and that goal limits its future development. The elite-based parties in North America, Western Europe, Australia, and New Zealand were established with one goal in mind: to form a government by winning a large number of votes. Over time, the means to that end have changed; the structures and activities of those parties adapted to the new incentives set by bigger and more diverse electorates, changing technologies, and institutional change (e.g., the adoption of a new electoral system in New Zealand). But because the goal remained the same, the change from elite-based to electoralist parties was relatively modest and easily accomplished.

Peter MacKay and Stephen Harper create the new Conservative Party of Canada.

CP Photo/Fred Chartrand

In contrast, it is very difficult (and sometimes impossible) for a party to abandon its original goal—for a personalistic party to survive the departure of its leader, or for a mass-based party which wants to destroy the political status quo (e.g., a Leninist party) to embrace democratic pluralism. Even the relatively minor shift from an electoralist-programmatic party to a catchall party can be painful and divisive, especially if it occurs over a short period of time and at the behest of the party leadership (as opposed to being initiated by the "grassroots"). Some party members may welcome a greater emphasis on electoral success, even at the cost of downplaying cherished ideological principles; others, who were attracted to the party by those very principles, feel betrayed by ambitious party elites. A recent example of this phenomenon is the transformation of the Reform Party of Canada—a programmatic party with strong populist and conservative principles—into the Canadian Alliance, and the subsequent merger of the Alliance with the catchall Progressive Conservative Party to create the new Conservative Party of Canada (Box 11.2).

Voters in established democracies can choose among one or more electoralist parties, and a variety of smaller parties representing the various "species." On the surface, this plurality of political options supports the IDEA's assertion that parties are essential to a healthy and stable democracy. But problems lurk beneath the surface. As the IDEA points out, "In all sustainable democracies the party system must be deeply and durably entrenched in specific substructures of the specific society. *Parties link the institutions of government to the elements of civil society.*"[29] In contrast, electoralist parties are almost wholly preoccupied with controlling the institutions of government. Their links with civil society are intermittent at best. Electoralist parties have few members, and even fewer committed activists. They derive their funding from the state, rather than seeking tangible support from individuals and groups. Their leaders pay close attention to the grassroots only at election time, and even then they are likely to communicate with the membership via television (and increasingly through the Internet). The dominance of electoralist parties in established democracies has contributed to a widespread and worrisome loss of **party identification**—especially, but not exclusively, among young voters.[30] As long-standing party loyalties disappear, so does much of the motivation for citizens to become engaged in the political process: to join a party, to volunteer for campaign work, or even to cast a vote.[31] While it is difficult to disentangle cause and effect, it is reasonable to assume that the dominance of electoralist parties has contributed to public disengagement from politics.

The Conservative Party of Canada was founded in late 2003, as the product of a merger between the old Progressive Conservative Party of Canada and the Canadian Alliance. The latter was created in 2000 by Preston Manning, who had founded the programmatic Reform Party of Canada in 1987. Manning believed that Reform could not provide a serious electoral challenge to the governing Liberals, because its genesis as a Western-based populist party limited its appeal in eastern Canada. The solution, as he perceived it, was to unite Reformers and other conservatives in a more broadly based political coalition. Unfortunately for Manning, Progressive Conservative leader Joe Clark refused to consider a merger. So the Alliance was essentially the Reform Party rebranded, albeit with some high-profile new supporters in the provincial PC parties in Alberta and Ontario. It won only two seats in Ontario in the 2000 election. Meanwhile, the PCs were struggling to stay alive; in the same election, they barely won the 12 seats needed for official party status in the House of Commons.

By June 2003, both parties had new leaders. Stephen Harper and Peter MacKay began secret negotiations to merge their organizations as quickly as possible. The major impetus for a merger was their shared fear of Paul Martin, the popular former Finance Minister who was certain to become the next Liberal leader (and Prime Minister) by the end of the year. He had promised to call an election in spring 2004, and the Liberals seemed likely to win a huge majority under his leadership. Harper and MacKay were also motivated by their parties' poor financial situation, which could only be alleviated

by attracting large donations from corporations that had long demanded a single conservative party. New election-finance laws, set to take effect on the first day of 2004, would prohibit businesses from giving money to national parties. The clock was ticking.

In October 2003 the two men announced that their parties would unite into a new Conservative Party of Canada. The announcement was greeted with dismay by many PC members, including former leader Joe Clark. One group even went to court to try (unsuccessfully) to block the merger. Harper won the leadership of the new party in March 2004. Within a few months, the Conservatives had to put their fragile unity to the test in a general election. The newly combined constituency associations managed to nominate a full slate of 308 candidates, and the party mounted a surprisingly smooth campaign—at least for the first few weeks. In the end, however, lingering doubts about the new party seem to have hurt its electoral chances. The Conservatives won 99 seats, 21 more than the two parties had won separately in 2000. But their combined percentage of the national vote dropped by almost eight points, and their hopes of winning enough seats to form a government evaporated in the late stages of the campaign.

One reason for the disappointing election result was public uncertainty about the goals and principles of the new party. Was it a catchall party, with a centrist and flexible ideology, or a programmatic party committed to social conservative principles? The Conservatives answered that question in March 2005, when the party's first national convention endorsed moderate policies.[32] Harper and his team learned additional lessons from the 2004 campaign. His efforts to present the party as a safe alternative to the governing Liberals had been thwarted by a handful of MPs from the Alliance wing of the party, who "freelanced" on touchy issues like abortion, same-sex marriage, the *Charter of Rights*, and official bilingualism. Ontario voters who might have voted for a conservative "catchall" party appear to have changed their minds when confronted by the more programmatic rhetoric from some candidates. The 2006 campaign was very different: Harper imposed strict "message discipline" on his MPs and candidates. Together with a savvy media strategy and a clear, focused platform, this discipline helped to secure an election victory. The Conservative Party of Canada formed a minority government a little more than three years after its creation.

How Are Political Parties Organized?

At its founding, a political party may consist of a self-appointed leader and a handful of committed members. If it is an elite-based or personalistic party, it may persist in that form for a while. But if it is to survive for more than a few years, especially in a competitive electoral environment, the party must establish some kind of stable organizational structure. The specific form that a party takes will depend, in large measure, on the political system in which it operates (as we will see shortly). However, certain structural features are common to all political parties—or at least those parties that have succeeded in electing a few candidates to public office, and have existed long enough to establish a formal division of responsibilities.

The weak links between electoralist parties and civil society can be explained, in part, by the current relationship among these three elements. In parties which are oriented toward winning votes, the party in public office (and, in many cases, the party in central office) dominates the organization. There is little effort to build, maintain, and mobilize the party on the ground.[33] Unlike mass-based parties, electoralist parties neglect their members—the people who can get their friends and neighbours directly involved in the democratic process—relying instead on

| The Three Elements of Party Organization | BOX 11.3 |

Every established political party contains three distinct structural elements: the party in public office, the party in central office, and the party on the ground.[34]

- The party in public office comprises the leader, his or her entourage, and the elected officials who represent the party in the legislature (and, for parties in power, in the executive branch of government). The **parliamentary wing** of the party is often called the *caucus*.

- The term party in central office refers to the paid permanent staff at the party's headquarters, the professional consultants and temporary employees who are hired before and during campaigns, and caucus employees.

- Finally, the party on the ground includes the volunteer members.

paid professionals and technology-intensive methods of campaigning. (However, there seems to be modest revival of local face-to-face campaigning, as we will see later.) When their funding comes from the state, and most of their communication with the voters is mediated by television and the Internet, parties seem distant and perhaps irrelevant to many voters.

The growing dominance of the party in public and central office appears to be widespread, if not universal, regardless of party type.[35] Looked at in another way, it seems that parties are forced to become electoralist if they wish to compete for power. Despite this reality, the official description of a party organization—its written constitution—usually identifies the party on the ground as the real locus of power. While this is rarely if ever true, it is particularly inaccurate when the party is in government. The party in public office is even more dominant, because its leader is the prime minister (or a senior cabinet minister, in the case of a junior coalition partner) and other MPs are members of the political executive.

The presence of these three elements does not imply that all party organizations are identical. Even among parties of the same type, there are striking variations arising from the unique political institutions that operate in each democratic state. The institutional factors that most directly affect party structures are the electoral system, the relationship between the legislative and executive branches of government (Chapter 7), federalism (Chapter 6), and the laws which regulate party competition.

Electoral Systems and Party Structures

The method used to elect members of the national legislature has a direct impact on the parties which compete in those elections. (Table 10.2 summarizes the major types of electoral system.) The **first-past-the-post system** used in Canada, the United Kingdom, and the United States divides the country into districts, each of which elects one member of the legislature.

Within a district, the members of each party—or, in some American states, the voters at large—nominate a single candidate. Consequently, a national party must establish and maintain a local association in every district. The party on the ground is divided into hundreds of separate clubs. In contrast, the Netherlands uses a list-proportional representation system; the entire country is one huge district. The parties are not required to divide their ground organization into separate clubs. Unlike most electoral systems, the single transferable vote (STV) pits candidates from the same party against each other; every party nominates as many candidates as there are seats in the district, and those candidates must compete among themselves and against their rivals from different parties. This feature of STV can divide local party organizations.[36] (We will discuss the procedures for nominating candidates later in this chapter.)

The Relationship Between the Legislative and Executive Branches of Government

Political systems in which the legislative and executive branches are fused, as they are in most parliamentary democracies, tend to reinforce the dominance of the party in public office over the party on the ground. Responsible Cabinet government requires a disciplined majority in Parliament, which in turn requires the party in public office to speak with a single voice, not to reflect the diversity of the party on the ground. On the other hand, the separation of legislative and executive powers (as in the presidential–congressional systems of the United States and Mexico) permits a looser, less coherent party organization; individual legislators enjoy somewhat more autonomy from the caucus leadership.

In the United States, for example, the President is elected by the voters.[37] He (or she?) serves a four-year term in office, whether or not his party controls a majority of the seats in the

House of Representatives and the Senate. Partly for this reason, American parties are highly decentralized.[38] Each candidate campaigns independently of the others. Nor are American candidates dependent on local party associations for their nominations; as we have seen, candidates for Congress (and for executive offices including governorships and the presidency) are nominated by the voters in primary elections (as opposed to local party members in nominating conventions). The cumulative result is that American parties are less cohesive organizations than those in parliamentary systems such as Canada or Australia. The party in public office is divided between the executive branch (the White House) and the legislative branch (Congress). This division is reflected in the party in central office and the party on the ground.

Where the authority of the executive branch depends on the cohesion of the legislative wing(s) of the party or parties in the cabinet, as it does in parliamentary systems, party discipline within the caucus is considerably stronger. The leader of the (senior) governing party is simultaneously the head of the political executive (the cabinet) and the dominant figure in the legislature. Because the effectiveness of the government depends, in part, on the qualities of the men and women in public office, the leader has good reason to encourage the nomination of capable candidates. The caucus is united behind a single leader, as is the party in central office. The party on the ground can focus its efforts on one goal—the election of as many MPs as possible, ideally a majority or plurality of the legislature—instead of dividing its scarce resources between separate presidential and congressional campaigns.

Federal Versus Unitary States

In many constitutional democracies, powers are divided between as well as within governments. (See the discussion of federalism in Chapter 6.) It is easy to see how **federalism** shapes party structures. The presence of separate state or provincial governments requires political parties to establish distinct national and subnational organizations to contest for power at both levels. In the United States, for example, the Democratic and Republican parties monopolize the executive branches (and, for the most part, the legislative branches) in Washington and in the 50 state capitals. This does not mean, however, that all federal parties have the same structure. We can distinguish among three models of party organization in federations:[39]

- *Integrated* parties are electorally competitive at both levels of government, and "the relations between the two levels are generally close."
- *Confederal* parties are present at both levels of government, but the links between the national party and one or more of its subnational organizations are strained (and sometimes openly hostile).
- *Truncated* parties operate only at one level of government, in whole or in part (e.g., the Conservative Party, which has no provincial organization in British Columbia, Saskatchewan, or Quebec, or the Bloc Québécois, which only exists inside Quebec).

The degree to which a particular party resembles one or another of these three models depends on at least three factors: the nature of the party itself; the degree of centralization in federal institutions, and the intensity of conflict among the component parts of the federation. A programmatic party usually tries to maintain a unified organization across the two levels of government. Its national and subnational organizations are tightly integrated, and its ideology may provide the glue which holds the various local associations together. A catchall party is more likely to be confederal or truncated. Its fuzzy ideology is rarely a sufficient unifying force to hold the party together. Each separate wing of the party is dominated by its leader. Personal or political clashes between national and subnational leaders may provoke splits between the two levels of party organization, as the members on the ground choose sides in the dispute. A prolonged failure to win power at one level of government may induce party officials and members to concentrate on the other, more promising level. In regions where it cannot compete effectively, a party's provincial wing may fade away altogether—hence the truncated structure of Canada's Conservative Party.

The impact of different federal systems on party structures is illustrated by comparing Canada and Germany. Canada has a highly decentralized federal system, in which the two levels of government pursue distinct (though often coordinated) policy agendas. Most aspiring politicians devote their efforts to either federal or provincial politics.[40] It is relatively rare for Canadian legislators to serve at both levels of government, although there are important exceptions. Former federal cabinet minister Sheila Copps was a member of the Ontario Legislature before her election to Parliament in 1984; Conservative cabinet minister (and former Canadian Alliance leader) Stockwell Day was Treasurer of Alberta before he entered federal politics in 2000. Nonetheless, the fact that most politicians lack experience at both levels of government may exacerbate the political divisions within the federation. The German federal system is considerably more centralized, and the two levels of government—the national government, or *Bund*, and the states, or *Länder*—are tightly integrated. The upper house of the national parliament is the *Bundesrat*, which is composed of delegations from the *Land* governments. All national legislation which directly affects the *Länder* must be passed by a majority of the state delegations in the *Bundesrat*. The state governments are responsible for implementing much of the legislation passed by the national parliament, in addition to executing their own local laws. The design of Germany's federal institutions creates strong incentives for the national and *Land* party organizations to work closely together, and for individual politicians to move back and forth between the two levels of government. Hence, "In sharp contrast to Canada or the United States, [Germany] can be said to have nationally integrated party organizations."[41]

Intense or prolonged conflict within the federation can turn an integrated party into a confederal party, or even a truncated party. When the national government enacts policies which arouse anger and hostility in a particular region, its party organization in that region suffers the political consequences. For example, the Liberal governments of Lester Pearson (1963–68) and Pierre Trudeau (1968–1984) pursued a centralizing agenda which alienated the party's Alberta and Quebec wings.[42] Those provincial Liberal organizations are formally separate from the national party, with distinct personnel, central offices, and memberships. The alienation of a particular region from a national party is intensified by Canada's electoral system, which distorts the translation of each party's vote share into its proportion of seats in the House of Commons. The Liberals elected only a handful of MPs from the four western provinces between 1972 and 1993, despite winning respectable shares of the regional vote in most elections; consequently, their policies have not always been sensitive to western concerns, which further alienated voters in that region.

In like manner, the patriation of the Constitution in 1982 over the objections of the Quebec government produced a widespread dealignment of voters in that province. In 1984, nationalist Québécois turned to the Progressive Conservatives; after two attempts to meet Quebec's constitutional demands failed (in 1990 and 1992), they shifted en masse to the Bloc Québécois. The BQ has profited from the electoral system, because its vote is concentrated in a limited number of constituencies.

Our electoral system also encourages each party to focus its campaign in geographic regions where it expects to do well,[43] which exacerbates feelings of resentment in the "neglected" provinces. Over time, provincial wings that cannot rely on organizational support from the federal party either disappear or separate themselves from a national organization that has become a political liability.

Election Laws and Party Structures

Finally, the legal regime that regulates party activities shapes their internal structures. A minority of states have adopted party laws, which explicitly define the role and functions of political parties.[44] Several of these statutes permit the state to outlaw particular parties (those whose goals or activities are considered threatening to the constitution), or to prohibit the formation of certain types of party (e.g., ethnic or ultranationalist). Some party laws also prescribe requirements for the organization of parties: restricting membership to citizens of that country, prohibiting active soldiers from joining parties, or requiring that internal party officials be elected by a secret ballot of the membership. Explicit party laws are more common in new and emerging democracies than in established democracies, although two countries in the latter category, Canada and the United Kingdom, have recently adopted similar provisions.[45]

A second type of statute, which exists in a majority of democratic states, regulates the financing of parties and their electoral campaigns.[46] Such laws are often accompanied by public subsidies to party organizations, which take a variety of forms in different countries.

- Direct subsidies include annual funding of parties between elections; reimbursement of campaign expenses incurred by parties and/or candidates; and the provision of research and staff budgets to the party in public office.
- Indirect subsidies include the creation and maintenance of voters' lists; the provision of free and/or cut-rate broadcast time on publicly regulated television and radio networks; and the issuing of tax credits for political donations.[47]

Some of these benefits are available to all of the recognized parties in the specific country; others are restricted to the parties with the largest vote shares or those represented in the legislature. Parties that qualify for public subsidies have become increasingly dependent on them in recent decades, as their social bases have dwindled and the costs of campaigning have escalated.[48]

Most of these subsidies are provided to (and used by) the party in central office or the party in public office. Consequently, they enhance the power of the party leader and headquarters relative to the volunteers on the ground.[49] The major exception, in Canada, is the provision of partial reimbursements to candidates who won at least 10 percent of the votes in their respective constituencies. Because surplus funds remaining in the candidate's campaign account after all the bills have been paid must be turned over to the party's constituency association, the candidate reimbursement often benefits the local party organization.[50] Canadian parties, which began as private "clubs" of local notables, have now become "public utilities"—state-funded and regulated bodies that perform a useful public service, like their counterparts in Western Europe.[51]

To summarize the discussion to this point: While political parties in Western democracies are organized along broadly similar lines—especially those which we have characterized as "electoralist"—there are important structural differences among them. Those variations are imposed by the varying political institutions and laws in each country, and by the relative positions of each party within parliament. In other words, while the party in public office and the party in central office dominate the party on the ground in all cases, the degree of that dominance in any given party varies with external factors.

What Do Political Parties Do?

As we have seen, the IDEA argues that newly democratizing states need to establish strong political parties if they are to remain free and stable over the long term. The primary reason is that parties "are the only institutions that carry out *all* [the] functions which are necessary for the democratic process."[52] These functions include

Sen. Barack Obama secured the U.S. Democratic Presidential Nomination after a long primary battle with Sen. Hillary Clinton.

REUTERS/Allen Fredrickson/Landov

- "[mediating] between a pluralistic society and its political institutions of government"
- "recruit[ing] political personnel by selecting and nominating candidates who stand for public office in an election"
- "organiz[ing] political campaigns in order to mobilize voters to participate in an election"
- organizing the government and the legislature
- making public policy[53]

As we suggested at the beginning of this chapter, parties in Western democracies are no longer as successful in mobilizing voters as they once were. Their role as mediators between the state and society, and their capacity to make policy, is diminished by their eroding bases in the electorate. On the other hand, parties still organize the government and the legislative branch, and they monopolize the recruitment of political leaders. (The United States is a partial exception; most of its party candidates are nominated in primaries regulated by state laws, some of which allow non–party members to vote.) The recruitment function can be divided into two separate tasks: leadership selection and candidate nomination. Parties are also primarily responsible for election campaigning, which we will also discuss in this section.[54]

Selecting Leaders

The choice of a new leader is a crucial decision for a party, for at least four reasons.

First, the leader is the public face of the party. He or she features prominently in media coverage of the party's activities, both inside and outside the legislature. Increasingly, he or she is also the primary visual focus of the party website.[55] Therefore, he or she must be an effective communicator in person and through the news media.

Second, the leader has the last word, and sometimes the only word, on party policy. He or she decides the party's position on the issues of the day, usually in consultation with fellow caucus members and policy experts inside and outside the party. The leaders of catchall and personalistic parties have the most flexibility in this regard; those who lead programmatic, mass-based, ethnic, and movement parties are more constrained by preexisting principles.

Third, the leader of a parliamentary party is the general in the daily legislative battle. He or she must be able to rally the troops in caucus, keep their fighting spirit up, and unite them against the slings and arrows of the competing parties. In a single-party government, the leader is the prime minister. In a coalition cabinet made up of two or more parties, the prime minister is the leader of the largest party, and the leader of the junior party is normally a senior minister.[56] On the opposition side, the leader of the largest party is designated leader of the official opposition (at least in British-style parliamentary systems). He or she leads the verbal assault on the government, while trying to act like a potential prime minister. The leaders of the smaller opposition parties have more freedom to attack the government aggressively, without worrying about portraying themselves to the public as alternative governments. The ability to keep a caucus united under intense political pressure is one of the most important skills a party leader can demonstrate. It requires an intimate knowledge of parliamentary procedure and the ability to build and maintain strong personal relationships with fellow legislators. The task of a party leader in a congressional system, such as that of the United States, is somewhat different. The majority leader has the votes to ensure that his party's proposed legislation passes, but the norm of party discipline is weaker; therefore, the leader and his staff may have to compromise on the details of legislation, both within the majority party and with the minority party across the aisle. The minority leader in the U.S. House of Representatives or the Senate cannot hold the executive branch (the president and cabinet) directly accountable on the floor of the legislature, because of the separation of powers in the American constitution. This is a significant difference from the role of the leader of the official opposition in a Westminster-style parliamentary system.

Fourth and finally, the leader is ultimately responsible for keeping the party organization in a state of election-readiness. He or she chooses the professional consultants whom the party employs before and during election campaigns. The leader must inspire the volunteers in the local party organizations, motivating them to devote their time and energy to party tasks. Where political parties are funded by individual and corporate donors, the leader must also be an effective fundraiser; this task is less important in states where parties are heavily subsidized by public money. In some cases, the leader is also the chief inducement for prospective candidates: if he or she can persuade prominent local or national figures to run for office under the party banner, the party's prospects in the next election may be enhanced.

To summarize: The party leader must be an excellent communicator. He or she must be well versed in the policy issues of the day, and in the imperatives of party organization. And the leader must project an aura of competence and optimism at all times; a consistent failure to do so alienates voters, party workers, and potential donors.

A party leader must be selected according to a clear and consistent set of rules, to avoid divisive conflicts over the fairness of the process. In rough terms, we can say that the methods for selecting leaders vary according to party type. (Leadership succession is rarely an issue for personalistic parties, which usually fade away when the charismatic founder leaves.) Elite-based parties leave the choice of leader to the parliamentary wing, which generally selects one of its own members. There are at least two advantages to this "caucus selection" system. First, the men and women who work closely with the leader every day possess the necessary knowledge—both of the political system and of the various contenders—to choose wisely. Second, a candidate with extensive parliamentary experience is better qualified for the job than one who has never held public office, particularly when the party is in government.

The logic of the elite-based party legitimates a relatively closed selection process. In contrast, mass-based parties, whose members are central to the party's activities, usually hold conventions to select their leaders. Delegates elected (or appointed) to represent various elements in the party organization gather to choose among the various candidates by voting on successive ballots. Delegated conventions allow the party to control the number of votes from each group within the party—the constituency activists, the affiliated organizations (e.g., labour unions), women and youth wings, and so forth.

In general, electoralist parties, including those which began as elite-based or mass-based parties, choose their leaders via some sort of **one-member-one-vote system (OMOV)**.[57] Although the widespread use of OMOV appears to contradict earlier claims about the shift of power from the party on the ground to the caucus, it is consistent with the logic of electoralist parties. First, the transformation from elite-based into electoralist parties diminishes the value of an extended parliamentary apprenticeship, and encourages the party to seek the most appealing leader—which the party in public office may not be able to supply. Second, the growing public demand for "democratic" methods of decision-making puts pressure on parties to bring their internal procedures up to date—including pressure from their own members.[58] This is consistent with the determination of electoralist parties to appeal to as many voters as possible.[59] Third, Katz and Mair argue that the switch to OMOV only *appears* to empower the party membership. In reality, replacing delegated conventions with OMOV diminishes "the position of the party activists and the organized party on the ground."

The Liberal Party of Canada selects Stéphane Dion as leader.

CP Photo/Tom Hanson

Almost by definition, the often disorganized and atomized mass membership of the party . . . is likely to prove more deferential to the party leadership, and more willing to endorse its proposals. It is in this sense that the empowerment of the party on the ground remains compatible with, and may actually serve as a strategy for, the privileging of the party in public office.[60]

Additionally, OMOV can "open the door to groups or individuals from outside the party entirely, who may wish to use these institutions as an arena in which to promote a particular issue, candidate or cause."[61] Such incursions can alienate the party on the ground, driving out long-time members in favour of "instant" members whose attachment to the party may be short-lived. This is a further example of the tension between the logic of electoralist parties and the maintenance of loyal, motivated local volunteers.

Candidate Nomination

As previously described, the type of electoral system used in a particular country affects the organization of its parties. It also helps to determine the procedure for nominating candidates. In all PR-list systems, the parties nominate slates of candidates in large multimember districts.

Some parties leave the task of compiling and ranking the lists to the central office, depriving the party on the ground of a meaningful role in choosing candidates. Others permit the party members in each district to vote for their preferred nominees—although the leader usually retains the final say over choice and the ranking of party candidates.[62] Traditionally, a first-past-the-post system gave the local party members complete autonomy over candidate nomination.

Today, the party in central office plays a bigger role regardless of the type of electoral system used to determine which of the candidates will be elected to the legislature. For example, British parties nominally leave the choice of candidate to the members of the local associations; but in practice, the party in central office screens the aspirants and can veto a particular nomination.[63] In Canada, where the constituency associations traditionally enjoyed complete autonomy over candidate nomination, the party in central office has recently acquired similar screening powers. The erosion of local control began in 1970, when the *Canada Elections Act* was amended to provide for the registration of political parties and the identification of party candidates on the ballot. To verify a candidate's claim to be the party's standard-bearer in the riding, the party leader must endorse his or her nomination papers. In the past, a few controversial or discredited candidates have been disallowed, but more recently, Canadian party leaders have used their veto power to impose central authority over the nomination process.[64] In advance of the 2006 general election, for example, aspiring Conservative candidates had to fill in detailed questionnaires about their professional and personal activities; their answers were reviewed by a central committee, which turned down some applicants (a few of whom sued the party in response). Similar practices have recently been adopted by Canada's other major parties.[65]

This determination to ensure quality control illustrates the importance of candidate nomination in an electoralist party. When ideology is downplayed in favour of broad appeal, and content-free campaigns are built around the leader and a few "star" candidates, much depends upon the selection of party standard-bearers. Even in non-electoralist parties, the intense media coverage of election campaigns raises the stakes and makes it more tempting for the party in public and central office to seize or retain the power to choose.

In general, parties look for strong candidates: men and (increasingly) women with professional qualifications, high public profiles, good communication skills, and clean personal reputations. Historically, the party in public office reproduced itself, which produced a preponderance of white male candidates; but as electorates have become more diverse in most Western democracies, electoralist parties have tried to recruit candidates who fulfill particular representational criteria, such as ethnicity, gender, or language.[66] Parties that are expected to do well in the next election usually find it easier to recruit strong candidates than those that are likely to win few legislative seats.[67]

Election Campaigns

The nature of party campaigns has changed dramatically in the past half-century, largely because of the growing importance of television in national politics. In the first half of the 20th century, election campaigns were heavily labour-intensive: volunteers went door to door, speaking directly to the voters on behalf of their parties and candidates. Since the 1960s, campaigns have become increasingly capital-intensive: parties hire experts to craft sophisticated advertising campaigns, relying on analyses of opinion data gathered by pollsters and interpreted by political strategists.[68] Party members still go door to door—although today, they are more likely to contact voters by telephone and computer—but the emphasis has shifted from local mobilization to national persuasion. This shift is both cause and consequence of shrinking party memberships and the growing dependence of parties on public resources. It also reflects the growing power of the party in central office, where the professionals work, relative to the party on the ground.

In principle, party campaigns provide important cues to voters. Party leaders try to win over the public, selling their platforms on the nightly news and through paid advertising. Strategists identify voters who might be predisposed to support their party, working to solidify that support by crafting narrowly targeted appeals. For example, Labour and Social Democratic parties often use the rhetoric and symbols of class struggle to mobilize their target audience: they speak of "working people" and "average citizens," implicitly contrasting "their" voters to the "elites" or the "fat cats" who support the more conservative parties. The U.S. Democratic Party strives to maximize its support base among African-Americans by encouraging them to register to vote, and by highlighting prominent figures (e.g., Illinois Senator Barack Obama) at their presidential nominating conventions.

In practice, as noted earlier, parties appear to be losing their capacity to mobilize voters. Turnout levels in Western democracies have fallen sharply in recent elections, although voters in new democracies usually embrace the franchise with enthusiasm. The decline in electoral participation is particularly marked in countries where weakly organized parties have lost their connections with the electorate—in short, countries with dominant electoralist parties.[69] Today some parties are rediscovering the value of the old-fashioned labour-intensive campaign, although they have fewer resources now to put it into practice. Recent research has demonstrated that vigorous local campaigns can make a significant difference to the outcome of an election, especially in tight races between two or three parties.[70] The recognition that local campaigns still matter has prompted electoralist parties to revive some of their old practices. Norris distinguishes between three phases of campaigning: "pre-modern," in which local activists mounted labour-intensive campaigns of personal contact and persuasion; "modern," characterized by capital-intensive

Hillary Clinton rides the fence.

Ed Hall/Artisans

campaigns run out of party headquarters; and "post-modern," which combines targeted media appeals with local personalized contacts.[71] An Australian scholar reports "evidence of just such a rediscovery of the importance of local-level campaigning, albeit a grass roots electioneering tightly controlled by the central party and confined to certain key seats."[72] Despite this trend, party mobilization of voters has a long way to go. The continuing decline in voter turnout suggests that Canadian parties, like electoralist parties elsewhere, are neglecting their local organizations and, by extension, the vital democratic functions extolled by the IDEA.

Parties in Government

Despite the erosion of parties on the ground, government in every democratic country is party government. In the legislature, the division between the government and the opposition is along party lines. In Canada and Britain, whose FPTP electoral systems usually produce single-party governments (majority or minority), the largest party forms the government; the smaller parties are relegated to the opposite side of the House of Commons. Most democracies use proportional electoral systems; it is rare for one party to win enough seats to form a government on its own. Under those circumstances, a stable political executive requires the creation of a parliamentary majority by combining two or more parties in government. The leaders of those parties are included in a coalition cabinet, whose legislative program is constructed through negotiations among the various party leaders.

Most coalitions are dominated by a single party, which holds a majority of the cabinet posts, with the remaining ministries assigned to the "junior partner(s)." Examples include the pre-1994 Italian coalitions, which were anchored by the Christian Democratic Party, and the Christian Democrat–Free Democrat coalition that governed Germany from 1949 until 1969. In a single-member electoral system, which tends to give the largest party a majority of the seats in parliament (usually with less than half the vote), coalitions are rarely required. Even when the largest party fails to win a majority, it usually governs alone as a minority government with informal support from one or more opposition parties (e.g., the Conservative minority government in Ottawa, elected in January 2006).

Parties and Public Policy

It is often assumed that parties create **public policy**. Party leaders claim that their election *platforms*—the collection of specific promises which they issue during campaigns, also called "manifestoes"—are based on resolutions passed by their members. The truth is often rather different. We have already seen that party leaders enjoy considerable influence over policy and principle, and that election campaigns are crafted by the permanent staff and contract consultants who work in central office. More often than not, parties rely for policy innovation on interest groups, think tanks, public servants, and other external sources. In other words, the policies of governing parties do not necessarily reflect the priorities of their members. Even if the membership of an electoralist party wanted its caucus to pursue a particular policy objective, it has few if any means of controlling the party in public office.[73] In theory, the members of mass-based parties set the policy agenda according to the party's stated principles; in practice, the imperatives of governing increasingly diverse societies enhance the autonomy of the party leadership from the grassroots.

Party Systems

In democratic states, a political party does not operate in a political vacuum; it belongs to a **party system**. A party system can be defined as "the system of interactions resulting from inter-party competition."[74] It consists of the parties within a particular jurisdiction that compete with each other for scarce resources, particularly money and votes.

Comparative studies often focus on the number of parties in each system, although this tells us little about the politics of a particular country. For example, both Country A and Country B have two large parties which compete for power at each national election. This might lead us to conclude that the two countries are quite similar in some way. In reality, A has a diverse electorate but its electoral system makes it very difficult for smaller parties to win legislative seats, while B has a proportional system and an electorate divided by a single cleavage. So a simple count of the parties represented in the legislature yields relatively little useful information.

To fully understand the differences among party systems, we must examine three sets of factors:[75]

- *Sociological:* The voting pattern in the national electorate (politically salient cleavages and subcultures)
- *Institutional:* The type of electoral system, the relationship of the legislative and executive branches of government
- *Competitive:* The degree of ideological polarization in the party system; the presence or absence of political entrepreneurs—politicians willing to create new parties to fill an unmet need in the electorate, or to modify an existing party for political advantage

The sociological and institutional approaches treat individual parties and party systems as dependent variables. Put differently, they attribute the number and size of the parties in a given country to factors beyond the control of any one party or politician (despite the fact that some institutions, notably electoral systems, can be chosen and manipulated by the party in power at a given time). On the other hand, the competitive approach recognizes that the creation or adaptation of a political party is at least partly a matter of choice, and acknowledges the power of parties to shape their own environments. All three approaches contribute to our understanding of party politics in democratic states.

The Sociological Approach

The number and relative size of the parties in a given jurisdiction are determined, to a greater or lesser degree, depending on the institutional factors discussed below, by the demographic and ideological composition of the electorate. In some countries, the population is divided by a single **cleavage** into two subcultures; other electorates are divided by multiple cleavages into a range of subcultures.

The number and the political salience of subcultures associated with a particular cleavage pattern depend on whether the cleavages cut across or reinforce each other. Simply put, two overlapping cleavages—say, language and religion—may produce only two subcultures, but the members of each group are more likely to vote for a party which reflects both their linguistic and their religious identities. On the other hand, two cross-cutting cleavages (e.g., class and religion) may produce a large number of subcultures, but the impact of each on voting behaviour may be weakened. If working-class Catholics have a choice between voting Labour and voting Christian Democrat, and the middle-class members of their congregations can choose between a secular Conservative Party and the Christian Democrats, none of these parties can take the support of its particular electoral base for granted.

It is generally accepted that sociological factors no longer influence voting patterns, and consequently party systems, as strongly as they once did.[76] As we have seen previously in this chapter, class-mass parties in Western Europe watched the erosion of their working-class bases in the second half of the 20th century; the more extreme left-wing parties have largely disappeared, while the moderate social democratic parties were forced to adopt electoralist structures and appeals in order to survive. Similarly, Christian Democratic parties have lost much of their Catholic base over the years; they became catchall parties, downplaying the explicitly religious character of their policies and rhetoric.

However, this should not be taken to mean that demographic differences among voters are now irrelevant. Even in Canada, which has long been regarded as an exception to the sociological model, voters in different demographic categories tend to cast their ballots for different parties. Other things being equal, a Canadian Catholic is significantly more likely to vote Liberal than Conservative or NDP, as is a Canadian of Latin American, Asian, or African origin.[77] Gender also influences voting, although to a lesser extent: women are more likely than men to vote Liberal or the NDP, and less likely to vote for the Conservative Party (or its Reform/Alliance predecessor; see Box 11.1 above).[78]

The Institutional Approach

We have seen that individual parties are strongly affected by the institutions within which they operate. The same is true for party systems. Most important, the number and relative size of the parties in a given jurisdiction are influenced by the way in which the electoral system translates votes into seats in the legislature. In a proportional electoral system, smaller parties can win enough seats in parliament to satisfy their members and voters that their views are being expressed in national politics. A single dominant cleavage—for example, the class cleavage in Austria—will translate into two large parties in parliament; a more complex cleavage structure, such as that in Belgium, will produce several parties (regional, linguistic, working-class, religious, and Green).

A disproportional electoral system, like those in Canada, the United States, and Britain, makes it difficult for smaller parties to win seats in parliament. There are exceptions: regionally based nationalist parties such as the Bloc Québécois and the Scottish National Party tend to do very well under such systems, especially where, as in Canada, federalism provides a strong regional basis for mobilization.[79] Over time, the supporters of smaller parties which do not enjoy these institutional advantages become discouraged by their failure to gain parliamentary representation; they gradually fade away, leaving one or two large parties to contend for power. These "mechanical" and "psychological" effects on the number of parties are less pronounced in countries which use proportional electoral systems, because it is easier for small parties to win at least one seat in the legislature. However, the difference should not be exaggerated. In 1996, New Zealand switched from FPTP to a proportional "mixed" electoral system. Before the switch, between two and four of the five active parties were represented in the New Zealand parliament at any given time; in the 1996 election, 6 of the 19 active parties won seats. The two parties that had dominated New Zealand politics for decades (Labour and National) continued to do so, although their combined share of both votes and seats fell significantly.[80] The point is that institutional factors shape the party system, but they do not determine the number or the respective size of the parties.

The Pattern of Party Competition

The pattern of party competition is made up of three elements: the frequency of party alternation in government; the consistency of government composition; and the openness of access to government.[81] If we combine these characteristics with the number of parties, we come up with four types of party system. These are listed in Table 11.2, together with examples of each.[82]

Table 11.2 Four Types of Party System

Type of Party System	Description	Example(s)
Two-party	Two major parties compete for power; they alternate in government more or less frequently	United States; New Zealand (pre-1996)
Two-and-a-half party	In addition to the two parties described above, there is a "third" party that rarely challenges for power but that may support one of the major parties during periods of minority government	Canada (1963–1993); Britain
Multiparty system with a dominant party	Four or more parties contest national elections, only one of which has a realistic chance to either form a single-party majority government or become the senior partner in a coalition	Italy (pre-1994); Canada (1993–2004); Japan (pre-1993); India (pre-1977); Mexico (pre-2000); West Germany (1949–1969)
Multiparty system with no dominant party	Four or more parties compete for inclusion in governing coalitions, with fairly regular alternation in power; after each election, the composition of the new government depends on bargaining among all of the parties, not just the incumbents	The Netherlands; Italy (post-1994); Canada (post-2004); Norway

As the table suggests, the concept of party competition brings together several key concepts: the number of parties in the system; the relative size of the parties (in terms of both voting support and legislative representation); the willingness of the parties to overcome their differences when required (e.g., to create and sustain a coalition cabinet); and the degree of competitiveness among the parties.

As we suggested earlier, the number of parties, by itself, tells us little about the politics and government of a particular country. A useful categorization of party systems emerges when we combine the number of parties with the other factors just mentioned. Systems in which one party remains in power for long periods of time, either alone or with one or more junior coalition partners, produce different patterns of government and politics from highly competitive systems, which feature two major parties or two (or more) possible coalitions that regularly alternate in power. At the very least, the possibility of a meaningful choice between alternative governments implies a more vibrant democracy than exists when the outcome of an election is determined well before voters go to the polls. Public policy may also be affected by the type of party system: significant changes in the party composition of a government may produce major changes in policy direction, at least in those fields (such as law and order) least affected by globalization and fiscal constraints.

CONCLUSION

While political parties remain central to democratic politics and government, they have become less effective in mobilizing the electorate and linking citizens to their governments. As their ties to civil society weaken, their organizational capacities have been enhanced by growing public subsidies and the increasing professionalization of their personnel. In other words, the party in public and central office has flourished while the party on the ground has withered. As a result, "the gap between the citizenry and the established political class"[83] grows ever wider.

> . . . the problem is not one of party decline per se, as is often imputed to be the case; rather, it appears to be one in which the parties are at once stronger, but also more

remote; at once more in control, but also less powerful; and at once more privileged, but also less legitimate.[84]

It is unlikely that the ties between parties and civil society in Western democracies will be fully reestablished. We cannot turn back the clock to the days when mass-based parties commanded the loyalty of cohesive political subcultures, voters flocked to the polling booths, and local party associations mobilized large numbers of citizens into participating in the political process. Electoralist parties respond to the imperatives of political competition within their particular countries. If these continue to favour the party in public and central office over the party on the ground, a significant revival of the latter is unlikely. A party that can win seats with fewer votes has little reason for concern about falling turnout rates;[85] similarly, a party that can win seats with a smaller but more efficient local campaign has no incentive to invest in the recruitment and training of members.[86] As long as public subsidies account for a significant and growing proportion of party income, the widening gap between the political class and the rest of society will have few tangible consequences for the former.

Given this bleak prognosis, it is tempting to dismiss the IDEA's rosy portrayal of political parties as unrealistic. But before we do so, we should consider the practical reasons behind the IDEA's advocacy of party organization in new democracies:

> *There has been no mass democracy without parties during the past two centuries. . . . Over the decades the basics have remained unchanged. Wherever non-partisan elections have been held they were either partisan in all but name or non-democratic despite the name. Obviously, for the near future there will be no democracy without parties. If parties in general wither away, as has been predicted for some of the most advanced democracies, the institution called "party" will be replaced by some other type of political organization which will have to perform many similar functions.*[87]

As this quotation suggests, political parties are still key players in the democratic game. They will likely persist, in some form, as long as there are differences of political opinion and representative institutions through which to express them. The real question is whether, given the political and social environments within which they operate, today's electoralist parties are willing and able to rebuild the linkages between civil society and the state. If they do not, they will survive as "public utilities" long after they have ceased to represent their respective political constituencies in any meaningful way.

While this is not a particularly hopeful picture, neither is it entirely pessimistic. Table 11.1 proves that political parties are remarkably adaptable institutions. If the citizens of Western democracies demand more from their parties than an empty ritual of leadership recruitment and election campaigns, then the parties, old or new, will provide it. This is the moral of the story: instead of blaming the parties for all of the problems discussed in this chapter, we should ask how much of the responsibility lies in the citizens (and especially the young citizens) who have turned their backs on politics. Whether or not we get the political parties that we want, we do seem to get the parties we deserve.

DISCUSSION QUESTIONS

1. Do you pay close attention to national or provincial party politics? Why or why not?

2. If you wanted to influence public policy on a particular issue, which do you think would be more effective: joining a political party, or participating in a public protest? Explain your choice.

3. Do you plan to vote in the next federal or provincial election? Why or why not?

4. Should a party in government keep all of its election promises? Why or why not?

KEY TERMS

CLEAVAGE: A persistent division among two groups of voters, based on long-term demographic or economic characteristics. Examples include language, religion, class, and region. One or both of the groups on either side of a cleavage may be mobilized into a **subculture**: a long-lasting and cohesive political organization that shapes the voting patterns and political perceptions of its members. In some countries, such as the Netherlands, each of the major subcultures has historically supported its own political party. Examples are trade unionists, linguistic or religious minorities, and distinct regional populations. When a subculture is fully mobilized, it can produce a mass-based party (e.g., a Social Democratic Party), an ethnic party, a nationalist party, or a movement/party. (335)

ELECTORALIST PARTY: A type of political party, increasingly common in Western democracies over the past 50 years, that is almost exclusively concerned to maximize its electoral support. It emphasizes the political attractiveness of its leaders and candidates rather than its policies or platform, and it relies on media appeals rather than on a large, active membership. (321)

ONE-MEMBER-ONE-VOTE (OMOV): A method of leadership selection in which party members vote directly for the candidate of their choice, instead of electing delegates to make the choice on their behalf. Popular OMOV methods include telephone voting, mail-in ballots, and voting in person at a local polling place. Some parties have created hybrid or two-stage OMOV systems, in which delegates are bound to vote according to the preferences of the members whom they represent (e.g., the Liberal Party of Canada). (331)

PARTY SYSTEM: "[T]he system of interactions resulting from inter-party competition"; the parties within a particular jurisdiction (country, state, or province) that compete with each other for scarce resources, particularly money and votes. The word "system" refers to a set of distinct but interrelated objects. When an individual party changes in some way—by appealing to a new group of voters, or by altering its internal structures—that change affects all of the other parties in the system. (335)

POLITICAL PARTY: An organization of volunteers and paid professionals who work together to achieve shared political goals, one of which is the election of candidates to public office. The nomination of candidates is the defining characteristic of a political party—as distinct from an interest group. For many parties, the primary goal is to elect enough candidates to the legislature to form a government. Other parties are more concerned with the advocacy of particular ideas or policies. (320)

WEB LINKS wℳw

For constitutions of most major parties (click on "Political Parties Around the World"):
http://www.polisci.nelson.com

International Foundation for Electoral Systems:
http://www.ifes.org

International Institute for Democracy and Electoral Assistance:
http://www.idea.int

For directory of electronic resources on political parties:
http://toby.library.ubc.ca/subjects/subjpage1.cfm?id=169#canadianpolitics

For links to political party websites from around the world (click on "Government and Politics on the Web," then "Political Parties Around the World"):

http://www.polisci.nelson.com

For up-to-date information about government and politics from around the world, with emphasis on parties and elections:

http://www.politicalresources.net

FURTHER READING

Austin, Reginald Austin, and Maja Tjernström, eds. *Funding of Political Parties and Election Campaigns*. Stockholm: International Institute for Democracy and Electoral Assistance, 2004.

Dalton, Russell J., and Martin P. Wattenberg, eds. *Parties Without Partisans: Political Change in Advanced Industrial Democracies*. New York: Oxford University Press, 2002.

Duverger, Maurice. *Political Parties: Their Organization and Activity in the Modern State*. London: Methuen, 1964.

Gunther, Richard, and Larry Diamond. "Species of Political Parties: A New Typology," *Party Politics* 9(2) (2003): 167–99.

Gunther, Richard, José Ramón Montero, and Juan J. Linz, eds. *Political Parties: Old Concepts and New Challenges*. New York: Oxford University Press, 2002.

Harmel, Robert, and Kenneth Janda. "An Integrated Theory of Party Goals and Party Change," *Journal of Theoretical Politics* 6(3) (July 1994).

Katz, Richard S., and Peter Mair, eds. *How Parties Organize: Change and Adaptation in Party Organizations in Western Democracies*. London: Sage, 1994.

Lawson, Kay, and Peter H. Merkl, eds. *When Parties Fail: Emerging Alternative Organizations*. Princeton: Princeton University Press, 1988.

LeDuc, Lawrence, Richard G. Niemi, and Pippa Norris, eds. *Comparing Democracies 2: New Challenges in the Study of Elections and Voting*. Thousand Oaks, CA: Sage, 2002.

Maor, Moshe. *Political Parties and Party Systems: Comparative Approaches and the British Experience*. London: Routledge, 1997.

Panebianco, Angelo. *Political Parties: Organization and Power*. Cambridge: Cambridge University Press, 1988.

Reynolds, Andrew, et al. *Electoral System Design: The New International IDEA Handbook*. Stockholm: International Institute for Democracy and Electoral Assistance, 2005.

van Biezen, Ingrid. "Political Parties as Public Utilities," *Party Politics* 10(6) (2004): 701–22.

Ware, Alan. *Political Parties and Party Systems*. Oxford: Oxford University Press, 1996.

ENDNOTES

1. Gerald M. Pomper, "Concepts of Political Parties," *Journal of Theoretical Politics* 4(2) (1992): 143.

2. Mark Tran and agencies, "Iraqi Elections: The Key Parties," *Guardian Unlimited*, January 27, 2005 (available at http://www.guardian.co.uk).

3. Karl-Heinz Nassmacher, "Introduction: Political Parties, Funding and Democracy," in *Handbook on Funding of Political Parties and Election Campaigns* (Stockholm: Institute for Democracy and Electoral Assistance, 2004), p. 2.

4. Neil Nevitte, "Introduction: Value Change and Reorientation in Citizen–State Relations," in Neil Nevitte, ed., *Value Change and Governance in Canada* (Toronto: University of Toronto Press, 2002), pp. 3–35.

5. Ronald Inglehart and Christian Welzel, *Modernization, Cultural Change, and Democracy: The Human Development Sequence* (Cambridge: Cambridge University Press, 2005), p. 262.

6. Russell J. Dalton, "Political Cleavages, Issues, and Electoral Change," in Lawrence LeDuc, Richard G. Niemi, and Pippa Norris, eds., *Comparing Democracies 2: New Challenges in the Study of Elections and Voting* (London: Sage, 2002), pp. 190–211.

7. For a discussion of the British case, in which the decline of class voting has been particularly marked, see Anthony King, "The New Electoral Battleground," in Anthony King et al., eds., *New Labour Triumphs: Britain at the Polls* (Chatham, NJ: Chatham House, 1998), 219–23, and Richard Rose and Ian McAllister, *Voters Begin to Choose: From Closed-Class to Open Elections in Britain* (London: Sage, 1986). On the general decline of cleavage voting in Western democracies, see Russell J. Dalton, *Citizen Politics: Public Opinion and Political Parties in Advanced Western Democracies*, 2nd ed. (Chatham, NJ: Chatham House, 1996), ch. 8.

8. Russell J. Dalton and Martin P. Wattenberg, "Unthinkable Democracy: Political Change in Advanced Industrial Democracies," Russell J. Dalton and Martin P. Wattenberg, eds., *Parties Without Partisans: Political Change in Advanced Industrial Democracies* (New York: Oxford University Press, 2002), p. 11.

9. David M. Farrell and Paul Webb, "Political Parties as Campaign Organizations," in Dalton and Wattenberg, eds., pp. 102–28.

10. Richard S. Katz and Peter Mair, "The Ascendancy of the Party in Public Office: Party Organizational Change in Twentieth-Century Democracies," in Richard Gunther, José Ramón Montero, and Juan J. Linz, eds., *Political Parties: Old Concepts and New Challenges* (New York: Oxford University Press, 2002), pp. 113–35.

11. Jon H. Pammett and Lawrence LeDuc, "Explaining the Turnout Decline in Canadian Federal Elections: A New Survey of Non-Voters" (Ottawa: Elections Canada, March 2003), pp. 25 (Table 17) and 28; available at http://www.elections.ca/loi/tur/tud/TurnoutDecline.pdf; accessed June 13, 2008.

12. *Ibid.* See also Benny Geys, "Explaining Voter Turnout: A Review of Aggregate-Level Research," *Electoral Studies* 25 (2006): 637–63; Andrew Ellis et al., *Engaging the Electorate: Initiatives to Promote Voter Turnout From Around the World* (Stockholm: International Institute for Democracy and Electoral Assistance, 2006), Section I.

13. Katz and Mair, "The Ascendancy of the Party in Public Office," p. 123; Farrell and Webb, pp. 118–19; Ingrid van Biezen, "Political Parties as Public Utilities," *Party Politics* 10(6) (2004): 701–05.

14. Louis Massicotte, "Electoral Legislation Since 1997: Parliament Regains the Initiative," in Jon H. Pammett and Christopher Dornan, eds., *The Canadian Federal Election of 2006* (Toronto: Dundurn, 2006), p. 262.

15. For a thorough discussion of party goals, see Robert Harmel and Kenneth Janda, "An Integrated Theory of Party Goals and Party Change," *Journal of Theoretical Politics* 6(3) (July 1994): 259–87.

16. See, for example, Maurice Duverger, *Political Parties: Their Organization and Activity in the Modern State* (London: Methuen, 1964); Angelo Panebianco, *Political Parties: Organization and Power* (Cambridge: Cambridge University Press, 1988); Giovanni Sartori, *Parties and Party Systems: A Framework for Analysis*, vol. 1 (Cambridge: Cambridge University Press, 1976); Otto Kirchheimer, "The Transformation of the Western European Party Systems," in Joseph LaPalombara and Myron Weiner, eds., *Political Parties and Political Development* (Princeton, NJ: Princeton University Press, 1966).

17. Richard Gunther and Larry Diamond, "Species of Political Parties: A New Typology," *Party Politics* 9(2) (2003):167–99.

18. *Ibid.*, p. 175.

19. *Ibid.*

20. The Welfare Party was banned by the courts in 1998, under the Turkish Party Law; it was regarded as a potential threat to the officially secular state. Some moderate elements re-formed as the Justice and Development Party (AKP) shortly afterward.

21. Gunther and Diamond, p. 185.

22. *Ibid.*, p. 187.

23. *Ibid.*, p. 187.

24. *Ibid.*, p. 185.

25. These points are a paraphrased summary of Gunther and Diamond, p. 171.

26. The history of Canada's national parties is well summarized in David E. Smith, "Government, Representation and National Integration in Canada," in Peter Aucoin, ed., *Party Government and Regional Representation in Canada*, volume 36 of the Collected Research Studies for the Royal Commission on the Economic Union and Development Prospects for Canada (Toronto: University of Toronto Press, 1985), pp. 1–68, and R.K. Carty, "Three Canadian Party Systems: An Interpretation of the Development of National Politics," in George Perlin, ed., *Party Democracy in Canada: The Politics of National Party Conventions* (Scarborough: Prentice-Hall Canada, 1988), pp. 15–30.

27. Susan Harada, "Great Expectations: The Green Party of Canada's 2006 Campaign," in Pammett and Dornan, eds., *The Canadian Federal Election of 2006*, pp. 143–70.

28. The DNA metaphor is taken from Panebianco, ch. 2, pp. 49–68.

29. Nassmacher, "Introduction," p. 3; emphasis in original.

30. On the extent of voter "dealignment," see Russell J. Dalton, "The Decline of Party Identifications," in Dalton and Wattenberg, eds., pp. 19–36.

31. Russell J. Dalton, Ian McAllister, and Martin P. Wattenberg, "The Consequences of Partisan Dealignment," in Dalton and Wattenberg, eds., pp. 60–61.

32. Faron Ellis and Peter Woolstencroft, "A Change of Government, Not a Change of Country: The Conservatives and the 2006 Election," in Pammett and Dornan, eds., pp. 63–65.

33. The names for the three sections of the party organization are taken from Peter Mair, "Party Organizations: From Civil Society to the State," in Richard S. Katz and Peter Mair, eds., *How Parties Organize: Change and Adaptation in Party Organizations in Western Democracies* (London: Sage, 1994), p. 4.

34. Richard S. Katz and Peter Mair, "The Ascendancy of the Party in Public Office: Party Organizational Change in Twentieth-Century Democracies," in Richard Gunther, José Ramón Montero, and Juan J. Linz, eds., *Political Parties: Old Concepts and New Challenges* (New York: Oxford University Press, 2002), pp. 113–35; David M. Farrell and Paul Webb, "Political Parties as Campaign Organizations," in Dalton and Wattenberg, eds., pp. 102–25.

35. Katz and Mair, "The Ascendancy of the Party in Public Office," pp. 122 and 130.

36. Andrew Reynolds et al., *Electoral System Design: The New International IDEA Handbook* (Stockholm: International Institute for Democracy and Electoral Assistance, 2005), pp. 73 and 77; Law Commission of Canada, *Voting Counts: Electoral Reform for Canada* (Ottawa: Minister of Public Works and Government Services, 2004), p. 81.

37. Note, however, that the president is not directly elected by the voters; he (someday she) is chosen by the Electoral College, made up of delegates from the various states.

38. Richard S. Katz, "Party Organization as an Empty Vessel: Parties in American Politics," in Katz and Mair, eds., *How Parties Organize*, pp. 28–29.

39. Rand Dyck, "Links Between Federal and Provincial Parties and Party Systems," in Herman Bakvis, ed., *Representation, Integration, and Political Parties in Canada*, volume 14 of the collected research studies for the Royal Commission on Electoral Reform and Party Financing (Toronto: Dundurn, 1991), pp. 129–32.

40. Dyck, p. 155.

41. William M. Chandler, "Federalism and Political Parties," in Herman Bakvis and William M. Chandler, eds., *Federalism and the Role of the State* (Toronto: University of Toronto Press, 1987), p. 160.

42. Dyck, pp. 138–39.

43. Alan C. Cairns, "The Electoral System and the Party System in Canada, 1921–1965," in Douglas E. Williams, ed., *Constitution, Government, and Society in Canada: Selected Essays by Alan C. Cairns* (Toronto: McClelland and Stewart, 1988), pp. 111–38.

44. Lauri Karvonen, "Legislation on Political Parties: A Global Comparison," *Party Politics* 13(4) (2007): 437–55.

45. The British law is entitled *Political Parties, Elections and Referendums Act*; it was adopted in 2000. The *Canada Elections Act* was amended in 2004 to define a political party as "an organization one of whose fundamental purposes is to participate in public affairs by endorsing one or more of its members as candidates and supporting their election." This type of definition is consistent with the party laws in other democracies. It became necessary to define a "political party" in Canadian law when the Supreme Court struck down a restriction on the registration of parties as a violation of the *Canadian Charter of Rights and Freedoms*; in order to protect the political finance regime from potential fraud, Parliament had to find a way to distinguish "real" parties from organizations established purely to take advantage of the tax credit regime. See Heather MacIvor, "The Charter of

Rights and Party Politics: The Impact of the Supreme Court Ruling in *Figueroa v. Canada (Attorney General)*," *Choices* 10(4) (May 2004).

46. Of 111 democracies studied by the IDEA in 2003, 71 (64 percent) regulate party finance. See Maja Tjernström, "Matrix of Political Finance Laws and Regulations," Table 1, in Austin and Tjernström, eds., pp. 185–87.

47. For more information, see the "Matrix of Political Finance Laws and Regulations."

48. Moshe Maor, *Political Parties and Party Systems: Comparative Approaches and the British Experience* (London: Routledge, 1997), pp. 110–13.

49. Katz and Mair, "The Ascendancy of the Party in Public Office," p. 127; van Biezen, pp. 701–02. For a contrary view on the impact of public subsidies on party organizations, see Michael Pinto-Duschinsky, "Financing Politics: A Global View," *Journal of Democracy* 13(4) (2002): 79. The financial power of the party in central office grew in 2004, when the *Canada Elections Act* was amended by Bill C-24. Corporate and union donations to national party organizations were banned, and replaced with annual allowances of public money. Because the allowances are paid directly to the national party headquarters, this change in the law will likely enhance the power of the party in central office and reduce the autonomy of the constituency associations on the ground. Bill C-24 permitted small contributions to registered constituency associations and candidates by individuals, corporations, and unions. All remaining corporate and union donations were prohibited in late 2006, when the *Federal Accountability Act* took effect; at the same time, the cap on individual donations was lowered by $5,000 to $1,000 per year. The 2006 amendments further reduce the capacity of the constituency associations to raise money, and make them even more dependent on the party in central office. Heather MacIvor, "A Missed Opportunity: Political Finance and the Federal Accountability Act," paper presented to the 2006 Law and Parliament Conference "Accountability as a Pillar of Democratic Governing," Ottawa, November 2, 2006.

50. Canada, House of Commons, *Canada Elections Act*, 48–49 Elizabeth II, Chapter 9; sections 464–70. On the value of candidate surpluses, see John Laschinger and Geoffrey Stevens, *Leaders and Lesser Mortals: Backroom Politics in Canada* (Toronto: Key Porter, 1992), pp. 146–48.

51. John C. Courtney, "Recognition of Canadian Political Parties in Parliament and in Law," *Canadian Journal of Political Science* 11(1) (March 1978): 33–60; van Biezen, "Political Parties as Public Utilities," p. 705.

52. Nassmacher, "Introduction," p. 2; emphasis in original.

53. *Ibid.*, p. 2.

54. In most countries, election campaigns are organized by political parties. However, parties and their candidates are not the only participants. Interest groups of various stripes also get involved, by advertising their political views to the electorate and by asking their members to vote for or against a particular party or candidate.

55. For an interesting comparison of party websites in Western Europe, see Pippa Norris, "Preaching to the Converted? Pluralism, Participation and Party Websites," *Party Politics* 9(1) (2003): 21–45.

56. For example, in the SPD–Green coalition that took power in Germany in 1999, SPD leader Gerhard Schroeder was Chancellor (Germany's term for "prime minister"); Joschka Fischer, the Green leader, was Foreign Minister.

57. R.M. Punnett, *Selecting the Party Leader: Britain in Comparative Perspective* (London: Harvester Wheatsheaf, 1992), p. 18; Heather MacIvor, "From Emergence to Electronics: Explaining the Changes in Canadian Party Leadership Selection, 1919–1995," *National History* (1995), 173–85.

58. Lisa Young and William Cross. "The Rise of Plebiscitary Democracy in Canadian Political Parties," *Party Politics* 8(6) (2002): 673–99.

59. On the adoption of OMOV by British, American and Canadian parties, see Lawrence LeDuc, "Democratizing Party Leadership Selection," *Party Politics* 7(3) (2001): 323–41.

60. Katz and Mair, "The Ascendancy of the Party in Public Office," pp. 128–29.

61. LeDuc, "Democratizing Party Leadership Selection," p. 326.

62. Reuven Y. Hazan, "Candidate Selection," in LeDuc, Niemi and Norris, eds., *Comparing Democracies* 2, pp. 117–21.

63. Rahat and Hazan, p. 303.

64. In 1992, former Liberal leader Jean Chrétien used his veto power to wring a major concession from delegates to a party convention: the power to appoint candidates over the objections of local associations. Chrétien appointed several candidates in the 1993 and 1997 campaigns, angering Liberals in the affected constituencies. In self-defence, he claimed that this was the only way to ensure enough female and/or visible minority candidates. Paul Martin revived the practice in the 2004 campaign, although most of his hand-picked "star" candidates (including Ken Dryden) were male. His decisions angered many Liberals, especially those who had spent months organizing their nomination bids.

65. William Cross, "Candidate Nomination in Canada's Political Parties," in Pammett and Dornan, eds., pp. 176–80.

66. Recent trends in candidate selection within electoralist parties are described in Susan E. Scarrow, Paul Webb, and David M. Farrell, "From Social Integration to Electoral Contestation: The Changing Distribution of Power Within Political Parties," in Dalton and Wattenberg, eds., pp. 138–42.

67. R. Kenneth Carty, D. Munroe Eagles, and Anthony Sayers, "Candidates and Local Campaigns: Are There Just Four Canadian Types?," *Party Politics* 9(2) (2003): 621.

68. This distinction between "capital-intensive" and "labour-intensive" campaigning is taken from David M. Farrell, "Campaign Strategies and Tactics," in LeDuc, Niemi, and Norris, eds., *Comparing Democracies*, pp. 160–83.

69. Martin P. Wattenberg, "The Decline of Party Mobilization," in Dalton and Wattenberg, eds., pp. 64–76.

70. See, for example, Paul F. Whiteley and Patrick Seyd, "The Labour Vote and Local Activism: The Impact of Local Constituency Campaigns," *Parliamentary Affairs* 45 (1992): 582–95; Carty and Eagles, ch. 8.

71. Pippa Norris, *A Virtuous Circle: Political Communications in Postindustrial Societies* (Cambridge: Cambridge University Press, 2000), pp. 137–49.

72. Ian Ward, "'Localizing the National': The Rediscovery and Reshaping of Local Campaigning in Australia," *Party Politics* 9(5) (2003): 587.

73. The exception is the members' ability to indirectly reshape policy by choosing candidates or leaders who share their particular preferences on key issues. R. Kenneth Carty, "Parties as Franchise Systems: The Stratarchical Organizational Imperative," *Party Politics* 10(1) (2004): 20.

74. Sartori, p. 44.

75. Alan Ware, *Political Parties and Party Systems* (Oxford: Oxford University Press, 1996), p. 184.

76. Dalton, pp. 190–91.

77. André Blais, "Accounting for the Electoral Success of the Liberal Party in Canada," *Canadian Journal of Political Science* 38(4) (December 2005): 821–40.

78. Lynda Erickson and Brenda O'Neill, "The Gender Gap and the Changing Woman Voter in Canada," *International Political Science Review* 23(4) (2002): 373–92.

79. John Gerring, "Minor Parties in Plurality Electoral Systems," *Party Politics* 11(1) (2005): 79–107.

80. Fiona Barker and Elizabeth McLeay, "How Much Change? An Analysis of the Initial Impact of Proportional Representation on the New Zealand Parliamentary Party System," *Party Politics* 6(2) (2000): 131–54.

81. Mair, "Party Systems and Structures of Competition," p. 90.

82. The information in this box is taken from Peter Mair, "Party Systems and Structures of Competition," in LeDuc, Niemi, and Norris, eds., *Comparing Democracies*, pp. 86–92.

83. Mair, "Party Organizations: From Civil Society to the State," p. 19.

84. *Ibid.*

85. Wattenberg, "The Decline of Party Mobilization," p. 76.

86. Some experts argue that a smaller membership base makes party campaigns more efficient, and could potentially empower the members who remain involved. Susan E. Scarrow, "Parties Without Members? Party Organizations in a Changing Electoral Environment," in Dalton and Wattenberg, eds., pp. 79–101.

87. Karl-Heinz Nassmacher, "Introduction: Political Parties, Funding and Democracy," in Austin and Tjernström, eds., p. 3.

Chapter Twelve

CIVIL SOCIETY: Interest Groups and Social Movements in Politics

Miriam Smith

CHAPTER OBJECTIVES

After you have completed this chapter, you should be able to:

■ understand what interest groups and social movements are

■ enumerate the differences among the major subtypes of interest groups and social movements

■ discuss the most common ways in which such groups influence the political system

■ engage in the debate over whether such groups are too powerful

Introduction

Protestors take to the streets of Toronto, Montreal, Vancouver, and other cities to demonstrate against the wars in Iraq and Afghanistan. Amnesty International coordinates urgent action campaigns in defence of political prisoners by letter and e-mail. Greenpeace activists occupy treetops in Argentina to stop logging. Pro-life groups appear before the Supreme Court in the United States to claim that life begins at conception. Oil companies protest the Alberta government's decision to raise the royalty rate on oil and gas. Laid-off workers stage factory occupations and sit-ins in China. What these incidents have in common is that they are expressions of protest based on non-territorial interests, identities, and values: antiwar protestors, peace campaigners, environmentalists, business, and pro-life groups.

Much of our everyday discussion of politics is defined by territory. The ideas of government and the state are based on the assumption of a certain geographical region. When we think of Canada or China, we are thinking of a defined geographical territory around which politics is organized. In democratic political systems, voting is often organized around constituencies or districts in which voters elect a representative.

While the electoral system provides for the territorial representation of citizens, groups and movements organize citizens according to non-territorial interests and identities. In the electoral system, voters choose a representative of the geographical area in which they live. In group and movement politics, citizens get together with likeminded citizens to form a group or movement that reflects political cleavages such as economic interests, gender, language, or simply political opinions.[1]

Democratic freedoms are very important for the organization of movements and groups. Without freedom to assemble, freedom of the press, and freedom of expression, it is very difficult for citizens to form groups and movements. Yet, even in nondemocratic systems, group politics may operate. Authoritarian states may permit certain types of political groups to exist, or may not be able to expend the resources necessary to stop such groups from forming. And movements of political protest may bring people into the streets, leading to the downfall of an authoritarian regime and the transition to democracy.

What Are Interest Groups and Social Movements?

Interest groups and **social movements** bring together people with common interests and/or a common sense of identity for the purpose of influencing the political process. Groups and movements are not part of the state, although in some cases they may have very close relationships with the state. Groups and movements are different from political parties because they do not seek public office. They may seek to influence **public policy** or they may primarily aim to influence the beliefs and values of their fellow citizens.

Groups and movements form part of **civil society**—that is, social institutions and organizations that are independent of the state and in which citizens pursue their interests, express their beliefs, and live in communities. Examples of institutions of civil society are churches, schools, professional associations, trade unions, companies, and families.

This chapter discusses both interest groups and social movements. Interest groups are formally organized, while social movements function as informal networks of activists. Further, social movements often engage in **contentious politics**—strikes and demonstrations—as a means of achieving their goals, while interest groups usually pursue their goals through conventional means such as lobbying.[2]

An example of social movement politics is provided by Greenpeace, mentioned at the beginning of this chapter. The organization began in the 1970s as a small group of environmentalists in Vancouver brought together by a sense of common values and identities. In order to stop U.S. nuclear testing in the South Pacific, they sailed their ship, the *Rainbow Warrior*, directly into the testing area both to stop the tests and to provide witnesses for the testing. Greenpeace is premised on the effectiveness of direct action and witnessing to achieve their goals. These strategies are typical of social movement organizations, which often use direct action and demonstrations to draw attention to public issues and as a means of effecting change.

The social movement politics of Greenpeace can be contrasted with the interest-group politics of, for example, the National Rifle Association (NRA) in the United States. The NRA is well organized with thousands of members and a large budget; it also has spinoff organizations that fund litigation in gun control cases, defend shooting sports, and alert members to upcoming legislation in Congress. The NRA has been heavily involved in lobbying members of Congress on gun control legislation. Moreover, the organization is well known to the public and has a high media profile. It is said that it is almost impossible to change gun control legislation in the United States because of the influence of the NRA on Congress.[3]

The politics of interest groups and social movements can also be distinguished from the activities of lobbying or consulting, in which groups or companies hire professionals to contact and influence government on their behalf. For example, tobacco companies might hire professional lobbyists to influence legislators' and public servants' views on their products and advertising. Typically, lobbyists and consultants are paid well to protect the interests of their

Activists camp in the treetops, demanding the implementation of the "Law of the Forests."

© Greenpeace/Infoto

clients in government policy. This type of activity is common in most democratic countries; it is a very sizable industry in the United States and increasingly in Canada as well.

Interest groups and social movements are sometimes called **nongovernmental organizations (NGOs)**. This term is particularly common in the fields of international relations and development, but NGOs are also active in domestic politics. Such organizations are part of neither the state nor international organizations such as the United Nations (UN). In addition to targeting states and trying to change domestic policies, they aim to influence international organizations such as the UN and the World Trade Organization (WTO).

Functions of Interest Groups and Social Movements

Interest groups and social movements serve a number of functions in the political system. The four main types of functions of interest groups and social movements are

- to provide a means for citizens to express their views to government and to participate in the political system
- to influence the policies followed by governments, international organizations, and corporations
- to influence views held in society
- to provide information and legitimacy to governments and to international organizations

First of all, group and movement politics provide a link between citizens and government and allow citizens an alternative means of expressing their views. Group and movement organizations allow for the articulation of political opinions that are much more specific than those that can be expressed through voting periodically in an election or even by actively participating in party politics. Some voters may feel none of the political parties represents their views on issues important to them.

Environmentalists, for example, might feel that party politics is a waste of time and that their activism might be more effectively channelled through participation in the environmental movement. People who support the pro-life side of the abortion debate might join a pro-life organization that reflects their specific viewpoint. People might belong to religious and cultural organizations; while these organizations do not exist primarily to influence government, they might from time to time involve themselves in politics and aim to influence policy. Some citizens might feel government is not serving their interests and might organize in their own communities to provide needed services. Many women's organizations such as rape crisis lines and battered women's shelters started out as community-based organizations intended to fill gaps in public services. In this sense, then, group and movement politics provide a means for citizens to express their views to government and to participate in the political system.

In authoritarian systems, some forms of group political activity might be permitted and might provide a vehicle for some citizens to express their views to government in a limited fashion. In Box 12.1, you can see an example of the range of interest groups that currently exists in China, which has an authoritarian regime.

Interest Groups in Nondemocratic Systems: The Example of China

BOX 12.1

According to Chinese politics experts George Gilboy and Eric Heginbotham, the following important interest groups exist in China, despite the fact that it is not a democratic country:

- *Farmers.* With increasing frequency, Chinese farmers are organizing to protest corrupt local officials, onerous and arbitrary taxes, and extreme poverty. In recent months, farmers have attacked tax collectors, blocked roads, and fought with officials and police.

- *The unemployed.* As economic reform continues, millions of Chinese workers are being laid off each year with little hope of reemployment or adequate social welfare support. In some cities, unemployed workers are now coming together in large-scale protests involving as many as 20,000 people at a time.

- *Consumers.* Today's Chinese consumers frequently speak out and organize against defective products, financial scams, and official corruption.

- *Industry associations.* Because China's official industry associations are weak and dominated by the Communist Party, they are unable to mediate effectively between industry and government. Yet some industry leaders have coalesced to force the central government to change policies on taxes, international trade, and price reforms.

- *Religious and spiritual movements.* The rise of Falun Gong is only the most visible indication of resurgent spiritualism in China. Traditional religions, mystical movements, and cults have attracted millions of followers in recent years.

- *Special-interest groups.* A variety of nascent special-interest groups, ranging from environmental and animal-rights organizations to regional soccer clubs, now place new demands on the state for resources and attention. For example, environmental groups—some with nationwide reach—have sponsored direct actions such as tree-planting programs and petitions calling for better municipal waste management.

SOURCE: Excerpted from George Gilboy and Eric Heginbotham, "China's Coming Transformation," *Foreign Affairs* 80(4) (July/August 2001): 31–33. Reprinted by permission of *Foreign Affairs* 80(4) (July/August 2001). Copyright 2001 by the Council on Foreign Relations, Inc.

Yet interest-group and social movement politics raise the problem of collective action and the question of why people join such groups. According to rational choice theorists such as Mancur Olson, people will not join groups, especially ones devoted to goals that will benefit everyone in society. Olson assumes that citizens are rational self-maximizing individuals; that is, they are interested in pursuing their own interests. Given that the individual is primarily concerned with the satisfaction of personal interests and needs, why should he or she join a group or social movement organization? After all, if the group is devoted to goals that benefit everyone, such as clean air, why join? If the goal is achieved, one will benefit regardless of the extent of one's participation.

Because of this, Olson argues that the individual is more likely to *free-ride*—that is, to avoid participating. This creates the problem of collective action: if everyone free-rides, how will groups form? Olson argues that groups will form through the provision of incentives to members.

While many groups do use incentives to encourage membership and participation, many forms of collective action are difficult to explain in terms of incentives for participation. Interest groups and social movements tap into collective identities. For example, nationalist, ethnic, and linguistic groups may form on the basis of a sense of common interests and identity. Historically, business, labour, and farmer groups in Canada have created unity by appealing to a shared sense of political identity and interests.

Second, group and movement politics influence the policies followed by governments, international organizations, and in some cases corporations. Citizens banding together may convince government to follow one course of action rather than another. Protesters against the Multilateral Agreement on Investment (MAI) had some effect on causing the Organisation for Economic Co-operation and Development (OECD) and the WTO not to go ahead with the treaty. Farmers in Britain who banded together managed to influence the government's stance on the treatment of the foot-and-mouth disease affecting British cattle.

Third, groups may aim to influence society as much as or more than they may aim to influence the state. For certain types of groups, it may be more important to change what citizens believe about an issue or to change the core political values of citizens than to change public policy. For example, business groups may attempt to use the media to put forth the point of view that free-market policies are superior to state intervention as a means of ensuring economic development and growth. For business groups, it may be just as important to convince citizens to believe in a free-market perspective as to convince governments to undertake a certain policy decision. This is increasingly the case as certain types of decisions by corporations become subject to democratic scrutiny. Whether in the economic or environmental areas, corporations may be scrutinized by groups of citizens and may find it more productive and useful to expend their "political" resources in media and public relations strategies.

Similarly, social movements may find it more important to influence society than to influence the state per se. The women's movement in many countries has fought for equality with men, a battle very far from over, especially in certain areas of the world. While the state's actions are important in this respect, the movement has also aimed to change public opinion on this issue. Governments may mandate gender equality, but legal rules and regulations are unlikely to make a difference unless citizens believe in them.

Finally, group and movement organizations may provide information and legitimacy to governments and to international organizations. Government may encourage the formation and establishment of groups and movements. Even where governments and organizations have not actually encouraged the establishment of groups or movements, they may promote their involvement in the policy process.

Why? There are two main reasons governments and international organizations might actually welcome input, even pressure, from group and movement organizations. First, in both democratic and nondemocratic states, governments need to know what their citizens think. Groups may provide a barometer of public opinion. Further, precisely because interest groups and social movements bring together citizens with a sense of common interests or a common identity, they are in a position to provide targeted information to governments or international organizations regarding the views of their constituencies on given policies or issues. Governments may wish to know what a given group thinks about a specific issue. If a government wished to know farmers' views on an international trade agreement that was under negotiation, the fastest way would be to ask farmers' groups.

Group and movement organizations may also provide technical information to government and international organizations. In some cases, it may be cheaper for governments and organizations to obtain information from groups and movement organizations than to collect the data themselves.

While such data might be tainted by the groups' putting their own claims in the best possible light, governments and international organizations could still find such information useful.

For example, if the government of Botswana wanted to update its information about water availability and quality in villages, it could send out its own inspectors to obtain this data. One could imagine that the task of sending such inspectors to villages would be very expensive and labour-intensive. So instead, the government might seek this information from farmers' organizations and from traditional village leaders. Such civil society organizations and networks would have access to excellent information on water availability and quality, as might NGOs working in the field of development. An NGO that had worked in many parts of the country at the village level might be able to give the government updated information on water. Although NGOs, farmers' groups, or village leaders could provide information that reflects their interests and experience, it might be cheaper and more efficient for government to use the information provided by these groups rather than to collect the information from scratch.

A second reason governments and international organizations might encourage the formation and participation of group and movement organizations in the policy process is that such participation may enhance the **legitimacy** of governments or international organizations. When group or movement organizations participate in the process of policy formation, they send the message that the governments or international organizations with whom they are collaborating are legitimate political actors. If governments can secure the agreement of group or movement organizations to specific policies, those policies will more likely be viewed positively by the public. For example, in almost any democratic system, a government that brings down a budget or economic plan will provoke reactions from economic groups such as business, labour, and farmer groups, as well as from others. If every economic group in the country from farmers to business condemns the budget or plan, it is unlikely the public will support it. The same phenomenon exists in other policy areas. President George W. Bush's plan to open up the Arctic National Wildlife Reserve to drilling was condemned by environmental groups, undermining Bush's support among Americans who cared about the environment.

These dynamics are reinforced by the media, which tend to seek out groups and movement organizations that can provide reactions to government initiatives. In this process, some groups—those with economic and media expertise and resources—are better able to exert such influence. Also, the media tend to reinforce existing definitions and concepts of the interests and identities at stake in any given area. For example, economic policy is defined as being of interest to groups that are clearly economic, such as business, labour, and farmers. However, development NGOs, antipoverty groups, and women's groups might all argue that they have a stake as well.

Furthermore, how well a particular group or movement organization can lend legitimacy to government depends in turn on its own legitimacy and visibility in the public eye. Legitimacy and visibility depend on the characteristics of the group or movement organization and the political, social, and economic context in which it operates. In any given context, opponents may attempt to de-legitimate or undermine the group or movement through a wide variety of tactics, from questioning how well it represents the constituency it champions to accusing its leaders of political corruption.

Types of Interest Groups and Social Movements

Interest groups and social movements may be classified into types. When considering these, it is important to remember that such typologies are just approximations of the complex and rich reality of group politics in diverse contexts.

At the beginning of this chapter, we saw that interest groups are more organized than social movements and tend to use more conventional means to achieve their goals; social movements are looser networks of activists who may use unconventional methods such as demonstrations (see Table 12.1). One way to imagine the variety of possible groups and movements is to use a continuum, with social movements on one end and interest groups on the other.

Interest Groups

The continuum is based on degree of organization. At one end, we have groups, known as *latent groups*, that have no formal organization whatsoever. For example, no organization represents "all taxpayers" collectively. Some organizations might claim to represent their interests and put forth goals and values that purportedly serve them; but "all taxpayers" are not, as such, organized into a formal group in any country. Hence, the category "all taxpayers" is a latent group. Other important latent groups are consumers and the unemployed. Although members of both groups have significant interests in common, neither is organized.

In contrast, some groups are highly organized. In most countries, people that have a stake in business, farming, or labour are organized into **institutionalized groups**, which represent the interests of their members and attempt to influence government policy. In democratic countries, such groups may have very long histories. In many European countries, the employers' federations (or business groups) date back to the late 19th century.

Institutionalized groups are characterized by a permanent organization. This means they have the economic and other resources necessary to sustain ongoing organization. In many cases, institutionalized groups employ professionals to carry out some of the work of the group. In some institutionalized groups, political goals may be secondary to their primary function. For example, religious organizations might have as their first purpose spiritual or religious goals. Yet they may also have political goals, such as to protect the status of their religion within the state, to pursue particular tax or legal advantages in the education system, or to promote strong views on family and gender-related policies such as abortion and birth control or strong preferences in foreign policy. Institutionalized groups also tend to use conventional means to achieve their goals—for example, lobbying politicians or entering into consultations with governments. At times, groups may press their case through legal action or by joining forces with political parties.

The more institutionalized interest groups are also characterized by the nature of their goals. Because these groups use conventional strategies, their goals also tend to follow a pattern. In general, they pursue goals that are easily negotiable: they seek more or less of something rather than profound change. For example, regulation and tax policies are divisible—they can be increased or decreased marginally—and hence negotiable; an institutionalized group might

Table 12.1 Types of Groups and Movements

Institutionalized Groups		Social Movement Organizations
	General Features	
Division of labour		Networked
Narrow goals		Broad goals
Well organized		Loosely organized
Formal structure		Informal structure
Many resources		Few resources
State-oriented		Society-oriented
	Examples	
Canadian Federation of Agriculture		Égale (gay and lesbian rights)
Canadian Council of Chief Executives		National Action Committee on the Status of Women (NAC)

advocate a specific regulatory or tax policy that will benefit its constituency. If the group is demanding that certain types of taxes be lowered, taxes can be reduced by a greater or lesser amount. Governments can at least go partway toward meeting the group's aspirations. In this sense, the goals of the group fit with the language and assumptions of government and can be dealt with by politicians and civil servants.

In order to support all of this organization, institutionalized groups tend to have access to a stable base of economic resources. Business and professional groups charge their members a substantial fee to join and are able to sustain themselves in this manner. Groups that represent less affluent constituencies may create a stable base of funding by charging a large group a smaller membership fee. Farmers' groups and trade unions are good examples of such groups.

In some cases, groups may receive funding from governments that are interested in the creation and maintenance of organizations representing certain societal interests. In many European countries, for example, governments fund community groups at the local level in hopes that they will help spark urban renewal in areas with social problems and high crime rates. These community organizations become part of consultative processes with governments over urban policy and problems. In other cases, funding may be withdrawn from groups that disagree with the governments. For interest groups and social movement organizations, government funding may be a double-edged sword. While providing a stable base for the organizations' work, it may also hinder their ability to speak freely and influence policy in the best interests of their members.

In Canada, there has been a lively debate over whether the federal government should fund groups that disagree with it.[4] Politicians in the Canadian Alliance and Progressive Conservative parties had argued that government should not fund interest groups that were critics of the government. In this view, it only gives the governments' critics more ammunition to disagree with and undermine policy. When the Conservatives were elected in January 2006, one of their first acts was to cut funding to the Court Challenges Program, which funds litigation on *Charter* issues, and to review funding to other social groups. On the other hand, the Canadian government under the leadership of the Liberal Party had become interested in the idea of institutionalizing links with certain civil society groups with the aim of strengthening their place in society. During a period in which government had been expected to do less, not more, and in which large-scale state intervention was out of favour, it was thought government might benefit from downloading tasks to interest groups and from developing a consultative partnership with such groups. In Canada, Australia, and most of the European democracies, state funding of group life is practised to some extent. In the United States, in contrast, groups do not benefit from such systematic state funding.

Social Movements

Moving to the other end of our continuum, social movements tend to be less organized, to use less conventional means, and to have less easily negotiable goals than institutionalized groups. In place of the permanent and professional organization of the institutionalized group, social movements are often composed of networks of activists. These networks may be linked in part by informal ties rather than by large professional organizations.

Social movements often begin life with very broad goals, which may be based on assumptions that are very different from the assumptions of policymakers and power holders. Movements may demand democracy from authoritarian regimes (e.g., democracy movements in the former Eastern bloc and across many developing countries during the 1980s and 1990s), an end to foreign occupation and domination (e.g., anticolonial movements and the Palestinian *intifada*), an end to race-based laws (e.g., the South African anti-apartheid movement), an end to rampant economic growth (e.g., the deep ecology and radical environmental movements in industrialized countries), or peace in a time of war (e.g., the movement against the wars in Iraq and Afghanistan). In these cases, the goals are often not easily negotiable with governments or elites. Even in stable democracies, demands for human rights (e.g., made by the women's movement) or environmental protection may be difficult to negotiate with governments and power holders. In many cases, the goals sought are not easily divisible.

Social movements may have goals that differ profoundly from those of governments. In particular, such movements commonly aim to influence society as well as the state. As mentioned, the women's movement has been concerned with influencing social attitudes as much as changing policy. Further, as politics increasingly moves out to the global level, some organizations have goals that reach beyond the borders of the nation-state—they may aim to influence the policies of other states. Human rights groups such as Amnesty International organize themselves across borders in order to do so. Other groups may try to influence the policies of international organizations. The antiglobalization movement has had an effect on opening up the WTO and the International Monetary Fund (IMF) to greater involvement by NGOs.

Over time, social movements may be tempted to moderate their goals to gain influence with states and international organizations. Some environmental groups may even try to make common cause with government to influence policy. Of course, in addition to influencing states or international organizations, social movements may also aim to influence civil society. For example, some environmental groups might choose to try to change consumer or corporate behaviour directly.

Social movement organizations often use unconventional means to achieve their goals. These means may include demonstrations, such as those that have occurred in recent years in the antiglobalization movement. The civil rights movement in the United States, drawing its inspiration in part from the anticolonial struggles in India and elsewhere, used the strategies of nonviolence to achieve its goals. Civil disobedience, sit-ins, and marches were used to dramatize and challenge the segregationist laws of the southern U.S. states during the 1950s and 1960s. At times, governments may react with violence to such protest, as when state authorities in the United States attacked civil rights protesters in southern cities or police forces used tear gas and arrests against antiglobalization protesters.

Another means of influence that may be employed by social movements is direct action, as we saw in the example of Greenpeace. The technique is based on the assumption that changing government policies may not be the most efficient way to achieve a political goal. Direct action has been common in the environmental movement over the past 30 years and, as a strategy, has been publicized best by Greenpeace. The organization has intervened directly to stop environmental damage across the globe as in the case of logging. Other environmental organizations, such as Earth First!, have engaged in tree spiking, that is, hammering a spike into, and then marking, a tree to prevent it from being cut down. At times, such tactics can veer into the realm of violence. Most commentators view organizations that systematically engage in violence as not really social movements but ones engaged in armed struggle.

Social movements are also organized differently from institutionalized interest groups. They tend to function as networks of activists, who may be brought together by shared interests, identities, and values but may not actually belong to formal organizations. Where organizations form, their members may overlap with those of informal networks. Social movement organizations are typically smaller than those of institutionalized interest groups and have fewer economic resources.

The two ends of our continuum of group and movement organizations represent different **organizational cultures**. Social movements and their attendant social movement organizations spring from a political culture that is populist, emphasizing democratic participation in the decisions and actions of the group or network. An important and sizable sector of social movement organizations springs from progressive or left-wing politics; as a result, they share the political cultural heritage of such politics. For example, social movement organizations may make decisions by consensus, allowing each member of the group or each member of the decision-making cadre to approve or veto group decisions.

In contrast, some institutionalized groups share an organizational culture that is markedly different in many ways from the social movement culture. This culture emphasizes majoritarian decision-making rather than consensus decision-making; that is, decisions are made by majority rule rather than by consensus. Further, institutionalized groups, by their very nature, embrace the division of labour. Members may play a passive rather than a participatory role, and professionals often dominate the organization.

The differences between institutionalized interest groups and the social movements that have been highlighted on our continuum represent generalizations about the real-world shape and behaviour of civil society actors. The reality of associational life is much more complex. For example, over time, social movement organizations may take on some of the characteristics of the institutionalized interest group. Some environmental groups have been involved in extensive consultation with government and have developed many of the professional attributes of the institutionalized group, despite their origins in social movement organizing. At times, institutionalized groups may even deploy the tactics of the social movement. Farmers' organizations, for example, have been known to engage in direct action, demonstrations, and occupations in pursuit of their goals. This last example shows the importance of viewing civil society actors in historical context. In most countries, farmers' organizations began as social movements. Similarly, trade unions, usually defined as part of the universe of the stable, institutionalized groups, began as social movements and often deploy the ultimate weapon of direct action—the strike—in pursuit of their goals. The U.S. civil rights movement used the sit-in, demonstration, and other tactics of civil disobedience to bring segregation to an end. Similarly, the anti–Vietnam War movement of the 1960s and the anti–Iraq War movement of today have both used massive demonstrations as means of bringing public attention to their point of view. In the map here, BBC News Online shows the sites and numbers of people involved in the global protest against the Iraq War in 2003.

Anti-War Protests on February 15-16, 2003.

Source: BBC News Online (http://news.bbc.co.uk/2/hi/ europe/2765215.stm#map)

Groups and Movements in Public Policy

It is now time to discuss more systematically the means groups and movements have at their disposal to influence government and society.

Influencing Politicians

Perhaps the most obvious and visible way groups may influence the shaping of public policy in democratic systems is through bringing pressure to bear on politicians. In most democratic countries, the legislature is by definition the key forum for lawmaking; hence, it might seem natural for groups to seek out politicians to champion their views.

However, the influence groups are able to exercise through the legislature depends on the legislature's role within the political institutions of the country. As noted in preceding chapters, legislatures are more important in some democratic systems than in others. In parliamentary systems, which are common in much of the democratic political world, legislative and executive power are fused, in the sense that the executive (prime minister and cabinet) is responsible to the legislature and must have the support of the legislature in order to govern. In practice, however, the members of the legislature are loyal to their political parties. The political party that wins the general election forms the government, and for most of the duration of the government's term in office, the prime minister and the cabinet are able to dominate the business of the legislature.

The extent to which prime ministers and their cabinets dominate legislatures in parliamentary systems does vary. In some cases, such as Britain, MPs tend to serve long terms in office and to develop policy expertise; parties allow their MPs some latitude so that the MP can actually play an independent role in lawmaking. In other systems, such as Canada's, there is a higher turnover of MPs and a great concentration of power in the hands of the prime minister and the cabinet; MPs do not have much influence in lawmaking, at least in a majority government situation.

Yet another important difference among parliamentary systems is the type of electoral system used. In the first-past-the-post system, used in Canada and Britain, the candidate with the most votes wins the election, which tends to favour one-party majority governments. In Germany, Italy, and many of the northern European democracies, the system of proportional representation allocates seats in the legislature in part according to the proportion of votes received by each party. In this system, it is rare for one party to have a majority on its own; most of the time, these countries are governed by coalitions.

In presidential systems, such as that of the United States, there is a separation of powers between the legislature and the executive. In contrast to the parliamentary model, the president and the congress are elected independently, and the tenure of the president does not rest on his or her party's dominance of the congress. President Bill Clinton, a Democrat, ruled with a Republican-dominated Congress, while President George W. Bush governed with a Republican House of Representatives and a Senate that changed hands between the two parties. After the Democratic Party's success in the midterm elections of 2006, President Bush had to serve out the final two years of his presidency with a Congress dominated by Democrats. This system of divided government means that **party discipline** is not as strong as in parliamentary systems. Cross-party coalitions between Democrats and Republicans often form, and individual members of Congress have much more latitude to make their own decisions about lawmaking.

These political institutional differences play a very important role in determining how interest groups and social movement organizations lobby members of the legislature or the executive. In first-past-the-post parliamentary systems, such as those of Britain and Canada, attempting to influence the legislature is not a very effective strategy for interest-group and social movement organizations, since MPs do not have much independence in the development of public policy. In the proportional representation system, similarly, lobbying individual MPs is not likely to have a direct influence on policy formation. In such a system, the parties reach agreement by negotiating among themselves behind closed doors, which tends to decrease the possibility of direct group influence on individual members of the legislature.

In the presidential system, such as the U.S. system with its separation of powers, the situation is quite different. Because of the freedom from party discipline of the individual members of Congress, that body is ripe for group influence. Indeed, the United States is the home of pressure group politics, as groups and organizations vie with each other to exercise influence in the Congress.

Another means by which interest groups and social movement organizations may influence politicians is through exerting pressure in electoral politics. In the U.S. system, there is a lack of regulation of campaign finances, which means that groups and social movement organizations can influence the political process by giving money to politicians for their reelection campaigns. Groups often do this through the formation of **political action committees (PACs)**, whose express purpose is to donate to political campaigns and to influence the views of parties and politicians on issues of import to the group (see Figure 12.1). Such a system obviously favours groups with plenty of resources.

Because of the influence wielded by groups in election campaigns, campaign finance reform is a major issue in U.S. politics. There have been lively debates about the selling of access to decision-makers. Bill Clinton was accused of selling off guest invitations for overnight visits to the White House (e.g., in the Lincoln bedroom) in return for donations from groups that contributed to his campaigns, while George W. Bush was beholden to a variety of corporate interests.

In parliamentary systems, influence through the electoral system takes different forms. In some cases, groups have formed parties to put forth their views. Trade

"MY GREATEST ASSET IS I'M SO RICH, I CAN'T BE BOUGHT BY ANY INTEREST GROUP."

Rich candidate can't be bought by lobby groups.

Harley Schwadron/Artizans

Figure 12.1   Top 20 PAC Contributors to Federal Candidates, 2005–2006*

PAC Name	Total Amount	Democrat Percentage	Republican Percentage
National Association of Realtors	$3,752,005	49	51
National Beer Wholesalers Association	$2,946,500	31	69
National Association of Home Builders	$2,900,000	26	73
National Auto Dealers Association	$2,821,600	30	70
International Brotherhood of Electrical Workers	$2,796,875	97	3
Operating Engineers Union	$2,784,435	78	21
American Bankers Association	$2,748,299	36	64
Laborers Union	$2,687,150	85	15
American Association for Justice	$2,558,000	96	3
Credit Union National Association	$2,412,853	45	54
AT&T Inc.	$2,341,683	34	66
Carpenters & Joiners Union	$2,293,923	74	25
United Parcel Service	$2,239,128	32	67
United Auto Workers	$2,220,350	99	1
American Federation of Teachers	$2,113,448	99	1
Teamsters Union	$2,085,100	91	8
American Federation of State/County/ Municipal Employees	$2,048,683	98	1
American Medical Association	$2,011,634	31	69
Plumbers/Pipefitters Union	$1,946,100	91	9
International Association of Fire Fighters	$1,872,105	72	27

* For ease of identification, the names used in this section are those of the organization connected with the PAC, rather than the official PAC name. For example, the "Coca-Cola Company Nonpartisan Committee for Good Government" is simply listed as "Coca-Cola Co." Totals include subsidiaries and affiliated PACs, if any. Based on data released by the FEC on Monday, June 4, 2007.

Source: "Top 20 PAC Contributors to Federal Candidates, 2005–2006" (table), OpenSecrets.org (The Center for Responsive Politics); available at http://www.opensecrets.org/bigpicture/toppacs.php?cycle=2006; accessed June 4, 2008.

unions in many countries played an important role in the creation of socialist and social democratic parties such as the British Labour Party. Business groups often have close but informal ties with right-of-centre political parties. Green parties have been formed in many democracies to put forth the environmental point of view, and in some countries (e.g., Germany), these parties have been quite successful. In Iceland, the Women's Party was formed to advocate **feminist** views. Groups may also attempt to gain influence within an existing political party. Pro-life and evangelical Christians play an important role in the Republican party in the United States and to some extent played one in the Canadian Alliance.

Influencing the Bureaucracy

In most societies, the **bureaucracy** plays a very important role in the formation and implementation of public policy. Civil servants often wield a decisive influence over government action, partly because civil servants in many states are experts in their fields. Even in democracies in which civil servants are expected to be accountable to democratically elected politicians, they may still have much influence because of their expertise, stability, and longevity in government positions. This is particularly true of the merit-based bureaucracy, in which civil servants are selected for their positions on their merits rather than on their political connections. In authoritarian systems, civil servants may be chosen in part for their political connections, particularly to the party in power.

In any case, in most contexts, influencing the bureaucracy is one of the most effective means for groups to influence public policy. It is important to note that this strategy works best for institutionalized groups, which have the resources, the money, and the expertise to develop stable relationships over time with government bureaucrats. In both democratic and authoritarian systems, governments may cultivate these relationships for the reasons outlined earlier, namely in order to obtain valuable political or technical information from these groups and to use the groups to legitimate the policies of government.

In many democratic systems such as Canada, the United States, and Britain, relationships between interest groups and bureaucrats are so close that these groups and the bureaucracy are involved in institutionalized patterns of relationships and form what scholars call a **policy community**. Groups and the bureaucracy mutually influence each other and collaborate in the formation of public policy. This does not necessarily mean that groups dictate public policy; in some cases, groups may be dominated by government priorities, while in others, groups may indeed play an influential part in policy formation.

The pattern of relationships between groups and the civil service varies depending on the type of regime and the type of political institutions in place. In authoritarian political systems and in new and fragile democracies, such as Russia, the civil service may be weakened or even corrupted by links to organized crime, making institutionalized group relationships of the type described here impossible. Access may depend solely upon elite connections. In other cases, the civil service may be dominated by appointees of a particular political party, as was the case in Mexico with the dominant party prior to the election of Vicente Fox in 2000. In this case, social groups were institutionalized within the party and dominated by party elites.

Influence Through Lobbying

Those who wish to influence government may choose to do so by hiring professional **lobbyists** to do the job on their behalf. Interest groups may choose this approach if they feel they are unlikely on their own to secure access to the relevant department of government or to the policies that will shape legislation. Corporations or groups of corporations with similar interests may choose this approach because they can afford to pay for lobbying by professionals.

Ottawa-based Hillwatch Inc., for example, provides a list of its current and past clients, as well as samples of its work, on its website at http://www.hillwatch.com/About_Us/Clients.aspx. The list shows the type of work lobbyists undertake; it includes different levels of government (e.g., the City of Ottawa), utilities from outside of Canada (e.g., the New York Power Authority), embassies of foreign governments (e.g., the Embassy of Japan), interest groups that represent particular economic sectors (e.g., the Ontario Lumber Manufacturers' Association), and large corporations (e.g., Nestlé Canada, Paramount Communications, and Honeywell Canada).

Lobbying is effective for those who have relatively narrow and well-defined goals with respect to issues that affect a specific industry, such as levels of taxation or regulations. Tobacco companies, for example, have hired professional lobbyists to influence the Canadian government on advertising. They have also hired lawyers to pursue their interests through the courts, arguing that restrictions on tobacco advertising constituted an unconstitutional limit on free expression under the *Charter of Rights and Freedoms*. Lobbying and the use of courts to advance policy goals are similar in that professionals (lobbyists, lawyers, or both) are hired for the express purpose of securing political influence.

Many observers have recognized that lobbyists pose a threat to the democratic process. Because lobbyists are hired by those with money, they may give corporations and well-funded interest groups an advantage in the political process. In recognition of this, some countries have regulated paid lobbying. In Canada, lobbying is regulated by the 1989 *Lobbyists Registration Act*. Lobbyists must register and provide information about each of their efforts undertaken to influence government. Unfortunately, the act does not have much in the way of enforcement mechanisms. Under the Chrétien government, the federal ethics counsellor might report on breaches of the code but, being appointed by the prime minister, he was under fire for failure to stand up to the government. In a most unsavoury demonstration of lobbyist behaviour, all major contenders for the Liberal party leadership in 2003 had lobbyists playing major roles in their campaigns, especially Paul Martin. At the same time, many of these lobbyists continued to agitate in their candidate's department on behalf of their clients. When the Conservatives were elected in 2006, they put into place the *Federal Accountability Act*, which created a new Commissioner of Lobbying as an independent officer of Parliament. Nonetheless, many critics argue that the act does not go far enough.

Influencing the Courts

In democratic societies, the courts also provide a venue for interest groups to exert influence. As in the case of politicians and the bureaucracy, the opportunities for influencing the courts depend on the specific shape of political institutions and the role courts play in the political system. In Britain, for example, groups traditionally have not had much influence on public policy through the courts. Without a written constitution and judicial review, groups did not have strong legal tools to force changes in government policies. Britain's membership in the European Union is changing the role of courts in the British political system, however. Increasingly, groups are turning to European courts, such as the European Court of Human Rights and the European Court of Justice, to influence the British political system. Recent issues in which British laws have been influenced by European court decisions include assisted suicide for the terminally ill and equality of the sexes in entitlement for government benefits.[5]

In the United States, judicial review has formed part of the constitution from an early period. Groups and social movement organizations in the United States often turn to the courts to influence public policies. There are many examples of such influence. Two of the most well-known are the women's movement securing the right to abortion in *Roe v. Wade* in 1973 and the African-American civil rights movement ending segregation of the school system in *Brown v. Board of Education* in 1954.[6]

In Canada, venues for group influence through the courts were weak before the entrenchment of the *Charter of Rights and Freedoms* in the Canadian constitution in 1982. Since then, many groups have turned to the courts, using the *Charter*'s rights guarantees and other provisions of the 1982 Constitution (such as Aboriginal rights' guarantees in Section 35) to achieve important policy objectives. Political scientist Gregory Hein has studied these group efforts to influence public policy through the courts, and his tabulation of frequency of recourse to the courts by different groups in society appears in Figure 12.2. The data show that recourse to the courts has increased across different groups in society, although corporations use the courts far more frequently than other groups. In fact, as noted above, corporations have persuaded the Supreme Court that such *Charter* rights as freedom of expression should be extended to themselves! Hein concludes that "interest group litigation is ... an established form of collective action"[7] in Canada.

Influencing the Media

The success of collective actors in challenging government policy or seeking to influence social norms and values may be greatly enhanced through the skilful use of the media. In particular, when groups seek to influence politicians and elections, the media provide a vehicle for drawing public attention to the groups' point of view. In the cases of gun control, abortion, and lesbian and gay rights, supporters and opponents on each issue attempted to capture the media's attention as a way of bringing pressure to bear on MPs. Because media such as television tend to focus on dramatic conflicts within a limited time frame, groups that can successfully produce quick sound bites tend to receive more attention than collective actors attempting to call attention to the structural forces that shape government policy or societal norms. In the case of environmentalism, for example, a wide variety of deep ecology perspectives emphasize that economic development in many parts of the world threatens humanity's survival. However, complex scientific and philosophical arguments

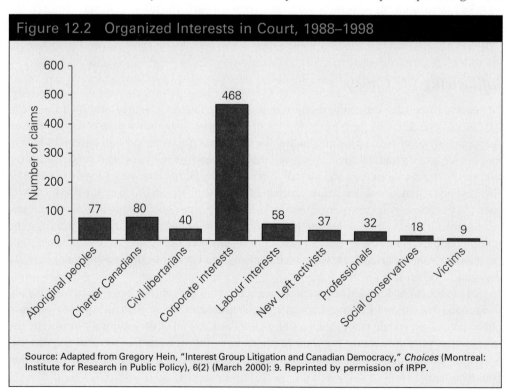

Figure 12.2 Organized Interests in Court, 1988–1998

Source: Adapted from Gregory Hein, "Interest Group Litigation and Canadian Democracy," *Choices* (Montreal: Institute for Research in Public Policy), 6(2) (March 2000): 9. Reprinted by permission of IRPP.

about deep ecology are unlikely to produce the quick media sound bites that television demands. Hence, successful environmental groups have often sought to dramatize environmental issues in ways that can be captured easily for global media consumption. As Stephen Dale has pointed out, Greenpeace is a master of media tactics. By sailing into the U.S. nuclear test site in the Aleutian Islands in 1971, a tiny band of protesters was able to draw worldwide media attention to the test. This was Greenpeace's start; from a few protesters in an old fishing boat, it grew to an international organization with a budget of US$28.3 million by 1994.[8]

Influence at the Transnational Level

Globalization has had important effects on the mobilization of groups and movements. More than ever, public policy is subject to pressures from beyond the borders of one country. Enhanced communications technology facilitates links between groups across borders, while international organizations ranging from the WTO to the UN play an increased role in the making of policy decisions. Regional economic and political integration, as in the European Union, create new transborder policies. Trade agreements, such as the North American Free Trade Agreement (NAFTA), limit the range of policy choices open to governments. This process of "decentring" the state, as Warren Magnusson has termed it, has been characterized by a marked increase in **transnational group** activity in recent years, as is shown in Table 12.2.[9] The table shows the extent to which various types of transnational advocacy groups have grown over the past few decades.

Interest groups and social movement organizations may appeal to international organizations to pressure their own state, or they may form alliances with other groups outside their own state. This may occur when groups have failed in their efforts to achieve positive results through domestic strategies alone. For example, pro-democracy and human rights activists in South Africa were successful in mobilizing international organizations and public opinion to overthrow the apartheid regime. In the last 20 years, First Nations in Canada have developed links with Indigenous peoples around the world, especially through the World Council of Indigenous Peoples. Another example of transnational linkages was the campaign to stop the OECD's Multilateral Agreement on Investment (MAI), a proposed investment treaty. Over 500 NGOs from 67 countries signed a joint statement condemning the MAI; this concentrated effort was widely credited with delaying the ratification of the accord in 1997.[10] Christina Gabriel and Laura Macdonald have demonstrated that, in the wake of NAFTA, incipient linkages are developing between feminist activists in Canada and Mexico, as women attempt to deal with the economic, social, and political consequences of North American economic restructuring.[11]

Interest groups and social movement organizations within one country may mobilize to influence politics elsewhere in the world, targeting foreign states or international organizations in an effort to influence the behaviour, policies, and practices of foreign states and international actors. One of the best examples of this was mentioned above: the campaign against South Africa's apartheid regime, in which many solidarity groups from other states, international organizations, private companies, and other institutions in developed democracies sprang up to put pressure on South Africa. For example, the divestment campaign in North America and Europe pressured social institutions such as universities to cancel their investments in companies doing business with the country. International pressure played a key role in instituting change.[12]

The antiglobalization protests of the past few years have had important effects on how multilateral economic institutions function. According to Robert O'Brien and his colleagues, the labour, women's, and environmental movements have all had a very important impact. Organizations such as the IMF, the WTO, and the World Bank have responded to such pressure. Scholars argue that transnational social movement advocacy is creating a new and complex form of global governance as political issues move from the domestic to the

Table 12.2 International Nongovernmental Social Change Organizations

Issue Area	1953		1963		1973		1983		1993	
	Number	Percentage*	Number	Percentage	Number	Percentage	Number	Percentage	Number	Percentage
Human rights	33	30.0	38	27.0	41	22.4	79	22.7	168	26.6
World order	8	7.3	4	2.8	12	6.6	31	8.9	48	7.6
International law	14	12.7	19	13.4	25	13.7	26	7.4	26	4.1
Peace	11	10.0	20	14.2	14	7.7	22	6.3	59	9.4
Women's rights	10	9.1	14	9.9	16	8.7	25	7.2	61	9.7
Environment	2	1.8	5	3.5	10	5.5	26	7.5	90	14.3
Development	3	2.7	3	2.1	7	3.8	13	3.7	34	5.4
Ethnic unity/group rights	10	9.1	122	8.5	18	9.8	37	10.6	29	4.6
Esperanto	11	10.0	18	12.8	28	15.3	41	11.8	54	8.6

* The percentages in any one decade do not add up to 100 because groups that champion other causes have not been included.

Source: Adapted from Margaret E. Keck and Kathryn Sikkink, eds., *Activists Beyond Borders: Advocacy Networks in International Politics* (Ithaca and London: Cornell University Press, 1998), p. 11. © 1998 by Cornell University. Used by permission of the publisher, Cornell University Press.

international and global levels.[13] In this sense, the contestation and social movement tactics we have seen on television at antiglobalization protests such as those in Seattle in 1999 and Quebec City in 2001 are counterbalanced by the actions of more institutionalized groups, which serve some of the same functions for international institutions and for multilateral economic organizations as we have identified at the domestic level. While the social movements protest in the streets and put pressure on such organizations through the media, the more established groups are developing institutionalized relationships with these organizations. As on the domestic level, interest groups at the international level provide international organizations and institutions with information about complex areas of public policy. Also at the domestic level, transnational advocacy groups lend legitimacy to the actions of international organizations such as the World Bank and the IMF. In an era of heightened and increasingly competitive and globalized media scrutiny, special-interest social movement groups are valuable potential allies for such international organizations.

Box 12.2 shows how a domestic crisis with external causes—the September 11 tragedy in the United States—can affect domestic interest-group behaviour. On the other hand, now that the less-than-unanimous U.S. invasion of Iraq has somewhat superseded 9/11 on the presidential agenda, such groups are less inhibited in their activities.

Are Interest Groups Too Powerful?

Are interest groups and social movement organizations too powerful? In the media, one often hears the view, at both the domestic and the international level, that special-interest groups should not be able to dominate policymaking. This debate revolves around the question of democratic legitimacy. Are groups and social movements legitimate representatives of citizens, thus advancing the process of democratization? Or do they pervert and distort the process by using money and other illegitimate means to pursue their interests? Do such groups and movements reflect or impede the spirit and practice of democracy?

Which side we take on this question may well depend upon the context. In an undemocratic system such as Mexico's before the Fox election, we might favour the mobilization of societal interests to facilitate the transition to democracy. In recent years many mobilizations have pushed forward democratic transitions, as noted in Chapter 14. In Eastern Europe's struggle against communism, in the Philippines' "people power" movement, and in South Africa's anti-apartheid movement, we see street power, demonstrations, and other tactics of social movement protest bringing about democracy. Even in existing authoritarian regimes, groups may play an important role in permitting channels for the expression of public opinion between citizens and the state. Such channels, though likely narrow and circumscribed, are even more important in the absence of free elections.

Furthermore, many scholars believe interest groups and social movement organizations are essential to the healthy functioning of democratic political institutions, and a prerequisite to the establishment of democracy. In the 19th century, observers such as Alexis de Tocqueville (in his famous book, *Democracy in America*) and French sociologist Émile Durkheim argued that democratic political institutions required the healthy soil of associational and group life in order to flourish. Some scholars have argued that societies in which interest groups and social movements do not exist or in which they have been weakened by a strong and repressive state (e.g., Russia) may find it difficult to make democracy work.[14]

On the other hand, in capitalist democracies, the power of groups and movements may in part depend upon their access to money. Left-wing and populist critiques of group involvement in democratic politics emphasize how business groups may use their financial resources to access and influence political elites. By this view, in a market society the playing field is not

Following the September 11, 2001, attack on the World Trade Center and other U.S. targets, interest groups in the United States began to back off from the business-as-usual approach, as the following article shows.

> Several influential U.S. environment groups have silenced their criticism of the U.S. government and stopped lobbying for conservation measures because of the terrorist attacks on New York and Washington.
>
> The Sierra Club, one of the largest U.S. environmental groups, last week dropped all of its work challenging Bush administration policies. Greenpeace, known for its high-profile environmental campaigns using civil disobedience, has also decided to take a lower profile.
>
> The terrorist attacks have rattled the leaders of environmental organizations and made them wary of being viewed as divisive and unpatriotic while the country faces a national trauma.
>
> As well, the attacks have swept environmental issues off the political agenda.
>
> "We lost the stomach, both personally and individually, for some of the fights we had been engaged in prior to that," Craig Culp, a spokesman for Greenpeace in the United States, said.
>
> The decision by the groups to play down activism could have implications on a number of pressing public-policy issues, including the U.S. response to global warming, the opening up of Alaska's Arctic wildlife reserve to oil drilling and the development of the Star Wars missile-defence system.
>
> Until the attacks, environmentalists had been on a roll. They had launched highly effective attacks on the Bush administration on issues ranging from the higher arsenic levels allowed in drinking water to the government's failure to endorse the Kyoto pact on global warming.
>
> The administration had inadvertently become a boon to conservation groups, which were successfully using the government's anti-environmental policies as tools to raise funds and to mobilize their members.
>
> But with the terrorism crisis, those campaigns became unexpected collateral damage.
>
> The head of the Sierra Club, Carl Pope, issued a statement shortly after the attacks saying his group was going to pause because of the country's national-security crisis and unsettled public mood....

SOURCE: Martin Mittelstaedt, "Environmental Groups Drop Campaign Criticizing Bush," *The Globe and Mail*, September 21, 2001, p. A8. Reprinted with permission from *The Globe and Mail*.

level for interest-group and social movement activity; certain groups have more power than others because of their ability to mobilize economic resources. Many argue that interest-group activity during election campaigns should be limited because of the fact that monied groups (such as the PACs in the United States) can circumvent election spending laws and influence election outcomes. From a right-wing perspective, it is sometimes argued that certain minority groups have too much power and have been able to influence public policy against the interests of the democratic majority. Right-wing critics of interest-group and social movement activism often point to feminism as an example of a negative identity politics that has produced public policy outcomes that ignore the wishes of the majority.

CONCLUSION

Debates over the power of groups and movements as political actors go to the heart of the question of the nature of political power itself. How is such power exercised? Who has it and who doesn't? Who should have it? Should politics be restricted to politicians? How can citizens engage in democratic deliberation, and how can group politics and associational life facilitate citizen engagement? There are no easy answers. These questions extend from the realm of political debates in any one country into the international arena as groups increasingly overlap across borders in the new political spaces of our globalized world.

DISCUSSION QUESTIONS

1. Choose one social movement organization or interest group. Trace its attempts to influence public policy.

2. Are demonstrations and civil disobedience a legitimate means of influencing public opinion and public policy?

3. Should interest groups and social movement organizations have the right to spend money during election campaigns?

4. What are the main similarities and differences between institutionalized interest groups and social movement networks?

KEY TERMS

CIVIL SOCIETY: Social institutions and organizations that are independent of the state and in which citizens pursue their interests, express their beliefs, and live in communities. (349)

CONTENTIOUS POLITICS: Protests that take the form of disruption of the normal activities of society, such as demonstrations and civil disobedience. (349)

INTEREST GROUP: A group that brings together people with common interests and/or a common sense of identity for the purpose of influencing the political process. (349)

LEGITIMACY: The degree to which citizens accept and tolerate the actions and decisions of social and political actors such as governments, states, international organizations, and civil society groups themselves, usually based on the notion that the decision-makers have a right to such power. (353)

NONGOVERNMENTAL ORGANIZATION (NGO): A non-profit organization that is not part of the state and is not a private corporation. Usually, the term is used to describe organizations that operate across borders in areas such as peace, development, human rights, and international affairs. (350)

ORGANIZATIONAL CULTURE: Clusters of beliefs about the way groups should be organized. Examples are a belief in hierarchy or in internal democracy. (356)

POLICY COMMUNITY: A collection of groups and individuals (including both state bureaucrats and interest groups or social movement organizations) who influence each other in an effort to shape policy outcomes in their area of interest. (360)

SOCIAL MOVEMENT: An informal network of activists who seek to transform the values of society. (349)

TRANSNATIONAL GROUP: A group that organizes across the borders of nation-states with the aim of influencing national governments, international organizations, or public opinion. (363)

WEB LINKS

The U.S. Civil Rights Movement:
http://www.msnbc.com/onair/modules/selma.asp

Greenpeace:
http://www.greenpeace.org

The Confederation of British Industry:
http://www.cbi.org.uk/home.html

An American-style interest group, NRA
http://www.mynra.com

Mexico Solidarity Network:
http://www.mexicosolidarity.org

Political Action Committees in U.S. electoral politics:
http://www.opensecrets.org/bigpicture/toppacs.php?cycle=2006

FURTHER READING

Broder, David S. *Democracy Derailed: Initiative Campaigns and the Power of Money*. New York: Harcourt Brace, 2000.

Graziano, Luigi. *Lobbying, Pluralism and Democracy*. London: St. Martin's Press, 2001.

Keck, Margaret E., and Kathryn Sikkink. *Activists Beyond Boarders: Advocacy Networks in International Politics*. New York: Cornell University Press, 1998.

Roberts, Alexander, ed. *The Classics of Interest Group Behavior*. New York: Wadsworth, 2004.

Smith, Miriam. *A Civil Society? Collective Actors in Canadian Political Life*. Peterborough: Broadview Press, 2005.

Smith, Miriam, ed. *Groups and Movements in Canadian Politics*. Peterborough: Broadview Press, 2008.

Soule, Sarah, et al. *The Blackwell Companion to Social Movements*. Oxford: Blackwell, 2004.

Tarrow, Sidney. *The New Transnational Activism*. Cambridge: Cambridge University Press, 2005.

ENDNOTES

1. John Agnew, *Geopolitics: Re-visioning World Politics* (London and New York: Routledge, 1998).

2. Sydney Tarrow, *Power in Movement: Social Movements, Collective Action and Politics* (Cambridge: Cambridge University Press, 1994).

3. Osha Gray Davidson, *Under Fire: The NRA and the Battle for Gun Control* (Iowa City: University of Iowa Press, 1998).

4. Leslie A. Pal, *Interests of State: The Politics of Language, Multiculturalism and Feminism in Canada* (Montreal and Kingston, ON: McGill-Queen's University Press, 1993).

5. *Pretty v. the United Kingdom* (European Court of Human Rights, January 18, 2002); *Fielding v. the United Kingdom* (European Court of Human Rights, January 29, 2002).

6. Charles Epp, *The Rights Revolution* (Chicago: University of Chicago Press, 1998).

7. Gregory Hein, "Interest Group Litigation and Canadian Democracy," *Choices* (Montreal: Institute for Research in Public Policy) 6(2) (March 2000): 9.

8. Stephen Dale, *McLuhan's Children: The Greenpeace Message and the Media* (Toronto: Between the Lines, 1996), pp. 4, 15ff.

9. Warren Magnusson, "Decentring the State," in James Bickerton and Alain G. Gagnon, eds., *Canadian Politics* (Peterborough, ON: Broadview Press, 1994).

10. Council of Canadians, "Joint NGO Statement on the Multilateral Agreement on Investment (MAI) to the Organization for Economic Cooperation and Development"; available at http://www.canadians.org/ngostatement.html; accessed June 13, 2008.

11. Christina Gabriel and Laura Macdonald, "NAFTA, Women and Organizing in Canada and Mexico: Forging a Feminist Internationality?," *Millennium* 23(3) (Winter 1994): 535–62.

12. Audie J. Klotz, *Norms in International Relations: The Struggle Against Apartheid* (New York: Cornell University Press, 1996).

13. Robert O'Brien, Anne Marie Goetz, Jan Aart Scholte, and Marc Williams, *Contesting Global Governance: Multilateral Economic Institutions and Global Social Movements* (Cambridge: Cambridge University Press, 2000).

14. Robert Putnam, *Making Democracy Work* (Princeton: Princeton University Press, 1994), pp. 163–86.

Part 6

Political Development and Change

JONATHAN ROSS

Jonathan Ross graduated with a double-major B.A. in Political Science and Communications from Simon Fraser University. Politics had been a lifelong interest and dream, and Jonathan's university experience coincided with active involvement in the Canadian political scene. Political participation as a student included such experiences as attending national political conventions, serving as a cabinet minister in several university model parliaments, and writing opinion pieces for various daily newspapers. Jonathan also had the opportunity to work in Ottawa as a summer student in the office of the Minister of Fisheries and Oceans after his second year.

Soon after graduating, Jonathan began to work for the Minister of National Resources as a Special Assistant responsible for regional communications for western Canada. Tasked with setting up a British Columbia communications strategy to mitigate the sensitive and complicated issues attached to the moratorium for offshore oil and gas exploration, Jonathan engaged in extensive stakeholder relations across the province on behalf of the department and the Minister. Throughout his time as part of the Minister's staff, Jonathan's work portfolio grew to be quite wide-ranging, encompassing speech writing, media relations, policy position papers, newspaper editorials, briefing notes, community outreach, advertising and website content, and official correspondence.

After leaving the government, Jonathan started up a boutique public affairs company that specializes in professional writing, communications and public awareness campaigns, government relations, and public policy development. Over the next couple of years, Jonathan was able to amass a diverse group of clients including the Urban Development Institute, the City of Vancouver, the West Vancouver Police Department, the Government of Canada, and 2010 Legacies Now, an organization committed to creating sustainable legacies that will benefit all British Columbians as a result of hosting the 2010 Olympic and Paralympic Winter Games.

Running a small business, TDH Strategies, continues to be a labour-intensive endeavour, but the rewards attached with creating his own entity and seeing it blossom and succeed have been hugely satisfying for Jonathan. Work highlights have included having an academic paper commissioned for and presented to the 2006 World Urban Forum, and helping to design a province-wide strategy on how to make British Columbia the most accessible and inclusive jurisdiction in the world for people with disabilities and the entire community as a whole.

Jonathan is still deeply committed to the calling of public service, and plans on eventually running for office in the not-too-distant future.

AP Photo/Kent Gilbert

Chapter Thirteen

THE POLITICS OF DEVELOPMENT AND UNDERDEVELOPMENT

James Busumtwi-Sam

CHAPTER OBJECTIVES

After you have completed this chapter, you should be able to:

- identify some of the dimensions of global inequality, including inequality between men and women

- discuss the history and sources of development as a global issue and the evolution of the dialogue between rich countries and poor countries over how best to achieve development

- identify some of the main explanations offered for patterns of development and underdevelopment

- outline the contemporary issues and debates that arise from processes of development and change

Introduction

Economic growth and industrialization, as well as advancements in science and technology, have resulted in a level of prosperity and material well-being unparallelled in human history. But these very same forces of development and change have generated deepening imbalances among countries, individuals, and groups, between men and women, and between human civilization and the natural environment. These imbalances have been a source of past and continuing political conflict and disagreement. In this chapter, we examine "development" as an international issue and discuss some key questions arising from processes of development and change. What does development entail? Why do some countries and peoples enjoy very high standards of living while others live in poverty? What are the consequences of underdevelopment, and what prescriptions are available for addressing these consequences? The phrase "politics of development and underdevelopment" in the title of this chapter draws attention to the fact that the answers to these questions are not straightforward, but have been and continue to be highly contentious.

We begin with an overview of some key challenges to development globally, highlighting the dimensions of the gap between the "haves" and "have-nots" of the world, and then proceed to examine the question of what "development" entails by investigating the different circumstances of countries classified as "developing." Having a good sense of the relevant history helps our understanding of the present, and thus this chapter discusses, under "Colonialism in the Americas, Asia, and Africa," the history and legacy of colonialism in those parts of the world. The countries in these regions were subject to European colonial expansion between the 17th and early 20th centuries. In the contemporary period, as a group, they generally fall into the "have-nots" category. The efforts by these countries to effect change in international economic and political relations is examined in the next section, "Decolonization and the Politics of North–South Relations, 1950–2008." The next two sections, "Measuring Development: Economic, Social, and Political Dimensions" and "Political, Economic, and Social Development: Issues of Debate" consider the difficulties in, and controversies surrounding, the measurement and explanation of patterns of development and underdevelopment. Here we examine different ways of looking at development—political, economic, and social—as well as some of the theories and explanations offered for development and the lack thereof. Worldwide, women fare comparatively less well than men on various indicators of development, and this section also examines aspects of the debate over women in development including the gender dimensions of global inequality.

The final sections, "The Causes of Development and Underdevelopment" and "Contemporary Issues and Debates," explore some contemporary issues and debates arising from processes of development and change, including the debate over the role of foreign aid in development and that over the environment and development captured by the term "sustainable development." Also examined is the role of democracy and "civil society" in development, as well as problems of political violence and civil strife in many poorer countries.

Challenges of Global Development

Development entails the transformation of human, natural, and material resources at various levels of social interaction (local, national, regional and international/global) in order to enhance the quality of life of individuals and groups.[1] Challenges to development globally are manifest in a number of ways. These can usefully be grouped into three broad categories: challenges arising from global poverty and inequality, challenges in the area of human security, and challenges arising from environmental stress and degradation.

Global Poverty and Inequality

Since the early 1960s considerable advances have been made in improving living standards for people around the world. Overall production of wealth has increased sevenfold globally since the early 1960s. However, out of an estimated world population of about 6 billion in 2000, approximately 1.1 billion people lived below the income poverty line (less than US$1 per day). While the proportion of the world's population living in poverty decreased (from about 28 percent in 1990 to about 21 percent in 2001), the absolute number of poor people actually increased in many regions of the world, particularly in sub-Saharan Africa and parts of Latin America, Eastern Europe, and the Middle East (see Table 13.1). The majority are women and children. Income disparities between the richest 20 percent and the poorest 20 percent have also more than doubled since the early 1960s. The richest 50 individuals in the world have a combined income greater than that of the poorest 416 million. Almost half the world's population lives on less than $2 a day and receives only 5 percent of global income, while 54 percent of global income goes to the richest 10 percent of the world's population.[2] The assets of the 200 richest people exceed the combined income of 41 percent of the world's total population.

Table 13.1 Population Living on Less Than $1/Day (projected to 2015)

REGION	POPULATION (MILLIONS)			SHARE OF POPULATION (%)		
	1990	2001	2015	1990	2001	2015
East Asia/Pacific (excluding China)	472	271	19	29.6	14.9	0.9
Eastern Europe/Central Asia	2	17	2	0.5	3.6	0.4
Latin America/Caribbean	49	50	43	11.3	9.5	6.9
Middle East/North Africa	6	7	4	2.3	2.4	0.9
South Asia	462	431	216	41.3	31.3	12.8
Sub-Saharan Africa	227	313	340	44.6	46.5	38.4
Totals/average	**1,218**	**1,089**	**624**	**27.9**	**21.3**	**10.2**

Source: World Bank, *Global Monitoring Report 2005*, Table 2.1, p. 22.

Human Security

Another major challenge to global development lies in the insecurities faced by large numbers of individuals and groups around the world. Traditional interstate wars (i.e., wars between two or more states) affected the security of the state or nation, but modern forms of warfare and political violence largely affect the security of individuals and communities. Many of these armed conflicts, the majority of which have occurred in poorer developing countries, were accompanied by some of the most gruesome violations of human rights and humanitarian law, including the use of child soldiers and the direct targeting of civilian populations. The proportion of civilian casualties soared from 5 percent of total casualties in World War I to 80 percent in armed conflicts that occurred during the 1990s.

The concept of **human security** was first introduced through a publication of the United Nations Development Program (UNDP) in 1994, and has since become a central theme in discussions of international development and international security. The evolving discourse on human security, in which Canada has played a leading role, represents an attempt to focus attention on threats to the safety of individuals and groups, and to link insecurity to problems of underdevelopment. Here, factors such as political repression and violence, abuse of human rights, extreme poverty and deprivation, and environmental degradation, are seen as prime sources of the large number of political and social systems around the world that are fragmenting. Human security is said to have two main components: *safety* (of individuals and groups) from such chronic threats as hunger, disease, and repression; and *protection* from sudden and hurtful disruptions in patterns of daily life. More than one-half of the 35 poorest countries experienced a major armed conflict in the past 15 years. The 1990s also saw a dramatic increase in displaced persons (internal refugees) and international refugees—over 70 million people. Mass migrations of people across borders seeking better economic conditions can also be a source of conflict. Also on the increase is the incidence of violent crime, within nations as well as internationally. This has led to recognition of the phenomena of transnational organized crime and terrorism as global issues. The issue of political violence and warfare is discussed in a later section of this chapter and in more detail in Chapters 14 and 15.

Environmental Stress and Degradation

Challenges to development are also evident in the area of increased pressure on the earth's natural environment. According to the United Nations Environment Program's (UNEP) *Global Environment Outlook-4* report, one of the most authoritative scientific reports on the global environment, climate change, the collapse of fish stocks, and the extinction of species have reached a point where they threaten the survival of humanity.[3] Only 1.7 million out of an estimated 30 million species living on the planet have been identified. However, natural habitats including forests and wetlands, where many of the unidentified species live, are disappearing at a rate of 0.5 to 1 percent per year. World population, which reached 6.75 billion in 2006, is increasing by approximately 800 million people per decade and is expected to reach an estimated 8 billion by the year 2030. To keep pace with this growth, world food production will need to double in the next 30 years. Approximately 1.3 billion people world wide have no access to safe drinking water or basic sanitation, while 800 million people, 200 million of them children, are at risk of disease and malnourishment. More than 2 million people are possibly dying prematurely from air pollution, and close to 2 billion are likely to suffer absolute water scarcity by 2025. Resource scarcity, including declines in arable land, compounds the insecurities faced by individuals and groups around the world, and can contribute to the incidence of violent conflict, both within and between nations.

Development and Underdevelopment: Problems of Classification

Considerable differences exist among the 192 sovereign states in the world today in terms of their levels of development. Generally, discussions of development internationally have focused on how to improve the conditions or circumstances of people living in a group of countries variously described as *developing countries, less developed countries, underdeveloped countries,* the *Third World,* or the *South*. This group is said to include all countries in Central and South America and the Caribbean, Africa, Asia and the Middle East (excluding Japan), and the Pacific islands excluding Australia and New Zealand. In all, about 32 countries are represented here (see Figure 13.1). These various terms are used to differentiate this group from the *developed* countries (also called the *North*) which includes Canada and the United States, Europe, Australia, New Zealand, and Japan.

Some analysts question whether such classifications and generalizations are still relevant today.[4] They point to the fact that the term *Third World* was originally a political classification to describe

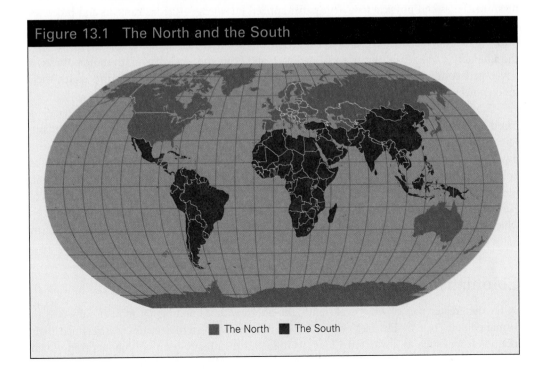

Figure 13.1   The North and the South

■ The North   ■ The South

one of the "three worlds" that existed during the Cold War—a "first world" of western industrialized states; a "second world" comprising the Soviet Union and its allies in eastern Europe; and a "third world" that included all other countries that were not aligned with either of these groups. Now that the Cold War is over, the argument goes, this classification is no longer relevant.

Some postmodernist critics, noting the Cold War context within which "development" first came to be used, reject the very notion of development as a discourse of power, imposing on the world a modernity that many in it do not necessarily want or need.[5] Others point to the increased diversity within the group of developing nations. For example, the group includes countries such as Singapore and South Korea that are among the fastest-growing economies in the world. On some economic indicators of development, these countries are comparable to many developed western states. Singapore, for example, had an average national income (US$29,230) slightly higher than New Zealand (US$27,280) in 2006.[6] While these criticisms have merit, the fact remains that diversity within the group of developing countries tends to be exaggerated when the focus is mainly on economic indicators of development. When the concept of development is disaggregated into its economic, social, and political dimensions, it becomes evident that the developing countries as a whole tend to score lower on all three dimensions than developed countries. These dimensions are explored in greater detail below.

Other critics object to the terms *underdeveloped* and *less developed* on normative grounds. They are essentially negative concepts that describe and classify a group of countries and people by what they do not have in comparison to what another group of countries has (i.e., they are not developed).[7]

In deference to some of these negative connotations, the subsequent discussion in this chapter will use the terms "South" or "developing" countries interchangeably. As Figure 13.1 indicates, most of the countries that make up the "developing world" are located in the southern hemisphere or to the south of the developed countries. Most developed states, with the notable exceptions of Australia and New Zealand, are located in the northern hemisphere.

Another important factor that unites the developing countries of the South vis-à-vis the developed North is a technological gap or dependence. "Technology" as used here does not simply mean machines and physical tools, but rather applied knowledge—the instruments and processes used to solve social, economic, and political problems. For much of the post–World War II period, "development" in practice has been virtually synonymous with modernization and Westernization—the adoption of Western forms of social, political, and economic organization. Even non-Western developed countries such as Japan owe their success in part to their ability to adapt their indigenous practices to Western forms of technology and organization.

For example, although bureaucracy may have originated in China, the modern bureaucracy—based on rational-legal authority and an efficient technocracy—is very much a Western invention. As the discussion later in this chapter shows, the emergence of such rational-legal authority is seen by some as a key to successful political development. Furthermore, the most dominant form of political organization in the world today, the sovereign territorial **state**, is also a Western invention. Almost all present-day developing countries in Africa, Asia, and the Americas were once colonies of European states, and all are the product of a process that began in the late 15th century in Europe by which scattered peoples throughout the world were brought together into a single society of sovereign states and a single global economy.[8] The history and legacy of colonialism is examined below.

Colonialism in the Americas, Asia, and Africa

By far the greater part of what is currently the South was at one time or another subjected to formal colonial rule by European states.[9] Even those non-Western societies that retained their independence, such as Japan and China, were forced to come to terms with a world in which

European technology and influence were dominant, and to adapt their own domestic political structures to meet the European prerequisites of statehood. European **colonialism** took different forms depending on the colonizing state itself, the reasons for which it undertook colonialism, and especially, the sociopolitical organization and response of the colonized peoples. In many cases, colonialism was part of a broader process of European **imperialism** that resulted in the establishment of large European empires.

Colonialism in the Americas

European colonialism in the Americas was distinguished from Africa and Asia by the thoroughness with which it displaced indigenous societies. In the islands of the Caribbean, the first point of contact in the Americas, indigenous populations almost entirely disappeared within a few generations. In Central and South America, strong indigenous empires such as the Aztec and Inca could not resist European expansion. However, the extent to which indigenous populations were displaced varied in the Americas. In the northwest portion of the South American continent and in Central America, indigenous populations still account for a significant proportion of the population—Bolivia (70 percent), Peru (46 percent), Ecuador (39 percent), and Mexico (30 percent). In the southern part of South America and the Caribbean islands, however, they have all but disappeared. Although substantial indigenous populations still exist in Canada and the United States, they remain socially, politically, and economically peripheral.

The displacement of local populations in the Americas was due to the following factors. Many of these territories, which had a more temperate climate similar to that in Europe, were designated "white settler" lands—especially in Canada, the United States, Argentina, and Chile. The more tropical areas of the Americas (the Caribbean, Brazil, southern U.S., etc.) were designated for the production of "cash crops" for the European market—sugar, cotton, tobacco, and coffee. For various reasons, the indigenous populations were deemed "unsuitable" for the production of cash crops, and the solution was to import people from the African continent to work as slaves. This led to the trans-Atlantic slave trade, which began in the mid-16th century, continued for 300 years, and poured millions of Africans into the Americas, some estimates putting the figure as high as 100 million people. A renewed demand for plantation labour in the 19th century after the demise of the slave trade led to the importation of indentured labourers from India and China.

Colonialism in Asia

What distinguished colonialism in Asia from the Americas was the comparative strength and resistance of its indigenous cultures and societies. In no case (except for small islands in the Indian Ocean such as Mauritius) could these be destroyed or completely subordinated to a predominantly European settler society. Even though Asia had been the prime target for European mercantilist expansion even prior to the "discovery" of the Americas (in the late 15th century), the cohesiveness of Asian societies restricted European incursions to coastal trading posts. The formal imposition of colonial rule in Asia occurred mainly in the 19th century, and was made possible by European technological advances; however, a number of political entities such as Iran, Afghanistan, and Thailand were never subject to formal colonial rule.

European colonialism in Asia proceeded by taking over existing political systems, including preserving their political leaders (e.g., in India). Societies were taken over in their entirety and the new, fixed colonial territorial frontiers roughly coincided with the un-demarcated boundaries within which the pre-colonial rulers had ruled. The Middle East also experienced a unique brand of colonialism. This region had been subject to European expansion since the time of the crusades (5th–10th centuries), and by the mid-17th century had come under the control of the Ottoman Empire. At the end of World War I, European powers such as France and the United Kingdom ruled most of the territories formerly controlled by the Ottoman Empire under the League of Nations Mandate system in conjunction with local dynasties. The impact of European incursions here was limited by the strength of the local dynasties and by the force of "pan-Arabism" that produced a very strong sense of regional identity.

Colonialism in Africa

Unlike Asia, Africa was initially perceived to have little economic worth (except for its people to be exported as slaves); it had an interior that was difficult to penetrate, and was perceived to have a climate inhospitable for European settlement. Thus, except for a few coastal trading forts and settlements that were used primarily for slave raids and storage of slaves for export, formal imposition of colonial rule did not occur until the end of the 19th century (except Algeria, colonized by France in 1830). By the time Africa began to be formally colonized in the late 1800s most colonies in the Americas (except the Caribbean) had already become independent states.

Colonialism in Africa, like Asia but unlike the Americas, did not involve the displacement of indigenous peoples. But unlike Asia, no attempt was made to create colonial boundaries that broadly coincided with existing cultures and political systems. Instead, colonial boundaries in Africa were demarcated by European powers at the Berlin Conference of 1884–85. Only one existing African state (Ethiopia) retained its independence for much of the colonial period (save for a brief period in the 1930s when Mussolini of Italy attempted to colonize it). By 1914, all of Africa (except Liberia—created as an independent state in 1822 for freed slaves from the USA, Lesotho, Ethiopia, and South Africa) was made up of colonies of the European powers.

Decolonization and the Politics of North–South Relations, 1950–2008

The collapse of European colonialism was rapid, and with very few exceptions is virtually complete today. **Decolonization** began in Central and South America in the 1820s with the independence of Brazil and Mexico. The relative decline of Spain and Portugal—the main colonizers of the region—as major European powers contributed to this early start in the process. In most of Africa and Asia, however, decolonization did not begin until after World War II, with the independence of India and Pakistan in 1947. (As a result, the term *post-colonial era* usually refers to the period after 1945.) A number of factors contributed to decolonization on these continents, including the weakening of European colonial powers as a result of the war, the rise of nationalist movements in the colonies demanding political independence, and the emergence and institutionalization of new norms in international relations that de-legitimized colonialism.[10] These norms centred on a new interpretation of the principle of **self-determination**.

The resolution adopted by the United Nations General Assembly in 1960, called the Declaration on the Granting of Independence to Colonial Countries and Peoples, sums up the new views on self-determination: "All peoples have the right to self-determination; by virtue of that right they freely determine their political status and freely pursue their economic, social and cultural development. . . . Any attempt aimed at the partial or total disruption of the national unity and the territorial integrity of a country is incompatible with the purposes and principles of the Charter of the United Nations" (UN General Assembly Resolution 1514—XV, December 14, 1960).

Prior to 1945, the international system was very much a European state system (with countries such as the United States and Japan emerging in the early 20th century). The founding of the **United Nations** in 1945 involved only 51 states as members. By 2007, the UN had a total of 192 member states. This phenomenal growth is largely due to decolonization. Once political independence was attained, the countries of the South, through a series of international conferences and negotiations beginning in the mid-1950s, sought to achieve changes in the international political and economic order. These demands often brought the interests of the South into conflict with the interests of the North. Five stages or phases can be discerned in the evolution of the dialogue between North and South.

Phase One: The 1950s and 1960s

The first phase of decolonization, which occurred in the 1950s and 1960s, was characterized by the South's attempt to carve out a separate identity in world politics. Two international conferences served to highlight these efforts: the Afro-Asian Conference held in Bandung (Indonesia) in 1955, and the first meeting of the Non-Aligned Movement (NAM) held in Belgrade (Yugoslavia) in 1961.

By the early 1960s a more focused strategy to influence international events began to emerge on the part of the South. This involved an attempt to extend the international normative consensus that had emerged in favour of decolonization and political independence into international support for development. Prior to the 1960s, the issue of development assistance—the notion that resources should be mobilized internationally to assist poorer nations to develop—was not on the international agenda. Through the UN system and the creation of new institutional frameworks, such as the UN Conference on Trade and Development (UNCTAD), the countries of the South were successful in bringing the issue of development onto the international agenda. Their objectives during this period were defined mainly in terms of "closing the gap" with the North.

Phase Two: The 1970s

At the beginning of the 1970s, a series of events occurred that produced a change in strategy of the South. These events included the quadrupling of oil prices by the Organization of Petroleum Exporting Countries (OPEC) after the 1973 Middle East war. This new strategy was more explicitly redistributive and combined the threat of negative sanctions (on the North) with the promise of mutual gains for both North and South. This strategy, known as the **New International Economic Order (NIEO)**, represented an attempt by the South to affirm a "right to development," and to convince the North that reform of existing institutions and practices in the global political economy was needed (see Box 13.1).[11] The call for the NIEO, however, failed to produce the results that developing countries expected.

Phase Three: The 1980s

During the 1980s, several events displaced the NIEO from the top of the international agenda including the worldwide recession of the early 1980s precipitated by a second round of oil price increases in 1979, and the emergence of the first developing country debt crisis in 1982 (see Box 13.2). These events undermined the unity of the South and weakened its bargaining position vis-à-vis the North.

In view of these developments, a new strategy began to emerge in North–South relations. This strategy deemphasized redistribution and focused on common problems and the interdependence between North and South. The premise was that the development problems of the South and their political, social, and environmental consequences were very much a concern for the North, and hence the efficient working of the international system as a whole required cooperation between North and South. This new emphasis on interdependence and multilateralism was articulated through a series of reports commissioned by the UN.[12]

The New International Economic Order (NIEO)

BOX 13.1

The New International Economic Order refers to a set of proposals made by the South for reform of the international economic order. The idea for the NIEO took shape first within the Non-Aligned Movement and subsequently in the United Nations. Two resolutions adopted by the UN General Assembly (UNGA) in 1974 launched a series of global negotiations between North and South. These were UNGA Resolution 3202, "The Program of Action on the Establishment of the New International Economic Order," and Resolution 3281, "The Charter of Economic Rights and Duties of States." Three sets of reforms were proposed:

1. the self-reliance reforms, designed to increase the control of developing countries over their natural resources

2. the resource-transfer reforms, designed to achieve greater and more regular flows of financial resources from North to South (e.g., an increase in grants and concessional foreign aid)

3. the international influence reforms, designed to increase the participation of developing countries in the central institutions that regulated international economic and political interactions

Some modest changes occurred as a result of these negotiations but the fundamental reforms sought by the South did not occur. By the early 1980s, negotiations for the NIEO were effectively over.

The First Developing Country Debt Crisis

BOX 13.2

The causes of the first debt crisis can be traced to the impact of the 1973 quadrupling of oil prices that resulted in severe deficits in oil-importing developing countries.[13] Many of these countries, faced with a choice between a swift but painful adjustment that would have entailed a reduction in imports and strict austerity measures, chose instead to finance their deficits by borrowing money from the "offshore" private capital markets (branches of commercial banks in the North located offshore). The second round of oil price increases in 1979 led governments of industrialized countries, particularly the United States, to make controlling domestic inflation a key priority. These policies were deflationary and resulted in a reduction in the demand for and prices of exports from developing countries, increased protectionism, and a steep rise in interest rates to unprecedented levels.[14] The export earnings of countries in the south declined relative to the prices of their imports. Debt-service obligations rose while the income to meet them declined. At the same time, commercial bank lending dried up, and by late 1982, there were widespread difficulties in servicing the mountain of accumulated debt. The actual onset of the crisis is dated from August 1982, when Mexico announced a moratorium on repayments. By the end of 1983, over 30 countries had suspended repayments of their debts. Total external debt of low- and middle-income developing countries increased from US$480 billion in 1980 to over US$1.3 trillion in

1990. By 2005 it had reached over US$2.8 trillion.[15]

In the mid-1980s the **International Monetary Fund (IMF)** and the **World Bank** became major players in the management of the international debt problem, because of the leverage they had over countries seeking to refinance and reschedule their debts. The source of this leverage lay in the conditionality attached to their lending facilities. The linchpin of the debt management system was a package of policies known as "structural adjustment," in which debtor countries had to agree to restructure their economies according to market-oriented principles (more on this in the section on the "Washington Consensus" later in this chapter). In addition, through the Consultative Groups, chaired by the World Bank, which brought together the major foreign aid donors in the international community, and the Paris Club of debt rescheduling chaired by the IMF, all other forms of assistance and aid were linked to IMF and World Bank programs. As a result, developing countries today as a whole face a much tighter system of conditionality than ever before.

Phase Four: The 1990s

For most of the 1980s, issues arising from the (1982) debt crisis dominated North–South relations. Debt problems of developing countries continued into the 1990s, with a number of currency and financial crises including the Mexico Peso crisis in 1994 and the Asian financial crisis that began in 1997. Thus a key issue in the 1990s was how to manage the mountain of debt accumulated by countries in the South. One initiative was the Highly Indebted Poor Countries Initiative (HIPC), launched in 1996, which offered some debt-relief to low-income developing countries. An enhanced version of the HIPC (the EHIPC) was introduced in September 1999 to strengthen the link between debt relief and poverty reduction. Although managing debt problems was dominant, a number of other significant issues were added to the agenda of North–South relations, aided by the end of the Cold War in 1990, which created the space for these newer issues to emerge. One of the most prominent of these was the increased concern over the relationship between development and the natural environment, encapsulated in the concept of "sustainable development." Other significant issues that emerged include the debates on the role of foreign aid and trade in development, and debates over democracy, human rights, and development. Also in the 1990s, increased attention was paid to the issue of gender and development. In addition, the end of the Cold War focused attention on problems of human security in the context of civil war, state failure, and ethnic conflict in various regions of the world. Each of these contemporary issues is explored in more detail later in this chapter.

Phase Five: The Millennium Development Goals (MDGs)

The new century appeared to usher in a new era of cooperation between North and South marked by a determination to meet some of the challenges of global development outlined at the beginning of this chapter. In September 2000, 189 countries at the largest-ever gathering of heads of state signed the United Nations Millennium Declaration, which led to the adoption of the Millennium Development Goals (MDGs). This declaration committed all countries, rich and poor, to eradicate poverty, promote human dignity, achieve greater gender equality, and achieve peace, "good governance" and environmental sustainability (see Box 13.3). They also include actions to reduce debt and increase aid, trade, and technology transfers to poor countries. Since the adoption of the MDGs in 2000, a number of other international conferences have sought to provide a framework for a partnership between North and South to help achieve the MDGs, including the

The MDGs are set of eight goals for which a number of numerical targets have been identified.[16] These goals and targets are to be achieved by the date of 2015 or earlier.

Goal 1: Eradicate Extreme Poverty and Hunger

Halve by 2015 the proportion of people whose income is less than $1 a day and the proportion of people who suffer from hunger.

Goal 2: Achieve Universal Primary Education

Ensure that by 2015 children everywhere, boys and girls alike, will be able to complete a full course of primary schooling.

Goal 3: Promote Gender Equality and Empower Women

Eliminate gender disparity in primary and secondary education, preferably by 2005 and in all levels of education no later than 2015.

Goal 4: Reduce Child Mortality

Reduce by two-thirds the under-five mortality rate.

Goal 5: Improve Maternal Health

Reduce by three-quarters the maternal mortality ratio.

Goal 6: Combat HIV/AIDS, Malaria, and Other Diseases

Reverse the spread of HIV/AIDS.

Goal 7: Ensure Environmental Sustainability

Integrate sustainable development into country policies and reverse loss of environmental resources. Halve the proportion of people without access to potable water. Significantly improve the lives of at least 100 million slum dwellers.

Goal 8: Develop a Global Partnership for Development

Raise official development assistance. Expand market access in international trade.

November 2001 Doha Declaration, the March 2002 Monterrey Declaration, the September 2002 Johannesburg Declaration on Sustainable Development, and the 2005 Paris Declaration on Aid Effectiveness.

Assessing Outcomes of the North–South Dialogue

At the beginning of the new millennium, assessing the outcomes of the over 50-year dialogue between North and South is difficult. On the whole, the fundamental changes in international political and economic relations that the South wanted have not been achieved. Nevertheless, some changes have occurred. Perhaps the most visible impact of the South has been normative and institutional. In normative terms, countries of the South have been successful to a degree in placing issues on the international agenda that, arguably, would not be there otherwise, such as the very notion of "development" as an international issue. Even more important has been the impact of the South on international institutionalization, especially within the United Nations system. While the Millennium Declaration does appear to signify a new era of cooperation between North and South, it remains to be seen whether the specified targets of the MDGs are indeed achieved by 2015.

Measuring Development: Economic, Social, and Political Dimensions

The study of development is the study of social transformation or change, particularly those changes that affect the *quality of life* of individuals and groups. The synopsis of North–South relations above shows that the question of "development" is a highly contentious one. Defining exactly what "development" entails is, like many other concepts in the study of politics, subject to much debate. While analysts agree that development involves processes of change, considerable debate has revolved around specifying who or what the target or object of "development" is, exactly what these processes of change involve, and what the desirable goals of such development processes are. Despite these disagreements, the practice of development internationally as it has evolved over the past 50 years has generally included economic, social, and political dimensions. These three aspects of development are analyzed below.

Economic Development

The economic dimension of development refers to the *production* and *distribution* of wealth and income in a country.[17] Perhaps the most widely used measure of the production of wealth in a country is the *gross domestic product (GDP)* or *gross national product/gross national income (GNP/GNI)*.[18] The GDP or GNP/GNI can also be expressed as a ratio of a country's population to provide a representation of that country's average national income (the GDP or GNI per capita). Less economically developed countries tend to produce less wealth and income than more economically developed countries. For example, in 2006, the per capita GNI for the United States, one of the wealthiest countries in the world, was over US$44,970. In comparison, Ethiopia, one of the poorest countries, had a GNI per capita of only US$180. The 18 richest countries in the world—the United States, Japan, and Canada, plus the 15 countries of the European Union (EU) prior to its May 2004 enlargement—accounted for about 47 percent of total global GDP in 2003.

The World Bank, the leading institution charged with promoting development internationally, has developed a fourfold classification of countries to distinguish their level of economic growth. See Table 13.2.

In addition to GDP per capita and GDP growth, levels of economic development are measured by how that wealth and income are distributed. Not only do developing countries tend to produce less wealth and income, but whatever they do produce is often poorly distributed. One way of measuring inequality is the *Gini Index*, which measures the extent to which the distribution of income (or consumption) among individuals or households within a country deviates from a perfectly equal distribution. The Gini is expressed on a scale between 0 and 1, zero representing perfect equality and one perfect inequality. No country ever scores a perfect 0 or 1, and generally countries with Ginis closer to 0 are considered to have lower income inequality (see Table 13.3). Most developed countries have Ginis below 0.4.

Social Development

The social dimension refers to the development of a country's human resources.[19] Indicators such as levels of education, school enrolments, literacy rates, life expectancy, and levels of nutrition are often used as measures of a country's social development. The United Nations

---

Table 13.2   The World Bank's Classification of Levels of Economic Growth

Classification	GNI per Capita (US$)	Example (US$ 2006)
Low income	$905 or less	Cambodia ($480)
Lower middle income	$906–3,595	Egypt ($1,350)
Upper middle income	$3,596–11,115	South Africa ($5,390)
High income	$11,116 or more	United Kingdom ($40,180)

Source: World Bank, *World Development Report 2008*, p. 333, and Annex Table 1, p. 334.

Table 13.3 Gini Index of Income Inequality Within Countries

LOWER INEQUALITY		HIGHER INEQUALITY	
Country	Gini	Country	Gini
Finland	0.25	Haiti	0.68
Denmark	0.27	Botswana	0.63
Norway	0.27	Brazil	0.59
Canada	0.33	Bolivia	0.58
United States	0.38	Columbia	0.54

Source: World Bank, *World Development Report 2006*, Table A2, p. 280.

Development Program (UNDP), an agency of the UN, has developed a **Human Development Index (HDI)**, a composite index that contains three variables: longevity (measured by average life expectancy); knowledge (measured by adult literacy and combined primary, secondary and tertiary enrolment); and standard of living (measured by the real GDP per capita).

The HDI is calculated for each country and expressed on a scale between 0 and 1 to allow for comparisons. A score of one indicates that a country has attained the highest possible quality of life for its citizens. HDI scores of less than one indicate how far a country must go to reach this ideal. All countries are ranked from "high" (scores of 0.81 and above) to "medium" (0.51 to 0.80) and "low" HDI (less than 0.50). Since the HDI was introduced in 1990, no state has ever scored a perfect 1. Generally, developed countries of the North tend to score higher than developing countries of the South. For example, in 1998 Canada achieved the highest HDI score of 0.960. The lowest was Sierra Leone with a HDI of 0.185. In effect, Canada was rated the "best country in the world to live," while Sierra Leone—a country afflicted with civil war and extreme poverty—was the "worst country in the world to live." In 2006, however, Canada was 6th in the HDI rankings (see Table 13.4). Singapore at 25th was the highest-ranked country in the South in 2006.

Political Development

Measuring **political development** is far more difficult than measuring economic and social development.[20] Because no widespread agreement on the suitable indicators of political development exists, political variables—dealing with values and beliefs, institutions, and power— cannot be quantified as readily as economic and social variables. Ideological and cultural differences also further complicate the debate. Despite these disagreements within the literature, several

Table 13.4 Human Development Index Rankings, 2006

TOP 10		BOTTOM 10	
Country Rank	HDI	Country Rank	HDI
1. Norway	0.965	168. Mozambique	0.390
2. Iceland	0.960	169. Burundi	0.384
3. Australia	0.957	170. Ethiopia	0.371
4. Ireland	0.956	171. Chad	0.368
5. Sweden	0.951	172. Central African Republic	0.353
6. Canada	0.950	173. Guinea-Bissau	0.349
7. Japan	0.949	174. Burkina Faso	0.342
8. United States	0.948	175. Mali	0.338
9. Switzerland	0.947	176. Sierra Leone	0.335
10. Netherlands	0.947	177. Niger	0.311

Source: UNDP, *Human Development Report, 2006*, Table 1, pp. 283–86. Used by permission of Oxford University Press.

influential views on measures of political development may be discerned. These include the degree of state capacity and the degree of political stability. More recently, issues of governmental responsiveness and representation have been added as criteria.

Degree of State Capacity Political development involves the creation of specialized and differentiated government institutions that have the capacity to effectively carry out the functions of government—making (legislative functions), implementing (executive functions), and adjudicating (judicial functions) public policy and laws. The idea here is that political development entails the institutionalization of rational-legal authority and the establishment of an effective state **bureaucracy**. Although they possess all the attributes of statehood such as population, demarcated territories, and so on, many states in the South do not have governments that can discharge these functions effectively. In some extreme cases—what are known as *failed states*—government capacity is virtually nonexistent. Examples include Somalia and Afghanistan.

Degree of Political Stability Countries that are politically developed enjoy a degree of political stability. The notion of political stability addresses the issue of how political conflicts and disputes are resolved. Stable polities are those in which political conflicts can be resolved in a peaceful manner without recourse to widespread violence. In contrast, less developed polities are plagued by instability—civil strife, communal violence, military coups, and sometimes outright civil war. Generally, developed countries of the North tend to be more stable than those in the South. Indeed, as shown under "Contemporary Issues and Debates" in this chapter, since 1945 almost all major armed conflicts in world have been located in the South.

Degree of Governmental Responsiveness and Representation In addition to state capacity and political stability, some observers include the degree of governmental responsiveness and representation as indicators of political development. The idea here is that politically developed countries have governments that are responsive to broad segments of society, and show respect for that population's fundamental rights and freedoms. Representative governments reflect the wishes of their populations, and govern with the consent, or at least the acquiescence, of that population. Responsive and representative governments would enjoy a high degree of **legitimacy**, they would allow their citizens to pursue their values, interests, and goals peacefully, have mechanisms and procedures in place to prevent the abuse of power, and allow for a peaceful change in government.

The criteria of responsive and representative government sound very similar to those associated with the form of government known as *democracy*. Does this mean political development is synonymous with democratization? Early works on political development gave ambiguous answers to this question to avoid the accusation that they were attempting to impose Western values. However, today the widespread view is that political development does entail the emergence and consolidation of some type of democratic political institutions and procedures, for democratic governments tend to have greater political capacity, are more responsive and representative, and tend to be more stable than authoritarian governments. This issue of democracy and development is examined in greater detail later in this chapter and in Chapter 14.

Using the three broad measures of economic, social, and political development, we can generally say that more developed societies have achieved higher levels of economic growth with a degree of equity in their income distribution; have a relatively high level of social development; and have a higher degree of state capacity and political stability, with governments that are responsive to and representative of their populations. In Box 13.4, we look at the interesting case of Ghana.

Ghana is a relatively small country located on the west coast of Africa with a population of about 18 million. It was one of the first sub-Saharan African countries to achieve political independence (from Britain) in 1957. In the immediate post-independence period, Ghana's future development prospects looked bright. It was relatively well endowed with natural resources (gold, manganese, timber, bauxite) and by the standards of colonial Africa at the time (generally very low) it had a relatively well-educated population. In 1960, Ghana had a GNP per capita that was similar to that of South Korea. But in 1998 the GNP per capita of South Korea (US$10,550) was more than 20 times greater than that of Ghana (US$400). South Korea is generally seen as a "success story" of development (see Box 13.5 for more on South Korea and other Asian countries), having achieved marked improvements in the economic, social, and political dimensions of development. The experience of Ghana between 1960 and the early 1980s, on the other hand, appeared to demonstrate everything that might go wrong in the development of a country.

For example, between 1970 and 1982, GNP per capita in Ghana fell by 20 percent, and almost every social indicator of development, including school enrolments, declined. Politically, Ghana's post-independence history has been unstable, having experienced five successful military coups d'état, in which incumbent governments were violently overthrown. The country has also experimented with a wide range of governments, civilian and military-authoritarian. By the early 1980s, the central institutions of the state were near collapse. However, at the end of 1981, an authoritarian military leader took power who was determined to break the cycle of economic, social, and political decay, and set the country on a path to development. He rigorously implemented policy reforms. These reforms appear to have reversed the cycle of decline, and resulted in improvements in economic, social, and political development.

From the mid-1980s and throughout the 1990s, for example, the rate of GNP growth in Ghana exceeded the average for sub-Saharan Africa (about 5 percent per annum as against the continental average of about 2 percent). Ghana has also shown signs of political development. In 1992, Ghana made a transition from authoritarian to democratic government, and since then a degree of political stability has been achieved, and the capacity of state institutions has been strengthened. Four successful rounds of democratic elections have been held (1992, 1996, 2000, and 2004), the 2000 election resulting in a peaceful transfer of power. This represented one of the few instances in Africa in which an incumbent government accepted defeat in an election. As a result of the dramatic turnaround in the country's political, economic, and social development, Ghana today is considered to be one of the countries in sub-Saharan Africa that is on a road to recovery and development.

Political, Economic, and Social Development: Issues of Debate

The relationship among the three dimensions of development has generated considerable debate on whether they might be achieved simultaneously. Influential works have identified important tradeoffs and tensions within each dimension as well as between the economic, political, and social dimensions of development. In terms of political development, for example, some analysts have argued that to achieve the goal of political stability, a country in the early stages of development has to forgo a degree of political participation and representation. The argument was that for many of the new countries in the South, democracy was incompatible with order and stability—indeed, that premature democratization created political instability. Thus, from this perspective, priority was to be given to stability at the expense of democracy.[21]

Some versions of this argument went further, positing a tension between political and economic development, such that premature creation of democratic governments in developing societies would impede economic growth. Or, to put it another way, strong authoritarian government was necessary for economic growth. Only a strong authoritarian government free from particular interests in society could take the necessary measures. This was the so-called "liberty–growth" tradeoff. To support this argument, they pointed to the successes of the Asian newly industrialized countries (NICs)—Singapore, South Korea and Taiwan—each of which achieved impressive rates of economic growth in the 1970s and 1980s under authoritarian governments. More recently China has adopted elements of this approach and is also recording impressive rates of economic growth (see Box 13.5). However, the empirical record supporting a direct correlation between type of government and economic growth is mixed. While the Asian NICs did achieve impressive rates of economic growth under authoritarian governments, they were the exception, not the rule. The majority of such governments elsewhere in the South—in most Latin American and African countries—failed to achieve sustained growth. With respect to democratic government, the historical record is also mixed. While some democratic governments (such as Botswana) have been able to manage impressive rates of economic growth, others such as Bolivia have not.

The East Asian Export-Oriented "Development-State" Approach BOX 13.5

For much of the early post-colonial period in the 1950s and 1960s there was little variation in the domestic economic structures throughout the South—in Asia, Latin America, and Africa. The period from the 1970s onwards, however, began to see significant variations in domestic economic performance, especially between those in Southeast Asia (and a few Latin American states on one hand) and the rest of the South. Observers have argued that the explanation of these differences lies in a particular model of development adopted by the south East Asian countries—the "development state" model.

The success of the East Asian newly industrialized countries (NICs), including Singapore, South Korea, and Taiwan, is attributed to an outward-oriented growth strategy based on export growth and a strong private sector. Centralized and authoritarian economic management was a major ingredient in this model. In each of these NICs, state agents and administrators, backed by government-financed "think-tanks," played a key role in the direction of economic policy, with little public debate and input. Government intervention was directed at ensuring an efficiently working market economy, including policies of trade liberalization, currency devaluations, reductions in wasteful government spending, and the reduction of barriers to foreign investment. In contrast to this outward-oriented set of policies, the majority of countries in Latin America, Africa, and the rest of Asia pursued inward-oriented growth strategies involving extensive state interventions, economic nationalism, and import-substitution, which distorted markets and discouraged production.

In summary, the three key ingredients of the Development State model, first developed by Japan and subsequently adopted by East Asian NICs, include:

1. *Strong centralized economic management.* This is essentially a market economy; however, the government intervenes into and controls the operation of the economy in the areas of finance, foreign investment, and industrial and export development.

2. *Emphasis on the promotion of exports*, with preferential access to credit for exporters, investment incentives, and other trade interventions (e.g., the use of trade tariffs).

3. *Emphasis on industrialization*, but also support for more efficient agricultural production.

Much debate continues on whether the success of the East Asian countries can be replicated elsewhere in the South. Those who question the transferability of this model point to the changed international environment of today compared to that of the late 1960s and 1970s when these NICs began their phenomenal growth. They note, for example, that the NICs received large amounts of foreign aid, particularly from the United States and Japan, which assisted in their economic growth. However, foreign aid to many other countries in the South has declined considerably since the early 1990s. Also, the financial crises that hit several East Asian countries in 1997 have led to questions about the durability of this model.

Another important tension that has been identified is between economic growth and equity. This view argued that economic growth should be accorded priority over income distribution and equity. One influential theory that became known as the "trickle-down" doctrine posited that income inequality was indeed necessary to provide incentives for investment. If investors were allowed to reap differential rewards for their entrepreneurial efforts, total societal income would be maximized and the benefits would eventually trickle down to those less well off in that society. However, here again the empirical record to support the trickle-down theory is mixed. For example, rapid economic growth in South Korea and Singapore was achieved together with a marked reduction in levels of poverty and income inequality. In contrast, other countries that pursued growth-first strategies, such as Mexico and Brazil, did so at the cost of widening income disparities and increased inequality. Furthermore, countries such as Cuba and Costa Rica, which recorded comparatively slow rates of economic growth, nevertheless recorded impressive gains in the area of social development, including marked improvements in literacy, school enrolments, and the reduction of infant mortality rates.

Thus, the relationship among the three dimensions of development (especially between political and economic development) is very complex and continues to be the subject of much debate. These debates, in turn, have been influenced by strong disagreements among analysts on the causes of development and underdevelopment.

The Causes of Development and Underdevelopment

Debates over development have revolved not only around how best to measure levels of development, but also around how to understand and explain the present condition of poorer countries and societies, and possibly shape and predict the future direction of change. The kinds of answers to these questions have depended on the type of theoretical framework or *paradigm* employed. A paradigm can be defined as a model or a worldview from which springs a coherent tradition of research. Paradigms include collections of theories that rely on a common set of assumptions, and a common set of questions and methodological tools that shape the way they diagnose the problem to be investigated and the solutions or prescriptions they offer.

We will examine early views on development provided by modernization theories, and then explore the dependency and world system theories that put forth an alternative explanation of development. That will bring us to the view called the "Washington Consensus" that became dominant in the 1990s, as well as to some of the critical perspectives on gender and development.

The Modernization Paradigm

As the name implies, theories within the modernization paradigm, which emerged in the 1950s and 1960s, saw development as a process of progressive transformation in which societies moved from "traditional" through a series of stages to "modern" (see Box 13.6).[22] In effect, this meant that present-day developing countries were at an earlier stage in the historical trajectory of development through which all states had to pass. The obstacles to development thus lay within the countries of the South—in the nature and operation of their political institutions and processes, and in their economic and social systems. These political institutions were still steeped in ancient traditions and cultures and had not yet acquired the rational institutions and processes found in the North.[23]

In their prescriptions for change, modernization theories emphasized the creation of institutions and processes within poorer countries that would allow for more rational and efficient public-policy making and administration, by doing away with practices such as nepotism and corruption. A more efficient system for allocating and distributing economic resources (the operation of competitive market forces) was also needed to allow economic growth to occur. The diffusion of technology, skills, capital, and other values from North to South, through trade and other international transactions, was also seen as a key instrument of change. In this respect, modernization theories drew on the works of Max Weber (1864–1920) on political organization, authority, and bureaucratic rationalization, as well as the ideas of classical economists such as Adam Smith (1723–1790) who championed *laissez-faire* economics, in which the "invisible hand" of the market was the best mechanism to allocate economic resources for development.

Modernization theories were criticized on a number of fronts, including their view of what development entailed, their diagnosis of development problems, and their prescriptions for change. With respect to the first, modernization theories were accused of being ethnocentric because of the notion that development was synonymous with Westernization. Their view of history was also criticized for being "linear"—they assumed there was only one path to development and that path was the one followed by the present-day developed states. Modernization theories also came under criticism for, in effect, blaming the poor for their poverty. They implied that the poor were poor because they were inefficient. They were also criticized for placing too much emphasis on domestic changes within developing countries and ignoring the international aspects of the problem such as the protectionist practices of developed countries in international trade relations that discriminated

The work of Walt W. Rostow is considered to be a classic in the modernization paradigm. In 1960 he identified five stages through which all countries had to pass on the path to modernization and development.

1. *Traditional society.* Characterized by an agrarian economy, the existence of traditional authority structures, a high level of subsistence, and low levels of technological and scientific knowledge.

2. *The preconditions for takeoff.* This is a period of transition from tradition to modernity, and is characterized by the development of new ideas and processes, and advances in education. A change occurs in the balance of social forces, away from traditional authority structures toward new elites. This period also sees the creation of a centralized state.

3. *The takeoff.* This is the stage where the old traditional pre-modern ways of doing things are finally overcome. Technology plays a key role. Rapid increases in agricultural productivity and industrialization occur, together with the emergence of elites who champion modernization of the economy.

4. *The drive to maturity.* This is a period of fluctuating but sustained progress. Here a society and economy demonstrate the ability to move beyond the original industries that fuelled takeoff. Rostow argued it took roughly 60 years from the stage of takeoff for an economy to reach maturity.

5. *The high mass-consumption society.* At this stage an economy and society move toward the production of consumer goods and provision of services, and away from a reliance on heavy industry. It is characterized by a rapid rise in per capita incomes and overall living standards. Also at this stage we see the development of social welfare programs.

against exports from the South. In response to these criticisms, various attempts were made to modify modernization theories, by rejecting the linear view of history, identifying important tradeoffs in the development process, and attempting to acknowledge the special political and historical circumstances of developing countries.[24]

Dependency and the World Systems Paradigm

By the beginning of the 1970s, the influence of modernization theories began to wane. The initial optimism that countries in the South recently emerged from colonialism would rapidly modernize was soon replaced by pessimism. This pessimism in part reflected events in the real world such as the fact that a majority of states in Africa, Asia, and Latin America had adopted various types of military and authoritarian governments; and the fact that although some economic growth had been achieved throughout the developing world, less progress had been made in reducing poverty.

The most serious challenge to the modernization paradigm came from theories in an alternative paradigm of development—theories of **dependency** and the world system—that provided a very different explanation of problems of poverty and underdevelopment in the south. World system theories were broader in scope. They provided an explanation of the evolution and impact of imperialism and capitalism on political and economic organization throughout the globe since the 16th century. Dependency theories had a narrower focus. They examined the consequences of imperialism, colonialism, and global capitalism for the development of countries in the South.[25] Dependency theories may thus be seen as a subset of world system theories.

Theories of dependency and the world system, despite considerable differences among them, saw a causal relationship between the historical expansion of western European political and economic influence, beginning with the industrial revolution and the expansion of European colonial empires on the one hand, and the progressive impoverishment of countries in Africa, Asia and the Americas on the other. Unlike modernization theories, which saw underdevelopment as a natural stage or condition on a linear process of development, for theorists of dependency there was nothing natural about underdevelopment. It was a specific historical creation, a product of unequal political and economic relations between developed countries located at the "core" of the world system and underdeveloped countries located at its "periphery." In the words of one prominent dependency theorist, "underdevelopment was developed."[26]

The central concern for dependency theories in their diagnoses of the problems of underdevelopment was an analysis of how power was used to allocate and distribute resources, especially economic resources. Two broad positions emerged, the neo-Marxists and the structuralists. The neo-Marxists, who drew on the earlier works of Karl Marx (1818–1883) focused on the internal class structure within countries on the periphery, while the structuralists focused on the international linkages between core and periphery. For the structuralists, in the contemporary period, the unequal relationships between core and periphery were described in terms of an "international division of labour" created by core states. This international division of labour was the prime determinant of economic and political outcomes in the developing countries. In effect, the poor were poor not because they were inefficient, but because of their exploitation by the rich and powerful.

Such dependency relationships were maintained by the cooperation of classes and elites in the periphery who profited from their economic links with the core, and whose common identity and survival as a class derived from subordination to the international economy. In effect, although formal political independence had been achieved, exploitative economic relationships were maintained by former colonial and imperial powers—a situation described by some analysts as "neocolonialism." The neo-Marxists, on the other hand, while acknowledging the exploitative international linkages between rich and poor countries, diagnosed the problem of underdevelopment primarily in terms of the weaknesses of domestic classes within poor states and their failure to play their "historic role" of overturning traditional elites and practices and spearheading economic and political development.

Theories of dependency and the world system were criticized for being too deterministic by overemphasizing the role of international and global forces on countries in the South. Other critics rejected them as little more than "conspiracy" theories for implying that rich countries deliberately kept the poor impoverished. One of the most serious criticisms was that dependency theories were better at explaining why countries did not develop than they were at explaining how countries actually did develop. In other words, unlike modernization theories, dependency theories had no explanation of how development occurred, and thus no vision of the future. In response to these criticisms a "soft" variant of dependency emerged. It argued "dependent capitalist development"—a form of development that did not fundamentally alter the unequal relationship between core and periphery—was possible, but only when it was in the interests of the developed core states.[27]

The ideas developed by dependency and world system theories were embraced by many developing countries. Here was a paradigm that had been developed in large part by scholars from developing countries themselves, and that reflected their sense of exploitation going back to the era of European colonialism. Indeed, the demands by the South for the NIEO that were outlined above were strongly influenced by theories of dependency and the world system.

The Washington Consensus on International Development

The influence of dependency theories was relatively short-lived. By the mid-1980s a newer perspective on development called the "Washington Consensus" began to take hold.[28] In part, the shift occurred in response to the series of international crises that occurred during the 1970s and 1980s that produced important changes within the South and in their relations with the North. They included the oil crises of 1973 and 1979, the international recession of the early 1980s, and the debt crisis that emerged in 1982.

The *Washington Consensus* is so named because it was strongly endorsed by agencies within the United States government and by the two central institutions of the global economy, the International Monetary Fund (IMF) and the World Bank, both having their headquarters in the capital of the United States, Washington, DC. This view is based on the classical economic principles developed by Adam Smith, which put emphasis on a free and competitive market in which rational economic agents could make choices to overcome scarcity and efficiently utilize productive resources. Government intervention in the economy is to be minimal ("*laissez-faire*") and is to focus on stimulating savings, investment and production by the private sector. This would ensure that the economy produced the desired goods in the most efficient manner. Market instruments are supposed to encourage greater allocative efficiency, increased investment, faster economic

growth, and increased standard of living. From this perspective, the obstacles to development in the South lie in government interventions into the market, which result in an inefficient allocation of resources.

In some respects, then, the Washington Consensus can be seen as a contemporary restatement of some of the ideas that informed earlier works in modernization theory. The influence of the Consensus has been extended in part through the lending conditions of the IMF and World Bank to countries in the South that required assistance in managing their debts. These loans come with a package of conditions linked to specific economic and institutional reforms known as *structural adjustment* (see Box 13.7). The neoclassical economic principles on which the Consensus is based have also become an integral part of the contemporary phenomenon known as **globalization**. This issue is explored in greater detail in Chapter 16.

Perspectives on Women and Gender in Development

For most of the post–World War II period, scholars and policymakers were largely oblivious to the role of women in development. In the past two decades, however, the rise of gender-related social science research led to the emergence, in chronological order, of *women in development (WID)*, *women and development (WAD)* and most recently, *gender and development (GAD)* perspectives. The inclusion of gender-related issues in the study of development draws attention to the sources and dimensions of gender inequality and the victimization of women, the analysis of structures of power and patriarchy, and the ways to empower women and increase their participation in development processes.[29]

For example, with respect to the dimensions of gender inequality and victimization, women tend to be relegated to particular occupations. In Africa and South Asia, women dominate in the informal sector and in agricultural labour. In Southeast Asia and parts of Central and South America, women (and children) are largely found in low-wage, labour-intensive industry. Even in developed countries, a "gendered division of labour" is evident in the overrepresentation of women in the so-called "nurturing professions" such as teaching, nursing, social work, and so on. Furthermore, women tend to be underrepresented in the public sphere of politics and business. With a few notable exceptions throughout the developing world, women hold fewer government positions and their representation decreases

---

Some Typical Reforms Under Structural Adjustment   BOX 13.7

- Currency devaluation and market-determined exchange rate adjustments

- Anti-inflationary demand management measures, reduction in rate of growth of money supply, and wage restraints

- Reduction in the state's role in the economy through retrenchment and divestment of state-owned enterprises, and elimination of subsidies

- Restoration or construction of market mechanisms through price liberalization and deregulation

- Privatization

- Trade and financial sector liberalization

- Redirection of public expenditure toward infrastructure (schools, hospitals, etc.), and more recently, to poverty reduction

as one moves up the ladder of political power. In addition, women worldwide are subject to a litany of abuses, injustices, and acts of violence.

Most official statistics on economic activity have tended to overlook women's participation and contribution. Informal sector activities and production for household consumption, where women tend to dominate, for example, are not normally included in official GDP accounts. The UNDP has created a *Gender Development Index (GDI)* to complement the HDI. The GDI measures the gap between scores obtained by women and men on the HDI. In 2006, the country with the highest GDI (i.e., the lowest gap between men and women) was Norway followed closely by Iceland and Australia (see Table 13.5). In general, countries of the North score higher on the GDI than countries in the South. The highest-rated country in the South in 2006 was South Korea (rated 25). However, in every country in the world, developed and developing, women generally fare less well than men in virtually all indicators of development.

Sources of gender inequality in the South include traditional beliefs and cultural practices such as the preference in many parts of Africa and Asia for male children over females. Colonialism also compounded women's inequality by changing some traditional patterns of authority and economic activity. In some west African societies, for example, matrilineal patterns of lineage enabled women to play important political roles as clan elders, in the selection of traditional chiefs and kings, and even as chiefs. This system was eroded under British colonialism. Other factors affecting women's inequality include social class, ethnicity, religion, urbanization, and levels of education.

Studies on gender and development also identify ways to enhance women's participation in development processes. This has led to a focus on the issue of women's empowerment, designed to meet "strategic gender needs" of women in addition to their "practical gender needs." Practical gender needs include the basic necessities of survival such as health care, water, housing, food, and employment. Strategic gender needs are designed to address the structural inequalities between men and women, and the processes that have served to keep women in an inferior position. The premise underlying empowerment is that rights are not given, but won through political action. Greater equality for women will only come about through mobilization, activism, and participation.[30]

Contemporary Issues and Debates

A number of issues and debates arising from processes of development and change have become prominent in our period: the role of foreign aid and the impact of globalization on national development, sustainable development, democratization and development, and the management of political violence and war.

Table 13.5 Gender Development Index Rankings, 2006

TOP 10		BOTTOM 10	
Country Rank	**GDI**	**Country Rank**	**GDI**
1. Norway	0.962	127. Malawi	0.394
2. Iceland	0.958	128. Mozambique	0.387
3. Australia	0.956	129. Burundi	0.380
4. Ireland	0.951	130. Congo, Democratic Republic of	0.378
5. Sweden	0.949	131. Chad	0.350
6. Luxembourg	0.949	132. Central African Republic	0.336
7. Canada	0.947	133. Burkina Faso	0.335
8. United States	0.946	134. Mali	0.329
9. Netherlands	0.945	135. Sierra Leone	0.317
10. Switzerland	0.944	136. Niger	0.292

Source: UNDP, *Human Development Report,* 2006, Table 24, pp. 363–366. Used by permission of Oxford University Press.

Foreign Aid, Globalization, and Development

Foreign aid might be defined as the administered transfer of resources from rich to poor countries ostensibly to promote the latter's welfare and development.[31] The term *foreign aid* is usually reserved for official (i.e., government-to-government) transfers and resource flows as distinct from private resource flows. Foreign aid is also known as *official development assistance (ODA)*. ODA can be provided as *bilateral aid*, in which the assistance flows directly from a donor to a recipient government, and as *multilateral aid*, in which the assistance flows from donor governments through international organizations (such as the World Bank) to recipients. The largest source of Bilateral ODA comes from the 22 member states of the Development Assistance Committee of the Organization for Economic Cooperation and Development (DAC-OECD).

The practice of giving aid emerged mainly in the post–World War II era, and was driven by a mixture of self-interest and altruism on the part of donors. Aid was used to promote the strategic and political interests of donors (e.g., to counter the threat of communism) as well as to promote long-term growth of countries in the South. The amount of foreign aid increased steadily from the 1960s, peaking in 1991 at $69 billion, but declined during the 1990s. Table 13.6 provides a summary of foreign aid as a percentage of the GNPs of a selected group of the major donor countries in the North. In 1974, the UN recommended that donor countries devote a minimum of 0.7 percent of their GNP/GNI to development assistance. However, as the table shows, most of the major aid donors including Canada have not met the target.

Table 13.7, which shows long-term trends in ODA, reveals that some of the richest countries in the world, including the United States and Japan, devoted a smaller proportion of their national income to development assistance in 2004 than in 1960.

The reasons for the decline in foreign aid from the early 1990s to and into the early 2000s include the end of the Cold War, which reduced the strategic importance of the South to aid donors, and the emergence of unfavourable public attitudes within donor countries to foreign aid reinforced

Table 13.6 ODA/GNI Rankings of the Major Aid Donors, 2004

Country	ODA/GNI (%)
1. Norway	0.87
2. Luxembourg	0.85
3. Denmark	0.84
4. Sweden	0.77
5. Netherlands	0.74
0.7% GNI TARGET	
6. Portugal	0.63
7. France	0.42
8. Belgium	0.41
9. Ireland	0.39
10. Switzerland	0.37
11. United Kingdom	0.36
12. Finland	0.35
13. Germany	0.28
14. Canada	0.26
15. Spain	0.26
16. Australia	0.25
17. Austria	0.24
18. Greece	0.23
19. New Zealand	0.23
20. Japan	0.19
21. United States	0.16
22. Italy	0.15

Source: Adapted from OECD, *Development Cooperation*, 2005.

Table 13.7 Long-Term Trends in ODA, 1960–2004 (selected countries)

Country	ODA AS PERCENTAGE OF GNP/GNI*					
	1960	1970	1980	1990	1997	2004
Canada	0.19	0.43	0.43	0.44	0.31	0.26
Denmark	0.09	0.38	0.74	0.94	0.97	0.84
Germany	0.31	0.32	0.44	0.42	0.28	0.28
Japan	0.24	0.23	0.32	0.31	0.22	0.19
Netherlands	0.31	0.63	0.97	0.92	0.81	0.74
Sweden	0.05	0.37	0.78	0.91	0.76	0.77
United Kingdom	0.56	0.37	0.35	0.27	0.26	0.36
United States	0.53	0.31	0.27	0.21	0.08	0.16

* After 2000, figures are per expressed as a percentage of GNI.

Source: OECD, *Development Cooperation*, various years.

by the perception that aid was wasted and supported corrupt regimes in the South. Other important factors that contributed to the decline in ODA included the emergence of the Washington Consensus described above and the expansion and integration of global financial markets and expansion in private capital flows. Worldwide, private capital invests about $4 trillion annually, of which about $1.5 trillion is invested in developing countries. This figure is six times greater than the amount invested by governments. These factors have led to serious questions about the relevance of foreign aid in a globalized world. The new slogan is "trade not aid."

Indeed, some have characterized the contemporary period as a "post-aid" world—that globalization has rendered redundant the kinds of official financial transfers between governments that we call foreign aid. Supporters of this view argue that instead of receiving aid from donor governments in the North, countries in the South should adopt the policy prescriptions of the Washington Consensus, "get their houses in order," and thereby attract foreign private capital investment. Such private investment plus increased trade opportunities, they argue, are more effective avenues for achieving development than official government-to-government aid transfers.

Supporters of increased foreign aid, however, take a very different view. They observe that aid played a large role in the successful development of many countries in the postwar era. For example, they point to the Marshall Plan, named after U.S. Secretary of State George C. Marshall, in which the U.S. government provided aid to Western Europe that played a significant role in reconstruction and development after 1945. At its peak, the Plan represented about 2.0 percent of U.S. GNP. However, U.S. aid in 2004 was 0.16 percent of its national income. Furthermore, foreign aid, as noted in Box 13.4, was a key ingredient in the development of some of the East Asian NICs.

Supporters of foreign aid point to the paradox of "globalizing poverty amidst global prosperity" evident in the increased levels of poverty and inequality worldwide noted at the start of this chapter. Other critics question the ability of private capital to foster stable development. For example, they note the volatility and instability of such investment, evident in the major financial and debt crises that occurred in the South in the 1980s and 1990s. The major aid donors pledged to increase aid to help achieve the MDGs, and have sought ways to make aid more effective. However, debates about the role of foreign aid in development are likely to continue as processes of globalization intensify and global inequities widen.

Sustainable Development

The concept of **sustainable development** emerged in the 1980s, and was popularized through the publication of a report *Our Common Future* by the World Commission on Environment and Development (WCED) in 1987.[32] According to the WCED report, sustainable development is "development that meets the needs of the present without compromising the ability of future generations to meet their needs." It is "a process of change in which the exploitation of natural resources, the direction of investments, the orientation of technical development, and institutional change are all in harmony and enhance both current and future potential to meet human needs and aspirations." Since the report's publication, the concept of sustainable development has become a vital feature in discussions of development, and debates have centred on how to solve the "environmental paradox"—the mismatch between the demand placed on Earth's resources and what Earth is capable of supplying. A healthy natural environment is the lifeblood of successful development. However, many contemporary development practices are unsustainable, because they create numerous environmental problems including the depletion of natural resources, destruction of ecosystems, and air and water pollution. In the quest for economic growth, the environment had traditionally been seen as little more than a resource to be used and exploited. When environmental problems arose, they were seen as discrete technical problems requiring technical solutions, rather than as interconnected problems producing wide-ranging and often unforeseen consequences that required political as well as technical solutions.

Two broad views on how to solve the environmental paradox and achieve sustainable development have emerged in the literature. The first, "weaker sustainability" (or "shallow environmentalism") sees the solution in the expansion of the stock of resources by, for example, developing renewable resources, creating substitutes for non-renewable resources, and applying new technologies to solve problems such as resource depletion and pollution. The second view, "stronger sustainability" (or "deep ecology"), argues that nature is finite and thus rather than attempting to adapt the natural environment to meet the increased demands of the world's population, the demands made on the world's resources need to be changed and reduced.[33]

Since the late 1980s, international conferences have been convened (and agreements signed) with the objective of implementing sustainable development programs worldwide. These include the 1992 United Nations Conference on the Environment and Development (UNCED) also known as the Earth Summit held for the first time in Rio de Janeiro in Brazil. The second conference was held at UN headquarters in 1997. The third Earth Summit was held in Johannesburg in 2002. While a measure of international agreement exists on the desirability of environmentally sound development, there are considerable disagreements on how to implement sustainable development programs. These disagreements have assumed a distinct North–South dimension, and revolve around questions of who should bear the costs of cleaner and more environmentally friendly products and development processes.

For example, many countries in the South take the position that the North has contributed disproportionately to global environmental degradation. Relative to its population, the North produces a disproportionate amount of pollutants and consumes a disproportionate amount of global resources. At the Rio Summit in 1992, concerns were expressed that the emphasis on sustainable development may place too strong an emphasis on the environment at the expense of development in the South. Furthermore, some of the issues at the core of the environment–development debate, such as population growth, are among the most divisive political issues. They have reflected differences between North and South and between the "neomalthusians" who see dire negative consequences arising from unchecked population growth, and "cornucopians" who look to technology, increased production, and economic growth to meet demands of increased populations. Issues arising from women's rights and reproductive health are also at the centre of the debate. In addition, matters of national power and prestige, culture, race, and religion further complicate the debate over population growth.

Democracy, Civil Society, and Development

The term **democratization** describes the processes involved in the creation of democratic governments. This process entails the relaxation of authoritarian political control by political leaders, the expansion of political and civil liberties, and the creation of institutional mechanisms that open up a political system to greater representation and participation. On the basis of this definition, analysts have identified three "waves" of democratization, as discussed in more detail in the following chapter.[34] The "first wave" occurred between the 1820s and the 1920s with the expansion of the franchise and the creation of universal adult suffrage. The "second wave" occurred between 1945 and the early 1960s. This was largely due to decolonization in Asia and Africa. By the end of the 1960s, however, the trend toward democratization was reversed. Many of the newly emergent democratically elected governments in these countries were replaced by military dictatorships and single-party authoritarian systems. The current or "third wave" of democratization began in the mid-1970s, continued in the 1980s with democratic transitions in South and Central America, and intensified in the 1990s with the collapse of authoritarian communist governments in the Soviet Union and Eastern Europe, and the emergence of democratic forms of government in Africa and Asia.

Democracy and democratization have become important issues in discussions of development, and have generated a number of interesting debates. One of these debates centres on identifying the conditions that promote "democratic transitions" and the consolidation of democratic systems of government. One of the factors identified as playing a central role in processes of democratization is the role of **civil society**. Civil society is seen as the realm of organized private social life represented by nongovernmental actors and associations, which emerges through the organization of individuals and groups in society in pursuit of their interests.

Another aspect of the debate centres on the role of democracy in development. Some of the key issues informing this debate were outlined above where we discussed the relationship between political and economic development. While the empirical record does present inconclusive results, the widely held view today, influenced in part by the Washington Consensus, is that some form of democratic government is conducive to economic growth, if not an essential prerequisite for such growth. The reason is that the procedural aspects of democratic government are more likely to produce "good governance"—upholding the rule of law, ensuring transparency in the administration of justice, and allowing for citizen participation in decision making. These are seen as essential for private capital investment and market-driven economic growth.

The issue of democracy is important in discussions of development for yet another reason—the apparent relationship between democracy and peace and stability. This idea is captured in the notion of "democratic peace" that suggests that democratic governments tend to be more peaceful, because they have institutional and procedural safeguards that make it difficult to go to war, and because democratic norms encourage negotiation, compromise, and the peaceful settlement of disputes. This issue is of particular importance in view of the problems of civil war and state failure in many regions of the developing world, examined briefly below and in more detail in the following chapter.

Political Violence and Civil Strife

While the incidence of interstate war declined since the end of World War II in 1945, the incidence of various types of such war and other forms of organized group political violence within states increased. Almost all the major wars since 1945 have been in the developing world, with the exception of those that erupted in central and eastern Europe following the breakup of Yugoslavia

Table 13.8 Countries Experiencing Major Armed Conflicts, 1970–2000

Africa	The Americas	Asia/Middle East	Europe
Algeria	Colombia	Afghanistan	Armenia
Angola	El Salvador	Burma (Myanmar)	Azerbaijan
Burundi	Guatemala	Cambodia	Bosnia & Herzegovina
CAR	Haiti	Indonesia	Croatia
Chad	Nicaragua	Iraq	Georgia
Congo	Peru	India-Pakistan	Russia (Chechnya)
DR Congo		Israel/Occupied Territories	Yugoslavia (Kosovo)
Djibouti		Lebanon	
Eritrea		Sri Lanka	
Ethiopia		Tajikistan	
Guinea Bissau		Vietnam	
Liberia		Yemen	
Mali			
Mozambique			
Namibia			
Niger			
Rwanda			
Sierra Leone			
Somalia			
South Africa			
Sudan			
Uganda			

Source: Carter Centre, *State of World Conflict Report*, 2000.

and the USSR in the early 1990s. That decade saw an average of 30 ongoing civil wars per annum, most of which were in developing countries especially in Africa, South and Central America, and South Asia. Many of these wars have had devastating consequences on the political, economic, and social development of the affected countries. Table 13.8 provides a list of countries that experienced major armed conflicts between 1970 and 2000.

Thus, one key debate has focused on identifying the factors that lead to civil war and other forms of political violence. Some have sought the sources of war in economic factors; others have looked to the legacy of colonialism, and to the role of external powers which have intervened openly or covertly in many countries in the South. Some analysts examine social factors such as ethnic, cultural, and religious differences, and yet others examine the political sources of war. Here, the concept of **state failure**—a situation that arises when central governmental authority breaks down—has emerged as a key variable in the study of war.[35] Other aspects of the debate have centred on how best to manage, resolve, and prevent various types of armed conflicts. As noted early in this chapter, the concept of human security attempts to locate the sources of and possible solutions to insecurity, state failure, and political violence in processes of development and change.

CONCLUSION

The comparative study of development is a broad subfield within the discipline of political science, and so a single chapter cannot hope to cover all of the topics, issues, themes, approaches, and methods that make it up. Nevertheless, we have provided an introduction to some of the main issues that arise from the politics of development and underdevelopment. We have outlined some of the dimensions of global inequality, introduced some key concepts, provided a brief history of the evolution of the dialogue between rich countries of the North and the poorer countries of the South, offered some of the major explanations for patterns of development and underdevelopment, and discussed some of the contemporary issues and debates that arise from ongoing processes of development and change.

DISCUSSION QUESTIONS

1. Why has democracy become important in the study of development?

2. Are the explanations offered for development and underdevelopment by modernization and dependency theories still relevant today? Why or why not?

3. Should rich countries provide more aid to poorer countries?

4. In what ways does the inclusion of gender-related issues alter the way we think about development?

5. Why have issues of development generated conflict between rich countries of the North and poorer countries of the South?

KEY TERMS

COLONIALISM: The ownership and administration of one territory and people by another, as if the former were part of the latter. (377)

DECOLONIZATION: The process in which a population and territory formerly under colonial domination achieve formal political independence and become a sovereign state. (378)

DEPENDENCY: A condition in which countries in the South lack any degree of autonomy in their political, economic, and social development by virtue of their reliance on countries in the North for access to capital, technology, and markets. (390)

HUMAN DEVELOPMENT INDEX (HDI): A composite index measuring longevity, knowledge, and standard of living, designed to give an indication of and a basis for comparing the quality of life in various countries. (384)

HUMAN SECURITY: A broadened concept of security focusing not only on national security and interstate war but also on threats to the safety of individuals and groups. (374)

IMPERIALISM: A broader term than colonialism that literally means "empire building." Imperialism occurs when one country dominates another with the aim of controlling and/or exploiting the latter. The domination can be economic, political, social, or cultural. (377)

NEW INTERNATIONAL ECONOMIC ORDER (NIEO): A set of proposals launched in 1974 for reform of the international economic order, with the goal of enhancing the self-reliance of the South and its influence over international institutions and events and achieving an increase in resource flows from the North to the South. (379)

POLITICAL DEVELOPMENT: A concept that describes how well a society has developed politically, usually measured by the degree of state capacity to effectively carry out the legislative, executive, and judicial functions of government; the degree of political stability, or ability to resolve political conflicts in a peaceful manner; and the degree of governmental responsiveness to public demands and respect for fundamental rights. (384)

SELF-DETERMINATION: A principle of international law that grants all peoples/nations the right to determine their political status, and pursue their economic, social, and cultural development free from external domination or interference. (378)

SUSTAINABLE DEVELOPMENT: An approach to development that makes environmental conservation and protection an integral part of development processes, in order to enhance the ability of current and future generations to meet their needs. (396)

WEB LINKS

The World Bank:
http://www.worldbank.org

The United Nations Development Program:
http://www.undp.org

The World Trade Organization:
http://www.wto.org

International Monetary Fund:
http://www.imf.org

International Development Research Centre (Ottawa):
http://www.idrc.ca

FURTHER READING

Chilcote, Ronald H. *Theories of Development and Underdevelopment*. Boulder, CO: Westview Press, 1984.

Escobar, Arturo. *Encountering Development: The Making and Unmaking of the Third World*, Princeton University Press, 1996.

Handelman, Howard. *The Challenge of Third World Development*, 4th ed. Pearson-Prentice Hall, 2006.

Huntington, Samuel P. *The Third Wave: Democratization in the Late Twentieth Century*. Norman: University of Oklahoma Press, 1992.

Kiely, Ray, and Phil Marfleet, eds. *Globalization and the Third World*. London: Routledge, 1998.

Moser, Caroline. *Gender Planning and Development: Theory, Practice and Training*. New York: Routledge, 1993.

Rostow, Walt W. *The Stages of Growth: A Non-Communist Manifesto*. Cambridge: Cambridge University Press, 1960.

Schurman, Frans J. "Paradigms Lost, Paradigms Regained? Development Studies in the Twenty-First Century." *Third World Quarterly* 21(1) (2000): 7–20.

Sen, Armatya. *Development as Freedom*. New York: Alfred Knopf, 1999.

Weatherby, Joseph N., et al., eds. *The Other World: Issues and Politics of the Developing World*, 2nd ed. New York: Addison Wesley Longman, 2005.

Weiner, Myron, and S.P. Huntington, eds. *Understanding Political Development*. Boston: Little, Brown & Co, 1987.

World Commission on the Environment and Development. *Our Common Future*. New York: Oxford University Press, 1987.

ENDNOTES

1. Statistical figures in this section are drawn from the following sources: World Bank, *World Development Report 2004, 2005, 2006,* and *2007* (New York: Oxford University Press, 2004; 2005; 2006; 2007); World Bank, *Advancing Sustainable Development: The World Bank and Agenda 21* (Washington, DC: World Bank, 1997); United Nations Development Program (UNDP), *Human Development Report,* New York: Oxford University Press, various years.

2. UNDP, *Human Development Report,* 2005, p. 4.

3. United Nations Environment Program, *Global Environment Outlook 4* (UNEP, 2007).

4. See, for example, Allen H. Meriam, "What Does 'Third World' Mean?," in J. Norwine and A. Gonzalez, *The Third World: States of Mind and Being* (Boston: Unwin Hyman, 1988); and Richard E. Bissell, "Who Killed the Third World?," *The Washington Quarterly,* 13(4) (Autumn 1990): 23–32.

5. See, for example, Arturo Escobar, *Encountering Development: The Making and Unmaking of the Third World* (Princeton: Princeton University Press, 1996) and Wolfgang Sachs, ed., *The Development Dictionary* (London: Zed, 1992).

6. World Bank, *World Development Report, 2007,* Annex Table 1, pp. 334–35.

7. See, for example, Meriam, "What Does 'Third World' Mean?"

8. See Christopher Clapham, *Third World Politics* (London: Croom Helm, 1985).

9. For more on colonialism in the Americas, Africa, and Asia, see Clapham, *Third World Politics;* Joseph N. Weatherby et al., eds., *The Other World: Issues and Politics of the Developing World* (New York: Addison Wesley Longman, 2000), pp. 113–25.

10. See Robert H. Jackson, *Quasi-States: Sovereignty, International Relations and the Third World* (Cambridge: Cambridge University Press, 1990).

11. For more on the NIEO, see Jagdish Baghwati and John Ruggie, *Power, Passions and Purpose: Prospects for the North-South Negotiations* (Cambridge: Cambridge University Press, 1984).

12. These included the Independent Commission on International Development Issues (Brandt Commission, 1980); the Independent Commission on Disarmament and Security Issues (Palme Commission, 1982); the World Commission on Environment and Development (Brundtland Commission, 1987); the South Commission (1990); and the Commission on Global Governance (1995).

13. For more on the debt crisis, see James Busumtwi-Sam, "International Financial Institutions, International Capital Flows, and Financial Liberalization in Developing Countries," in Stephen McBride and John Wiseman, eds., *Globalization and Its Discontents* (London: Macmillan & NY: St. Martin's Press, 2001), pp. 84–96.

14. *Report of the South Commission,* 1990, pp. 50–55.

15. World Bank, *World Development Indicators,* external debt tables, various years; *Recent Developments in External Debt,* Report of the United Nations Secretary-General, A/61/152, July 2006, p. 3.

16. For more on the MDGs, see World Bank, *World Development Report,* 2004, p. 2.

17. Figures in this section are from the World Bank, *World Development Report,* 2006 and 2007.

18. GDP measures the total economic output of a country for a given period, usually a year. This figure is then divided by the total population to obtain the GDP per capita. Production of wealth is also sometimes expressed as the gross national product (GNP) or the gross national income (GNI) which replaced the GNP in World Bank Classifications in 2000. The GDP excludes net income earned from abroad, while the GNP/GNI includes this income. Of the two, the GDP is more commonly used to compare economic production across countries.

19. Figures in this section are from the UNDP, *Human Development Report*, 2004 (New York: United Nations, 2004).

20. For more on political development, see Myron Weiner and S. P. Huntington, eds., *Understanding Political Development* (Boston: Little, Brown & Co, 1987); and Howard Handelman, *The Challenge of Third World Development*, 2nd ed. (Prentice Hall, 2000).

21. See, for example, Samuel P. Huntington, *Political Order in Changing Societies* (New Haven: Yale University Press, 1968).

22. See Walt W. Rostow, *The Stages of Growth: A Non-Communist Manifesto* (Cambridge: Cambridge University Press, 1960).

23. Notable works on modernization include Clifford Geertz, *Old Societies, New States: The Quest for Modernity in Asia and Africa* (New York: Free Press, 1963); Gabriel A. Almond and James S. Coleman, *The Politics of Developing Areas* (Princeton: Princeton University Press, 1960); Edward Shills, *Political Development in the New States* (The Hague: Mouton, 1966); David Apter, *The Politics of Modernization* (Chicago: University of Chicago Press, 1965); A.F.K. Organski, *Stages of Political Development* (New York: Knopf, 1965). For a recent discussion of modernization theory, see Samuel P. Huntington and Myron Weiner, eds., *Understanding Political Development* (Boston: Little, Brown, 1987).

24. See, for example, Samuel P. Huntington, *Political Order in Changing Societies* (New Haven: Yale University Press, 1968).

25. Prominent works in the dependency tradition include A.G. Frank, *Capitalism and Underdevelopment in Latin America* (New York: Monthly Review Press, 1966); Samir Amin, *Accumulation on a World Scale* (New York: Monthly Review Press, 1975); Ronald H. Chilcote, *Theories of Development and Underdevelopment* (Boulder, CO: Westview Press, 1984); F. Cardoso and E. Falletto, *Dependency and Development in Latin America* (Berkeley: University of California Press, 1979); Walter Rodney, *How Europe Underdeveloped Africa* (London and Dar-es-Salaam: Bogle L'Ouverture and Tanzania Publishing House, 1972); and Immanuel Wallerstein, *The Modern World System* (New York: Academic Press, 1974).

26. André Gunder Frank, *Capitalism and Underdevelopment in Latin America* (New York: Monthly Review Press, 1966).

27. See, for example, F. Cardoso, "Dependent Capitalist Development in Latin America," *New Left Review* 74 (1972) and Peter Evans, *Dependent Development: The Alliance of Multinational, State and Local Capital in Brazil* (Princeton: Princeton University Press, 1979).

28. For more on the Washington Consensus, see John Williamson, "What Washington Means by Policy Reform," in John Williamson, ed., *Latin American Adjustment: How*

Much Has Happened? (Washington, DC: Institute for International Economics, 1990); and Charles Gore, "The Rise and Fall of the Washington Consensus as a Paradigm for Developing Countries," *World Development* 28(5) 2000: 789–804.

29. See Caroline Moser, *Gender Planning and Development: Theory, Practice and Training* (New York: Routledge, 1993); Eva Rathgeber, "WID, WAD, GAD: Trends in Research and Practice," *Journal of Developing Areas* 24 (1990): 489–502.

30. Jane L. Parpart, "Rethinking Participation, Empowerment and Development from a Gender Perspective," in Jim Freedman, ed., *Transforming Development* (University of Toronto Press, 2000), pp. 222–34.

31. See Ray Kiely and Phil Marfleet, eds., *Globalization and the Third World* (London: Routledge, 1998).

32. World Commission on the Environment and Development, *Our Common Future* (Oxford University Press, 1987).

33. Colin C. Williams and Andrew C. Millington, "The Diverse and Contested Meanings of Sustainable Development," *The Geographical Journal*, 170(2) (June 2004): 99–104.

34. See Samuel P. Huntington, *The Third Wave: Democratization in the Late Twentieth Century* (Norman: University of Oklahoma Press, 1992).

35. Michael Brown, ed., *Ethnic Conflict and International Security* (Princeton: Princeton University Press, 1993), and I. William Zartman, ed., *Collapsed States: The Disintegration and Restoration of Legitimate Authority* (Boulder, CO: Lynne Rienner, 1995).

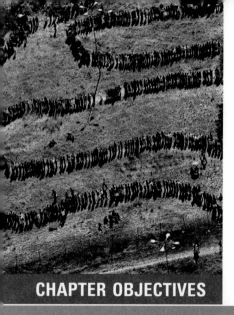

Chapter Fourteen

REGIME CHANGE IN AN ERA OF GLOBALIZATION

Peter A. Ferguson

CHAPTER OBJECTIVES

After you have completed this chapter, you should be able to:

■ describe how the state of global democracy has changed over the past 30 years

■ explain the causes and consequences of the regime breakdown process

■ discuss the implications of a democratic transition

■ discuss the impediments to and the consequences of democratic consolidation

Why Study Regime Change?

During your lifetime, the world has experienced a dramatic transformation in the way most people are governed. The number of democratic governments worldwide has surged over the past 30 years to the point that there are many more countries with democratic governments than with nondemocratic ones. This wave of democracy has extended across the globe from southern Europe to Latin America, Southeast Asia, Eastern Europe, and Africa. The implications of this change can be seen from things as simple as where you are now able to travel to where you may end up working or doing business when you graduate from school. On a national level, the countries with which Canada interacts have radically changed. Recent negotiations dealing with expanding the North American Free Trade Agreement (NAFTA) to include all the Americas—the Free Trade Area of the Americas (FTAA)—for example, included discussions about the importance of maintaining democracy throughout the Americas. On an international level, as the forces of globalization and interdependence "shrink" the size of the world we live in, the scope of incentives (and disincentives) for these new democracies to avoid nondemocratic change has greatly increased. Table 14.1 tracks the increase in democratic states between 1900 and 2000.

Why, then, should you be interested in the global democratic transformation? The answers are the same as the ones found in Chapter 1 when we discussed the reasons to study politics. Global democratization is fascinating—there are colourful characters and interesting stories about faraway places. Beyond that, democratization is very important. It has serious implications not only for the people who live in countries that experience such transitions, but also for people who come into contact with those countries, whether through family, business, or travel. The

Table 14.1 Tracking the Trend to Democracy in the 20th Century

	1900 Units	1900 Percent	1950 Units	1950 Percent	2000 Units	2000 Percent
Democracy	0	0	22	14	120	63
Restricted democratic practice	25	19	21	14	16	8
Constitutional monarchy	19	14	9	6	0	0
Traditional monarchy	6	5	4	3	10	5
Absolute monarchy	5	4	2	1	0	0
Authoritarian regime	0	0	10	7	39	20
Totalitarian regime	0	0	12	8	5	3
Colonial dependency	55	42	43	28	0	0
Protectorate	20	15	31	20	2	1
Total	**130**		**154**		**192**	

Source: Adapted from Freedom House, *Democracy's Century: A Survey of Global Political Change in the 20th Century* (New York: Freedom House, 1999); available at http://www.freedomhouse.org/reports/century.html#table1; accessed August 1, 2002. Reprinted by permission of Freedom House.

issues surrounding the questions of citizenship are galvanized around democratization. At a time when many Canadians no longer seem to care about politics, reading a story about people waiting in line for eight or nine hours while facing military forces bent on intimidation—simply to be able to exercise their right to vote—should help us all appreciate the importance of democratic citizenship. Finally, the wave of democracy that has transformed the world we live in holds great opportunities for political science graduates. In this era of globalization, companies, governments, and all sorts of organizations need to hire people knowledgeable about this expanding list of democratic countries—about which they lack a real understanding but are now forced to interact with on a variety of levels. Understanding the material in this chapter could lay the foundation for you to take one of these exciting jobs.

Regime Breakdown

Change is the one constant in politics, and this is especially evident in the examination of political **regimes**. Throughout history, one sees the rise and fall of regimes. This section examines issues surrounding regime breakdown. Why should we be interested in such breakdowns? If we are to understand why some countries become democracies and others do not, and why democracy persists in some countries and not in others, we must first understand the roots of such change. These are found in an examination of the breakdown of the prior nondemocratic regimes. One thing that is important to understand from the beginning is that the collapse of a nondemocratic regime does not necessarily result in a democratic regime coming to power. Down the ages, the most likely result of a nondemocratic regime breakdown has been the institution of another nondemocratic regime, not the establishment of a democracy. To understand why, we must first look at the various trigger events or causes of breakdown and then examine the various actors that play a part in such an occurrence. On that basis, we can turn our attention to the various consequences of these breakdowns.

Breakdown Causes

What are the events or situations that raise the possibility of regime breakdown? This chapter argues that the causes of breakdowns interact with the actors in a particular country to lay the foundation for breakdown. These causes set the table for change. Once the table has been set, we need to examine the various actors to determine not only if the regime will break down but also what outcome will be produced. For ease of understanding, the trigger events are divided into economic, social, and political explanations.

Economic Causes One of the most widely studied concepts in political science is the idea of modernization. Seymour Martin Lipset advanced the argument that socioeconomic development is a prerequisite for democracy. In order for nondemocratic countries to become democratic, they must achieve a certain level of development. The idea is that as a country modernizes, its social structures become increasingly complex and a variety of new groups emerge; this produces a system that can no longer be effectively governed by command, and democracy emerges.[1] This theory makes sense in that poor countries tend to be nondemocratic, whereas rich countries tend to be democratic. The fate of middle-income countries, however, varies widely. The search for an economic threshold for democracy continues to be a highly contested idea in political science.

A second potential economic explanation examines the economic performance of regimes. Unlike the modernization theory, this approach argues that enduring levels of poor economic performance trigger regime changes. As the economy in a country deteriorates, the resources available are reduced, making it harder to maintain the regime's bases of support. One way of thinking about this is that political regimes usually have a group of allies. The regime receives support from its allies, which allows it to continue to run the country. In exchange for this support, the regime's allies receive benefits, many of which cost the regime money (tax breaks, subsidies, and so on). As the economy deteriorates, the amount of money available to the regime is reduced, resulting in a reduction of the regime's ability to deliver benefits to its supporters. At some point, benefits are reduced to such an extent that support is withdrawn and the regime collapses.[2]

Social Causes A variety of explanations for regime breakdown revolve around social (and psychological) issues in a country. The theory of rising expectations recognizes that people have a set of expectations about their future and that significant events, such as a regime change, can cause people to raise their expectations. These expectations are commonly economic in nature but can also include things such as human rights. The difficulty with such expectations arises when they go unmet, causing people to agitate for change. When a new regime comes to power, such as when Nelson Mandela was elected in South Africa, people expect that their economic situation will improve. In this case, as in others, they expected that jobs would be more plentiful, that they would earn more money, and that they would be able to buy more goods. As the euphoria surrounding the demise of apartheid and Mandela's election began to fade from memory, the people of South Africa started asking themselves if they were, in fact, better off than they had been before these changes. Many observers of South Africa believe these unmet expectations hold the seeds for significant tensions in the future.

A second theory, that of relative deprivation, looks at situations in which the conditions people have come to understand as normal change for the worse. Unlike the rising expectations theory, this theory examines the circumstance where people have a relatively stable set of expectations that have been met over time. When these expectations are no longer met, people begin to support systemic change. A number of Eastern European countries saw communist parties return to power in the second round of elections following the demise of the Soviet Union. Many observers have argued that some of this shifting support can be explained by the idea that the initial post-Soviet regimes were forced to cut back on commodity price supports and to slash the size of the public sector. As a result, concerns and expectations that people had regarding issues ranging from the price of food to job security significantly worsened and caused them to throw their support behind parties that had maintained acceptable levels of these values in the past. Such a shifting of support back to past nondemocratic actors increases the chances of regime change.

A third set of theories relevant to regime breakdown surrounds the issue of ethnic conflict. Many countries throughout the world are now home to numerous ethnic groups. In some places, two main groups vie for power. In India, for example, the Hindu majority makes up more than 80 percent of the population, while the Muslim minority makes up a little more than 10 percent. Other countries face more severe **cleavages**. Nigeria contains people of more than 250 languages and tribes, of which the three main groups make up two-thirds of the population. Such cleavages do not always trigger serious problems, however, as the experiences of Canada and the United States attest. Donald Horowitz argues that ethnic divisions threaten regimes due to problems with inclusion and exclusion. Those included in power structures receive certain privileges, while those excluded from power receive penalties. The difficulty arises when groups begin to feel that the exclusions from power are permanent. If groups foresee that there is no possibility for them to receive the privileges of power, they may begin to cause problems for the regimes, especially through violent actions. The groups in power, likewise, feel the need to protect their power and often resort to violence in order to do so.[3] The postcolonial histories of the Central African countries of Burundi and Rwanda demonstrate that when ethnic divisions explode, in this case between the Hutu and the Tutsi, hundreds of thousands can die in the subsequent fighting.

Political Causes One of the most common explanations of regime breakdown is corruption. While a certain amount of political corruption is found everywhere, the level in some states is extremely high, and it is generally highest in developing countries. Almost without fail, when a regime is overthrown, the victors point to the endemic levels of corruption found in the old regime as a justification for taking power. Their argument is that such corruption creates economic inefficiencies that make it impossible for the country to develop. They also point out that it becomes increasingly difficult for the mass public to trust political leaders who are seen as personally benefiting from the fruits of corruption. Transparency International is an international nongovernmental organization devoted to studying the causes and consequences of and cures for corruption. Their website, http://www.transparency.org, contains a wealth of information on this issue.

A second set of political explanations can be found in the idea of institutional failure. When the institutions of government cease to function, it becomes increasingly difficult for a regime to sustain itself. Legislative assemblies that can no longer pass legislation because of fractionalized party systems make it virtually impossible for a regime to solve the problems it faces. Bureaucracies that have extensively relied on patronage appointments may no longer be capable of administering the country. This is especially problematic when the effectiveness of the tax (revenue) agency is compromised. The problems a regime faces when institutional failure begins to occur are manifold. In Turkey, for example, the military has intervened at least three times since independence because of institutional failure. In 1980, the situation reached such an extreme that the military argued the government could no longer control the spread of violence across the country, so they took over. Every time the Turkish military stepped into power, they vowed to return power to civilian governments as soon as they got the situation under control. And, every time, they did so, something that cannot be said of many other military regimes.

A final political explanation can be found in war. History is replete with examples of defeated regimes breaking down and being replaced by new ones. If a regime cannot maintain the integrity of its borders, it has little hope of surviving. Following World War II, political regimes in defeated Germany and Japan had new, democratic regimes imposed on them. Shortly after losing the Falklands War to Britain, the military regime governing Argentina collapsed. It is not always the case, however, that military defeat signals the demise of a regime.

Most would argue that the first Gulf War coalition led by the United States defeated Iraq, but that if anything, the regime led by Saddam Hussein emerged more fully entrenched. In general, though, military defeat signals to regime opponents that there is a vulnerability that can be exploited, raising the risk of regime breakdown.

Breakdown Actors

A variety of actors and groups are involved in and affected by any type of political regime. We will discuss here five sets of actors: political elites, business elites, the military, the mass public, and the international community. These rather large groupings are not necessarily mutually exclusive—a member of the military might also belong to the political elite, for example. Nor do these groups function as a unified whole; there is certainly no agreement within any one group across all issues and concerns. Such a basic division of actors, however, will provide us with an understanding of the set of players within a regime and help explain why one or more of these groups might seek to change the regime.

Political Elite The political **elite** is a group that is interested in the functioning and overall success of any regime. This group consists of more than just the political leader and his or her immediate advisors. Also included is the upper echelon of the various departments of the bureaucracy, members of the legislature, the leadership of any recognized "loyal" opposition, important regional and local leaders, and a variety of civilian leaders who play a vital role in the support and operation of the government. These people are powerful players in the country because of their ability not only to influence government policy but also to distribute the benefits of such policy. These benefits may include such disparate things as providing family and friends with jobs, securing public works projects for one's home region, and getting a tax policy approved to benefit an important domestic industry.

If these people are most directly responsible for the functioning of politics in a country, why would they ever take part in its demise? As in most sporting events, politics creates winners and losers. The winners seek to maintain or augment their power. If, for example, a finance minister in a country feels he has reached the apex of power under the current regime but has aspirations to be leader himself, he might conceivably support change, anticipating that he will become the leader of the new regime. If someone at such a high level in government could defect (withdraw support from the existing regime), it should be fairly easy to understand why those within the political elite who have not attained such powerful positions might also withdraw their support. Beyond the desire to improve personal or group position and power, there might also be concern about the direction in which important policy is heading or for the overall welfare of the country. Likely some combination of all of these factors is at play.

Business Elite The second important group of actors is the business elite. This group consists of the people outside of government involved in the functioning of the country's economy, including the leaders of the country's largest corporations, key associational groups (e.g., lawyers or engineers), and trade groups (such as major unions). These people and groups are important players in that they are responsible in large part for the health and direction of the country's economy: they provide the people with jobs, the government with tax revenues, and the country with regional or global prestige. Most obviously, the business elite may withdraw their support from a regime if the economy is performing poorly or if it is in the midst of a severe crisis. However, it may happen that regimes also break down during relatively stable or prosperous economic times. Why? It could be that certain groups feel left out of the political process (e.g., labour unions). Others may feel that while the economy is in good shape, in order for the country to experience real success government policies must be changed (such as opening the country to more global trade or restricting the flow of goods entering the country). The point is not the particular policy or problem; it is that sometimes the economic losers are willing to gamble to improve their position, while the winners feel they might do even better under a new regime.

The Military The group most often considered when examining regime change is the military. It is the military that executes coups and crushes rebellions. If, as Mao said, power grows out of the barrel of a gun, then surely the military will always be a key actor in regime breakdown. Unlike in Western democracies, the military in most nondemocratic regimes plays an important role in both external and internal security. Political leaders rely on the support of the military for their survival. There are numerous explanations as to why the military might withdraw its support from a regime. It is useful to divide such explanations into internal and external rationales. Internally, the military is usually concerned, first and foremost, with its institutional survival. Actions, events, and circumstances that the military perceives as threats to its survival can include things such as the dismissal of popular or powerful military figures, the undermining of military discipline, and severe budget cuts. Additionally, internal conflicts can arise when junior officers see no room for promotion, or when traditional elements perceive the institution as becoming too politicized. External rationales might include a perception that the civilian government is corrupt or unable to deal with economic or political crises, and the desire on the part of the military to seek a stronger role in influencing the direction the country is taking. Most often several reasons interact with one another and serve as justification for military intervention. The role of the military in Pakistan is discussed in Box 14.1.

Mass Public The mass public also has a role to play in the breakdown of nondemocratic regimes. Too often people think of such regime change as an elite-driven process, but as events ranging from the fall of the Berlin Wall to the "people power" movement in the Philippines

---

Case Study: Pakistan | BOX 14.1

To understand the role of the military as an obstacle to democratization in developing countries, we need look no further than the Pakistani model. In 1997, Nawaz Sharif, leading a 14-party coalition, was elected to the post of prime minister. Following his election Sharif sought to "undermine every institution capable of challenging him, including the judiciary and the press" (Freedom House, 2007). It was only after Sharif sought to undermine the primacy of the military, however, that his leadership was compromised. In October 1999, after Nawaz attempted to remove General Pervez Musharraf, the Chief of Army Staff, Musharraf returned to Pakistan and seized control in a bloodless coup, becoming the fourth Army chief to take control of the country. Musharraf ruled in a similarly authoritarian manner, suspending the constitution, dismissing or jailing several judges, and arresting political dissidents. Later elected President, he was forced to resign for his misdeeds in 2008.

SOURCE: Based on "Freedom in the World: Pakistan, 2007," *Freedom in the World* (New York: Freedom House, 2007).

demonstrate, the power of the mass public should not be ignored. The mass public consists of all the people in a country not included in the first three groups—the "regular" citizens. The raw numbers of people involved is what makes this group powerful. Nothing makes elite groups sit up and pay attention as 100,000 people, normally only marginally involved in politics, marching in the streets. As a result, the public can wield a lot of power; it also represents a significant source of potential power for other groups to use or threaten to use. Groups perceived to have the support of the masses can often increase their power simply by threatening to mobilize mass demonstrations. Likewise, groups occasionally may set out to mobilize the masses to push for reforms, but end up frightening other actors (such as the military) into much more extensive responses because of these actors' fear of such mobilization.

The public may withdraw its support for the old regime for a variety of reasons. Economic reasons span a wide spectrum, which includes factors such as poor economic performance, the onset of economic crisis, the failure to meet expectations raised by initial successes, and a lack of hope for the future among the rising middle classes. Political reasons can range from scandals involving key leaders to extensive levels of corruption to assassinations of sympathetic or popular figures. In November 2004, despite subzero temperatures, tens of thousands of citizens camped out in central Kiev, the Ukrainian capital, for several weeks in support of efforts to overturn the results of an obviously fraudulent presidential election. Bowing to this pressure (as well as that of opposition politicians and the international community), the government arranged for new elections to be held the day after Christmas. The vote reversed the previous result and elected opposition leader Viktor Yushchenko. This example aside, it is important to remember that there is a normal level of public activity in most countries that is usually not exceeded. It is rare for the public to be mobilized to an extent necessary to trigger regime change. While it does happen, the role the public more often plays is in the credible threat that another actor may gain its support and mobilize it.

During the WTO summit meeting in Seattle in late 1999, protestors stood in silent confrontation with a line of police officers who had closed the intersection after a demonstration at McDonald's.

CP Photo/Eric Draper

International Community The final player in regime change is the international community. This group includes any actors not resident in the country in question. It may include actors in neighbouring countries, in countries with economic or political involvement in the country, and in regional and international organizations. During the Cold War, the role of the international community was defined more by strategic interests than by other considerations. The international influence on regime breakdown was more a function of whom the regime (or its opponents) supported at the global level and how important its strategic position was to the superpowers. Immediately following the end of the Cold War, the international community became much more involved in expressing its support for democracy as the preferred regime type. The international community, owing in significant part to the influence of the United States and its closest allies, became decidedly more active and aggressive in the promotion of global democracy. Following the events of 9/11, the U.S. became more tolerant of nondemocratic regimes, such as Pakistan, in exchange for their support for the "war on terror." More recently, President Bush has made a concerted effort to tie support for democracy and opposition to terrorism together into one overarching test of whether a country deserves the support of the United States and its allies. Box 14.2 outlines the Bush Doctrine in more detail.

The Bush Doctrine   BOX 14.2

Addressing the graduating class of 2002 of the U.S. Military Academy at West Point, President Bush introduced what has come to be known as the "Bush Doctrine" when he announced the end of foreign policy based on containment and deterrence. In an era defined by the threat of terrorism, he argued, if you wait for threats to fully materialize, you have waited too long. Instead, the security of the United States requires all Americans to "be ready for pre-emptive action when necessary to defend our liberty and our lives." The policy of preemption was described more formally in the *National Security Strategy of the U.S.A.* released on September 17, 2002 (http://www. whitehouse.gov/nsc/nss.html).

This document points to a new vision of American interaction with the world: rogue states and terrorists will be confronted preemptively, the United States will not allow its military superiority to be challenged, and the U.S. will use its economic and military power to encourage the spread of freedom and democracy. Recognizing the potential for international resistance, the policy further states that when American vital interests are at stake, the United States will seek international approval for its actions but will go it alone if necessary.

In 1992, following the failure to oust Saddam Hussein from power during the first Gulf War, Paul Wolfowitz (the Pentagon's third-highest-ranking civilian at the time) drafted a set of guidelines titled "Defence Planning Guidance" calling for America to "talk loudly, carry a big stick, and use its military power to pre-empt the proliferation of weapons of mass destruction" (http://www.pbs.org/wgbh/pages/ frontline/shows/iraq). Further, he argued

that coalitions of the future would be ad hoc collections of states and that the United States should be prepared to act independently when collective action cannot be orchestrated. The document was leaked to the press, triggering controversy, and Secretary of Defence Dick Cheney was forced to rewrite it, removing all reference to preemptive action.

Nevertheless, the George W. Bush Administration put the policy of preemption to the test in Iraq during the second Gulf War. An evaluation of events surrounding this war remains premature. However, it should be noted that President Bush not only views it as a success but also as a template for further action. In his 2005 State of the Union address and in a number of subsequent speeches, he indicated that the United States continues to view preemptive military action as a viable strategy, specifically pointing to Iran and Syria as potential future targets. In meeting the objective of spreading democracy throughout the Middle East and the rest of the world, the president argues that no tools should be taken off the table.

When discussing such potential application of preemptive military strikes we should, at minimum, evaluate questions of imminence and globalism. In most societies, self-defence is justified if someone points a gun at you and threatens your life; there is no requirement to wait until after you are shot to act. The key to resolving the situation, legally and morally, is evaluating the credibility of the threat. Similarly, on the international level, the key is to understand both whether there is a threat and, if so, whether it is imminent. If the threat is not judged imminent, "just war" theory would counsel consideration of nonmilitary solutions. In this regard, the globalization of

When attempting to influence regimes, a variety of tools are available, including, most importantly, aid and trade. Countries desiring aid from the West and from international organizations such as the **World Bank** and the **International Monetary Fund (IMF)** are much more likely to receive that aid if they are democratic or if they undertake democratic reforms (and/or support U.S. efforts against terrorism) than if they operate in a nondemocratic fashion (and/or oppose U.S. efforts against terrorism). Increasingly, democratic reforms are one of the main preconditions for such countries to receive economic assistance. Countries experiencing democratic reversals are much more likely to come under pressure to return to democracy or face the prospect of losing access to such assistance. Likewise, trade relations are increasingly becoming tied to democracy and democratic reform. Western countries have become more reluctant to trade with countries that are not democracies; when they do trade with such countries, they often attempt to use the expansion (or restriction) of trade as a tool to encourage democracy. As mentioned, the proposed FTAA treaty text includes provisions for the exclusion of countries that experience democratic reversals. Economic assistance and trade relations have, in short, become a powerful tool used to push for democratic reform in nondemocratic countries and to prevent democratic breakdown in existing democracies.

Breakdown Consequences

Having outlined the major actors in the regime breakdown process, we can now turn our attention to the consequences of such breakdowns. This section will address three basic consequences: nondemocratic change, liberalization, and democratization. As previously stated, the most common result of the breakdown of a nondemocratic regime is its replacement with another: one military government replaces another or one dictator replaces another. If one is able to identify the key actors and their interests, it is not difficult to see why they may not favour a democratic outcome. If the goal is to get rid of the old regime in order to take power, there is no real desire for open competition. In certain cases, however, regime breakdown holds the potential to start the democratization process.

A second potential outcome is liberalization. Liberalization occurs when a regime significantly expands civil and political liberties in the country or opens itself up, at some level, to more meaningful competition from opposition forces. This does not mean that it becomes a democracy, but rather that it takes on some of the trappings of democracy. Why would a regime do such a thing? First, a regime that finds itself in trouble may seek to stave off radical change and total loss of power by agreeing to ease off some of the restrictions it has in place. It may attempt to address problems of human rights violations; allow increased group formation (e.g., labour organizations); ease restrictions on freedom of the press, religion, association, or speech; or allow opposition parties to compete in a more meaningful fashion at the local, regional, or national level. It takes these actions not to begin the process of democratic change but rather to stave it off. The idea is to change certain policies to address the concerns of powerful opposition forces in order to guarantee the survival of the regime.

Second, regimes may pursue liberalization because they seek to expand their power and influence. Occasionally, very stable nondemocratic regimes pursue liberalization exactly because they feel secure and powerful. As the above discussion about the international community points up, a number of advantages (such as access to aid and trade) are available to regimes that undertake some type of democratic reform that are not available to nondemocratic regimes. Therefore, regimes that feel they can undertake some democratic reforms while continuing to maintain their control and power liberalize in an attempt to receive these extra benefits.

In both cases, the difficulty is that, once started, liberalization is difficult to control. As the different actors begin to get a taste of the advantages of change, they are often tempted to push for even more change. Such reforms also send unintended signals to opponents of the regime. Rather than seeing such reforms as a decision made from a position of strength, opponents often interpret them as a sign of weakness and redouble their efforts to overthrow the regime. This is especially true in regimes attempting to save themselves from mounting problems. Finally, almost all nondemocratic regimes overestimate their power and popularity. When the means to express dissatisfaction with the system are restricted long enough, leaders often (incorrectly) take silent acquiescence as a positive sign of support for the regime. This combination produces a situation in which the regime overestimates its power, while signalling to the opposition that it is vulnerable and providing an opportunity for all the actors (both its supporters and its opponents) to experience the benefits of reform. The bottom line is that while liberalization often seems to be a sound strategy for a regime to maintain its control over a country, it proves difficult to control in the end.

The final potential outcome of regime breakdown is some form of transition to democracy. Most often, this involves the announcement that democratic elections will be held at some future date. Depending on the circumstances and the degree of power the old regime still holds, several events follow from such an announcement. One has to do with the country's constitution. In order to accommodate democracy, countries often have to write an entirely new constitution or radically overhaul the old one. The terms of such constitutional reforms are a function of the power and desires of the old regime and the opposition. A second issue arises from the fact that the old regime has to make political room for the opposition, usually in the form of political parties. Again, the strength of the old regime dictates its ability to control this process. Outgoing regimes that maintain a significant power base often attempt to exclude popular leaders or parties that might threaten the success of their preferred candidate or party. Regimes with little power may attempt to exclude only anti-system parties, such as rebel groups or communists. A last issue surrounds the election itself. Regimes attempt to control such things as the timing of the election, voter eligibility and registration, access to the media, the runoff process, and the transparency of tabulating the results. As with the other issues, the ability to control the election is a function of the distribution of power of the players and their various objectives.

Nondemocratic Regime Change

The most common historical outcome of regime breakdown is nondemocratic change, of which there are three main forms. The first is *political dissent*, which can range from protest to domestic violence to international terror. The second is *rebellion*, which for purposes of this section refers to military coups and *autogolpes* (leaders' coups against themselves). The third is *state failure*, which can be understood by examining civil war and social breakdown.

Political Dissent

Political dissent involves some form of action taken to indicate a rejection of the existing order. Protest is one aspect of dissent that is both widespread and accepted throughout the world. People who feel they are unable to effect change through the mechanisms of government turn instead to protest. When groups feel that government is no longer paying attention, one option they have is to expand the scope of the conflict. By organizing rallies and demonstrations, they hope to inform a greater portion of the population about their cause and thus force the government to act. It is important to remember that protest can produce results ranging from no change to wider recognition of the issues to the initiation of regime change. The world has recently seen many protests surrounding the issues of globalization. The first major action in this regard took place in November 1999, when protesters attempted to disrupt the World Trade Organization's meetings in Seattle, Washington. One of the major difficulties with protest is that it may turn violent. While many protesters look to the likes of Gandhi and Martin Luther King for examples of nonviolent protest, others believe the only way to galvanize opinion (and media coverage) is through violent protest. Students protesting economic and human rights conditions in South Korea during the late 1980s routinely hurled rocks, bottles, and Molotov cocktails at the police. Anyone following the protests of Palestinian youths against Israel has probably seen similar pictures. The point here is that protest is undertaken for many different reasons, can take many forms, and can have a variety of effects. The importance of protest for our purposes is that it can signal that there is a potential for regime change.

A second form of political dissent can be found in domestic violence and terror. Groups seeking systemic change in a country sometimes turn to organized violence in an attempt to force change. The battle between the Irish Republican Army (IRA) and the British government is a prime example. Feeling that the British had no legitimate claim to rule Northern Ireland, the IRA, which was formed following the Easter Rebellion in 1916, undertook a sustained campaign of terrorism in both Ireland and England. The aim was to force change by constantly reminding the people of the IRA's cause and making them doubt their personal security. In December 1999, the political arm of the IRA (Sinn Fein) formally entered into the governing process in Northern Ireland in exchange for the disarmament of the IRA. Following a series of negotiations in 2006, both Britain and Ireland declared

The Grim Reaper takes on the United States and Afghanistan.

Carlucho, Cartoonists & Writers Syndicate/ cartoonweb.com

that the IRA no longer represented a terrorist threat. Another example of domestic terror involves the Shining Path (Sendero Luminoso) in Peru. This group was a communist guerrilla force that turned to domestic violence in the 1980s. By the late 1980s, the Shining Path found a great deal of success in targeting urban infrastructure so as to disrupt the lives of Peruvian citizens. The democratic regime broke down in 1992 when President Alberto Fujimori suspended the constitution, one of his justifications being the need to defeat the Shining Path and capture its leader, Abimael Guzmán Reynoso. Guzmán was captured within six months, which greatly diminished the activities of the organization. Once Fujimori fled the country in 2000, a fragile democracy was restored, but during 15 years of terror in Peru, more than 25,000 people (mostly civilians) died. The examples of both the IRA and the Shining Path should point to the potential importance of domestic terror in the regime change process.

A third form of political dissent can be found in international **terrorism** (see Box 14.3). The events of September 11, 2001 drove home the relevance of this phenomenon. The actions of the United States and its coalition partners in response to what came to be known as "9/11" aptly demonstrate the linkage between international terrorism and regime change. The ramifications of this act of terror went far beyond the deaths and injuries of a single day. For example, the global economy was seriously damaged. Illustrating the effects of interdependence, economies from Europe to Asia to North America turned down.

The question of what constitutes terrorism has been debated for decades without being definitively answered. The oft-heard comment that one person's terrorist is another's freedom fighter underlies the difficulty of achieving a consensus definition. Unable to unravel this problem, the United Nations continues to identify terrorism via 12 piecemeal conventions and protocols (http://www.unodc.org/unodc/en/terrorism/conventions.html). Rather than defining the term, they identify events that most agree constitute terrorist activities, such as taking hostages, harming diplomatic agents, and hijacking planes. The government of Canada is no more clear. The Supreme Court of Canada, in *Suresh v. Canada*, argued that there is no authoritative definition of terrorism, in large part because the term is open to "politicized manipulation, conjecture and polemical interpretation." Instead of undertaking such an effort, the *Anti-Terrorism Act* defines terrorism by recognizing 10 of the UN antiterrorism conventions and protocols. Some in the UN have proposed relying on AP Achmid's "short legal definition," which states an act of terrorism is "peacetime equivalents of war crimes." When evaluating any proposed definition, keep in mind the three elements of motive, identity, and method.

Terrorism has historic roots stretching back more than 2,000 years, but the first example within the last 100 years was the assassination of the Archduke Franz Ferdinand on June 28, 1914 in Sarajevo—an act carried out by an activist from a group known as the Young Bosnians. Following World War II, terrorism was mainly employed by non-state groups including nationalist and anticolonial groups in Asia, Africa, and the Middle East. The 1960s and 1970s witnessed the prominence of nationalist groups such as the Provisional IRA, the PLO, and the Basque ETA and of groups motivated by ethnic and ideological considerations, such as the Red Army Faction and the Italian Red Brigade. During the 1980s, state-sponsored terrorism, backed by countries such as Iran, Iraq, Libya, and Syria, reemerged in the form of attacks against American and other Western targets in the Middle East. More recently, the world has witnessed the reemergence of religiously motivated terror culminating in the Al-Qaeda attacks of September 11, 2001.

While the United States has attempted to focus global attention on Al-Qaeda, it is important to remember that people in other parts of the world may be more concerned with other groups—FARC in Columbia, the Liberation Tigers of Tamil Eelam (LTTE) in Sri Lanka, Chechens in Russia, etc. That said, Al-Qaeda remains the focus on the U.S.-led "war on terrorism." *Al-Qaeda*, an Arabic word meaning "the base," was built on the foundation of the mujahideen resistance movement against the Soviet invasion of Afghanistan sometime around 1989 by Osama bin Laden and Muhammad Atef and was dedicated to opposing non-Islamic governments with force and violence. Prior to 9/11, Al-Qaeda was behind numerous terror attacks: 1992 bombings in Yemen targeting U.S. troops; training those responsible for attacks in 1993 on U.S. military personnel in Mogadishu, Somalia; the 1998 bombing of the U.S. embassies in Nairobi, Kenya, and Dar es Salaam, Tanzania; and the 2000 bombing of the USS *Cole* in Yemen.

Following the 9/11 attacks, the United States led a military campaign in

Afghanistan that ousted the Taliban from power, forcing the leadership of Al-Qaeda to flee its bases in that country. Subsequently, U.S. President George Bush advanced a foreign policy agenda based on the "war on terrorism." This policy was used, in part, to justify the U.S. invasion of Iraq. As well, most Western countries have passed legislation aimed at bolstering the domestic tools to fight terrorism including the *Patriot Act* in the United States, the *Anti-Terrorism Act* in Canada, and the *Anti-Terrorism, Crime and Security Act* in Britain. Such legislation usually aims to provide new investigation tools to law enforcement and intelligence agencies in areas such as tracking and intercepting communications, thwarting money-laundering efforts, and increasing control over border entries. Opponents of such legislation point out that such efforts to fight terrorism directly trade off with the civil and political liberties of citizens. They argue that while suspending constitutional rights of citizens certainly makes it easier to combat the threat of terrorism, it exacts a high democratic price. The tradeoffs between protecting individual rights and preventing terrorism are sure to remain at the core of future debates surrounding this issue.

Contrary to the intentions of the initiators of this act, at least one country, Afghanistan, experienced a regime change in the subsequent U.S.-led war on terrorism. While 9/11 certainly was not the first example of international terrorism, it demonstrated the vulnerability of even the United States, and it serves as a prime example of how such events can play a role in regime change.

Rebellion

The most common form of regime failure involves some form of rebellion. The two most salient examples of rebellion are military coups and *autogolpes*. A **coup d'état** is the mechanism most people understand as the cause of nondemocratic regime change; it is defined as the overthrow of a political regime or leader by military force.

A quick reference to the motivations of the military as an actor in the regime change process should indicate why it may step in and overthrow a regime. While many motivations may appear reasonable, there are two basic sets of theories explaining why militaries seize power. The first revolves around the national interest of the country. This view sees the military as the nonpartisan adjudicator of politics in the country. As such, it will seek power when the existing government has lost legitimacy and can no longer govern effectively. Exactly when this point is reached is the subject of much debate. Typically, the military will point to economic crisis, a deadlocked or ineffective legislature, or widespread governmental corruption to indicate that the current regime has put the national interest at risk. The Turkish military is a prime example of this approach, having executed three military coups. Whenever it has stepped into politics in the form of bloodless coups, it has cited legislative deadlock that left the country unable to confront crises. It established control over the country, made constitutional changes, and then withdrew from power in favour of an elected civilian government.

The second theory explaining military motivation involves the corporate interest of the military. From this perspective, if it feels its very existence is at risk under the current regime, it fights to defend itself. What types of actions or events trigger such a feeling? For one, they may concern money. From this perspective, the chief corporate concern of the military is its budgetary support. If the institution's funding is endangered (or significantly reduced), it may feel it can no longer meet obligations to its members or to the nation. Another triggering factor has to do with autonomy. Threats to the military's autonomy can be found when the existing regime attempts to interfere in that body's internal affairs: for example, the education and training curriculum, the assignment of posts, the promotion of all but the most senior officers, and the crafting of national defence strategy. Militaries express concerns that such interference puts the chain of command at risk and thus threatens the entire institution.[4] When the Goulart regime in Brazil changed promotion patterns and then proclaimed amnesty for all involved in a sailors' revolt, the military took control of the country by coup.

A second example of rebellion is the *autogolpe*, a kind of self-coup in which a country's leader (usually elected) decides to rule by decree. This normally takes place when a country faces an economic crisis at the same time as an ambitious leader experiences institutional gridlock. A classic example was President Alberto Fujimori of Peru's forcible closure of the congress and suspension of the country's constitution in April 1992. This action was greeted with massive public support because of Peruvians' weariness with the corrupt and incompetent congress. The international community, on the other hand, overwhelmingly opposed the "coup," and moved to isolate Peru and force it back to democracy. Fujimori's success in dealing with the economic problems and defeating the Shining Path earned him reelection in 1995.[5] It was only when his right-hand man was caught on video bribing a member of congress that he was forced to flee to Japan, ending his rule.

State Failure

The third form of nondemocratic regime change involves **state failure**. State failure involves more than simply rebellion, coups, or riots; it refers to "a situation where the structure, authority (legitimate power), law, and political order have fallen apart and must be reconstituted in some form, old or new."[6]

The clearest example of such failure is civil war. When two or more factions within a country take up armed struggle against one another, it puts the state at risk. History is replete with examples of civil war and the threats they posed to regimes. The civil war in the United States threatened to tear the country apart and throw it into chaos; John A. Macdonald drew on the lessons of that conflict in arguing that Canada should not provide too much power to the provinces. The bloody civil war in El Salvador in the 1980s can be understood in light of the Cold War politics of the times. The civil war fought in Ethiopia really began after World War II as a result of the unification of two historically distinct groups by European powers. The effects of civil war extend well beyond body counts. The death and destruction are truly awful, of course, but such wars also serve to divide the loyalties of citizens and put the very survival of the state in jeopardy.

A second example of state failure is total social breakdown. Occasionally, events in a state reach such a point that the state basically ceases to exist. It is under these circumstances that humans find themselves closest to a Hobbesian "state of nature," in which life is "solitary, poor, nasty, brutish and short." In 1991, the leader of Somalia was ousted from power, which plunged the country into civil war. A significant portion of northern Somalia announced it had seceded. A devastating famine the following year killed an estimated 300,000 people, triggering an attempt by the United Nations to broker a truce that would allow peacekeepers and famine relief workers and supplies into the country. For all practical purposes, the truce was ignored. Attempts by the international community to prevent looting only served to draw it into the burgeoning tribal conflict. The escalating fighting, which resulted in deaths and casualties among the international peacekeeping forces, led to the departure of the UN by 1995. In the period that followed, the country was ruled by tribal warlords. There was no central government, and all services usually carried out by a state ceased to function. At that point, Somalia was close to anarchy. Since then, a ray of hope has emerged, but at the time of this writing the transitional federal government established in 2004 remains exiled in neighbouring Kenya.

The Transition to Democracy

The world has seen a remarkable wave of **democratic transitions** over the past three decades. Thus, it is important to have a more complete understanding of the issues surrounding the transition itself. To more fully understand democratic transition, we must first define "democracy." While it is possible to define it in terms of the roots of authority and the ideal outputs of democratic regimes, this chapter defines it in terms of the procedures for constituting government, and therefore focuses on free and fair **elections**. We then explore the historic evolution and the current state of global democracy. Finally, we turn our attention to the defining event of the transition—the election. For an election to be considered the end of a transition to democracy, it must be seen as "free and fair," so we examine what is meant by this phrase, and explore the limitations of the groups that arrive at such judgments—election observers.

Defining Democracy

The idea of democracy has meant different things to different people over the ages, as noted in other chapters in this book. One approach is to focus on the source of authority. From this point of view, democracy means government by the people. We might debate the question of whether history has ever witnessed a regime that operated as a true direct democracy, in which the people really govern. Certainly women and other people not offered the advantages of citizenship would disagree with even the "best" cases of ancient democracy. In the modern age, there are no examples of the people directly governing. Such a solution is simply not practical. So while this approach offers interesting food for thought, it does not provide guidance for discriminating between democratic and nondemocratic cases in today's world.

Another approach is to focus on the outputs of government. We all know that democracies are supposed to protect the common good: safeguard individual rights, provide equality, and guard against tyranny (see Figure 14.1). The question that must be asked is whether these are defining features of democracy as a form of government or objectives democracies are supposed to strive toward. Put another way, if a regime must accomplish the objectives set out in our list before being considered a democracy, how many democracies actually exist in the world? Surely we could come up with examples in which even Canada and the United States violate some of these requirements, such as their early treatment of women and their dealings with Aboriginal peoples. If we can use the terms of the definition to question even the most well-established democracies in the world, how useful is the definition in examining newly formed democracies? This approach does not allow us to distinguish between democracies and nondemocracies in the countries we are interested in during the post–World War II period.

The third approach is much more limited. It focuses on the procedures for constituting the government, arguing that we must examine the method of leadership selection. This definition, first advanced by Joseph Schumpeter, argues that democracy is "that institutional arrangement for arriving at political decisions in which individuals acquire the power to decide by means of a competitive struggle for the people's vote."[7] Several scholars have pointed out additional elements necessary to improve on this definition. Robert Dahl argued that democracy requires contestation, participation, and civil and political liberties. There must be meaningful competition (also called *contestation*) for the effective positions of power in government. This is accomplished through regular elections. These elections must allow for a highly inclusive level

Figure 14.1 The Map of Freedom, 2007

Map Legend

■ Free □ Partly Free ■ Not Free

Source: Reprinted by permission of Freedom House; available at http://www.freedomhouse.org/template.cfm?page=363&year=2007; accessed June 7, 2008.

of political participation that excludes no major social group. In order to carry out such elections, a minimum level of civil and political liberties such as those of speech, press, and association is necessary.[8] This is a *very limited* definition of democracy, but it is employed here because it allows for the inclusion of newly formed democracies and provides us with a reasonable list of factors to examine when determining whether a country is a democracy.

The State of Global Democracy

Samuel P. Huntington has advanced a widely cited theory that there is an observable historical pattern of global political change. He refers to the patterns of change as waves, and notes that history is not unidirectional: countries can experience transitions *to* democracy but they can also experience transitions *away* from democracy. Transitions away from democracy are referred to as *reverse waves*. While recognizing that the events of history are messy and therefore difficult to sort into nice, neat boxes, Huntington argues that there have been three waves of **democratization** and two reverse waves in modern history.[9] See Table 14.2.

Even a cursory examination of these dates reveals that the waves overlap; for example, the first wave did not end until 1926, but the first reverse wave began in 1922. This should reinforce the *inexact nature* of attempting to divide history into neat groupings. Nevertheless, Huntington's classification provides an easy way to conceptualize the ebb and flow of democracy over time.

The first wave is rooted in the American and French **revolutions**. Exactly when these countries became democratic is a subject of ongoing debate. Nevertheless, when we employ even a basic democratic qualification of 50 percent adult male suffrage and some type of responsible executive (either through parliamentary support or periodic election), we can see that the United States began this wave with the 1828 presidential election. By the end of the first wave, 33 countries, including Canada and most of Europe, experienced some form of democratic transition. The first reverse wave began in 1922 with Mussolini's rise to power in Italy, and continued with Hitler's rise to power in Germany. During this period, military coups resulted in the overthrow of democracy in numerous places across the globe, ranging from the Baltic states to a number of South American countries.

The second, short wave of democratization began during World War II but lasted only through the early 1960s. Countries such as West Germany and Japan adopted democratic forms of government following occupation by Allied forces. Others, such as a number of Latin American states, seemed to follow the lead of the Allied democracies, which facilitated improved aid and trade relations. In addition, a number of countries "created" during this period due to the decline of Western colonial rule began as democracies. Most of these postcolonial democratic experiments, however, were short-lived. The second reverse wave saw a return to nondemocratic regimes across the globe. From Latin America to Asia to southern Europe, democratic governments were swept from power through military force.

The third wave of democratization began in southern Europe with the end of dictatorial rule in Portugal, followed quickly by a return to democracy in Greece and Spain. This wave picked up steam

Table 14.2 Huntington's Waves of Democratization

First wave of democratization	1828–1926
First reverse wave	1922–1942
Second wave of democratization	1943–1962
Second reverse wave	1958–1975
Third wave of democratization	1974–present

Source: Samuel P. Huntington, *The Third Wave* (Norman: University of Oklahoma Press, 1990), p. 16. © 1990 by Samuel P. Huntington.

during the late 1970s in Latin America. Ecuador, Peru, and Bolivia all saw military governments attempting to withdraw from power. The movement to democracy subsequently spread throughout Latin America. At the same time, beginning with India and continuing from the Philippines to South Korea, Taiwan, and Pakistan, the democratic wave spread throughout Asia. The collapse of the Soviet Union triggered a surge of democracy across Eastern Europe. Beginning with Hungary in 1988, the world witnessed a rapid and dramatic spread of democracy across the countries formerly behind the Iron Curtain. The 1990s saw the third wave spread into Africa.

Most recently, the debate on democratic reform has spread to the Middle East. Putting aside the issues around weapons of mass destruction, one of the objectives of the most recent war in Iraq was to attempt to put a democratic government in control of the country. Despite an ongoing insurgency conflict, the Iraqi people went to the polls on January 30, 2005 in the country's first free election in at least half a century. Much work remains, however, as the newly elected National Assembly is merely tasked with writing a new constitution which, if ratified, will lay the foundation for electing a permanent government. Iraq was not the only Middle Eastern country to recently experience a democratic push. Following the February 14, 2005 murder of popular former prime minister Rafik Hariri, at least one million Lebanese citizens demonstrated in Beirut calling for the withdrawal of Syrian troops and democratic elections. Since then, the pro-Syrian Lebanese government was forced to resign and Syria has begun a military withdrawal. While it is too early to assess the democratic possibilities for either country, these events seem to indicate that the third wave may finally be reaching the Middle East.

Free and Fair Elections

The defining moment of the democratic transition is the initial election. Whether the regime is ultimately viewed by the international community as a democracy comes down to a judgment on whether the transition election is free and fair. In this context, the word *free* gets at the element of participation, whereas the word *fair* refers to contestation. The idea of civil and political liberties underpins both the "free" and the "fair." Therefore, the first question we must ask is: How are these two things determined? When evaluating this question, keep in mind the discussion in Chapter 10, particularly the information in Box 10.1.

Whether an election is free usually comes down to the issues of suffrage and coercion. Is there universal suffrage? To determine this, we examine whether virtually all of the adult citizens in the country are eligible to vote. Are women excluded? Are significant minority groups—especially ethnic and religious—excluded? If there is universal suffrage, then the question of whether the election was also generally free from coercion must be examined. To determine this, we usually ask whether voters were intimidated, either when registering or when actually voting. A certain degree of intimidation is allowed for; however, turning large numbers of voters away from polling stations or widespread, especially targeted, violence during the election period is usually grounds for declaring an election to have been not free.

Whether an election is fair usually comes down to restrictions placed on candidates and parties, as well as to the level of corruption throughout the process, especially in the tabulation of votes. While some restrictions on contestation are accepted—for example, excluding anti-system and communist parties—we have to examine whether the major opposition leaders and parties were, in general, allowed to have candidates run in the election in an open fashion. If they were, then we turn to the issue of corruption. It is widely recognized that no election is totally free from corruption. The questions become how pervasive the corruption was and whether it affected the outcome. While minor indiscretions during the campaign may be tolerable, stuffing the ballot box or not counting ballots from opposition strongholds is usually not. Of course, out-and-out fraud in the reporting of election results, assuming such fraud can be identified, results in a declaration that the election was not fair.

The issue of civil and political liberties, while recognized as important to the definition of democracy, does not extensively come into play when examining the issue of free and fair elections. It is generally accepted that significant restrictions on such liberties will exist. As long as the outgoing regime loosens them to some extent, such restrictions rarely result in a declaration that the election was not free or fair. Aside from the elements of the free-and-fair determination that overlap with such liberties, the question usually comes down to media access. In most countries experiencing transition elections, the major media in the country are state-owned and thus dominated by those loyal to the old regime. If the opposition forces are excluded from all media access, the election risks losing the free-and-fair determination. But as long as they have some degree of access, issues such as the state media's bias against the opposition are generally ignored.

There is one outcome that always results in a declaration that the election was free and fair: if the opposition wins the election. Regardless of any violations mentioned above, such a victory is seen as prima facie evidence that it was a democratic election. If the opposition does not win, analysts examine whether the opposition forces were provided with a chance to win. They may not take advantage of such opportunities, of course, and even if they do they may still not win. In the end, the real question is simply the existence of such opportunities.

An important question to keep in mind when considering the issue of free and fair elections is, Who decides? The problem with making such a determination is that it is almost entirely subjective. Elections are inherently imperfect, even in developed democracies. Answering questions dealing with the allowable degree of exclusions, intimidation, and corruption is ultimately a judgment call. Who then is making this call? The answer varies over time and across countries. As the third wave of democratization has matured, a system of international election observers has developed. Observer missions operate under the umbrella of international organizations such as the United Nations or the Organization of American States; think tanks such as the Carter Center at Emory University and the National Endowment for Democracy; and individual countries such as Canada and the United States.

While generally well intentioned, election observation missions face numerous difficulties. The first is the issue of *access*: Will the government allow observers access to the entire country during both the campaign and the election itself? If so, can these observers be offered a reasonable guarantee of safety? Will the government allow access to party officials, candidates, party headquarters, and domestic media? What about outside observation of the vote count? The second is the issue of *money*. Assuming reasonable access is granted, can observer missions afford to take advantage of it? This is usually a function of the size of the country, its location, the infrastructure (travel and telecommunications), and the importance the international community attaches to the election. The bigger, the farther away from the West, the poorer, and the less important a country is, the harder it is to gather even minimally sufficient funds to observe the election. Finally, there is the question of *timing*. As the world has moved to real-time communications, people have become much less patient about receiving judgments on international events. If missions wait several weeks to gather all the data they believe to be necessary to judge the election, the media have either already passed judgment without their input or are no longer interested in the story. On the other hand, if observer missions attempt to make judgments according to the news cycle of the Western media, how informed can such decisions actually be? The best most missions can usually hope for is to have people covering a small sample of the important or controversial polling stations, some form of limited access to the vote count, and enough clear information to make their best guess in time to receive international media attention. These are important yet difficult tasks indeed.

People line up to vote in the black township of Soweto, South Africa, in April 1994.

AP/Wide World Photos

Democratic Consolidation

Once an election that is certified as free and fair occurs, does the world have another democracy? Is that the end of the story? No. At this point, all that has happened is this: the nondemocratic regime experienced a breakdown, and subsequently there was a democratic election. If you compare a country that has just gone through this process to Canada, it is difficult to make the case that they should be considered equal in terms of democracy. Canada has well-developed democratic political institutions, a vibrant democratic political culture, and minimal prospects of reverting to a nondemocratic form of government in the foreseeable future. In comparison, we should remember that countries such as Iraq have only succeeded in concluding a single free and fair election. Rather than indicating an attainment of the democratic condition, such an event is really indicative of the beginning of a long challenge. In political science, the issues surrounding this challenge are known as **democratic consolidation**.

Consolidation Definition

Now that a fledgling democracy has been put in place, what needs to happen for that country to remove the "fledgling" tag? Democratic consolidation exists when none of the major political actors, parties, organized interests, forces, or institutions consider that there is any alternative to democratic processes to gain power, and when no political institution or group has a claim to veto the action of democratically elected decision-makers.[10]

A consolidated democracy may have small antidemocratic actors and groups. The important idea here is that the major actors in the regime, especially in times of crisis, do not turn to such groups for assistance. Rather than seeking such support, groups embrace the uncertainty of democracy—the idea that winners and losers are temporary and prone to change from election to election. It is this uncertainty that tempers the interactions and competition of groups both in and out of power. Out-of-power groups recognize that the uncertainty of democracy guarantees them a chance to regain power during the next election; rather than attempting to take power by force, they put their energies into attempting to turn this uncertainty to their advantage. Likewise, groups in power recognize that the uncertainty of democracy means they may lose the next election; rather than planning to stay in power by force, they plan for how to maintain their power through elections—and, if they lose, how to regain it next time. Because of this ebb and flow of groups in power and the likelihood that even though a party is a winner today, it may not be a winner after the next election, it behooves each group to treat its opposition with some level of respect at all times. The objective of the post-transition period is to get actors to embrace the advantages of uncertainty. Thus, as Juan J. Linz put it, a democracy is consolidated when democracy becomes "the only game in town."[11]

Consolidation Challenges

How do democracies become consolidated? New democratic regimes face at least four common challenges: asserting civilian control over the military, reforming the institutions of government, fostering the growth of civil society, and improving relations with the international community.

Asserting civilian control over the military is likely the most important challenge confronting a new democratic regime. Given that new regimes often face numerous threats and contenders for power, they may require more from the military than simply a "return to the barracks." Newly formed democracies often find themselves turning to the military to actively assist them in defeating challengers. For this to take place, the civilian government has to achieve some level of control over the military. A number of problems stand in the way of such control. The first is the issue of what to do about past human rights violations. The government is often left in a no-win situation: if it prosecutes the military it greatly increases the risk of a coup, but if it ignores past violations it may anger the mass public. Countries such as South Africa have tried to deal with this problem via "truth and reconciliation commissions." Such commissions attempt to uncover information about past injustices, but they do not aim to prosecute the people behind the acts.

Another issue confronting civil–military relations in new democracies revolves around the military's budget. Most third-wave democracies have sprung up in relatively poor countries, which face severe economic problems and pressure from international lenders (such as the IMF and World Bank) to drastically reduce government spending. Generally speaking, governments can cut military budgets in countries where the military has lost a significant amount of prestige and influence, but they try to insulate the military from cuts where it still retains significant power. However, it may be that just the opposite should occur: powerful militaries should be confronted if the civilian government ever hopes to gain dominance, while defeated militaries should not be pushed into a corner where they feel they have nothing else to lose.

Given these and other challenges, how should the new regime respond to the military? The overarching object must be democracy's survival. In the short term, this may require the regime to appease the military. In the long run, however, the civilian regime must assert its control over the military. Democracies must figure out how to send the military back to the barracks and how to keep them there. What this means is that military professionalism must be increased. The military must come to understand that its job exists in the military realm, not in the political or economic realms.

A second major challenge that transitional democracies face is how to build and reform the democratic institutions of government. The most obvious targets are the legislature, the courts, and the bureaucracy. Outside of the executive, these three institutions are most responsible for the functioning of government—for making, enforcing, and carrying out the law—and are crucial to the government's ability to operate as a democracy. The root of the problem is that these same institutions were also responsible, in some manner, for the operation of the previous, nondemocratic regime. As such, we should expect them to experience difficulties making the transition to a completely new set of rules. Specifically, these institutions must somehow confront issues surrounding responsiveness and corruption.

The legislature must learn how to function in a democracy. New rules must be established to allow the legislature to actually legislate. This demands attention to everything from how to form committees to how question period will work. A variety of challenges also surround funding necessary to undertake new responsibilities ranging from constituency service to legislative research to public communication. In addition, the legacy of corruption must be confronted. The list of necessary reforms is almost endless, but the legislature has to undergo a radical makeover before the people come to see it as a democratic institution.

Similar challenges are found when examining the courts. For a consolidated democracy to function properly, the courts must be able, at minimum, to check abuses that occur in the rest of the government. Instead of relying on the desires of the executive, the courts have to be put in a position to rely on the law. Here, too, the legacy of corruption must be overcome. To accomplish this, the courts will require additional funding for the recruitment of new judges and staff members. The corrupt judges of the old regime must be retrained or retired.

Finally, the bureaucracy also faces challenges. Citizens are much more likely to have direct interactions with the bureaucracy than with the legislature or the courts. One of the toughest tasks in reforming the bureaucracy is the implementation of merit-based hiring practices. In most nondemocratic (and even many democratic) regimes, staffing in the bureaucracy is used as a way to reward followers. An important job allows one to employ family and friends, regardless of qualifications. Such jobs are powerful, not because of the missions or objectives of the position but rather as a function of their ability to deliver goods. The most straightforward solution to the problem is to hire civil servants on merit, although such reforms are likely to receive resistance from within the institution.

The proper functioning of government is not enough to push a democracy toward consolidation; democracy also requires a functioning **civil society** (see Box 14.4). Civil society refers to nongovernmental groups in society, but in nondemocratic political systems the term goes beyond the definition provided in Chapter 12.

Civil Society in Transitional Democracies   BOX 14.4

Civil society is a set or system of self-organized intermediary groups that: 1) are relatively independent of both public authorities and private units of production and reproduction, that is, of firms and families; 2) are capable of deliberating about and taking collective actions in defence or promotion of their inter-ests or passions; 3) do not seek to replace either state agents or private (re)producers or to accept responsibility for governing the polity as a whole; and 4) agree to act within pre-established rules of a "civil" nature, that is, conveying mutual respect.

SOURCE: Philippe C. Schmitter, "Civil Society East and West," in Larry Diamond, Marc F. Plattner, Yun-han Chu, and Hung-mao Tien, eds., *Consolidating the Third Wave Democracies: Themes and Perspectives* (Baltimore: Johns Hopkins University Press, 1997), p. 240.

The idea is that as more groups are created and as more people join them, the chances of democratic consolidation increase. At an individual level, membership in such groups helps develop people's understanding of the way democracy functions and therefore serves as an incubator for democratic political culture in the country. At a group level, such organizations offer a check against the abuse of power and a backstop support for democracy. These two points make it clear that democratic consolidation is dependent, not only on the groups that make up civil society, but also on how these groups interact with their members, each other, the business sector, and the government. While such groups are more likely to form spontaneously in a democracy, anything transitional governments can do to foster their formation and survival will assist in the consolidation process.

A final element to consider is the role of the international community. As the forces of the Cold War have faded and the forces of **globalization** have spread around the world, the role the international community plays in democratic consolidation has greatly increased. During the 1990s, it became clear that the international community, especially the Western world, favours democracy and actively works to foster and maintain it. The West relies on economic tools to accomplish its objectives. Western-backed international organizations, such as the World Bank and the International Monetary Fund, condition aid packages to new democracies on a set of economic reforms theoretically aimed at making these fledgling democracies more competitive. Individual donor countries often tie aid not only to meeting conditions set out by the World Bank and the IMF but also to consistent progress toward democratic consolidation. The effectiveness of conditioning aid on the achievement of democracy (or democratic progress) is still much disputed.

The other tool employed in this respect is international trade. Given that the world is becoming more interdependent, countries that desire economic success must become more open and active in the realm of international trade. Aid and trade are also used to foster consolidation by delivering needed short-term assistance, which helps countries get their economic houses in order, and then to offer these new democracies prospects for long-term success by putting them in a position where they can take advantage of globalization and world markets.

Unconsolidated Democracy

An understanding of the challenges facing countries during the consolidation period should lead one to understand that consolidation is not easily achieved. In fact, depending on how one defines and measures democratic consolidation, it is more typical for a country that experiences a democratic transition *not* to achieve consolidation. Throughout Latin America and Asia, countries that have experienced democratic transitions have more often than not found a sort of semi-democracy persisting in their country, rather than a move to eventual consolidation. One way of looking at this is to consider such states so-called "electoral democracies." These states have experienced one or more free and fair elections but have failed to consolidate. There are still serious nondemocratic actors in the country, and the levels of civil and political freedoms common in Western democracies have not materialized. This is not to say that electoral democracies can never consolidate. Rather, their condition should serve as a reminder that there is no natural pattern of regime evolution. Not only is it possible for countries to experience a democratic transition that never results in democratic consolidation; it is also important to remember that democracies can and do break down.

Consolidation Consequences

Having laid out the issues surrounding the challenge of democratic consolidation, we will now consider its consequences. What are the practical effects of consolidation? Life in a country that has experienced a nondemocratic regime breakdown, an initial democratic transition, and the successful completion of the democratic consolidation will be much different at the end of the process. The domestic and international implications vary across individual countries and across time, but it is possible to isolate some common consequences of a successful democratic consolidation. Political rights, including things such as the right to vote, the fairness of electoral rules, the principle that votes endow actual power, the ability to organize political parties, and the existence of meaningful opposition are the norm and are almost taken for granted. Civil liberties, encompassing the freedoms to hold views, maintain institutions, and possess personal autonomy apart from the state, are widespread.[12] While they may come under attack from time to time, society recognizes their importance and strives to protect the core set of liberties. The political elite sees democracy as the only possible regime and spends its time trying to take advantage of the rules in order to gain power. The military takes its orders from the civilian government and is now considered professional and divorced from politics. Civil society has blossomed as people are more engaged in group activities and government is more responsive to and inclusive of outside groups' views. The socioeconomic situation of the country has gradually improved and gross distributional problems such as famine have become much less frequent. On the international level, the country is much more fully involved in the globalized world. Aid donors and trade partners no longer question whether they should be engaged with the country. While there may be disagreements as to the degree or type of engagement, the regime is no longer questioned over democratic legitimacy. While this is obviously an idealized picture, and even consolidated democracies will have trouble achieving all of the benefits just described, it does provide the rationale for attempting the consolidation process.

CONCLUSION

During the past three decades, the world has undergone a radical transformation toward democracy. The third wave of democratization began in the early 1970s and continues today. For this reason, the study of democratization has never been more important. In order to understand this process, it is essential to begin with an examination of the key actors: political elites, business elites, the military, the mass public, and the international community. With an understanding of their interests and strengths, the reasons why some of these groups may withdraw their support from nondemocratic regimes and thus break those regimes down become more apparent.

It is important to remember that the consequence of such breakdowns is, more often than not, the installation of another nondemocratic regime. Sometimes, however, the result is a transition to democracy. The defining moment of any transition is the election itself. In the end, whether a country is considered by the international community to be democratic depends on the judgment of election-monitoring teams on whether the election was free and fair. Having completed a free and fair election, the democratic regime enters into the consolidation phase of democratization, in which the objective is to make democracy the only game in town. Once this is accomplished, a country can expect the benefits of democracy to take on a more permanent status.

DISCUSSION QUESTIONS

1. Identify and discuss the importance of the different actors in the democratization process.
2. Identify and discuss the importance of the different consequences of the breakdown of nondemocratic regimes.
3. Compare and contrast the different approaches to defining democracy.
4. What is meant by "free and fair" elections?
5. Discuss the challenges regimes face during the democratic consolidation process.

KEY TERMS

COUP D'ÉTAT: The overthrow of a political regime or leader by military force. (418)

DEMOCRATIC CONSOLIDATION: The achievement of a situation in which none of the major political actors, parties, organized interests, forces, or institutions consider that there is any alternative to democratic processes to gain power, and in which no political institution or group has a claim to veto the action of democratically elected decision-makers. (425)

DEMOCRATIC TRANSITION: The change from nondemocratic to democratic government, usually indicated by the existence of at least one free and fair election. (420)

DEMOCRATIZATION: A group of transitions from nondemocratic to democratic regimes, involving the relaxation of authoritarian political control by political leaders, the expansion of political and civil liberties, and the creation of institutional mechanisms that open up a political system to greater representation and participation. Democratization can be seen to occur in waves. A reverse wave occurs when some of the countries that had previously made the transition to democracy revert to nondemocratic forms of government. (422)

REGIME: The whole decision-making apparatus of the state; the constitutional principles and arrangements according to which government decisions are made; the fundamental rules of the game. (407)

STATE FAILURE: A situation in which the structure, authority, law, and political order have fallen apart and must be reconstituted in some form. (419)

TERRORISM: The threat or use of violence, usually directed at civilian populations, in order to effect some form of political change. (416)

WEB LINKS

Freedom House:
http://www.freedomhouse.org

World Audit:
http://www.worldaudit.org

Election World:
http://www.electionworld.org

International Foundation for Election Systems:
http://www.ifes.org

The National Endowment for Democracy:
http://www.ned.org

International Institute for Democracy and Electoral Assistance:
http://www.idea.int

National Democratic Institute for International Affairs:
http://www.ndi.org

Transparency International:
http://www.transparency.org

Stanford University's Comparative Democratization Project:
http://democracy.stanford.edu

FURTHER READING

Diamond, Larry. *Developing Democracy: Toward Consolidation*. Baltimore: Johns Hopkins University Press, 1999.

Haggard, Stephan, and Robert R. Kaufman. *The Political Economy of Democratic Transitions*. Princeton: Princeton University Press, 1995.

Huntington, Samuel P. *The Third Wave*. Norman: University of Oklahoma Press, 1990.

Mainwaring, Scott, Guillermo O'Donnell, and J. Samuel Valenzuela, eds. *Issues in Democratic Consolidation: The New South American Democracies in Comparative Perspective*. Notre Dame, IN: Notre Dame University Press, 1992.

Przeworski, Adam, et al. *Democracy and Development: Political Institutions and Material Well-Being in the World, 1950–1990*. Cambridge: Cambridge University Press, 2000.

ENDNOTES

1. Seymour Martin Lipset, "Some Social Requisites of Democracy," *American Political Science Review* 53 (1959): 69–105; Adam Przeworski, et al., *Democracy and Development: Political Institutions and Material Well-Being in the World, 1950–1990* (Cambridge: Cambridge University Press, 2000), pp. 78–80.

2. Stephan Haggard and Robert R. Kaufman, *The Political Economy of Democratic Transitions* (Princeton: Princeton University Press, 1995), pp. 25–32.

3. Donald Horowitz, *Ethnic Groups in Conflict* (Berkeley: University of California Press, 1985).

4. Eric A. Nordlinger, *Soldiers in Politics: Military Coups and Governments* (Englewood Cliffs, NJ: Prentice-Hall, 1977).

5. Maxwell A. Cameron and Philip Mauceri, eds., *The Peruvian Labyrinth: Polity, Society, Economy* (University Park: Pennsylvania State University Press, 1997).

6. I. William Zartman, "Introduction: Posing the Problem of State Collapse," in I. William Zartman, ed., *Collapsed States: The Disintegration and Restoration of Legitimate Authority* (Boulder: Lynne Rienner Publishers, 1995), pp. 1–11.

7. Joseph Schumpeter, *Capitalism, Socialism, and Democracy*, 2nd ed. (New York: Harper, 1947), p. 269.

8. Adapted from Samuel P. Huntington, *The Third Wave* (Norman: University of Oklahoma Press, 1990), p. 6; and Georg Sorensen, *Democracy and Democratization* (Boulder, CO: Westview Press, 1993), pp. 12–13.

9. Huntington, pp. 15–26.

10. Juan J. Linz, "Transitions to Democracy," *Washington Quarterly* 13(3) (1990): 158.

11. *Ibid.*

12. See the checklist of political rights and civil liberties employed by Freedom House for their *Freedom in the World* reports, available at http://www.freedomhouse.org.

Part

7

International Politics

KATRINA BURGESS

Katrina Burgess graduated with an honours bachelor of arts degree in politics at Queen's University. In the course of taking that degree, she spent one year as an exchange student at L'Institut d'Études Politiques at Lyon, France. While at Queen's, Katrina participated in the Model Parliament and Model United Nations, volunteered in a number of extracurricular causes, and became involved in many athletic activities.

Immediately after graduating from Queen's, Katrina accepted a position as an English teacher in Japan for a year, and after that she studied for a master's degree in international relations at the London School of Economics. In London, she learned about both international security threats and the dangers that arise from drinking with the Brits!

Katrina joined Foreign Affairs Canada in September 2004. She began her work there as a policy advisor in the federal–provincial–territorial relations division, dealing with the provinces' role in Canada's international affairs. She followed that with a position in the Human Security Policy Division working on war-affected children and the Human Security Network. This involved representing Canada at ministerial meetings in Bangkok, Ljubljana, and New York.

Katrina took a six-month leave from the Human Security work to undertake a special assignment in Rome, reporting to Canada's

ambassador to Rome and the Prime Minister's Personal Representative for Africa (a G8 designation) who was also head of the Sudan Task Force. In Rome, Katrina liaised between the Ambassador and Ottawa on Canada's response to Darfur and participated in the Canadian delegation to the annual G8 Africa Partnership meeting in Maputo, Mozambique. The highlight was a project site visit trip to Malawi to evaluate Canada's development aid and ascertain how to better respond to what is referred to as Malawi's triple threat: famine, HIV/AIDS, and poor governance.

Katrina began a two-or-three-year posting in Venezula in August 2007, where she is the Second Secretary responsible for political reporting on domestic issues, human rights, and the administration of a small project fund, as well as managing the education and academic affairs program at the embassy. Thus far, she has been able to observe and report on the December constitutional reform referendum and is anticipating another exciting year ahead in Venezuela with ongoing milk and sugar shortages and an increasingly active opposition student movement.

Katrina excels at both languages and athletics. She is fluently bilingual in English and French and getting there in Spanish. As an athlete, she participates in skiing, soccer, running, and diving, and has recently taken up surfing.

Chapter Fifteen

WORLD POLITICS: Global Anarchy, Global Governance

Kim Richard Nossal

CHAPTER OBJECTIVES

After you have completed this chapter, you should be able to:

- discuss the nature and scope of world politics

- put contemporary global politics into a broader historical perspective

- discuss the impact of anarchy on the nature of politics at a global level

- understand the nature and limitations of global governance

Introduction

Politics at a global level, like all politics, is about the management of conflict and the creation of community. This chapter focuses on politics at this broader and wider political level. Its purpose is not to serve as a mini-text on international relations that seeks to provide a capsule summary of that rich field of scholarly enquiry, but rather to provide an overview of the nature of world politics and in particular the primary problems of politics at a world level: the causes of war, the conditions of peace, and the difficulties of governance in an anarchical world.

The Nature of World Politics

Many people, when they think about politics at a global level, use the term *international relations* or *international politics*. The etymology of the word—*inter* + *nation*—suggests that we are interested only in the politics (or relations) between nations, but in fact we are interested in more than the politics between *nations* and we are interested in more than the politics *between* nations.

First, we do not want to restrict our attention merely to the nation. Rather, we are interested in looking at politics involving a much wider range of actors and agents. Moreover, using *inter* + *national* might just as reasonably refer to "domestic" politics as to "international" politics. After all, the politics between the Scottish and English *nations*, the Québécois and Canadian *nations*, or the Catalan and Spanish *nations* might be considered *inter* + *national*— even though these politics are not normally considered "international," since they occur within the boundaries of Britain, Canada, and Spain.

However, finding a more apt generic description is difficult. The word *polity* (a political community) is one possibility, though "inter-polity politics" does not exactly roll smoothly off the tongue. Nor do generic synonyms work any better: inter-group, inter-country, or inter-unit. "Independent political community" is a reasonably accurate generic descriptor for all the political formations mentioned above—and more besides. However, "inter-independent-political-community politics," while it might be more accurate, is unlikely to find a place in common usage.

The *inter* in "international" is also problematic. We should be interested in more than how independent political entities—be they empires, states, nations, fiefdoms, kingdoms, chiefdoms, tribes, or villages—interact politically *between* each other. The relationships between different countries today are all *international* and often highly *political*, but international politics is more than the sum of the 18,000 possible bilateral relationships between the 192 states in the world today. While we are interested in the bilateral relationships of different countries, we are also interested in looking at much broader political processes.

That is why modifying the word *politics* by specifying the domain with which we are concerned is useful. We all have a sense of "politics by domain" that can begin with units as small as the family, the clan, or the tribe. As the aperture widens, the domain expands: for example, urban politics is about the politics of the city, both inside the city and outside, in its relations with a broader sociopolitical environment. "National politics" includes all the lower layers as well as the relations between the nation-state and the outside—or what is usually called foreign policy. And beyond the nation are two further levels of politics. The next step is **supranational** politics, where a separate and independent political community exists "above" the nation-state. At present, there is only one active site of supranational politics: the **European Union (EU)**. It is a supranational community of 27 European nation-states that have come together to create a higher level of government, based in Brussels (see Box 15.1). Consequently, the politics of the EU is a mixture of national and international politics, similar to the politics one finds in a federal state, in which different levels of government share political authority over the same territory and people.

The next step up from supranational politics is politics at the level of the whole world. We might call this *global politics*, *planetary politics*, or *Earth politics*, but *world politics* is both a common and a commonsense way of naming this level. By its very nature, then, world politics seeks to provide an account of politics at a global level, which is the broadest domain of politics.

We also need to focus on the noun and ask: What is the *politics* of the world? For some, politics is the pursuit of the good. For others, politics is the struggle for power; for others still, politics is the art and science of governing. For yet others, politics is, to use Harold Lasswell's classic definition, about who gets what, when, and how (and why).[1] Although it might be tantalizing to be able to capture the essence of a huge sphere of human activity in a single phrase, such simple definitions cannot convey the multifaceted nature of the political realm. One can count at least five related facets of politics at a global level: community, economic structures, interests, power, and governance.

Community

Politics is first and foremost about the communities into which human beings have always organized themselves. Political communities come in markedly different shapes, sizes, and types, and they exist for varying amounts of time: tiny clan-based hunter-gatherer bands, small agricultural villages, the small *poleis* (or city-states) of ancient Greece, the vast empires of antiquity, nomadic tribes such as the Vandals or the Mongols, the feudal fiefdoms of medieval Europe, the kingdoms of West Africa, the continental-sized contemporary states with hundreds of millions of members, or the supranational community of the European Union. As the other

The Original Six, 1957
Belgium
France
Germany
Italy
Luxembourg
The Netherlands

1973
Denmark
Ireland
United Kingdom

1981
Greece

1986
Portugal
Spain

1995
Austria
Finland
Sweden

2004
Cyprus
Czech Republic
Estonia
Hungary
Latvia
Lithuania
Malta
Poland
Slovakia
Slovenia

2007
Bulgaria
Romania

chapters in this book make so clear, politics focuses on the community and its nature as well as the relationship of individuals and groups to the community.

But people are also capable of conceptualizing the existence of community at a level above their own political community and of seeing their polity as part of a broader community. For example, ancient Greeks believed that they constituted a single community—the Hellenes. Although divided into various *poleis*, they saw themselves as a united singularity against others, particularly Persians, and developed numerous community institutions. These included common spiritual institutions, such as the oracle at Delphi; the inter-*polis* games, held in four-year cycles; and a system of lawsuits for settling contractual disputes. *Poleis* would even hold civilized debates with one another about inter-*polis* affairs—before engaging each other in brutal and bloody wars. Likewise, as Kalevi J. Holsti points out, we can point to Christendom in Europe during the feudal period or to the conceptualization of "Europe" in the 17th century, when phrases such as "the tranquillity of Europe," "the health of the European community," and *"le repos général de la Chrétienté"* (the general repose of Christendom) dotted the discourse of international politics—at the very same time that the armies of European kings and princes were fighting a series of hugely destructive wars.[2] And in the contemporary period, we conceptualize the world in community terms with the widespread use of the phrase "the international community." This phrase is invariably used in a way that means much more than "192 governments and what they are doing." Rather, it usually refers to an inchoate unity—*all governments and peoples in the world*.

While world politics is about the capacity of humans to conceive of some kind of community at a global level, it is also about the boundaries that human beings have always erected to divide themselves from one another—boundaries that intensify the physical distances created by geography and the cultural distance created by language. From the earliest civilizations to the contemporary nation-state, humans have divided themselves on the basis of language, race, class, tribe, religion, gender, culture, nationality, ideology, and wealth. And division may also come simply from the heavy hand of history—that which has gone before but which is remembered and passed down, reinforcing patterns of difference and perhaps even enmity and hatred.

Economic Structures

Politics also focuses on the economic structures that each political community creates for itself. These structures do not just spontaneously occur, but are heavily dependent on ways of thinking—and acting—about economic exchange: what is of value, what is treated as a commodity, what money is, and how property is to be regarded. Economies are *determined*: for example, political ideas and political activity determine whether the economy is barter-based or monetarized, or whether land and labour are commodified (i.e., treated as commodities that can be bought and sold). Ideas and actions govern how markets within communities operate, if they operate at all; they determine how wealth is generated and distributed and how much of the production or labour of individuals and groups is appropriated by the community as taxation.

Just as political communities have economic structures that are determined by ideas and political decisions, the larger world has certain economic structures that operate on a wider scale. These differ considerably depending on time, place, level of technological development, and ideas about wealth and how it should be organized, created, and distributed. For example, before the year 1500, the world was marked by a number of different localized economies, largely self-contained systems of barter exchange that involved localities such as villages, towns, and even larger political units. Local economies were almost always nested within a broader economic structure. Thus, for example, each Greek *polis* had its own economy, but all *poleis* were intimately connected in a broader system of economic exchange. Moreover, economic exchange between Greeks occurred in the context of a broader economic relationship that existed between the Greeks and their neighbours around the Mediterranean and the Aegean Seas.

Beginning around 1500, we see the emergence of an internationalized economy—a single international marketplace connecting the local economies of the world. European states expanded out into the world during the eras of mercantile imperialism and nationalist imperialism, fuelled by the technological innovations of the Industrial Revolution. European expansion consolidated regional economies into a single global economy that linked the centre, in Europe and the United States, with a vast periphery that extended around the world. The descent of the world into a prolonged period of general conflict—marked by two world wars and an interwar period of economic and political crisis—strained the European-dominated international economy.

In the half-century after the end of World War II, the international economy enjoyed a period of considerable growth. There were dramatic increases in trade in goods and services, investment, finance, agriculture, and other primary products. The changes in the international economy during the last quarter of the 20th century formed the beginnings of what some have called a **globalized** economy. As William D. Coleman demonstrates in the next chapter, no longer is the economy at the world level merely a marketplace for the exchange of goods and services between local economies; rather, all of the elements of wealth creation—finance, investment, production, distribution, marketing—are beginning to be organized on a global scale.

Like economic structures within countries, economic structures at the global level are determined by ideas about the economy and the way economic exchange should be organized. Through the ages, those who wielded political power and authority have sought to use the marketplace for political purposes. The shape of the international marketplace and how it operates, the nature of wealth creation, and the complexity and dynamism of international exchange are all determined by the various communities that operate in the global arena. As James Busumtwi-Sam shows in Chapter 13, political decisions determine the global distribution of wealth and thus determine who is rich, who is poor, who lives a marginal existence, who lives in luxury and plenty, who has access to cheap medical services, and who cannot afford medicines or medical help.

Interests

Human beings have the capacity to know what they like, what they want, what they think is good and righteous and just, and what they think is bad and unjust; in other words, to know what their interests are. Political philosophers have long sought to identify universal political interests—what humans seek at all times and in all places. The Greek historian Thucydides identified a classic trio: safety (security), gain (possessions or wealth), and reputation (honour and standing). He put the following words into the mouths of some Athenians who happened to be in Sparta in 432 BCE when that *polis* was debating whether to declare war against Athens. The Athenians sought to defend their *polis* against charges that they were being too aggressive. Thucydides had the Athenians say,

> *We have done nothing extraordinary, nothing contrary to human nature in accepting an empire when it was offered to us and then in refusing to give it up. Three very powerful motives prevent us from doing so—security, honour, and self-interest.*[3]

Such a trio of goals was echoed some 2,000 years later in *Leviathan*, in which English philosopher Thomas Hobbes sought to explain the logical consequences of the natural equality of humankind. Arguing that there were three principal causes of quarrel between humans—competition, diffidence (or insecurity), and glory—Hobbes suggested that

> *The first, maketh men invade for Gain; the second, for Safety; and the third, for Reputation. The first use Violence, to make themselves Masters of other mens persons, wives, children, and cattell; the second, to defend them; the third, for trifles, as a word, a smile, a different opinion, and any other signe of undervalue.*[4]

One can usefully apply this classic trio of interests to actors in world politics. **Security** is that peace of mind that comes with a sense of safety, a freedom from threats of harm to all that one values; insecurity is one's fear that harm will come to that which one values (see Box 15.2). Gain is the desire of humans to possess and control. It can refer to the desire to own things of value and to accumulate desirable possessions (wealth); efforts to provide safety through gain can also be characterized as efforts to provide welfare, an objective that overlaps with both security and wealth. Welfare normally refers to a sense of well-being, including the sense of well-being that comes from freedom from threats to one's security (economic, physical, environmental). Honour, reputation, or prestige involve the desire of actors in global politics to be well regarded by others and seen as legitimate, valued members of the international community. They tend not to take kindly to characterizations of themselves by others that are contemptuous or "undervaluing." They dislike being described in negative terms, and they generally respond defensively to criticisms or insults levelled against them.

While much of the activity of global actors can be understood by reference to safety, gain, and reputation, one other universal interest can also be identified—**independence**. Actors in

Students of security remind us that we have to specify (a) what is to be made safe, (b) against what threat, and (c) for whom the security is to be provided.

These facets of security and insecurity must be analyzed on the individual level. Individuals have markedly different conceptions of their own security, even when they occupy the same space at the same time. While individual definitions of security vary considerably, we can generalize about what is likely to create peace of mind in individuals. First, security begins with a sense of personal safety: in other words, the ability to live in and move around one's own community without fear of being interfered with, mocked, hassled, robbed, assaulted, raped, taken away, imprisoned, expelled, "ethnically cleansed," or killed; as well, one must be assured that no one is going to break into one's home and do the occupants harm. Security is also concerned with a sense of community safety—a sense that some other group is not going to try to seize the community's land, occupy its property, or imprison or harm the community in which one lives. Security involves a sense that one's property is safe against robbery, seizure, and destruction. Finally, security is a sense of well-being that can have economic, environmental, social, linguistic, and cultural dimensions.

Threats to security come in a wide variety of forms—some natural, some as the consequence of human agency. Living on a geological fault line, in the shadow of a volcano, in a frequently deluged river delta, or at the fringe of a desert subject to desertification are examples of sources of natural insecurity. Insecurity can come from a fear about the future of one's language or culture. Insecurity can also result from the consequences of human action: not knowing where one's next meal will come from; worrying whether one will be infected with HIV; or not knowing whether the fish stocks on which one relies for a living have been depleted. Or insecurity can come from not knowing whether you will be robbed on the streets of Johannesburg, or whether the car driving by you on a Karachi street is about to be exploded by a suicide bomber, or whether the soldiers sent to disperse a protest in Rangoon will open fire on the crowd.

If we look at security in this multifaceted way, we can see that individuals can in fact have a mixture of insecurities and securities at the same time. Individuals may have secure employment, but live in neighbourhoods where personal insecurity is high; or they may live in a community that is completely free from any concern about being overrun by the country next door, but nonetheless may be worried about the fact that they are of a different religious faith than the majority of their neighbours, who have shown a propensity to attack minorities. Or they may have no fear of their neighbours, but may worry that the state security forces will take exception to their union organizing. Or they may have no fear of any other member of the community, but may worry about the enmity of others across the border.

We can extrapolate these observations to different aggregates of individuals— families, groups, organizations, and even political communities. But with every aggregation, the complexity of the pattern of security and insecurity deepens. Often, supposedly secure units can hide deep insecurities of members of the unit.

For an excellent discussion of security in international affairs, see David A. Baldwin, "The Concept of Security," *Review of International Studies* 23 (January 1997): 5–26.

world politics have always demonstrated an interest in seeking autonomy, or freedom from control by others. The desire for an independent existence is manifested everywhere at a personal level, and usually gives rise to deeply seated social structures of dominance and control: parents over children, men over women, landowners over peasants, capital over labour, elites over masses, governments over peoples. But it is also manifest at the level of political community.

Consider how few communities have voluntarily decided to surrender their independence so that they could be ruled by others: the Scottish parliament more or less voluntarily joined England in 1707; in 1845, Texans gave up the independence they had gained from Mexico in 1836. In the contemporary era, those living in Puerto Rico and Bermuda have decided not to pursue independence. But these are the few exceptions to an otherwise virtually universal norm that people prefer to govern themselves. "What nation likes to be oppressed by a stronger power?" asks one of the Dead Sea scrolls, written about 2,000 years ago.[5] The question is rhetorical, for much of world politics is about the intense struggle of people eager to escape the rule of others and establish their own independent existence.

Indeed, the histories of many communities revolve around the story of struggles for independence. And so intense is the desire for autonomy that individuals will willingly die rather than surrender their independence. Melos, a colony of Sparta, refused to join the Athenian Empire in the great war between Athens and Sparta and their respective allies. In 416 BCE, Athens demanded that the Melians either submit or be destroyed. As was usual in ancient Greece, Athenian representatives visited the *polis* of Melos to argue their case. In the ensuing debate, known to history as the Melian dialogue, the Athenians argued, "We want you to be spared for the good both of yourselves and of ourselves." The debate went on:

Terrorism in New York City, September 11, 2001.

CP Photo/Todd Hollis

> *Melians: And how could it be just as good for us to be the slaves as for you to be the masters?*
> *Athenians: You, by giving in, would save yourselves from disaster; we, by not destroying you, would be able to profit from you.*

But in the end, the Melians decided to take their chances and fight, even though the Athenian forces were more powerful:

> *Our decision, Athenians, is just the same as it was at first. We are not prepared to give up in a short moment the liberty which our city has enjoyed from its foundation for 700 years. We put our trust in the fortune that the gods will send . . . and in the help of men— that is, of the Spartans; and so we shall try to save ourselves.*

But the outcome was never in doubt: the militarily superior Athenians eventually forced the Melians to surrender. They killed every male, sold the women and children into slavery, and repopulated the island with Athenians.[6]

The Intersection of Interests and the Relevance of Power

What happens when the interests we just discussed are actively pursued by almost seven billion individuals, whether individually, in groups, or in independent political communities? The interests and goals of individuals or groups can interact or intersect with one another in four possible ways. The first possibility is that interests may not intersect at all. They may be discrete interests, in the sense that there is no contact between the interests as they are being pursued. Second, interests may be different but compatible; these are called *complementary interests*. Third, interests may be convergent, with varying degrees of similarity that range from identical to similar. The final possibility is that interests, when they are pursued, may be conflicting.

When this framework is applied at the world level, we can get some sense of the huge harmonies and disharmonies that are produced by the intersections of interests as people seek their goals. Individuals, groups, organizations, and political communities all have their own conceptions of what their interests are—what they think is right and proper and just. Some of those interests are discrete: one can readily think of hundreds of examples where the pursuit of interests by some people does not affect the interests of vast numbers of others. Other interests are complementary or convergent: for example, much of the cooperation that we see between individuals, groups, organizations, and political communities is driven by the complementarity of interests of those many actors who crowd the global marketplace. Indeed, that cooperation makes the contemporary international political economy possible.

But a great deal of world politics is marked by conflicts of interest between individuals, groups, and political communities and their governments. Some of the disharmonies of interest are exceedingly deep. Consider two communities that claim that they own the same piece of territory: unless they agree to share it, there is no way that one can overcome that incompatibility. Or consider the huge disharmonies in interest that exist between those human beings whose lives are lived in deprivation and insecurity and those who live in luxury and security. Consider the disharmonies of interest about rules of the global game. Whether they are rules about funding **terrorist** organizations, disarmament, the control of weapons of mass destruction, the transborder flows of investments, the proper role of women in society, the application of human rights, or the flow of illegal drugs, there is considerable disagreement between individuals, groups, organizations, and political communities. This facet directs our attention to conflicts at the global level, their sources, and most importantly their resolution.

When the interests of actors conflict, what determines whose interests prevail? Briefly put, **power** is the ability to prevail over others in a conflict of interests—or, to put it more crudely, the ability to get your way. Not everyone can get his or her own way, but some people are always able to exercise power over others and get to ensure that *their* interests, wants, desires, and definitions of the "good" prevail over those of others. Power has been described as the central concept of world politics—and for good reason, since it determines so much of the political world.[7]

Governance Without Government: Anarchy and World Politics

Finally, world politics is about governance at a global level. Governance involves establishing rules for a community, making allocative decisions for the community as a whole, settling conflicts over the rules, and mediating disputes between individuals and groups. Governance also includes the exercise of authority, which involves that fascinating human capacity of obeying others without having to be forced, coerced, induced, or persuaded.

The governance of political communities takes many different forms: tribal systems of governance by elders, the singular rule of absolute monarchies, or the highly institutionalized structures of the 20th-century bureaucratic states. But in most political communities, institutional systems of governance that we call the **government**, or the **state**, have evolved, as discussed in Chapter 2. While the degree of institutionalization varies widely, this form always involves a basic hierarchy, a division between the governors and the governed, between those entitled to command and those obligated to obey. Generally, governments seek to establish laws, rules, policies, and day-to-day practices for the community. These rules cover not only the behaviour of individuals toward each other, but also the nature and operation of economic relationships within the community. Importantly, governments generally seek to impose these rules on the community as a whole, securing the obedience of the governed by legitimate authority if possible, but by brute force if necessary. Moreover, in many (but not all) communities, governments seek to monopolize the legitimate use of force, not only to make the task of ruling easier, but in many cases also to provide a safe and secure environment for the conduct of economic activity.

By contrast, governance at a global level occurs in the absence of government, for the world of world politics is an anarchical one. Coming to English from the Greek *anarchos*—without a chief or governor (*an + archos*)—the term **anarchy** describes a system of social, political, and economic relations without formal institutions of governance to define enforceable rules or exact obedience from the governed. In an anarchical condition, no hierarchy exists between governors and governed, nor is there any comparable entitlement to command or obligation to obey. In an anarchy, there is no institution with coercive powers (such as the state or the government) telling people what to do, defining what is right and wrong, or proscribing a whole range of forbidden acts.

Anarchy is an apt description for the setting of world politics. There is no government of the world—no institution with coercive powers to regulate the political relations among over six billion human beings, to make laws for all people that can be enforced over the whole globe, or to arbitrate and settle disputes. In short, in world politics there is neither entitlement to command nor obligation to obey. In this way, politics at the world level differs substantially from politics within communities.

Global Governance in World Politics

On the other hand, politics between political communities is similar to politics within communities precisely because it is marked by an effort to provide the structures of governance so that world politics is not marked by a chaotic and bloody war of all against all. **Global governance** is aimed at resolving the inevitable conflicts that arise from the effects of billions of individuals, organized in groups, pursuing their interests. Five broad areas of global conflict can be identified: conflicts over independence; conflicts over power and dominance; conflicts over conceptions of rightness and justice; conflicts over wealth and its distribution; and conflicts over the environment.

Entrenching Independence

It was argued above that world politics is very much about the different political communities that people create—under a wide array of different names and forms, from the huge empires of antiquity to the compact *poleis* of Hellas, to the vassal relations of the feudal period, to the contemporary sovereign nation-state. The ideal of an independent political community has inspired uprisings, revolts, and wars—across the world and across the centuries, from the periodic revolts of Iberian tribes against their Roman overlords to the struggles of the East Timorese against Indonesian domination in the late 1990s (the most recent war of national liberation resulting in the creation of a sovereign nation-state in May 2002). This ideal continues to manifest itself in the large number of peoples who think of themselves as a national community and who want to give their nation expression in a separate and sovereign state, be it Kurds in Turkey and Iraq, Palestinians in the Middle East, Chechens in Russia, or Québécois in Canada.

Once independence is achieved, maintaining it is often a struggle. It is thus not surprising that world politics has always been about the efforts of people to ensure that their communities are free from elimination, butchery, enslavement, absorption, exploitation, or domination by others. That desire to remain free has prompted numerous people to give up their lives in the cause of the independence of their communities: to put themselves in harm's way or even to commit suicide.

Less dramatically, but no less importantly, there is the ongoing struggle for autonomy and freedom from the impositions and importunities of the more powerful, a struggle that continues to inspire much of the politics of the contemporary era. Examples include European concerns over American protectionism against foreign steel imports, the grumbling of the British over the disappearance of their pound, or Canadian complaints about the effects of the American war on terror on travellers between the two countries.

As is shown in the next chapter, the impact of globalization, and in particular the emergence of global financial markets, poses an even greater challenge to autonomy. Governments and peoples find their room to manoeuvre limited by the impact of the global economy and the necessity of pursuing a course that will not attract the discipline of the market. However, while globalization may threaten local autonomy, we can see that the governing structures at the global level are designed to privilege and entrench that local autonomy and the national communities that value it so highly.

The key institution here is the **United Nations (UN)**, a vast array of intergovernmental organizations, as Figure 15.1 shows. The UN, created during World War II, is dedicated to the idea of ensuring that the world remains divided into separate sovereign states. Even though the preamble of the UN's charter begins with the lofty phrase "We the peoples of the United Nations," the use of the word "peoples" is entirely metaphorical, for only governments of states are admitted as members of the UN, and only governments of states that have been recognized as sovereign by existing members. Moreover, the UN is dedicated to the idea that every state should retain the right to make its own decisions and decide its own fate, without interference by outsiders. Article 2.7 of the UN Charter makes it explicit: "Nothing contained in the present Charter shall authorize the United Nations to intervene in matters which are essentially within the domestic jurisdiction of any state." The UN's rules and procedures, its mission, and its institutional energies have all been devoted to the maintenance of a system of separate sovereign nation-states.

Managing Conflict

The widespread desire for independence produces frequent struggles between political communities: some seek to dominate others, and others seek to avoid domination. Thomas Hobbes's description is still the most evocative of this dynamic:

> In all times, Kings, and Persons of Soveraigne authority, because of their Independency, are in continuall jealousies, and in the state and posture of Gladiators; having their weapons pointing, and their eyes fixed on one another; that is, their Forts, Garrisons, and Guns upon the Frontiers of their Kingdomes; and continuall Spyes upon their neighbours.[8]

To be sure, this does not describe the condition of every political community toward every other. However, even when neighbours do not have "weapons pointing" at each other, they invariably have them pointing at someone else. And the rest of Hobbes's description remains accurate. There are continual jealousies—conflicts, tiffs, annoyances—between governments and peoples; that is the day-to-day stuff of world politics. Frontiers are everywhere "fortified"; even if the front lines consist of agents who swipe passports through their computers, interrogate foreigners, and x-ray luggage, the coercive power of those "Persons of Soveraigne authority" are there to ensure that the frontiers are as impermeable as possible. And there are indeed spies everywhere.

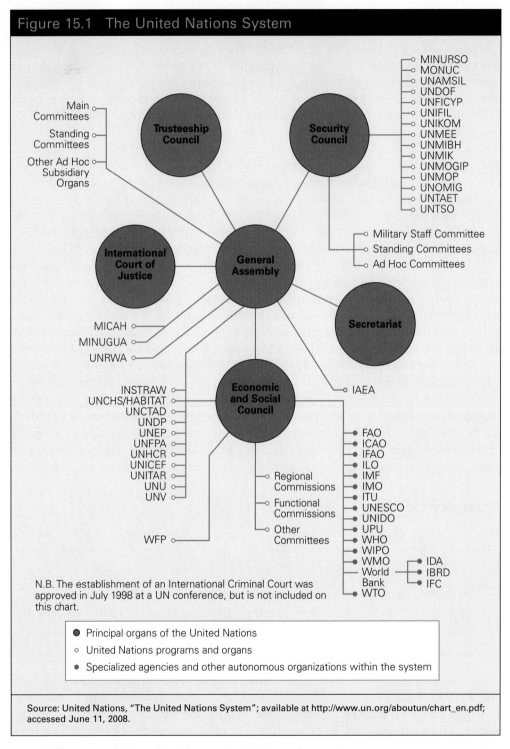

Figure 15.1   The United Nations System

N.B. The establishment of an International Criminal Court was approved in July 1998 at a UN conference, but is not included on this chart.

● Principal organs of the United Nations

○ United Nations programs and organs

● Specialized agencies and other autonomous organizations within the system

Source: United Nations, "The United Nations System"; available at http://www.un.org/aboutun/chart_en.pdf; accessed June 11, 2008.

More importantly, over the long stretch of history, those jealousies on occasion erupt into a struggle for dominance, an attempt to widen control, to achieve the security that can (but need not always) come with control. Those struggles for dominance tend to be periodic rather than omnipresent. Efforts to achieve dominance (or undermine the dominance of others) are more pronounced at some times than others. Thus, for example, the period between 1945 and 1989—the

Cold War era—was marked by a deep rivalry between the United States and the Soviet Union that saw the expenditure of trillions of dollars and rubles in an effort to prevail. By contrast, the years after the Soviet Union was disbanded in 1991 have been marked by no comparable struggle for dominance. And while it is clear that some governments, notably the Chinese and Russian governments, are not entirely comfortable with the dominance of the United States as the sole remaining superpower, the only actors in world politics who have openly sought to upset the dominance of the United States have been transnational Islamist radicals, not other governments. As a result, in the post-9/11 era, Americans and their enemies have adopted the posture of gladiators, but the frontiers between them are not as clear-cut as they were during the Cold War era.

The persistence of the struggle for dominance, combined with the anarchical nature of world politics, also mean that war and the use of force are inevitable features of politics at a global level (see Box 15.3). The history of the world is dominated by the story of wars of different types: civil wars, guerrilla wars, wars of secession, wars of independence, wars of national liberation, wars of absorption, wars of attrition, wars of elimination, humanitarian wars, colonial wars, hot wars, cold wars, dirty wars, limited wars, general wars. Some wars are driven by desire for land, resources, or dominance. Some are fought between political communities of various sizes; some affect a large number of people—indeed, the wars of the 20th century engulfed the majority of humankind. And much of the story of world politics is about the consequences of war, for every war fought, large or small, leaves long-lived traces, affecting all who lived through the horror, terror, pain, and deprivation that go with it.

Global politics is as much about the efforts of political communities to regulate, manage, and limit the destructiveness of war as it is about the efforts by some to use war and force as means of prevailing in conflicts of interest over others. A great deal of expense, energy, and effort are devoted to the prevention of war, whether by deterrence—that is, accumulating enough power that an enemy does not deem it worthwhile to attack—or by the management of conflict through diplomacy or negotiation. Over the course of the 20th century, a number of international organizations were created to try to prevent war. The League of Nations, established after the end of World War I (1914–18), which claimed some 11 million lives, was designed to ensure that the global system would never again experience the destructiveness of such a war by putting in place a system of **collective security**, which involved all nations in the world agreeing that they would jointly attack any country that violated the Covenant of the League. In the end, however, the League proved to be an ineffective instrument of global

---

War and the Use of Force in Contemporary World Politics — BOX 15.3

Recent Invasions
American-led invasion of Iraq, 2003
American-led invasion of Afghanistan, 2001–02
Iraqi invasion of Kuwait, 1990
American invasion of Panama, 1989
American invasion of Grenada, 1983
Israeli invasion of Lebanon, 1982
Argentinean invasion of Falkland Islands, 1982
Soviet invasion of Afghanistan, 1979

Tanzanian invasion of Uganda, 1979
Vietnamese invasion of Cambodia, 1978
Indonesian invasion of Timor, 1975

Recent Armed Humanitarian Interventions
East Timor, 1999
Kosovo, 1999

Recent Interstate Wars
Eritrea versus Ethiopia, 1998–2000
Iraq versus Iran, 1980–88
China versus Vietnam, 1979

governance in the interwar period: the struggle for dominance between the Axis powers (Germany, Italy, and Japan) and the other states in the international system eventually led to the second major war of the 20th century, one even more destructive than the first. The United Nations was designed by the victors of World War II to correct the imperfections of the League, but the essential purpose of this global institution remained unchanged: to provide a mechanism for attempting to resolve conflicts between states before war breaks out—or to bring warring states to a condition of peace.

Thus, an important international mechanism for the achievement and maintenance of peace during the Cold War era (1945–89) was **peacekeeping**, the practice of putting forces of a third party between warring parties who have come to a ceasefire, in order to encourage them to keep the peace. In the post–Cold War period (1991–2001), we saw the transformation of peacekeeping. In the 1990s, the number of interstate wars declined dramatically; most wars were internal. In civil war situations, no longer could third-party armed forces be inserted only after there was peace to be kept. Instead, in what was dubbed "second-generation peacekeeping," or **peacemaking**, the armed forces of a third party intervened, directly or indirectly, in a war to bring peace to an area, as was done in Somalia in 1992—an intervention captured in the 2002 film *Black Hawk Down*—or in the former Yugoslavia. And after peace has been achieved, there was a third process, **peacebuilding**, which refers to the efforts of the international community to create the structures of a peaceful society, as in Bosnia after the Dayton Accords in 1995 and in Kosovo after the defeat of Serbia in 1999, and as was done after the ouster of Indonesia from East Timor in 1999–2000, or at present in Afghanistan.

In the post-9/11 period, however, we have a dramatic decline in traditional peacekeeping. Rather, we have seen the emergence of the idea that there is an intimate relationship between the defence forces needed to bring stability to a conflict situation, the diplomatic resources necessary to negotiate the conditions of peace, and the development resources needed to rebuild and reconstruct wartorn societies—or the *3D approach* (defence, diplomacy, development). In addition, in the post-9/11 era, armed forces are increasingly organized to engage in what is known as the *three-block war*, in which armed forces might be engaged in combat in one city block, in stabilization efforts in an adjacent block, while, a couple of streets over, they are engaged in such reconstruction efforts as building schools, hospitals, or reconnecting electricity. In Afghanistan, for example, the countries of the North Atlantic Treaty Organization and other Western countries are seeking to assist the Afghanistan government of Hamid Karzai to fight a local insurgency, and at the same time develop social, political, and economic institutions in the country—a complex process that has led to the deaths of hundreds of American, Australian, British, Canadian, and Dutch soldiers.

Even if the institutional structures put in place to prevent war or maintain peace do not work—and in the years since 1945 there have been numerous wars that have cost millions of lives—the international community has always been keen to put in place rules and understandings to regulate the use of force. The various **Geneva Conventions** agreed to over the course of the 20th century provide a comprehensive and detailed set of rules to try to ensure that warfare is conducted in a predictable and orderly way. And the rules of war are always being updated to take into account the most recent war: for example, after the Yugoslav civil war in the 1990s, rape was finally made illegal as a tool of war.

Children drive a donkey cart through the Otash refugee camp in Darfur, Sudan. Having fled there to avoid violence, they were under increasing pressure to leave.

AP Photo/Alfred de Montesquiou

Seeking Justice

Everyone has a sense of justice, and this creates considerable political conflict, for definitions of right and wrong—of justice—are always deeply contested, regardless of the level of politics we examine. This is because individuals are prone to come to different conclusions about matters of morality, notions of goodness, and conceptions of righteous behaviour. Indeed, for Thomas Hobbes, that is why words such as *right, wrong, justice,* and *injustice* are devoid of meaning unless and until there is a "common power"—a Leviathan, a supreme authority, or a government. Hobbes's formula is succinct: without government, "nothing can be Unjust. The notions of Right and Wrong, Justice and Injustice have there no place. Where there is no common Power, there is no Law: where no Law, no Injustice."[9] But with a common power, these words can be given meaning by defining *through* law what is right and what is wrong; with a common power, there is a means to insist that everyone abide by those laws.

In many political contexts, we do indeed have a Leviathan that makes laws defining wrong and right and possesses the coercive power to try to impose those definitions on all the people under its authority. But at the level of global politics, there is no institution comparable to local or national governments.

The absence of government in no way dampens the concerns for justice at the global level. People push hard to see justice done, and actors, organizations, and institutions are concerned with the standard used. Individuals and governments do not hesitate to express themselves on their views of right and wrong. This has been particularly true on issues such as **human rights** (including women's rights, children's rights, and the rights of Aboriginal peoples), the economic and sexual exploitation of children, nuclear proliferation and disarmament, environmental protections of all sorts, slavery, the use of child soldiers, and global poverty.

Moreover, while there is no global Leviathan, international organizations such as the United Nations have proved willing to try to articulate commonly held views of justice and rightness on a range of matters. The **International Court of Justice (ICJ)** seeks to develop and apply formal rules. Governments of countries bring disputes over what is just and unjust to the ICJ, and panels drawn from 15 judges (who are elected to the Court by the United Nations Security Council) hear cases and render their decisions on the basis of the huge accumulated body of **international law** that has evolved over hundreds of years.

The ICJ deals only with governments of countries, but the international community also has institutionalized means for dealing with organizations and individuals. For example, under the provisions of the North American Free Trade Agreement between Canada, Mexico, and the United States, multinational corporations from one country that have investment disputes with one of the other governments can submit such disputes to an independent tribunal for decision. Likewise, since 1950, Europeans have had access to the European Court of Human Rights; its rulings are widely obeyed by governments of states, even when this means changing national laws.

In addition, the international community has developed means of dealing with individuals deemed to be international criminals. After World War II, the victorious powers established courts to try individuals accused of **crimes against humanity**. Following the civil wars in the former Yugoslavia and in Rwanda in the 1990s, the United Nations established special international tribunals to try individuals accused of war crimes, including Slobodan Milosević, the former president of Yugoslavia, who was ousted from power and turned over by the new government to the special tribunal in The Hague and put on trial for **genocide** and crimes against humanity. An effort to make such tribunals a permanent feature of the international political landscape resulted in the creation of a permanent **International Criminal Court (ICC)** to deal with individuals accused of a specific range of war crimes or crimes against humanity. While the ICC received enough signatures to come into force in July 2002, it is notable that it has not been endorsed by the United States, China, or the Russian Federation, a function of the profound skepticism those countries have about giving an international organization this kind of judicial authority. As a result, the work of the ICC has tended to focus on cases in smaller countries: the ICC is currently pursuing charges against individuals in Sudan, Democratic Republic of the Congo, and Uganda for various crimes.

It is true that the search for justice at a global level is constrained by the absence of a global Leviathan to define right and wrong and impose that definition on all actors. As a result, the underlying structure of the search for justice at the global level has not changed much since Thucydides was writing 2,500 years ago. At the outset of the Melian dialogue, the Athenians claimed that they would use no "fine phrases" about rights in trying to persuade the Melians to surrender. Instead, they suggested that the Melians "look the facts in the face" and decide how to save their *polis* from destruction. As Thucydides had the Athenians say,

> *You know as well as we do that, when these matters are discussed by practical people, the standard of justice depends on the equality of power to compel and that in fact the strong do what they have the power to do and the weak accept what they have to accept.*[10]

And so it remains today: justice everywhere and at all levels, national and international, is heavily dependent on the "equality of power to compel." The powerful usually manage to evade the mechanisms that exist to enforce rules; the less powerful "accept what they have to accept." Power explains why Milosević was put on trial in The Hague while other political leaders who had given orders that also resulted in the deaths of thousands of human beings went free. Power explains why the governments of Cuba, Burma, and North Korea—all small and relatively marginal actors in the international political economy—tend to be targets for international punishment while injustices by countries that are more powerful tend to go unchallenged.

However immature international law must be in an anarchical system, many people continue to be impelled to impose their standard of justice on others. This has been (and will likely continue to be) a source of tension between communities, and in particular between their governments, for there is little agreement on those issues. Hence "the standard of justice [will depend] on the equality of power to compel," just as Thucydides said some 2,500 years ago.

Managing the Global Economy

Global governance is also about managing the global economy. In the absence of an overarching authority capable of economic regulation and management, it is left to the governments of the international system to seek mechanisms for overcoming the political problems that arise from the allocations of the marketplace. So global economic management is concerned not only with relations among industrialized countries, but also with the management of the basic division between the rich and the poor in the contemporary international system.

The first concentrated global efforts at economic management emerged toward the end of World War II, when the Allied governments met to plan the postwar international order, drawing on what they regarded as the lessons of the Great Depression of the 1930s. In the interwar era—that is, between 1919 and 1939—governments had tried to solve the economic problems that followed the crash of the New York stock market in October 1929 by offloading their economic problems to neighbouring countries, using what have become known as beggar-thy-neighbour policies: raising tariffs, restricting imports, and subsidizing exports. Moreover, many governments tried to correct their balance of payments deficits by abandoning the gold standard. By allowing their currencies to float—that is, to be no longer tied to gold—governments could engage in currency devaluations, making imports more expensive and exports more attractive to foreigners. However, this merely triggered competitive devaluations by other governments, deepening the cycle of depression.

In July 1944, the Allies met at Bretton Woods, a resort in New Hampshire, to find ways of avoiding these problems. The United States government in particular sought to put in place a system for the conduct of international trade and the management of international finance that would provide stability and growth, which had been so lacking in the 1930s, at the same time forcing nation-states to forfeit their independence.

The result was what John Gerard Ruggie has called the compromise of embedded liberalism. A tradeoff was involved: countries would agree to forgo some of the benefits of pursuing their own economic policies without regard for others by cooperating with one another in liberalizing the system; on the other hand, countries would be free to pursue their own economic and social policies at home.[11] The key institutions to provide coordination and liberalization were to be the **World Bank**, the **International Monetary Fund (IMF)**, and the International Trade Organization (ITO). The World Bank and the IMF would regulate the international monetary system with fixed interest rates linked to gold and a limited pool of capital to ensure international liquidity; the ITO would seek to lower tariff barriers to trade. The ITO was never created: the United States Senate decided not to ratify it, and it was replaced with the General Agreement on Tariffs and Trade (GATT). And while the Bretton Woods system never worked precisely as those who met in 1944 had envisaged, it did produce the effects intended by its framers. The European countries and Japan recovered, their economies increasingly robust and diversified. World trade grew. Confidence in the U.S. dollar remained strong.

Over time, however, the system grew unstable. By the end of the 1950s, such a quantity of dollars had flowed out of the United States that it overwhelmed the capacity of the U.S. government to meet its commitment to convert dollars into gold. Through the 1960s, efforts by the United States and its major trading partners to correct this system created new organizations for multilateral management, such as the Group of Ten. But a number of underlying problems were not resolved. These included an increase in the gap between foreign dollar holdings and U.S. reserves of gold; a massive increase in financial transactions involving Japan and Europe; the rise of multinational corporations moving money around the international system; and the rise of a market in Eurodollars—U.S. dollars deposited in and traded by foreign banks (mostly but not necessarily in Europe, the name notwithstanding) without being converted to local currency, and hence not subject to domestic controls. By the early 1970s, these related elements of financial integration were creating monetary problems for the United States government, notably a continuing outflow of capital and a worsening trade balance.

The desire of a number of administrations in Washington to spend increasing sums on domestic social welfare programs while pursuing a costly war in Vietnam only exacerbated these economic problems. In the spring of 1971, there was a high demand for the dollar, causing a sharp decline in American gold reserves. This coincided with the announcement that the United States had experienced its first trade deficit. The response of the administration of President Richard Nixon was to abandon the Bretton Woods system. On August 15, 1971, the United States government announced that it would no longer convert dollars into gold. In addition, Nixon imposed a 10 percent surcharge on all dutiable items in an attempt to bring American trade back into balance. These measures were known as the "Nixon shocks."

These measures led to a transformation of the world economy, as borrowing on international capital markets started to grow—from US$96.6 billion annually in the late 1970s to US$427.4 billion by the late 1980s. By 1993, borrowing amounted to US$818.6 billion a year—approximately 10 times what it was 15 years earlier. Over the past 20 years, world trade has also grown explosively. Much of that growth can be explained by the progressive liberalization of trade—the efforts to remove barriers to the trans-border movement of goods and services. Liberalization aims to first lower and then eliminate tariffs and duties. It seeks to replace discriminatory practices, such as trading preferences, with nondiscriminatory approaches, such as most-favoured-nation (MFN), in which all states are treated as though they were indeed the "most favoured." It seeks to eliminate dumping—the selling of goods in a foreign market at a price below that charged in the home market. It also seeks to eliminate **nontariff barriers**, the policies that governments put in place besides tariffs and duties to favour their goods and services over those of foreigners.

The key multilateral forum for the negotiated dismantling of barriers to trade has been at the GATT, in a series of multilateral negotiations called *GATT Rounds*: the Dillon Round (1961–62, named after the U.S. secretary of the treasury who initiated it, C. Douglas Dillon); the Kennedy Round (1963–67, named after President John F. Kennedy); the Tokyo Round (1973–79); and the Uruguay Round (1986–93), which resulted in the creation of the **World Trade Organization (WTO)**, the key global organization for the management of trade between and among nations. The WTO agreements provide a set of rules negotiated and signed by over 140 states to promote liberal trading practices and to reduce **protectionism**.

Today there is a dense web of international institutions for the management of the global political economy besides the WTO. The core international financial institutions include the World Bank and the IMF, as well as a range of regional development banks. In addition to intergovernmental organizations, there are a number of essentially private groups who meet to organize economic affairs on a global scale. There are regional economic institutions, the most highly integrated of which is the EU. There are also institutions designed to facilitate the discussion of global economic affairs. A major intergovernmental event is the annual summit meeting of the **Group of Eight (G8)**, which began life as a group of leaders of six industrialized countries at Rambouillet, France, in 1975: the United States, Japan, Britain, France, Germany, and Italy. The meeting was so successful that the leaders decided to meet again the following year, hosted by the United States. U.S. president Gerald Ford decided to invite Canada, and thus the G7 was born. It has met annually since then, joined by the European Community (the forerunner of the European Union) in 1978. In 1991, just before the Soviet Union was disbanded, Moscow was invited to the G7 meeting; the Russian Federation became a full member at the Birmingham summit of 1998.

An important nongovernmental venue for the discussion of global economic problems is the World Economic Forum, an elite annual meeting of leaders of governments, corporations, and international institutions held in Davos, Switzerland. In 2001, a group of nongovernmental organizations organized a counterpoint forum in Porto Alegre, Brazil to discuss ways of opposing the **neoliberalism** embraced at the Davos forum. Since then, the World Social Forum has met in a number of locations in the South: four times in Porto Alegre, in Mumbai and Nairobi. Its 2006 meeting was polycentric, with meetings in Caracas, Bamako, and Karachi; the 2008 forum was global, with thousands of local organizations holding simultaneous meetings.

Managing the Global Environment

In 1968, Garrett Hardin, a biologist at the University of California, argued that people should give up their "freedom to breed" as a response to the global problems that he believed would come with population increases.[12] His argument about population was based on the idea of the commons, the land in medieval English villages that was set aside for common use, usually pasture, where all farmers could send their animals to graze. Hardin noted that the idea of a commons works well enough if the number of animals owned by farmers is less than the carrying capacity of the land. But what happens when that carrying capacity is reached? Hardin argued that the benefits to an individual farmer of adding one animal to the commons far outweigh the negative costs of overgrazing, since those costs are borne by all farmers using the land. Thus the rational farmer will add as many animals as possible. But, as Hardin pointed out, this conclusion is reached by all farmers. If they are all rational, they will all try to add animals, counting on the costs being borne by the collectivity. The result is that the commons is overloaded and overgrazed.

For Hardin, the *tragedy of the commons* was a tragedy in two senses. First, it was a tragedy that the commons suffered a disaster. But more importantly, Hardin was using the word in its literary sense. A tragedy is a form of drama in which the main character is brought to ruin or suffers extreme sorrow. Moreover, the essence of tragedy is the remorseless and inevitable way calamity unfolds: tragedy demands that the audience be gripped by an understanding that there is no way out for the central character, no escape from what they understand must be that character's fate. For Hardin, the tragedy of the commons described perfectly the dynamic of the global environment. All human beings and each political community to which they belong are like the farmer: they have every incentive to treat the "global commons" in a way that spreads the negative consequences of their treatment over the entire collectivity. This involves "taking out" of the commons (the way a grazing sheep takes out grass)—extracting nonrenewable resources (such as oil, gas, and minerals) or renewable resources (such as trees and fish) and decreasing biodiversity through development (such as urban growth). But it also means spreading the costs of what is "put into" the commons: the pollution, the effluents discharged into the water, and the noxious gases released into the air.

The tragedy of the commons arises from the fact that the threats posed by overpopulation, overexploitation, and pollution are virtually impossible to deal with in the absence of an authority to dictate the behaviour of individuals in such matters—and the capacity to enforce those decisions. By definition, the globe does not have such an apparatus. Appeals to morality or conscience have limited effects: without the prospect of punishment, there will always be those who follow their interests, exploiting or polluting, and shifting the burden to the collectivity. There is only one option: negotiation between the users of the commons with an eye to limiting use to the carrying capacity.

Global governance involves the attempts to grapple with this problem. Among the successful efforts to establish global rules have been the Convention on International Trade in Endangered Species (CITES) and the Basel Convention on the treatment, movement, and disposal of hazardous wastes. But overcoming the tragedy has been difficult. Some argue that the solution is a global agreement on keeping "loadings" down to sustainable levels to ensure that the carrying capacity of the global ecosystem is not strained beyond repair.

However, as we have seen in the case of the Kyoto Protocol to the UN Framework Convention on Climate Change, the obstacles to global management of the commons are significant. The Kyoto Protocol, signed in 1997, was an international agreement on **greenhouse** gas emissions. However, the agreement has significant structural flaws. Most importantly, under Kyoto, there is no incentive to agree to forgo one's sovereign rights to exploit and develop—and pollute. Indeed, two of the countries whose GHG emissions are increasing most dramatically, India and China, are not required under the Kyoto Accords to reduce emissions. In addition, two other countries, the United States and Australia, decided not to ratify the agreement. And while some countries worked to meet their Kyoto commitments, many other countries signed the Kyoto Accords but then did nothing to implement them. For example, Canada's Kyoto commitment requires Canadians to reduce their greenhouse gas emissions to a level 6 percent below 1990 emissions by 2012. However, the Canadian government spent the 10 years after Kyoto studiously avoiding taking any serious measures to implement that commitment; as a result, by 2007, Canada's GHG emissions had actually *increased* 24 percent.

As 2012—the target date established by Kyoto for reducing GHG emissions—draws closer, the problems inherent in the Kyoto Protocol have been increasingly exposed. But there is widespread recognition that the problem of GHG emissions should be addressed, reflected for example in the awarding of the 2007 Nobel Peace Prize to the Intergovernmental Panel on

Climate Change and Al Gore, Jr., for their efforts to increase knowledge about human-made climate change. In January 2006, six of the countries who were either outside the Kyoto emission-reduction regime or skeptical about Kyoto met to form the Asia-Pacific Partnership on Clean Development and Climate. At their inaugural meeting in Sydney, the six governments—Australia, China, India, Japan, Korea, and the United States—committed to accelerate the development of clean energy technologies. In October 2007, the Canadian government of Stephen Harper joined the group. While the Asia-Pacific Partnership may have no more success than Kyoto in lowering GHG emissions, its very emergence demonstrates the propensity to try to solve global problems through global governance.

CONCLUSION

This chapter has painted a rather grim picture of politics at a global level. It has suggested that the global political realm is always marked by conflict. The pervasiveness of raw power as a determinant of political outcomes, the horror of war, the use of force, the pain of poverty and deprivation, and the debilitation of disease—all are consequences of an absence of government that could give justice a meaningful definition on a global scale.

At the same time, global politics is not unremittingly bleak. While conflict, war, deprivation, environmental degradation, and pandemics are endemic and pervasive, there has also been both a desire and an ability to forge a sense of community at the global level—despite the obvious and clear divisions that have marked humankind. We saw such a compulsion at work most clearly in the aftermath of the Indian Ocean tsunami in 2004, but historically it has manifested itself in numerous ways: the efforts of the ancient Greeks from *poleis* with deep-seated enmities to fashion community; the attempts by merchants, traders, and producers to create security and predictability in order to lower risk and raise profit; the propensity of governments to engage in global governance and establish "rules of the game"—and an equal willingness to abide by those rules a significant part of the time.

This desire to cooperate has resulted in the spread of peace over huge areas of the globe, allowing billions of people to live their lives free from the devastation of war. It has also permitted commerce to spread over virtually every part of the earth, with all the positive effects that the growth of wealth tends to bring. In short, there has always been a willingness to conceive of politics as extending beyond the confines of the political communities into which humans have always divided themselves.

DISCUSSION QUESTIONS

1. What are some of the solutions that have been advanced to deal with the anarchical condition of world politics?

2. What is the role of the ideology of nationalism in maintaining divisions between peoples?

3. In what ways is war "thinkable" and thus possible?

4. Can the tragedy of the commons be overcome without dismantling the system of sovereign states?

KEY TERMS

CRIME AGAINST HUMANITY: A wrongful act deemed to be not a violation of any particular nation's laws, but rather a violation against humankind as a whole. (447)

GLOBAL GOVERNANCE: The process by which different actors—governments, organizations, firms, groups, and individuals—try to make common decisions about and for the global community. (442)

HUMAN RIGHTS: Rights enjoyed by individuals simply because they are human beings, primarily including the prevention of discrimination or coercion on grounds of ethnicity, religion, gender, or opinion. (447)

INDEPENDENCE: The state of being free from the control of others; the ability to make one's own decisions, not having to rely on anyone else. (The term comes from the Latin word *pendere*, meaning "to hang," so independence is not having to "hang" on others.) In the context of world politics, it is the ability of a political community to govern itself rather than be governed by others. (438)

NONTARIFF BARRIER: Any measure or practice that puts a barrier in the way of "free" commerce between nations, ranging from the obvious, such as procurement policies that favour one's nationals, to the not-so-obvious, such as the imposition of strict health and safety standards on imports in order to make the goods of other countries more expensive. (450)

POWER: The capacity of one actor to prevail in a conflict of interests with other actors, normally through force, sanction, coercion, or manipulation. Power resources are any of the things needed in order to exercise power. (441)

PROTECTIONISM: The use of various policy tools, such as subsidies, tariffs, and quotas, to protect goods and services produced within a country against competition from producers in other countries. (450)

SUPRANATIONAL: A sphere of politics and political institutions that exists "above" the nation-state but usually "below" the global level. The only supranational polity in the world is the European Union. (435)

WEB LINKS

Department of International Politics, University of Wales, Aberystwyth:
http://www.aber.ac.uk/~inpwww

Canadian International Council:
http://www.igloo.org/canadianinternational

Canadian Institute for Strategic Studies:
http://www.ciss.ca

Europa: Gateway to the European Union:
http://europa.eu/index_en.htm

International Alert:
http://www.international-alert.org

International Criminal Court:
http://www.icc-cpi.int/home.html

United Nations:
http://www.un.org

FURTHER READING

Bull, Hedley. *The Anarchical Society: A Study of Order in World Politics*. London: Macmillan, 1977.

Doyle, Michael W. *Ways of War and Peace: Realism, Liberalism, Socialism*. New York: W.W. Norton, 1997.

Morgenthau, Hans J. *Politics Among Nations: The Struggle for Power and Peace*. New York: Alfred A. Knopf, 1948.

Sens, Allen, and Peter J. Stoett. *Global Politics*. 3rd ed. Toronto: Thomson Nelson, 2005.

ENDNOTES

1. Harold Lasswell, *Politics: Who Gets What, When, How* (New York: Meridian Books, 1958).

2. Kalevi J. Holsti, *Peace and War: Armed Conflicts and International Order, 1648–1989* (Cambridge: Cambridge University Press, 1991), p. 45.

3. Thucydides, *The Peloponnesian War*, trans. Rex Warner (Harmondsworth, U.K.: Penguin, 1954), p. 80.

4. Thomas Hobbes, *Leviathan, or the Matter, Forme, & Power of a Common-Wealth Ecclesiasticall and Civill*, ed. C.B. Macpherson (Harmondsworth, U.K.: Pelican, 1968 [1651]), p. 185. The echo should not be surprising: Hobbes's first published work was a translation of Thucydides into English, published in 1628.

5. Quoted in Hans J. Morgenthau, *Politics Among Nations: The Struggle for Power and Peace*, 5th ed. (New York: Alfred A. Knopf, 1973 [1948]), p. 36.

6. Thucydides, pp. 402, 407.

7. For an excellent discussion of the concept of power, see Steven Lukes, *Power: A Radical View* (London: Macmillan, 1974).

8. Hobbes, pp. 187–88.

9. Hobbes, p. 188.

10. Thucydides, p. 402.

11. John Gerard Ruggie, "International Regimes, Transactions, and Change: Embedded Liberalism in the Postwar Economic Order," *International Organization* 36 (Spring 1982): 379–415.

12. Garrett Hardin, "The Tragedy of the Commons," *Science* 162 (December 13, 1968): 1243–48.

Chapter Sixteen

THE POLITICS OF GLOBALIZATION

William D. Coleman

Introduction

Over the past several decades, processes now termed *globalization* have been steadily reshaping how many of us live and relate to others across the globe. They are reducing many limits on the interactions between individuals and communities once imposed by physical location. They are destabilizing existing centres of authority and security such as nation-states, with new centres emerging at various scales of social life, from global down to local levels. The organization and scope of markets and the production and diffusion of cultural forms like movies and literature and practices like the choices of foods eaten have taken on even more global dimensions. Many concerned citizens the world over have mobilized politically in order to oppose or reshape some of the changes involved. The changes are potentially so profound that they may be altering some of the basic elements of the human condition.

One of the most basic of these elements is autonomy. The term *autonomy* is used in two ways. First, it refers to the situations of individual persons and usually to their capacity to shape the conditions under which they live.[1] It is also used in connection with collective bodies, such as nation-states, minority groups within states, indigenous peoples, and religious movements. In this collective sense, autonomy usually means something closer to the Greek roots of the term: the capacity to give oneself laws. Individual and collective autonomy are linked and globalization shapes these linkages in important ways. Protesters have gathered in the streets at meetings of major global institutions over the past few years to register their worries about a loss of control over their lives. These worries extend, however, well beyond these street protests. Concerned about collective autonomy, African political leaders note the increased marginalization of their economies and societies in the world system. Peasants throughout the developing countries and many workers in manufacturing sectors such as auto-making in wealthy countries see international trade rules as inevitably bringing an end to what individual autonomy they might have had. Ministers responsible for culture in countries outside the United States have formed a worldwide alliance in pursuit of the preservation of collective autonomy in the cultural realm in the face of such U.S. corporations as Disney and McDonald's. Fears have become more widespread about climate change and about the growing inability of communities to have any control or say in how such change might affect their futures. Ethnic nationalist movements and religious fundamentalist communities have sought new forms of collective autonomy as they have become more anxious and even violent as "modernity" is globalized in ways that threaten "traditional" practices.

Others speak of new possibilities. Changes in communications and information technology have created surprising openings in high-technology industries in developing countries, as the software sector in India illustrates, and with them new avenues for individual autonomy. Aspects of culture such as music, literature, and films produced in one part of the world are increasingly accessible to large numbers of people in other parts, thanks to some of these same technologies. Attempts to establish an international human rights regime have helped some individuals and communities to imagine autonomy in different ways, breathed new life into cosmopolitan thinking, and encouraged the growth of such notions as global justice and global citizenship.

This chapter examines the politics of globalization. It is divided into three sections. The first focuses on the meaning of globalization and explores the several dimensions of the concept. It shows how globalizing processes bring about new linkages between what happens globally and what occurs locally in our communities and in our daily lives. The second section builds on this definition by examining the kinds of changes to politics that have come about with globalization. These changes involve new forms of **global governance** as was noted in previous chapters, novel ways of life in local communities, changes in what nation-states can and cannot do, and new regional structures such as the **European Union (EU)** and the **North American Free Trade Agreement (NAFTA)**. The final section investigates the relevance of these kinds of changes for democracy. Democracy is a form of governance that rose to prominence together with the nation-state as a political structure. Most of the time when we speak of democracy, we are referring to political practices in nation-states. If nation-states are ceding sovereign powers to new global centres of authority or are pooling these powers with other nation-states, what happens to democracy as we know it?

What Is Globalization?

Often in political science, we work with concepts that are highly charged with political meaning. On the one side, they are used in everyday political practices and discourse, while on the other, scholars debate them and adapt them for the analysis of politics. Globalization has become one of these kinds of concepts. Social movements, corporate executives, politicians, and public intellectuals writing in popular magazines or appearing on television refer to it often. In these public usages, globalization takes on a number of different meanings. When many social movements say that they are "antiglobalization" (see Chapters 3 and 12) or seek an alternative globalization ("alter-globalization"), they usually mean they are opposed to unchecked power of **transnational corporations**. Sometimes, they mean simply that they are opposed to capitalism becoming entrenched as the sole approach for organizing economic activity. Others use "globalization" synonymously with Americanization. They see the growing economic and military dominance

KFC in Beijing.

Photo: Yanqiu Rachel Zhou, Photographer

of the United States, whether through the spread of American movies and fast food outlets, through the global role taken on by U.S. multinational corporations such as Monsanto, KFC, and Disney, or through the extensive reach of U.S. military power. Still others see globalization as another way of saying that capitalism is extending itself on a global scale.

Like other social scientists, political scientists examine carefully the way terms are used by various persons and organizations in society. They reflect upon these usages and seek to distil the core ideas and concerns implicit to them. Building on these core ideas and concerns, they begin to develop an analytic definition of the phenomenon. This analytic definition then takes on a life apart from how the concept might be used by political actors in broader society. It becomes a tool for analyzing politics. Eventually, such a definition might, in turn, become adopted by people more generally, changing their behaviour and attitudes toward globalization. Social scientists refer to this process as *reflexivity*.

Many social scientists have engaged in this careful process of reflection when it comes to **globalization**. After examining the competing definitions of globalization, political scientist Jan Aart Scholte suggested that globalization involves "the spread of transplanetary—and in recent times also more particularly supraterritorial—connections between people."[2] *Supraterritorial* refers to relations that are "above" territory or relatively unconstrained by one's physical location. John Tomlinson characterizes this "empirical condition" of supraterritoriality as one of "complex connectivity," a set of "connections that now bind our practices, our experiences and our political, economic and environmental fates together across the modern world."[3] Associated with this change in the character of social relationships for both authors is "de-territorialisation." The relative importance of physical location as a basis for building social relationships is declining as supraterritorial ties grow in significance. In this respect, globalization is bringing far-reaching changes to the nature of social space: it is less and less defined by the physical place in which we live.[4]

Following David Held and his colleagues, we can begin to assess the scope of these changes by looking at three properties of supraterritorial relations.[5] First, we can observe shifts in *extensity*, the degree to which cultural, political, and economic activities are stretching across the whole world thus taking place in a global space. For example, suppose we are interested in global environmental problems such as the climate change triggered by increased human creation of greenhouse gases. We can ask whether the human production of excessive greenhouse gases has extended to include more parts of the world than it did 20 years ago. If the answer is yes, we can argue that the propagation of greenhouse gases is becoming more extensive over time. Second, we can assess *intensity*—changes in the magnitude and regularity of interconnectedness. To continue with our climate change example, if we observe that more and more presumed effects of climate change such as intense, destructive storms and higher temperatures are affecting the everyday lives of more persons in the world, we can argue that the effects of climate change are becoming more intensive. Third, Held et al. draw our attention to the property of *velocity*—changes in the speed of global interactions and processes. If the increasing levels of greenhouse gases are leading to a faster rise in temperatures and a greater increase in the number of destructive storms than historical averages, we can say that the velocity of global climate change is increasing. Some of these processes are captured in the graph of temperature changes over time shown in Figure 16.1.

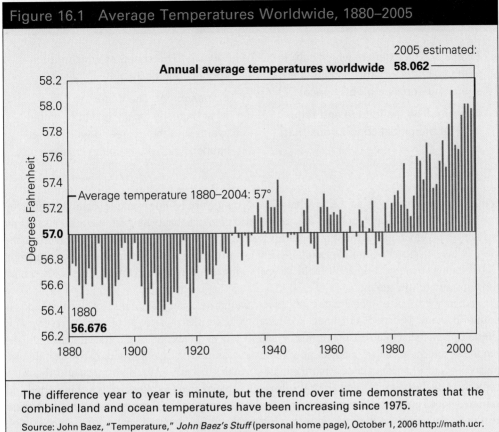

Figure 16.1 Average Temperatures Worldwide, 1880–2005

Annual average temperatures worldwide

2005 estimated: **58.062**

Average temperature 1880–2004: 57°

1880
56.676

The difference year to year is minute, but the trend over time demonstrates that the combined land and ocean temperatures have been increasing since 1975.

Source: John Baez, "Temperature," *John Baez's Stuff* (personal home page), October 1, 2006 http://math.ucr. edu/home/baez/temperature; accessed June 13, 2008.

Together these three properties contribute to a fourth: *enmeshment*—changes in the interdependence of the global and the local (see Box 16.1). Suppose we look at small villages in the Canadian Arctic. If temperatures have risen significantly over the past 20 years, and if these changes have consistently led to a melting of polar ice, making it more difficult to do traditional subsistence activities like hunting and fishing, we can say that the people living in this rather remote region of the world are more enmeshed in global economic and environmental processes today than they were two decades ago. What happens in the small settlements in the Canadian north is more closely linked to what is happening globally in the creation of greenhouse gases, the so-called **greenhouse effect**.

Contrary then to what might have happened in the past, globalization is not just a matter of the rich and the famous travelling the globe. Rather, it involves changes to the lives of more people in all walks of life, living in an even more diverse range of local communities. Robertson offers the concept of "global unicity" for understanding how these changes are linked to one another.[6] Unicity comes first from a global context of trading rules, of international regimes, including those related to the environment (see Chapter 15), of cultural transmission, and of corporate activities that has an ever-increasing impact on how individuals and groups relate to one another in their local settings. Second, it arises from the creation of global frames of reference within which social actors increasingly understand who they are and how they should orient their activities. Accordingly, even acts of resistance, whether these be attempts to prevent massive depopulation of agricultural areas or to secure the traditional family in a strong religious

- *Extensity.* The extent to which cultural, political, and economic activities are stretching across a global space.

- *Intensity.* The magnitude and regularity of the global connections that occur.

- *Velocity.* The speed at which global connections occur.

- *Enmeshment.* The degree to which what happens locally is tied to global events and the degree to which what happens globally is tied to local events.

community, are done with an eye to what is happening globally. For example, demonstrations by farmers about agricultural policies are targeted to what is happening at negotiations on an Agreement of Agriculture at the World Trade Organization (WTO). Religious fundamentalists make effective use of current communications technologies to send out their message about resisting secularization, thereby seeking to build alliances with other religious communities with similar concerns around the globe.

When we speak of globalization, therefore, we are referring to a complex phenomenon. It occurs in many aspects of our lives. We have spoken earlier about global climate change and cultural phenomena like religious fundamentalism. There are examples in other domains. In the economy, foreign exchange markets now reach fully around the globe (more extensive); involve trades of about $1 trillion per day (more intensive), trades that take place almost instantly, thanks to computers (higher velocity); and affect the lives of people in many localities (prices of imported and exported goods go up and down depending on the exchange rate). Of course, associated with these economic activities we find the growth of globally active, transnational banking companies. Transnational banks have expanded into new areas of finance such as derivatives, the trade in which grew from $47 trillion per year in 1995 to over $197 trillion by 2003 (see Table 16.1).

In the social realm, migration to Canada now draws from all parts of the globe and not just Europe (more extensive); we have been admitting between 200,000 and 250,000 immigrants per year since the 1980s (more intensive); people can get here more quickly by airplane than in the past (higher velocity); and many of our cities are becoming much more culturally diverse (more enmeshment of the local and the global) (see Chapter 3). See Figure 16.2.

In politics, the rules of the international trade regime at the WTO now bind the activities of 150 states including China (more extensive); these rules affect a large range of policies (more

Table 16.1 Global Over-the-Counter (OTC) Derivatives Markets, 1995–2006 (billions of U.S. dollars)

	Notional Amounts,* June 1995	Notional Amounts, Dec. 1998	Notional Amounts, June 2000	Notional Amounts, Dec. 2003	Notional Amounts, Dec. 2006
Foreign exchange contracts	13,095	18,011	15,494	18,068	40,179
Interest rate contracts	26,645	50,015	64,125	141,991	291,987
Equity-linked contracts	579	1,488	1,671	3,787	7,485
Commodity contracts	318	415	584	1,406	6,935
Other	6,893	10,388	12,433	31,925	68,593
Grand total	**47,530**	**80,317**	**94,307**	**197,177**	**415,179**

* Notional amounts outstanding provide a measure of the market risk faced by counterparties.

Source: Bank for International Settlements (BIS), *OTC Derivatives Market,* various years.

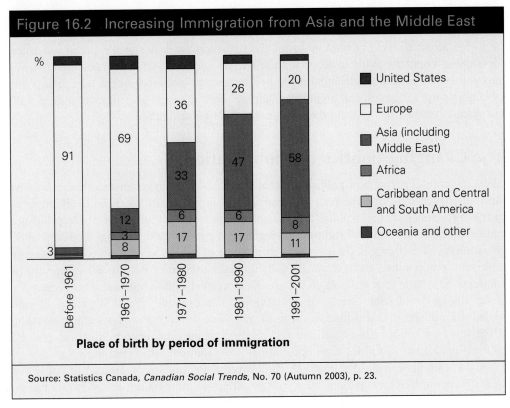

Figure 16.2 Increasing Immigration from Asia and the Middle East

Legend:
- United States
- Europe
- Asia (including Middle East)
- Africa
- Caribbean and Central and South America
- Oceania and other

Place of birth by period of immigration

Source: Statistics Canada, *Canadian Social Trends*, No. 70 (Autumn 2003), p. 23.

intensive); meetings on the interpretation and implementation of these rules go on almost constantly (higher velocity); and the economic fates of a larger number of workers and firms are affected by these rules (greater enmeshment of local production with global rules). The international agreement on trade is just one of an increasing number of international treaties in the economic arena.

Across the world, however, people do not participate equally in these processes. Scholars emphasize the importance of communication and information technologies for supporting growing extensity, intensity, and velocity. These technologies facilitate the development of the supraterritorial relations particularly characteristic of contemporary globalization. Table 16.2 provides a snapshot

Table 16.2 Diffusion of Information and Communication Technologies

	TELEPHONE MAINLINES (PER 1,000 PEOPLE)		CELLULAR SUBSCRIBERS (PER 1,000 PEOPLE)		INTERNET USERS (PER 1,000 PEOPLE)	
	1990	2003	1990	2003	1990	2003
Developing countries	29	113	—	134	—	53
Poorest developing countries	3	8	0	16	0	4
OECD* countries	365	494	7	644	3	403
High-income OECD countries	439	567	9	705	3	480

* OECD: Organization for Economic Co-operation and Development (an organization of the wealthiest countries of the world).

Source: United Nations Development Programme, Human Development Report, 2005 (New York: UNDP, 2005), p. 265. Used by permission of Oxford University Press.

of the inequalities of access to these technologies across the world, inequalities often referred to as the "digital divide." It shows that the persons living in the wealthier countries of the world have far higher access to these technologies than their counterparts living in the poorer, so-called "developing" countries. Without access to these technologies, individuals and communities will have less power to contest globalization and to shape it in ways they might wish. Thus, this table points up a more general argument made by some scholars: globalization is deepening inequalities between the rich and the poor, rather than reducing them.

The Changing Politics of Globalization

Globalization is changing how politics works at all levels of human governance: the global, the local, the nation-state, and the regional, illustrated in Box 16.2. At the global level, an ever-increasing number of international organizations, more informal arrangements of principles and norms called international regimes, and regularized coordination meetings of nation-states' governments have emerged. These cover a broad range of human activity, from how countries trade with one another, to how much equity capital banks must hold as a backup against failure, to how states treat refugees, to the way we label food, and to how countries prepare for global disease pandemics. Some are quite strong. For example, the WTO has a dispute settlement mechanism that is binding on its member states. If a country loses a dispute at the WTO, it must stop the offending activity and compensate the other country. If it does not, the country lodging the complaint can impose a financial penalty on the offending state.

Others are quite weak. For example, the Universal Declaration on Human Rights of the United Nations has been ratified by many countries, including Canada. Such ratification, however, does not necessarily mean that these countries always respect human rights. The UN Commission on Human Rights ruled in the late 1990s that Ontario's refusal to give people involved in "workfare" programs the right to unionize was a violation of the right to freedom of association. The Ontario government at the time simply ignored the ruling, and there is no mechanism to require a government to comply with it.

Perhaps the most significant examples of global governance come in the economic area. We have already had several opportunities to mention the **World Trade Organization (WTO)**. There are other prominent examples as well. At the Bank for International Settlements in Basel, Switzerland, a host of nested committees and organizations has grown up since 1974 to define rules for the global banking sector and for financial markets. Previous chapters have mentioned the **Group of 8** (the United States, Japan, France, Germany, Italy, the United Kingdom, Canada, and Russia). The heads of government from these countries meet once a year to discuss how they might coordinate their economic activities so as to ensure that the global economy functions well. Their

Levels of Political Authority		BOX 16.2
Local	Vancouver City Council or Frankfurt City Council	
Subnational	British Columbia Legislative Assembly or the Landestag (State Assembly) of Bavaria	
National	Parliament of Canada or the Bundestag (Federal Parliament in Germany)	
Regional	Dispute settlement under the North American Free Trade Agreement (NAFTA) or the European Parliament	
Global	Dispute settlement mechanism of the World Trade Organization or the International Criminal Court	

Reprinted with permission from *The Globe and Mail*

ministers of finance and governors of their central banks (e.g., the Bank of Canada or the Federal Reserve System in the United States) meet twice a year, and have drawn up more detailed procedures for assessing how their economies are performing and for coordinating their macroeconomic policies. The **International Monetary Fund (IMF)** has evolved into an organization that moves in to help countries when instabilities in the global financial system threaten to destroy their economies. In the process, sometimes it pushes countries to implement "structural adjustment" programs and these have often had disastrous social impacts in these countries. Its partner organization, the **World Bank**, finances projects to assist in the "development" of poorer countries in the world (see Chapter 13).

Many dispute the value of such organizations, however, arguing that they inevitably impose a **neoliberal** orthodoxy on developing countries that is highly inappropriate and harmful to the most disadvantaged. They also argue that liberalization of trade and investment increases inequalities within countries. As those critical of the forms of contemporary globalization become more aware of one another and as they build networks to link their activities, many observers see them as forming a "global civil society." Global **civil society** actions have become more important in resisting unfettered liberalization. They also have generated a rather strong reaction from governments, as the cartoon suggests.

These economic governance mechanisms coexist with other international institutions and regimes that seek to provide rules for other domains of social activity (see Box 16.3). The **United Nations (UN)** provides an umbrella for some of these institutions. The UN supported the drawing up of the Universal Declaration on Human Rights and set up an organization to promote the declaration: the United Nations High Commission on Human Rights. All UN

Group of 8 (U.S., Japan, Germany, France, U.K., Italy, Canada, Russia)
World Trade Organization
United Nations Framework Convention on Climate Change (Kyoto Protocol)
International Monetary Fund

World Bank
World Health Organization
International Labour Organization
Universal Declaration of Human Rights
United Nations Human Rights Council

members who sign the Declaration are agreeing, in effect, to ensure that those rights are respected within their borders. Many UN members have also signed a Convention on the Prevention and Punishment of Genocide, whereby they define what **genocide** means and commit themselves to act when genocides are being committed. In some instances, such as the mass killings in the former Yugoslavia and in Rwanda, the UN has set up binding international courts to try the perpetrators for their crimes of genocide. If the new **International Criminal Court (ICC)**, which became active in 2002, functions as many hope it will, the reach of binding international law will extend even further. Global civil society actions have been important in supporting the protection of human rights and in pressuring some of these institutions to respect their mandates.

Politics at the local level are also changing with the progression of globalization. Three examples will illustrate the kinds of changes taking place. First, let us think a little about Aboriginal peoples. The United Nations agreed in 2007 on a covenant defining the rights and responsibilities of Indigenous peoples. In becoming involved with the UN in this work, the identity of many Aboriginal communities is changing. Rather than considering themselves only as Cree, Haida, Mohawk, Sami (Scandinavia), Torres Strait Islanders (Australia), or Maori (New Zealand), they now also see themselves as Indigenous peoples linked to one another. By adding a global component, their identity becomes more complex. The United Nations becomes a point of political reference for them when they find themselves unjustly treated. The Grand Council of the Cree in Northern Quebec followed this route when they were fighting against the Quebec government's hydroelectric development in their territories.

Diaspora and transnational communities provide a second example. In Chapter 3, these were described as ethnic groups who experience dislocation in multiple states yet typically nurture narratives about their specific "homeland," held out as a place of possible return. For example, we might speak of part of a Tamil diaspora or transnational community living in Canada. Tamils are a minority ethnic group living in Sri Lanka, and they have been fighting the majority Sinhalese group for many years in pursuit of more political autonomy. The fierce fighting in their "homeland" has forced many to leave Sri Lanka for Canada, the United Kingdom, the United States, and other countries. Many of these emigrants remain attached to Sri Lanka and would like to return when political autonomy has become a reality or when the fighting has ended.

With the onset of contemporary transportation and communication technologies, these local, often marginalized, communities can become global political actors. Members can travel back and forth to the "homeland" or to other states hosting their ethnic group more easily than before. Using the Internet, they can communicate with their relatives, friends, and political allies on a daily basis. They can import clothing and food more easily, thereby reproducing more aspects of the lives they were familiar with in their homeland. The international right of freedom of conscience gives them more room to practise their religion, with perhaps less fear of persecution or discrimination. With all of these changes, they can imagine their local group as part of a global community of Tamils, Jains, Chinese, or Serbians more easily than in the past. Moreover, their local politics tends often to reflect politics in the homeland, which in turn is reproduced in local communities of these groups around the world. When Pakistan and India clash over Kashmir, for example, dimensions of this same struggle may surface simultaneously in the Pakistani and Indian transnational communities living in Toronto, Hamilton, Vancouver, New York, London, Manchester, and Sydney.

A third example of changing local politics can be drawn from British Columbia. Forest companies in that province long used an approach to logging called "clearcutting." They simply went in and cut down every tree in a given tract of land. Local ecologists and Indigenous peoples' communities protested these practices as highly destructive of old-growth forests and as a threat to some endangered species. Gradually, international environmentalist movements, notably Greenpeace, joined these protests. As noted in Chapter 12, Greenpeace is a transnational **interest group** with national branch organizations in many countries around the world. Angry at the effects of clearcutting, several of Greenpeace's European branches organized a boycott of exports of British Columbia lumber products. These European boycotts proved quite effective and put immense pressure on the forest companies to change their practices. Visits to clearcutting sites by such prominent ecologists as Robert Kennedy, Jr. added to the international dimension of this protest. Once again, local politics had global effects and led individual ecologists with local identities to couple these to an ecological identity that transcended national borders.

These changes in global governance on the one side, and in local politics on the other, raise difficult questions about whether nation-states are losing some of their powers to respond to the demands of their citizens. With the loss of such powers, some see nation-states as losing relevance. These questions are not at all easy to answer and have sparked some of the strongest debates in contemporary political science. These debates have shown us that there is no "one size fits all" answer to this question. The impact of globalization on the United States may be somewhat less than it is on a middle power like Canada and considerably less than it might be on developing countries like Honduras or Ghana. What is clear is that for some policy problems, such as the rate of growth of the national economy or the quality of the environment within a state's boundaries, nation-states cannot find solutions unless they cooperate with other states and perhaps even coordinate their policies with these states. Reinicke refers to this development as "global **public policy**."[7] States no longer have sufficient power to act effectively on their own; they must "pool" their sovereignty with other states to accomplish their domestic objectives.

The rapid growth of formally binding international rules such as those overseen by the World Trade Organization or informally binding ones such as those associated with the international regime for banking and financial markets has clearly restricted many states' regulatory powers. If Canada provides a subsidy to Bombardier to help it export its small jet planes, it can be overruled by the World Trade Organization when a competitor like Brazil complains. For these reasons, some political scientists like Stephen Clarkson say that such rules are now part of an "external constitution" that is as binding on national governments as the "internal constitution" (see Chapter 6). International rules have also curbed other traditional areas of state regulation such as protecting intellectual property, erecting tariff barriers to trade, the pricing of agricultural commodities, using state corporations to provide services like telecommunications and electrical power, and giving their own citizens priority in the use of natural resources, all of which are examples of **protectionism**.

Globalization has also reshaped domestic politics by adding to the power of some parts of the government while reducing the power of other parts. As noted in Chapter 7, globalization tends to require a strengthening of **central agencies** such as the offices serving the prime minister or the president and ministries of finance and trade. These agencies have to coordinate policymaking horizontally within states, and do it quickly and efficiently, if they are to be effective in global policy discussions and negotiations. Conversely, departments whose mandates are heavily shaped by developments in global public policy—environment, culture, industry, labour—tend to lose influence and to become more subject to these central agencies. In many democracies, there are rising complaints about the increased powers of the head of government, whether it be the prime minister, chancellor, president or the finance minister—the Secretary of the Treasury (U.S.), Minister of Finance (Canada, France, Germany), or Chancellor of the Exchequer (U.K.).

Even while nation-states are being drawn into multilevel governance arrangements to accomplish their domestic policy goals, the "national" identities of their citizens are becoming more fluid (see Chapter 3). In the 18th and 19th centuries, when the nation-state was rising to become the dominant organizational form in the world, states invested considerable energies in constructing a national identity. In the United Kingdom, a "British" identity was forged out of the identities of peoples living in England and in the Celtic regions of Scotland and Wales. France melded the Celtic Bretons, the Provençal in the south, and the German-speaking Alsatians in the east into a single, universalistic French identity. Canada adopted a slightly different approach by building a political nationality composed of two supposedly complementary identities: those of English and French Canadians. All persons were pushed to adopt one of these identities, whether these be the original settlers in the area (Aboriginal peoples), or new arrivals (immigrants).

These same national identities are now weakening and becoming part of more complex senses of citizenship. In the United Kingdom, a Scottish identity has strengthened over the past 20 years, as has a sense of being European. This idea is captured in the slogan of the Scottish nationalists, "An independent Scotland in a united Europe." Similar developments may be seen in France as the Breton language (Breizh) has resurfaced at the same time as discussions of European citizenship are increasingly important. In Canada, the former French-Canadian identity has evolved into a Québécois one, which is much less complementary to the traditional English Canadian identity. The latter identity has fractured with the onset of cultural pluralism and as the identities based in transnational and diaspora communities receive limited legitimacy from a policy on multiculturalism. In all parts of Canada, Aboriginal peoples have asserted an identity based on their being the "first peoples" in North America and on their recognition as "peoples" by the United Nations. All these developments mean that the traditional national identity constructed in the past 300 years in many nation-states has declined in importance. Simultaneously, it has become coupled to new identities that transcend national borders or that are unique to ethnic minorities within those borders.

Globalization and Democracy

If we are to understand the impact of globalization on democracy, we must first take note of the relationship between democracy and the nation-state. The principles of democracy and the procedures developed based on those principles assumed the territorial integrity of the nation-state and the idea of sovereignty that was emerging in the system of states. Behind the concept, therefore, there lie two crucial assumptions (see Box 16.4):

1. Citizens are able to hold *accountable* all the political leaders who make decisions affecting their daily lives. For example, if citizens are concerned about air pollution, they can express these concerns to, and hold to account, all the political leaders governing the territories and firms that are the source of the air pollution.

2. Citizens can bring about changes in the political factors affecting their daily lives by using democratic procedures to pressure or to change their political leaders. We refer to this aspect of democracy as *popular sovereignty*. For example, if citizens are unhappy about the quality of the air they breathe, they can choose new leaders who will have the necessary power and authority to respond to their concerns.

- *Accountability.* Citizens can make demands on, and hold accountable, the political leaders making decisions that affect them in their everyday lives.

- *Popular sovereignty.* Citizens can bring about changes in the political factors affecting their daily lives by using democratic processes to influence or to change their political leaders.

These assumptions are important because globalization appears to be placing both of them into doubt.

Since the conception of liberal democracy was developed in tandem with the nation-state as a unit of territorial organization, theorists of democracy assumed that the nation-state would be the principal, if not the only, body in a given territory with the powers to affect the daily lives of citizens inhabiting that territory. In the present era, this assumption no longer holds. Other organizations operating at the international level now have decided impacts on our lives, whether they be the World Trade Organization, the International Monetary Fund, or various and numerous smaller, but no less vital, international regimes. Accordingly, we have a problem. How do we speak of democracy when the matters of concern to us are beyond our political reach? If we look at the notion of globalization as outlined in this chapter and some of the effects of globalization discussed in other parts of this book, we can identify four challenges to democracy that come from globalization. Let us now look at each of these.

A Changing Demos or People Within the Nation-State

Political scientists use the Greek term *demos* to refer to the idea of a people who have a sense of community and of common purpose. The *demos* (or sovereign people) within the nation-state has changed drastically over the past 150 years. Let us think back to 1867, when the Dominion of Canada came into being. Who constituted the *demos* at that time—that is, the people who exercised some measure of democratic rights? First of all, it was men only. Women were not considered to be part of the people for the purpose of political decisions. And this group of men itself was a highly restricted one. It certainly did not include the men in First Nations communities, nor did it include men who had lower incomes and little personal property. At the time of Confederation, only those men who possessed a certain amount of property and wealth actually exercised democratic rights. Historians estimate that about 13 percent of the male population of the Dominion had the vote in 1867.

So the Canadian *demos* has travelled a long way from the small, relatively wealthy group of principally British and French men who exercised power in 1867. Women began to get the vote beginning in 1916 in Manitoba and ending in 1940 in Quebec. Chinese and Japanese Canadians *lost* their right to vote in the interwar period, and only regained it in the late 1940s. Aboriginal peoples did not obtain the vote until 1960. In addition, as we have seen, the addition of women and First Nations peoples is not the only complicating factor to the Canadian political community. Since 1960, our political community has become much more heterogeneous in terms of visible minorities and religions (see Table 16.3). If we add to these categories the **identity politics** associated with the second wave of the women's movement, the gay and lesbian movement, and various **social movements** interested in the environment and

Table 16.3 Religious Affiliation of Immigrant Population, Non-immigrant Population, over Time

Religion	Non-immigrant Population	Immigrant Population	Before 1961	1961–1970	1971–1980	1981–1990	1991–2001	1991–1995	1996–2001
Catholic	46.2	32.8	40.6	43.8	34.1	33.4	23.6	27.4	20.1
Protestant	31.4	20.1	39.2	26.9	21.1	14.5	10.7	11.4	10.2
Christian Orthodox	0.9	4.8	3.8	6.3	3.8	3.0	6.3	5.4	7.1
Muslim	0.6	7.6	0.2	1.3	5.4	7.5	15.1	11.5	18.3
Jewish	0.9	1.9	2.7	2.0	2.2	1.9	1.2	1.2	1.3
Buddhist	0.3	4.0	0.4	0.9	4.8	7.5	4.6	5.7	3.7
Hindu	0.3	3.9	0.1	1.4	3.6	4.9	6.5	6.7	6.3
Sikh	0.4	3.2	0.1	1.1	3.9	4.3	4.7	4.8	4.5
Aboriginal spirituality	0.1	0.0	0.0	0.0	0.0	0.0	0.0	0.0	0.0
No religious affiliation	16.3	17.2	11.3	13.8	16.9	17.5	21.5	20.2	22.7
Other	2.5	4.3	1.5	2.5	4.2	5.6	5.8	5.8	5.8
	100.0	**100.0**	**100.0**	**100.0**	**100.0**	**100.0**	**100.0**	**100.0**	**100.0**

Source: Statistics drawn by author from Statistics Canada, "Religion (95) and Immigrant Status and Period of Immigration (11) for Population, for Canada, Provinces, Territories, Census Metropolitan Areas and Census Agglomerations, 2001 Census—20% Sample Data," available at http://www.statcan.ca/bsolc/english/bsolc?catno=97F0022XCB2001004; accessed June 8, 2008.

world peace, we have a much more complex political community. And as we have argued above, globalization intensifies these complications because it enables the construction of identities that transcend borders more easily.

Should we be worried about such developments? The problem is that our whole conception of democracy within the nation-state involved the development of a common political identity as Canadians, or Americans, or French. Nation-states have worked to develop a common understanding of a shared history, a common political culture. They have sought to cultivate identification with common symbols such as the Maple Leaf flag or "O Canada" or common practices such as universal health care. They have stressed the institutions we have in common—parliament, a public education system, modern hospitals, and so on. Behind these efforts to develop this sense of national community and identity are two qualities assumed to be important to democratic governance: *trust* and *solidarity*.

It is important, many will argue, that citizens trust one another. If I have faith in my co-citizens that they will fulfill their duties, then I will fulfill mine. I will obey the laws and follow the general rules of my political community, because I trust that others will do the same. Solidarity is also important. Citizens must believe that their compliance with laws, including the paying of taxes, is important even if it does not bring them direct personal benefit. They must feel sufficient sense of solidarity with their co-citizens that they are willing to help improve the situations of others who are elderly or ill or disabled or temporarily without work.

The problem then is that the cultivation of trust and solidarity becomes ever more difficult the more different we citizens become from one another. Differences based on gender, religion, or ethnicity can be thought so deep that women may not trust men, or that Muslims and Christians do not trust one another, or that immigrants from Sri Lanka may find it difficult to feel solidarity with immigrants from Jamaica. What steps can we take to improve solidarity and trust? We have adopted a *Charter of Rights and Freedoms*, other countries have similar charters, and the UN also has covenants on political, civic, and human rights. Are these steps enough? Do we need to do more? If so, what should we be doing? If we want to preserve the principles of democracy within the nation-state, we are going to have to work much harder at trust and solidarity in this globalizing era.

Accountability

Working hard at trust and solidarity may become more difficult, however, because globalization is shrinking somewhat the areas of public policy to which citizens can hold their political leaders to account. Democracy requires that citizens are able to hold accountable all the political leaders who make decisions affecting their daily lives. Such accountability is diminishing in certain key areas:

1. Important changes in the value of our money are taking place very far away, and there is little that our political leaders can do about it. For example, as the Canadian dollar appreciated in value by close to 20 percent against the U.S. dollar in 2007, our politicians did not take action, and there was virtually nothing they could do. Nevertheless, this change had a significant impact on the economic situation of thousands of Canadians. For example, thousands of automobile and forestry workers lost their jobs.

2. It is very difficult for a country like Canada to have its own autonomous policy favouring economic growth and full employment. With the liberalization of capital movements, we lose important degrees of freedom in this realm. This change is important, because the postwar economic order postulated that countries would have control over their own macroeconomic policies so they could promote full employment and provide a social safety net for those in need: the ill, the elderly, the disabled, the unemployed. Have Canadians and citizens in other countries asked that their healthcare budgets, their education budgets, and other, related social policies be cut or held constant while needs for such services increase? Probably not, and yet their politicians have gone ahead and done these kinds of things in response, in part, to external financial pressures. Such political outcomes indicate, in turn, a decline in accountability.

3. Developments in the area of the environment illustrate the problem as well. Virtually everyone is familiar now with the fact that the size of the ozone layer that protects us from some of the harmful consequences of the sun's radiation is gradually retracting. Over the past 20 years, there has been a steady decline in levels of ozone. Again, we have here a global problem that requires a set of global political decisions. It is also an area where accountability is low. Decisions about ozone depletion that are affecting us as Canadians are being made by governments and others who are well beyond our capacity to hold accountable. The possibility of a nuclear accident is in the same category. Think of the accident in Chernobyl in the Ukraine in the 1980s as the radioactive fallout drifted over Western Europe and other parts of the globe with the winds. How could the citizens of Sweden, for example, hold any politicians to account for the radiation found in the vegetables growing in their backyard gardens?

4. Let us think of still another area of public policy: security. Since the end of World War II, there has been a steady growth in the number of countries with research into, potential for, and possession of nuclear weapons. Not only are these weapons terrifying technologies, but they are also ones whose use has global ramifications. If even a small nuclear war were to break out virtually anywhere on the globe, the radioactive fallout and other disastrous consequences would have very significant effects well beyond the territorial borders of the states involved. In February 1945, when the German city of Dresden was firebombed, the effects were felt principally in that city alone. If Pakistan and India were to begin dropping nuclear bombs on one another tomorrow, the radiation produced would have direct, immediate impacts well beyond the territorial borders of those states. Citizens of Sri Lanka or Iceland or Canada, however, have little capacity to affect such matters.

Popular Sovereignty

Can we as citizens bring about changes to our life circumstances through political action directed at the relevant decision-makers? The previous discussion will already have raised questions about this possibility. Many of the key decisions, it would appear, are being made either by other states or by international organizations. So it is difficult for citizens to have any impact on the kinds of political outputs that they might want in their lives.

Leaders of nation-states are discussing policy options and reaching decisions in international organizations much more than in the past. As the importance of these discussions has increased, it has brought about changes in the organization of government. Certain officials (prime ministers and ministers of finance and trade) have grown in importance, as have the bureaucracies underneath them. What is more, because they are making policy beyond the framework of the nation-state and they have to make decisions relatively quickly, the usual institutions for holding political leaders to account do not work well. This kind of decision-making does not fit easily into cabinet government in a parliamentary system, nor does it provide much of a role for the parliament or legislature. In fact, in the United States, the president usually seeks "fast track" authority from Congress so that he does not need to consult the elected representatives until the very end, when an international deal has already been struck. In short, as political decisions become globalized, citizens seem to be losing control over the persons making those decisions, even though the decisions might have an impact on their lives in crucial ways. Such a development is inconsistent with popular sovereignty—the idea that the "people" have the ultimate power and authority over their lives.

International Organizations and Democracy

In the face of these kinds of problems, a concern for the future of democracy brings us to focus more on the growing number of international organizations and how they might be made to conform to democratic principles. International agreements affecting such policy areas as the environment and trade have increased significantly during the most recent period. Associated with many of these agreements is the development of international secretariats or committees that oversee the agreements and provide a site for ongoing decision-making. Other international organizations have developed without the signing of formal agreements. And as we have noted, a global civil society has evolved in response to the growth of these organizations.

It is important to recognize, however, that these international institutions are increasingly parts of systems of multilevel governance that in many instances include decision-making, not only by regional organizations or national governments, but also by subnational governments. Democratic governance requires, therefore, that democratic principles be followed and inform policy processes at *all levels of decision-making*. Accountability at the supranational level becomes a hollow concept if it is lacking at the regional, national, or subnational level. Legitimacy will only result if democracy is entrenched throughout the system. For example, in a country with a federal system, such as Canada, the United States, or Germany, it would not make sense to have a democratic federal government and autocratic provinces or states. Similarly, it is no use reforming international institutions if some of the problems in domestic governance we have noted are not also addressed.

At this point, we are some distance away from institutions at the global level that might conform to democratic principles. What we can do at this stage is to identify some criteria that might be used to assess democracy in existing institutions. Applying these criteria does not amount to the full realization of democratic principles; but it is a start, until these institutions are replaced or supplemented by more democratic structures. The criteria proposed below extract key underlying principles of democracy that have emerged within nation-states. They are applied, however, in a way that does not tie them to political institutions, such as legislatures, that do not (yet) exist globally.

Assessing Levels of Democracy in International Institutions[8]

There are six main criteria by which we can assess the levels of democracy in international institutions. They are listed in Box 16.5.

Transparency Can all interested observers inform themselves fully on the core questions and tradeoffs under consideration? Often policies are developed in locations or technical languages that remove them from the scrutiny of citizens. Transparency can be enhanced by such techniques as the posting of policy documents and other reports in technical and lay language on websites. The World Trade Organization has adopted these kinds of practices more and more.

Openness to Direct Participation Global governance only becomes democratic when political influence within processes of deliberation and decision-making is equally accessible or available to affected or concerned parties. Similarly, because the interests at stake in an issue area may change as it develops, it is problematic to restrict access permanently to a specified set of actors. Evidence that international institutions are satisfying this criterion, therefore, will be found primarily when they let citizens' organizations have some access to the policy process. Many of the global civil society movements argue that the WTO and the IMF are closed off to such citizens' organizations.

Quality of Discourse Democracy requires the existence of public arenas or spaces where open, informed debates can take place about possible policy options. Such public spaces are often absent at supranational levels. Accordingly, public spaces where debates can take place must be created for supranational governance arrangements. These debates must permit the "translation" of technical issues into language for a lay public, so that as many citizens as possible can inform themselves about the stakes involved and about the advantages and disadvantages of choosing one policy option over another. For example, if intellectual property rules at the WTO are to govern the duration of the patents that transnational pharmaceutical companies can hold on their medicines, all countries and the WTO itself should have a "place" where citizens can debate the pros and cons of different proposals.

Representation Representation is a formal means of aligning the interests of citizens at large with the smaller number of actors required if bargaining, deliberation, or decisions are to be effective. Practices well established at the domestic level, such as electing representatives on the basis of majority voting in territorial constituencies, are often inapplicable or not yet available at supranational levels. Although its application may be complex, the idea is simple: all those

Criteria for Assessing Levels of Democracy in International Institutions	BOX 16.5

1. Transparency
2. Openness to direct participation
3. Quality of discourse and its accessibility to all interested citizens
4. Degree of representativeness
5. Capacity to make decisions (effectiveness)
6. Fairness (procedural and substantive)

potentially affected by policymaking in a given supranational institution should be represented in some way in the policy process. In the area of global finance, representation is often a problem. For example, even though the actions of the IMF and the World Bank are directed primarily toward developing countries, these institutions are led by persons from the wealthy countries. The managing director of the IMF is always nominated by the member states of the European Union, and the president of the World Bank has always been an American recommended by the U.S. president. Rules that have global effects are too often devised by leaders from a limited number of highly developed states. Citizens in developing countries have no voice or representation in these organizations.

Effectiveness There is little value in having open, transparent, representative institutions if they cannot make decisions and implement them. Effectiveness refers to the ability of institutions to do these things, and normally involves the creation of an executive-like grouping for taking decisions and a bureaucracy for implementing them. This bureaucracy may, in fact, be located at the nation-state level, provided that participating governments have agreed upon rules for implementing decisions taken at a higher level. In the absence of effectiveness, the legitimacy of institutions may come into question, thereby undermining democracy. For example, if political leaders operating in open, transparent, and representative institutions cannot reach agreement on rules to reduce the pollution responsible for climate change, they are not effective and the democratic institutions within which they are working may be questioned. Or if they can agree on the rules but have no bureaucracies with the needed expertise to implement them, decision-making is again not effective, and the legitimacy and value of democratic institutions might be questioned.

Fairness Political theorists talk about fairness in two ways. *Procedural* fairness refers to the types of considerations that have been discussed in the first four criteria listed earlier. *Substantive* fairness refers to the distribution of benefits from policy outcomes. Are some nation-states and some citizens systematically excluded from the distribution of benefits by given institutions? For example, if the WTO becomes more open, more transparent, and more representative and still the citizens of developing countries receive little benefit from stronger international trade rules, then the criterion of substantive fairness is being compromised.

CONCLUSION

If individual citizens wish to continue to preserve and build democracy in this globalizing era, they will need to be more demanding of their political leaders at the nation-state level. They must work to ensure that democratic principles are not marginalized by the growth of supranational decision-making. Further, they must resist closed-door decision-making at the international level. Individual citizens may need to join organizations that are active on the international level and that are seeking more democracy along the lines described in this chapter. Whatever the nation-state in which they find themselves governed, citizens may no longer have the luxury of keeping their political activity within their own national borders. Too much crucial to their lives is now being decided elsewhere.

It took at least two centuries of struggle to realize some of the potential of democracy within the nation-state. Now that globalization has given rise to centres of power and authority outside the control of the nation-state system, those believing democracy is important will have to target some of their energies on these centres if they are to have any hope of controlling the conditions under which they will live.

DISCUSSION QUESTIONS

1. Can you identify areas of the economy or culture where there is increasing extensiveness, intensity, and velocity in human social relationships?

2. Is globalization a welcome process or an unfortunate development?

3. Some scholars argue that globalization has been going on for 500 years or more. What factors might differentiate contemporary globalization from globalizing periods in the past?

4. What is the significance of the large "global civil society" protests taking place at meetings of world political leaders and at meetings of such organizations as the WTO?

5. Give some examples of where nation-state governments have lost power as a result of globalization. Give some examples of where nation-state governments remain very powerful, if not more so. How do we explain these apparently contradictory changes?

6. Take an international organization such as the United Nations Human Rights Council or the World Trade Organization. Use the criteria presented in this chapter to assess where they are democratic and where they are lacking in democracy.

KEY TERMS

GLOBALIZATION: Globalization is the transformative growth of connections among people across the planet. In the contemporary era, many of these connections take a supraterritorial form. In ever more profound ways, globalization ties together what people do, what they experience, how they perceive that experience, and how they reshape their lives. In short, individuals and communities begin to see the world as one place and to imagine new roles for themselves within it. (458)

GREENHOUSE EFFECT: A warming of the surface and lower atmosphere of the earth caused by the increased presence of various pollutants that break down the ozone layer of gases that protects life from harmful rays from the sun. The process leads to rising temperatures and climate change; it is also known as global warming. (459)

NORTH AMERICAN FREE TRADE AGREEMENT (NAFTA): An agreement ratified by the United States, Canada, and Mexico that contains rules to promote the freer movement of goods, capital, and services between these countries. (457)

TRANSNATIONAL CORPORATIONS: Business firms that are headquartered in one country but have plants or places of operation around the world permitting them to integrate their business activities on a global scale. (457)

WORLD TRADE ORGANIZATION (WTO): An organization created during the Uruguay Round of GATT negotiations whose goal is to promote liberal trading practices and to reduce protectionism through the development and enforcement of global laws and regulations. (462)

WEB LINKS W(W)W

United Nations System:
http://www.unsystem.org

Rights and Democracy (a Canadian organization interested in globalization issues):
http://www.ichrdd.ca

The Globalization and Autonomy Compendium (an online resource designed with students in mind):
http://www.globalautonomy.ca

The Open Democracy Network (addresses issues related to globalization and democracy on a daily basis):
http://www.opendemocracy.net

World Trade Organization:
http://www.wto.org

FURTHER READING

Pauly, Louis and William Coleman, eds. *Global Ordering: Institutions and Autonomy in a Changing World.* Vancouver: University of British Columbia Press, 2008.

Scholte, Jan Aart. *Globalization: A Critical Introduction*, 2nd ed. Basingstoke, U.K.: Macmillan/ Palgrave, 2005.

Woods, Ngaire. *The Globalizers: The IMF, the World Bank and Their Borrowers.* Ithaca, NY: Cornell University Press, 2006.

ENDNOTES

1. David Held, *Democracy and the Global Order* (Stanford: Stanford University Press, 1995), p. 145.

2. Jan Aart Scholte, *Globalization: A Critical Introduction*, 2nd ed. (Basingstoke, U.K.: Macmillan/Palgrave, 2005), p. 59.

3. John Tomlinson, *Globalization and Culture* (Chicago: University of Chicago Press, 1999), p. 2.

4. William D. Coleman, Louis Pauly, and Diana Brydon, "Globalization, Autonomy and Institutional Change," in Pauly and Coleman, eds., *Global Ordering: Institutions and Autonomy in a Changing World* (Vancouver: University of British Columbia Press, 2008).

5. David Held, Anthony McGrew, David Goldblatt, and Jonathan Perraton, *Global Transformations* (Palo Alto, CA: Stanford University Press, 1999).

6. Roland Robertson, *Globalization: Social Theory and Global Culture* (London: Sage, 1992).

7. Wolfgang Reinicke, *Global Public Policy* (Washington, DC: Brookings Institution Press, 1998).

8. William D. Coleman and Tony Porter, "International Institutions, Globalisation and Democracy: Assessing the Challenges," *Global Society* 14(3) (2000): 377–98.

Glossary

Note: Numbers in parentheses refer to the chapters in which the term in question is discussed.

Aboriginal self-government A demand by Aboriginal or Indigenous groups that they be able to govern themselves, as they did before colonial rulers removed such power. (2, 6)

absolute monarchy A system of government ruled, at least in name, by one individual whose authority is unchecked, final, and permanent. (2)

administrative tribunals Boards or commissions established by the government to adjudicate certain disputes by applying laws to the facts; also called quasi-judicial tribunals or regulatory agencies. These tribunals are not proper courts presided over by judges. (9)

affirmative action Policies that seek to overcome historical patterns of systemic discrimination against groups of individuals, primarily in employment practices; the giving of preferential treatment to targeted groups in such areas as employment, promotion, housing, or education to redress the effects of past discrimination. (3, 5)

agents of political socialization Those groups of people or institutions that convey political attitudes and values to others in society. (4)

amending formula The procedure by which a constitution may be amended; in most states, it is a more onerous procedure than that which applies to the amendment of ordinary legislation. (6)

anarchism A political ideology that sees no need to impose government order on a society, because of the essential goodness of human beings; it assumes harmony will naturally prevail when free individuals participate equally in mutually beneficial decisions. (5)

anarchy A system of social, political, and economic relations without formal institutions of governance to define enforceable rules or exact obedience from the governed; as such, it is more characteristic of world politics than of politics within communities. (2, 15)

aristocracy A system of government ruled by a few, namely "the best," which is commonly interpreted as the nobility. (2, 5)

authoritarian government A nondemocratic government that rules without public input, glorifies the leader, allows no dissent, strictly controls the mass media, relies on the police and military to root out opposition, and is dedicated to remaining in power at all costs. (2)

authority The imposition of one's will on another by reason of legitimacy—because the subject regards the decision-maker as having a right to make such a binding decision. (1)

backbenchers Members of parliament who, if they are in the governing party, are not cabinet ministers, or, if in an opposition party, are not among the important party critics. (8)

bicameral legislature A legislature that has two separate houses, or chambers, each with its own set of members. (8)

bill The formal text of a proposed law before it has been enacted into law. When it has completed all stages of the legislative process, it becomes a law and is known as a *statute* or an *act*. (8)

bourgeoisie In Marxist theory, the ruling class in capitalist society consisting of those who own the means of production, such as factories or mines. This capitalist class rules over the proletariat or working people. (5)

bureaucracy The expert, permanent, nonpartisan, professional officials employed by the state to advise the political executive and to implement government policies. (1, 2, 7, 12, 13)

cabinet The group of people chosen by the prime minister or president to provide political direction to government departments; in Canada, cabinet members act collectively to make the key government decisions. (7)

cabinet government A system of government in which the major political decisions are made by the cabinet as a whole, as opposed to one in which the prime minister or president acts with considerable autonomy. (7)

cabinet solidarity The constitutional duty of ministers to publicly support the policy of the government. Ministers who openly dissent from government policy must resign from the government. (7)

capitalism An economic system in which the means of production are privately owned and operated according to the profit motive. Decisions about investment, production, and distribution are determined according to market forces, rather than direct government control. (5)

caucus A group composed of all members of a legislature that belong to a particular party or legislators who meet to further a specific policy interest. (8, 11)

central agencies Those agencies of the state that assist the political executive to coordinate and control overall government operations. They provide both policy advice and administrative support. (7, 16)

checks and balances A constitutional system of power-sharing under which powers are assigned to different branches of government (especially executive, legislative, and judicial) so as to enable each branch to curb the unilateral exercise of power by the others. (7)

citizenship Legal membership in a political community, especially in a nation-state, entailing rights and responsibilities. (1)

civil rights and liberties Those legal and constitutional guarantees, such as freedom of speech, the right of *habeas corpus*, and nondiscrimination rights, that govern the conduct of the state, and some private power holders, in relation to citizens and certain minority groups. (6)

civil society Social institutions and organizations that are independent of the state and in which citizens pursue their interests, express their beliefs, and live in communities. (2, 4, 5, 10, 11, 12, 13, 14, 16)

class A concept that describes hierarchical groupings within societies based on social and economic factors such as income, occupation, education, and status. (4, 5)

class consciousness An awareness of the divisions in society based on social and economic differences and a sense of identification with the appropriate division. (4)

cleavage A persistent division among two groups of voters, based on long-term demographic or economic characteristics. Examples include language, religion, class, and region. Groups on either side of the cleavage may be mobilized into a subculture which shapes the voting patterns and political perceptions of its members. (4, 11, 14)

closure Application of procedural rules that permit the majority to put an end to debate on a motion and require that a vote on the matter be held; also known as *cloture* or *the guillotine* or *time allocation* in various countries. (8)

coalition government A government that occurs when two or more parties hold seats in cabinet supported by a combination of parties that forms a majority in the legislature. (8)

coercion The imposition of one's will on another by the use of penalty, force, or the threat of force. (1)

collective responsibility In Westminster parliamentary systems, members of the political executive are collectively responsible to parliament for government policy and for the overall administrative performance of the government. (7)

collective security A commitment by a number of states to join in an alliance to defend themselves militarily against any threat to the peace and jointly attack any aggressor. (15)

colonialism The ownership and administration of one territory and people by another, as if the former were part of the latter. (2, 3, 13)

common law A system of law in which precedents from relevant cases in the past are applied to current cases. Judges are bound by precedent and should decide like cases alike. (9)

communism A political ideology based on eliminating exploitation through nearly total public ownership, full state control, and central planning of the economy. (2, 5)

concurrent powers Those fields of shared jurisdiction under a federal constitution in which both the national and the subnational government may act and pass laws. (6)

confidence (or non-confidence) vote (1) An explicitly worded motion indicating that the legislature either has or does not have confidence in the government. (2) A vote on a matter that the government has previously declared to be a matter of confidence. (3) A vote on important measures central to the government's plans, such as the whole budget. (7, 8)

conservatism The ideology of defending the status quo against major social, economic, and political change. Today conservatism is often used to label anyone on the political right, especially those who want to conserve the free-market capitalist system against radical demands for progressive reforms. (5)

constituency A geographical electoral district or the group of people represented by a member of a legislature. (8)

constitution The body of fundamental laws, rules, and practices that defines the basic structures of government, allocates power among governmental institutions, and regulates the relationship between citizens and the state. (1, 6)

constitutional convention An unwritten rule of constitutional behaviour that fills in gaps in the written constitution and conditions the exercise of legal powers under the constitution. (6)

constitutionalism The idea that the constitution should limit the state by separating powers among different branches of govern-

ment and protecting the rights of individuals and minorities through a bill of rights. (6)

contentious politics Protests that take the form of disruption of the normal activities of society, such as demonstrations and civil disobedience. (12)

coup d'état The overthrow of a political regime or leader by military force. (14)

crime against humanity A wrongful act that is deemed to be not a violation of any particular nation's laws, but rather a violation against humankind as a whole. (15)

Crown corporation A corporation owned by the government that assumes a structure similar to that of a private company and that operates semi-independently of the cabinet. (7)

cultural pluralism The coexistence of many ethnic and cultural groups within a country. Such diversity is the starting point in arguing that all groups in a society can maintain their linguistic, cultural, and religious distinctiveness without being relegated to the economic or cultural margins, and is achieved through the creation of a common set of values and institutions. (3, 4)

decolonization The process through which a population and territory formerly under colonial domination achieve formal political independence and become a sovereign state. (13)

democracy See *liberal democracy*.

democratic consolidation The achievement of a situation in which none of the major political actors, parties, organized interests, forces, or institutions consider that there is any alternative to democratic processes to gain power, and in which no political institution or group has a claim to veto the action of democratically elected decision-makers. (14)

democratic transition The change from a nondemocratic to a democratic government, usually indicated by the existence of at least one free and fair election. (14)

democratization A group of transitions from nondemocratic to democratic regimes, involving the relaxation of authoritarian political control by political leaders, the expansion of political and civil liberties, and the creation of institutional mechanisms that open up a political system to greater representation and participation. (2, 13, 14)

department of finance The department referred to as the government's chief economic advisor, responsible for overall economic management, raising revenue, preparing economic forecasts, and determining government expenditure levels. In Britain, it is called the Treasury. (7)

dependency A condition in which countries in the South lack any degree of autonomy in their political, economic, and social development by virtue of their reliance on countries in the North for access to capital, technology, and markets. (13)

deputy minister The minister's chief policy advisor, the department's general manager, and a key participant in the collective management of the government; known in Britain as the permanent secretary. (7)

devolution The delegation of administrative or limited legislative powers by a central government to regional or local governments. (6)

diaspora An ethnic group that has experienced or currently experiences dislocation across multiple states, yet typically nurtures narratives and political projects about a specific "homeland" as a place of eventual return. (3, 16)

dictatorship of the proletariat A Marxist concept that refers to the interim period immediately after the *proletariat* (the working class) has triumphed in revolutionary class war over the *bourgeoisie* (capitalists). The rule of the proletariat is expected to later give way to the classless society in the final stage of history when full communism is realized. (5)

digital democracy A broad term meant to encompass the application of technological innovation to politics and political participation; also called *e-democracy* or *e-politics*. (10)

direct democracy A political system in which citizens hold power directly rather than through elected or appointed representatives. (2, 10)

dominant conformity A model of ethnic group integration that holds that all groups in a society should conform to the language and values of the dominant group. (3)

dual executive A form of executive in which the posts of head of state and head of government are divided and each is held by a separate officeholder. In parliamentary systems, the head of state is a constitutional monarch or an elected president and the head of government is the prime minister. (7)

egalitarianism The doctrine that advocates equal social and political rights for all citizens, regardless of class, sex, religion, ethnicity, etc. Reform-oriented liberals emphasize the need for an equality of opportunity, which guarantees to all the equal chance to compete for the social, economic, and political benefits available in society. Socialists often interpret egalitarianism to require an equality of condition, so that all goods and resources in a society would be distributed equally. (5)

election A mechanism by which the expressed preferences of citizens in democratic states are aggregated into a decision regarding who will govern. (1, 10, 14)

electoralist party A type of political party, increasingly common in Western democracies over the past 50 years, that is almost exclusively concerned to maximize its electoral support. It emphasizes the political attractiveness of its leaders and candidates rather than its policies or platform, and it relies on media appeals rather than on a large, active membership. (11)

elite A small group of individuals who have significantly more power than other members of their community. They are either in a position to make authoritative decisions or have privileged access to decision-makers. (4, 10, 11, 14)

enumerated powers Those areas of legislative authority in a federal state that are specifically listed in the constitution and assigned to one level of government or the other, or to both. (6)

ethnic cleansing The removal of one or more ethnic groups from a society, by means of expulsion, imprisonment, or killing. The term entered the political lexicon in reference to the former Yugoslavia; it was first used to describe the violent measures and policies designed to eliminate or dramatically reduce the Muslim and Croat populations in Serb-held territory. (3, 4)

European Union A unique supranational organization made up of 27 European states characterized by increasing economic and political integration. (2, 3, 6, 15, 16)

executive That branch of government concerned with the implementation and enforcement of laws and other authoritative decisions of the state. The executive also formulates public policy and provides political leadership. (1, 7)

Executive Office of the President Offices and agencies attached directly to the President of the United States that provide advice on decisions and help develop and implement policies and programs. (7)

fascism The political system of the extreme right, based on the principles of the leader (dictator), a one-party state, nationalism, total control of social and economic activity, and arbitrary power, rather than constitutionalism. In 1922 in Italy, Benito Mussolini created the first fascist regime, emulated by Adolf Hitler in Germany. Today there are numerous neofascist movements advocating ultranationalist, racist, and anti-immigrant political positions. (2, 5)

federalism A form of government in which the sovereign powers of the state are formally divided under the constitution between two levels of government, neither of which is subordinate to the other. (4, 6, 11)

feminism A belief in the full equality of men and women and the insistence that all barriers to such equality be removed. (5, 10)

filibuster A device used by a member or group of members who take advantage of the procedural rules of a legislature that allow members to speak for extended periods of time in order to stall proceedings. (8)

first-past-the-post (FPTP) An electoral system that requires the winning candidate to receive more votes than any other in order to win the seat—that is, to receive a plurality of votes. The majority of first-past-the-post systems employ single-member electoral districts. (8, 10, 11)

fiscal imbalance In federal states the constitutional responsibilities of the provincial or state governments to deliver a wide range of public services often greatly exceed the financial capacity of such governments. This gulf between public expenditures and public finances usually requires the central government to provide cash and other transfers to the provinces. (6)

flexible amending formula A constitution whose provisions may be amended with relative ease. (6)

FPTP See *first-past-the-post (FPTP)*.

franchise The right to vote in public elections. (10)

fusion of powers In parliamentary systems, the joint exercise of legislative and executive powers by the prime minister and members of the cabinet who simultaneously hold office in both the legislative and executive branches of government. (7)

Geneva Conventions A comprehensive and detailed set of rules put in place over the course of the 20th century to try to ensure that warfare is conducted in a predictable and orderly way. (15)

genocide The deliberate and systematic extermination of a national, ethnic, or religious group. The term was developed in response to the horrors of the Holocaust. (3, 4, 15, 16)

global governance The process by which different actors—governments, organizations, firms, groups, and individuals—try to make common decisions about and for the global community. (2, 15, 16)

globalization (1) The transformative growth of connections among people across the planet. In the contemporary era, many of these connections take a supraterritorial form. In ever more profound ways, globalization ties together what people do, what they experience, how they perceive that experience, and how they reshape their lives. In short, individuals and communities begin to see the world as one place and to imagine new roles for themselves within it. (2) The movement of goods, capital, ideas, and people across geopolitical boundaries today and in the past. Contemporary patterns of globalization involve a deepening constellation of economic, technological, and cultural changes that are worldwide in scope and that challenge the sovereignty of the state. (1, 2, 3, 10, 12, 13, 14, 15, 16)

government The set of institutions and practices that make and enforce collective public decisions for a society. (1, 2, 15)

greenhouse effect A warming of the surface and lower atmosphere of the earth caused by the increased presence of various pollutants that break down the ozone layer that protects life from harmful rays from the sun. The process leads to rising temperatures and climate change; it is also known as *global warming*. (15, 16)

Group of 8 (G8) Canada, France, Germany, Italy, Japan, Russia, the United Kingdom, and the United States, whose leaders meet once a year to discuss how they might coordinate their economic activities to ensure that the global economy functions well. (15, 16)

HDI See *Human Development Index (HDI)*.

head of government The person in effective charge of the executive branch of government, namely the prime minister in a parliamentary system. (7)

head of state The person who symbolizes and represents the state but does not exercise effective political power, namely the monarch in a parliamentary system. (7)

Human Development Index (HDI) A composite index measuring longevity, knowledge, and standard of living, designed to give an indication of and a basis for comparing the quality of life in various countries. (1, 13)

human rights Rights enjoyed by individuals simply because they are human beings, primarily including the prevention of discrimination or coercion on grounds of ethnicity, religion, gender, or opinion. (2, 15)

human security A broadened concept of security focusing not just on national security and interstate war but also on threats to the safety of individuals and groups. (13)

identity politics Political activity of particular groups for recognition of their status and identity, as well as of the ways their beliefs and value systems differ from those of others. (4, 16)

ideology A reasonably consistent system of political beliefs that aspires to explain the world, to justify certain power relationships, and to maintain or transform existing institutions; a fairly coherent set of beliefs that not only explains what may be wrong with society, but also provides a vision of what society should be like. (1, 4, 5)

IMF See *International Monetary Fund (IMF)*.

imperialism The domination of one country by another with the aim of controlling and/or exploiting the latter. This domination can be economic, political, social, or cultural. Imperialism literally means "empire building." (3, 13)

independence The state of being free from the control of others; the ability to make one's own decisions, not having to rely on anyone else. In the context of world politics, it is the ability of a political community to govern itself rather than be governed by others. (15)

influence The imposition of one's will on another through persuasion and voluntary compliance. (1)

initiative A mechanism that allows citizens to petition the government to introduce or adopt specific pieces of legislation or force a referendum on an issue. (10)

institutionalized group A highly organized interest or pressure group that has a permanent, professional staff. (12)

interest group A group that brings together people with common interests and/or a common sense of identity for the purpose of influencing the political process. (1, 12, 16)

International Court of Justice A branch of the United Nations consisting of 15 judges elected by the Security Council that hears disputes between governments of countries and renders decisions on the basis of the accumulated body of international law. (15)

International Criminal Court A branch of the United Nations created on a permanent basis in 1999 to deal with individuals accused of a range of war crimes or crimes against humanity. (15, 16)

international law A complex body of rules, derived principally from the treaties, covenants, and declarations signed by the governments of various countries. The resolutions of international organizations, the writings of academics, and rulings of domestic and international courts can also be sources of international law when the rules are not otherwise clear. (9, 15)

International Monetary Fund (IMF) A sister of the World Bank and a branch of the United Nations that regulates the international monetary system in order to stabilize national currencies, and that, subject to certain conditions, makes loans to developing countries. (13, 14, 15, 16)

JCPC See *Judicial Committee of the Privy Council (JCPC)*.

judicial activism A style of judges' decision-making that involves an active use of their discretion to create new policies. (9)

Judicial Committee of the Privy Council (JCPC) A British court that was the final court of appeal for Canada until 1949, when the Supreme Court of Canada took over this function. (9)

judicial impartiality A state of mind in which judges preside over and decide cases with an open mind toward the parties and issues involved. (9)

judicial independence A relationship between the courts and the other branches of government that allows judges to function without interference from other government officials. (9)

judicial review A function of the courts in which judges examine actions of the government to determine whether they are authorized by law. This may also include a determination of whether statutes and regulations are contrary to the constitution. (6, 9)

judiciary The term used to refer to all the judges collectively in a country. It can also mean the whole judicial branch of government, including juries and the courts' administrative staff. (1, 9)

laissez-faire Literally "Let do" (French). An economic theory that provides the intellectual foundation for the system of free-market capitalism. *Laissez-faire* rejects state ownership or control, advocates a free market, values individualism, and promotes free trade. (5)

law A type of rule that has been formally approved by the legislature or the executive or declared by the courts and that people are obliged to obey. (9)

left That part of the ideological spectrum that believes in equality in society and the intervention of government via such collectivist measures as taxation, regulation, redistribution, and public ownership to effect such equality. (5)

legislature An institution with primary responsibility to enact laws. (1, 8)

legitimacy A measure of the degree to which citizens accept and tolerate the actions and decisions of social and political actors such as governments, states, international organizations, and civil society groups themselves, usually based on the notion that the decision-makers have a right to such power. (1, 2, 6, 10, 12, 13)

liberal democracy A form of government common to Western political systems in which there is a combination of the "liberal" right to individual freedom and the "democratic" right to representative government. Hence, the ability of the elected representatives to exercise decision-making power is subject to the rule of law as established by a constitutional system that recognizes fundamental rights and freedoms along with certain legal rights to property, privacy, equality under the law, etc. Liberal democracies also include protection for minorities against possible encroachment on their rights by the majority, open and free elections with multiple party systems, civilian rule, separation of powers between the executive and legislative branches, an independent judiciary, and a political culture of tolerance and pluralism. (5)

liberalism The ideology based on the paramount value of individual liberty. Liberals regard the individual as a rational creature who can use his or her intelligence to decide how best to live life and maximize his or her own well-being; liberals also believe all humans are free and equal by nature. (5)

list system The most commonly adopted form of proportional representation, employing relatively large multimember electoral districts and a ballot that requires voters to choose from among party lists or candidates on party lists. (10)

lobbyists Those professional, private sector firms and individuals that are paid by companies or groups to influence and access government. (12)

Maastricht Treaty A 1993 European treaty that created an economic and monetary union for the countries joined in the European Union, specifying that they have a single currency (the Euro) and one common central bank (the European Central Bank); it also introduced a citizenship of the European Union. (3, 6)

majoritarian system An electoral system that requires the winning candidate to receive a majority of votes to win the seat. The majority is normally achieved through a second ballot or by an alternative voting system. (10)

majority government A government in which one party holds all the seats in the cabinet as well as the majority of seats in the legislature (or lower house in bicameral legislatures). (7, 8)

mass-based party A political party with a large, involved membership, often based on a distinct subculture, with a central set of principles that it promotes at the same time as it seeks electoral support. (11)

mass media The methods of mass communication, such as television, radio, and newspapers, designed to reach large numbers of people. (1, 2, 4, 10)

merit principle A system of hiring or promoting public servants on the basis of their merit (education, training, experience, and so on), rather than on the basis of party preference or other considerations. (7)

ministerial responsibility The responsibility of individual ministers to answer to parliament for the administration of their departments, including the actions of public officials employed in such departments. (7)

minority government A government in which one party holds all the seats in the cabinet but has less than 50 percent of the members in the legislature. (8)

multiculturalism A policy sometimes adopted in a state characterized by cultural pluralism that supports ethnic and cultural groups in maintaining their customs and traditions, often with public financial assistance. (2, 3)

multination state A state that contains more than one nation. (2, 3, 4)

multinational corporations See *transnational corporations*.

NAFTA See *North American Free Trade Agreement (NAFTA)*.

nation A community of people, normally defined by a combination of ethnicity, language, and culture, with a subjective sense of belonging together. (2, 3)

nationalism An ideology that holds that certain populations are nations, that the world is divided into nations, and that a nation should be self-determining (i.e., able to establish its own institutions, laws, and government and to determine its future). (3, 5)

neoconservatism A social ideology that advocates a traditional, hierarchical, patriarchal, authoritarian, and inequitable society; it usually overlaps with neoliberalism in economic terms. (5)

neoliberalism An economic ideology that advocates an economic arena free of government regulation or restriction and free of government participation in the marketplace via public ownership; usually overlaps with neoconservatism in economic terms. (5, 7, 15, 16)

New International Economic Order (NIEO) A set of proposals launched in 1974 for reform of the international economic order, with the goal of enhancing the self-reliance of the South and its influence over international institutions and events and achieving an increase in resource flows from the North to the South. (13)

New Public Management A bureaucratic transformation occurring in many states over the past 15 years involving downsizing government, technological change, providing public services in new (alternate) ways, and forming partnerships with private sector agencies (7).

NGO See *nongovernmental organization (NGO)*.

NIEO See *New International Economic Order (NIEO)*.

non-confidence vote See *confidence (or non-confidence) vote*.

nongovernmental organization (NGO) A nonprofit organization that is not part of the state and is not a private corporation. Usually, the term is used to describe organizations that operate across borders in areas such as peace, development, human rights, and international affairs. (1, 12)

nontariff barrier Any measure or practice that places a barrier in the way of "free" commerce between nations, ranging from obvious measures, such as procurement policies that favour one's nationals, to not-so-obvious practices, such as the imposition of strict health and safety standards on imports in order to make the goods of other countries more expensive. (15)

North American Free Trade Agreement (NAFTA) An agreement ratified by the United States, Canada, and Mexico that contains rules to promote the freer movement of goods, capital, and services between these countries. (6, 16)

oligarchy A system of government ruled by a few and, according to Aristotle, in their own interests. (2)

OMOV See *one-member-one-vote (OMOV)*.

one-member-one-vote (OMOV) A method of leadership selection in which party members vote directly for the candidate of their choice, instead of electing delegates to make the choice on their behalf. Popular OMOV methods include telephone voting, mail-in ballots, and voting in person at a local polling place. Some parties have created hybrid or two-stage OMOV systems, in which delegates are bound to vote according to the preference of the members whom they represent, for example, the Liberal Party of Canada. (11)

opposition In parliamentary systems, those members of the legislature who do not belong to the party or parties that form the government and cabinet. (8)

organizational culture Clusters of beliefs about the way groups should be organized. Examples are a belief in hierarchy or a belief in internal democracy. (12)

PAC See *political action committee (PAC)*.

parliamentary wing The wing of a political party that includes the leader, the elected legislators, and the people who work in their offices. Also called *caucus* or party in public office. (11)

party discipline The practice that all members in a legislature belonging to the same political party should normally vote the same way, in accordance with their party's stand on the issue at hand. (8, 12)

party identification An individual's long-standing identification with a particular political party. (10, 11)

party system The system of interactions resulting from interparty competition; the parties within a particular jurisdiction (country, state, or province) that compete with each other for scarce resources, particularly money and votes. The word "system" refers to a set of distinct but interrelated objects. When an individual party changes in some way—by appealing to a new group of voters or by altering its internal structures—that change affects all of the other parties in the system. (11)

patriotism A sense of pride in one's country. (4)

PCO See *Privy Council Office (PCO)*.

peacebuilding An extension of *peacekeeping* that refers to the efforts of the international community to create the structures of a peaceful society, as was done in Bosnia in 1995, Kosovo in 1999, and East Timor in 1999–2000. (15)

peacekeeping An undertaking by any group of governments, usually under the sponsorship of the United Nations, to put the forces of a third party between warring parties who have come to a ceasefire, in order to encourage them to keep the peace. (15)

peacemaking An extension of *peacekeeping* that involves the armed forces of a third party intervening in a war to bring peace to an area, as was done in Somalia in 1992. (15)

PMO See *Prime Minister's Office (PMO)*.

policy community A collection of groups and individuals (including both state bureaucrats and interest groups or social movement organizations) who influence each other in an effort to shape policy outcomes in their area of interest. (12)

political action committee (PAC) A political committee organized for the purpose of raising and spending money to elect and defeat a candidate, especially in the United States. (12)

political alienation A sense of detachment or resentment that arises in people who have little trust in political leaders and feel unable to influence political decisions that affect their own interests. (4)

political culture The collection of the understandings, values, attitudes, and principles of a community or society that relate to its political organization, processes, disputes, and public policies. Out of a society's political culture come important beliefs and values that structure the citizens' attitudes and expectations toward such basic political concepts as legitimacy, power, authority, and obedience. (1, 4)

political development A concept that describes how well a society has developed politically, usually measured by the degree of state capacity to effectively carry out the legislative, executive, and judicial functions of government; the degree of political stability, or ability to resolve political conflicts in a peaceful manner; and the degree of governmental responsiveness to public demands and respect for fundamental rights. (13)

political dissent Any form of action taken to indicate a rejection of the existing order, such as peaceful protest, domestic violence, or terrorism. (14)

political efficacy The belief that we as individuals can have some influence upon the political decisions that affect our lives. (4)

political participation Actions taken by individuals and groups in an attempt to influence political decisions and decision-makers. (10)

political party An organization of volunteers and paid professionals who work together to achieve shared political goals, one of which is the election of candidates to public office. The nomination of candidates is the defining characteristic of a political party—as distinct from an interest group. For many parties, the primary goal is to elect enough candidates to the legislature to form a government. Other parties are more concerned with the advocacy of particular ideas or policies. (1, 11)

political patronage The awarding of benefits to individuals or companies on the basis of their support for the governing political party. (7, 9)

political science The systematic study of government and politics. (1)

political socialization The process through which attitudes toward and knowledge about political matters are passed on within a society. (1, 4, 5)

political trust The belief that political leaders act in the best interests of society. (4)

politics That activity in which conflicting interests struggle for advantage or dominance in the making and execution of public policies. (1)

polity A system of government ruled by the many but not, as in a democracy, by all; according to Aristotle, this was the most stable system of government when it was able to balance the interests of the wealthy with those of the poor. (2)

power The ability of one actor to impose its will on another, to get its own way, to do or get what it wants; the capacity of one actor to prevail in a conflict of interests with other actors, normally through force, sanction, coercion, or manipulation. (1, 15)

PR See *proportional representation (PR)*.

prime minister The head of government in a parliamentary system who provides political leadership and makes the major decisions, usually in concert with a cabinet. (7)

Prime Minister's Office (PMO) In Canada, the office that provides political advice to and is staffed by close partisan advisors of the Prime Minister, and whose overriding concern is to safeguard his or her political fortunes. (7)

private law A branch of law dealing with relationships between private parties such as individuals, groups of people, and corporations; it includes laws governing contracts, property, and personal injury. (9)

privatization Transferring a government program, agency, or Crown corporation to the private sector, for example, by selling shares in the corporation to the public at large or to a private firm. (7)

Privy Council Office (PCO) In Canada, the office that links the Prime Minister and Cabinet to the world of administration and provides logistical and decision-making support to the government; it is made up of nonpartisan career public servants. (7)

propaganda An organized attempt to spread beliefs through a communications campaign. It implies the use of exaggerated facts. (4)

proportional representation (PR) An electoral system that attempts to award seats to parties in proportion to the share of votes earned. Such systems must be combined with multimember constituencies. (10)

protectionism The use of various policy tools, such as subsidies, tariffs, and quotas, to protect goods and services produced within a country against competition from producers in other countries. (15, 16)

public law A branch of law involving governments and public authorities; it includes constitutional, administrative, and criminal law. (9)

public opinion polling The use of survey interviews, often conducted over the telephone, with a representative, randomly selected sample of people, providing an accurate description of the attitudes, beliefs, and behaviour of the population from which the sample was drawn. (10)

public policy A course of action or inaction selected by public officials, usually in response to a specific problem or set of problems. (1, 3, 7, 8, 9, 11, 12, 16)

Question Period A set period of time in a parliament when members can put questions directly to the prime minister and other cabinet ministers. (8)

race Historically, the term *race* was used to speak about differences between people that were supposedly biologically based. Today social scientists completely reject the idea that there are any significant biological differences between people that warrant the use of the term "race." While some suggest that, in the light of this, the term should not be used at all, many contemporary social scientists use the term in quotation marks to refer to differences that, while merely socially constructed, are historically specific and have important consequences in the form of racism. Contemporary discussions of racism highlight the fact that it involves a biological and/or cultural assertion of superiority by one group over another. (3)

rational voting A model that seeks to explain voting decisions by emphasizing the rational evaluation of alternatives (parties and candidates) and the retrospective assessment of the governing party. (10)

recall A mechanism that allows citizens to petition to remove their political representative before the next election period. (10)

referendum A mechanism that provides citizens with the ability to vote directly on pieces of legislation or constitutional changes. (10)

regime The whole decision-making apparatus of the state; the constitutional principles and arrangements according to which government decisions are made; the fundamental rules of the game. (2, 14)

representation by population The principle suggesting that the allocation of seats in assemblies should occur in a manner that encourages an equal division of the population across electoral districts, so that each vote is of equal weight. (10)

representative democracy A political system in which citizens hold power indirectly by selecting representatives who render public decisions on their behalf in popular assemblies. (2, 10)

republic A system of government ruled by a head of state who is not a monarch (generally, in modern times, a president), in which citizens are entitled to participate in decision-making. (2, 6)

residual powers Powers to pass laws in relation to any matters that the constitution does not expressly assign to any level of government; these powers typically belong either to the federal government or to the state or provincial governments. (6)

responsible government A defining principle of Westminster-style parliamentary governments, which states that the cabinet may only hold office as long as it has majority support in the legislature (or lower house in a bicameral parliament) for votes of confidence. (7, 8)

revolution A sudden, drastic, and usually violent change in the government of a state; the overthrow and replacement of existing political institutions and principles, not merely the forcible removal of the current ruler or government. (2, 4, 5, 6, 14)

right That part of the ideological spectrum which cherishes individualism and believes in leaving the private sector to operate with minimal government intervention. (5)

rigid amending formula A constitution whose method of amendment is relatively onerous. (6)

security The peace of mind that comes with a sense of safety from harm of what one values; a sense of well-being that can have economic, environmental, social, linguistic, or cultural dimensions. It can be seen in terms of both individual and community safety. (15)

self-determination A principle of international law that grants all peoples/nations the right to determine their political status and pursue their economic, social, and cultural development free from external domination or interference. (13)

separation of powers A principle of constitutional government usually taken to mean that legislative, executive, and judicial functions of the state should be carried out by separate branches of government, and that no one may hold office in more than one branch at the same time. (7)

single executive A form of executive in which the posts of head of state and head of government are combined and held by a single officeholder. This arrangement is characteristic of presidential systems, such as those of Argentina, Mexico, and the United States. (7)

single transferable vote (STV) A proportional electoral system that elects candidates in multimember ridings and provides voters with significant freedom by allowing them to rank-order their choices within and across party lines. (10)

social movement An informal network of activists who seek to transform the values of society. (1, 12, 16)

socialism The doctrine advocating economic equality of the classes and the use of government to serve the collective good of the whole society. Socialists value the collective good over the private interests of individuals and emphasize cooperation over competition. (5)

sovereignty The final or ultimate power over a population and a piece of territory, commonly claimed by the government of a state but ultimately sanctioned by the international system of states. In other contexts, sovereignty can be said to reside in the people or in parliament; in all cases, however, it has probably been eroded by global forces. (2)

Speech from the Throne The document prepared by the prime minister and cabinet and read by the head of state at the opening of each session of parliament; it outlines the government's legislative proposals for the session to follow. (7)

stare decisis The principle of common law systems by which courts are bound to follow prior decisions that involved similar issues of law. A judgment by one member of a court binds other members, and lower courts are bound to follow the decisions of higher courts. (9)

state A modern form of organizing political life that is characterized by a population, territory, governing institutions, and a government that claims a monopoly of legitimate force; recognition by the international community of states (most often by the United Nations) may also be key. (2, 3, 13, 15)

state failure A situation in which the structure, authority, law, and political order have fallen apart and must be reconstituted in some form. (2, 13, 14)

STV See *single transferable vote (STV)*.

subculture A cluster of people who share the same basic political values and attributes distinct from those of other groups in society and from the predominant values and attributes of society as a whole. (4, 11)

supranational A sphere of politics and political institutions that exists "above" the nation-state but usually "below" the global level. The only supranational polity in the world is the European Union. (15)

Supreme Court of Canada Canada's highest court and final court of appeal since 1949. (9)

sustainable development An approach to development that makes environmental conservation and protection an integral part of development processes, in order to enhance the ability of current and future generations to meet their needs. (13)

terrorism The threat or use of violence, usually directed at civilian populations, in order to effect some form of political change. (2, 10, 14, 15)

totalitarian government A nondemocratic form of government—most notably Nazism, fascism, and Soviet communism—that is based on a single party and ideology, takes control of all aspects of political, social, economic, and intellectual life, and mobilizes its mass public into active support of the government. (2)

transnational corporations Business firms that are headquartered in one country but have plants or places of operation around the world permitting them to integrate their business activities on a global scale. (1, 3, 16)

transnational group A group that organizes across the borders of nation-states with the goal of influencing governments, international organizations, or public opinion. (12)

tyranny of the majority Abuse of the minority by the majority through excessive use of power; it can occur in social settings (when, for example, members of an ethnic minority feel oppressed by the actions of the ruling majority) or in political settings (when, for example, members of a legislature feel influenced in their decision-making by the majority group). (5, 8)

UN See *United Nations (UN)*.

unicameral legislature A legislature with only one house, or chamber, to which all members belong. (8)

United Nations (UN) An international organization, formed in 1945 as a successor to the League of Nations, that has become the largest and most ambitious international governmental organization in world history, consisting of a vast array of organs and agencies. Its membership now includes almost every country in the world. Less than a world government, it attempts to promote peaceful relations among states and economic and human rights for all people. (2, 13, 15, 16)

unwritten constitution A constitution whose subject matter is dispersed across a variety of statutes, court rulings, and unwritten political practices known as constitutional conventions. (6)

veto The authorized power to block a decision or piece of legislation, especially of a president to reject a law passed by congress or of a province to reject a proposed constitutional amendment. (7, 8)

welfare state A concept that stresses the role of government as a provider and protector of individual security and well-being through the implementation of interventionist economic policies and social programs. (1, 5, 7)

World Bank A bank closely linked to the IMF that is one of the world's largest sources of development assistance. Through loans, policy advice, and technical assistance, it aims to improve the living standards in the developing world. (13, 14, 15, 16)

World Trade Organization (WTO) An organization created during the Uruguay Round of GATT negotiations whose goal is to provide liberal trading practices and to reduce protectionism through the development and enforcement of global laws and regulations. (2, 6, 15, 16)

written constitution A constitution whose fundamental provisions have been reduced to a single document or limited set of documents. (6)

WTO See *World Trade Organization (WTO)*.

Index

Boxed material is indicated by *box*. Tabular material is indicated by *table*. Pictorial material is indicated by *figure*.

New International Economic Order (NIECO), 380 *box*

New Public Management (NPM), 214

Newspapers. *See also* Mass media

daily Canadian market, 101, 101 *table*

Nietzsche, Friedrich, 118, 120, 124, 127

Nigeria, 408

"Night-watchman state," 130

Nisga'a, 50

Nixon, Richard, 196, 197, 205, 449

Nomination of candidates, 332–333

Non-confidence vote in cabinet, 225

Nongovernmental organizations (NGOs), 10–11, 350. *See also* Interest groups; Social movements

Non-state governments, 47, 49–53

Normative studies, 122 *box*

North American Free Trade Agreement (NAFTA), 406, 457

Northern Cyprus, 51

North Korea, 48 *box,* 128

free speech in, 133

North–South relations, 378–379

the 1950s, 379

the 1960s, 379

the 1970s, 379

the 1980s, 379

the 1990s, 381

development/underdevelopment in, 375–376, 375 *figure*

Millennium Development Goals, 381–382, 382 *box*

outcomes of, 382

Nozick, Robert, 119 *box,* 130

Obama, Barack, 4, 330 *figure,* 333

O'Brien, Robert, 363

O'Donnell, Terrence, 267 *box*

Official development assistance (ODA), 395–396

long-term trends in, 396 *table*

major donors of, 395 *table*

"Official" ideologies, 140–141

Oligarchy, 35

Olson, Mancur, 351, 352

One-member-one-vote system (OMOV), 331–332

Open-list system, 298

Ozone depletion. *See* Global warming

Pakistan

military as obstacle to democratization of, 411 *box*

Musharraf's crackdown on the courts, 255, 256 *box*

"Palestine" territory, 64 *box*

Parliamentary government, 194–195

advantages of, 195

British parliament, 226–227

cabinet government, 199–200

coalition government, 226

disadvantages of, 195–196

dual executive, 190. *See also* Prime minister(s)

Question Period, 225

responsible government, principle of, 225–226

Parliamentary wing of a party, 325 *box*

Parties. *See* Political parties

Party discipline, 358

Party identification, 301, 323

Pateman, Carole, 92

Patriation Reference case, 257

Patriotism, 108

Peacebuilding, 446

Peacekeeping, 446

Peacemaking, 446

Pearson, Lester, 328

Peer groups, political socialization through, 106–107

Pericles' funeral oration, 34 *box*

Peron, Eva, 5

Personal attitudes, 88

Personal identity, 91 *box*

Pinochet, Augusto, 5

Plant, Geoff, 274

Plato, 13, 34, 35, 118 *box,* 124, 135, 136, 141, 149

Policy community, 360

Political action committees (PACs), 359

top 20 contributors to federal candidates, 359 *figure*

Political alienation, 88

Political cleavage(s), 93–94, 335

Political culture, 13, 85–86

subcultures, 86–88

Political development, 18–19, 21, 384–385. *See also* Developing world

governmental responsiveness and representation, 385

issues of debate, 387–388

political stability, 385

state capacity, 385

Political dissent, 415–418

Political efficacy, 88

Political ideas, 13–14. *See also* Political theory

Political ideologies, 14

attitudes toward the state, 146 *figure*

function of, 138

"left–right" continuum, 141–148, 145 *figure*

nature of, 138–139

"official," 140–141

style of thought, "ideology" as, 139–141

Political institutions, 14

Political participation, 302–305